Migrating to
Windows® 95

LIMITED WARRANTY AND DISCLAIMER OF LIABILITY

Migrating to Windows® 95

A Programmer's Guide to What's New

Mark Andrews

AP PROFESSIONAL

Boston San Diego New York
London Sydney Tokyo Toronto

This book is printed on acid-free paper. ∞

AP PROFESSIONAL
1300 Boylston Street, Chestnut Hill, MA 02167
World Wide Web site at http://www.apnet.com

An Imprint of ACADEMIC PRESS, INC.
A Division of HARCOURT BRACE & COMPANY

United Kindom Edition published by
ACADEMIC PRESS LIMITED
24–28 Oval Road, London NW1 7DX

Library of Congress Cataloging-in-Publication Data
Andrews, Mark.
Migrating to Windows 95: programmer's guide to what's new / Mark Andrews.
p. cm.
Includes index.
ISBN 0-12-058525-1
1. Microsoft Windows 95. 2. Operating systems (Computers)
I. Title.
QA76.76.063A53494 1995 95-41466
005.265—dc 20 CIP

Printed in the United States of America
96 97 98 99 IP 9 8 7 6 5 4 3 2 1

To Marilyn

Acknowledgements

This book could not have been written without the help of Carole McClendon, my agent; Chuck Glaser, Dave Hannon, and Karen Pratt of AP Professional, Boston; Tandy Trower, director of user interface design at Microsoft; Donald Johnson, program manager of the Microsoft Visual C++ product group; Dean D. McCrory, Microsoft Foundation Class library development lead for Visual C++; Adam Demming, MFC program manager at Microsoft; John Elsbree, Visual C++ software design engineer at Microsoft; Kraig Brockschmidt, program manager of the OLE team at Microsoft and author of *Inside OLE*; and everyone at Microsoft who worked so hard to create and develop Windows 95, Visual C++ 4.0, and Version 4.0 of the Microsoft Foundation Class library. Thanks, everybody!

Contents

8 Programs and Processes 343

9 Multithreading and Multitasking 409

Preface

To developers of Windows 95 applications, the release of Visual C++ 4.0 is almost as important as the release of Windows 95. Why? Because Visual C++ 4.0 is the first Windows development environment with full support for Windows 95 built in.

For millions of Windows users, the age of Windows 95 began on August 24, 1995. Developers of Windows 95 applications had to wait a little longer.

Windows 95 made its debut on August 24, 1995. Version 4.0 of Visual C++—the first development system designed especially for Windows 95—was not introduced until a little later in the fall. But for several months before Visual C++ 4.0 was officially released, Microsoft distributed beta and even pre-beta copies of the product to a small number of developers and reporters and held a number of conferences and press briefings to disclose some of the new features of Visual C++ 4.0 to Windows programmers.

Several of these meetings and press briefings were held at the Santa Clara Convention Center in Santa Clara, CA, about a five-minute drive from my house. That made it easy to keep track of what was happening—or soon would be happening—in the world of Windows 95 and Visual C++ software development.

As it turned out, there was much more going on than most people had anticipated. Once Windows 95 was officially released and Microsoft got a chance to start shifting its focus to Visual C++, the news began to leak out that Visual C++ would be changing substantially with the release of Version 4.0. And when Visual C++ was officially released, the scope of its changes turned out to be more dramatic than most Visual C++ had imagined.

Not only did Visual C++ come with a new interface and a host of new common controls designed especially for Windows 95—there was also a new Component Gallery (for instant access to reusable code objects called components); full Visual C++ and ClassWizard support for OLE controls and OLE control containers; and, of course, many new features supporting 32-bit programming and the multithreading and preemptive multitasking capabilities that had previously been available to Windows developers only in Windows NT.

As Visual C++ 4.0 grew and changed during the pre-beta and beta stages of its development, this book changed, too. On more than one occasion, a chapter was about ready to go to the publisher when a new pre-beta or beta version of Visual C++ arrived by messenger and the chapter had to be rewritten. Often I felt like a newspaper reporter who was assigned to a big story that kept changing every day.

It was hectic but it was fun. And the result was what you're reading now. Because this book and Visual C++ 4.0 grew up together, I think you'll find a lot of material in these pages that is new, exclusive, and not yet available anywhere else—yet. This book is not only one of the first books on the shelves to provide in-depth coverage of many of the advanced new features of Visual C++—it also contains a generous amount sample code that shows you exactly how those new features work, and exactly how you can incorporate them into your own Windows 95 programs.

User-Interface Features of Windows 95

Some of the new features of Windows 95 are apparent as soon as you turn on your computer, and some aren't. The most obvious feature of Windows 95 is, of course, that slick new user interface that everyone was talking about long before Windows 95's official premiere. But Windows 95 has many other features are more subtle. These almost invisible new features of Windows 95 are capabilities that you don't become aware of them right away. In fact, if you aren't a developer, you may never become aware of some them at all.

This book covers both categories of new Windows 95 features: those that are immediately apparent—and, perhaps even more important, those that aren't.

Here are just a few of the new features of Windows 95 covered in this volume:

- In Windows 95, the screen is no longer considered just a visual backdrop. Now it has become a *container*—a term you'll see over and over in this book. It means that in Windows 95, the screen is not just a graphical interface for DOS, but is a container of *objects* represented by icons. By using Windows 95's drag-and-drop capabilities, you can pick up objects from the Windows 95 desktop with the mouse and deposit them into other objects. For example, you can pick up an object that represents a document and drag it into another object that represents a folder. When you do that in Windows 95, you're making use of a relatively new and rapidly expanding Windows 95 technology called *object linking and embedding*, or *OLE*. OLE is used in many ways in Windows 95, and that's just one of them. In fact, Microsoft has linked the future of Windows so closely to OLE that you'll be hearing a lot about OLE over the months and years ahead—and you'll read quite a bit about it in this volume.

- The Windows 95 interface lets users open documents by simply double-clicking on their icons, without having to open the applications that created documents. That is another operation that is made possible by OLE, and it is another feature that you can incorporate into your own Windows 95 programs.
- Windows 95 offers a host of new *common controls* to software designers. They are called common controls because they are used by the system as well as by applications. Common controls offer an easy way for you to give your applications the same kind of look and feel that Windows 95 itself has. This kind of consistency makes the user of your applications immediately comfortable with them—and therefore more likely to like your programs and want to use them. And, because common controls have already been user-tested and debugged, you can use them without being concerned that they'll break or behave in unexpected ways while the customer is using your application. In Chapter 6, "Windows 95 and Visual C++," you'll find full coverage of common controls—including a sample application that shows how you can use common controls in your Windows 95 applications.
- With the release of Windows 95, Microsoft has updated the common dialog boxes used in earlier versions of Windows and has increased the number of common dialog boxes available. Common dialog boxes available in Windows 95 include a **Find and Replace** dialog box, a **Page Setup** dialog box, a **Font** dialog box, and a **Color** dialog box. You'll learn all about them in Chapter 1, "Introducing Windows 95."
- Objects on the Windows 95 desktop have attributes, or *properties*, that can change dynamically as the user manipulates them. By right-clicking on a desktop icon, the user can display a popup menu that can then be used to open a page in tabbed dialog box called a *property sheet*. Then, by typing text and clicking buttons on that property sheet, the user can view and change the properties

of an object—for example, the user can change a logon password or activate a property that allows a disk to be shared across a network. When you develop Windows 95 applications, the most important fact about properties is that you can use them in your own applications—in exactly the same way they are used by system-generated objects on the Windows 95 desktop. Chapter 7, "OLE 95," shows how to write property pages and presents a sample application showing how you can equip objects with property sheets in your own Windows 95 programs.

- For many developers, the best new feature of Visual C++ 4.0 is its support for OLE controls—Microsoft's 32-bit successors to VBX controls. In Visual C++ 4.0, every Windows object you create is automatically an OLE control container, and ClassWizard now offers full interactive support for developing OLE controls. In Chapter 7, "OLE 95," you'll learn how to create and implement OLE controls in your Windows 95 applications. There's even an example program and a step-by-step tutorial that can help you get started developing your own OLE controls.

Features for Developers Only

Some of the most important new features of Windows 95 are those you can't see. Important features you might miss if someone didn't point them out include these:

- The *system registry*. In Windows 95 (and also in Windows NT), the registry is a tool that replaces most of the text-based configuration and initialization files such as CONFIG.SYS and AUTOEXEC.BAT that Windows relied on back during the days of Windows 3.1. Chapter 1, "Introducing Windows 95," explains what the registry is and presents a sample application that will give you an inside look into the system registry.
- Support for 32-bit hardware. Both Windows NT and Windows 95 have left the Intel 80286 processor in the dust. To run Windows 95 on an Intel-based computer, you must have a machine equipped with at least an Intel 386—and that requirement enables Windows 95 to use many advanced features of the 386/486/Pentium family of processors that earlier versions of Windows did not have access to. Chapter 2, "Underneath Windows 95," tells you about the hardware that Windows 95 relies on—and guides you through a step-by-step tutorial that shows you exactly what happens inside your computer's memory when you start up Windows 95.

- A hybrid 16-bit/32-bit operating-system architecture (Windows NT has a 32-bit architecture from the ground up, while the Windows 95 operating system is a cross between a 16-bit OS and a 32-bit OS.) Chapter 3, "Windows 95 Architecture," shows you exactly how the Windows 95 operating system is designed and how its parts all work together—knowledge you must have if you want to become an expert Windows 95 programmer.
- Reliance on a brand-new version of the new Win32 API (application programming interface). The Win32 API, the successor to the old 16-bit Windows API, made its debut with release of Windows NT. Now, along with the release of Visual C++ 4.0, Microsoft has introduced a new Win32 API that's compatible with both Windows NT and Windows 95. This new Win32 API offers enhanced support for multithreading, multithreaded DLLs (dynamic-link libraries), networking, and many other new features supported by Windows 95. You'll learn all about the new features and capabilities of the new Win32 API in Chapter 4, "The Win32 API," and in subsequent chapters.

Visual C++ 4.0 and MFC 4.0

When Windows 95 was officially released on August 24, 1995, very little software had been written specifically for the new operating system. And no one had written any Windows 95 software at all on development systems designed specifically to create applications for the Windows 95 environment.

That's why the release of Visual C++ 4.0 was so important Windows 95 developers—it was the first Windows development system with full support for Windows 95 built in. Some of the most important new features of Visual C++ 4.0 are:

- Support for Version 4.0 of the Microsoft Foundation Class (MFC) library, which contains dozens of new classes and hundreds of new member functions designed specifically to support the many new features of Windows 95.
- Full support for OLE controls and OLE control containers. (OLE controls, as previously mentioned, are Microsoft's 32-bit successors to VBX controls—and OLE containers are windows with built-in support for OLE controls.) When you develop Windows 95 applications with Visual C++ 4.0, every window you create is automatically a container for OLE controls. Furthermore, in Visual C++ 4.0, the graphically based ClassWizard class-manage-

ment utility supports the interactive creation of OLE controls and OLE control containers.

- ControlWizard, a new Visual C++ tool created especially for designing and implementing OLE controls. ControlWizard works much like the AppWizard application generator that Visual C++ programmers are familiar with. With ControlWizard, you can create a fully functioning OLE control using only menu buttons and dialog controls. Then you can customize your OLE control by adding code that gives it whatever functionality your application requires. When you've done all that, you can store your OLE control away in yet another new Visual C++ utility called Component Gallery. Once you have made your control available to yourself or any licensee by storing it in Component Gallery, you can use ClassWizard to incorporate your new control automatically into any Visual C++ application.
- With Component Gallery, you can create reusable code objects—called components—and you can then store those components in source-code form in a central repository. Then, at any time you like, you can retrieve any component from Component Gallery and use it in any Visual C++ application. When you import a component into an application from Component Gallery, the Visual C++ Developer Studio inserts the component you have selected into the source code of the application you're working on. Then the Visual C++ editor automatically jumps the spot in your source code where Component Gallery has inserted your component. When that is done, you can tweak the component (if necessary) to suit the particular needs of your application.
- A set of extensions to ClassWizard that are designed specifically to support OLE controls. ClassWizard, as Visual C++ programmers know, is a graphics-based Visual C++ tool for creating and implementing C++ classes. With ClassWizard, you can set up mechanisms that pass data back and forth between your application and the controls in dialog boxes. With the OLE extensions to ClassWizard, you can do the same thing with OLE controls.
- A whole new set of tools called *custom AppWizards*. AppWizard, which has been around since the first version of Visual C++, is a Visual C++ tool for creating a working Windows application at the touch of a menu button. With Visual C++ 4.0's custom AppWizard extensions, you can design a customized AppWizard that will automatically create any kind of framework you like when the Visual C++ user clicks the appropriate button on the Visual C++ editor's menu. So if AppWizard's default application framework doesn't fill your needs, you can create a custom

AppWizard that creates application frameworks better suited to your requirements.

- Finally, Visual C++ 4.0 supports a new set of custom extensions to the MFC library. With these new MFC extensions, you can create your own MFC classes and add them to the Microsoft's MFC DLL. Then, when your application loads the standard MFC DLL into memory, the classes you have added to MFC will be added, too.

Chapter Outline

Now that you know something about you'll be reading about in this book, here's a chapter outline that shows how the book's contents are arranged:

- Chapter 1, "Introducing Windows 95," describes the features of the Windows 95 user interface and shows how you can use them in your Windows 95 applications. It also describes the system registry and presents a sample application that shows how you can retrieve information from the registry.
- Chapter 2, "Underneath Windows 95," lifts the hood of the Intel 386/486/Pentium processor. It shows you how Microsoft engineers harnessed all the processing power built into the 386 family of chips and put it to work in the Windows 95 interface. Chapter 2 also shows how you can get that same power to work for you in your own Windows 95 programs.
- Chapter 3, "Windows 95 Architecture," examines the architecture of the Windows 95 operating system. This chapter shows you how the all the parts of the Windows 95 OS work together, so you can design applications that work well with Windows 95. Chapter 3 tells you what you need to know about the Windows 95 virtual machine, the Windows subsystem, the Windows 95 MS-DOS virtual machines, the Windows 95 core DLLs, Windows 95 virtual device drivers, and much more.
- Chapter 4, "The Win32 API," introduces you to the new Win32 application programming interface (API). The Win32 API is the generic name for the code that implements all the system function calls used in both Windows 95 and Windows NT. The Microsoft Foundation Class (MFC) library—the C++ class library that Visual C++ relies on—does its work by calling functions implemented in the Win32 API. In Chapter 4, you'll learn about the newest features and capabilities built into the Windows API, and you'll learn how to use them in your own applications.

- Chapter 5, "Windows 95 and the MFC Library," introduces you to Version 4.0 of the Microsoft Foundation Class library and shows how you can use the advanced new features of MFC 4.0 in your Windows 95 applications. In this chapter, you'll learn about all the new interface gadgets and common controls that are built into Windows 95, and you'll get a step-by-step, hands-on introduction to an example program that actually implements a common control.
- Chapter 6, "Windows 95 and Visual C++," introduces Version 4.0 of Visual C++ and gives you a first look at what you need to do to create and implement OLE controls. This chapter focuses on four of the most important categories of new features of the Visual C++ 4.0:
    - Developer Studio, the new Visual C++ user interface that has replaced the old Visual C++ 2.*x* Programmer's Workbench
    - Component Gallery, the new Visual C++ tool that makes it easy in incorporate OLE controls into your Visual C++ applications. Components are reusable controls, classes, and other objects that you can drop into any Visual C++ program. In this chapter, you'll see exactly how Component Gallery works, and you'll get a chance to step through a hands-on tutorial that shows how to install a control in Component Gallery.
    - OLE controls—one of the most significant new features of Visual C++ 4.0—are Microsoft's 32-bit successors to VXB controls. And they are much better tools for Windows programmers than VBX controls ever were. This chapter introduces OLE controls, and Chapter 7, "OLE 95," covers them in much more detail.
- Chapter 7, "OLE 95," shows how you can use OLE controls in your Windows 95 applications. This chapter introduces both the OLE component (COM) object and the ControlWizard tool, which automatically creates and implements OLE controls in Visual C++. The chapter concludes with an example program and a step-by-step tutorial that shows you exactly how to create OLE controls, OLE property sheets, OLE methods, and OLE event handlers in your Visual C++ applications.
- Chapter 8, "Programs and Processes," shows how Windows 95 creates and manages *processes*—a word used to refer to what used to be called tasks under earlier versions of Windows. Chapter 8 also shows how Windows 95 implements *preemptive multitasking*, a new (for Windows) technology that divides processes into threads and allocates each thread an individual share of CPU time, depending upon preallocated thread priorities. Chapter 9,

"Multithreading and Multitasking," explores the creation and implementation of multithreaded programs in more detail.

- Chapter 9, "Multithreading and Multitasking," shows how Windows 95 uses multithreading and synchronization objects to implement preemptive multitasking. It presents several example programs that demonstrate the use of multithreading, preemptive multitasking, and the use of synchronization objects such as wait objects, mutexes, and semaphores.
- Chapter 10, "Windows 95 DLLs," introduces DLLs—object-code libraries that let multiple programs share code, data, and resources. DLLs are so important in Windows that the Windows 95 operating system owes its very existence to them; the Windows OS is implemented as an enormous set of DLLs. In this chapter, you'll learn how to write three different kinds of DLLs that are used in different kinds of Windows programs—including, of course, Windows 95. Sample applications show how you can use all three kinds of DLLs in your Windows applications.
- Chapter 11, "Windows 95 Networking," shows how Windows 95 supports the TCP/IP communications protocol. TCP/IP, the most direct gateway to the Internet, is built into Windows 95—and this chapter shows how to use it. Chapter 11 also introduces the Windows Sockets API, which you can use to equip your Windows 95 applications with support for TCP/IP and other communications protocols. The chapter concludes with a pair of example programs that demonstrate how you can use TCP/IP to set up networked communications between a pair of Windows 95 systems, a pair of Windows NT systems, or a mixture of Windows 95 workstations, Windows NT workstations or servers, and other nodes (even UNIX nodes) on a network.

Summary

This book focuses not just on what's new and different in Windows 95, but on what's new and different and most useful to developers of Windows 95 applications. If you develop your programs using Visual C++, or plan to start using Visual C++, you'll find this book even more helpful and even more interesting. I even think you'll have fun with it; I know I did.

So happy programming!

Mark Andrews
Santa Clara, CA
August 24, 1995

Chapter 1

Introducing Windows 95

Until Windows 95 made its debut, Windows wasn't much more than a graphical user interface for DOS, and the screen when you fired up Windows was not much more than a visual backdrop. Now, in Windows 95, the screen has become a container—a Windows 95 word that means a container of objects represented by icons.

Windows 95 has more new features than you can click a mouse at.

Some of these new features are apparent as soon as you turn on your computer. The new Windows 95 user interface is slick and impressive, but many other important features of Windows 95 are more subtle; you don't become aware of them right away.

This chapter focuses on the Windows 95 features that you can see, but also introduces a few that you can't. The remainder of this book goes into more detail about the more subtle features of Windows 95 and shows you how you can make use of them in the applications you write for Windows 95.

The major topics covered in this chapter are:

The chapter concludes with a hands-on example program that demonstrates the use of an important Windows 95 tool called the system registry. The Windows 95 registry stores initialization and configuration information about applications and can be used to initialize and configure both applications and computer systems.

The example program at the end of this chapter is named REGDEMO.EXE. It presented in the section titled "Online Help in Windows 95" on page 30. Figure 1.1 shows the program's output.

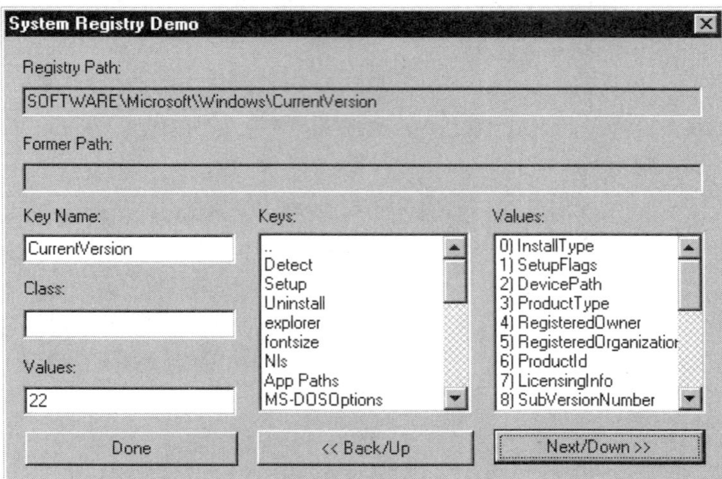

Figure 1.1 Output of the REGDEMO example program

Behind the Windows 95 Interface

Many of the new features of Windows 95 are reflected in its impressive new user interface (Figure 1.2). This section introduces some of the most important features of the Windows 95 interface, and reveals some of the details of how those features are implemented. Later in this chapter, you'll learn how to implement the new features of the Windows 95 interface in your own Windows 95 applications.

Figure 1.2 The Windows 95 user interface

Containers in Windows 95

Back in the days of Windows 3.*x*, Windows was really just a graphical user interface for DOS. Now, in Windows 95, the screen has become a *container*—a Windows 95 word that means a container of *objects* represented by icons.

In Windows 95, you can drag objects that appear inside a container and drop them into other objects, which then become containers themselves. For example, you can drop objects that represent documents into objects that represent folders. Also, by double-clicking on an icon that represents a document, you can open that document without having to open the application that created it.

Even more remarkably, you can drag a document created by one application into a document created by another application and edit it on the spot, without opening the application that created the first document. When you do that in Windows 95, you're making use of one of the features of *object linking and embedding*, or *OLE*.

OLE is used in many ways in Windows 95, and that's just one of them. OLE is introduced in Chapter 6, "Windows 95 and Visual C++," and is described in more detail in Chapter 7, "OLE 95."

Popup Menus and Property Pages

Objects on the Windows 95 desktop have attributes, or *properties*, that can change dynamically as the user manipulates them. For example, the name of each folder and document displayed on the desktop is a property.

To change the name of a folder or a document displayed on the desktop, all you have to do is select the document's name (beneath or beside its icon) and type in a new name. The name property of the selected file or folder then changes to the name the user has typed in.

You can also change an object's properties by right-clicking the mouse over its icon and then choosing the **Properties** item from a popup menu. Windows 95 then displays a property page that you can use to change the object's properties. For example, if you right-click over the **My Computer** icon on the Windows 95 desktop, the menu shown in Figure 1.3 pops up.

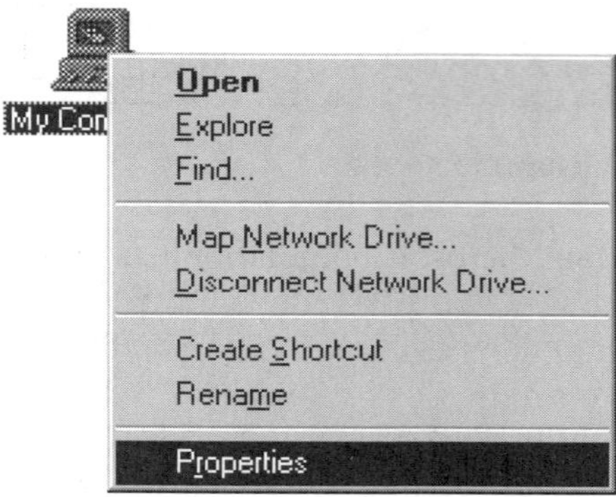

Figure 1.3 Opening a popup menu on the Windows 95 desktop

When the popup menu shown in Figure 1.3 appears, you can display the **Properties** dialog box shown in Figure 1.4 by choosing the **Proper-**

ties menu item. In Windows 95 jargon, a **Properties** dialog box is implemented as a tabbed dialog box called a *property sheet*. A property sheet, as you might guess, lists the properties of a Windows 95 object.

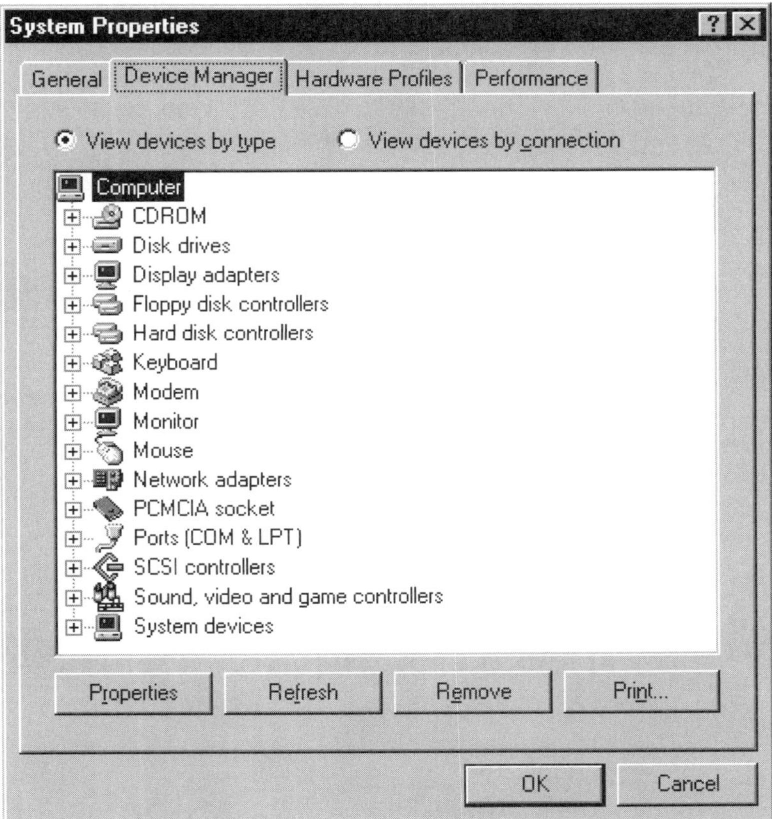

Figure 1.4 A property sheet

Version 4.0 of the Microsoft Foundation Class (MFC) library, which was introduced along with Windows 95, provides C++ classes that make it easy for you to equip OLE objects with property sheets. Users of your applications can then change the properties of objects you use in your applications very easily. You'll learn more about property sheets, and how to use them in your applications, in "Property-Sheet Dialog Boxes" on page 224.

Popup Menus and Contextual Commands

The commands that appear in a Windows 95 popup menu are called *contextual commands*: that is, commands that are related to the object over which the user right-clicks. By using popup menus, the user of your application can obtain very quick access to menu commands. You can use this same feature in your own Windows 95 applications.

In your Windows 95 applications, you should keep your popup menus as simple as possible. They should not be long lists of rarely used menu items, but should instead provide the user with access to frequently used commands that are directly related to the object over which they pop up.

One guideline to remember when you implement popup menus is that they should always pop up when the user releases the mouse button, not when the button goes down. If you always display popup menus when a right-button-up message is dispatched, your application will a follow a consistent model that is compatible with Windows 95 drag-and-drop commands.

Common Controls

The Windows 95 interface offers a host of new *common controls* that are used extensively by the Windows 95 system, and are also available to you for use in your Windows 95 applications. These controls are called common controls because they are used by the system as well as by applications.

By using common controls, you can give your applications the same kind of look and feel that Windows 95 itself has. This kind of consistency is good both for you and for the users of your applications. It benefits you because it offers an easy way for you to incorporate standard-looking Windows custom controls into your applications. It benefits users of your applications because your programs work the same way as the Windows 95 interface, so there's no need to learn about a new kind of interface to operate them.

Another benefit of using common controls is that they are user-tested and debugged, so they'll have less chance of breaking while your customers are using your application.

Common Dialog Boxes

With the release of Windows 95, Microsoft has updated the *common dialog boxes* used in earlier versions of Windows and has added more. Common dialog boxes, like common controls, are devices that are used extensively by Windows 95 and are also available to you for use in your applications. Common dialog boxes available in Windows 95 include a **Find and Replace** dialog box, a **Page Setup** dialog box, a **Font** dialog box, and a **Color** dialog box. All these dialog boxes have the new Windows 95 look, and they are very easy to incorporate into your Windows 95 applications.

Under Windows 95, as you might expect, all common dialog boxes look and work just like dialog boxes in Windows 95. For example, in Windows 95, the **Open** common dialog box looks like the one shown in Figure 1.5.

Figure 1.5 The Open common dialog box

In Windows 95, common dialog boxes that display file and folder icons have a look similar to that of the system's **Open** window and other windows used by the system, and they work in a similar fashion.

Along with the makeover that familiar common dialog boxes such as **Open** have received, several new common dialog boxes have been added in Windows 95. They include:

- A **Find and Replace** dialog box for finding or replacing text.
- A **Page Setup** dialog box for setting up pages for printers.
- A **Font** dialog box for selecting fonts.
- A **Color** dialog box for setting colors.

For more details about new and updated common dialog boxes in Windows 95, see Chapter 5, "Windows 95 and the MFC Library."

The Windows 95 Task Bar

At the bottom of the Windows 95 desktop, there is now a *task bar* (Figure 1.6). The task bar displays buttons that tell the user what objects are currently open on the desktop.

Figure 1.6 The Windows 95 task bar

For the user, the task bar is a home base for starting programs, switching between applications, quitting programs, and obtaining general information about desktop objects.

The Windows 95 task bar has several properties you can set by choosing the **Start | Settings | Taskbar** menu item. For example, if you check the **Auto hide** button in the task bar's property sheet, Windows 95 makes the task bar invisible until the mouse touches the bottom edge of the desktop window. Then the task bar pops up and becomes visible. You can use the task bar's auto hide feature to increase the size of the client area of the Windows 95 desktop window.

The task bar makes it easy for the user to navigate from one application to another and from one kind of window to another in a multiwindow applications. It can even eliminate the need for the MDI programming model in Windows 95 applications (for more on that topic, see "Returning to the SDI Model" on page 26).

What the New Look of Windows 95 Means to You

As you will see in this chapter, all those new gadgets and gizmos on the Windows 95 desktop are not just there for their looks. They offer the Windows 95 user—and the Windows 95 programmer—an enormous amount of functionality that earlier versions of Windows did not provide.

Furthermore, the new features and capabilities built into the Windows 95 interface were not created for the exclusive use of Microsoft's interface designers. They are also available to you, for use at any time you like in your own applications.

In fact, you should not see the Windows 95 user interface as just a desktop interface. Microsoft hopes that you will use the streamlined new features built into the Windows 95 interface in all the Windows applications you create from now on.

This chapter introduces the most important new features of the Windows 95 interface and explains how you can incorporate them into your own Windows 95 applications.

How the Windows 95 Interface Was Designed

According to Microsoft marketers interviewed just before the release of Windows 95, these were the main goals of the team that developed Windows 95:

- To improve the overall ease of use of Windows 95.
- To provide a more consistent interface.
- To clear up confusion that existed in earlier versions of Windows about the differences between the roles of the Program Manager and the File Manager. In Windows 95, the Program Manager and the File Manager have been merged into a single entity called the Windows 95 *desktop*.
- To make Windows a more document-centered interface (that concept is consistent with Microsoft's current OLE-based design philosophy; for more about that, see Chapter 7, "OLE 95").

The "ultimate goal" of Windows 95 designers, one Microsoft spokesperson explained, was "to help developers to design software that would allow users to focus more on their tasks—more on what they were doing—rather than on all the different ways of doing things" that they had faced in earlier versions of Windows.

Toward a Data-Oriented Interface

From a more technical standpoint, said this Microsoft exec, one of the most important goals of the Windows 95 design team was "to create an environment that would continue the evolution toward a more data-oriented, or document-centered user interface." A data-oriented interface, he explained, is one that lets the user manipulate documents directly, instead of being concerned with the files in which the documents are stored.

For example, the Windows 95 interface lets the user create and open documents directly from the desktop, without taking the intermediate step of starting the application that created the document. (This approach is explained in more detail later in "Opening Documents without Their Applications" on page 13.)

The spokesman also emphasized that the Windows 95 user interface "focuses on the metaphor of objects." He explained: "You can use all the object tools in the world that exist right now and still have what I call the standard GUI (graphic user) interface." On the other hand, he said, the "underpinnings" of an application do not have to be object-oriented for the application itself to have a document-centered user interface.

The Object Metaphor in Interface Design

Tandy Trower, director of user interface design at Microsoft, described and demonstrated the Windows 95 interface at a developer's conference in Santa, Clara, CA. The conference was held shortly before Windows 95 made its commercial debut.

Trower explained that a program written in any language can use the object metaphor because it is "a very natural metaphor. It's a concept that we all become familiar with at a very early age. We know how to interact with objects around us; there are certain concepts that we develop about objects."

Three of these concepts, he said, are *methods, operations*, and *relationships.*

Methods

Computer users naturally understand properties of objects, Trower explained, because objects have properties such as weight, color, and size. So "users naturally understand the concepts of attributes, or properties of an object. We understand that there are things you can do to objects; you can hold them, manipulate them. There are operations—or, in object terminology, there are *methods* that you can use to describe interactions with objects."

Relationships

"Finally," Trower concluded, "there's a very important concept that you can bring into the interface: that of relationships. Objects don't exist without some context; they exist in some situation. And sometimes that situation has a very powerful effect on the object's implementation—on the way it's presented to the user. For example, one of the most important examples that you'll find in the Windows 95 user interface—and in OLE—is the concept of *containment*: the notion that one object exists in a place, and that place is its *container*." To put it another way, said Trower, the container of an object is the place where the user goes to access the object.

Containers of Objects

Containment is an important concept in the Windows 95 user interface, said Trower, because a container often influences what can be done with an object.

For example, a container can:

- Add commands to an object.
- Hide commands from an object.
- Add properties to an object.
- Hide properties from an object.

These capabilities of containers parallel the capabilities of containers in the natural world. If you put something in a container and then move the container, the object in the container moves with the container. So containment is "a very powerful notion in the interface," said Trower. "It's a very simple relationship that people understand, so there are ways to take advantage of it in the interface."

User-Interface Components

"Another thing you get from the metaphor of objects," said Trower, "is the ability to look at the interface and break it down into component pieces. Just as the material world is built out of atoms and their components, we can describe things in sort of a self-describing, self-repeating fashion and come up with concepts in the interface that allow us to repeat at any level.

"We can look at objects—whether we're talking about a character, up to a full document, up to a full file system—and see that they all share similar aspects to the user interface. They all can have actions; they all can have properties."

So the object metaphor provides a way of referring to objects in the interface without having to provide multiple kinds of interfaces for multiple kinds of objects.

When you add all this up, said Trower, "these aspects are the way people differentiate one thing from another. And we call that the notion of *type*."

User-Interface Object Types

Although "there's a more technical notion of type," said Trower, a different notion of type is used in connection with the Windows 95 user interface terminology. In Windows 95, Trower explained, type is what determines the way the user differentiates one object from another thing in the interface.

"And what you're going to see more and more in the user interface," he said, "is that type is less defined by what you as a developer see as type, and is more defined by what the user sees in terms of how the user interacts with a particular object, and how the user uses that object. That defines more what the type is to the user."

Persistence of Objects

Trower concluded: "The final thing that we get out of the metaphor of objects that's important to reflect in the interface is that of *persistence of state*. In the real world, when an object is created, it automatically exists and persists. And it maintains its state unless another agent, or another object, comes along and changes it. But that's not the model we've had over the past few years in this industry.

"We require users to *save* files because the technology otherwise just assumes that they just go away, because we maintain things in RAM.

"But more and more, what you're seeing—and it's a more natural model for users to understand—is that the action of creation causes an object to *persist*, and that it takes an overt action by the user to make it no longer exist. We're trying to change the model around to a much more natural model for people."

The many new features of the Windows interface pose many new challenges for the designers of Windows 95 applications. The remainder of this chapter describes some of those challenges and outlines some of the methods Microsoft proposes for meeting them.

Managing Objects in Windows 95

Windows 95 has many new features that can simplify the ways in which users work with objects that appear on the desktop. For example:

- The Windows 95 interface lets users open documents by simply double-clicking on their icons, without having to open the applications that created them.
- Objects on the Windows 95 desktop can display popup menus when the user presses the right mouse button.

Along with the new object-management features of Windows 95 comes a new user-interface guideline called the *single-instance model*.

The single-instance guideline says you should allow the user to open only one instance of an application whenever that is possible.

Properties of Objects

Properties of objects are important in Windows 95, and Microsoft suggest that you provide appropriate properties for the objects you create in your application. When you design an object, think about how the user will interact with the object. If the object has attributes that the user can change, write your application in such a way that the user changes the object's attributes by changing its properties.

Opening Documents without Their Applications

One of the most important changes in Windows 95 shifts away from the traditional application-oriented model of opening documents. In previous versions of Windows, documents had to be opened within the applications that created them. In Windows 95 applications, users should be able to open any document from the desktop by double-clicking on its icon. The document should then open by itself, without forcing the application that created it to open first.

Letting documents open by themselves is, of course, the OLE way of doing things—and just in case you don't know this already, Microsoft has decreed that OLE is the only way to go from now on in Windows programming. As you'll see in Chapter 7, which covers OLE in more detail, OLE allows the user to insert an object into a container without forcing the application that created the object to open. Instead, the object simply merges itself into the interface of the existing container.

Similarly, the Windows 95 user interface lets you right-click anywhere on the desktop and choose an item from the menu that pops up. Windows 95 then automatically executes the menu option you have chosen. If the menu item you have chosen is connected with a particular application, Windows 95 does not have to open that application to execute the menu option you have chosen.

To demonstrate how that operation works, here's how you can create a new text document from the desktop, without opening any text-editing application: Simply right-click anywhere on the desktop, choose **New** from the menu that pops up, and then choose **Text**

Document from the hierarchical menu that appears beside the **New** item (Figure 1.7).

Figure 1.7 Opening a popup menu on the Windows 95 desktop

A new **Notepad** icon then appears on the desktop, right in the location you have chosen (Notepad is a simple text-editing application provided by the desktop).

When you double-click the Notepad icon, a new **Notepad** window opens (Figure 1.8). But the Notepad application never actually opens—at least, not in the way that ordinary Windows applications used to open—and you are spared both the inconvenience and the overhead that would be required to open the Notepad application in the conventional way.

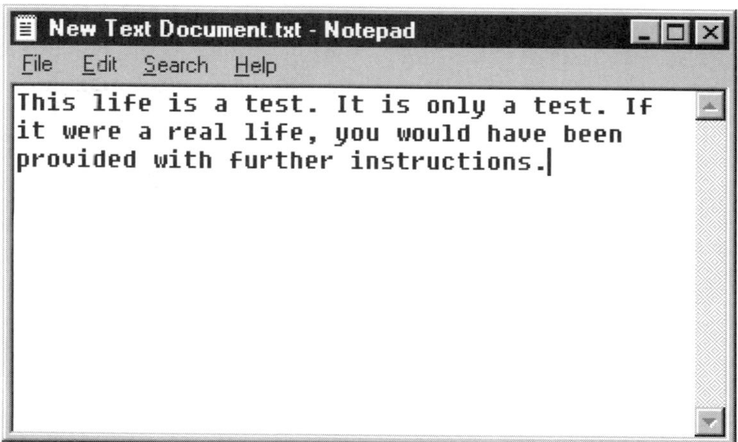

Figure 1.8 A Notepad Document

The Single-Instance Model

The user-interface guideline that proposes the single-instance model grew out of extensive user testing conducted at Microsoft. During user tests, Microsoft found that users sometimes did not understand what was happening when they found that multiple instances of an application were running at the same time. Sometimes a user would inadvertently open a new instance of an application, see an empty window, and mistakenly believe that a document that he or she had been editing had disappeared.

To prevent this kind of confusion, Microsoft now suggests that you allow the user to open only one instance of an application whenever that is possible. When a user attempts to open an application that is already open, Microsoft suggests that you simply bring the existing window to the top instead of opening another window, provided that technique makes sense in your application. If it doesn't, Microsoft suggests that you at least open a dialog box asking the user if he or she really wants to open a second instance of your application.

Transfer Operations in Windows 95

Transfer operations are one of the most important interactive capabilities of Windows 95. A transfer operation is a procedure that can be broken down into three basic operations: *moving*, *copying*, or *linking* an object.

All commonly used editing procedures are transfer operations. And some procedures that are not normally considered editing operations can also be viewed as transfer operations. For example, printing is in a sense a copying operation, so it can be considered a transfer operation. Sending mail is usually either a moving or a copying operation, depending upon how it is set up in an application, so it, too, can be categorized as a transfer operation.

The Windows 95 supports transfer operations in two different ways:

- Through the *command model*—the cut-and-paste model that has long been familiar to users of Windows applications.
- Through the *direct manipulation model*—a Windows 95 term used to refer to the dragging and dropping of objects. Dragging and dropping has been available in the Windows shell since the days of Windows 3.1, and has now been expanded into an important transfer-operation model for Windows 95 applications.

Cutting and Pasting Objects

Until now, data was transferred from one application to another in Windows using the familiar **Cut/Copy/Paste** menu commands. In Windows 95, **Cut/Copy/Paste** has become a universal paradigm for moving objects around.

In an application that supports OLE (see Chapter 7), the user can select a data object, move to the desktop, and paste the object on the desktop. The object then becomes what Windows 95 calls a *scrap object*.

Alternatively, a Windows 95 application can *link* an object to the desktop, or place it in a particular folder or any other kind of file container that the Windows 95 system supports.

As a result, the **Cut/Copy/Paste** paradigm is no longer one that supports transfer operations just between applications. Now it has been made universal across applications, and even within the Windows 95 shell itself. That means that there's now only one command model that users need to know about to perform transfer operations.

Dragging and Dropping Objects

Another transfer-operation technique that's important to support in Windows 95 is the *direct manipulation model*: a Windows 95 term that refers to the ability to drag an object from one location to another.

One of the most common examples of a direct-manipulation drag-and-drop operation is the act of dragging a document into a folder on the Windows desktop (Figure 1.9).

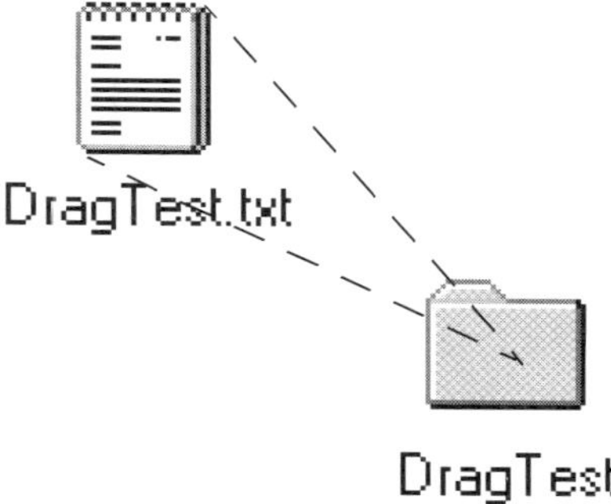

Figure 1.9 Dragging and dropping an object in Windows 95

You can also implement that kind of drag-and-drop functionality in your own applications. The trick is to learn to use OLE, which is introduced in Chapter 6, "Windows 95 and Visual C++," and examined in more detail in Chapter 7, "OLE 95."

Default Drag and Drop

During user testing of the Windows 95 user interface, Microsoft discovered that there was a troublesome problem with dragging and dropping. The problem was this: How do you define what the interpretation of a drag-and-drop operation should be when the user drops the object?

The first solution to this problem that Microsoft engineers came up with was to decide that the container into which an object is dragged has the job of determining what the nature of the operation is. That solution worked in some situations, but in other situations there was still a problem, because the container offered several alternative ways of handling objects dragged into it. For example, a container receiving an object might support both the moving of objects and the copying of objects, and perhaps the linking of objects, too. So the problem of what should be done with an object dragged into the container remained unsolved.

Microsoft engineers then devised a new drag-and-drop mode called *default drag and drop*. The right mouse button supports this kind of dragging and dropping in the Windows 95 shell, and Microsoft hopes that software developers will implement right-mouse-button drag-and-drop operations in their Windows 95 applications.

Here's how right-button dragging and dropping works: When the user presses the right mouse button to drag an object into an OLE container, a menu pops up at the point where the right mouse button is released. This popup menu lets the user choose an option to determine how the receiving container should handle the dropped object. The appearance of the popup menu can vary from application to application. Figure 1.9 on Page 16 shows one example.

If there is an operation that the container carries out by default when an object is dropped, that operation is printed in boldface type in the popup menu.

This is the basic guideline for using right-mouse-button dragging and dropping: If a container in an application can handle a dragged object in only one way—for example, placing it in a folder—the application has no need to implement a right-mouse-button drag-and-drop capability. But if the container offers a choice of operations on the dropped option, right-button dragging and dropping should be used.

The Microsoft Foundation Class (MFC) library—described in Chapter 5, "Windows 95 and the MFC Library"—provides a number of C++ classes that support drag-and-drop operations. Chapter 7, "OLE 95", covers drag-and-drop operations in more detail.

Managing Properties of Objects

Document properties, which OLE fans already know about, have taken on new importance in Windows 95. As mentioned earlier in this chapter (in "Popup Menus and Property Pages" on page 4), when you activate a popup menu on the Windows 95 desktop by right-clicking an icon, one command on the menu is the **Properties** command.

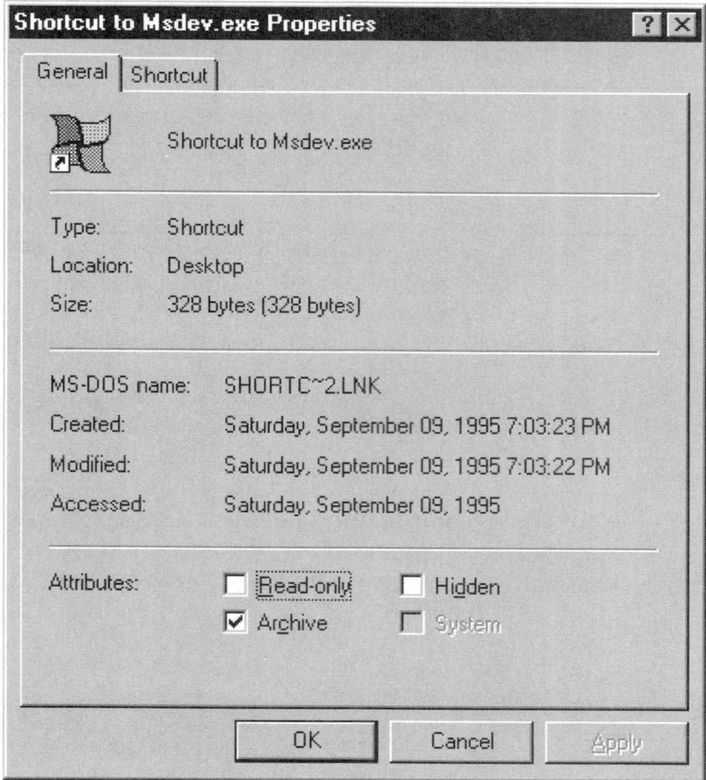

Figure 1.10 A property sheet

When you choose the **Properties** command, Windows 95 displays a *property sheet*—one mechanism for presenting the attributes of an object to the user in Windows 95.

Property Sheets

As you may recall, a property sheet is a dialog box that is designed especially to present a list of an object's properties to the user. Figure 1.10 on page 18 is a typical property sheet for a Windows 95 application.

Generally speaking, a property sheet should be implemented as a modeless dialog box (as shown in Figure 1.10) so the user can make multiple changes in an object's properties without facing the annoyance of a dialog box that keeps disappearing.

Property Pages and Property-Sheet Controls

A property sheet can be equipped with tabbed *property pages* for showing different categories of properties, and it can offer controls such as drop-down lists for moving up and down hierarchies of properties. Finally, a property sheet is usually equipped with the kinds of *transaction buttons* seen in most dialog boxes: that is, a standard row of buttons with labels such as **OK**, **Cancel**, and **Apply**, as shown in Figure 1.10.

The MFC library supplies two Visual C++ classes that you can use to implement property pages in your applications: CPropertyPage and CPropertySheet. Property sheets and property pages are covered in more detail in Chapter 5, "Windows 95 and the MFC Library."

Using Icons in Windows 95

Icons have a more important role in the Windows 95 interface than they had under previous versions of Windows. As mentioned earlier in this chapter, icons are no longer just representations of minimized windows. In Windows 95, an icon is a representation of an object that can be manipulated by the user and can cause operations to be performed on the associated object.

Another important change is that a single icon size is no longer sufficient in Windows 95. Besides the standard 32-bit by 32-bit icon that is familiar to Windows 3.*x* users, Windows 95 supports a 16-bit by 16-bit icon that can appear both in desktop windows (when you click the **Small Icon** menu item) and inside the title bars of windows. (For more about icons and title bars in Windows 95, see the next section, "Window Design in Windows 95.") In addition, Windows 95 supports a giant-size 48-bit by 48-bit icon designed specifically for very high-resolution screen displays.

If you want to make your Windows 95 applications as robust as possible from a user-interface point of view, you should make sure that they support all three sizes of Windows 95 icons.

Another important new change in Windows 95 is that it is no longer enough for you to provide a single icon for each application you create; now you should also design icons for each kind of document that each application creates. That's because Windows 95 users must be able to differentiate between data objects and application objects when both kinds of objects can appear on the desktop.

Window Design in Windows 95

Windows have taken on a whole new appearance in Windows 95. In Windows 95, document windows can be (and should be) equipped with task bars and other useful kinds of gadgets, and application and document icons can appear inside the title bars of windows. Figure 1.11 shows a typical Windows 95 desktop window.

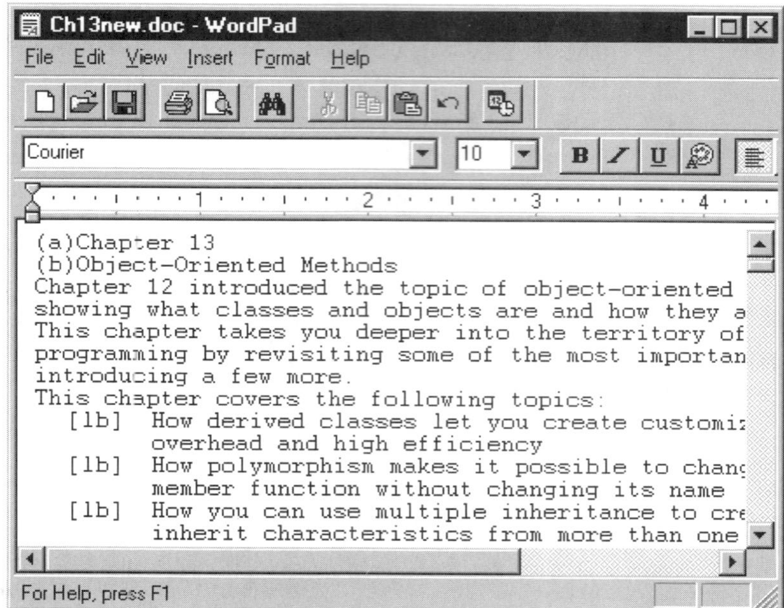

Figure 1.11 A Windows 95 window

Using Title-Bar Icons

As mentioned a couple of pages back, Windows 95 supports a 16-bit by 16-bit icon that can appear inside the title bars of windows. In Windows 95, when a window is associated with an object, a 16-by-16 version of the object's icon appears in the upper left-hand corner of the window's title bar (Figure 1.12).

Figure 1.12 A Windows 95 title-bar icon

It's important to remember that in Windows 95, the icon shown in a window's title bar is not always an application icon. When the user opens a window that displays a document (or data file), the icon that appears in the window's title bar is usually an icon associated with the displayed document—not with the application that created the document.

There are exceptions to this rule, however. For example, the desktop calculator application has no data file, so the icon that appears in the calculator window's title bar is the application's icon.

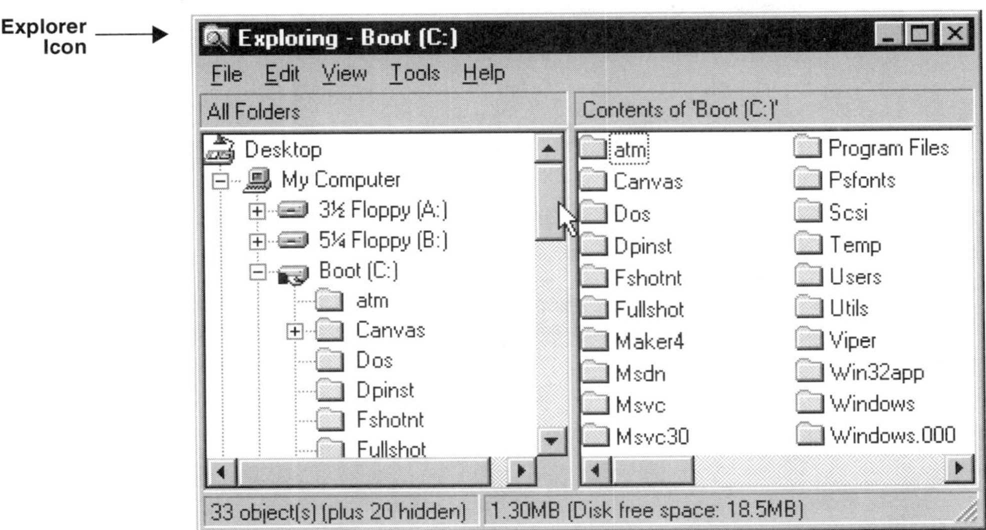

Figure 1.13 The Explorer icon

When the user runs an MDI (multiple-document interface) application, the title bars of different windows associated with the application might display different icons at the same time. Some windows might be associated with data files opened by the application, and they might display document icons. Other windows might be associated with the application itself and might display application icons.

Still another kind of icon that can appear in a title bar is a *tool icon*—that is, an icon that does not represent an application or a data file, but attempts to represent what an application does. For example, when you open the Windows 95 Explorer application, the icon you see in the **Explorer** window's title bar (Figure 1.13 on Page 21) shows a magnifying desk in front of a folder—a graphic representation of one of the Explorer's main functions, which is to browse through the contents of folders.

Formatting Title-Bar Text

Because some windows are associated with data files and others are associated with applications, the formatting of the text in title bars has changed in Windows 95. At first glance, the rules for placing text in title bars in Windows 95 look complicated—even a little arbitrary. Sometimes text in a window's title is the name of document, and sometimes it's the name of a folder. And there are times when it's neither of the above, but is the name of an application.

Figure 1.14 shows three different kinds of titles that can appear in a Windows 95 title bar. The top title bar contains the name of a folder, the middle bar contains the name of an application, and the bottom bar contains the name of a file.

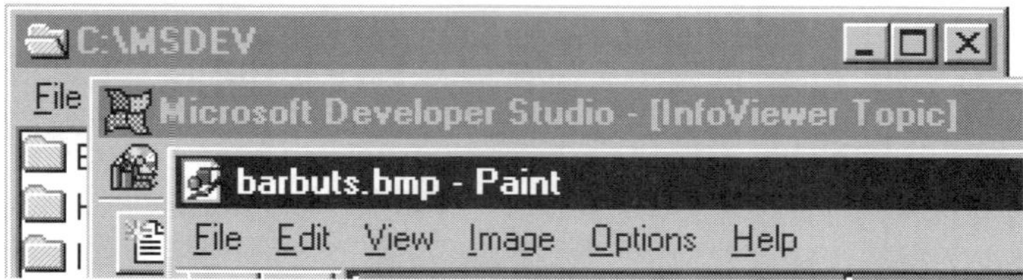

Figure 1.14 Icons and text in title bars

If Figure 1.14 looks confusing, this may be a handy rule to remember about text in Windows 95 title bars: In the title bar of a window, the icon that is displayed should match the first entry that appears in the title bar's text. So, if a data-file icon appears in a title bar, the first name that appears in the title bar's text should be the name of that data file.

Similarly, if an application's icon appears in the title bar, the first name in the title bar's text should be the name of the application.

Title-Bar Popup Menus

Another change you may notice in the design of windows is that there is no longer any such thing as a **System/Control** menu in Windows 95. (The **System/Control** menu, as you may recall, is the menu that popped up when you pressed **Alt+Space** in Windows 3.1. With the **System/Control** menu, you could perform such actions as moving, sizing, or closing a window.)

In Windows 95, what used to called the **System/Control** menu is now simply called a popup menu for the window being displayed—Microsoft sort of wants to forget about it, so it no longer has the dignity of even having a particular name. To activate a window's popup menu, you can still press **Alt+Space**, and the menu that pops up still offers the same functionality (Figure 1.15).

Figure 1.15 A popup menu for a window

The reason Microsoft would like to forget about the menu shown in Figure 1.15 is that it's a holdover from the past; Windows 95 supports the menu mainly for backward compatibility with earlier versions of Windows. It represents a window—not an application, a document, or a tool—so it is not considered a useful part of the Windows 95 system because it does not fit in well with the document-centered model that is so important to Windows 95. So you should just let it remain there and not try to do anything special with it in your Windows 95 applications.

Instead of being concerned with the kind of popup menu shown in Figure 1.15 on Page 23, Microsoft suggests that you provide your application's windows with a Windows 95-style popup menu that opens when the user right-clicks the mouse on the title-bar icon. You should not see a Windows 95 popup menu as being directly associated with the window being displayed. Instead, you should see it as being associated with the *object* that's represented by the window being displayed.

For example, when you click the **Network Neighborhood** icon on the Windows 95 desktop, the popup menu that appears is the one shown in Figure 1.16. This popup menu is associated with networking properties, not with any particular window. Generally, this is the kind of menu that should come up when the user right-clicks a desktop icon that opens a window.

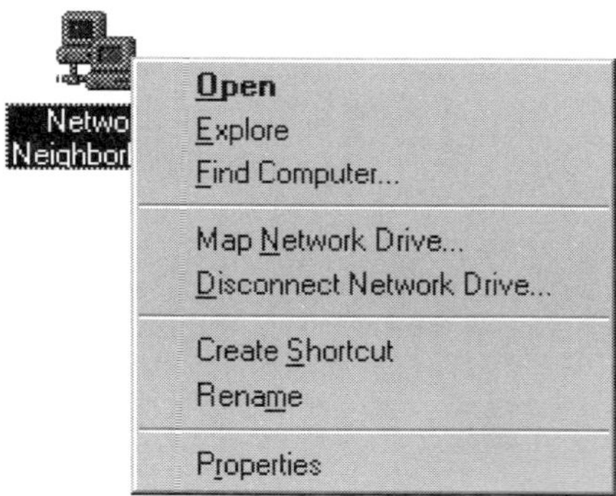

Figure 1.16 A popup menu associated with an object

Title-Bar Buttons

The Windows 95 makeover has brought about some changes in the conventions for the buttons that appear in window title bars. In primary application windows, the minimize and maximize windows have been updated to provide what Microsoft considers a clearer representation of what those operations do (Figure 1.17 on Page 25).

A close box—a welcome addition to a window when a dialog box lacks a **Close** button—has been added to the right-hand end of windows 95 title bars Window Management in Windows 95.

When Windows 95 was in the testing stage, one question that software designers often asked Microsoft designers was: "Can I still do MDI?"

Officially, the answer is yes—but it sounds very much like a qualified yes when you question Microsoft engineer/management/marketing folks closely about MDI.

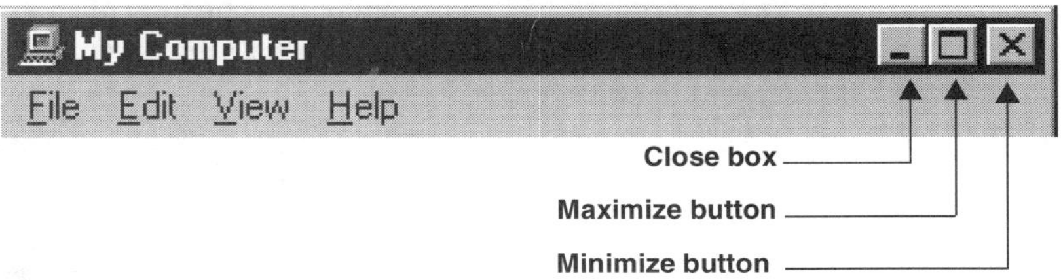

Figure 1.17 Improved title-bar buttons in Windows 95

MDI, as you may know, stands for *multiple-document interface*. In Windows 95, as in earlier versions of windows, an MDI application is an application that supports the use of multiple windows—specifically, a main frame window and as many child windows as an application requires.

An SDI application, in contrast, is an application with a *single-document interface*. An SDI application, as you might guess, supports only a single window.

Is MDI Dead? No, But . . .

In Windows 95, MDI was considered the best kind of architecture for most applications because its windows-within-a-window structure was quite versatile and very powerful; it allowed the user to load data into an application easily and in various ways. But, because the Windows 95 interface is designed to be document-centered rather than application-centered, some software developers have raised doubts over whether the MDI model is well suited to Windows 95.

In Windows 95, MDI continues to offer some benefits, but it now has some drawbacks, too. The main potential drawback is that MDI is a very application-centered interface. In an MDI application, the user often loads things—such as text files, pictures, or data—into the application.

That, of course, is a typical characteristic of an application-centered interface. In a data-centered interface, as mentioned earlier in this chapter, the user can open data objects directly, without having to open an application.

Alternatives to MDI

Because of the differences between the way Windows 3.1 applications work and the way Windows 95 applications work, Microsoft has proposed that developers consider some alternatives to the traditional MDI interface. So far, Microsoft evangelists have presented this proposal as a very gentle suggestion.

Developers who feel that the MDI model still works well for them can continue to use it, asserts Microsoft. "We don't frown on it," said one Microsoft manager. At this stage in the evolution of Windows, this manager explained, Microsoft merely proposes that developers also look at the alternatives to MDI.

Returning to the SDI Model

And what are those alternatives? One is simply to return to the SDI model, which has fallen out of wide use as application developers have increasingly used MDI.

Microsoft believes that the Windows 95 desktop, with its task bar (Figure 1.18), does a better job of organizing documents for the user—while allowing the user to switch back and forth between them—than any MDI application can do.

Now that a task bar has been added to the Windows interface, you may find that many applications you create work just fine with a single window. When that is the case, it may be better to design your application as an SDI application than to confront the user with the complexity of an MDI program.

Figure 1.18 The Windows 95 task bar

Microsoft has confirmed its newly rediscovered commitment to SDI by using the SDI approach in the design of many shell applications (such as WordPad and Paint) that have been designed or redesigned in Windows 95. Experiment with WordPad, Paint, and some of the other shell applications provided with Windows 95, and you will see that they have shed their MDI complexity and have returned to the simpler days of SDI.

Implementing Parent Windows as OLE Containers

In some cases, even with the navigational help offered by the Windows 95 task bar, an application really does require the kind of multiple- window support that straight SDI support does not provide. When you create such an application, there are alternatives to the MDI approach.

One alternative is to create an SDI window that is an OLE-style *container*, rather than a traditional MDI parent, of other windows. (Yes, this is still another way in which Microsoft is promoting the use of OLE. For more about OLE, see Chapter 7.)

Suppose you implement an SDI window as an OLE container. Then, when the user opens a window inside your application's main window, the new window is an OLE object that the main window contains.

This approach makes your application data-centered rather than window-centered, because it automatically resolves the question of whether the user has opened an object inside your application's main window, or has merely opened a window. In traditional MDI applications, the user can easily become confused about a child window that appears inside a parent window, because only the child window is really there—the object that it represents is not.

When a user opens a child window that is also an OLE object, this confusion disappears; the new window that the user opens is a real object that the user can manipulate directly, not merely a representation of an object.

The Workbook Model

Another way to build MDI-like functionality into a non-MDI application is to create a mechanism called a *workbook* (see Figure 1.19 on page 28). A workbook is an interface element that lets the user of your application page between different views. A workbook can be designed in various ways; it can offer a set of views of the same document, or it can offer views of different documents that are loaded into memory at the same time.

A workbook, like an OLE-based parent window, is a kind of container. Furthermore, it is a more structured kind of container than a traditional MDI parent window is.

When you base a Windows application on a workbook model, the user can easily page from one view to another (using tabs, menu items, or other interface devices) without having to be concerned with all the point-and-click operations that it takes to manage a hodgepodge of MDI windows displayed on a screen.

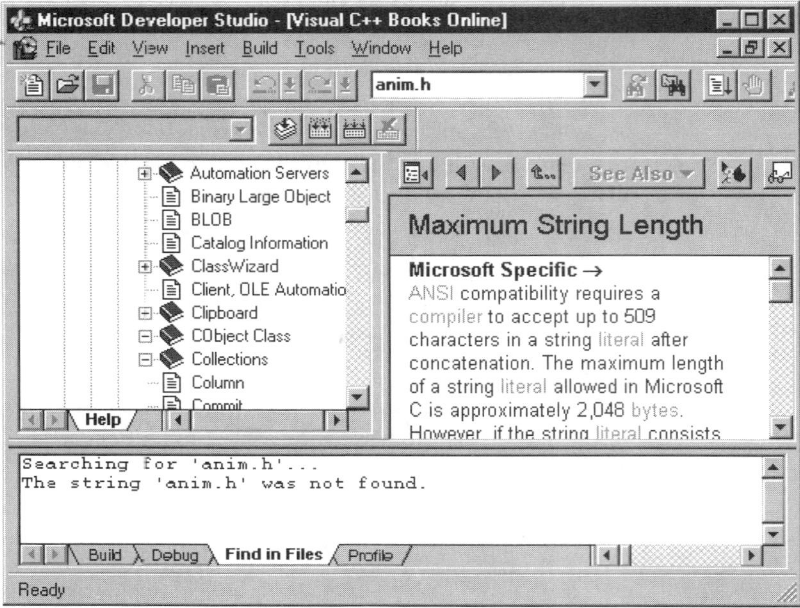

Figure 1.19 Example of a workbook interface (Visual C++)

Workbook-based applications can be designed in many different ways. Figure 1.19 is one example of what a workbook can look like in a Windows 95 application.

New Controls in Windows 95

Windows 95 offers a host of new controls to the software designer. In fact, Version 4.0 of the Microsoft Foundation Class (MFC) library gives developers access to many of the same controls that are used in the Windows 95 user interface. That means they are pretested, and it also means that you can use the Windows 95 interface as a model for using them in your own applications.

One example of a system control that is now available to developers is the standard docking toolbar that the Windows 95 system uses in its applications (see Figure 1.20 on page 29). Along with its docking feature, this new toolbar supports button-wrapping (automatic adjustments in the numbers of columns and rows of button, depending on the user resizes the window). That makes it an ideal palette window, as well as a toolbar.

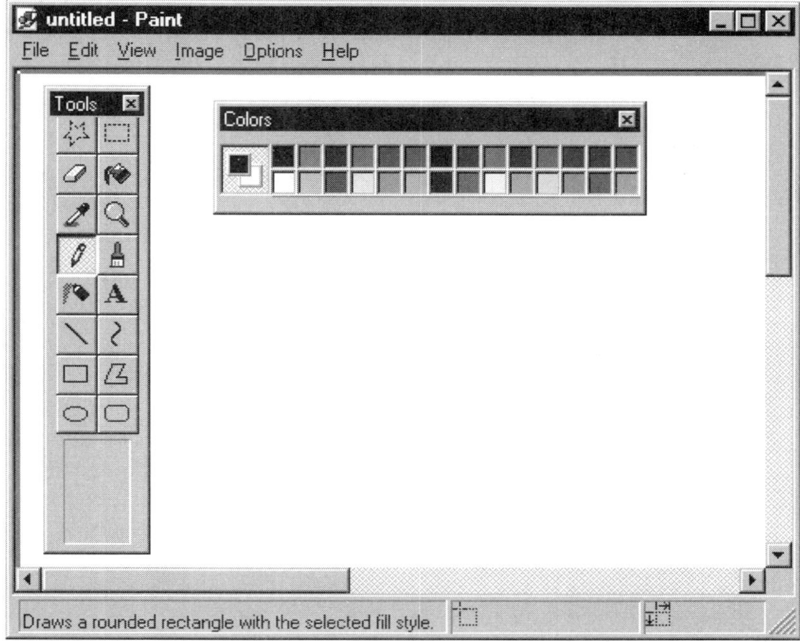

Figure 1.20 Windows 95 toolbars

The Windows 95 toolbar control also supports *tool tips*—small text windows that pop up as the mouse moves over toolbar buttons to inform the user of each button's functionality. (Figure 1.21). You can customize the tool tips displayed by a toolbar, or you can let the system automatically provide default tool tips, which merely display the name of each button.

Figure 1.21 A tool tip

These are other new controls made available to developers in MFC 4.0:

- *Status bars*, which can be placed at the bottom of windows to provide the user with important messages and notifications of events.
- A *tree-view control*, which creates a hierarchical view for navigating through various icons. Tree views are often used in

browser-style applications such as the Explorer, and can also be used to display other kinds of other hierarchical views such as outlines.

- A *list-view control*, which can display lists of graphics objects such as icons.
- A *column heading control*, which can be used to place column titles at heads of lists. The column heading control supports automatic resizing and can trap events—including user events—so you can reformat list boxes when necessary.
- A *slide control* with a pointer that you can move back and forth (or up and down) to move to a specific location in an object—for example, to a particular shot in a video movie or to a particular part of a waveform sound.
- A handy *progress-bar control* that you can use to track the progress of time-consuming operations. Windows programmers have been designing their own slide controls for years now. Now they don't have to any more.
- *Property sheets* that can be used to construct tabbed dialog boxes.
- *Tab controls* that can be used to equip dialog boxes and other objects with tabs.
- A *rich text box* that supports RTF (rich text format) files, multiple fonts and some fairly complex text-editing and find-and-replace operations. The WordPad application that you can activate from the desktop uses the rich text box control—and now this same control is available for you to use in your own applications.

For a closer look at these and other new controls, see Chapter 5, "Windows 95 and the MFC Library."

Online Help in Windows 95

Windows 95 provides a much more consistent model for online help than earlier versions of Windows provided. New help features offered to Windows developers include:

- Context-sensitive help
- Task help
- The Help Topics Browser
- Help wizards
- Reference help.

Context-Sensitive Help

In secondary windows—such as dialog boxes, property sheets, and the like—you can provide a special kind of button. It looks like a small question mark (Figure 1.22). When the user clicks on the question-mark button, the command that the user is executing is called the "What's this?" command.

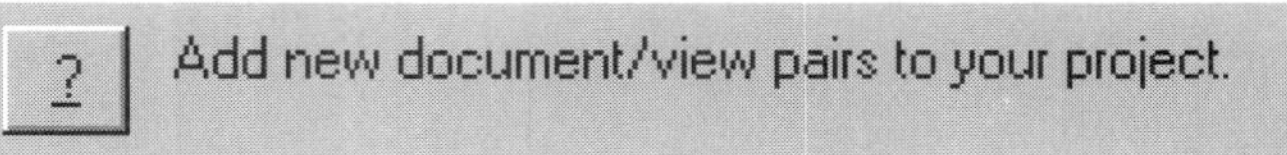

Figure 1.22 A 'What's this?' button

When the user clicks a "What's this?" button in a secondary window, the next object that the user clicks on does not perform the action that would otherwise be expected. Instead, Windows displays a *contextual help window* that describes the object the user has clicked on, as also shown in Figure 1.23.

You can use the **Shift+F1** key as a shortcut key for popping up a contextual help window.

Figure 1.23 A contextual help window

Task Help

Another kind of online help offered in Windows 95 is *task help*—a method of making online help available in a more conventional kind of window (Figure 1.24).

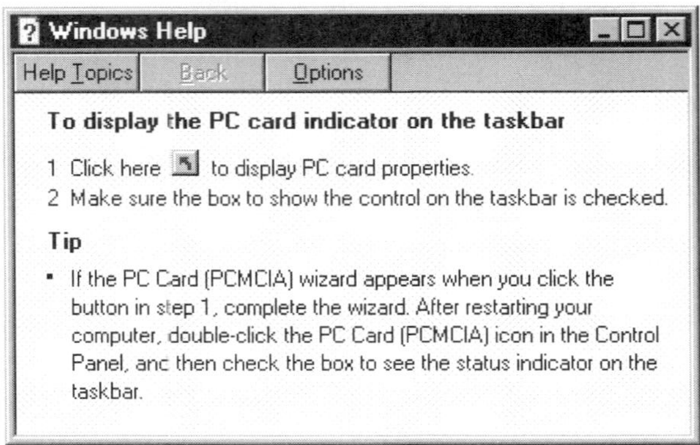

Figure 1.24 The task help window

Microsoft decided to build a task-help feature into Windows 95 because user tests showed that one question frequently asked by users was, "How do I do this?"

Windows 95 task help attempts to answer this question by displaying a help window like the one shown in Figure 1.24. As you can see, a task-help window can contain various kinds of buttons, including a small arrow button that the user can click to display additional help windows.

One way to provide task-help windows in Windows 95 is to have the user access them through the Help Topics Browser, introduced under the next heading.

The Help Topics Browser

The help topics browser (Figure 1.25 on Page 33) is a generic-style interface that the user can access by simply selecting a **Help** menu item or by using other kinds of interfaces that your application may provide. In Windows 95, the help topics browser is the central location where users go most often to obtain general help.

The help topics browser is a property sheet (tabbed dialog box) that is designed especially to respond to user requests for help. It provides two different property sheets for locating help topics: a *context view* (shown in Figure 1.25) and an *index view* (Figure 1.26 on Page 33).

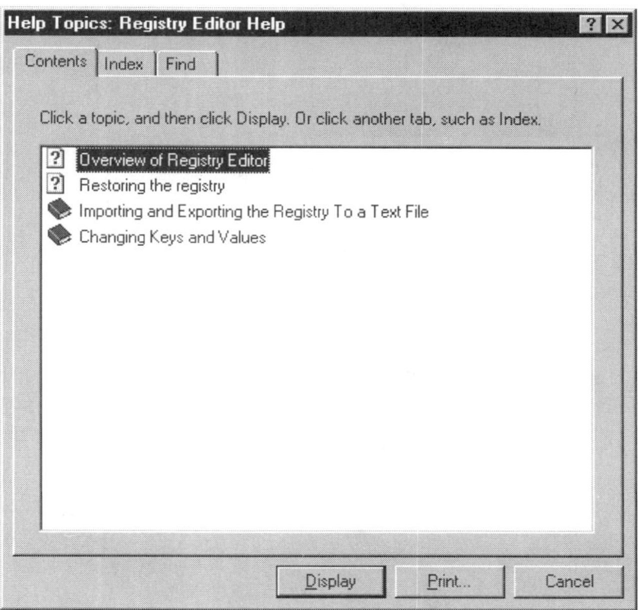

Figure 1.25 The help topics browser

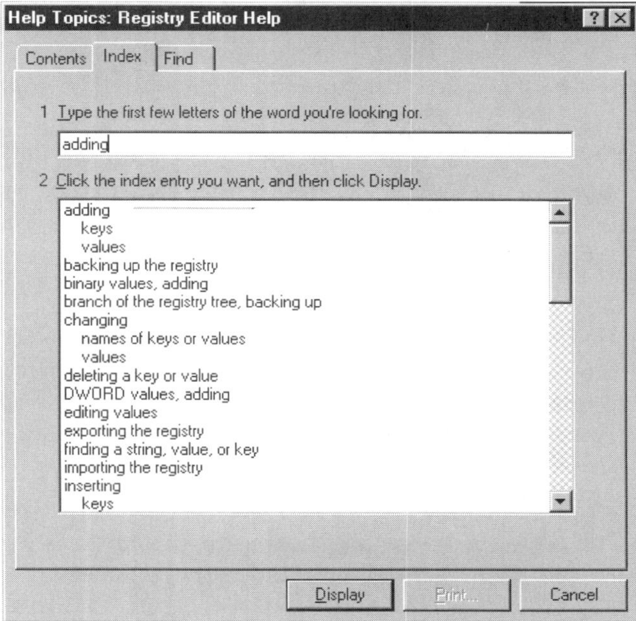

Figure 1.26 The help topics browser's Index view

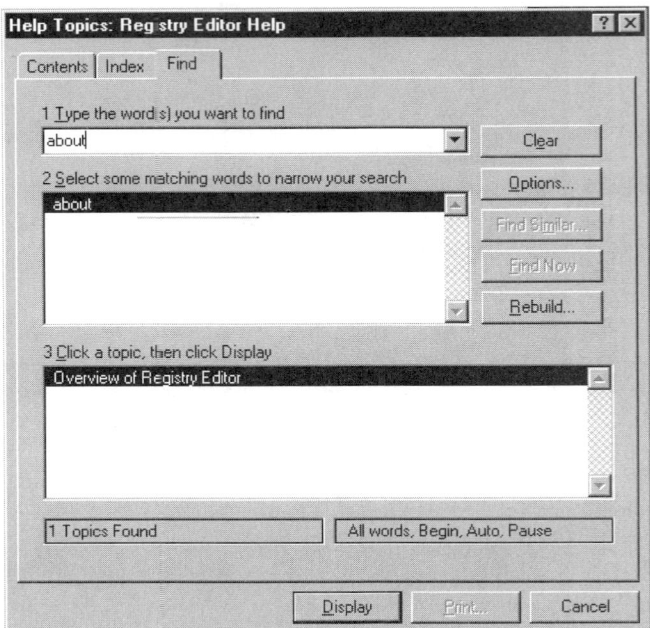

Figure 1.27 The help topics browsers Find view

An index view (Figure 1.26 on page 33) is a kind of outline view that allows the user to find topics easily using an index of topics offered in a help file.

The help topics browser also offers a *find view* property sheet (Figure 1.27) where the user can go to track down help topics listed in the index.

Help Wizards

In Windows 95, wizards are special kinds of dialog boxes designed to simplify multi-step procedures that users have to perform. When users are required to take multiple steps to perform an action—for example, to set up the configuration of an application they are installing—Windows 95 often uses a wizard to help the user out. Visual C++ provides a *help wizard* that is especially designed for setting up help tools.

One example of a help wizard is the dialog box shown in Figure 1.28 on page 35. It opens when Windows 95 is about to compile an index of help topics. The first time the user clicks the **Find** tab in the help topics browser, Windows 95 displays a help wizard like the one shown in

Figure 1.28. The user can then select options offered by the help wizard to complete the index-compilation task.

Figure 1.28 A help wizard dialog box

The Windows 95 Registry

One tool that has taken on major new importance in Windows 95 (and in Windows NT, too) is the *system registry*. Although the system registry (usually referred to simply as the *registry*) has many powerful and versatile capabilities, it is probably best known as the tool that will eventually replace the CONFIG.SYS and AUTOEXEC.BAT files.

But that is not nearly all that the system registry can do, as you'll see in this section. The more you learn about the system registry, the more you'll understand that it is one of the most important features of Windows 95.

Besides serving as a replacement for CONFIG.SYS and AUTOEXEC.BAT, the registry can be used to store:

- Important information about your application, such as the name of the program, its version number, your company's name, and other information about your company.
- Information about the kinds of documents or files your application can create. When you store that kind of information in the

registry, the Windows 95 user does not have to start up your application in order to open a document that it has created. Instead, the user can simply click on the document's icon. Your application will then open the document. That saves the user the trouble of explicitly opening your application.

- A command line that is executed when the user of your application uses the Windows 95 shell to open a file associated with your program.
- Uninstall information that allows your application and all its data to be removed from the user's Windows 95 system safely and easily, without interfering with any other software running on the system.
- Path information that allows your application to run under Windows 95.

This section introduces the Windows 95 registry and shows how you can create applications that support the use of the registry. An example program named REGDEMO.EXE, presented at the end of this chapter, shows how the registry works and can help you learn to write Windows 95 programs with registry support built in. Figure 1.29 shows the output of the REGDEMO program.

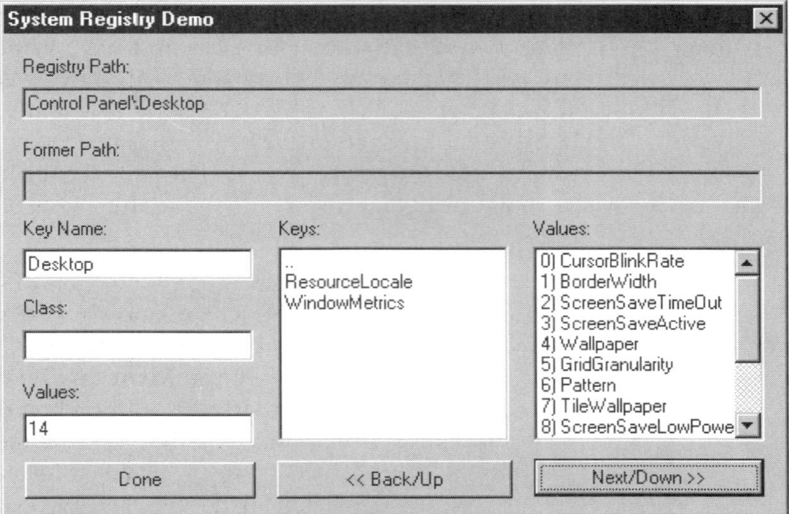

Figure 1.29 Output of the REGDEMO program

Initializing the System with the System Registry

From the point of view of a system administrator, the Windows 95 registry is a kind of turbocharged combination of the old CONFIG.SYS and AUTOEXEC.BAT files used by MS-DOS and Windows 3.*x*. The CONFIG.SYS and AUTOEXEC.BAT files, as Windows 3.*x* programmers know, are a pair of text-based executable files that run automatically every time you start MS-DOS (with or without also starting Windows).

The CONFIG.SYS file configures the user's computer for various kinds of hardware devices that might be installed in the system. The AUTOEXEC.BAT file can perform functions similar to those performed by CONFIG.SYS, and also performs other kinds of initialization tasks.

Windows 95 reluctantly supports the use of the CONFIG.SYS and AUTOEXEC.BAT files, but only for the purpose of backwards compatibility—that is, because many 16-bit device drivers and many 16-bit applications that are still in use rely on information stored in CONFIG.SYS and AUTOEXEC.BAT and wouldn't run without them. But Windows 95 itself has no need for CONFIG.SYS or AUTOEXEC.BAT.

If you install Windows 95 from scratch, and from then on use only 32-bit Windows 95 software and plug-and-play Windows 95 device drivers, your Windows 95 system will never create or use a CONFIG.SYS or AUTOEXEC.BAT file. If you don't if you have any old 16-bit software or 16-bit devices hanging around, your Windows 95 system will run perfectly well—in fact, it will boot up and run faster—without having to bother about any CONFIG.SYS or AUTOEXEC.BAT files.

Although the registry can do a much better job of configuring and initializing a system than CONFIG.SYS and AUTOEXEC.BAT can do, most Windows 95 users won't be throwing out the CONFIG.SYS and AUTOEXEC.BAT files for a while yet. Many 16-bit Windows applications—and many 16-bit device drivers—depend on the CONFIG.SYS and AUTOEXEC.BAT files, and wouldn't work without them. Applications and device drivers that rely on information stored in CONFIG.SYS and AUTOEXEC.BAT will probably be around for some time, so Windows 95 has not yet done away with these two infamous files quite yet.

Eventually, though, as old applications that require CONFIG.SYS and AUTOEXEC.BAT fade out of existence, their usefulness will begin to diminish. And maybe one day they'll be gone forever.

Because the days of CONFIG.SYS and AUTOEXEC.BAT are numbered, you definitely should stop using them to configure and initialize your applications. Instead, you should become familiar with the system registry and use it to configure the user's system to run all your applications.

Other Important Functions of the System Registry

As mentioned earlier, the system registry does much more than just replace CONFIG.SYS and AUTOEXEC.BAT. It also configures and initializes applications that are designed to run under Windows 95, and it provides a storage area for the kinds of data that many Windows 3.x applications used to stow away in other kinds of ASCII files such as WIN.INI and SYSTEM.INI. Most important, the registry manages various kinds of interactions between Windows 95 applications and the Windows 95 system.

Overall, the system registry is so important in the world of Windows 95 programming that applications must support the use of the registry to qualify for Microsoft's Windows 95 logo.

Capabilities of the System Registry

In Windows 95, the system registry is a binary file (not an ASCII file) that can do everything that CONFIG.SYS and AUTOEXEC.BAT used to do, and much more. For example, if several people use the same Windows 95 workstation, the registry can configure the workstation differently for each individual user, depending on who has logged on.

If you're a system administrator, you can also use the registry to configure different workstations connected across a network. Workstations connected across a network can be configured in different ways, depending on what kind of job each workstation performs. The registry can even recognize an individual user (for example, the system administrator) who may log on from time to time on different machines. By recognizing an individual user's logon name and password, the registry can set up a correct profile for the user, no matter what workstation he or she uses to log on.

Using the Registry in Windows 95 Applications

The Windows 95 registry is also an important tool for software developers. In fact, if you want your applications to qualify for Microsoft's "Windows 95 compatible" logo, they must fully support the use of the registry.

An application that supports use of the registry must register itself on the user's system at installation time and must store any startup information that it needs—such as communications passwords, fonts, and information about the kinds of files it generates—in the system registry. A registry-friendly application written for Windows 95 should not store data in CONFIG.SYS, in AUTOEXEC.BAT, or in initialization files reserved for use by the system, such as WIN.INI or SYSTEM.INI. (WIN.INI and SYSTEM.INI are still present in Windows 95, but are strictly off limits to applications; they are reserved for use by the system. Instead of cluttering up WIN.INI or SYSTEM.INI with application-specific information, a well-behaved Windows 95 application must stay away from them store its configuration and initialization data in the registry.)

Your application can use the registry as a long-term storage area for any kind of information that it needs to keep on file in the user's system when the system is not running. For example, if your company sells games, you can design each game you create in such a way that it stores the current score and the current level in the registry each time the user quits. You can then retrieve that information from the registry the next time the user starts up the game.

Of course, if you store that kind of information in the registry, you should make sure that your storage needs aren't too great. Storing too much information in the registry can make it grow much larger than it should be and, and can even slow down the whole system. If your application needs to store large amounts of information—for example, a database of system users and their e-mail addresses—you shouldn't even think about storing that data in the registry. Instead, you should create your own database file out on a disk somewhere and store the information there.

Using the Registry Properly

By storing the right kind of information in the registry, you can automate the way Windows 95 handles your applications and their documents and data when the user takes certain actions that Windows 95 supports. For example, when you register a Windows 95 application, you can place DOS-style filename extensions in the registry to show what kinds of documents your application create. A Windows 95 user can then open any document your application has created by simply double-clicking on document's desktop icon, without having to go through the intermediate step of opening your application.

You can also store machine-configuration information in the registry—for example, information about user preferences such as screen colors, screen wallpaper, and screen savers. When you have stored preferences such as these in the registry, they are activated as soon as the user starts up your application.

Placing Information in the Registry

One of the most important things to know about the registry is that it stores system information in *binary* files instead of in text-based files such as CONFIG.SYS and AUTOEXEC.BAT. That means you can't open registry files and read them directly with an ASCII text editor. To view and edit the contents of your workstation's registry, you must use a special tools such as the REGEDIT editor (described in "Using the REGEDIT Editor" on page 43).

Similarly, you can't place initialization or configuration information about your Windows 95 application into the registry by simply writing data to an ASCII file. Instead, you must use special registry-related functions provided in the Win32 software development kit, or Win32 SDK. (The Win32 SDK is provided with Visual C++, Symantec C++, and other Windows 95 software-development packages. It is described in more detail in Chapter 4, "The Win32 API.")

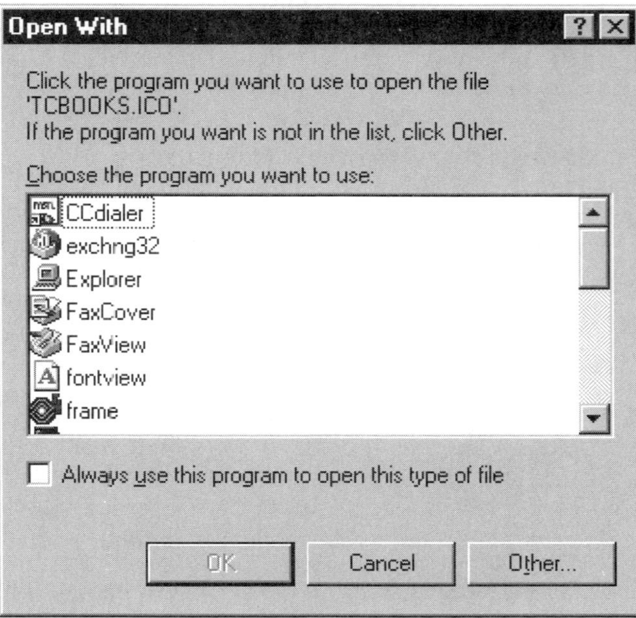

Figure 1.30 The Open With dialog box

You can store many different kinds of configuration data in the Windows 95 registry. For example, the registry is a good place to store the *type* of data that your application creates and uses. (In Windows 95 jargon, *type* is what determines the way the user differentiates one object from another thing in the interface; for more details, see "User-Interface Object Types" on page 11.)

If you store information about your application's type in the registry, Windows 95 can execute your application when the user double-clicks the icon of a document your application has created. If you don't register your application's type, your application is more of a clunker; Windows 95 assigns generic icons to you program's documents because the system has no way to associate them with any stored icons. More important, if you don't register your program's type, Windows 95 does not have the information it needs to open a document automatically when the user clicks on the document's icon. Instead, the system displays an **Open With** dialog box like the one shown in Figure 1.30 on page 40, prompting the user to type in the name of the application that created the document.

To register the types associated with your application and its documents, all you have to do is record their filename extensions in the registry. (In Windows 95, as in MS-DOS, a filename extension is a three-letter extension following a dot.) Windows 95 can then find your application and open it when the user clicks on an appropriate document icon.

Registering an Application's Resources

You can store information about an application's resources, as well as information about its associated data types, in the system registry. It is especially important to record your application's icons in the registry. Then the system can display your program's icons properly on the Windows 95 desktop and can use them in a neat and consistent way when the user is executing your application.

Along with your program's icon, you can also register other kinds of resources that your application uses. Registered resources can include bitmaps, menus, and any multimedia resources your application uses, such as video clips and sounds. The system can then help you manage your program's resources while it is running.

There are several ways to provide your applications with resources that the system registry recognizes. You can embed them in your application's executable (.EXE) file, or in your application's resource (.RES) file. And you can store icons in icon files (.ICO), Windows metafiles (.WMF), or as device-dependent or device-independent bitmap (.BMP) files. The system can create icons using any of these file types, as long as you register your icons and their file types properly with the system registry.

Ways to Place Information in the Registry

There are three main ways to place information in the system registry:

- To store registry information about an individual computer, an individual computer user, or a particular group of computers connected across a network, you can use an interactive tool such as the REGEDIT editor, which is supplied with Windows 95. The REGEDIT tool is designed primarily for use by system administrators. It is not intended for casual Windows 95 users, and it is not documented in entry-level user manuals. But when you are designing Windows 95 applications, REGEDIT can be a useful tool for testing your software to see how it interacts with the registry. REGEDIT is also a useful tool for learning about the registry.
- To help you build registry support into your applications, the Win32 SDK provides a number of registry-related functions. For example, you can place information in the registry by calling the `RegCreate` key function or the `RegSetValue` function, and you can retrieve information stored in the registry by calling functions such as `RegEnumKeyEx`, `RegEnumValue`, or `RegQueryInfoKey`. The example program presented later in this chapter (see "Example Program: Exploring the Registry" on page 48) shows how you can use these and other registry-related functions in your Windows 95 programs.
- The easiest way to make your application registry-friendly is to create an installer program using an installation-generator package that supports the use of the Windows 95 registry. If you write your Windows 95 application using Visual C++, you can create registry-ready installers for your program by using the InstallShield package that is provided with Visual C++. With InstallShield, you can easily register your applications and their resources with the user's Windows 95 system at install time. InstallShield can automatically equip your application with an "uninstall" program that can remove your program and all its data from the user's system on demand. (You'll need to provide uninstall tools with your applications if you want your programs to qualify for the Windows 95 logo.)

Using the REGEDIT Editor

One good way to start learning about the registry is to run the REGEDIT.EXE program. When REGEDIT starts, it opens a GUI (graphical user interface) editor that you can use to examine your system's registry and experiment with it.

The REGEDIT.EXE application is supplied with Windows 95, but Microsoft has hidden it from ordinary users quite efficiently by not providing any documentation and making the program accessible only from an MS-DOS command. To execute REGEDIT.EXE, you must open a Windows 95 console window (console windows are described in Chapter 8) and execute the DOS command

```
REGEDIT
```

Windows 95 then opens a window like the one shown in Figure 1.31.

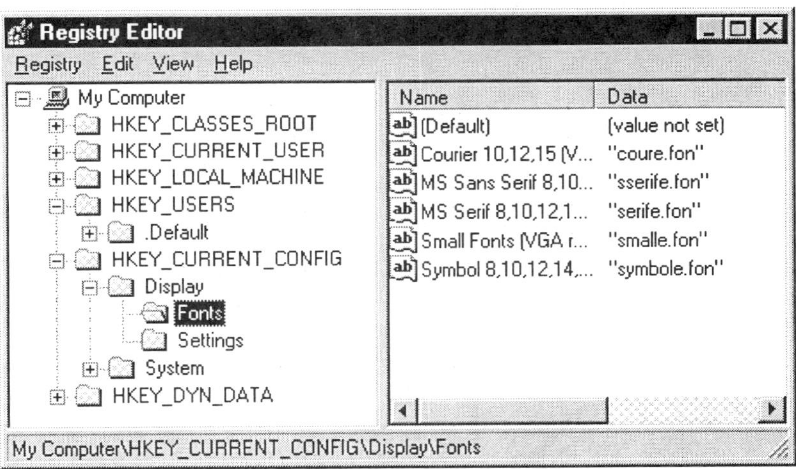

Figure 1.31 The REGEDIT editor

Structure of the Registry

As you can see, the REGEDIT editor displays registry information in a two-panel window. The left panel contains a directory-like tree structure that will be explained in a moment. The right panel shows a list of icons associated with objects that have been registered with the system. In the REGEDIT window shown Figure 1.31, the right panel contains a list of registered fonts.

The REGEDIT window is also equipped with a menu bar. By selecting items from the registry menu, you can import and export registry files, print registry files, and connect to the registry files of remote computers. From the Edit menu, you can add new information to the registry and delete information from the registry.

The left panel of the REGEDIT window can be confusing because it appears to show a hierarchy of folders. However, the icons in that panel are not folders. Instead, they are containers that are specially set up by the system to hold information about objects stored in the registry. Because they are not really folders, the only way you can access the information they contain is by using special tools such as the REGEDIT editor or by embedding registry support in your program.

As Figure 1.31 on Page 43 illustrates, the data containers used by the registry are arranged in a tree-like hierarchy. All the containers that reside at the root level of this hierarchy have names that begin with the characters HKEY_ and are called *keys*. Each key in the registry has a set of subcontainers called *subkeys*.

Every Key Has a Handle

Why do the names of registry keys begin with the characters HKEY_? To show software developers that key names are handles that can be used in programs. (A handle, as you may know, is a value used to identify a resource uniquely so that a program can access it. Handles are widely used in Windows programming; if you don't know what they are, you might want to read a good book on Windows programming such as *Programming Windows 3.1* by Charles Petzold or one of the other Windows programming books listed in the Bibliography.)

The registered objects displayed in the right panel of the REGEDIT window are called *value entries*, or simply *values*. When you select a subkey icon in the left panel by clicking the mouse, any value entries that the selected subkey contains appear in the right panel of the REGEDIT window.

In Figure 1.31, for example, a subkey icon named **Font** is selected in the left panel of the REGEDIT window, and a list of font information that the **Font** subkey contains is visible in the right panel.

As you can see, the Windows 95 registry is a database with a tree structure similar to that of a traditional directory-and-file system. The Windows 95 registry, like a traditional directory-and-file system, a pathname-style system to assign unique names to keys and values stored in the registry. In the same way that a fully qualified filename can be used to access a particular file in a file-and-directory system, a registry key can be used to access a particular value stored in the registry.

Registry Keys

Each key in the Windows 95 registry is used as a container for a different kind of registration information. Information stored in each key can be subdivided into subcontainers called *subkeys*.

Windows 95 provides six predefined keys that can contain standard kinds of configuration information. Figure 1.31 on Page 43 lists these six predefined keys. At any time you like, you can use tools such as the REGEDIT editor to define keys of your own and add them to your system's registry.

These are the six predefined keys recognized by Windows 95, and the kinds of information they can contain:

- HKEY_CLASSES_ROOT—Contains object linking and embedding (OLE) information and information about the relationships that exist among file classes.
- HKEY_CURRENT_USER—Contains a user profile of the user who is currently logged on. This information includes environment variables set by the current user and the user's personal program groups, desktop settings, network connections, printers, and application preferences.
- HKEY_LOCAL_MACHINE—Contains information about the local workstation currently in use, including startup control data and hardware and operating system data. Hardware information stored in the HKEY_LOCAL_MACHINE key includes data about the local workstation's bus types, the system's memory, and device drivers used by the system.
- HKEY_USERS—Contains all currently loaded user profiles, including the one maintained in the HKEY_CURRENT_USER key. The HKEY_CURRENT_USER key is always a subkey of the HKEY_USERS key and is always the default profile. On a server, the HKEY_USERS key does not maintain profiles for users who access the server remotely. Instead, their profiles are loaded into the registries on their own local computers.
- HKEY_CURRENT_CONFIG—A new key predefined specifically for Windows 95 (not predefined for Windows NT). The HKEY_-CURRENT_CONFIG key is mapped to a branch inside HKEY_LOCAL_MACHINE. Applications should use this tree to store non-user-specific configuration information that pertains to

hardware. For example, an application might store a different server name for its data, depending on whether the system is attached to a network.

- HKEY_DYN_DATA—Another new Windows 95-specific key that contains up-to-date values used by the registry itself and by the Windows 95 *configuration manager*. The configuration manager is a keeps track of the current system configuration and maintains a set of performance statistics that show how the system is running.

Extending the Registry

One of the most useful features of the registry is its extensibility. You can add commands to the registry for your files and for other file types that are in the system. For example, suppose you write a special piece of code to modify files created by a particular application.

Because the registry is extensible, you can associate your applications and documents they create with popup menu commands that are easily accessible to the Windows 95 user. Using registry functions provided by the Windows SDK, you can add menu commands to the popup menu that appears each time the user right-clicks on a document created by your application. You can then write code that executes each time the user chooses the popup menu command that you have provided.

You can also write code that provides property pages for objects associated with applications you have registered. If you wish, you can create specific properties for objects associated with your applications and store those properties in the registry. Then you can place information about those properties on a property sheet associated with your application. When you have done that, the Windows 95 user can display your property sheet by right-clicking on a document associated with your application and then choosing the **Properties** item from the document's popup menu. When the document's property sheet opens, the user can change its properties using whatever property-sheet items you have provided.

Finally, you can use the registry to create special views for registered objects. One registry-related Win32 command is the `QuickView` command. With the `QuickView` command, you can display a summary view of what an application's output looks like without opening the application. The registry supports several different kinds of `QuickViews` that you can use to view the outputs of applications. You can also create your own custom viewers.

Registry Keys You Should Know About

As mentioned earlier in this section, there are two ways to create a Windows 95 program that supports the system registry. One way is to build registry support into your application using Win32 functions that interact with the registry. The other method is to create an installation program that automatically registers your application and its data and resources. The easiest way to do that is to design an installer using a commercial installer generator such as the InstallShield package provided with Visual C++.

The Application Information Key

No matter which method you use, there are certain fundamental principles about the registry that you should be familiar with. For example, you should know about an important registry key called the *application information key*. The application information key identifies your application by its name, its version number, and your company's name. The general format of the application key is:

```
[ HKEY_LOCAL_MACHINE]\Software\Company\Product\Versi
   on
```

For example, the following is the application information key entry for Version 1.0 of an application called Creation manufactured by a company named The Game Lab:

```
[ HKEY_LOCAL_MACHINE]\Software\TheGameLab\Creation\1
   .0
```

The Uninstall Information Key

Another key that is critical for any installation is the *uninstall information key*. The uninstall information key stores information that lets the Windows 95 user remove your program and all its data from his or her system easily and safely.

Uninstall information, when it exists is stored in an application-specific key under the general key:

```
[ HKEY_LOCAL_MACHINE]\Software\Microsoft\Windows\
   CurrentVersion\Uninstall
```

In the following example, the key "SampleAppV3" identifies the location of two values. The `[ DisplayName]` value is the name that appears in the Windows 95 **Add/Remove Programs** applet in the control panel. The `[ UninstallString]` value identifies the exact locations and names of the uninstall executable file and the log file containing uninstall data.

```
[ HKEY_LOCAL_MACHINE] \Software\Microsoft\Windows\
   CurrentVersion\Uninstall\SampleAppV3
   [ DisplayName] = Sample App
   [ UninstallString] =C:\WINDOWS\deinst.exe
            C:\Program
Files\Company\SampleApp\Deislog.1
```

The Per Application Paths Information Key

A third important key is the *per application paths information* key. This key stores path information that enables Windows 95 to find your application's executable files. In Windows 95, path information is stored in the registry under an application-specific key located under the general key:

```
[ HKEY_LOCAL_MACHINE] \Software\Microsoft\Windows\
   CurrentVersion\App Paths
```

The following example is a per application paths key entry that shows the [Path] and [Default] values stored under an application-specific key named designer.exe:

```
[ HKEY_LOCAL_MACHINE] \Software\Microsoft\Windows\
   CurrentVersion\App Paths\designer.exe
       [ Path] = C:\Program
   Files\Company\SampleApp\PROGRAM;
                 C:\Program
   Files\Company\SampleApp\System
       [ Default] = C:\Program
   Files\Company\SampleApp\PROGRAM\designer.exe
```

Example Program: Exploring the Registry

The example program named REGDEMO, in this chapter's directory on your bonus disk, is a simple program you can experiment with to see how the registry works in Windows 95. The REGIS application demonstrates the use of registry functions including RegEnumKey, RegEnumValue, and RegQueryInfoKey functions.

REGDEMO is a dialog-based program that was created using the Visual C++ AppWizard utility. A dialog-based application is one that is not equipped with any document windows, but simply displays a dialog box when it is executed.

✔ To create a dialog-based program, follow these steps:

1. Select the **File | New** menu item from the Developer Workshop menu, and then create a new project by selecting the **Project Workspace** item in the **New** dialog box and clicking the **OK** button.
2. When the **New Project Workspace** dialog box opens, choose **MFC AppWizard (exe)** from the **Type** list box
3. Close the **New Project Workspace** dialog box by clicking the **Create** button.
4. When the AppWizard opens window (Figure 1.32) opens, select the radio button labeled **Dialog based**.
5. From this step on, follow normal procedure for creating a Visual C++ project. (For details, see online help or your Visual C++ documentation.)

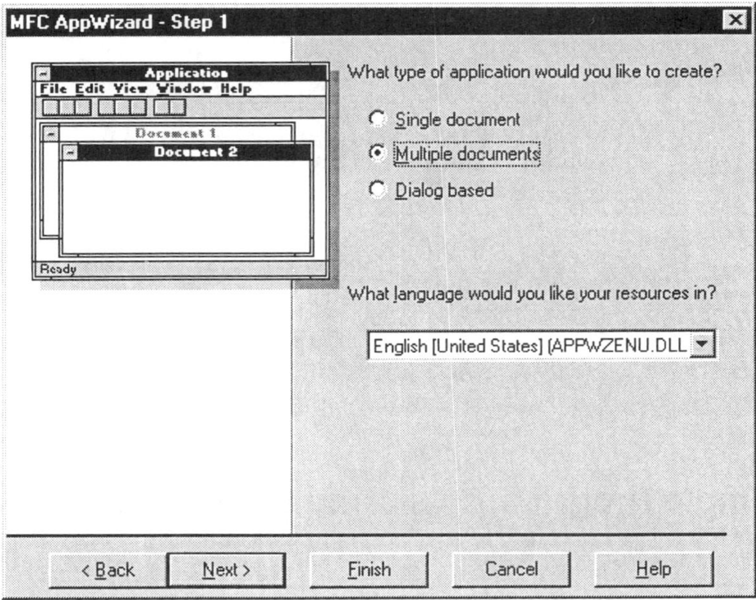

Figure 1.32 Creating a dialog-based application

Features of the REGDEMO Program

The REGDEMO program is a Visual C++ adaptation of the example program named MONKEY program that is provided with Visual C++. The MONKEY program is written in C, not in Visual C++, and is beginning to show its age. REGDEMO was written using Version 4.0

of Visual C++ and updates the MONKEY program by making use of many of the advanced features of Visual C++.

The REGDEMO program also has a neater and more intuitive user interface than its C-language predecessor. The buttons labeled **Back/Up** and **Next/Down**, which display information in the program's two list boxes, are placed directly under the list boxes they're associated with and are provided with arrows that show the two directions in which data is moved.

More important, both buttons are implemented as C++ classes so they can be equipped with member functions that give the program designer more control over their functionality. For example, the **Back/Up** button is disabled when it is not functional; the button grays out when you reach the root level of the registry's keys and can't back up any farther. That's a more user-friendly design than the MONKEY program's solution, which is to display a dialog boxes that pops up and chastens you for clicking the Back button when it isn't functional.

Retrieving Dialog-Box Data with the DDX Mechanism

Instead of using complicated callbacks to access the information in dialog-box controls—a traditional headache until Visual C++ made things easier—the new member functions added to REGDEMO use the Visual C++ DDX (dialog data exchange) system for passing the values of variables back and forth between dialog-box controls and program functions. (Some of the original callbacks in the MONKEY program have not been updated to use the DDX mechanism, but have been left just as they were originally. They work fine just the way they are, so there was no reason to change them. Leaving these callbacks in the program demonstrates an important fact about Visual C++; you can make Windows API calls from a Visual C++ program, just as you always could. So when you port a non-Visual C++ application to Visual C++, you can update only the API calls that need updating; you don't have to spend the time or energy it would take to update all of them.)

To use the Visual C++ DDX system, all you have to do is create member variables for your dialog-box controls using ClassWizard, and then call the MFC member function `UpdateData` to transfer information back and forth between your dialog box's controls to their corresponding member variables.

If you call `UpdateData` with a `FALSE` parameter, it copies data from all member variables associated with a dialog box's controls to their corresponding controls. The same function, called with a `TRUE` parameter, copies data the other way: from all controls associated with member variables to their corresponding variables.

It's difficult to remember that UpdateData(FALSE) copies data from variables to controls, while UpdateData(TRUE) copies data in the opposite direction. So, in the DLGDEMO.H file, I have provided these two #define directives to make things a little easier to remember:

```
#define VAR2CTRL FALSE
#define CTRL2VAR TRUE
```

With these two definitions in place, it's easy to remember that in the following function in the DLGDEMO.CPP file, the REGDEMO program copies a string that the user has selected from a list box into a text box:

```
UpdateData(CTRL2VAR);
m_ideName = m_lbStr1;
UpdateData(VAR2CTRL);
```

In the first line of the preceding code fragment, the UpdateData function is called to copy the data from all dialog-box controls associated with member variables into their corresponding data members. The second line copies the contents of a member variable named m_lbStr1, which is associated with a list-box entry, into another member variable named m_ideName, which is associated with a text-box string). The third line calls UpdateData function again, this time to copy the contents of all member variables associated with dialog-box controls into their corresponding controls.

To make the preceding code fragments work properly, you must use ClassWizard to associate the m_ideName and m_lbStr1 variables with the appropriate dialog-box controls. To see how ClassWizard can be used to create members variable and associate them with controls, see "Connecting a Common Control to an Application" on page 193.

To learn still more about associating member variables with controls and making variables and controls work together, work through the dialog-box section of the sample application named Scribble that comes with Visual C++.

You can also learn a lot about the DDX mechanism—and about a companion mechanism, DDV (dialog data verification)—by consulting Visual C++ Books Online and other Visual C++ documentation.

How the REGDEMO Program Works

With the REGDEMO application, you can navigate up and down the various branches of the registry tree and observe as the program displays the data values of individual keys.

When you start the program, it displays a dialog box that contains a pair of list boxes and a number of other dialog-box controls. The list box on the left, labeled **Keys**, always displays the child keys of the current key. The list box on the right, labeled **Values**, displays values stored in the selected key—provided, of course, that the local key has any values. When the program starts, the **Keys** list box contains four entries, representing the four key handles that are predefined in both Windows 95 and Windows NT: HKEY_LOCAL_MACHINE, HKEY_CURRENT_USER, HKEY_USERS, and HKEY_CLASSES_-ROOT.

If you select any of these four entries and click the **Next/Down** button, the name of the key that you have selected appears in the **Key Name** text box and the program calls a helper member function named `EnumerateLevel`. The `EnumerateLevel` function calls the Win32 function `RegOpenKey` to open a handle to a registry key, and then calls another member helper function named `QueryKey`. The `QueryKey` function then calls the Win32 function `RegQueryInfoKey` to obtain registry information about the selected key.

All this happens in a file named DLGDEMO.CPP, which is provided in this chapter's folder on your bonus disk. The program's source code is listed in Listing 1.1 on page 53.

When you select the name of key in the Keys list box and then click the **Next/Down** button, the names of the children of the key you have selected replace the entries in the **Keys** list box. For example, if you select HKEY_LOCAL_MACHINE, the name HKEY_LOCAL_MACHINE appears in the **Key Name** text box and the children of the HKEY_LOCAL_MACHINE key—HARDWARE, SECURITY, SOFTWARE, and SYSTEM—appear in the **Keys** list box. To move deeper into the tree, double-click another child key.

You can back out of the registry clicking the **Back/Up** button.

If the currently selected key is associated with any values, the names of those values are listed in the **Values** list box when you click the **Next/Down** button. If the current key is not associated with any values, nothing is displayed in the **Values** list box and a zero appears in the **Values** text box.

If the current key is associated with a class type, the key's class appears in the **Class** text box.

Source Code of the REGDEMO Program

Listing 1.1 is the REGDEM.CPP file, which implements the dialog-box portion of the REGDEMO program. The objects and member functions in the listing are defined in the REGDEM.H header file.

Listing 1.1 Using the system registry

```
// dlgdemo.cpp : implementation file
//
#include "stdafx.h"
#include "RegDem.h"
#include "dlgdemo.h"
#include "BtnBack.h"
#include "BtnNext.h"
#ifdef _DEBUG
#undef THIS_FILE
static char BASED_CODE THIS_FILE[] = __FILE__;
#endif
#define _UNICODE
//////////////////////////////////////////////////////////////////////
    ///////
// CDlgDemo dialog
CDlgDemo::CDlgDemo(CWnd* pParent /*=NULL*/)
   : CDialog(CDlgDemo::IDD, pParent)
{
   //{{AFX_DATA_INIT(CDlgDemo)
   m_ideACL = _T("");
   m_ideClass = _T("");
   m_ideName = _T("");
   m_lbStr1 = _T("");
   m_lbStr2 = _T("");
   m_ideTextOut = _T("");
   //}}AFX_DATA_INIT
   m_pStrList = NULL;
   m_btnBack = NULL;
}
CDlgDemo::~CDlgDemo()
{
   ASSERT_VALID(m_pStrList);
   delete m_pStrList;
   ASSERT_VALID(m_btnBack);
   delete m_btnBack;
}
```

```
void CDlgDemo::DoDataExchange(CDataExchange* pDX)
{
  CDialog::DoDataExchange(pDX);
  //{{AFX_DATA_MAP(CDlgDemo)
  DDX_Text(pDX, IDE_ACL, m_ideACL);
  DDV_MaxChars(pDX, m_ideACL, 128);
  DDX_Text(pDX, IDE_CLASS, m_ideClass);
  DDV_MaxChars(pDX, m_ideClass, 128);
  DDX_Text(pDX, IDE_NAME, m_ideName);
  DDV_MaxChars(pDX, m_ideName, 128);
  DDX_LBString(pDX, IDL_LISTBOX, m_lbStr1);
  DDX_LBString(pDX, IDL_LISTBOX2, m_lbStr2);
  DDX_Text(pDX, IDE_TEXTOUT, m_ideTextOut);
  DDV_MaxChars(pDX, m_ideTextOut, 128);
  //}}AFX_DATA_MAP
}
BEGIN_MESSAGE_MAP(CDlgDemo, CDialog)
  //{{AFX_MSG_MAP(CDlgDemo)
  ON_BN_CLICKED(IDB_BACK, OnIDBBack)
  ON_BN_CLICKED(IDB_NEXT, OnIDBNext)
  ON_LBN_DBLCLK(IDL_LISTBOX, OnDblclkListbox)
  ON_LBN_DBLCLK(IDL_LISTBOX2, OnDblclkListbox2)
  //}}AFX_MSG_MAP
END_MESSAGE_MAP()
//////////////////////////////////////////////////////////////////////
    ///////
// App-specific member functions.
// Override CDialog::OnInitDialog();
BOOL CDlgDemo::OnInitDialog()
{
  m_pStrList = new CStringList;

  // Rectangle coordinates for 'Back' button.
  RECT btnBackRect = { 166,266,310,290 };

  // Construct 'Back' button.
  m_btnBack = new CBtnBack;

  // Create 'Back' button.
  BOOL bRetVal = m_btnBack->Create("<< Back/Up", BS_PUSHBUTTON |
    WS_VISIBLE
    | WS_CHILD, btnBackRect, this, IDB_BACK);

  // Make 'Back' button's font match this dialog's font.
  CFont *thisDlgFont = new CFont;
  thisDlgFont = GetFont();
  m_btnBack->SetFont(thisDlgFont);
```

```
    // When program starts, m_btnBack button is disabled
    // because we're at Level 0 and can't back up any
    // further.
    m_btnBack->EnableWindow(FALSE);

    // Fill in the 'Keys' list box with its initial values.
    ListBox1().AddString("HKEY_LOCAL_MACHINE");
    ListBox1().AddString("HKEY_CURRENT_USER");
    ListBox1().AddString("HKEY_USERS");
    ListBox1().AddString("HKEY_CLASSES_ROOT");

    m_hKeyRoot = 0;// Initialize m_hKeyRoot.
    m_regPath = ""; // Registry path.
    m_fullBranches = TRUE; // Initialize m_fullBranches (see
                           // dlgdemo.h for details).

    return TRUE;
}
//////////////////////////////////////////////////////////////////////
// CDlgDemo message handlers

// This function  executes when the user clicks the 'Next' button.
void CDlgDemo::OnIDBNext()
{
    // Get the index number of the item the user has selected
    // in the 'Keys' list box.
    int index = ListBox1().GetCurSel();

      // We're no longer at Level 0, so enable the 'Back' list box.
    m_btnBack->EnableWindow(TRUE);

    // Prompt user for a selection if there is none.
    if (index == LB_ERR) {
      MessageBox("Please select an item in the left-hand list box.");
      // m_btnBack->EnableWindow(FALSE);
      return;
    }

    // If list-box item 0 is selected, user wants to move
    // back (up), so execute OnIDBBack (below).
    if (index = 0 && m_hKeyRoot) {
      OnIDBBack();
      return;
    }
    // Copy user's list-box selection into the Name text box...
    UpdateData(CTRL2VAR);
    m_ideName = m_lbStr1;
```

```
    // ... and clear both list boxes.
    ListBox1().ResetContent();
    ListBox2().ResetContent();

    // The EnumerateLevel() member function is defined later
    // in this file.
    char *sTemp = m_ideName.GetBuffer(128);
    char *sTemp2 = m_regPath.GetBuffer(128);
    EnumerateLevel(sTemp, sTemp2, &m_hKeyRoot);

    // Add the new path to the string list
    m_pStrList->AddTail(m_regPath);
    UpdateData(VAR2CTRL);
}

// This function  executes when the user clicks the 'Back' button.
void CDlgDemo::OnIDBBack()
{
    HWND hDlg = m_hWnd;
    CString s;
    int index;
    char NameLBSelect[ 256] ;
    CString regPath = m_regPath;

    // Get the item the user has selected in the 'Keys' list box.
    ListBox1().GetText(256, NameLBSelect);

    // If !m_hRootKey, we're already at the top level.
    // So we'll inform the user and then return. (Actually,
    // this should never happen in this version of the
    // program because the 'Back' button should be disabled
    // at this point. But I'm leaving this 'if' statement in,
    // just to make sure everything is working properly.)
    if (!m_hKeyRoot) {
      MessageBox ("Top Level; you can't back up any further.",
      "RegDemo Application", MB_OK);
      return;
    }

    //For all remaining cases, clear the list boxes.
    ListBox1().ResetContent();
    ListBox2().ResetContent();

    // If hRootKey has a value, but the pathname is blank,
    // then we must be one level deep. So we'll reset to
    // Level 0.

    if (m_regPath == "") {
```

```
    m_ideName = "";
    UpdateData(VAR2CTRL);
    ListBox1().AddString("HKEY_LOCAL_MACHINE");
    ListBox1().AddString("HKEY_CURRENT_USER");
    ListBox1().AddString("HKEY_USERS");
    ListBox1().AddString("HKEY_CLASSES_ROOT");
  // We're back at Level 0, so disable the 'Back' button.
  m_btnBack->EnableWindow(FALSE);

  m_hKeyRoot = 0;// Initialize m_hKeyRoot.
  return;
  }

  // Just two cases left: Either (a) the path has only one
  // key name in it, and there's no backslash character in that
  // name, or (b) there is more than one key name in the path
  // and there is at least one backslash in the name.
  // If this is case (a), we will fool EnumerateLevel
  // into thinking we have picked one of the predefined keys.
  // Then EnumerateLevel will re-enumerate the child key's
  // parent key, taking us back to Level 0. If this is case (b),
  // we will retrieve the last key name from m_pStrList and
  // then call EnumerateLevel.

  // First we check to see if (a) the path has only one
  // key name in it, and there is no backslash in that name.
  // If so, we will fool EnumerateLevel into thinking we have
  // picked one of the pre-defined keys. Then EnumerateLevel
  // will re-enumerate the child key's parent key, taking us
  // back to Level 0. .

  // If there is no backslash, m_regPath.Find
  // returns -1.
  if ((index = m_regPath.Find('\\')) == -1) {
    m_regPath = "";
    switch ((DWORD)m_hKeyRoot) {
      case (DWORD)HKEY_LOCAL_MACHINE:
        strcpy (NameLBSelect, "HKEY_LOCAL_MACHINE");
        break;
      case (DWORD)HKEY_USERS:
        strcpy (NameLBSelect, "HKEY_USERS");
        break;
      case (DWORD)HKEY_CURRENT_USER:
        strcpy (NameLBSelect, "HKEY_CURRENT_USER");
        break;
      case (DWORD)HKEY_CLASSES_ROOT:
        strcpy (NameLBSelect, "HKEY_CLASSES_ROOT");
        break;
```

```
    }

    ::SetDlgItemText (hDlg, IDE_NAME, NameLBSelect);
    m_hKeyRoot = 0;
    EnumerateLevel (NameLBSelect, m_regPath.GetBuffer(256),
      &m_hKeyRoot);

    // We're at Level 0, so clear the string list.
    m_pStrList->RemoveAll();

  } else {

    // This must be case (b) (see preceding comment),
    // so we can retrieve the last key namde from
    // the string list and then re-enumerate the
    // resulting level.

    // First, copy user's list-box selection into the
    // m_ideName variable.
    // (The old way was:
    // ::SetDlgItemText (hDlg, IDE_NAME, NameLBSelect);)
    m_ideName = NameLBSelect;
    UpdateData(VAR2CTRL);

    // If the string list isn't empty, retrieve the
    // last item from the string list. This will be
    // our new key selection.
    CString tempStr;
    if (!m_pStrList->IsEmpty()) {
      tempStr = m_pStrList->GetTail();
      // We've now retrieved the last item in the string
      // list, so discard it.
      m_pStrList->RemoveTail();
    } else {
      // MessageBox("The string list is empty!");
    }
    // Enumerate level for new key string.
    char *s = tempStr.GetBuffer(128);
    m_regPath = tempStr;
    EnumerateLevel (NameLBSelect, s, &m_hKeyRoot);
   }
}
void CDlgDemo::OnDblclkListbox()
{
  // TODO: Add your control notification handler code here
  // Decided not to do this; see the original MONKEY program.
}
void CDlgDemo::OnDblclkListbox2()
```

```
{
    // TODO: Add your control notification handler code here
    // Decided not to do this; see the original MONKEY program.
}
// The EnumerateLevel() Function
//
// The following function gets a valid key handle (either to
// determine if the one sent to the function was one of the
// six pre-defined keys, or to open a key specified by the
// path), and to pass that key handle along to QueryKey().
//
// To enumerate the children of a key, you must have
// an open handle to it. Four top-level keys of the
// registry are predefined and open for use:
// HKEY_LOCAL_MACHINE, HKEY_USERS, HKEY_CURRENT_USER,
// and HKEY_CLASSES_ROOT. These keys can be used to call
// RegEnumKey as is, but to RegEnumKey on any of the
// children of these you must first have an open key
// handle to the child.
//
// If hKeyRoot != 0, assume that you are lower than the
// first level of the Registry and that the user is trying
// to enumerate one of the children.  First calculate
// the name of the child, and then use RegOpenKey to
// get an open handle.
//
// If hKeyRoot == 0, assume that you are at the top level
// of the Registry, and set the hKey to be enumerated
// to be one of the 4 predefined values, the specific
// one indicated by the ListBox selection.
//

void CDlgDemo::EnumerateLevel (/* HWND hDlg, */
    LPTSTR NameLBSelect,
    LPTSTR RegPath, HKEY *hKeyRoot)
{
    HKEY hKey;
      UINT  retCode;
      CHAR   Buf[ 255] ;
    if (*hKeyRoot) {
      // If RegPath is not NULL, you must add a backslash to the
      // path name before appending the next-level child name.
      if (strcmp (RegPath, "") != 0)
        strcat (RegPath, "\\");
      // Add the next-level child name.
      strcat (RegPath, NameLBSelect);
      // Call RegOpenKeyEx() with the new registry path
      // to get an open handle to the child key you want to
```

```
    // enumerate.
    retCode = RegOpenKeyEx (*hKeyRoot, RegPath, 0,
      KEY_ENUMERATE_SUB_KEYS | KEY_EXECUTE |
      KEY_QUERY_VALUE, &hKey);
    if (retCode != ERROR_SUCCESS) {
      if (retCode == ERROR_ACCESS_DENIED)
        wsprintf (Buf,
        "Error: Can't open key, probably for security reasons.");
      else
        wsprintf (Buf,
          "Error: Can't open key, RegOpenKey = %d, Line = %d",
          retCode, __LINE__);
      MessageBox (Buf, "", MB_OK);

      // PostMessage (hDlg, WM_COMMAND, IDB_BACK, 0);
      OnIDBBack();

      return;
    }
  } else {
    // Set the *hKeyRoot handle based
    // on the text taken from the ListBox.
    if (strcmp (NameLBSelect, "HKEY_CLASSES_ROOT") == 0)
      *hKeyRoot = HKEY_CLASSES_ROOT;
    if (strcmp (NameLBSelect, "HKEY_USERS") == 0)
      *hKeyRoot = HKEY_USERS;
    if (strcmp (NameLBSelect, "HKEY_LOCAL_MACHINE") == 0)
      *hKeyRoot = HKEY_LOCAL_MACHINE;
    if (strcmp (NameLBSelect, "HKEY_CURRENT_USER") == 0)
      *hKeyRoot = HKEY_CURRENT_USER;
    hKey = *hKeyRoot;      // hKey is used in RegEnumKey().
  } //end if/else *hKeyRoot
  QueryKey (/* hDlg, */ hKey);
  RegCloseKey (hKey);    // Close the key handle.
  m_ideTextOut = m_recPath;
  UpdateData(VAR2CTRL);
}

// The QueryKey() Function
//
// This function displays the key's children (subkeys
// and the names of the Values associated with them.
// This function calls RegEnumKey, RegEnumValue, and
// RegQueryInfoKey.
//
void CDlgDemo::QueryKey (/* HWND hDlg, */ HKEY hKey)
{
  HWND hDlg = m_hWnd;
```

```
CHAR      KeyName[ MAX_PATH] ;
CHAR      ClassName[ MAX_PATH]  = ""; // Buffer for class name.
DWORD     dwcClassLen = MAX_PATH;     // Length of class string.
DWORD     dwcSubKeys;                 // Number of sub keys.
DWORD     dwcMaxSubKey;               // Longest sub key size.
DWORD     dwcMaxClass;                // Longest class string.
DWORD     dwcValues;                  // Number of values for this
  key.
DWORD     dwcMaxValueName;            // Longest Value name.
DWORD     dwcMaxValueData;            // Longest Value data.
DWORD     dwcSecDesc;                 // Security descriptor.
FILETIME ftLastWriteTime;             // Last write time.
DWORD i;
DWORD retCode;
DWORD j;
DWORD retValue;
CHAR  ValueName[ MAX_VALUE_NAME] ;
DWORD dwcValueName = MAX_VALUE_NAME;
CHAR  Buf[ 255] ;
// Get Class name and Value count.
RegQueryInfoKey (hKey, // Key handle.
  ClassName,          // Buffer for class name.
  &dwcClassLen,       // Length of class string.
  NULL,               // Reserved.
  &dwcSubKeys,        // Number of subkeys.
  &dwcMaxSubKey,      // Longest subkey size.
  &dwcMaxClass,       // Longest class string.
  &dwcValues,         // Number of values for this key.
  &dwcMaxValueName,   // Longest Value name.
  &dwcMaxValueData,   // Longest Value data.
  &dwcSecDesc,        // Security descriptor.
  &ftLastWriteTime); // Last write time.
::SetDlgItemText (hDlg, IDE_CLASS, ClassName);
::SetDlgItemInt  (hDlg, IDE_CVALUES, dwcValues, FALSE);
::SendMessage (::GetDlgItem (hDlg, IDL_LISTBOX),
  LB_ADDSTRING, 0, (LONG)"..");

// Loop until RegEnumKey fails. Then get the name of
// each child and place it in the list box.
// Enumerate the Child Keys.
SetCursor (LoadCursor (NULL, IDC_WAIT));
for (i=0, retCode = ERROR_SUCCESS; retCode ==
  ERROR_SUCCESS; i++) {
  retCode = RegEnumKey (hKey, i,
    KeyName, MAX_PATH);
  if (retCode == (DWORD)ERROR_SUCCESS)
    ::SendMessage (::GetDlgItem(hDlg, IDL_LISTBOX),
```

```
      LB_ADDSTRING, 0, (LONG)KeyName);
    }

    SetCursor (LoadCursor (NULL, IDC_ARROW));
    // Enumerate the Key Values
    SetCursor (LoadCursor (NULL, IDC_WAIT));
    if (dwcValues)
      for (j = 0, retValue = ERROR_SUCCESS;
        j < dwcValues; j++) {
        dwcValueName = MAX_VALUE_NAME;
        ValueName[ 0] = '\0';
        retValue = RegEnumValue (hKey, j, ValueName,
          &dwcValueName,
          NULL,
          NULL,               //&dwType,
          NULL,               //&bData,
          NULL);              //&bcData);
        if (retValue != (DWORD)ERROR_SUCCESS &&
          retValue != ERROR_INSUFFICIENT_BUFFER) {
          wsprintf (Buf,
        "Line:%d 0 based index = %d, retValue = %d, ValueLen = %d",
            __LINE__, j, retValue, dwcValueName);
          ::MessageBox (hDlg, Buf, "Debug", MB_OK);
        }
        Buf[ 0] = '\0';
        if (!strlen(ValueName))
          strcpy (ValueName, "<NO NAME>");
        wsprintf (Buf, "%d) %s ", j, ValueName);
        ::SendMessage (::GetDlgItem (hDlg, IDL_LISTBOX2),
                        LB_ADDSTRING, 0, (LONG)Buf);
        // We're at the top level, so disable the 'Next' button.
        // m_btnNext->EnableWindow(FALSE);

      } // end for(;;)
  SetCursor (LoadCursor (NULL, IDC_ARROW));
  }
```

Summary

This chapter explored the technology behind the Windows 95 interface and explained how you can use some of the features of the interface in your own Windows 95 applications. Many of the topics introduced in this chapter are covered in more detail in later chapters.

By mastering and using the Windows interface features introduced in this chapter, you can start building better Windows interfaces right now. To mention some examples:

- Your Windows 95 applications should make use of *contextual interfaces* such as popup menus, properties and property sheets, and contextual help interfaces.
- When a window displays a data file or a document type, the name of the displayed object is the name that should usually appear in the title bar.
- Create icons not only for your applications, but also for your data files—and register your icons (and other application resources) with the system registry.
- Consider writing applications that support the single-instance model—that is, consider letting the user open only one instance of your application at a time.
- Support OLE. This is one of the most important tips that anyone can give a Windows programmer. If you understand OLE, you understand where Windows is headed, and you can support all the new OLE-related features built into Windows 95 and future versions of Windows.
- Microsoft does not exactly frown on the continued use of MDI (the multiple document interface), but does suggest that you consider alternatives that can make your applications more document-centric. You found out about some of these alternatives in the section titled "Is MDI Dead? No, But . . ." on page 25.
- To enhance and streamline your Windows 95 applications, consider using some of the interface gadgets and controls that are used in the Windows 95 interface and are made available to you in the Microsoft Foundation Class (MFC) library. These gadgets and controls include common dialog boxes, popup menus, and the many new controls available in Windows 95, including toolbars, status bars, tree views, and rich text controls.
- Learn to use the system registry. You must know how to use the registry to create really well-behaved applications for Windows 95.

Chapter

2

Underneath Windows 95

This chapter puts the pedal to the metal and reveals not only what's new in Windows 95, but what's new underneath it. In this chapter, you'll learn how the designers of Windows 95 harnessed the capabilities of the 386 and its successors and made them available to developers of Windows applications.

In Chapter 1, "Introducing Windows 95," you learned all about the new features of the Windows 95 user interface and picked up some tips about how you can incorporate those same features into your own applications.

In this chapter, you'll learn more about the magic built into the Windows 95 interface and you'll get an inside look at how it happens. You'll get a chance to take a look inside the Intel 386/486/Pentium processor and see how Microsoft engineers harnessed all the processing power built into the 386 family of chips and put it to work in the Windows 95 operating system. And you'll learn how you can get that same power to work for you in your own Windows 95 programs.

This chapter puts the pedal to the metal and focuses not only on what's new in Windows 95, but also on what's new underneath it. In this chapter, you'll how the original 8080 chip evolved into the 386, the

486, and the Pentium, and you'll see how the Windows 95 designers have turbocharged Windows 95 processing by leaving the limitations of earlier chips behind. You'll get an insider's look at how Windows 95 memory management works, starting at the microprocessor level. You'll learn how the registers in the 80X86 family of processors work, and how they are used in 16-bit and 32-bit Windows programs.

You'll also learn how Windows 95 programs use the features built into the 386 chip and its successors to prevent applications from overwriting each other's code and data and from corrupting used by the operating system. That will be an important topic to know about when you get to Chapter 9, "Multithreading and Multitasking."

Finally, at the end of this chapter, you'll get a chance to run a diagnostic MS-DOS program that shows exactly what goes where in memory when you boot up Windows 95.

The following topics are covered in this chapter:

The chapter concludes with a hands-on exercise that shows you exactly what happens in your computer's memory when you boot up Windows 95.

32-Bit Memory Addressing

One of the most important features of Windows 95 is its flat 32-bit memory map—an advancement that finally frees Windows programmers from having to bother with such contrivances as memory models, memory segments, and far pointers.

Many people think that 32-bit memory mapping is a brand-new Windows technology made possible by the design of the Windows NT and Windows 95 operating system. And Microsoft has not gone to any great lengths to correct that illusion.

Actually, though, flat memory maps for 80X86-based computers have been around since the earliest days of the MS-DOS era. As many longtime DOS programmers have almost forgotten, the Intel 8080 processor—an early ancestor of today's 386, 486, and Pentium chips, had a memory map as flat as a tortilla. Programs written for the 8080 accessed memory in exactly the same way that 32-bit Windows applications access memory today.

There is one big difference, of course; a Windows 95 application can access many times the memory that an 8080 program could. The 8080, being an eight-bit chip, could address only 64K of memory. The 386, in contrast, is a 32-bit processor that can access up to 4GB of memory.

Nevertheless, the addressing mechanism used by 32-bit Windows 95 programs is just like the basic addressing mechanism used by the earliest IBM PC applications written for the 8080 processor.

To understand the similarities between 8080 addressing and 386/486/Pentium addressing, you have to understand that the original 8080 chip did not access memory locations using later innovations such as segment:offset addressing, multiple memory models, or near and far pointers. Every address in an 8080 program was an actual physical address, so you could access any address accessible to the 8080 without having to convert a logical addresses to a physical address.

When the 8080 processor was succeeded by the 8086, then by the 80286, and still later by the 386, the 486, and the Pentium, the addressing mechanisms of its successors grew increasingly complex. Intel created segment and offset registers to help the 8080's successors access more and more memory, and other innovations such as memory models and near and far pointers made 80X86 addressing even more complex.

Things grew ever more complicated until Windows 95 came along. And now we have returned to a simpler age of flat memory mapping.

Although today's 80X86 chips still have segment registers, you can almost entirely ignore them when you write 32-bit applications for Windows 95. Just make all your segment registers as large as available memory allows, start all of them in the same place, and forget about them. Then you can write applications for the 4GB address space of the 386/486/Pentium chip in exactly the same way that early programmers wrote programs for the 8080 and other 8-bit chips—only bigger.

Tech Talk

In case you aren't familiar with assembly language, this chapter introduces just enough 80X86 assembly language to help you to understand something about Windows 95 addressing at the chip level. You don't have to be an assembly-language whiz to write Windows 95 programs in C++ and other high-level languages. But to understand how Windows 95 memory addressing works, it helps to have at least a read-only knowledge of some of the most common elements of 80X86 assembly language.

Another reason for being at least a little familiar with assembly language is that even a rudimentary knowledge of assembly language can help you immensely when you start debugging your Windows 95 programs. Most debuggers, including the source-line debugger built into Microsoft Visual C++, can be operated in an assembly-language mode. The debugger then displays an assembly-language listing of the object code your compiler has actually generated instead of displaying the source code you originally wrote. If you can read that kind of display, it can provide you with much more information about what your application is doing than a C or C++ readout can.

Another reason for having some familiarity with assembly language is that assembly-language patches are often inserted into programs written in higher-level languages to increase their speed and efficiency. For example, the fast bit-transfer operations used in computer animation are often implemented as assembly-language routines patched into programs written in higher-level languages. While you might never have to write an assembly-language routine yourself, it's nice to know a little something about how assembly-language routines work when you find it necessary (or just helpful) to patch some assembly-language code into your own C or C++ programs.

Because a little knowledge of assembly language can be so handy, this chapter includes a very basic introduction to some of the most important elements of 80X86 assembly language. The material in this chapter won't make you an assembly-language expert overnight, but on the other hand, it won't put too much strain on your brain if you decide you have absolutely no interest in learning assembly language.

Of course, if your aim is to become a really top-notch Windows 95 programmer, you'll eventually want to obtain an assembler (the Borland Turbo assembler and the Microsoft MASM assembler are both good choices) and learn assembly language.

16-Bit Memory Addressing

If the Windows 95 operating system were a pure 32-bit OS, it would use a flat memory map exclusively and its memory addressing would be very easy to understand. Windows 95 programmers would be able to forget about segments, offsets, and memory models, and write all their programs using flat, 32-bit memory mapping.

Unfortunately, things aren't quite that simple. Although the designers of Windows 95 were given the authority to forget about the 80286 chip, and to design their new operating system solely for the 386 and its successors, they had no such latitude when it came to *software*. One important design requirement for Windows 95 was that it had to be compatible with applications written for earlier, 16-bit versions of Windows. And that requirement made it necessary for the designers of Windows 95 to come up with a kind of hybrid operating system—one that would run 16-bit software originally designed for the Windows 3.*x* operating system, as well as a new generation of software designed exclusively for newer, 32-bit Windows operating systems: specifically, Windows 95 and Windows NT.

As a result of this design decision, there are two ways to write applications for Windows 95. If you want to create a program that will run under Windows 3.*x* as well as under Windows 95, you can simply write an ordinary 16-bit Windows program. The disadvantage of choosing that option is that your program won't be able to make use of the advanced new features of Windows 95 that are described in this volume.

Alternatively, you can now write a 32-bit application that take advantage of all the new features of Windows 95. Choosing this option is what programming in Windows 95 is all about. You can forget about the hassles of keeping track of segment registers, and you can close the door forever on such troublesome mechanisms as tiny, small, medium, and large memory models and near and far pointers. Every pointer becomes just a pointer—not a near or far pointer—and every memory address becomes a real memory location, not an address calculated using segment:offset addressing.

Windows 95 Hardware

Inside every computer, there is a smaller computer called a microprocessor chip—the vital computer component that Intel proudly refers to as "Intel inside" (when Intel had some widely publicized problems with the Pentium chip in 1994, one industry pundit called that a "warning label"). Windows 95 is designed to run on computers equipped with the Intel 386 microprocessor and its successors, the 486 microprocessor and the Pentium.

As noted in the previous section, Windows 95 is specifically designed *not* to run on computers powered by the 80286 or 8086 processors, the ancestors of the 386. Intel had to sacrifice backward compatibility with these older computers to provide Windows 95 users with the benefits of a flat 32-bit memory map and many other new features built into Windows 95.

Because Windows 95 is designed to run on the Intel 386 chip or better, older computers built with Intel 8086 and 80286 processors won't run Windows 95. And if you want to design programs that take advantage of all the great new features of Windows 95, you'll want to write your applications specifically for systems equipped with386, 486, and Pentium processors.

Does that mean you'll have to throw away all software written for pre-386 PCs when you install Windows 95? The answer is: Certainly not. Windows 95 can *run* software designed for every 386-family chip ever built—even ancient applications designed to be run under DOS on an Intel 8080 microprocessor.

That's one of the neatest features of the Windows 95 operating system: It can run any well-behaved DOS or Windows program written for any Intel chip, all the way back to the 8086 and 8088 chips that powered the earliest Intel-based PCs.

The 80X86 Processor Family

The Intel 8080 chip mentioned at the beginning of this chapter was introduced in 1974. In 1978, the 8080 was succeeded by a 16-bit chip dubbed the Intel 8086. Two years later came the 16-bit 8088, the first microprocessor used in the IBM PC.

Later IBM PCs were equipped with the 8086, a more powerful chip than the 8088 despite its lower model number. So the 8086 is regarded today as the first real member of the Intel 80X86/Pentium family.

The 8086 Processor

The 8086 chip had a 20-bit address bus. That meant that it could access 1,048,576 different memory addresses, or 1MB of RAM. Every address that the 8086 could access corresponded to an actual physical memory location. That straightforward addressing technique is known today as *real mode*.

Although the 8086 had a 20-bit address bus, it had only a 16-bit data bus. In other words, the 8086 stored and manipulated information using 16-bit registers. A 16-bit register can hold a value of up to 64K. So each internal register in the 8086 was capable of handling numbers ranging from 0 to 65,535 (or 0 to FFFF in hexadecimal notation). To store or manipulate larger values, additional registers were required.

Segment:Offset Addressing

To access 1MB of memory, the 8086 used a mechanism called *segment:offset addressing*. In segment:offset addressing, a memory address is stored in two registers: a *segment register* and an *offset register*. To access a memory location, the 8086 processor combined the contents of a segment register and an offset register to calculate an actual physical address.

Segment:offset addressing derived its named from the way in which segment:offset addresses were expressed in 8086 assembly language programs. In an 8086 assembly-language program, a segment:offset address can be written in the form

segment:offset

—where *segment* is the starting address of a 64K memory segment and *offset* is the offset within that segment at which the desired address can be found. For example, the notation

```
DS:266
```

specifies the 266th memory location in whatever block of memory starts at the address stored in an 8080 register called the data segment register, or DS register.

The DS register and other 80X86 registers are described in more detail in "80X86 Registers" on page 72.

Microprocessor Registers

As you may know, an assembly-language program manipulates data by moving it back and forth between memory locations and various kinds of registers. Registers are essential to the operation of a computer chip because they can both store and process data. Ordinary memory locations, in contrast, can store data but can't process it.

As an illustration of how registers work, consider an addition operation in an assembly-language program. To add two numbers, an assembler program typically copies both numbers into registers, adds them together, and then moves the sum of the two numbers back into memory. This is what a typical addition operation looks like in an assembly-language program:

```
MOV      AX, VALUE1
ADD      VALUE2, AX
```

The example shown above contains two assembly-language instructions—one instruction in each line.

In the first instruction, an integer stored in a memory location that has been assigned the name **VALUE1** is copied into a special kind of register called the accumulator, or AX register. In the 80X86 chip, the AX register is the principal register used for arithmetic operations.The memory location from which the value is moved is specified in the third column of the instruction, and the target of the move is specified in the second column. In the second line of the example, the value that has just been moved into the AX register is added to the value of another memory location that has been assigned the name **VALUE2**. This operation overwrites the original value of **VALUE2**.

When the addition operation shown in the example is complete, the memory location named **VALUE2** holds the sum of the integer stored in **VALUE1** and the integer originally stored in **VALUE2**.

80X86 Registers

As the preceding example shows, a register can store or manipulate only a small amount of data. For example, each register in the 8086 chip holds just 16 bits of data. (As you'll see later in this chapter, the 386 chip and its successors are equipped with a mixed set of 16-bit and 32-bit registers. But a 32-bit number is still not a whole lot of data.)

Every chip in the 80X86 family has two kinds of registers: four *segment registers* that are used to specify the starting addresses of memory blocks, and eight other *general-purpose registers* that are used for other purposes, such as storing and manipulating data and storing pointers to memory locations.

Five of the general-purpose registers in the 8086 chip are *offset registers* that are used together with the processor's segment registers to calculate memory addresses. Figure 2.1 on page 73 shows the registers built into the Intel 8086 processor.

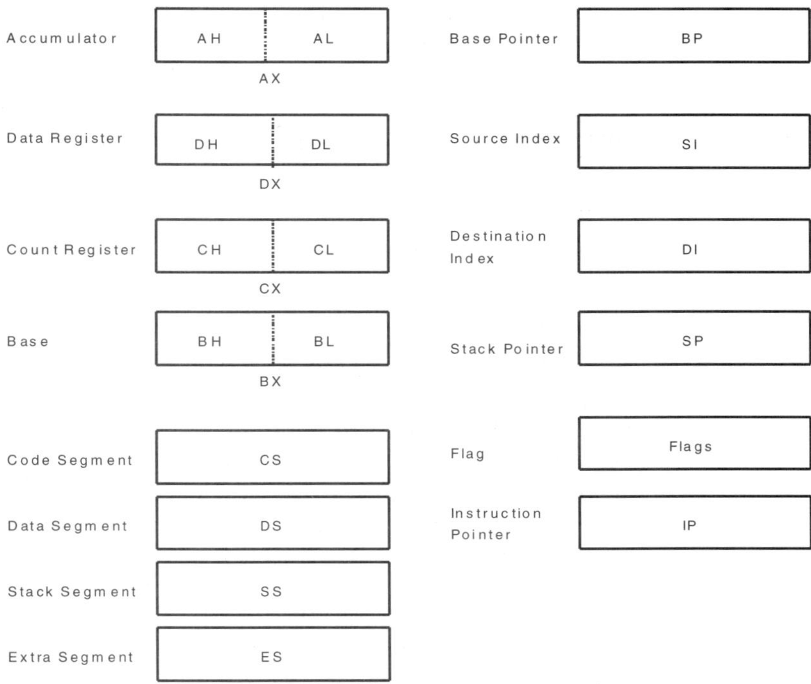

Figure 2.1 8086 registers

80X86 Segment Registers

Every chip in the 80X86 family has four *segment registers*:

- **The CS register** holds the starting address of the currently executing program's code segment.
- **The DS register** holds the starting address of the current program's data segment.
- **The stack segment register (SS)** keeps track of values stored on the stack.
- **The extra segment register (ES)** helps keep track of program data and helps process data transfers between memory segments.

When a program is running in protected mode, it can be divided into multiple segments, and the 80X86 chip can keep track of the program's segments using the CS, DS, SS, and ES registers. By adding the value of the offset register to the contents of the appropriate segment register (or selector), the 80X86 can determine any segment's physical address.

If the segment is a code segment, its base address is stored in the CS register. If the segment is a data segment, its base address is stored in the DS register. The ES register is also used to hold base addresses of data segments. The SS register is used to store the base address of the next accessible value on the stack.

How Segment:Offset Addressing Works

Segment:offset addressing was introduced with the 8086 chip and is still used by all processors in the 80X86 addressing. The easiest way to show how it works is to start with the 8086 processor.

Although the 8086 had segment and offset registers that could store values ranging from 0 to 65,535, it powered a line of computers that could address up to 1GB (1,048,576 bytes) of memory. So there was no way that any combination of 8086 segment and offset registers could hold numbers long enough to access all available memory locations. That is why Intel introduced *segment:offset addressing*.

Segment Registers and Offset Registers

To provide the 8086 with all the addressing capability it needed, Intel engineers divided the 1MB address space of a 8086-equipped computer into 64K segments.

To access the contents of a memory location that lies within any segment, the 8086 stores the starting address of the segment that contains the memory location in a segment register. An offset to the memory location's position inside its memory segment is then stored in an offset register.

When the number stored in the segment register is combined with the number stored in the offset register, the result is the physical address of the memory location.

In the 8086 processor, any 64K block of memory that starts at an address evenly divisible by 16 can be used as a memory segment. Because hexadecimal numbers are based on the number 16, a number that is evenly divisible by 16 always ends with a zero. So an 8086 memory segment always starts at an address that ends with a zero in hexadecimal notation.

Because the hexadecimal address of a memory segment always ends with a zero, the 8086 can squeeze a 20-bit segment address into a 16-bit register by simply dropping the final zero from the segment address and storing the rest of the location's segment address in the segment register.

Subsequently, when the 8086 needs to use a segment address to calculate a physical memory location, it can restore the segment address's final zero by simply rotating the segment address four bits to the left. Then the 8086 can add the contents of the segment register to the contents of an offset register to calculate a physical address. And that is exactly how the 8086 calculates memory addresses.

Table 2.1 shows how shifting a 16-bit value four bits to the left multiplies the value by 16 and results in a 20-bit value.

Table 2.1 Bit-Shifting and Segmented Addressing

	Binary Value	Hexadecimal Value
Before shifting	0011 1110 1011 0100	3EB4
After shifting	0011 1110 1011 0100 0000	3EB40

By examining Table 2.1, you can see what happens when the hexadecimal value 3EB4 is shifted four bits to the left. The result is that 3EB4 is multiplied by 16, for a product of 3EB40.

In this case, 3EB40 is the physical address, or *linear address*, that is obtained by combining the contents of a segment register with the contents of an offset register.

Illustration of a Bit-Shifting Operation

Figure 2.2 on Page 76 provides more details about how the 8086 uses bit-shifting to calculate a 20-bit linear address. In Figure 2.2, a memory location with a segment:offset address of 3EB0:0064 is converted to a linear address of 3EB64. The operation takes place in six steps:

1. A value stored in a segment register (3EB0) is shifted four bits to the left, resulting in a value of 3EB00.
2. The bit-shifted value 3EB00 is added to the value stored in the offset register, which is 64.
3. The result of this operation is a 20-bit linear address. In this example, the linear address is 3EB64.
4. A value stored in a segment register (3EB0) is shifted four bits to the left, resulting in a value of 3EB00.
5. The bit-shifted value 3EB00 is added to the value stored in the offset register, which is 64.
6. The result of this operation is a 20-bit linear address. In this example, the linear address is 3EB64.

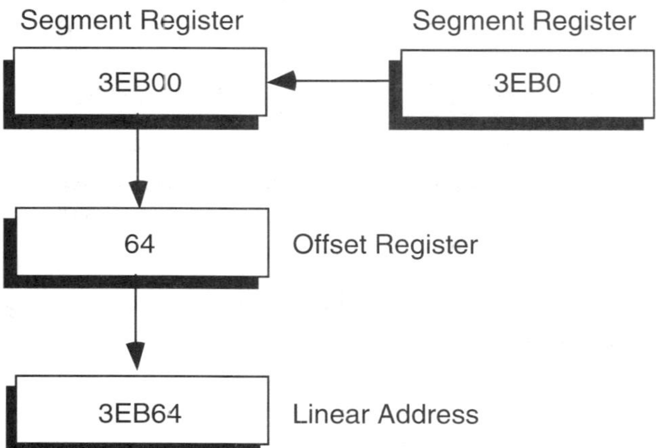

Figure 2.2 Segment:Offset Addressing

When a chip in the 80X86 family is running in real mode—that is, emulating a 8086 processor—there is no difference between the physical address of a memory location and its linear address. When more advanced 80X86 chips run in protected mode, however, there can be significant differences between the physical address and the linear address of a memory location. These differences are spelled out under the next heading.

A More Complex Bit-Shifting Operation

The operation shown in Figure 2.2 works out neatly because the value in the segment register does not end in a zero and the value in the offset register is only two hexadecimal digits long. In real-world segment:offset addressing, this situation is not the norm.

Figure 2.3 on page 77 shows how segment:offset addressing works when the value in the segment register does not end in zero and the value in the offset register is more than two hexadecimal digits long. There is no real difference in the way the operation works, but the figures look more complicated because the hexadecimal arithmetic involved is a little more complex.

In Figure 2.3, observe what happens when the value stored in the segment register—in this case, 1234—is shifted four bits to the left. The value that results (12340) is then added to the contents of the offset register (5678), yielding the linear address 179B8.

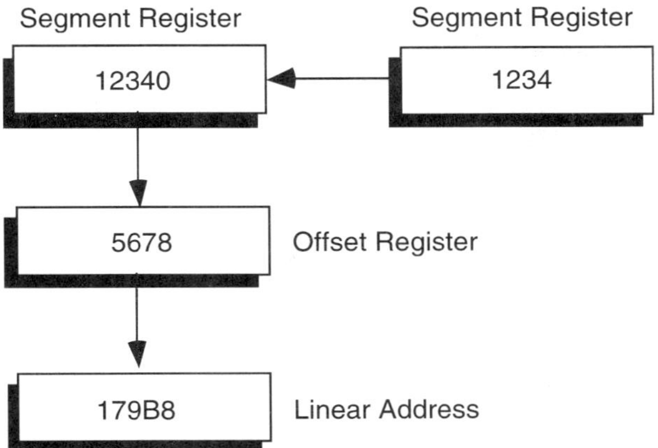

Figure 2.3 A more complex example of segment:offset addressing

Ambiguities of Segment:Offset Addressing

To achieve their goal of chip compatibility, segment:offset addressing works well; the 386 and its successors use CPU registers efficiently, and the 8086 chip can use it effectively. But the scheme has one confusing feature.

Because the system calculates linear addresses using base addresses that can be situated anywhere in a computer's memory, many different linear addresses can represent the same physical memory address. To see how, examine Figure 2.4 on Page 78.

Figure 2.4 illustrates an operation similar to those shown in the preceding two illustrations. Notice that the value stored in the segment register—179B—is shifted four bits to the left. The value that results is 179B0. This value is then added to the contents of the offset register (0008), yielding the linear address 179B8.

One unusual feature of the preceding operation may not be immediately obvious. Even though the values in the segment and offset registers shown in Figure 2.4 are different from the values in the segment and offset registers shown earlier in Figure 2.3, the linear address that is generated in Figure 2.4 is identical to the linear address generated in the preceding illustration.

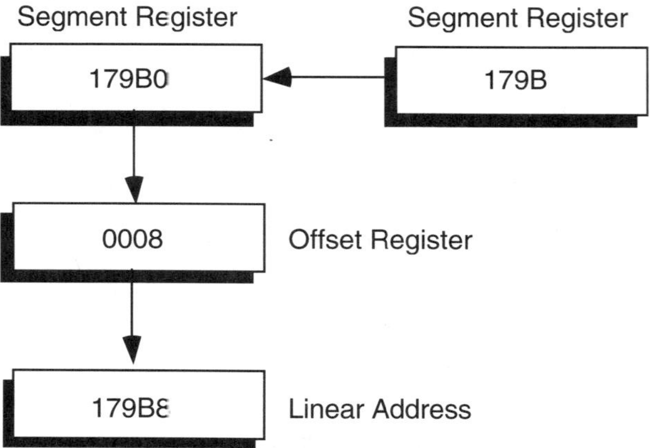

Figure 2.4 Segment:offset addressing ambiguities

This kind of occurrence is not unusual in 80X86 programming; in fact, it happens quite often. The reason is that in 8086 segment:offset addressing, any memory address that is divisible by 16 can be used as the starting address of a 64K memory segment. That means, of course, that memory segments overlap.

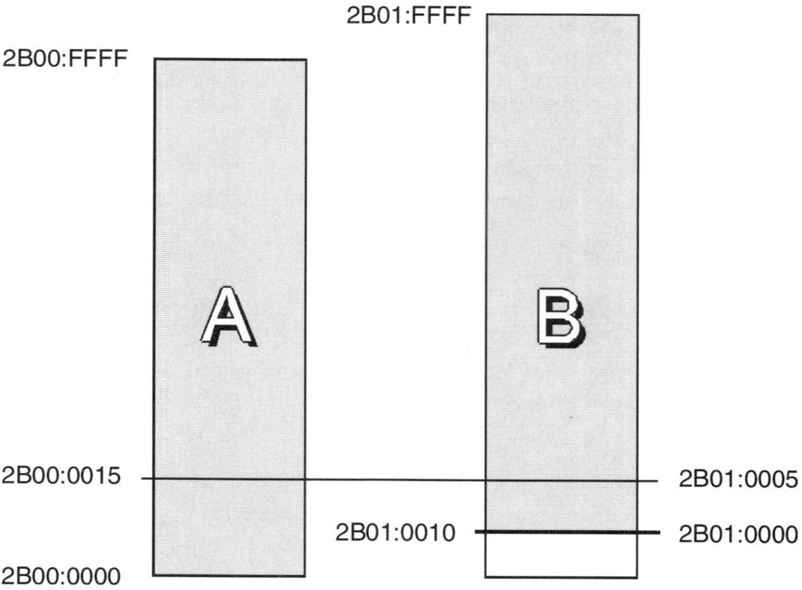

Figure 2.5 How memory segments can overlap

Figure 2.5 on Page 78 shows how this is possible. In Figure 2.5, a pair of memory segments are labeled A and B. Memory segment A starts at memory address 2B00:0015. Memory segment B starts at 2B01:0010.

Because the starting address of memory segment B is 2B01:0010, memory address 2B00:0010 can also be referred to as 2B01:0000. Each of these segment:offset addresses is made up of a segment address and an offset address. If you move each segment address four bits to the left and then add it to its corresponding offset address, you'll see that both physical addresses are the same.

As Figure 2.5 also illustrates, the segment:offset addresses 2B00:0015 and 2B01:0005 equate to the same physical addresses.

Even though Figure 2.5 shows only two segment:offset addresses for each physical address shown, every physical memory address in an 80X86 computer can be represented by many segment:offset addresses in a similar manner.

A little basic arithmetic is all you need to figure out how many segment:offset addresses a single physical memory location can have. Every 16th bit in memory marks the start of a new 64K memory segment, so there are 65,536 memory segments in lMB of memory.

Similarly, in each memory segment, there are 65,536 addresses, for a combination of more than four billion segment:offset combinations. So every physical address accessible by an 8086-equipped computer can be represented by 4,096 different segment:offset addresses.

The 80286 Processor

The 8086 processor was succeeded by the 80286, a 16-bit chip with a 24-bit data bus. The 80286 processor has a set of 16-bit *general-purpose* registers, a set of 16-bit *segment registers*, and two other registers called a flags register and an instruction pointer. Four of the 80286's general-purpose registers are used as offset registers in addressing operations.

The 80286 could address up to 16MB of memory—a significant improvement over the 8086's 1MB addressing capability—but there was no way to address 16MB of memory using real-mode addressing.

To deal with that limitation, Intel devised a new addressing mode called *protected mode*. The purpose of 80286 protected mode was to extend the addressing capabilities of it 80X86 line a little further.

Protected-mode addressing derives its name from another important new feature: a set of built-in safeguards that prevent applications from overwriting each other's code and data and from corrupting the code and data used by the operating system.

80286 Protected Mode

In 80286 protected mode, when an application needs to perform a delicate operation—such as accessing I/O devices—it must request permission from the operating system. The operating system can then check to see what other applications are doing before it grants permission to perform the requested operation.

From the standpoint of memory addressing, protected mode added some new complexities to 80X86 programming. For example, for the sake of backward compatibility with the 8086 chip, the 80286 could be operated in real mode as well as protected mode.

When the 803286 executed software designed to be run on an 8086-equipped computer, the ran in real mode—a mode that precisely emulated the operation of the 8086 processor. In real mode, the 80286—like its predecessor, the 8086—used a form of segment:offset addressing that could access only 1MB of memory.

When the 80286 was operated in protected mode, it could access 16MB of memory using a more complex kind of segment:offset addressing. In protected-mode addressing, a segment:offset address does not point to an actual memory location. Instead, it points to an entry in a table called a descriptor table, and each entry in the descriptor table points to an actual physical address.

Protected-Mode Memory Segments

In 8086-style addressing, as you may recall, any 64KB memory block of memory can be used as a memory segment, as long as it begins on a 16K boundary and starts within the first 1MB of a computer's memory.

In 80286 protected mode, a segment does not have to be 64K long; segments can be of variable length and can start anywhere in memory.

To access memory addresses, 80286 protected mode makes use of a technique that programmers call *indirection*. In protected mode, the value stored in the segment register is not part of an address, as it is in real mode. Instead, the segment register contains a number that points to a value stored in a *descriptor table*. The value located in the descriptor table is then combined with a number stored in an offset register to calculate a physical address.

The 80286 Segment Register

In 80286 protected mode, indirection adds some new complexities to address calculations. For example, the 80286 does not use its segment register to store a 16-bit offset address. Instead, it uses 13 bits of the segment register (bits 3 through 15) as an index into a descriptor table. That frees three bits of the segment register to store other kinds of information.

Two of these extra bits (bits 0 and 1) were used to store privilege information that protected operating-system code and data from being accessed by ordinary applications. The third bit (bit 2) was used to specify whether the descriptor table being used was a local descriptor table or a global descriptor table. (Local descriptor tables were tables used by applications. There was also a global descriptor table that was used by the system.)

This arrangement is shown in Figure 2.6.

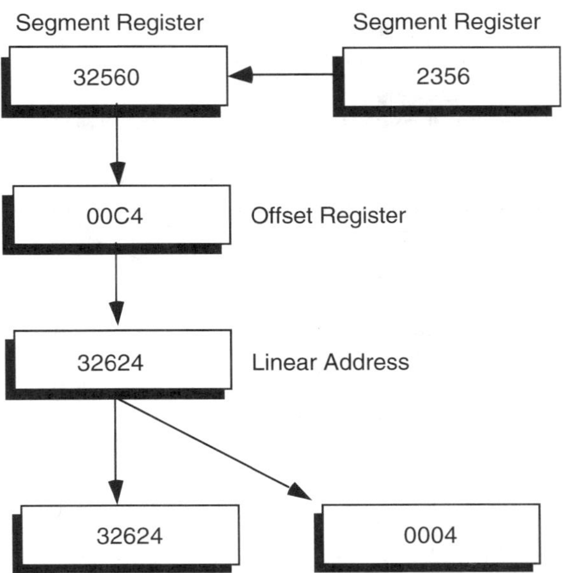

Figure 2.6 Calculating an address in 80286 protected mode

The 80286 Selector

When the 80286 started using bits 0 through 3 of the segment register to hold information not related to addressing, the part of the segment register in which address information was stored came to be known as a *selector*. This name distinguished the part of the register that was used to select a descriptor-table entry from the three bits that were used to store other kinds of information.

To calculate an address in a protected-mode application, the 80286 first adds a number stored in an offset address to the value in the selector. The result of this calculation is an address known as a *base address*. The 80286 then adds this base address to the value stored in the selector. The result of this second calculation is called a *logical address*, or a *virtual address*.

The 386 Processor

The successor to the 80286 chip was the 386—the first true 32-bit processor in the 80X86 lineage. The 386 has both a 32-bit address bus and a 32-bit data bus, so it can address 4GB of memory. Figure 2.7 shows the architecture of the 386 chip. (The architecture of the 8086 chip appears in Figure 2.1 on page 73.)

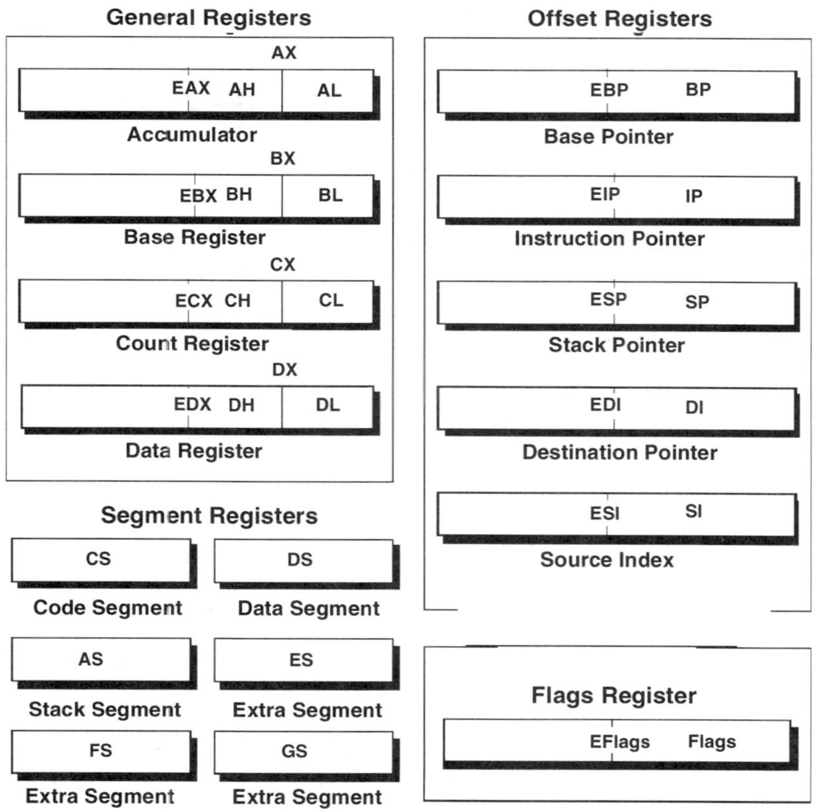

Figure 2.7 Architecture of the 386 chip

The segment register in a 386 chip, like the segment registers in the 8086 chip, is 16 bits long. But its offset register is 32 bits long, so it can access up to 4GB of memory.

To calculate an address in a protected-mode application, the 386 processor—like its 80286 predecessor—first adds a number stored in an offset address to the value in the selector. In 386 protected mode, the result of this calculation is a 32-bit *base address*. The 386 then adds this base address to the value stored in the selector. The result of this second calculation is a 32-bit *logical address*, or *virtual address*.

The 386 chip, like its 80286 predecessor, can operate in both real mode and protected mode. When you operate the 386 in real mode, it works just like an 8086. In real mode, the 386 processor uses 8086-style segment:offset addressing to access a maximum of 1MB of memory. In protected mode, however, the 386 processor can address as much memory as a fully loaded 386 computer can hold: up to 4GB of RAM.

Virtual 8086 Mode

Earlier in this chapter, you saw how 80X86 chips can be operated in either real mode or protected mode. Now it's time to reveal that chips in the 80X86 family can also be operated in a third mode, called *virtual 8086 mode*.

Virtual 8086 mode is similar to real mode; it's an operating mode in which a 32-bit 80X86 processor emulates the operation of an 8086. The biggest difference between real mode and virtual 8086 mode is that virtual 8086 mode is an MS-DOS emulation mode that operates under protected mode.

An 80286, 386, or Pentium processor can move into and out of virtual 8086 mode without leaving protected mode. In fact, the term real mode is often used interchangeably with the term virtual 8086 mode. When 80X86 programmers talk about running DOS programs in real mode, what they often really mean is virtual 8086 mode.

80286 Architecture and 386 Architecture

The protected mode used by the 386 chip—known, logically enough, as 386 protected mode—is different from the 80286 variety of protected mode that was created for the 80286 processor. The 80286 had a 20-bit address mode, so it could access only 16MB of memory when it was operated in protected mode. In contrast, the 386 has a 32-bit address bus that can access up to 4GB of memory in protected mode.

The 486 and Pentium Processors

The successor to the 386 chip was the 486, a faster chip with more built-in support logic, a built-in math coprocessor, and a memory cache. Next came the Pentium, a still faster successor to the 486 with even more on-board processing power and even more sophisticated memory-caching capabilities. Windows 95 is designed to run on computers equipped with the 386, 486, and Pentium processors.

The 486 and Pentium chips, like the 386 chip, are 32-bit microprocessor. The addressing mechanisms they use are identical to those used by the 386 processor.

386 Protected-Mode Addressing

Windows 95 can operate in real mode, but it does so only when no other mode will do—for example, when it has to execute a 16-bit DOS device driver that insists on running in real mode. In all other cases—and that means almost all the time—Windows 95 runs in 386 protected mode. 386 protected mode is an updated version of the kind of protected mode introduced with the 80286 processor.

In 386-style protected mode, a segment can begin anywhere in the 386's 4GB of address space and can have any size up to 1MB. (Alternatively, you can set a flag called a *granularity bit* to make the segments in your application any multiple of 4KB, and a segment can then be up to 4GB long. For an explanation of the granularity bit, see Table 2.2 on page 87.)

Base Addresses and Linear Addresses

In 386 protected mode, just as in 80286 protected mode, the value in the segment register does not point to the starting address of a memory segment. Instead, it points to a number stored in a descriptor table. In 386 protected mode, a number retrieved from the descriptor table is a 32-bit value called a *base address*.

In 386-style address calculations, the 32-bit base address retrieved from the descriptor table is added to the value of the CPU's offset register—another 32-bit number. The result of this calculation is a linear address.

When the 386 retrieves a base address from an entry in a descriptor table, it uses the same 13 of the segment register's 16 bits to point to the descriptor-table entry it is seeking—just as the 80286 did. The other three bits in the segment register are also used the same way they were used in the 80286 processor.

Linear Addresses

When you retrieve an address in this fashion in 386 protected mode, the address you wind up with is called a *linear address*. This linear address, sometimes known as a *virtual address*, is not the same thing as a physical address. But programs running on the 386 and its successors can track down a linear address quite easily using a mechanism called *paging*.

Paging can create virtual memory addresses that do not physically exist in RAM. So, when paging is in use, physical addresses and linear addresses are not necessarily the same. To learn more about paging, see Chapter 4, "The Win32 API."

In the 386 chip, just as in the 80286 chip, the 13 segment-register bits that are used to retrieve a descriptor-table entry are called a *selector*. The base address stored in the selector is 16 bits long, just as it was in the 80286 processor.

But the 386 offset is 32 bits long. So, by adding the value stored in the selector to a base address, the 386 processor can access up to 4GB of memory.

Because the descriptor table was originally designed for the 80286 chip and was later modified to suit the requirements of the 386 chip, the 386 descriptor table does not have the world's most elegant architecture. Fortunately, its ugliness doesn't affect its efficiency, since any bit works as well as any other as far as a microprocessor is concerned.

Segment Descriptors

The 386 selector—like the 80X86 selector—points to a number in a descriptor table instead of to a physical address. Each line of a descriptor table is called a *segment descriptor*.

When a 386 runs a program in protected mode, every entry in a descriptor table is a base address that is added to an offset address to form a linear address of a code or data segment.

A descriptor-table entry also includes such information as the size of the segment, whether it contains code or data, and privilege information. Every line in a descriptor table has three columns, as shown in Figure 2.8 on page 86.

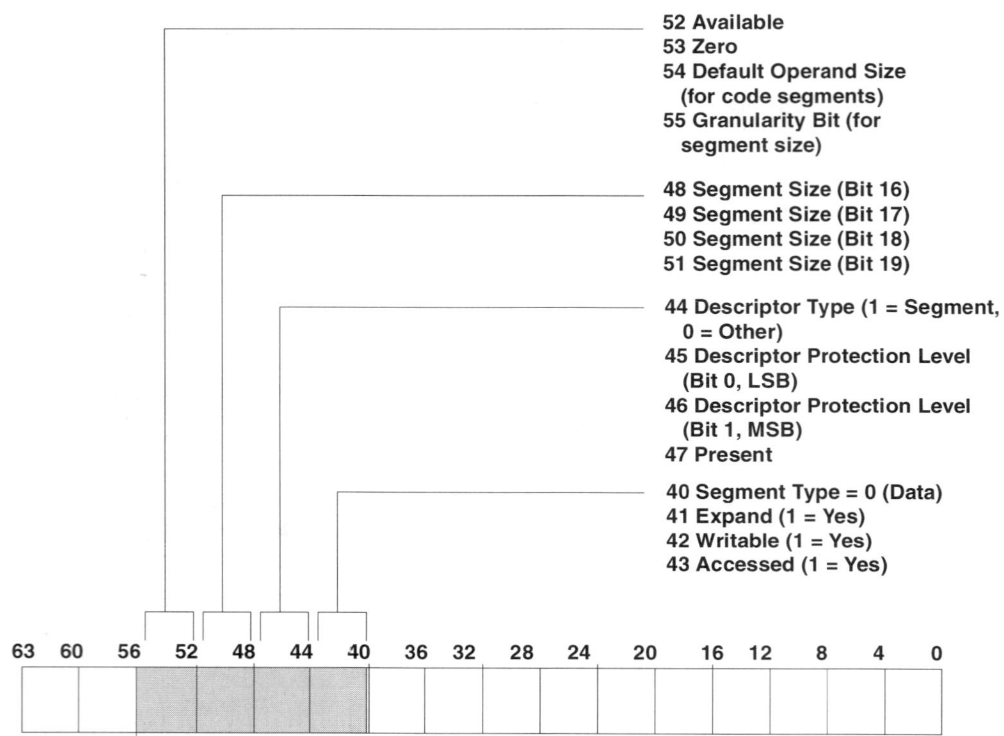

Figure 2.8 Descriptor-table entry

Descriptor-Table Entries

Table 2.2 on page 87 lists and describes the fields in a descriptor-table entry and shows its layout. The first column contains a three-byte base address for every memory segment referenced in the table. The second column is a two-byte entry that contains the size of each segment. The third column is a one-byte value that specifies the user-access rights needed to access each segment.

Memory-Segment Access Rights

Every time a program attempts to access a memory location in protected mode, the request is checked to see if it is valid.

A request is considered valid if it is seeking access to a location within a segment to which that program has appropriate access rights. (As Table 2.2 shows, the access rights to a segment are determined by the third column in the segment's entry in the descriptor table.)

Table 2.2 Components of a descriptor-table entry

Component	Function
Base address	These four fields combine to form a 32-bit address.
Limit	Specifies the upper limit of the memory segment referenced by the descriptor.
Granularity bit	When this bit is cleared to 0, the referenced segment can begin at any linear address in the processor's 4GB memory range and can have any size up to 1MB. That setting is used for 80286-style processing. When the granularity bit is set to 1, the segment size is multiplied by 4K, and then segments can be any multiple of 4KB, up to a limit of 4GB. This setting is used for 386/486/Pentium operations.
D bit or B bit	If the referenced segment contains code, this is the D bit. In this case, if the value is 1, the segment contains native (386) instructions, and if the value is 0, the segment contains 80286 code. If the referenced segment contains data, this is the B bit and a setting of 1 means the segment is larger than 64K.
Present bit	Set to 1 if the referenced segment is present in physical memory. Cleared to 0 if the segment is in virtual memory.
Descriptor privilege level	Specifies the privilege level for the referenced segment (0 to 3). Privilege level corresponds to the protection ring in which the segment runs.
Segment bit	Set to 1 for a memory segment. If this bit is cleared to 0, the referenced segment is reserved for a data structure used by the operating system. The OS can reserve segments for such uses as device interrupt-handling and memory protection.
Type field	Specifies the type of the referenced memory segment—for example, an execute-only code segment or a read-only data segment. This field helps the operating system enforce memory protection.
Accessed bit	Specifies whether any program has referenced the memory segment. Any reference to this segment causes the access bit to be set to 1. The operating system uses this bit to determined what segments are in line to be swapped out to disk using a least-recently-used algorithm.

If any portion of a computer system's memory address space does not lie within one of the segments described in a program's descriptor table, that portion of memory does not exist for that program. As long as this system works properly, one program cannot overwrite another program's data or code because no program can even "see" any other program.

Global and Local Descriptor Tables

To manage the descriptor tables used by all applications in memory, the 80X86 processor maintains a master descriptor table. This master descriptor table is often referred to as the *global descriptor table*. Each application table managed by the global descriptor table can be referred to as a *local descriptor table*.

Every program that is executed in protected mode has access to two descriptor tables: its own local descriptor table and the CPU's global descriptor table.

Every 80X86 that can run in protected mode has an internal register that points to the global descriptor table and a separate internal register that points to the current local descriptor table.

The register that points to the global descriptor table is called the GDT register, or GDTR. The register that points to the local descriptor table is called the LDT register, or LDTR.

The Task State Segment

Every time a new program starts running in protected mode, a local descriptor table for the program is built and the LDTR is set to point to that table. Subsequently, if another program becomes active, the processor saves the values of all the current program's registers in a special memory segment called a *task state segment*, or TSS. Then the CPU reloads its registers to match the settings last used by the newly reactivated program. (Those settings are also stored in the TSS.)

When all that is done, the CPU sets its program counter to the next instruction to be run in the new program, and sets its local descriptor table register to point to the reactivated programs local descriptor table. Then the CPU is ready to start executing the newly reactivated program.

The result of all this processing is that in protected mode, there is no longer just one linear address space for the 80X86 processor to access. Instead, there are two kinds of address spaces to deal with:

- One global address space, specified by all the selectors in the global descriptor table (plus those in another table called the *interrupt descriptor table*)
- One local address space for each program stored in memory, specified by all the selectors in each program's local descriptor table.

Each of these address spaces is a subset of the whole linear address space that can be accessed by the 80X86 processor.

For more about interrupt descriptor tables, see "Interrupt Gates" on page 98.

What this all boils down to is that in the 386 and its successors, a segment can begin at any linear address in the processor's 4GB memory range and can have any size up to 1MB. Alternatively, when the granularity bit in a segment's descriptor-table entry is set to 1, the segment size is multiplied by 4K, and then segments can be any multiple of 4KB, up to a limit of 4GB. (Table 2.2 on page 87 outlines the architecture of a descriptor-table entry, including the granularity bit.) You'll learn more about protected-mode addressing, and how it is used in Windows 95, later in this chapter.

Memory Paging

As mentioned earlier, the 386 chip and its successors can access up to 4GB of memory. But your average garden-variety PC is not equipped with nearly that much RAM.

So where do all those gigabytes of address space come from?

The answer: memory paging.

Briefly, this is how paging works: The portion of a 386 (or later) chip that calculates addresses and processes data is sometimes referred to as the chip's *execution unit*. Once the execution unit of an 386 calculates a linear address, that address is passed to another part of the chip called the *paging unit*.

The paging unit is one of the most powerful features of the 386 chip. In the 386's paging unit there is a flag that specifies whether paging is enabled.

If paging is not enabled, the 386 interprets the linear address that has been passed to the paging unit as a physical address. The processor then treats that address as an actual physical memory location.

If paging is enabled, the 386 treats the linear address that has been passed to the paging unit as a *virtual address*. The 386 processor can access up to 4GB of address space, whether the computer it's running on has that much actual address space or not.

If a virtual address that is passed to the paging unit does not fall within the physical address space of the computer being used, the paging unit knows where to find it. If everything is working correctly, any virtual address that is not available in physical memory can be found on some external storage device—usually a hard-disk drive.

Virtual Device Drivers

In Windows 95, a virtual device driver (or VxD, which means "virtual anything driver") is a 32-bit program that has the highest privilege level—Privilege Level 0. The .386 files that are stored in the /WINDOWS/SYSTEM directory and are provided by many Windows applications are VxDs.

A virtual device driver is not the same as an ordinary device driver. A traditional device driver is usually an interface to a hardware device such as a printer, a keyboard, or a disk drive. A virtual device driver merely simulates a device. For example, a VxD can support an add-on hardware device or provide some systemwide software service.

VxDs are used extensively by the Windows 95 operating system. In Windows 95, VxDs support existing terminate-and-stay-resident programs (TSRs), implement shared memory between virtual machines, provide low-level services to Windows-based applications, and provide 32-bit memory to virtual machines.

One important characteristic of a VxD is that it has a 32-bit address—even under Windows 3.*x*. That's one of the features that gives a VxD its power to go just about anywhere and do just about anything in a Windows environment.

Windows 95 allows applications to install new virtual device drivers. A VxD always runs in Ring 0, and if a VxD fails, it can cripple the entire system. Windows 95 does not isolate failed VxDs and allow the system to continue operation because it was decided that the code required to do that would bog the system down with a lot of processing that was not really necessary.

Instead of developing such a system, the Win95 team decided to build a debug kernel that would test VxDs at the design stage rather than at run time. Such a debug kernel was developed and is available in the Windows 95 Device Driver Kit (DDK).

For more information on VxDs, see "Virtual Device Drivers" on page 139.

Paging support has always been available in the 386 chip and its successors, but Windows 3.*x* did not take full advantage of the 386's paging capabilities. Both Windows NT and Windows 95 do.

Windows NT is designed to run on various kinds of microprocessors, and in programs running under Windows NT, the size of a page is platform-specific. However, Windows 95 is engineered to run on 80X86 computers, and a Windows 95 page is always a 4K block of memory.

It's important to note, however, that any block of physical memory—including lower (system) memory—can be mapped anywhere in the 4GB of virtual address space that a 386 chip can access.

Memory mapping lets you perform many different feats of memory magic. You can map low memory into otherwise empty places in upper memory. If you know what you're doing, you can even make data that is actually stored in memory seem to vanish—by simply mapping it out of memory. Then you can refill those linear addresses with RAM from other places in physical memory.

Page Protection

Along with providing Windows 95 applications with virtual-memory capabilities, paging adds a form of code-and-data protection called *page protection* to Windows 95 programs.

Page protection lets the Windows 95 operating system flag any 4K memory page as either a *user page* or a *supervisor page*. Operating-system code and VxD (virtual device-driver) code can access supervisor pages as well as user pages. But ordinary applications—which run at a lower privilege level—cannot access supervisor pages. Furthermore, applications can write only to pages that are specifically marked as being read-and-write pages.

Page protection is described in more detail in the next section, "Privilege Levels and Protection Rings."

Privilege Levels and Protection Rings

To protect applications kept in memory at the same time from corrupting each other's code and data, Intel built four *privilege levels* into the 386 chip and its successors. To implement these privilege levels, Intel engineers created a hardware mechanism called *protection rings*.

The protection-ring system prevents low-privilege programs, such as ordinary applications, from corrupting code and data used by higher-privilege programs, such as operating systems.

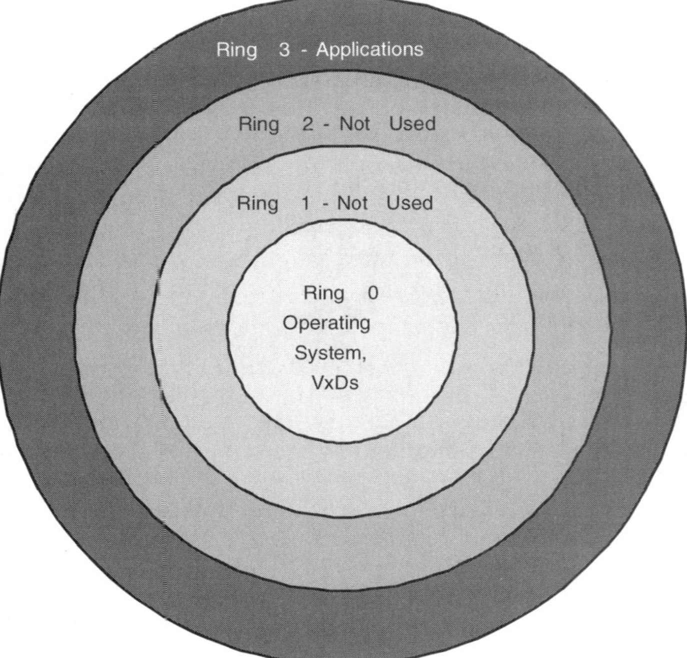

Figure 2.9 Protection rings in the Windows 95 operating system

Here's how the system works: Four protection rings, numbered consecutively from 0 to 3, are designed into the architecture of the 80X86 processor. Similarly, every program designed to be run on an 80X86 processor is assigned a privilege level ranging from 0 to 3. And the ring in which a program runs always corresponds to the privilege level of the program.

Because the privilege level assigned to a program always matches the protection ring in which the program runs, the terms *privilege level* and *protection ring* are often used interchangeably.

The protection ring in which a code segment runs determines what kind of code can access its data. The data in a program running in a particular ring can be accessed only by code that has the same privilege level or a higher one. Thus, data in a program running in Ring 2 can be accessed only by a program running in Ring 0, 1, or 2.

Attempting to access data from a code segment with a lower privilege level causes a GP fault (a general protection fault, exception 0DH).

Figure 2.9 shows how Windows 95 makes use of the four protection rings built into 80X86 processors.

How Protection Rings Work

Intel had some very specific aims in mind when it designed the four-ring protection system. Ring 0 was supposed to be used only for the highest level of programs—programs such as operating systems, which have access to everything. Ring 1 was to be used by operating-system service routines, Ring 2 was meant for various extensions to the operating system, and Ring 3 was designed for user-written programs.

But that is not exactly how things turned out. Most operating systems—including DOS, Windows 3.*x*, and Windows 95—make use of only two of the four rings that are available.

In Windows 3.0, operating-system software ran in Ring 0, while Windows applications and the core Windows DLLs (the Kernel, User, and GDI modules) ran in Ring 1. Rings 2 and 3 were not used.

With the introduction of Windows 3.1, this system changed. In Windows 3.1, the three core Windows DLLs were moved from Ring 0 to Ring 3. Applications were also moved out to Ring 3. Operating-system software and VxDs (see "Virtual Device Drivers" on page 139) remained in Ring 0. Rings 1 and 2 were not used.

How Rings Work in Windows 95

In Windows 95, rings work just as they did in Windows 3.1. Operating-system software, which has a privilege level of 0, still runs in Ring 0. Ring 0 is also available to high-privilege user-written programs such as virtual device drivers. Applications, which have a privilege level of 3, run in Ring 3.

In Windows 95, the three core Windows DLLs (the Kernel, User, and GDI libraries) also run in Ring 3. (In Windows 95, as explained in Chapter 3, these three components were known as the Windows subsystem.)

Rings 1 and 2 are not used in Windows 95.

The Missing Rings

Why doesn't Windows 95 use all four of the protection rings that Intel has provided? For two reasons.

First, the two-ring model (sometimes called "kernel and user modes") works well for most programming needs. Second, ring transitions are very expensive in terms of execution time and program efficiency. A direct subroutine call to code in another segment takes 20 clock cycles on a 486 processor. But it costs 69 clock cycles if a ring transition is needed.

What Privilege Levels Determine

The privilege level assigned to a code segment (and, consequently, the ring in which it runs) determines

- What assembly-language instructions the segment can use
- What kind of code the segment can transfer control to
- What kind of code can access the segment's code and data
- What kinds of data segments the segment can access.

Rings and Assembly-Language Instructions

The ring in which a program runs determines what assembly-language instructions the program can use. A program running in Ring 0 can legally execute any instruction that the 386 processor recognizes. Code running in any other ring causes a GP fault if it tries to execute certain instructions that are considered too dangerous to be executed by ordinary applications.

Dangerous assembly-language instructions include instructions that change the descriptor tables, perform I/O port operations, halt the processor, or switch the CPU into and out of protected mode.

If the operating system (which runs in Ring 0) wishes to allow less-privileged code to execute instructions reserved for Ring 0 code, it can intercept the GP fault, examine the faulting instruction, and if desired, simulate the instruction using Ring 0 code.

That is how Windows virtualizes devices such as the system timer which are accessed via port I/O instructions, and which could be used by more than one program.

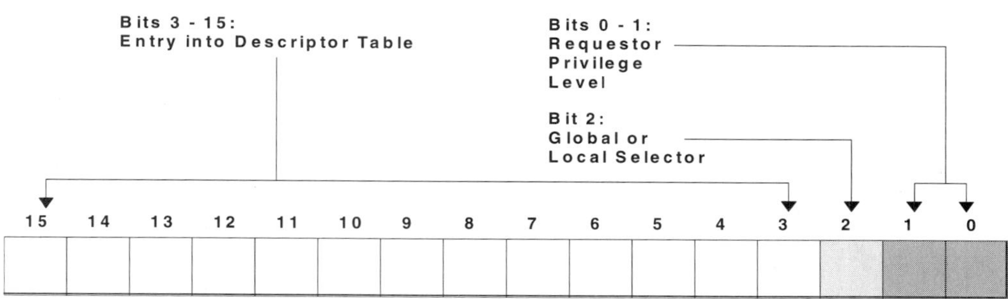

Figure 2.10 Privilege levels and the CS register

Descriptor Tables and the CS Register

In the pre-Win95 era, the Windows 3.*x* system allocated just one local descriptor table that was shared by the operating system and all Windows tasks. Windows 3.*x* did not make any use of the third least significant bit of the selector, but by convention, every selector used in Windows 3.*x* has its third least significant bit set to 1.

In Windows 95, every process running on the system has a local descriptor table. So Windows 95 uses Bit 3 of the CS-register selector to specify whether a global descriptor table or a local descriptor table is being used.

Also, in Windows 3.*x*, the two lowest-order bits of the selector were *not* used for storing privilege levels. Instead, they were set to the binary value 10 for a moveable memory segment or to the binary value 11 for a fixed (unmovable) memory segment.

Because Windows 95 is a 32-bit operating system with a built-in memory manager, it does not require applications to distinguish between moveable and unmovable memory segments.

So, in Windows 95, the two lowest-order bits of the selector are used for a different purpose: to designate the current privilege level (CPL).

Transferring Control

The privilege level of a code segment also determines what kind of code the segment can transfer control to. A code segment running in a particular ring can transfer control only to code segments running in same ring or in a ring with less protection.

Rings and Data Access

Finally, the privilege level of a code segment determines what kinds of data the segment can access. Code segments can transfer execution only to another code segment running in a ring with an equal or less protected privilege level.

For example, if a code segment is running in Ring 3, it can **JMP**, **CALL**, or **RET** only to a code segment running in Ring 3. Any attempt to transfer control to a code segment privilege level of 0 causes a GP fault.

At the machine-language level, the 386 processor is always operating at one of its four privilege levels. As Figure 2.10 illustrates, the privilege level of a code segment is determined by the settings of Bits 0 and 1 in the selector of the CS register. The setting of these two bits is sometimes referred to as the *current privilege level*, or *CPL.*

The third least significant bit in the selector specifies whether the code segment uses the global descriptor table (GDT) or a local descriptor table (LDT). The third least significant bit in the selector is set to 0 if it uses the GDT or to 1 if it uses an LDT.

Ring-to-Ring Communications

Rings are useful protection mechanisms, but sometimes it's necessary for code in one ring to communicate with code in another ring. If some means didn't exist for passing information between rings, the Windows 95 operating system wouldn't be able to communicate with applications—or even with the Windows 95 subsystem—and your computer system wouldn't be able to do anything useful at all.

Another time when communication between rings becomes essential is when a program calls code in another program to perform some subtask. For example, ordinarily an application that runs in Ring 3 sometimes needs to communicate with a virtual device driver (see "Virtual Device Drivers" on page 139) running in Ring 0. When that kind of need arises, there has to be a way for the application to get through to the VxD it requires.

The 80X86 chip provides two different mechanisms for letting less privileged programs communicate with more privileged ones. One method is called the *conforming segment* mechanism. The other technique is to use *gates*.

Conforming Segments

Some program segments, such as certain VxDs, run in Ring 0 (right along with the operating system) but are known not to contain any dangerous instructions such as I/O operations. These segments can be flagged in their descriptor tables as *conforming segments*. When a Ring 0 segment has been flagged as a conforming segment, it can be directly accessed by code running in Ring 3.

How Gates Control Operating-System Access

A more common method for setting up ring-to-ring communications is to use *gates*. A gate is a mechanism that the operating system uses to allow less privileged code to transfer to more privileged code in a strictly controlled way. The Windows 95 operating system sets up the gates and is responsible for monitoring them, so it has strict control over the access that applications are granted to operating-system code.

There are four kinds of gates:

- **Task gate**—lets a task (or, in Windows 95 terms, a process) instruct the CPU to save the current task's state and to switch to another task
- **Trap gates**—used by the operating system to implement exception handlers
- **Interrupt gates**—used by the operating system to implement interrupt handlers
- **Call gates**—used by applications to transfer control to the operating system or to device drivers.

A gate is a special kind of entry that can appear in a descriptor table. Call gates can appear in both local descriptor tables and global descriptor tables. Interrupt gates and trap gates can appear only in the interrupt descriptor table (see "Interrupt Gates," below). Task gates are legal in all three kinds of descriptor tables.

Every gate descriptor except the descriptor for a task gate contains the address of the code to which it should transfer control. This is the only address the operating systems allows access to through the gate.

To use a call gate or task gate, an application makes the gate's selector the target of a **CALL** or **JMP** instruction. Interrupt and trap gates are not called by applications, but are triggered automatically by interrupts or exceptions.

When an application invokes a call gate or a task gate by issuing a **CALL** or **JMP** instruction, the CPU recognizes from the content of the CS register that the descriptor is a gate, and transfers control to the address stored in the gate descriptor.

When an application invokes a gate, the operating system uses a special instruction pointer and a special stack pointer and stores some sensitive data in a protected area of memory. When access to Ring 0 code ends and processing of less privileged code resumes, the operating system returns the context of the less privileged code.

Interrupt Gates

When an application running in Ring 3 application needs to communicate with a virtual device driver (VxD) running in Ring 0, the application uses an interrupt gate. Here's how the system works:

In real mode, as DOS programmers know, every *interrupt service routine*, or ISR, has a number. The 80X86 can calculate the address of any ISR by multiplying the ISR's number by 4. The 80X86 processor then goes to the address that has been calculated and retrieves the address of the ISR.

This system does not work in protected mode. In protected mode, the CPU looks up ISR addresses using a *interrupt descriptor table*, or IDT.

An interrupt gate works much like a local or global descriptor table. An IDT can store up to 256 descriptors, one for each type of ISR allowed by 80X86 architecture. The CPU keeps the address of the interrupt descriptor table close at hand in a register called the IDT register, or IDTR.

When an interrupt or an exception occurs, the 80X86 uses the number of the ISR as an offset into the interrupt descriptor table. The IDT entry found at that offset provides the address of the requested ISR and tells the CPU how long the interrupt service routine is. The CPU then goes to the appropriate address and executes the interrupt service routine.

A call to a virtual device driver, or VxD (VxDs are described in "Virtual Device Drivers" on page 139) is really just a call into a Ring 0 code segment that contains INT 30H instructions. When an INT 30H instruction in a VxD is encountered, an interrupt gate in the interrupt descriptor table transfers control to the appropriate code in the WIN386.EXE VxD.

When an application calls other interrupts, such as INT 2FH or INT 31H, similar privilege-level transitions occur, but through different gates in the IDT. External hardware interrupts (such as the timer) also cause privilege level transitions to Ring 0 through a gate.

Call Gates

The call gate is the kind of gate most often used by applications. Applications can use call gates to transfer control to the operating system or to device drivers. Call gates allow stack-based parameters to be used even though the destination of the gate is at a different privilege level and use of a different stack is required.

Call gates let applications communicate directly with the operating system so they can ask the operating system to perform I/O or other tasks that require higher privileges than an application has.

Writing 32-Bit Programs for Windows 95

Now that you're familiar with the addressing mechanisms of the 80X86 processor family, you may be interested in taking a look at how memory addressing works in a 32-bit Windows 95 program.

When Windows 95 runs a 32-bit application, the memory segments of the 80X86 chip are still there, but you can ignore them almost completely. You can make every segment as large as your system's—up to 4GB—and you can start each segment at the same address. Then you can write your application in the same way you would if memory segments didn't exist at all.

To help you create 32-bit applications, Windows 95 recognizes a new memory model called the flat memory model. The flat memory model now joins the five other memory models that were used in Windows 3.*x* programming: tiny, small, medium, large, and huge.

The flat memory model places all the address of the 386/486/Pentium processor inside a single 32-bit segment. A 32-bit program that uses the flat memory model can access up to 4GB of virtual memory. In a 32-bit Windows 95 program, all code, all data, and the stack reside in the same memory segment. So each segment register can hold the same value, and that value never has to change.

Except for the size of the segments it uses, the flat memory model works much like the tiny model that is familiar to Windows 3.*x* programmers; in a program written using the flat memory model, all code and data are placed in a single 32-bit segment.

Using 32-Bit Assembly Language

When you write a 32-bit application for Windows 95 using a high-level language such as Visual C++ or Borland C++, you don't usually have to be very concerned with memory addressing; if you specify at design time that you want the target of your source code to be a 32-bit application, your compiler will take care of the rest.

You may never have a need to write a Windows 95 program in assembly language, but in case you do, you'll be pleased to know that it isn't a difficult task—at least, it isn't quite as tough as writing an assembly-language program under Windows 3.*x*.

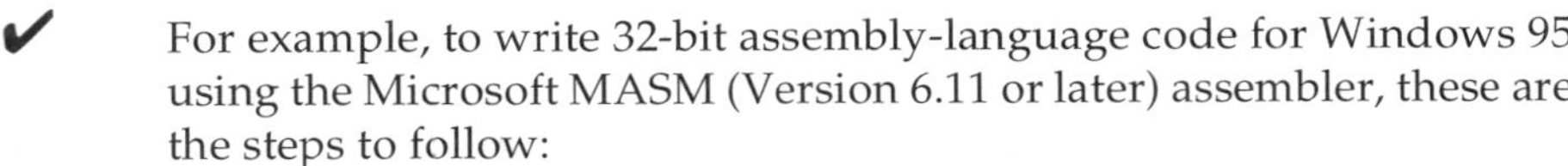

For example, to write 32-bit assembly-language code for Windows 95 using the Microsoft MASM (Version 6.11 or later) assembler, these are the steps to follow:

1. You must include in your code a **`.386`**, **`.486`**, or **`.586P`** directive, depending on whether your program is targeted toward machines using the 386, 486, or Pentium processor. (If you want your program to run on any Windows 95-compatible chip, use the **`.586P`** directive.)
2. When you have selected a target processor, you must place the **`.MODEL FLAT`** directive in your program. Windows 95 can then initialize the CPU's segments automatically at load time. The only time you have to be concerned with segment registers is when you mix 16-bit and 32-bit code in the same application.
3. Because code and data are placed in the same segment in assembly language, you must precede your data declarations with the **`.DATA`** directive and precede your executable instructions with the **`.CODE`** directive.
4. At the end of your source file, place an **`END`** directive.

Once you have specified a target processor and a flat memory model, you don't have to be concerned with near and far addresses. When a 32-bit program for Windows 95 is assembled, all addresses and pointers are recognized as 32-bit addresses and pointers and are treated in the same way near pointers are treated in the Windows 3.*x* tiny memory model.

What Happens when You Start Up Windows 95

When you start up Windows 95, one of the first things you see on your screen is a message that says:

```
Starting Windows...
```

It's an innocuous little message until you start thinking about it. Then it might seem like an odd line for Windows 95 to display at startup time. Why? Because Windows 95 has been widely touted as the first Windows system not to rely on MS-DOS. But that "Starting Windows . . . " message, despite its lack of any mention of DOS, looks suspiciously like an MS-DOS message. It's displayed in white letters against a black background, just as DOS messages are, and it's printed in a type font that' identical to the font used by MS-DOS. In fact, it has the same look and feel as the message you used to get when you booted a DOS-based computer. That message said:

```
Starting MS-DOS...
```

Remember?

What *Is* Starting Up, Anyway?

When you start checking into what that "Starting Windows . . . " message is all about, you can learn some interesting things about Windows 95.

By running some simple experiments, you can see for yourself that Windows 95 doesn't require a CONFIG.SYS file or an AUTO-EXEC.BAT file to get up and running. In fact, it doesn't even require the MS-DOS command interpreter, COMMAND.COM—which, under MS-DOS and Windows 3.*x*, was the file that made a boot disk bootable.

These same experiments can also demonstrate something else that's pretty interesting. They show that when you start up Windows 95, it executes quite a bit of 16-bit code that was originally written for MS-DOS.

DOS expert Andrew Schulman, in a book titled *Unauthorized Windows 95* (see bibliography) claims that Microsoft has misled us by claiming that Windows 95 runs completely independently of MS-DOS. Schulman, who also wrote *Undocumented DOS*, claims that Windows 95 does rely on MS-DOS because it starts up by executing a lot of real-mode code originally written for DOS.

Whether that is true or not, it is clear that Windows 95 does execute a number of real-mode procedures inherited from DOS at startup time. In this section, you'll see exactly what happens inside your computer when you start up Windows 95.

CONFIG.SYS, AUTOEXEC.BAT, and Windows 95

As noted in the section titled "The Windows 95 Registry," on page 35, Windows 95 doesn't require your system to have a CONFIG.SYS file or an AUTOEXEC.BAT file. If you're running software or hardware that does require CONFIG.SYS or AUTOEXEC.BAT, and if you have provided a CONFIG.SYS file and an AUTOEXEC.BAT file to meet your system's needs, Windows 95 quite happily makes use of these two files. But Windows 95 itself works perfectly well without them.

To understand why this is true, it helps to know what happens inside your system when you boot up a machine running MS-DOS. When MS-DOS starts up, the "Starting MS-DOS . . . " message that you see on your screen is produced by two hidden DOS files: one named IO.SYS and one named MSDOS.SYS.

When you start up Windows 95, the "Starting Windows . . . " message that is displayed on your screen is produced in a different way. It is not generated by IO.SYS and MSDOS.SYS, but by a longer and more complex file named WINBOOT.SYS.

The WINBOOT.SYS File

The WINBOOT.SYS file contains much of the same functionality—in fact, it reported contains much of the same real-mode code—that the IO.SYS and MSDOS.SYS files supplied back in the days of DOS. WINBOOT.SYS also contains a lot of new functionality required by Windows 95.

Besides displaying the "Starting Windows . . . " message, the WINBOOT.SYS file does a number of more important jobs that were performed by the IO.SYS and MSDOS.SYS files in MS-DOS systems. And WINBOOT.SYS does not require a CONFIG.SYS file or an AUTOEXEC.BAT file to run.

In Windows 95, WINBOOT.SYS is the file that contains the real-mode DOS INT21H handler (see "The INT 21H Interrupt" on page 137.) WINBOOT.SYS uses that handler to manage an assortment of DOS device drivers, including CLOCK$, PRN, CON, AUX, and others.

WINBOOT.SYS also loads a number of important system files, including HIMEM.SYS and IFSHLP.SYS—and, in some cases, SETVER.EXE and EMM386.EXE.

IFSHLP.SYS is an extremely important real-mode driver that handles the Windows 95 *installable file system manager*, or IFSMgr. The IFSMgr is the Windows 95 utility that manages 32-bit file access, long filenames, and Windows 95's built-in networking support.

The IFSHLP.SYS driver is an example of how important some real-mode drivers are in Windows 95. If the installable file manager cannot find the IFSHLP.SYS driver when you load Windows 95, your whole load fails and Windows 95 displays an error manager complaining that it cannot fine IFSHLP.SYS.

WINBOOT.SYS also handles an important driver named CONFIG$. The CONFIG$ driver is the software tool that supports the Windows 95 Plug and Play manager, the CONFIGMG VxD. (To learn about VxDs, see "Virtual Device Drivers" on page 139.)

WINBOOT.SYS and the COMMAND.COM File

Interestingly, when you start up Windows 95, WINBOOT.SYS does not always load COMMAND.COM—which, as you may know, is the DOS command interpreter. In an MS-DOS system, COMMAND.COM is the file that makes your boot disk bootable; you can't start a DOS system without it.

Under Windows 95, however, a COMMAND.COM file is not required unless your system uses hardware or software that requires the CONFIG.SYS and AUTOEXEC.BAT files to be executed. If your system doesn't have a CONFIG.SYS file or an AUTOEXEC.BAT file—or if you bypass CONFIG.SYS and AUTOEXEC.BAT by pressing the **f5** key at startup time—Windows 95 does not execute a COMMAND.COM file.

In the next section, you'll get a chance to experiment with an exercise that shows how Windows 95 can be started up without a CONFIG.SYS file or an AUTOEXEC.BAT file—and with a COMMAND.COM file.

Exercise: Starting Windows 95 Step by Step

To illustrate exactly what happens when you start Windows 95, try this experiment:

1. Start Windows 95 if it isn't already started.

2. If you have a CONFIG.SYS file and an AUTOEXEC.BAT file in your system, find them in the SYSTEM folder in your computer's root directory. From an MS-DOS console window or the Windows 95 desktop, temporarily rename these two files CONFIG.DAT and AUTOEXEC.DAT.
3. If you haven't yet opened an MS-DOS console window, open one by executing the **Start | Programs | MS-DOS Prompt** taskbar command.
4. Navigate to your system's root directory by executing the MS-DOS command

   ```
   C:\WINDOWS>cd \
   ```

5. Using the TYPE command, print the CONFIG.DAT and AUTOEXEC.DAT files on your screen to confirm that you have really saved your CONFIG.SYS and AUTOEXEC.BAT files under these new names.
6. Close your MS-DOS console window by entering the command

   ```
   C:\>exit
   ```

7. Using the **Start | Shut Down** taskbar command, shut down your system and restart it.
8. When your computer restarts, open an MS-DOS console window and execute the MS-DOS MEM command using the following syntax:

   ```
   MEM /C | MORE
   ```

   MEM is a DOS command that displays the contents of your computer's memory. When you execute **MEM** with the **/C** option, **MEM** not only lists the programs in memory, but also displays other information about them, such as whether they reside in conventional memory or high memory.

   The **MORE |** construct pipes the **MEM** command to the MS-DOS **MORE** command. The **MORE** command causes the **MEM** command to pause at the end of each screen when it is displaying its memory information. To move on to the next screen, you press **Return**.

   When you have executed the **MEM /C | MORE** command, your console window should resemble the one shown in Figure 2.11 on page 105. Notice that the WINBOOT.INI file (which MEM calls MSDOS) loads the HIMEM.SYS, IFSHLP.SYS, and SETVER.SYS files without the aid of a CONFIG.SYS file.

   Next, observe that WINBOOT.INI does not load the COMMAND.COM file into memory until *after* the **WIN** command is executed to start Windows 95. In fact, the only reason for loading the COMMAND.COM file at all is to display the MS-DOS window in which you are executing the **`MEM`** command. If you don't execute CONFIG.SYS or AUTOEXEC.BAT, and don't display an MS-DOS window, WINBOOT.INI doesn't bother to load COMMAND.COM.

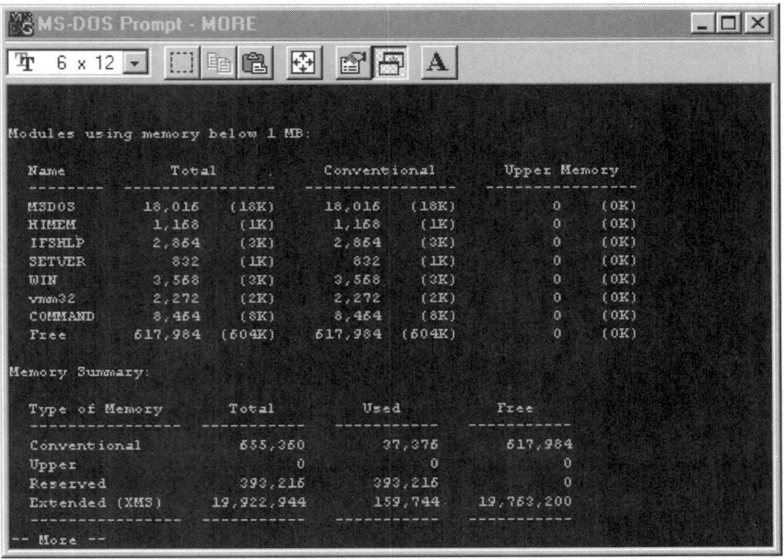

Figure 2.11 Running the MEM utility

Incidentally, another important file that is loaded after the **`WIN`** command is executed (you may have to press **Return** to see it) is a file named vmm32. That file implements the virtual machine manager, which is described in the section titled "The Windows 95 Virtual Machine" on page 109.)

9. If you had a CONFIG.SYS file and an AUTOEXEC.BAT file that you renamed in Step 2, navigate to your system's root directory and restore their original names.
10. Close your MS-DOS window by executing the **`EXIT`** command.
11. Using the **Start** taskbar item, shut down and restart your system.

Suggestions for Further Study

One potentially confusing feature of the previous exercise is that it requires WINBOOT.INI to load a copy of COMMAND.COM to execute the **`MEM /C`** command. So it doesn't really prove that

Windows 95 doesn't need a COMMAND.COM file. If you'd like to be convinced of that, you can run MEM from a Windows PIF file to eliminate the need for a COMMAND.COM file. You can also try executing the **`MEM`** command with the **`/D`** (debug) option, which provides a lot of additional details about your Windows 95 environment.

Even better, you can investigate Windows 95's startup sequence using a specialized tool such as the WINPSP program supplied with Andrew Schulman's book, *Unauthorized Windows 95*. The WINPSP utility provides information about program segment prefixes (PSPs), which identify real-mode DOS processes running under Windows 95. With Schulman's WINPSP program, you can demonstrate conclusively that Windows 95 can start up without a COMMAND.COM file. WINPSP and other utility programs supplied with *Unauthorized Windows 95* can also help you learn a lot of other interesting facts about the relationship between DOS and Windows 95.

Summary

In this chapter, you lifted the hood of the Windows 95 operating system and took a closeup look at the hardware that makes it go. Focusing on chip-level operations, you reviewed 16-bit addressing, learned about 32-bit addressing, and received an introduction to 386/486/Pentium features such as descriptor tables and memory paging. You also learned about privilege levels, protection rings, and flat-mode addressing. And you got a taste of how Windows 95 deals with assembly-language programs.

Finally, in the last major section before this one, you got a chance to use the MS-DOS MEM utility to show what happens inside your computer when Windows 95 starts up. This exercise demonstrated that Windows 95 doesn't require a a CONFIG.SYS file, an AUTOEXEC.BAT file, or even a COMMAND.COM file (the DOS command interpreter) to boot up and start running.

In Chapter 3, "Windows 95 Architecture," you'll see how the Windows 95 operating system makes use of the capabilities built into the 386 processor and its successors. Then you'll be ready to start writing your own C and C++ programs for Windows 95.

Chapter

3

Windows 95 Architecture

In this chapter, you'll see how the capabilities of the Intel 386 processor family have been incorporated into the design of the Windows 95 operating system.

In Chapter 2, "Underneath Windows 95," you got a closeup look at the hardware Windows 95 is built on—the Intel 386 chip and its successors, the Intel 486 and Pentium processors.

In this chapter, you'll see how the capabilities of the Intel 386 processor family have been incorporated into the design of the Windows 95 operating system.

The following major topics are covered in this chapter:

Components of the Windows 95 Operating System

The components that make up the Windows 95 operating system can be grouped into three major categories:

- The *system virtual machine,* under which all Windows and MS-DOS applications run
- The *Windows API layer,* which contains the core Windows libraries: the Kernel, User, and GDI (graphics device interface) DLLs
- The Windows 95 *base operating system.*

Figure 3.1 shows the overall architecture of the Windows 95 system.

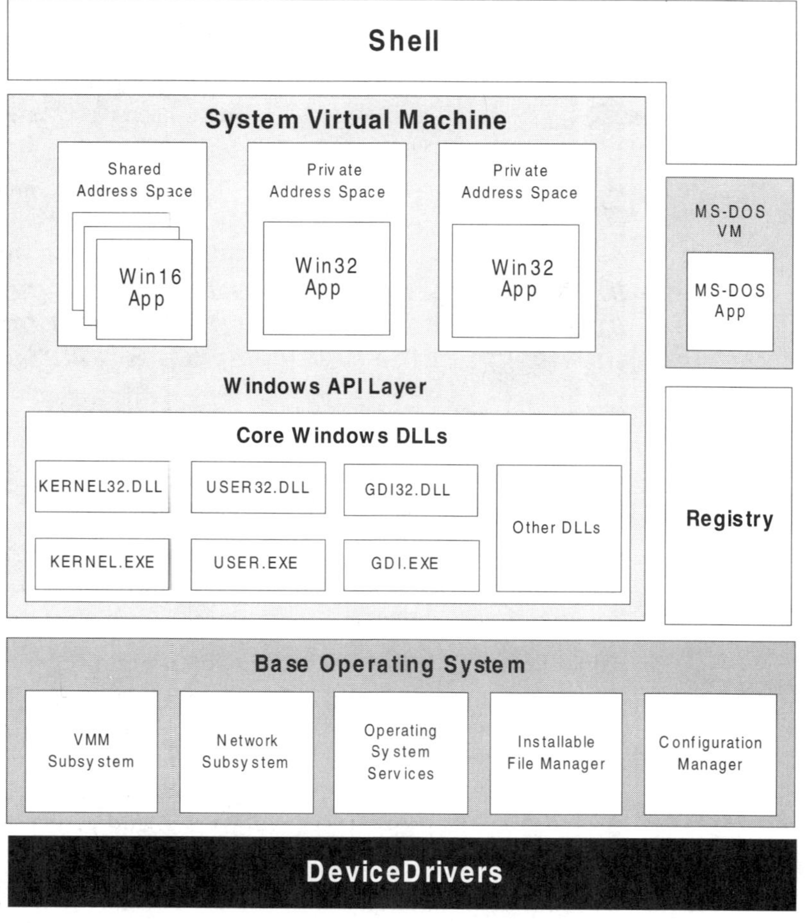

Figure 3.1 Windows 95 architecture

The Windows 95 Virtual Machine

Hardware and software designers seem to love the word *virtual.* You know about virtual reality. In Chapter 2, you learned about virtual 8086 mode and virtual memory. Now here comes still another kind of virtuality: the Windows 95 *system virtual machine.*

The system virtual machine, or *VM,* is the Windows 95 component that runs all applications—programs written for 16-bit Windows, 32-bit Windows, and MS-DOS. The system virtual machine derives its name from the fact that is a large and interactive collection of parts that really do work together much like the many parts of a big physical machine.

A Brief History of Virtual Machines

The term *virtual machine* is used so much in Windows 95 programming that you may think Windows 95 is the first operating system to make use of a virtual machine.

Actually, virtual machines have been around much longer than Windows 95. In both DOS and Windows 3.*x*—as well as in Windows 95—a virtual machine is an executable task with three well-defined components:

- Memory
- CPU registers
- Supporting software (such as ROM BIOS, MS-DOS, or the Windows 95 operating system).

The Virtual Machine Manager

Both MS-DOS and Windows 95 control all their operations using virtual machines. Under both DOS and Windows 95, the virtual machine is managed by a system service called the *virtual machine manager*, or VMM.

In both Windows 3.*x* and Windows 95, a virtual machine manager is a 32-bit protected-mode operating system. Its primary responsibility is to create, run, monitor, and terminate virtual machines. The VMM supports both Windows 3.*x* and Windows 95 by providing services that manage memory, tasks, interrupts, and protection faults.

When Windows 3.*x* is running under DOS (as you know, that's the way Windows 3.*x* *always* runs), the DOS VMM creates as many virtual machines as it needs for itself and for Windows. Specifically, the DOS

VMM creates one virtual machine for Windows 3.*x*, plus one additional virtual machine for each application started from the Windows Program Manager or other Windows applications.

As you learned in Chapter 2, *virtual 8086 mode* is a CPU mode in which a 386/486/Pentium processor can emulate the operation of a 16-bit 8086 chip. In Windows 3.*x*, applications running under the control of a virtual machine always run in virtual 8086 mode.

In virtual 8086 mode, sometimes referred to as V86 mode, Windows 3.*x* applications run as if they were being executed on an 8086 processor—or in real mode on an 80286 chip, a 386 chip, or a 486 or Pentium processor. V86 mode provides the registers, instructions, and 1 megabyte of address space that real-mode applications must have in order to run.

In the Windows 3.*x* environment, virtual machines emulate MS-DOS so well that they can run DOS applications under Windows without modification. In V86 mode, protected-mode applications can also run in virtual machines.

Virtual machines support Windows 3.*x* by providing memory protection, virtual memory, and privilege checking. If an application running in a virtual machine reads or writes memory addresses that have not been mapped into the virtual machine, an exception (a fault) is generated and the VMM regains control. An exception is also raised if an application or manipulates I/O ports to which it has not been allowed access. The VMM and virtual devices can then provide the requested memory, carry out the intended I/O operation, or terminate the application.

In a virtual machine, V86-mode applications run at privilege level 3; protected-mode applications run at privilege level 1, 2, or 3.

The System Virtual Machine

A virtual machine manager can create multiple virtual machines. When you start up a computer running, MS-DOS, the first virtual machine it creates is called the *system virtual machine*. In the Windows 3.*x* environment, the system virtual machine contains Windows and Windows applications.

The *system virtual machine* is also the processing environment of the core Windows DLLs: the Kernel, User, and GDI (graphical device interface) libraries. These core libraries, known collectively as the *Windows subsystem* in Windows 95, are the interface between applications and the Windows 95 operating system. They are examined in more detail in "The Virtual Machine Manager Subsystem" on page 123.)

Under Windows 95, the system virtual machine is managed by the virtual machine manager subsystem, which is part of the Windows 95 base operating system. The Windows 95 base operating system is described in "The Windows 95 Base Operating System" on page 135.

MS-DOS Virtual Machines

Once the system virtual machine has been created, MS-DOS can create other virtual machines for non-Windows applications as they are started. Each of these machines is known as an *MS-DOS virtual machine*.

MS-DOS can create as many MS-*DOS virtual machines* as it takes to manage the operation of DOS programs. In both Windows 3.*x* and Windows 95, every MS-DOS application that starts up runs in the context of its own individual MS-DOS virtual machine.

Each virtual machine has its own address space, its own I/O port space, and its own interrupt-vector table. The VMM also maps ROM BIOS, MS-DOS, device drivers, and TSRs (applications that remain in memory after they are terminated) to the address space of the virtual machine. This procedure provides each application with access to system functions provided by MS-DOS and to ROM BIOS routines. When protected-mode applications run under the control of a virtual machine, each protected-mode program also has its own local descriptor table (LDT).

Figure 3.1 on Page 108 shows how the virtual machine manager runs the *system virtual machine* and MS-*DOS virtual machines* under Windows 95.

How Programs Use the Virtual Machine

In Windows 95, all Windows and DOS applications run under what is known as the *context* of the system virtual machine. This context includes the following:

- A *memory map* that defines the virtual memory accessible to the currently executing application
- An *execution context* defined by the state of the 80X86 CPU registers
- *System resources*, such as window and graphics resources, that are accessible to the application running in the context of the VM.

Under the headings that follow, the three components of the system virtual machine are described in more detail.

The Windows 95 Memory Map

As explained in 2, the 386 processor provides a 4GB memory map, and Windows 95 uses almost all of it. Figure 3.2 shows what the Window 95 memory map looks like to the Windows 95 virtual machine.

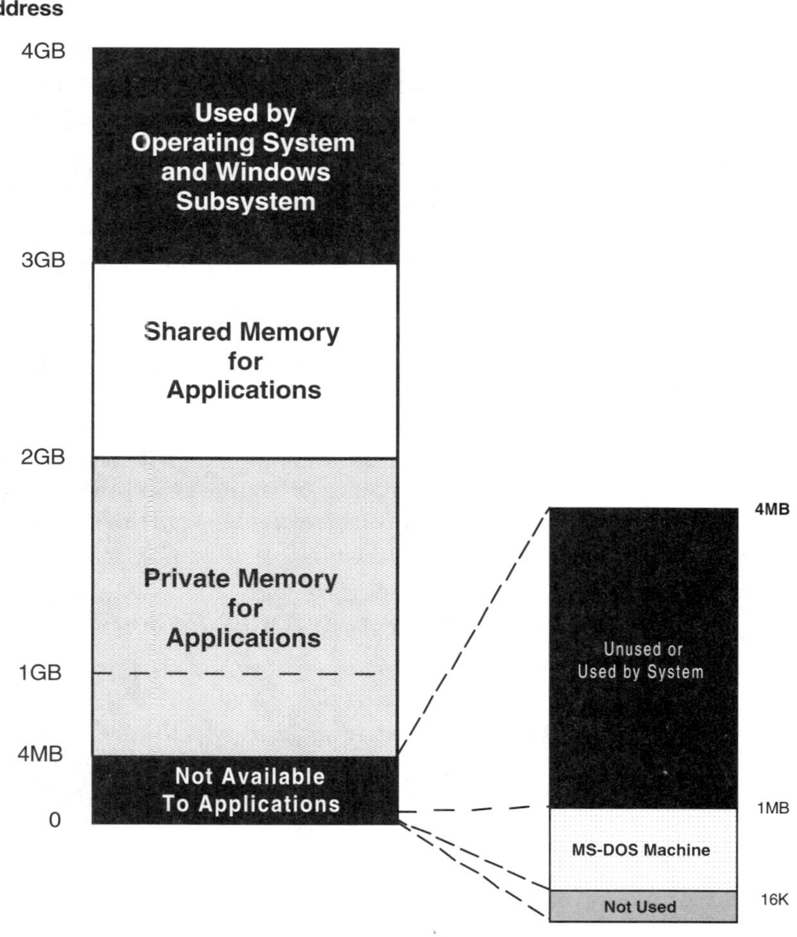

Figure 3.2 The Windows 95 memory map

Off-Limits Addresses

In the 4GB address space available to the Windows 95 system and the applications running under it, the lowest 16K of memory—virtual addresses 00000000 through 00003FFF—is unavailable for use. The Windows 95 design team declared this memory area off limits to trap a common programming error, the erroneous use of a null program pointer. Under Windows 95, a null pointer lands a program in the booby-trapped 00000000-00003FFFF area of memory and generates a memory fault, providing software developers with a chance to correct the error.

In an earlier era, leaving 16K of virtual memory space unused might have been considered wasteful. But with 4GB of virtual address space to parcel out, who's counting?

Memory for MS-DOS Machines

With the exception of the 0000-03FFFF no-person's-land, the lowest 1 MB of the 386's 4GB virtual address space is used by the currently executing MS-DOS virtual machine. So, when an MS-DOS VM is running, the operating system knows where to find it.

It's important to remember, though, that all the address space shown in Figure 3.2 is virtual. It can be mapped anywhere within a computer's physical address space, and can even be scattered around in whatever physical memory space is available. But it's unlikely in the foreseeable future that the whole 4GB of available virtual address space will be used in its entirety by very many computer systems.

Private Memory and Shared Memory

As Figure 3.2 shows, the virtual memory area that extends from 0004000(16K) to 00100000 (1MB) is reserved for use by Windows 95 and is not available to applications. But the enormous block of virtual memory that lies between 00100000 (1MB) and 0C000000 (3GB) is available for use by 32-bit applications.

Actually, there are two blocks of virtual memory between 1MB and 3GB. The 1MB-to-2MB range is private memory. As long as memory in that block is available, an application can claim any part of it for private use. Once an application has claimed a block of virtual memory in this range, other applications can't use it.

An application can reserve memory within its block of virtual memory space by calling a Win32 function named `VirtualAlloc`.

The range of virtual addresses that extend from 2GB to 3GB are available to be used as shared memory by Windows applications. Memory-sharing operations are explained in "Memory-Mapped Files" on page 114.

The virtual address space that extends from 3GB to 4GB is reserved for use by the Windows 95 operating system (see "The Windows 95 Base Operating System" on page 135) and the core Windows DLLs in the Windows subsystem (see "The Virtual Machine Manager Subsystem" on page 123). This virtual address space is off limits to Windows 95 applications.

Memory-Mapped Files

To share memory in the 2GB-to-4GB range, applications use a Windows 95 feature called *memory-mapped files*.

To create a memory-mapped file, an application obtains a block of memory addresses from the operating system and then maps a disk file into those addresses. Once a disk file is mapped into memory, applications can forget that it is a file and simply access it as if were actually stored in RAM.

To access a memory-mapped file, an application obtains a handle to the file by calling a Win32 function named **CreateFileMapping**. When an application has obtained a handle to a file-mapping object, it can call the **MapViewOfFile** function to obtain the object's address. Other applications can then obtain access to the file by calling **Open-FileMapping**, **MapViewOfFile**, or **MapViewOfFileEx**.

File mapping is examined more closely in the section titled "Memory-Mapped Files" on page 161.

Execution Context of a Windows 95 Application

When a Windows application is running under Windows 95, the application's *execution context* is defined by the current contents of all the CPU's segment and data registers as well as various flag settings.

These flag settings include the settings Bits 0 and 1 in the selector of the CS register, which specify the application's privilege level.

For more information about the 80X86 processor and its registers and flags, see Chapter 2, "Underneath Windows 95."

System Resources

The Windows subsystem libraries shown in Figure 3.1—the Kernel, User, and GDI DLLs—provide Windows applications with system resources. MS-DOS applications obtain access to the operating system by using the MS-DOS software interrupt (`INT`) interface. Sometimes MS-DOS programs also access hardware directly.

"The Virtual Machine Manager Subsystem" on page 123 describes the libraries in the Windows subsystem. "The MS-DOS Virtual Machine" on page 118 explains how DOS applications access the MS-DOS interrupt interface.

The Windows 3.*x* Virtual Machine

There are some significant differences between the way virtual machines work in Windows 3.*x* and the way they work in Windows 95.

Figure 3.3 shows the architecture of the Windows 3.1 virtual machine. In Windows 3.1, as in Windows 95, all Windows applications run in

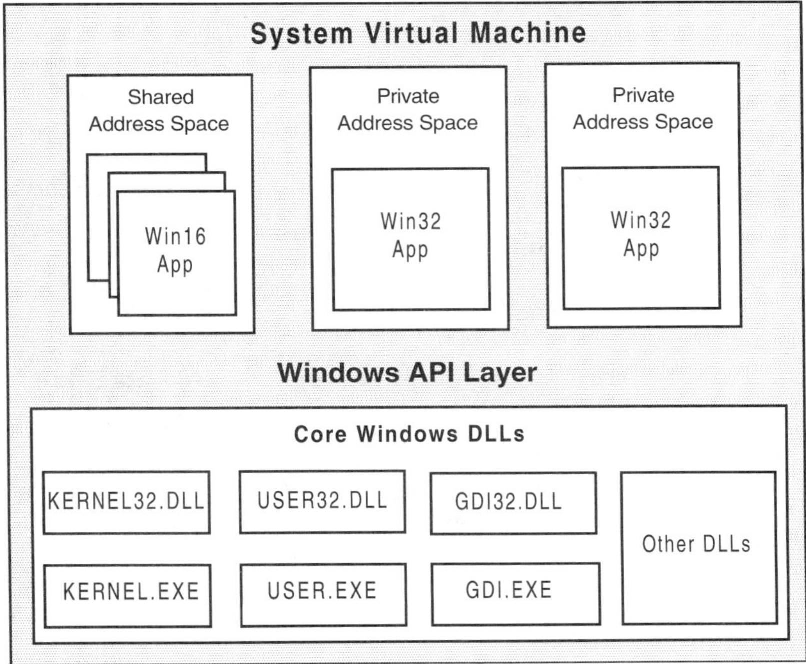

Figure 3.3 The Windows 3.1 virtual machine

the context of a single virtual machine, along with the Kernel, User, and GDI DLLs. Microsoft designed Windows 3.1 that way to mimic versions of Windows prior to Version 3.0, in which Windows tasks could freely pass data (such as addresses) back and forth to one another within the same address space.

The Windows 3.1 Core DLLs

In Windows 3.1, the three core Windows DLLs are named KRNL386.EXE, USER.EXE, and GDI.EXE. The KRNL386.EXE library, or the Kernel DLL, provides applications with low-level operating-system services. USER.EXE, the User DLL, handles window management. And GDI.EXE, or the GDI (graphical device interface) DLL, provides graphical capabilities to Windows programs.

In both Windows 3.1 and Windows 95, the Kernel, User, and GDI DLLs are managed by the operating system. (In Windows 95, the operating system is implemented in a file named WIN380.EXE.)

Because the core DLLs run in the context of the Windows virtual machine, just as applications do, they are in an ideal position to provide the interface between applications and the Windows 95 operating system. And that is just what they do. The core DLLs run at the same privilege level as applications, but they can call operating-system functions at will, so they can carry communications back and forth between applications and the operating system.

The interface provided by the core DLLs is the mechanism that lets Windows applications call operating-system services using named function calls rather than the numbered software interrupts that link applications and the operating system in MS-DOS applications. In both Windows 3.1 and Windows 95, the interface between applications and the operating system is provided by the core DLLs.

The Windows 3.1 MS-DOS Virtual Machines

When you start an MS-DOS application under Windows 3.1, the program does not execute in the context of the Windows 3.1 system VM. Instead, as Figure 3.3 illustrates, each DOS application launched under Windows 3.1 runs in the context of its own *MS-DOS virtual machine*. In turn, each MS-DOS machine runs in the context of the system virtual machine. (As you'll see in a few moments, this is the same way DOS applications run under Windows 95.)

The Windows 95 virtual machine works something like the Windows 3.1 virtual machine, but there are important differences.

The Windows 95 Virtual Machine

In Windows 95, just as in Windows 3.1, all Windows applications and the core Windows DLLs run in the context of the system virtual machine. And so do all MS-DOS applications.

This is a different arrangement from the virtual-machine architecture of Windows 3.1. In Windows 3.1, as noted earlier, MS-DOS applications run separately from the system virtual machine.

Running 32-Bit Applications under Windows 95

Another difference between the Windows 3.1 virtual machine and the Windows 95 VM is that Windows 95 supports a whole new class of 32-bit applications that operate by calling functions in the Microsoft Win32 API.

The Win32 API is an enormous collection of functions that Microsoft introduced along with Windows NT. Windows 95 uses a subset of functions in the Win32 API.

Many of the functions in the Win32 API are 32-bit versions of the 16-bit Windows API functions that are familiar to Windows 3.*x* programmers. But many other functions—some of which support the new features of Windows 95—are brand-new.

Most of the text and source code presented in this book explains and demonstrates the use of functions implemented in the Win32 API.

Code and Data Protection in Windows 95

In Windows 95, 32-bit applications run in the context of the System VM, just as 16-bit Windows applications do. But in Windows 95, every 32-bit application has its own private protected address space that other applications cannot access. This arrangement helps to prevent 32-bit applications from invading each other's memory spaces and corrupting each other's code and data.

Windows 95 does not provide 16-bit applications with this kind of protection. All 16-bit Windows applications share the same address space, so there are no guard rails to keep them from overwriting each other. However, Windows 95 does prevent runaway applications from corrupting operating-system code and data, as you'll see later in this chapter.

Preemptive Multitasking

Another important difference between the Windows 3.1 virtual machine and the Windows 95 VM is that the Win95 VM supports *preemptive multitasking*. Preemptive multitasking is a scheduling system that breaks processes down into *threads* and assigns each thread its own slice of processor time. Threads are assigned processor time in accordance with predetermined priorities, so low-priority process cannot steal time from higher-priority processes. This system speeds up processing and hastens response time when multiple applications are running concurrently.

The preemptive multitasking approach replaces the *cooperative multitasking* system used by Windows 3.1. Under cooperative multitasking, the operating system uses a single queue to hold all messages that perform Windows operations. This queue holds all messages that inform the system of new events—mouse clicks in one of the application's windows, new programs starting up, and so forth. As a result, one ill-behaved application can slow down message flow throughout the system or even bring the system crashing down.

To prevent such disasters, Windows 95 provides mechanisms that place messages destined for Win32 applications into private message queues, reducing the possibility of slowdowns and crashes when one application fails to service the message queue.

Threads, multithreading, and preemptive multitasking are the topics of Chapter 9.

The MS-DOS Virtual Machine

In Windows 95, just as in Windows 3.*x*, every MS-DOS application the user launches executes in the context of an *MS-DOS virtual machine*. Every time an MS-DOS application starts, Windows 95 creates a new virtual MS-DOS machine. So each MS-DOS application operates in the context of its own virtual DOS machine.

Virtual 8086 Mode

When a DOS application runs in the context of an MS-DOS virtual machine, the program doesn't execute in real mode. Instead, it runs in *virtual 8086 mode*. This is true in Windows 3.*x* as well as in Windows 95.

Virtual 8086 mode, often referred to simply as *virtual mode*, is the mode under which MS-DOS applications usually run when they are executed from Windows. Virtual 8086 mode is an operating mode that is built into the 386 processor.

Virtual 8086 mode operates within the context of protected mode, so the 386 and its successors can switch into and out of virtual mode without leaving protected mode. In fact, virtual 8086 mode was invented so the 80X86 processor wouldn't have to switch back and forth between real mode and protected mode to process different kinds of applications.

How Virtual Mode Speeds Up Processing

Because the 386 doesn't require a time-consuming mode-switch operation to start running in virtual mode, task switching between a Windows application and an MS-DOS application on the 386 is much faster than it was on the 286.

But to a DOS application, an MS-DOS VM running in virtual mode looks exactly like a real 8086 microprocessor, with a 1MB memory map that corresponds exactly to the memory map of a real 386 CPU. For example, a DOS VM has a standard block of directly addressable video display memory starting at memory address B8000H.

Code and Data Protection in Virtual 8086 Mode

Because virtual 8086 mode runs under 386 protected mode, MS-DOS programs running in virtual mode are protected by the same kinds of memory and device protection mechanisms that are provided to Windows programs running in protected mode. For example, the 386 privilege-level settings described in Chapter 2 apply to DOS programs running in virtual 8086 mode as well as to Windows programs running in protected mode.

In fact, DOS applications running in virtual 8086 mode receive a measure of protection that even 16-bit Windows programs do not have. Every MS-DOS VM runs in its own private address space, safe from interference by other applications and unable to corrupt other applications' code or data.

How Virtual 8086 Mode Works

Running an MS-DOS application in virtual 8086 mode is fairly straightforward. Once the program is loaded, the operating system flags it as a virtual-mode application by setting a single bit in one of the 386's control registers. All rules of 8086 program execution then apply to the virtual-mode program.

When a virtual-mode program is running, the 386 pretends that all its registers are 16-bit registers, and it generates 20-bit addresses exactly as it would if it were an 8086 processor.

Virtual Mode and Virtual Addresses

When the 386 executes a program in virtual mode, it keeps one big secret from the application. Although the program being executed doesn't know it, the 20-bit addresses that the 386 generates in virtual mode are not literal addresses, but virtual addresses.

Because virtual mode operates in the context of protected mode, the 386 calculates virtual-mode addresses using protected-mode rules. That means the Windows 95 operating system can load virtual-mode programs anywhere in memory. The 386 paging capabilities described in Chapter 2 are available in virtual mode, so the 386 can swap virtual-mode programs in and out of memory in the same way it can perform memory-swapping while running other kinds of protected-mode programs.

Opening Multiple DOS Windows

Another benefit of virtual 8086 mode is that users of Windows 95 don't have to leave Windows to run MS-DOS applications. When a user double-clicks the MS-DOS icon on the Win95 desktop, the Win95 virtual machine manager opens a console window and creates an MS-DOS VM that manages DOS I/O inside that window. Each time the user opens a new MS-DOS console window, Windows 95 creates a new DOS virtual machine.

DOS applications running under MS-DOS virtual machines use the software interrupt services of MS-DOS (mostly the INT 21H services; see "The INT 21H Interrupt" on page 137) to make system requests. Under Windows 95, these requests ultimately pass to the protected-mode code that implements the system services. In the case of file-system requests, the INT 21H call is passed to the new file-system manager to be handled together with other concurrent requests from applications that are running in the System VM.

How Windows 95 Initializes DOS and Windows

As you may have noticed, Windows 3.*x* and Windows 95 go through different loading procedures at startup time. When you boot a computer that has Windows 3.*x* installed, DOS starts up first and takes over control of the system. Windows doesn't start until the user executes the `win` command, either from a command line or from an

AUTOEXEC.BAT file. Then Windows starts, but under the control of DOS. (For more about how Windows 95 starts up, see "What Happens when You Start Up Windows 95" on page 101.)

Keeping Track of MS-DOS Applications

An easy way to see if any MS-DOS applications are installed in your Windows 95 system is to open a DOS console window and then enter the command dir /p. Windows 95 then lists all DOS .EXE files installed in your \WIN95\COMMAND director.

DOS VM Initialization under Windows 3.*x*

Under both Windows 3.*x*, and Windows 95, a system virtual machine handles the Windows initialization process. This system VM not only installs Windows, but also prepares the system's global context for any MS-DOS VMs that may be started later.

Under Windows 3.1, the system VM sets up a DOS environment by taking an electronic snapshot of MS-DOS at the moment when the user types the **`win`** command. Then Windows 3.*x* pushes DOS's real-mode operating-system code out of the way and takes over control of the system.

Later on, at any time the user decides to switch to DOS, the system is ready to create a new MS-DOS VM, using the snapshot taken at startup time to set up the new VM's context. This startup snapshot includes freeze frames of all terminate-and-stay-resident (TSR) applications, environment variables, and the like.

DOS VM Initialization under Windows 95

The initialization of DOS VMs is quite different under Windows 95. Instead of waiting for the user to enter a **`win`** command, Windows 95 immediately seizes control of the system and then switches right away to protected mode. The Windows 95 operating system then pushes DOS's real-mode code aside, just as Windows 3.*x* does, and takes control of the machine.

CONFIG.SYS and AUTOEXEC.BAT Are Optional

It's important to note that Windows 95 does not require any CONFIG.SYS or AUTOEXEC.BAT files. In fact, Windows 95 works better if there are no CONFIG.SYS or AUTOEXEC.BAT files to worry about. If those two files don't exist, Win95 configures itself automatically by reading its registry database (see "Online Help in Windows 95" on page 30) and using its plug-and-play capabilities to ferret out any new devices in the system or to track down any devices that have been changed since the last time Windows 95 was started.

Win95 grudgingly permits the existence of CONFIG.SYS and AUTOEXEC.BAT, but strictly for the sake of backward compatibility with Windows 3.*x*—mainly so owners of real-mode device drivers that haven't been updated yet can continue to run their equipment using existing CONFIG.SYS and AUTOEXEC.BAT files.

MS-DOS and the Mystery Virtual Machine

Windows 95 sets up MS-DOS VMs using a special virtual machine that you'll never see unless you go looking for it with a debugger. This special virtual machine never contains an application that actually runs. Instead, it contains the initial state of the MS-DOS environment once system booting and the processing of CONFIG.SYS and AUTOEXECI.BAT are complete.

This special hidden virtual machine is used to store all global information that applies to your computer system's MS-DOS environment when you start up your system. For example, if your AUTOEXEC.BAT runs a TSR program before it starts Windows, that TSR program is loaded into memory and becomes part of the global MS-DOS environment. This procedure makes it possible for your Windows 95 application to use CONFIG.SYS to load device drivers and AUTOEXEC.BAT to load TSRs as parts of the global MS-DOS environment.

Once this global initialization is complete, Windows saves a snapshot of the MS-DOS environment by setting up the context of the hidden VM context to be used as the initial state of every MS-DOS VM that is subsequently started. The saved hidden VM itself never runs because its only purpose is to provide a context for each virtual MS-DOS machine that subsequently starts.

Each time you start an MS-DOS application from within Windows 95, the system creates a new MS-DOS VM by allocating some memory and the appropriate control blocks within the system. Then Windows 95 copies into the new VM the entire global environment that is stored in the hidden VM. So the new MS-DOS VM has the same initial state that it would have if you had just turned the machine on and run through the startup procedure again.

Because each new MS-DOS virtual machine uses a context copied from the hidden VM—but does not change the context stored in the hidden VM—you can make changes in the state of any MS-DOS VM without affecting the states of other DOS VMs, and without affecting the saved global VM context that provides the initial states of each MS-DOS VM that starts.

The Virtual Machine Manager Subsystem

The virtual machine manager has been called the heart of the Windows 95 operating system. It manages vital Win95 operations such as task scheduling, virtual memory operations, program loading and termination, and intertask communication.

The VMM also controls various kinds of device drivers, including real-mode drivers, virtual device drivers (VxDs), and other kinds of drivers.

Microsoft and third-party manufacturers have worked together to create many new device drivers for products used with Win95, including mice, CD-ROM drives, and many kinds of printers, video monitors, and hard-disk drives. (To learn more about VxDs, see "Windows 95 Device Drivers" on page 139.)

How the Virtual Machine Manager Works

The virtual machine manager provides Windows 95 with many powerful new features that Windows 3.1 did not have.

In a nutshell, the VMM performs six kinds of functions:

- It schedules and manages the operation of all 16-bit and 32-bit Windows applications.
- It schedules the operation of threads, which make preemptive multitasking possible.
- It performs low-level memory-management services.
- It loads and terminates programs.
- It provides intertask communication.
- It creates virtual MS-DOS machines to run MS-DOS applications.

Figure 3.1, shown on page 108 at the beginning of this chapter, illustrates how the Windows 95 virtual machine manager operates within the context of the rest of the Windows 95 system. Each component shown in the diagram is described under a separate heading in this section.

Four kinds of code run in the context of the system virtual machine under the direction of the virtual machine manager:

- As many 32-bit Windows applications as memory (including virtual memory) allows, each running in its own address space
- The Windows 95 shell
- As many 16-bit Windows applications as memory (including virtual memory) allows, all running in a shared address space
- As many MS-DOS applications as memory (including virtual memory) allows, each running under the control of a separate MS-DOS machine.

The Windows Subsystem

In Windows 95, the core Windows libraries—the Kernel, User, and GDI DLLs—are grouped into a subsystem called the *Windows subsystem*. This subsystem is also known as the *Windows API layer* because the libraries it contains are implemented in the Win32 API.

As longtime Windows programmers know, most of the functionality of Windows 3.*x* is implemented in a set of three dynamic-link libraries named KERNEL.EXE, GDI.EXE, and USER.EXE. In the world of 16-bit Windows, these three libraries are sometimes referred to as the *core Windows DLLs*.

In Windows 95, there are two versions of each of the three core DLLs: one version that contains 16-bit code and another version that contains 32-bit code. Some calls to the Windows 95 subsystem are handled by the 16-bit versions of the core DLLs, some are handled by the 32-bit versions, and some are handled by both.

The Windows Subsystem DLLs

These are the six DLLs that make up the Windows 95 subsystem:

- **KERNEL.EXE**—handles 16-bit memory management, the loading and execution of programs, and scheduling.
- **KERNEL32.DLL**—handles 32-bit memory management, loading and executing programs, and scheduling.
- **GDI.EXE**—manages 16-bit graphics operations.
- **GDI32.DLL**—manages 32-bit graphics operations.
- **USER.EXE**—manages the 16-bit user interface and performs 16-bit window management.
- **USER32.DLL**—manages the 32-bit user interface and performs 32-bit window management.

The six DLLs in the in the preceding list contain most of the Windows 95 functions called by application and user-written libraries. They also pass communications back and forth between applications and subsystems that make up the Windows 95 operating system.

Figure 3.4 shows how the libraries in the Windows subsystem (or the Windows API layer) act as an interface between applications and the Windows 95 operating system.

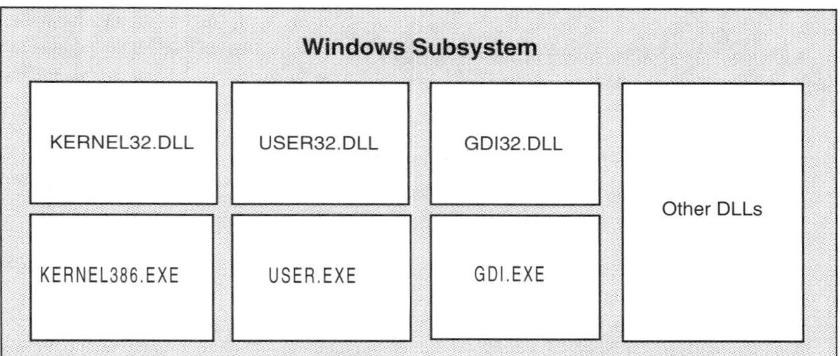

Figure 3.4 The Windows subsystem

Code and Data Protection in the Windows Subsystem

The DLLs in the Windows subsystem have a unique status in Windows 95 because they can communicate both with ordinary applications and with the subsystems that make up the base operating system.

The core DLLs enjoy their unique status because they run at the same privilege level as ordinary applications but are specially engineered to interface with operating-system functions that run at a higher privilege level.

Specifically, the core DLLs run at Privilege Level 3—also known as Ring 3—but can communicate with functions that run at Privilege Level 0, or Ring 0.

How the Core DLLs Span Privilege Levels

As you may recall from Chapter 2, four *privilege levels* are built into the 386 chip and its successors. In Windows 95, operating-system code has the highest privilege level, Level 0, and ordinary applications have the lowest privilege level, Level 3.

Privilege levels are built in the 80X86 family of processors in the form of a set of four *protection rings*. These rings are numbered consecutively from 0 to 3. The number of each ring corresponds to a privilege level.

In Windows 95, operating-system code has a privilege level of 0, so it is said to run in Ring 0. Applications have a privilege level of 3, so they are said to run in Ring 3.

However, unlike ordinary applications, the core DLLs can communicate with operating-system functions that run in Ring 0. That is why the core DLLs can operate as an interface between Windows 95 applications and the operating system.

How Protection Rings Work

The protection-ring system prevents low-privilege programs, such as ordinary applications, from corrupting code and data used by higher-privilege programs, such as operating systems.

A code segment running in Ring 0 code can execute any legal 386/486/Pentium instruction. But code running in any other ring generates a general protection (GP) fault if it tries to execute certain instructions that could adversely affect other programs or the operating system itself.

Instructions that can't be legally executed by code running outside Ring 0—unless the operating system specifically grants permission—include statements that change descriptor tables, perform I/O port operations, halt the processor, or switch the CPU into and out of protected mode.

How Applications Can Break the Ring Barrier

Although the Windows 95 operating system runs in Ring 0, it can allow code running in other rings to execute instructions that are ordinarily reserved for Ring 0 code.

To grant this special permission, the operating system intercepts the GP fault that less privileged code generates when it tries to execute an instruction reserved for a higher-privileged function. The operating system then examines the instruction that generated the fault.

If the operating system decides that the code should be executed, it re-executes the offending instruction using Ring 0 code. In this way, Windows 95 permits applications to access certain operating-system components such as the system timer.

Although this method of granting permission works, it would be too time-consuming for the operating system to examine a function call's credentials every time an application requests a system service. That is why the Kernel, User, and GDI libraries run in Ring 3.

Accessing the Operating System via Core DLLs

When an application needs to call a function provided by one of core DLLs, it can simply call the function. If the DLL that provides the function needs to obtain a service from the operating system, it obtains the service easily because core DLLs can always access Ring 0. In this way, applications can access system services without any costly ring-to-ring transitions.

The Kernel Module

In Windows 95, as in its 16-bit predecessors, the Kernel module handles Windows functions involving memory management, resource management, and multitasking. The Kernel DLL provides functions string management, local and global heap management, module management, task management, and even a mechanism for directly accessing physical locations in the first megabyte of your system's memory.

In Windows 3.*x*, memory management consisted mainly of the Kernel's heap management on the front end and the Windows virtual memory manager working in the background. In Windows 95, memory management is a bit more complicated, but the Kernel module is still responsible for low-level memory management.

The GDI Module

The GDI module handles all the painting, drawing, plotting, printing, and color functions that Windows 95 provides. Windows programs handle most graphics operations by calling functions provided by the GDI module (although some drawing functions actually have entry points supplied by the User module, described under the next heading).

The GDI DLL calls routines in various driver files—for example, it calls the video driver that accesses the hardware that is used to produce your system's video display. GDI can also call other kinds of drivers, such as drivers from printers and plotters.

The GDI module has a local heap in which it stores the overhead for all its graphics objects, such as bitmaps, icons, and cursors. In Windows 3.*x*, the GDI's local heap has a theoretical maximum size of just under 64K. The raw data for GDI objects is usually stored in the global heap, which has no such size limitation.

Because the space used to store GDI objects in Windows 3.*x* was limited, Windows 3.*x* programmers were always advised to discard GDI objects as soon as they were no longer needed. Although well-designed programs always manage memory resources carefully, the miserly management of GDI objects is not as critical in Windows 95 as it used to be in Windows 3.*x*.

The User Module

The User module controls everything in Windows 95 that involves communications, hardware, messaging, and window creation. The User module, like the GDI module, has a local heap in which it stores all class and window data. It has a second heap in which menu data is stored.

In Windows 3.*x*, the User DLL has even more severe memory limitations than the GDI DLL, because windows tend to have longer lives than GDI objects. In Windows, every window or dialog control is ordinarily regarded as an individual window. So, if several Windows programs are running simultaneously, it's easier than you might imagine to have 200 or 300 windows (both visible and invisible) running at the same time. And that can lock up your desktop.

In Windows 3.*x*, programmers used various techniques to avoid bringing processing to a halt by creating too many windows. But the easiest way to avoid the problem was also the most straightforward: Don't create so many windows.

In Windows 95, this memory headache has also gone away. Although it still isn't a great idea to create hundreds of windows just for the heck of it, you can generally use all the windows you need without worrying about their numbers in a Windows 95 program.

The 32-Bit Core DLLs

The code that implements the six core DLLs resides in four files in the \WINDOWS\SYSTEM directory. These are the contents of the 32-bit versions of core DLLs:

- KERNEL32.DLL contains the API entry points and support code for the 32-bit Windows kernel functions.
- USER32.DLL contains the API entry points and support code for the 32-bit window management functions.

- GDI32.DLL contains the API entry points and support code for the 32-bit graphics engine functions.

KERNEL32.DLL is completely independent of the 16-bit Windows Kernel. When Windows 95 is running, there is some communication from the 16-bit to the 32-bit side, but the 32-bit KERNEL never calls across to its 16-bit cousin.

This is not surprising, since most of the code in the 32-bit kernel (for example, the code that implements memory allocation and thread management) is quite different from the code that performs similar functions in the 16-bit kernel.

Most of the code in USER32.DLL amounts to no more than a wrapper that accepts 32-bit API calls and hands them to the 16-bit User DLL for processing. But this is a more complex procedure than you might imagine, as you'll see later in this chapter.

GDI32.DLL contains many new graphics functions, as well as many 32-bit versions of familiar 16-bit functions. Consequently, the 32-bit GDI DLL handles many function calls directly, without bothering to call older 16-bit functions that could be supplied by the 16-bit GDI library.

Mixing the 16-Bit and 32-Bit Core Libraries

Because Windows 95 is equipped with two versions of each core DLL—one 16-bit version and one 32-bit version—the designers of the Windows 95 operating system had to develop special techniques for using the Kernel, GDI, and User DLLs. In the simplest of all possible worlds, 16-bit applications would call the 16-bit versions of Kernel, GDI, and User, while 32-bit applications would call the 32-bit versions of the same DLLs, and everything would work just fine.

But that is not the way Windows 95 is designed. The main reason is speed.

If the Windows 95 design team had provided two complete copies of the Kernel, GDI, and User DLLs—one set written in 16-bit code and the other set written in 32-bit code—Windows 95 would be much too big to run on a 386 computer with 4MB of RAM. That's the minimum configuration that Windows 95 is supposed to require, and Microsoft could not stuff that much code into 4MB of RAM.

Instead, the Win95 development team created a set of code packages called *thunks* to make the Windows 95 subsystem compatible with both 16-bit and 32-bit applications. In Windows 95, a *thunk* is simply a piece of code that is used to call a 32-bit code segment from a 16-bit code segment or vice versa.

With the help of thunking technology, a 16-bit application can call a 32-bit function, or a 32-bit application can call a 16-bit function, through what is known as a *thunk layer*. When a 16-bit application calls a 32-bit function using a thunk, that is called *thunking up*. When a 32-bit function calls a 16-bit function using a thunk, that is called *thunking down*.

The Windows 95 subsystem uses both kinds of thunking. The 16-bit components of the Win95 subsystem thunk up to 32-bit code when they have to, and 32-bit functions thunk down to 16-bit code when necessary. They do that through a thunking layer, as shown in Figure 3.5.

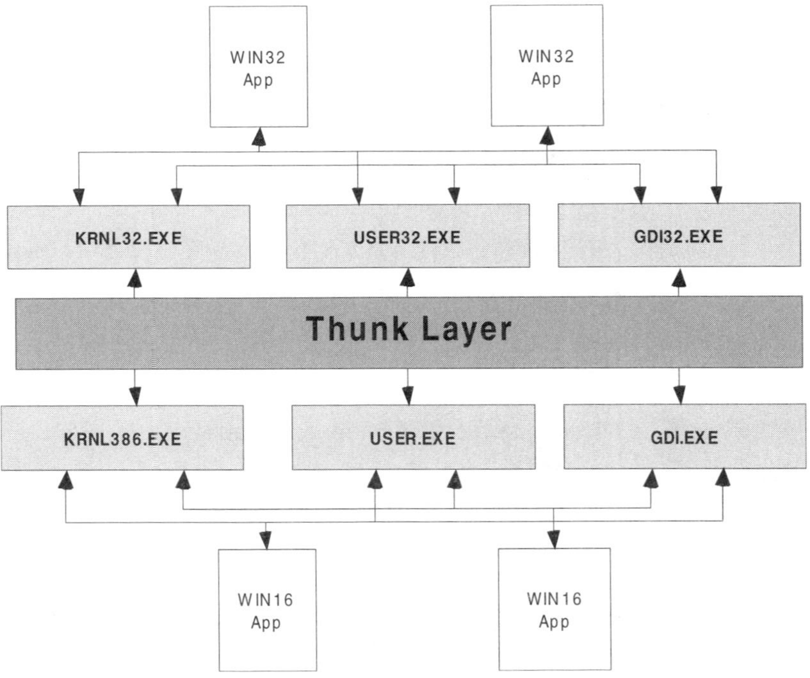

Figure 3.5 The thunking layer

Tech Talk

From an assembly-language point of view, Windows 95 handles stack-management during thunking by building a new stack frame during the transition between the different code types. A call from one code segment type to another translates parameter formats as they are pushed on top of the existing stack frame. The addressing of this new frame is then set up to conform to the rules of the target code type.

To Thunk or Not to Thunk

When 16-bit and 32-bit code segments communicate through a thunk layer, there is always a price to pay in terms of performance. But the price is not always inordinately high. When thunking degrades performance by only a small amount, it can be a good way to reduce code size. If the degradation is too great, the authors of the code can avoid the necessity of thunking by writing new code.

After considerable thought, the engineers who designed Windows 95 decided that there is a time to thunk and a time not to thunk. They calculated the performance price of each potential thunk, and used thunking only when it seemed to make sense. When it did not make sense, they avoided thunking by writing duplicate 16-bit and 32-bit functionality into their code.

As a result, some of the code in the Windows 95 subsystem is provided in both a 16-bit version and a 32-bit version. But some Windows 95 code is not.

When a Windows subsystem function needs to be accessed and performance is more important than code size, the Win95 subsystem thunks up or thunks down. Otherwise, the subsystem calls a function that supplies the same functionality, even though the extra code increases the overall size of the system. It's the same kind of tradeoff that programmers face every day in many other areas of software design.

Using Thunking in Windows 95 Application

Because Windows 95 is a cross between a 16-bit operating system and a 32-bit operating system, you may one day find yourself looking for a way to mix 16-bit code and 32-bit code in the same application. You may find that some parts of your application can be ported easily to the 32-bit Windows 95 environment, while other components are more tightly bound to the 16-bit environment.

For example, while porting your application to a 32-bit environment, you may encounter an existing DLL that relies on segment:offset addressing or has been specifically optimized for Windows 3.1's 16-bit architecture. Instead of gritting your teeth and wasting time and effort rewriting the offending DLL, you might find it easier to connect it to the rest of your code through a thunking level.

Fortunately, there is a way to do that. Windows 95 is equipped with two tools that are especially designed to help you mix 32-bit components and 16-bit components in the same application. One of these tools is called the *Microsoft thunk compiler*. The other is a set of functions called the *Windows generic thunks*.

The Microsoft Thunk Compiler

As noted in Chapter 2, "Underneath Windows 95," a pointer in a 16-bit Windows program has two parts: a selector and a 16-bit offset. In a 32-bit Windows program, a pointer essentially has just one part: a 32-bit offset.

When your computer is executing a 32-bit Windows 95 program, the selectors in your CPU's DS, ES, SS, and CS registers all hold the same base address. To put it another way, all pointers in a 16-bit program could be viewed as 16:16 pointers, while all pointers in a 32-bit Windows 95 program could be viewed as near 0:32 pointers.

Recall that to translate a 16:16 pointer to a 0:32 pointer, you determine the segment base for the selector portion of the pointer, and then you add an offset to that segment base. To go in the other direction, and translate a 0:32 pointer to a 16:16 pointer, you can allocate a selector and then calculate the offset from the base of the corresponding segment.

Sixteen-bit and 32-bit applications use the same mechanism to pass parameters to functions. Both kinds of programs pass function parameters on the stack.

There is a difference, however, between the way 16-bit programs place function parameters on the stack and the way 32-bit programs use the stack. Sixteen-bit applications address the stack using the SS:SP registers, while 32-bit applications use the SS:ESP registers. So, when your application thunks back and forth between 16-bit and 32-bit functions, you must use some kind of software interface for switching stacks. That's where the MFC thunk compiler comes in.

How the Thunk Compiler Works

The thunk compiler is simply a piece of software that translates 16-bit words to 32-bit words and vice versa. For example, suppose a 16-bit application contains the following function:

```
DWORD Func32(WORD value);
```

When a 32-bit function calls the preceding 16-bit function, the 32-bit function pushes a 32-bit argument on the stack. But when the time comes for the 16-bit function to execute, the 16-bit function pops only 16 bits off the stack. Conversely, when the function returns, the 32-bit calling function places the returned double-word value returned by the called function in the CPU's DX:AX pair of registers. Unfortunately, the 32-bit calling application expects the return value to be in the EAX register. The thunking compiler's job to negotiate these translations.

Thunk Scripts

The thunk compiler's input is a *thunk script*. A thunk script is a list of C-style function prototypes and typedefs. When you run a piece of source code through the thunk compiler, the compiler generates an assembly-language (.ASM) file that is really two .ASM files in one. One of the components of the file is a 16-bit to 32-bit thunk. The other component is a 32-bit to 16-bit thunk.

When the thunk compiler generates an .ASM file, the 16-bit component of the file contains a jump table containing the 16:16 address of each function named in the thunk scripts. The 32-bit half of the .ASM file contains a STDCALL function for each thunk. Each STDCALL function converts the parameters it receives to 16-bit values. Then the function makes use of some fancy internal processing provided by the thunk compiler to call the 16-bit target named in the jump table. When a 32-bit application invokes a thunked function, it calls these compiler-generated STDCALL functions directly.

When the thunk compiler generates an .ASM file, you can assemble the file with the Microsoft MASM assembler. If you assemble the file with the "-DIS_16" flag set, the result is a 16-bit .OBJ file that links your 16-bit code with your 32- bit code. If you then assemble the file with the "-DIS_32" flag set, the result is a 32-bit .OBJ file that links your 32-bit code with your 16-bit code.

Where to Find More Information

Thunking is a rather complex operation that requires the use of an assembler and is most likely to be used by advanced programmers with a lot of code to thunk. If you are interested in pursuing the topic further, you can find a more detailed explanation in the thunk-compiler documentation that comes with the Win32 SDK.

Using Generic Thunks in Windows 95

Windows 95 supports the Windows generic thunk functions, a set of thunking functions that were introduced in Win32 API along with the introduction of Windows NT.

The Windows generic thunk functions let you run 16-bit applications in a 32-bit environment using a technology known as *Windows on Windows*, or *WOW*. When you make a 16-bit Windows API call using WOW, the call is mapped to a corresponding Win32 API. You can find prototypes for the Windows generic functions in the WOWN16.H header file.

Windows 95 supports the following Windows NT generic thunk functions:

- **`LoadLibraryEx32W`**—Allows a 16-bit thunk DLL to load a 32-bit thunk DLL.
- **`FreeLibraryEx32W`**—Allows a 16-bit thunk DLL to free a 32-bit thunk DLL that has been previously loaded with **`LoadLibraryEx32W`**.
- **`GetProcAddress32W`**—Allows a 16-bit thunk DLL to get a value that corresponds to a 32-bit thunk routine.
- **`GetVDMPointer32W`**—Allows a 16-bit thunk DLL to translate a 16-bit far pointer into a 32-bit flat pointer for use by a 32-bit thunk DLL.
- **`CallProc32W`**—Used by a 16-bit thunk DLL to call an entry point in a 32-bit DLL.
- **`CallProcEx32W`**—Similar to **`CallProc32W`**, but with additional options.
- **`WOWGetVDMPointer`**—Converts a 16:16 address to the equivalent flat address.
- **`WOWGetVDMPointerFix`**—Functionally equivalent to **`WOWGet-VDMPointer`** in Windows 95 and Windows NT. In future releases of Windows 95, this function may call **`GlobalFix`** to prevent 16-bit code from moving around in memory when other 16-bit code is called.
- **`WOWGetVDMPointerUnFix`**—Calls **`GlobalUnFix`** and returns.
- **`WOWCallback16`**—Used in 32-bit code called from 16-bit code via generic thunks to call back to the 16-bit side (generic callback).
- **`CallbackRoutine`**—Also used in 32-bit code called from 16-bit code via generic thunks to call back to the 16-bit side (generic callback).

- **WOWCallback16Ex**—Allows any combination of arguments up to **WCB16_MAX_CBARGS** bytes total to be passed to the 16-bit callback routine.

Windows 95 also supports the following Windows NT generic thunk functions, which thunk 32-bit functions to the Win16 versions of the same functions:

- **WOWGlobalAlloc16**
- **WOWGlobalFree16**
- **WOWGlobalLock16**
- **WOWGlobalUnlock16**

In addition, Windows 95 supports these Windows NT generic thunk functions, which combine several common Win16 operations into one call across the thunk:

- **WOWGlobalAllocLock16**
- **WOWGlobalUnlockFree16**
- **WOWGlobalLockSize16**

Two Windows generic thunk functions supported by Windows 95 thunk down to the Win16 forms of the same functions to allow other tasks to run. These functions are designed to be used for thunks that perform lengthy operations:

- **WOWYield16**
- **WOWDirectedYield16**

Two other Windows generic thunk APIs map 16-bit handles to 32-bit handles, and vice-versa:

- **WOWHandle32**
- **WOWHandle16**

Along with the Windows NT generic functions it contains, the WOWNT32.H file contains macros that can be used to map handles between Win16 and Win32. For example, to map a Win16 HWND to a Win32 HWND, WOWNT32.H provides the HWND_32 macro.

The Windows 95 Base Operating System

In Windows 95, the Kernel, User, and GDI DLLs (see "The 32-Bit Core DLLs" on page 128) are known collectively as the Windows 95 subsystem. The Windows 95 subsystem and five other subsystems form the complete Windows 95 operating system, known in its entirety as the *base operating system*.

The base operating system is the only Windows 95 component that is assigned Privilege Level 0—the highest privilege level—and runs in the highest protection ring (Ring 0).

In contrast, the six DLLs in the Windows subsystem are assigned the lowest privilege level (Level 3) and run in the lowest protection ring (Ring 3).

Although the core DLLs run in Ring 3, special thunking mechanisms provided by Windows 95 give them access to the base operating system. Because they run in Ring 3, they also have access to ordinary Ring-3 applications.

That is an ideal arrangement because it allows the core DLLs to act as an intermediary between applications and the base operating system. And that is exactly what the core DLLs do. Because applications run at the same privilege level as the core DLLs in the Windows subsystem, applications can communicate with the subsystems in the base operating system through the DLLs .

Components of the Base Operating System

The Windows 95 base operating system is made up of five subsystems:

- The file-management subsystem
- The network subsystem
- Operating-system services
- The virtual machine manager subsystem
- Device drivers.

The File Management Subsystem

One important new component of Windows 95 is its *file management subsystem*—a completely redesigned subsystem that supports multiple file systems and makes them available concurrently.

The file management subsystem is a new 32-bit API that frees Windows 95 from the limitations of MS-DOS file management. The Win95 file management subsystem supports long filenames and lets applications access different kinds of filenames on networked computers simultaneously.

Windows 3.1 relies upon MS-DOS for file-system access. Although this is about the only significant reliance on MS-DOS within Windows 3.1, it is a weak point of the system. It creates a whole catalog of problems that the Windows designers have grappled with over the course of several releases. They finally fix the problems in Windows 95 by replacing the MS-DOS file-system services with a new protected mode subsystem.

The Windows 95 file-management system is completely different from the system used by Windows 3.1 and its predecessors. In Windows 3.1, file-system support for local disks was provided by MS-DOS. Support for SCSI devices such as CD-ROM drives did not come naturally to Windows 3.1 and was handled in different ways by different drivers.

This MS-DOS control impaired the performance of Windows, and the opportunity to improve file-system support didn't really exist while MS-DOS remained in control. Under Windows 95, the situation is entirely different. Notably, MS-DOS is no longer used for the management of files on local disks. The new file management subsystem provides a series of interfaces that allows all local disk file systems (including the CD ROM file system) and multiple network file systems to coexist.

The Plug and Play System

Windows 95, using a new approach known as plug-and-play, has considerably smoothed out the interface between Windows and hardware devices. Unless you have some old MS-DOS device drivers that are still hanging around to support particular devices, all Windows 95 file management is handled in protected-mode 32-bit code. This design supports local disks and CD-ROM devices, as well as network interfaces. So, when you run Windows 95, you can access hard disks, floppy disks, CD-ROM drives, removable hard disks, Windows NT-based servers, and even NetWare networks, without ever leaving protected mode.

For more details about the Windows 95 plug-and-play system, see Chapter 1, "Introducing Windows 95."

The INT 21H Interrupt

All MS-DOS file-system services are accessed by means of the INT 21H software interrupt. Within the system VM, the execution of the INT 21H instruction generates a general protection (GP) fault that the operating system intercepts and handles.

Windows 3.1 dealt with this fault by arranging for the System VM to switch temporarily to virtual 8086 mode so the MS-DOS INT 21H code could execute correctly. Once the file operation was completed, the Windows 3.1 system VM returned to protected mode and the Windows application code continues to execute.

Windows 95 intercepts the same fault and simply hands it to the protected-mode file-system manager for processing. No switch occurs from protected mode to virtual 8086 mode, and if there is a protected mode device driver in use for the target device, the system VM context remains a protected mode context throughout the entire operation.

The Networking Subsystem

The Windows 95 *networking subsystem* supports peer-to-peer networking as well as other networking protocols such as the NetBEUI protocol, the TCP/IP protocol, and Novell file services.

The networking subsystem built in Windows 95 is the latest incarnation of Microsoft's peer-to-peer network first seen in Windows for Workgroups in 1992 and later seen in Windows NT. The Windows 95 networking subsystem uses a new file-management subsystem to coordinate its access to remote files. Other network suppliers can also plug their products into the new file management services, allowing a user to simultaneously access more than one type of host network. Windows provides built-in support for SMB, Novell, and TCP/IP protocols.

Operating-System Services

In Windows 95, as in Windows 3.*x*, *operating-system services* provide applications with access to essential computer resources and operating-system components. In Windows 95, system services provide the following:

- Low-level memory-management services that allocate and deallocate memory and manage processes.
- Scheduling services that start and coordinate the operation of applications—or, in a preemptive multitasking environment such as Windows 95, multiple threads of execution in a single application.
- Access to files, directories, and input and output devices. The file I/O functions provided by system services give applications access to files and directories on disks and other the storage devices both on local computers and on computers in a network.

In Windows 95, as in Windows 3.1 and its predecessors, system services are provided primarily by the KERNEL, USER, and GDI DLLs. These DLLs are known as the Windows 95 *subsystem* or the *Windows 95 core DLLS* (see "The 32-Bit Core DLLs" on page 128). These core DLLs serve as interfaces between applications and the base operating system and therefore are technically not part of the Windows 95 operating system.

Operating system services also provide support for the plug-and-play capabilities of Windows 95 (described in Chapter 1, "Introducing Windows 95").

Finally, operating system services provide various kinds of miscellaneous functions such as those that respond to date and time requests.

Windows 95 Device Drivers

Because Windows 95 supports 32-bit device drivers, the only reason for using an old-fashioned 16-bit device driver to interface Windows 95 with a piece of hardware is because a 32-bit driver for the device is not yet available. Microsoft hopes that all hardware vendors will soon be offering 32-bit device drivers for their products, but no one knows how long it will be before all the hardware devices on the market come with 32-bit device drivers.

There are at least three good reasons for vendors to develop 32-bit device drivers: Windows 95, Windows NT, and the fact that 32-bit drivers are the only kind that are compatible with the Windows 95 plug-and-play system. When a device driver is designed to be compatible with plug-and-play, Windows 95 can install and configure the driver automatically (see Chapter 1, "Introducing Windows 95").

Windows 95 can't do that with old-fashioned 16-bit device drivers (sometimes referred to as "real-mode device drivers; see next heading).

Plug-and-play is an important feature of Windows 95, so one of the development goals of the Windows 95 design team was to help manufacturers develop protected-mode drivers for as many popular devices as possible.

Virtual Device Drivers

Along with 32-bit device drivers and 16-bit device drivers, there's another kind of driver—called a *virtual device driver*—that you may be hearing a lot about in connection with Windows 95.

That does not mean that VxDs are new—they've been around much longer than you may think. Virtual device drivers, like virtual machines, existed long before the introduction of Windows 95. In fact, WIN386.EXE file—which implements the Windows 3.*x* operating system—is implemented as a collection of VxDs.

In the era of Windows 3.1, VxDs were documented in a book called the *Virtual Device Adaptation Guide* (VDAG), which was provided with the Windows Device Driver Kit (DDK). Today, the best source of information about modern VxDs is the Win32 DDK.

The Windows 3.*x* DDK also came with a set of three software tools for building VxDs: MASM5B, LINK386, and ADDHDR. These same three tools still work with Windows 95, but they are obsolete. To build VxDs in a Windows 95 environment, it's easier to use the new VxD tools for Windows 95 provided in the Win32 DDK. (Those tools were still under development when this book was written; for details, see your Win32 DDK documentation.)

What Does the X Stand For?

What does the X stand for in the abbreviation "VxD"?

The same thing it stands for in algebra: whatever you want it to.

Because X can stand for something that is unknown, many of the VxDs used by the Windows 95 operating system (though not all of them) have names written in the form VxD, where *x* is the name of the device the VxD is "virtualizing," or simulating. For example, a VxD that simulates a DMA device is a VDMAD, a VxD that simulates a display device is a VDD, and so on.

How VxDs Work

To understand what a virtual device driver is, it first helps to understand what it is not. First of all, a virtual device driver VxD does not necessarily have any relationship with a hardware device—although the original purpose of a VxD was to provide a software emulation—or virtualization—of a physical device. That's how the virtual device driver got its name.

Today, VxDs are still used to virtualize hardware, but they have other jobs, too. For example, VxDs can be used to add extra functionality to VMM-aware (virtual-machine-manager–aware) applications. In the Windows 95 operating system, VxDs are used for such tasks as establishing communication between virtual machines and providing 32-bit memory access to MS-DOS–based applications.

Once you learn how to write a VxD, you can use VxDs in your own applications, too. For example, you could create a VxD that prints out the contents of your CPU's registers, or a VxD that accesses the Win95 Registry (a database that configures and keeps track of Windows 95 applications; see "Online Help in Windows 95" on page 30).

And why can VxDs can do these kinds of things? Because they run in Ring 0, the most privileged part of the Windows 95 operating system. That gives VxDs free access to the operating system, which also runs in Ring 0. An that means that a VxD, unlike an ordinary application, can go just about anywhere and do just about anything in the Windows 95 environment.

Creating and Using VxDs

As an illustration of how VxDs work, assume you wanted to create a VxD called a VPICD, which stands for "programmable interrupt controller device." In the Windows environment (Windows 3.*x* as well as Windows 95), VPICD is a Windows VxD that simulates the behavior of an actual device called a programmable interrupt controller (PIC). So, if you wanted to create a VxD that could serve as a software emulation of a real physical PIC, it would be logical for you to call your VxD the VPICD.

In its real physical form, a PIC is a hardware device built into the 386 chip. When the 386 is executing a DOS program in real mode, the PIC built into the 386 is tripped when a hardware interrupt occurs. The program being executed can then take whatever action is appropriate.

When Windows is running in enhanced mode, the PIC built into the 386 becomes useless. That's because DOS programs running under Windows in protected mode aren't directly controlled by DOS. Instead, DOS applications run under the control of the system virtual machine, which allocates each DOS program its own individual DOS virtual machine (see "The MS-DOS Virtual Machine" on page 118). That's how DOS programs run under Windows in protected mode; the effect is the same as if each DOS application were running under a separate CPU.

What the Problem Is

Although DOS programs work fine in individual DOS machines, the DOS virtual-machine setup does not support the use of the hardware-based PIC built into the 386 chip. The 386's hardware PIC knows nothing about virtual DOS machines, so when it is tripped by an interrupt, it has no idea which virtual machine to send the interrupt to. That's where your VPICD, or virtual programmable interrupt controller, comes in.

Because your VPICD is a *virtual* device driver, emulated in software that you write yourself, you can design it in such a way that it knows about virtual machines and knows how to work with them. When your VPICD is notified of a hardware interrupt, you can ensure that it creates a software version of a real interrupt controller and provides the appropriate virtual DOS machine with access to whatever fake controller you have created. For instance, when a program running in a virtual machine issues an end-of-interrupt (EOI), your VPICD can create a simulated software-based EOI signal and can make that signal accessible to the appropriate VM.

Other Jobs for VxDs

Another job a VxD might be called upon to handle is the job of interfacing a single hardware device with multiple Windows 95 applications. For example, when Windows 95 runs two MS-DOS applications in separate text windows on the same monitor screen, the system uses a VxD to create two MS-DOS virtual machines and to give each virtual machine access to the screen. You could call a VxD that does this kind of job a screen driver VxD.

Advantages of Using VxDs

One important characteristic of VxD virtualization is that it is transparent. For example, suppose an MS-DOS-based program running under Windows attempts to issue an EOI to a PIC by executing the assembly-language instruction OUT (see box, "What Does the X Stand For?," on page 140). The DOS program expects its OUT instruction to go to a physical PIC, but the instruction actually winds up going to a VPICD. So a VxD really does mimic the behavior of whatever device the *x* in its name—right down to *x*'s use of I/O ports when I/O ports are involved.

To mimic the behavior of devices transparently, a VxD must have far-reaching capabilities—for example, the ability to hook processor instructions such as IN and OUT. That is why VxDs run at Ring 0, the most privileged inner sanctum of protected mode. Essentially, at Windows startup VxDs become part of the Windows virtual machine manager (VMM), upon which everything else in enhanced mode relies. As a result, if something is "impossible" to do in Windows, you are allowed to do it in a VxD.

Besides running at Ring 0, several other aspects of VxDs give them privileged status in Windows 95. For one thing, because they are 32-bit executables, their memory address space consists of Windows in its entirety. In a VxD, CS and DS correspond to the same block of memory; this block of memory has a base address of 0 and a size of 4GB! Thus, any memory can be read or written using a simple 32-bit offset.

Writing Your Own VxDs

Back in the days of Windows 3.*x*, VxDs were generally written in assembly language. Today, thanks to new features that have been added to compilers and new, programmer-friendly features that have been added to VxD-building tools, you can write VxDs in C, or even C++. You can also write VxDs that are thread-aware and can make use of the multithreading features of Windows 95 and Windows NT.

But writing VxDs is still no sport for the weak-hearted. Creating VxDs is a complicated task that is well beyond the scope of this chapter. If you want to learn to write VxDs, a good way to start is to read the VxD documentation that comes with the Windows DDK. You may also want to take a look at articles on VxDs that have appeared in publications such as the *Windows Technical Journal*.

Even before you do that, you might find it helpful to study some of the other chapters in this book: particularly Chapter 2, "Underneath Windows 95"; Chapter 4, "The Win32 API"; and Chapter 9, "Multithreading and Multitasking." When you start writing VxDs for Windows 95, it might help if you have a solid knowledge of the 386/486/Pentium processor, the Win32 SDK, and multithreading.

Summary

In this chapter, armed with the hardware knowledge you acquired in Chapter 2, you got an introduction to the Windows 95 operating system. You learned what its components are, and how they work together. Then you learned what the system virtual machine does in Windows 95, and how Windows 95 runs DOS applications under individual MS-DOS virtual machines.

One important subject covered in this chapter was the Windows 95 subsystem, which is made up of the Windows 95 core libraries—the KERNEL, USER, and GDI DLLs. You learned how the core DLLs work (there are six of them in Windows 95), and you saw how they interface Windows 95 applications with the Windows 95 operating system.

This chapter also described the components of the Windows 95 base operating system, and introduced virtual device drivers (VxDs).

In Chapter 4, "The Win32 API," you'll learn how to put the information you learned in this chapter to work by tapping the power of the functions provided in the Win32 SDK. Then you'll be ready to start writing your own applications for Windows 95.

Chapter

4

The Win32 API

With the release of Windows 95, Microsoft has rolled two versions of the Windows API into a single Win32 API designed to work with both Windows NT and Windows 95. That step has eliminated the need to support two Win32 APIs.

The Windows application programming interface, or Windows API, is a mammoth set of functions and data structures that form the bedrock of all Windows software development systems. Until the advent of Windows 95, Microsoft supported two versions of the Windows API: a 16-bit version for Windows 3.*x* and Windows for Workgroups, and a 32-bit version—called the Win32 API—for Windows NT.

During the testing phase of Windows 95, developers also had access to a second, preliminary version of the Win32 API that was designed exclusively for use with Windows 95.

With the release of Windows 95, Microsoft has rolled those two versions of the Windows API into a single Win32 API designed to work with both Windows NT and Windows 95. That step has eliminated the need to support two Win32 APIs, one designed for Windows NT and the other designed for Windows 95. Now there is just one Win32 API, and you can use it with both Windows NT and Windows 95.

When Windows 95 was officially unveiled, further development of the original Win16 API halted, and Microsoft began encouraging Windows developers to concentrate their efforts on creating 32-bit software for Windows 95 and Windows NT.

Because the Win32 API is so important in the new world of 32-bit PC programming, it is the focus of this chapter. These are the main topics covered in this chapter:

What's in the Win32 API

In the Win32 API, you'll find just about any procedure you need to write 32-bit programs for both Windows 95 and Windows NT.

Along with all the old familiar features that are familiar to Windows 3.*x* programmers, the current version of the Win32 API—the version released with Windows 95—also contains many new functions, data structures, messages, and macros. The current Win32 API boasts many new improvements in the areas of window management, message-handling, and graphics. For example, the Win32 API now includes significant improvements in the following areas:

- Memory management
- Window management
- Multithreading (described in more detail in Chapter 9, "Multithreading and Multitasking")
- Message handling.

The Win32 API also contains several new categories of functions. For example, there are whole new sets of functions that support 32-bit memory management, 32-bit file management, multithreading, and network communications, and functions that support 32-bit graphics and multimedia programming.

Win32 Memory Management

One category of API functions that has changed dramatically in both Windows 95 and Windows NT is the category of memory management. Most of the changes in the memory-management functions of the Win32 API stem, as you might imagine, from the fact that the API is designed to produce 32-bit programs.

To understand the significance of this change, it is helpful to know something about how 32-bit Windows memory management evolved.

From the day the first IBM Personal Computer rolled off the assembly line to the day Windows NT was unveiled, the 64K memory barrier that was built into the Intel 8086 chip had plagued DOS and Windows programmers. Until the premiere of Windows NT, Microsoft made sure that every release of DOS and Windows was compatible with every 16-bit chip in the 80X86 family—a restriction that permitted DOS and Windows applications direct access to only 64K of memory (see Chapter 2, "Underneath Windows 95").

Windows NT changed all that, and Windows 95 has now driven the final nail into the 8086's coffin. To work around the limitations built into the 8086 (and into other Intel chips that predated the 386), DOS and Windows software developers resorted to all kinds of schemes, including memory extenders, memory expanders, memory segmentation, and various kinds of memory modes and memory models.

Virtual Memory, Heap Management, and File Mapping

With the advent of Windows NT—and now, with the premiere of Windows 95—life has become much easier for Windows programmers. Instead of forcing applications to perform much of their own memory management, Windows NT and Windows 95 provide applications with three built-in mechanisms that can handle most memory operations: *virtual memory*, *heap management*, and *file mapping*, an ingenious system of mapping disk files into RAM for easier handling. These three new memory-management features of Windows 95 are examined in more detail under separate headings in this section.

Virtual Memory and the Virtual Memory Manager

As noted in Chapter 3, "Windows 95 Architecture," Windows 95 is a cross between a 16-bit operating system and a 32-bit operating system. When Windows 95 is used as a 32-bit programming environment with a flat 32-bit memory map, applications are relieved from much of the responsibility for managing physical memory. Instead of accessing physical memory directly, a 32-bit Windows 95 application can entrust most memory management to functions built into the Win32 API. With these memory-management functions, applications can access up to 4 gigabytes of *virtual memory*—far more memory than any Windows application is likely to need today or in the foreseeable future. Windows 95 implements virtual memory by caching information into disk-based storage when applications need more memory space than RAM can provide. Thus, the memory that can be allocated to a Windows 95 application is limited only by the amount of disk storage space that is available.

In fact, the Win32 virtual-memory management system provides applications with access to much more virtual memory than the amount of real memory that is ever likely to exist in RAM—although the amount of actual memory that is available to an application at any one time is limited to the total amount of RAM and disk space that is available.

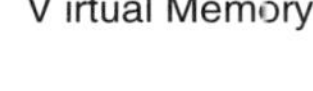

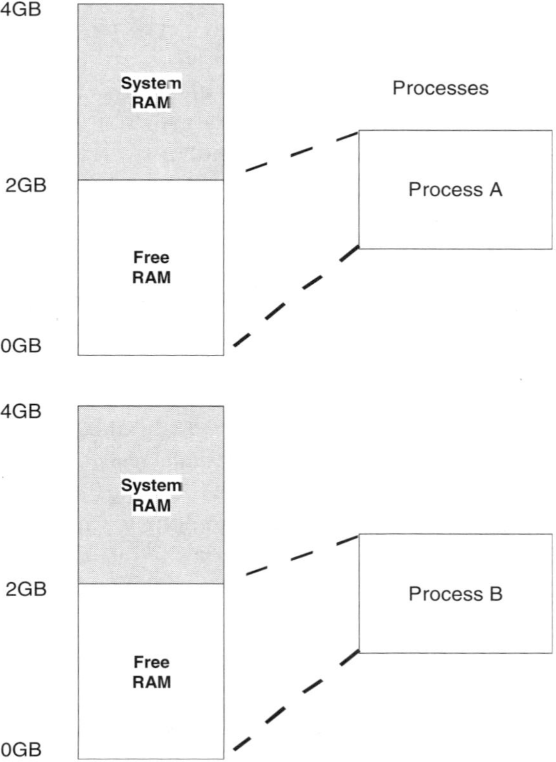

Figure 4.1 How processes see virtual memory

How 32-Bit Programs See Memory in Windows 95

To a 32-bit Windows 95 application, it always appears that 4GB of memory is available, regardless of how much physical memory is actually available in RAM and on the system's hard-disk drive. Figure 4.1 on Page 148 shows what the memory in a Windows 95 computer looks like to an executing application. The Win32 virtual-memory system is designed to work fast and transparently. To make the system as fast and efficient as possible, Win32 does not allocate physical memory when it is requested, but only when it is accessed. As a result, it takes about the same amount of time to allocate 5 megabytes of memory and that it takes to allocate 500 kilobytes.

To make the system transparent to executing processes, the Win32 operating system uses asynchronous threads (see box, "Processes and Threads in Windows 95") to allocate, free, and swap memory as needed. So Windows 95 applications rarely have to concern themselves directly with virtual memory management.

Processes and Threads in Windows 95

As explained in Chapter 9, "Multithreading and Multitasking," Windows 95 supports preemptive multitasking by dividing program operations into *processes* and *threads.*

In Windows 95, a *process* is an executable object-code module that can run independently as a program. (In Windows 3.*x* terminology, a process was known as a task.) Every process can be subdivided into *threads*, the small unit of executable code that can be allocated a share of CPU (central processing unit) time. Processes are covered at length in Chapter 8, "Programs and Processes,"

The Windows 95 operating system provides a service called a *scheduler* that schedules the operations of threads. The scheduler can allocate CPU time to each thread in accordance with predetermined thread priorities. Thread priorities can be set by both the Win32 operating system and Windows 95 applications.

For more information threads and preemptive multitasking, see the box "Multithreading" on page 164. Chapter 8, "Programs and Processes," explains and demonstrates the use of threads in Windows 95 programs.

Heap Management in Windows 95

Along with its virtual memory management system, Windows 95 is equipped with a heap management system that takes steps to prevent 32-bit applications infringing on memory areas owned by other applications. This system is not as foolproof as the memory-protection system built into Windows NT because Windows 95 lets applications share certain areas of memory, while Windows NT keeps memory used by every 32-bit program private (see my book, C++ *Windows NT Programming*, listed in the bibliography). But Windows 95 does go a long way toward preventing applications from corrupting memory used by the operating system.

The Win32 API helps Windows 95 manage memory by providing a number of heap-management functions. These functions are often used in Windows 95 programs to allocate, deallocate, move, and protect small blocks of memory such as strings, arrays, and short blocks of raw data. For larger memory blocks—blocks that are 4K or longer—it's usually more efficient to manage memory using virtual-memory functions or memory-mapped files.

File Mapping in Windows 95

One important Windows 95 memory-management tool is *file mapping*. File mapping is a clever and useful mechanism that lets Windows 95 manage files stored on disks in the same way it treats files that are stored in memory.

To create a memory-mapped file, a Windows 95 application obtains a block of memory addresses from the operating system and then maps a disk file into those addresses. Once a disk file is mapped into memory, applications can forget about the fact that it is a file and simply access it as if it were actually stored in RAM.

Free Home Demonstration

For a demonstration of how Windows 95 memory management affects system performance, pick out a robust Windows 95 application an launch it twice. The first time you start the program, Windows 95 must load it from a disk. The second time, the Windows 95 virtual memory manager searches for the image of the executable that has already been loaded into memory. If the image is still there—that is, if it hasn't been squeezed out of memory by some other application—the Win32 launches the executable again without having to access the disk.What's more, Windows 95 does all this without the need for a dedicated disk-caching mechanism, since virtual memory management is built right into the Win32 system.

Segmented Addressing in Windows 3.*x*

As explained in Chapter 2, "Underneath Windows 95," the 80X86 family of processors use a form of addressing called segmented addressing to calculate a linear address by bit-shifting the contents of a segment register, then adding the result to the contents of an offset register.

When you write a program for MS-DOS or Windows 3.*x*, you can choose between two memory modes: *real mode* and *protected mode* (for the hardware details, see Chapter 2, "Underneath Windows 95"). In real mode, which is compatible with the earliest 80X86 processors, a segmented memory address has a 16-bit segment identifier that is shifted to the left by four bits to produce a 20-bit base address. To reference a memory location, you add a 16-bit offset value to this 20-bit base address. Then you have an actual 20-bit memory address.

In protected mode, a memory mode supported by the 80386 chip and its successors, memory addresses can also be accessed using a system of paged virtual addressing. In real mode, applications access memory using a 16-bit segment selector and an offset that can be either 16 bits or 32 bits long.

In Windows 3.*x* programs, the 80X86 CPU retrieves addresses using address-translation hardware built into the chip. Depending on a value stored in a segment register, the CPU calculates an address using one of two tables: a local descriptor table (LDT) or a global descriptor table (GDT). The resulting address does not reference physical memory, but is a *paged address*—that is, a virtual address that the CPU can access using built-in paging hardware.

By using paged addresses—a technique often referred to simply as *paging*—the Windows 95 operating system can access virtual memory addresses. Virtual memory addresses are addresses that are maintained for data that is stored on a disk instead of being stored in any physical memory location.

Because virtual memory addresses do not physically exist in RAM, and because data is constantly being paged in and out of memory by the operating system, the physical address of a data item and the linear addresses of the same item are not necessarily the same. In fact, the item may be stored on disk instead of in memory, and consequently may have no memory address at all.

Memory Allocation and DLLs

With one exception, all memory that is allocated using Windows allocation functions is accessible only to the calling process.

The exception to this rule is memory allocated by a DLL. Memory allocated by a DLL is in the address space of the process that invoked the DLL and is not accessible to other processes using the same DLL. There is also an exception to this exception. By taking special steps, you can make it possible for processes that use a DLL to use memory allocated by the DLL.

The Win32 Paging System

The paging method used by the Windows 95 operating system is based on the paging system that Intel introduced with the 386 processor. However, the Win32 SDK ignores the segment registers built into the 386 and its successors. Instead of using these registers, Win32 defines two segment selectors that can address a total of 4 gigabytes of memory addresses (Win32 uses two selectors because Intel chips allow selectors to reference either code or data, but not both).

In the Win32 paging system, all available RAM is divided into equal-sized blocks called *pages*. The size of a page depends on the host computer. On computers equipped with 80X86 processors, each page is exactly 4 kilobytes (4,096 bytes) long.

The Win32 operating system places no restrictions on how the memory on any page is used. Everything in memory—code, data, resources, dynamic memory, and so on—is stored in pages.

Page Files

While applications are executing—particularly when multiple applications are executing simultaneously—there is a frequent need to shift pages around in memory as memory needs change.

For example, when the virtual memory manager needs to allocate a block of memory and discovers that there is not enough RAM available, it creates the RAM that it needs by moving pages of memory from memory to a hard disk.

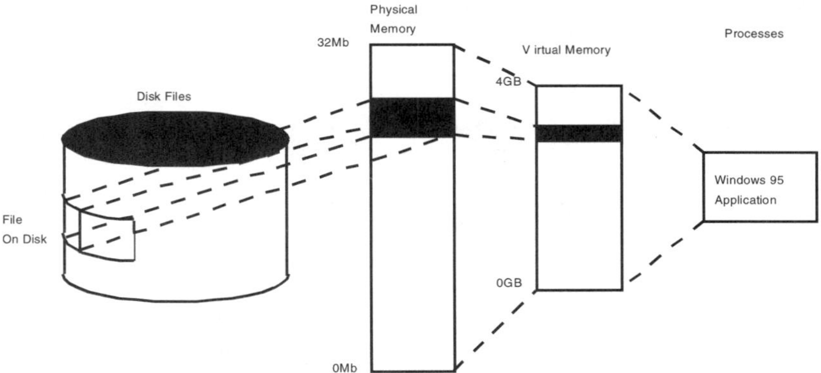

Figure 4.2 How Windows 95 uses page files

When information is cached to disk, it is stored in a file called a *page file*. A page file is an area of disk space that is reserved for use by the virtual memory manager.

The Win32 system can create up to 16 page files. The virtual memory manager allocates disk memory to page files dynamically, allowing them to grow as the demand for disk-based memory increases.

Figure 4.2 shows how Windows 95 uses a page file to swap information back and forth between memory and a hard disk.

The Virtual Memory Manager

In Windows 95, memory pages are managed by a service called the *virtual memory manager*. When the virtual memory manager needs space in physical memory, it moves the least recently used pages of physical memory to a page file.

When memory space in a page file is not being used and is needed for another paging operation, the virtual memory manager claims the space for the new paging operation.

Page Maps

When a thread accesses a virtual address that has been paged to disk, the virtual memory manager loads the information back into memory from disk. Then the virtual memory manager—with help from the host hardware—translates, or *maps*, the virtual addresses of the processes that are running into physical addresses where data is actually stored.

Paging data to disk frees RAM that is not currently being accessed so that applications and the Windows 95 operating system can use it for more immediate needs.

When a page is moved into or out of physical memory, the virtual memory manager records the operation by updating *page maps* that are associated with all executing processes.

By using this paged memory-management system, Win32 creates a flat 32-bit address space that can be freely accessed without any need for distinguishing between near and far pointers. Furthermore, the Win32 disk-caching mechanism is built into the system, so every application in memory automatically has access to up to 4GB of virtual memory space, with the addition of any special disk-caching software.

Memory mapping also ensures that individual processes do not corrupt each other's memory or (even worse!) overwrite memory used by the operating system.

How Win32 Translates Virtual Addresses

To the Win32 operating system, a virtual address is just a placeholder for information that is used to find an actual physical address. Windows 95 divides every 32-bit virtual address into three parts, as shown in Figure 4.3.

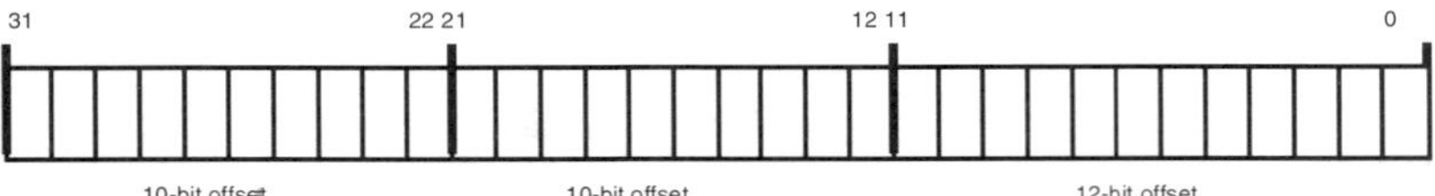

Figure 4.3 Format of a 32-bit virtual address

As Figure 4.3 illustrates, the lowest-order part of a virtual address is 12 bits long. Each of the other parts contains 10 bits. Each of the three parts that make up a virtual address is used independently as an offset into a page of memory. When a virtual address has been retrieved, it can be used to locate any address on any page that is being used by any process (application or task) stored in memory.

Page Directories, Page Tables, and Page Frames

This is how virtual addressing works in Windows 95: Each process has a single, unique page of memory called a *page directory*. A page directory, like any other page in memory, is simply a 4K block of RAM. Its one distinction is that it holds exactly 1,024 four-byte values called *page-directory entries*, or PDEs.

Each PDE is used to locate another page of memory called a *page table*. Every page table contains exactly 1,024 four-byte values called *page-table entries*, or PTEs. Finally, each PTE points to a page of memory called a *page frame*.

When the operating system has retrieved a virtual address, it uses the highest-order 10 bits in that virtual address to locate a page directory. Next, the second-highest 10-bit offset is used to locate a page table. Then the low-order 12 bits of the virtual address as used as an index to a page frame.

Page-Table Entries

Using these three layers of indirection, Windows 95 can locate any page of memory owned by any process. (A process is an application or a task; see the box titled "Processes and Threads in Windows 95" earlier in this chapter.) Every page in the system is a page directory, a page table, or a page frame. Figure 4.4 is a diagram of a page-table entry.

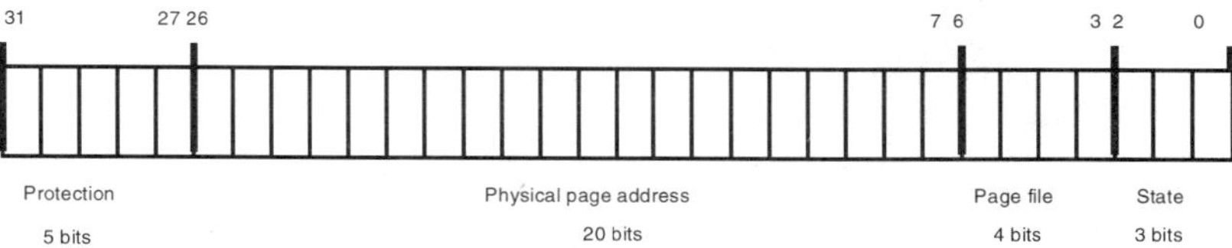

Figure 4.4 Format of a page-table entry

As Figure 4.4 illustrates, a page-table entry is divided into four parts:

- The five highest-order bits are used as a flag that specifies a level of protection for the page. This flag can be one of three constants: **PAGE_NOACCESS**, **PAGE_READONLY**, or **PAGE_READWRITE**.
- If the page associated with the page-table entry is stored in memory, the 20 next highest bits specify the page's physical address. A 20-bit address can access 4 gigabytes of memory, so a page-table entry can be used to locate any address within the 4-gigabyte address range that Windows 95 assigns to each process.
- Windows 95 uses 16 disk-based page files to cache memory. The second-highest four bits in a page-table entry specify the page file that can be used to cache the page of memory that is referenced by the page-table entry.

- The lowest-order three bits in a page-table entry are used to specify the protection level of the page that is referenced. A page can be in one of three states: present in memory (P), written to but not saved (D), and in transition (T). The Win32 system sets the value of these three bits automatically as pages are moved into and out of memory. You can also set these values, as explained in the following section.

Using Virtual Memory

The Win32 SDK provides six functions for managing virtual memory. The most common use for these functions is to allocate, deallocate, and protect large blocks of memory.

If most of your programming efforts are dedicated to writing new Windows 95 programs using Visual C++ or Borland C++, you may never need to call a memory-management function provided by the Win32 SDK. For the most part, the Win32 virtual memory system operates transparently, working quietly in the background to handle your application's memory needs. However, the Win32 SDK does provide the following functions to provide you with more direct control over virtual-memory operations:

- The **`VirtualAlloc`** and **`VirtualFree`** functions allocate and deallocate virtual memory.
- The **`VirtualLock`** and **`VirtualUnlock`** functions lock and unlock virtual memory.
- The **`VirtualProtect`** and **`VirtualProtectEx`** functions can set the level of protection of a block of virtual memory (see "Page-Table Entries" on page 155). The special feature of the **`VirtualProtectEx`** function is that can be used on processes other than the calling process (a process is an application or a task; see the box titled "Processes and Threads in Windows 95" on page 149.
- To obtain information about the virtual memory available to a process, an application can call **`VirtualQuery`** or **`VirtualQueryEx`**. The **`VirtualQuerEx`** function can retrieve information about virtual memory owned by processes other than the calling process.

For more details about these functions, see your development system's online help files or refer to Volumes 3 and 4 of the *Microsoft Win32 Programmer's Reference*.

Heap Management

Under Windows 3.*x*, programs managed memory using memory areas called *heaps*. Every Windows 3.*x* application had a single *global heap*, which the system and all applications share, and private *local heaps*, one for each application. To manage these two heaps, the Windows 3.*x* system provided two sets of functions: one for managing the global heap and another for managing local heaps.

For example, a Windows 3.*x* application could allocate memory from the global heap calling the SDK function **`GlobalAlloc`**, and it could allocate memory from the local heap by calling the **`LocalAlloc`** function.

When you run a 16-bit application under Windows 95, the **`GlobalAlloc`** and **`LocalAlloc`** functions are used in the same way they were used under Windows 3.*x*. But when you run a 32-bit application under Windows 95, there is no difference between these two functions because both local and global allocations return 32-bit virtual addresses.

Private Heap—Keep Out

The Windows 95 system actually does have a global heap—but it's private. Applications don't know about the global heap because they cannot access it. In Windows 95, functions such as **`GlobalAlloc`** affect only a process's local heap because the global heap is now inaccessible to applications.

Windows 95 has several safeguards to protect information stored on its private global heap. For example, processes can be granted either read-only access or read-and-write access to information in the global heap.

Even though applications do not have direct access to the global heap, they can access information stored on the global heap indirectly, through the Win32 operating system.

When a process is granted accesses to code or data stored on the global heap—for example, to code or data provided by a DLL—the code or data is mapped into the 4GB of virtual address space that is allocated to the process. The information that is mapped into virtual memory does not move; it remains on the global heap. However, to the process that has been granted access to the information, the information appears to have been moved into the process's address space.

Because the system maps information into virtual memory in this way, multiple processes can share code and data provided by a DLL, even though just one copy of the DLL has been loaded into memory—specifically, onto the global heap. For more about how this procedure works, see Chapter 10, "Windows 95 DLLs."

Global and Local Functions

Because 32-bit programs have a flat 32-bit address space when they are executed under Windows 95, they do not have to make a distinction between a global heap and a local heap. That's because Windows 95 makes no distinction between global memory-management functions such as **GlobalAlloc** and local memory-management functions such as **LocalAlloc** when a 32-bit application is running.

This is true because in a 32-bit Windows application, there is no difference between a long pointer and a short pointer. If you ever want to prove this, there is nothing to keep you from allocating a block of memory by calling **GlobalAlloc** and later freeing the same block of memory by calling the **LocalFree** function. That is not a recommended practice, of course; it would just make your application difficult to read. But there's nothing in the Win32 operating system that would prevent you from doing it such a thing if you wanted to.

Using C and C++ Memory Functions in Windows 95

Yes, you can use the C runtime library's **malloc** and **free** functions in Windows 95 programs—and you can feel much safer about using them than you may have felt back when you were writing Windows 3.*x* programs.

Microsoft Windows did not fully support the native memory-allocation functions provided by the C runtime library (CRT) until the Windows 3.*x* system was specially modified to support **malloc** and **free**. The designers of Windows 95 handled this issue at the outset, implementing the memory-allocation functions in the CRT library in the same way that the allocation of fixed memory is handled by the Win32 SDK. Furthermore, the CRT library's allocation functions are implemented using the same default heap manager that is used by the global and local SDK memory-management functions.

Because these design techniques were used, the **malloc**, **GlobalAlloc**, and **LocalAlloc** functions return pointers allocated from the same heap. The Win32 system treats all these functions the same, and their behavior is consistent.

Also, the distinction between near and far pointers that existed in Windows 3.*x* does not exist in Windows 95. So, when you write programs under Windows 95, you can use the family of functions that you're most familiar with. And if you want to port your programs to other operating systems, you can use CRT memory functions without hesitation.

It's also easy to mix the C++ operators **new** and **delete** with the heap-management functions provided by Windows 95. You can overload the **new** and **delete** operators in your applications, or you can use them without overloading. If don't overload new or delete, the Win32 system uses its own pair of default **new** and **delete** operators.

Default Heaps and Dynamic Heaps

Although 32-bit Windows 95 applications do not distinguish between global and local heaps, as Windows 3.*x* programs do, Windows 95 does recognize two kinds of heaps: *default heaps* and *dynamic heaps*.

When a Windows 95 process starts up, it is allocated a heap called a *default heap*. The Win32 subsystem uses this default heap for all global and local memory-management functions that affect the process. The C runtime library also uses the default heap for C-style memory-allocation (**malloc**) functions (see box, "Using C and C++ Memory Functions in Windows 95," on page 158).

Once a process is started, it can create as many *dynamic heaps* as it needs, allocating and deallocating them as needed. Applications can create dynamic heaps by calling either **GlobalAlloc** or **LocalAlloc**, and can free dynamic heaps by calling **GlobalFree** or **LocalFree**.

Applications can access default heaps and dynamic heaps using handles (indirect references to objects that are managed by the operating system). An application can obtain a handle to its default heap by calling the Win32 function **GetProcessHeap**.

When you call **GlobalAlloc** or **LocalAlloc**, you can set a flag that determines whether the memory you are allocating will be **FIXED** or **MOVEABLE**. If you allocate a block of memory with the **FIXED** flag set, Win32 returns a pointer that you can use to access the memory. If you set the **MOVEABLE** flag when you allocate a block of memory, Win32 returns a handle that you can safely use even if the system decides to move the block around.

You should set the **FIXED** flag only for memory blocks with short lifespans. If you allocate a lot of **FIXED** memory blocks and then fail to free them, you may fragment your computer's memory.

You can prevent **MOVEABLE** memory from being shifted around in memory by calling the **GlobalLock** or **LocalLock** function. When you call these functions, you should observe the same precautions that are advised for the **FIXED** and **MOVEABLE** flags. Keeping blocks of memory locked for too long can also result in memory fragmentation.

Using the Win32 Heap-Management Functions

In Windows 95, there are 18 heap-management functions—nine local functions and nine global functions. However, there is no meaningful difference between the nine global functions in Column A and the nine local functions in Column B. These functions are available:

- **GlobalAlloc** and **LocalAlloc** allocate memory.
- To discard a block of memory, call **GlobalDiscard** or **LocalDiscard**.
- **GlobalFlags** and **LocalFlags** return information about a specified block of memory. Each function returns a flag that tells if the specified memory object has been discarded, if it can be discarded, or if it is allocated for use by dynamic data exchange (DDE) functions.
- **GlobalFree** and **LocalFree** release a specified memory object and invalidate its handle.
- **GlobalHandle** and **LocalHandle** retrieve the handle of a specified pointer to a memory block.
- To lock a block of memory, you can call **GlobalLock** and **LocalLock**. When a block of memory is locked, it cannot be moved or discarded. The internal structure of every memory object contains a *lock count*, and each **GlobalLock** or **LocalLock** that is made to lock the object increments the object's lock count.
- **GlobalRealloc** and **LocalRealloc** can change the size or attributes of a specified memory block. The size of the block can be increased or decreased, and its attributes can be set to make it discardable, moveable, noncompactable, or zero-initialized.
- **GlobalSize** and **LocalSize** return the current size, in bytes, of a specified block of memory.
- **GlobalUnlock** and **LocalUnlock** decrement the lock count of a specified memory object. Each time a **GlobalUnlock** or **LocalUnlock** call is made, its lock count is decremented. The object is not actually unlocked until its lock count is decremented to zero.

Each of the functions in this list can access any 32-bit address, and therefore can allocate blocks of memory up to 4GB long. The only limitation is the amount of physical memory available, including storage space in the paging file stored on disk.

In practice, however, it is generally best to use Win32's heap-management functions to manage blocks of memory less than 4K long, and to use virtual-memory functions for larger blocks of memory.

For more about the syntax and use of heap-management functions, refer to your development system's online help or the *Microsoft Win32 Programmer's Reference*.

Memory-Mapped Files

Memory-mapped files (MMFs) are one of the most useful—and one of the easiest-to-use—memory-management mechanisms provided by the Win32 SDK. A memory-mapped file is a disk file that has been mapped into the 4GB virtual address space owned by a Windows 95 process. When a file has been memory-mapped into RAM, applications can access it using pointers, in the same way that they can use pointers to access any other memory location.

In Windows 95, memory-mapped files are more than just an easy method for managing memory in the Win32 API. They are also the only mechanism that multiple Windows 95 processes can use to share data stored in memory.

Memory-mapped files are often used for data-sharing in Windows 95 because every Windows 95 process runs in its own protected area of memory and cannot directly access data stored in memory areas owned by other processes. However, if a process is granted access to a disk file, it can map that file (or a portion of it) into a block of memory addresses within its own 4GB address space. Then it can use pointers to access memory locations in the file, just as if the file were actually stored in its address space.

This technique preserves the integrity of the private address spaces that are allocated to processes, while providing processes with access to shared files.

Figure 4.5 on Page 162 shows how memory-mapped files are used in Windows 95.

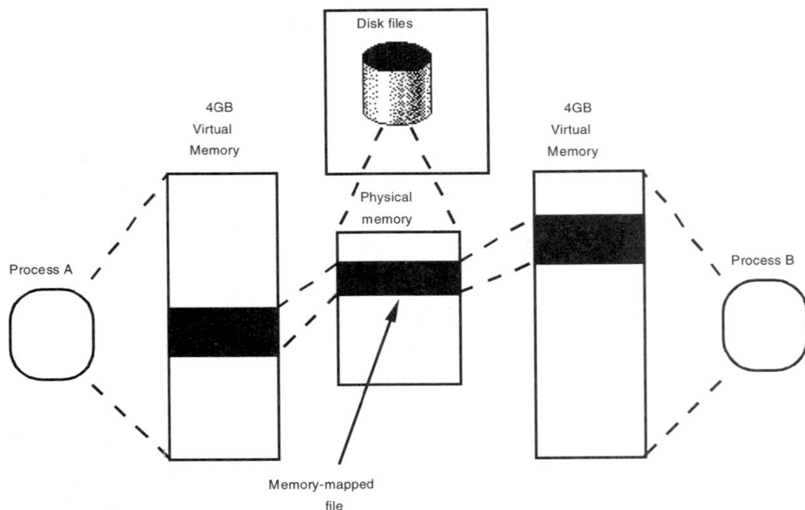

Figure 4.5 How memory-mapped files are used in Windows 95

How File Mapping Works

With memory-mapped files, a Windows 95 application can access files stored on disk in the same way that it accesses dynamic memory—through pointers. By using the file-mapping functions that are built into the Win32 operating system, a process can map any or all of a file stored on disk into its own 4GB virtual address space. Once that is done, the process can access information in the file by simply dereferencing a pointer, as in this example:

```
nAnInteger = *pMemLoc;
```

Conversely, modifying a location in a memory-mapped file is as easy as this:

```
*pMemLoc = 29;
```

In these examples, the ***pMemLoc** references an address somewhere in the 4GB range of virtual addresses that have been allocated to a process. When the Win32 system dereferences ***pMemLoc**, the address that it calculates is the actual memory location that is being addressed.

Memory-Mapping Large Files

Memory-mapped files are especially useful for manipulating large files. That's because a process can open a file for memory-mapping but delay the actual mapping of the file into memory until a later time.

Subsequently, when the process needs to access information in the file, the process does not have to map the entire file into memory at one time. Instead, it can map in a smaller portion of the file, called a *view*.

It takes hardly any physical resource simply to open a file for memory mapping, even if the file that is opened is extremely large. So opening a large file for memory mapping requires almost no overhead. Once a file is opened for memory mapping, smaller views of the file can be mapped into the process's address space just before I/O is performed. Then the process can access locations in the views that have been opened without loading the entire file into memory.

Quicker than the Eye

Although it appears that file-mapping takes place instantaneously, data in a memory-mapped file are not actually mapped into memory at the same time memory-mapping instructions are issued. Instead, much of the file input and output that is necessary to implement memory mapping is cached to improve system performance. You can override this behavior and force the system to perform disk transactions immediately by calling the Win32 function **FlushViewOfFile**.

Memory-Mapped Files and Memory Pages

Another advantage of using memory-mapped files is that the system performs all data transfers that are needed for memory-mapping operations using 4K pages of data. The virtual memory manager bases all its operations on memory pages, so it can perform memory mapping operations very efficiently. In memory-mapped file operations, disk read and write instructions are limited to sequences of 4K pages. When small reads or writes are needed, they are effectively cached into one larger 4K operation, reducing the number of times your hard-disk read-write head has to move.

Using File Mapping

To use file mapping, a process calls the Win32 function **CreateFileMapping**, passing the a filename to the function as a parameter. The **CreateFileMapping** function responds by creating a file-mapping object with the specified name. Other processes can then pass the object name to either the **CreateFileMapping** function or the **OpenFileMapping** function to obtain a handle to the mapped object.

An application can create a new file or open an existing file by calling the Win32 function **CreateFile**. When an application creates a file by calling **CreateFile**, it must specify the name of the file, and it must tell **CreateFile** whether it intends to read from the file, write to the file, or both.

The application must also tell the **CreateFile** function what to do if a file with the specified name exists. For example, an application can tell **CreateFile** to create a file with the specified name whether a file with that name exists or not. If this is the case, the **CreateFile** function creates the file if it does not exist and overwrites the file if it does exist.

When an application calls **CreateFile**, it can also provide the function with information about file sharing. The application that creates the file can give other users read access, write access, both read and write access, or no access at all.

For purposes of file sharing, the Win32 operating system assigns a unique identifier, called a file handle, to each file that is opened or created. An application can use the file's handle in parameters to functions that read from the file, write to the file, and obtain information about it. A file's handle is valid until the file is closed.

An application can close files when they are no longer needed by calling the Win32 function **CloseHandle**. If a file is open when an application terminates, Windows 95 closes it automatically.

The **DeleteFile** function deletes a file if the file is closed. If the file is not closed, **DeleteFile** returns an error.

In Windows 95, file-related functions such as **CreateFile** and **DeleteFile** can be used not only with files, but also with file-like objects. For example, file-related functions can open and close objects called *pipes*, which are used in Windows 95 programs to exchange data between threads and processes.

Multithreading

If improved memory management is the most important new feature of Windows 95, *multithreading* runs at least a close second.

Multithreading is the technique that Windows 95 uses to implement preemptive multitasking. As noted in Chapter 9, "Multithreading and Multitasking," preemptive multitasking is a feature that enables the Win32 operating system to apportion CPU time to individual applications so multiple applications can be executed on the same computer at the same time.

Multithreading can come in handy when you want an application to perform background processing or to be on the lookout for special events, such as messages arriving over a network or calls coming in on a serial port.

Chapter 9, "Multithreading and Multitasking," covers the topic of multithreading in much more detail.

The Windows 95 Core DLLs

Windows 95 uses a message-handling system that is based on the message-handling system used in Windows 3.*x*. But there are some significant differences in the way the two systems are implemented. To understand how Win32 message-handling works, it is necessary to have a basic understanding of how the operating system is implemented in Windows 95.

Windows 3.*x* DLLs and Windows 95 DLLs

Windows 95, like Windows 3.*x*, is implemented in a large and powerful set of dynamic-link libraries (see Chapter 3, "Windows 95 Architecture"). Recall that most of the functionality of Windows 95 is implemented in six DLLs: KERNEL.EXE, KERNEL32.DLL, GDI.EXE, GDI32.DLL, USER.EXE, and USER32.DLL.

In Windows 95, these six DLLs are sometimes referred to as the system's *core DLLs*. With a few important exceptions (described in Chapter 10, "Windows 95 DLLs,"), the responsibilities of the 32-bit core DLLs are similar to those of three similarly named DLLs (KERNEL.DLL, USER.DLL, and GDI.DLL) implemented in Windows 3.*x*.

One important difference between Windows 3.x and Windows 95 is that the Windows 95 core DLLs use multithreading to implement preemptive multitasking (see Chapter 9, "Multithreading and Multitasking").

The Windows 3.*x* operating system was not designed as a preemptive operating system, so it could not interrupt an application to give another application a chance to run. Thus, Windows 3.*x* had to perform all its message-handling using a single input queue. Under most circumstances, this one queue held all input from the user until the executing application removed the events from the queue.

Windows 3.*x* did support a simple form of multitasking; applications could call a **GetMessage** function or a **PeekMessage** function when they wanted to process a message, and applications could process user events and messages that resulted from non-user events. When an application executed a **GetMessage** or **PeekMessage** function, Windows 3.*x* performed any task-switching that might be necessary.

Under the Windows 3.*x* message-handling system, only one application could claim CPU time at any given time. Except for interrupts, which could be processed as the need arose, the application that had access to the CPU was always the last one that had issued a **GetMessage** or **PeekMessage** function. All other applications had to wait in line until that function returned. Then the next application in line could be served.

This kind of message-handling, as you know if you've ever tried printing in the background under Windows 3.*x*, does not make for a very robust multitasking system. If one application stops processing, the whole system can grind to a halt. This can happen when an application starts processing a long task such as printing, reading database records, repaginating, or performing disk I/O operations.

Some Windows 3.*x* applications took care of special messaging needs by placing statements that controlled long processes inside **PeekMessage** loops. An application could then call **PeekMessage** repeatedly and manually schedule other activities while the long process continues to run.

This was a lot of trouble for an application to have to go through to process messages—and most programmers would probably agree that it is not the kind of job that an application should be required to do. In the best of all possible worlds, message-handling should be the responsibility of the operating system, not the responsibility of applications running on the system!

Input Processing in Windows 95

Windows 95 solves these kinds of problems once and for all by using preemptive multitasking. When a process is created in Windows 95, the system also creates a high-priority thread called a *raw input thread*. As long as a process is alive, its raw input thread remains active to process the user's keyboard and mouse input.

When a process has started, it can create other threads. Every thread that is created can create still more threads.

When any thread calls a USER32 or GDI32 function, the system creates an input queue for the thread. If a thread does not call a USER32 or GDI32 function, no input queue is created.

Even if an input queue is created, the thread that obtains it does not have to use it. But that is no problem, because an input queue does not create any overhead merely by being allocated.

When Win32 detects a user event, the event is placed in the system queue, and the raw input thread immediately transfers the event to the thread input queue for which the input is intended.

Chapter 9, "Multithreading and Multitasking," explains and demonstrates how you can incorporate the message-handling features of Windows 95 into your own applications.

Windows and Processes

There are two kinds of Windows 95 processes: console processes and Windows processes. Console processes—described in Chapter 8, "Programs and Processes"—use text-based windows that are created by the Win32 operating system. Windows processes create their own windows.

When a Windows process is running under Windows 95, the Win32 operating system displays screen windows that look and feel just like Win16 windows. However, most of the window-management functions in the Win16 API Windows API have been rewritten, and many of them have been redesigned for Windows 95.

In developing the Win32 window-management system, the Windows 95 design team converted 16-bit code to 32-bit code where necessary, and added a number of new functions to meet the new requirements of Windows 95.

The Win32 Windows Hierarchy

When Windows 95 initializes, the operating system creates a *desktop window* that is sized to cover the entire screen display area. All other windows are displayed on top of the desktop window. Thus, the desktop window is at the top of the windows hierarchy.

Windows that are next in the hierarchy are called *top-level windows*. A window that has no parent, or whose parent is the Windows 95 desktop window, is called a *top-level window*. There can be more than one top-level window.

When a window creates another window, the new window is called a *child window* and the window that does the creating is called a *parent window*. Windows that descend from child windows are *descendant windows* of both the child window and the child's parent window.

Handles to all top-level windows that descend from the desktop window are stored in a linked list. This list is called a *child window list*. The desktop window stores a handle to its child window list in a variable called a *child window handle*.

Every window that can be placed on the desktop can be traced back to the desktop window through child window lists. The order in which windows are displayed when they become active is determined by a display order called the *Z order*.

(The Z order derives its name from the *z*-axis in the cartesian coordinate system. In the same way that the *x* and *y* axes of an object determine its horizontal and vertical placement on a screen or in a window, the *z* axis can be used to determine the distance of an object from the viewer.)

When a window is created or becomes active, the window manager places it at the top of the Z order. That means that the newly created or newly activated window appears on top of all other windows on the screen display.

Windows 95 adds one new level to the windows hierarchy used in Windows 3.*x*. Every computer that runs Windows 95 has an object called a *WindowStation* object. In Windows 95, the WindowStation object provides the first level of security for a Windows 95 workstation.

When Windows 95 is initialized, the WindowStation object displays a desktop window that does not exist in Window 3.*x*. This desktop window displays a modal dialog box that prompts the user to type CTRL+ALT+DELETE and then log on. The desktop window created by the WindowStation object stays on the screen until the user is properly logged on. Only then does the WindowStation object relinquish control of the desktop and allow the main Win32 desktop window to be displayed.

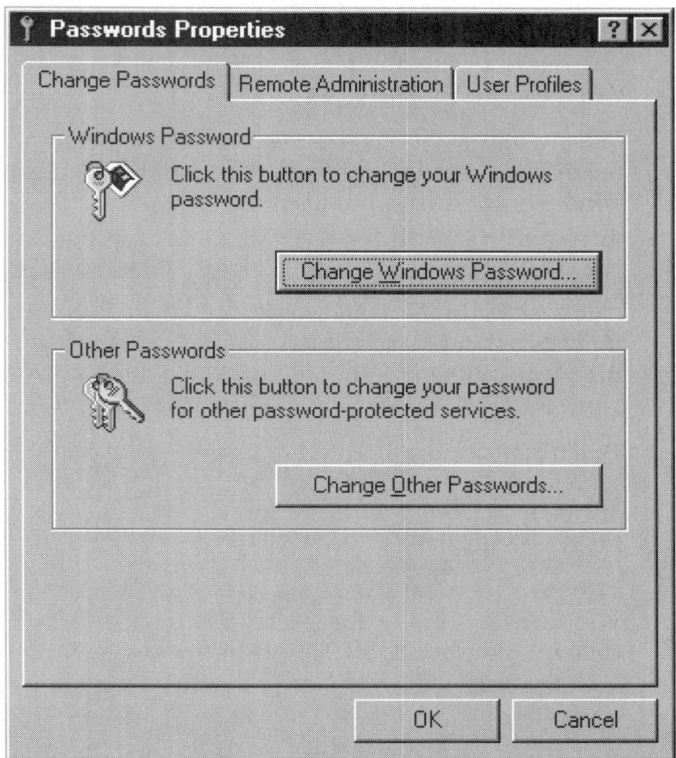

Figure 4.6 Property page for changing passwords

The WindowStation object keeps track of computer names, workgroups or domains, and user passwords that allow users to log on. You can select the **Network Neighborhood** icon on the Windows 95 desktop to change the computer name and the workgroup or domain that a workstation uses for logins.

To change a password, you double-click the **Password** icon on the control panel. Windows 95 then displays a property page that you can use to change your password (Figure 4.6).

Windows 95 defines two new window types that are not part of the standard window hierarchy: foreground windows and background windows. The foreground window is the window in which the user is currently working. All other windows are background windows.

Normally, it is not necessary for an application to find out whether a given window is a foreground window or a background window or to change this information; under most circumstances, the user of your application should make that decision. However, if an application does need to obtain or provide this information, it can do so by calling the Win32 function **SetForegroundWindow** or the Win32 function **GetForegroundWindow**.

Windows and Threads

Another new feature of the Win32 window manager is related to threading. In Windows 95, all windows that descend from a common parent share the same input queue. Under most circumstances, this means that windows behave the same way in Windows 95 and in Windows 3.*x*.

In Windows 95, however, it is possible for a process to spawn threads and for those threads to create windows that do not descend from a common parent and therefore do not share the same input queue. Under these circumstances, the Z order of windows displayed on the screen may not be the same as it would be in a non-threaded environment. If this situation arises, there are at least three corrective measures you can take:

- Modify the way your application handles threading.
- Call **PeekMessage** or **GetMessage** to detect window-related messages, and then change your application's window-related procedures manually.
- Change your expectations about what the Z order of windows should be when your application is running.

Besides the thread-related changes just mentioned, the Win32 SDK contains two new functions that support threading:

- To enumerate each window in a window hierarchy, and to call an application-supplied callback function for each window in the hierarchy, you can call the **EnumChildWindows** function.
- To obtain a handle to a specified thread's desktop window, you can call **GetThreadDesktop**.

Window Styles

Besides the main frame window, applications can create windows that have many different styles. The window styles that are available in Windows 95 are the same as the styles that are available in Windows 3.*x* programs. In Windows 95, as in Windows 3.*x*, you can create pop-up windows, windows with and without captions, windows with and without scroll bars, and so on.

An application determines a window's style by passing a style parameter to the **CreateWindow** or **CreateWindowEx** function that creates the window. Window styles available in Windows 95 are the same as those available in the Windows 3.*x* systems.

Windows 95 and the WinMain Function

The entry point of a Win32 console process is a standard C or C++ **main** function. A Win32 Windows process, like a Win16 Windows process, starts with the calling of a **WinMain** function. In Windows 95, as in pre-NT versions of Windows, the **WinMain** function has this form:

```
int WinMain(INSTANCE hInstance, HINSTANCE hPrevInstance,
    LPSTR lpszCmdLine, int nCmdShow)
```

Although the **WinMain** format just shown is used in Win32 applications as well as in Win16 applications, there are some important differences between the meanings of the parameters passed to the function in Win32 and the meanings of the parameters passed to the function in Win16. In fact, every **WinMain** parameter except one—**lpszCmdLine**—has a different meaning in Windows 95 and in Windows 3.*x*.

The hModule Parameter

In pre-NT versions of Windows, the **hModule** parameter specifies the module database for an .EXE or .DLL file. Even if multiple instances of an application are running, there is only one module database for the application. That means that a single **hModule** value is shared by all instances of the application.

This makes sense in 16-bit versions of Windows. Only one instance of a given DLL can be loaded under Win16, so there is only one **hModule** value for each loaded DLL.

The hInstance Parameter

In 16-bit versions of Windows, each running instance of a task also receives its own **hInstance** value. This value identifies the default data segment for the task. If, say, four instances of the task are running, there are four **hInstance** values—one for each instance.

In Windows 95, there is no distinction between a process's **hModule** and its **hInstance** values; they are exactly the same. Wherever the documentation for a Win16 API states that an **hModule** value is required, you can pass an **hInstance** value—and vice versa—when you are programming Windows 95.

When a Win32 process calls the **WinMain** function, the actual value that is passed to the function in the **hInstance** parameter is a base address that specifies the point where the .EXE file is mapped into the process's address space. By default, an .EXE file is mapped into a process's address space starting at 0x00010000 (you can change this default by using the **/BASE:address** linker switch). Thus, the default **hInstance** variable for an .EXE file is 0x00010000. This means that the **hInstance** value for all running processes is the same; specifically, 0x00010000.

A corollary of all this is that a process cannot load a resource—for example, a dialog-box template—from the resource file of another process that is currently executing. Even in Windows 3.*x*, this is not generally a wise thing to do—and in Windows 95, it is not possible. In Windows 95, when you make a call to an API that expects an **hInstance** value, the Win32 system interprets the call to mean that you are requesting information from an .EXE or a .DLL mapped into your own process's address space, at the address specified by the **hInstance** parameter.

The *hPrevInstance* Parameter

In a 16-bit Windows-based application, the **hPrevInstance** parameter specifies the instance handle to another instance of the same task. If no other instance of the task is running, a **NULL** value is passed in the **hPrevInstance** parameter. Applications frequently examine this value for two purposes:

- To determine if another instance of the same task is already running—and if so, terminate the instance that has just been invoked
- To determine whether window classes need to be registered.

DLL Entry Points in Windows 95

The Win32 system also allocates every DLL its own **hInstance** value—which, again, is identical to the DLL's **hModule** value under Windows 95. In Windows 95, DLL entry points look different. This is the format of a **LibMain** (DLL entry-point) function in Windows 95:

```
INT FAR PASCAL LibMain(HINSTANCE hInstance, WORD
    wDataSeg, WORD cbHeapSize, LPSTR lpCmdLine)
```

In a **LibMain** function in Windows 95, the **hInstance** parameter specifies the instance handle to the Win32 DLL. Just like the **hInstance** parameter passed to **WinMain**, the value of the **hInstance** parameter of **LibMain** specifies the address where the DLL is mapped to in the process's address space. If several different processes load the same DLL into their address spaces, these DLLs are all mapped into different addresses. In this case, each of the DLLs receives a different value for its respective **hInstance** parameter.

In a 16-bit Windows application, a module can call the **RegisterClass** function to register a particular window class only be once. This class is then shared by all instances of the application. If a second instance attempts to register the same window class a second time, the call to **RegisterClass** fails.

In Windows 95, each instance of an application must register its own window classes because different instances of the same application do not share window classes. Therefore, in a Win32 application, a **NULL** value is always passed in the **hPrevInstance** parameter to **WinMain**.

This characteristic can simplify the porting of Win16 applications to Win32. If a 16-bit application examines the **hPrevInstance** parameter when it registers a window class and finds a **NULL** value, all instances of the application discover that **hPrevInstance** is **NULL** and automatically re-register their window classes.

The *lpszCmdLine* Parameter

The **lpszCmdLine** parameter is the only parameter to **WinMain** that has the same meaning in Windows 3.*x* and Windows 95. The **lpszCmdLine** parameter points to a zero-terminated string containing the command line that is passed to the application to start it.

The *nCmdShow* Parameter

The **nCmdShow** parameter, the last parameter to **WinMain**, is usually **SW_SHOWNORMAL** or **SW_SHOWMINNOACTIVE** in applications written for Windows 3.x. In Windows 95, the value of **nCmdShow** is always **SW_SHOWDEFAULT**.

In Windows 95, when an application displays a window that has been created using **SW_SHOWDEFAULT**, the Win32 operating system examines the **nCmdShow** member of the window's **STARTUPINFO** structure to find out what process owns the window. Win32 then uses this value to determine how the window should be displayed.

Message-Handling in Windows 95

Windows 95, like its 16-bit Windows predecessors, is an event-driven, message-based system. When the user of an application performs an action such as pressing a key on a keyboard or moving or clicking the mouse, that action is an *event*. When Windows detects an event, it dispatches a *message* to the window associated with the event so the window can perform whatever action needs to be performed to respond to the event. Applications can also send messages to windows.

For example, when the user presses the left mouse button, Windows sends out a **WM_LBUTTONDOWN** message. When the user types a character on the keyboard, Windows dispatches a **WM_CHAR** message. When the user or the program being executed closes the window, Windows issues a **WM_CLOSE** message.

Events that are originated by the system rather than by the user can cause messages to be generated, too. For instance, a **WM_CREATE** message is generated when a window is being created, and a **WM_DESTROY** message is dispatched when a window is about to be destroyed.

Messages that are sent to an application window when the user selects a menu item are called *command messages*. An application can also define its own messages, which are known as *user messages*.

In a Windows application written in C, messages are dispatched from a **switch** statement that calls functions known as *message handlers*. (Visual C++ handles messages differently, as explained in Chapter 4, "The Win32 API.")

When a non-MFC program is executed, it continuously loops through an event-handling loop or *main event loop*, monitoring user input and dispatching messages to the appropriate functions when events of various kinds are detected. In MFC applications, messages are trapped.

Summary

This chapter explained how the Win32 API, application programming interface, implements the new features built into Windows 95. It showed how the Win32 SDK implements memory management, memory-mapped files, the Windows 95 DLLs, and window management in the Windows 95 environment.

Chapter 5, "Windows 95 and the MFC Library," introduces what some Microsoft executives have called the "new API"—Version 4.0 of the Microsoft Foundation Class library. In Chapter 5, you'll see how the many new features of MFC 4.0 streamline the use of the functions provided in the "old API" you read about in this chapter.

Chapter

5

Windows 95 and the MFC Library

If MFC 4.0 has really become the new Windows API, that means that from now on, all Windows applications will have to call functions implemented in the Microsoft Foundation Class library instead of calling functions implemented in the familiar Windows API. Furthermore, because the MFC library is a C++ class library, it means that the standard language for Windows developers has now shifted from C to C++.

When Microsoft unveiled Windows 95 and Version 4.0 of the Microsoft Foundation Class library, Microsoft evangelists declared that from that point on, MFC would be "the new Windows API."

That was a bombshell announcement for Windows programmers. The Windows API, or application programming interface, is the foundation of Windows programming. The "old" Windows API (described in Chapter 4, "The Win32 API,") contains the procedures that make Windows work. All Windows applications perform their tasks by calling functions defined and implemented in the Windows API.

If MFC 4.0 has really become the new Windows API, that means that from now on, all Windows applications will have to call functions implemented in the Microsoft Foundation Class library instead of calling functions implemented in the familiar Windows API. Furthermore, because the MFC library is a C++ class library, it means that the standard language for Windows developers has now shifted from C to C++.

The shift from C to C++ makes the new role of the MFC library even more extraordinary. A whole generation of Windows programmers has grown up on C, and an official shift to a C++-based Windows API would cascade down into myriad changes in Windows programming practices.

Why is this move from C to C++ so significant? Because the Windows API and the Microsoft Foundation Class library treat fundamental Windows concepts—such as program architecture and message handling—in very different ways. And the encapsulation of Windows functions into C++ classes—the basic building blocks of MFC programming—would force legions of Windows developers to learn C++ and to become familiar with object-oriented programming.

Is this all really happening? Indeed, it is. Still, all is not quite as scary as you might imagine. Once you learn C++—admittedly a major hurdle—you'll begin to see that the MFC library is really only a thin veneer (to use one Microsoft executive's description) over the Windows API.

Because the MFC 4.0 is such a thin veneer over the "old" Windows API, the vast majority of Windows functions provided in the MFC library do their jobs by simply calling Windows API functions—in fact, most MFC classes provide handles that you can use to access API functions directly whenever you like—so it still stands to reason that the more you know about the "old" Windows API, the better you'll be at using the new one.

This chapter introduces you to the new Windows API—MFC 4.0—and shows you how you can use it in your Windows 95 applications. Most of the new capabilities of MFC 4.0 are related to the new user-interface features of Windows 95, so the interface-related features of MFC 4.0 are the features examined most closely in this chapter.

The following are the major topics covered in this chapter:

- "Property-Sheet Dialog Boxes" on page 224
- "Common Dialog Boxes" on page 229
- "Example: Creating a Progress-Bar Control" on page 233
- "Summary" on page 238.

This chapter also presents a hands-on tutorial that shows how to create a progress bar: a thermometer-like common control that's often used to keep track of the progress of time-consuming operations, such as the installation of an application. The progress-bar control is one of many new common controls that are encapsulated into classes in Version 4.0 of the Microsoft Foundation Class library.

About MFC 4.0

Windows users are not the only people who got a bagful of new goodies when Microsoft introduced Windows 95. Shortly after Windows95 made its debut, Microsoft also unveiled two related products: Version 4.0 of the Microsoft Foundation Class library (MFC) and Version 4.0 of Visual C++. Both MFC 4.0 and Visual C++ 4.0 are packed with new features, many of them designed specifically for Windows 95.

Version 4.0 of the Microsoft Foundation Class library contains many new classes and member functions that were not available in earlier versions of MFC, plus many more classes and member functions that were introduced in beta form in MFC 3.1 but officially became available for the first time in MFC 4.0. Many of the classes that were provided with MFC 3.1 in a not-ready-for-prime-time version have been significantly enhanced for their official release with MFC 4.0.

Features of MFC that may be new to you (depending on what MFC version you've been using) include the following:

- Many new Windows controls (to be distinguished from OLE controls) that support the new user-interface features of Windows 95. The new controls available in Windows 95 are sometimes referred to as *common controls* because they are useful in many kinds of programs and are used by the system as well as by applications. New or enhanced common controls provided by MFC 4.0 include dockable toolbar controls; spin-button, progress-bar, and slider-bar controls; and many more. Each new or enhanced control in MFC 4.0 is described under its own heading in this chapter.
- New *common dialog boxes* that are used by the Windows 95 shell as well as by Windows 95 applications. The new common dialog

boxes available in MFC 4.0 include a new Windows 95-style **Open File** dialog box, and a new **Page Setup** dialog box that replaces the old **Print Setup** dialog box used by previous versions of Windows.

- New classes for creating and managing tabbed dialog boxes, which Microsoft calls *property-page* dialog boxes, or *property sheets*.
- New dialog boxes for creating and managing OLE objects.
- New support for OLE (object linking and embedding), including full support for OLE control containers. With the OLE classes in the MFC library, you can make your application an OLE visual editing container, an OLE visual editing server, or both. You can also add OLE automation to your application so other applications can use objects from your application or even drive it remotely. (The OLE-related features of the MFC library are covered in more detail in Chapter 7, "OLE 95.")
- Increased support for networking, including two new classes that support Windows sockets. (For more about Windows sockets, see Chapter 11, "Windows 95 Networking.")
- Enhanced support for multithreading, including new synchronization classes for creating mutexes, semaphores, and event objects (see Chapter 9, "Multithreading and Multitasking" for more details).
- An expanded set of database classes that simplify the writing of data-aware applications. Using the database classes provided in MFC 4.0, you can connect to local or remote databases using an open database connectivity (ODBC) driver, access data from databases provided by many different vendors, and manipulate the data you have accessed directly from Windows 95.
- New classes designed specifically to support new features of Windows 95, including classes that support the system registry.

The classes in the MFC library help to simplify the writing of Windows applications because they make it possible to use C++ programming tools—and a vast number of prewritten and pretested C++ classes—to write programs for Windows 95 and Windows NT.

Some of the classes provided by MFC encapsulate the functionality of the Windows API. Other classes encapsulate application concepts used in Visual C++, such as documents, views, and architectural models that represent complete Visual C++ applications. Still other classes encapsulate OLE features and data-access functionality.

By the Numbers

With the introduction of MFC 4.0, Microsoft made a welcome change in MFC and Visual C++ version numbers. Until MFC 4.0 was introduced, the version numbers of Microsoft's MFC and Visual C++ products were badly out of sync.

The 16-bit versions of Visual C++—Versions 1.0 through 1.52—used Versions 2.0 and 2.5, respectively, of the MFC library. The 32-bit versions of Visual C++—versions 2.0 and 2.1—used Versions 3.0 and 3.1 of the MFC library, respectively. Meanwhile, the most recent version of 16-bit Windows was Windows 3.1, and the latest version of Windows NT was Version 3.5.

By skipping over some unused version numbers—which will now remain unused forever—Microsoft finally brought the current version numbers of MFC and Visual C++ into sync. The current version of the MFC library is Version 4.0, and the current version of Visual C++ is also Version 4.0. And Microsoft pledges that the two products will stay on the same versioning track from now on.

Meanwhile, there will be no more releases of 16-bit versions of MFC or Visual C++. If you want to keep programming with Visual C++ 1.2 and MFC 3.0, you can do that indefinitely. Meanwhile, the rest of us will be developing software with Visual C++ 4.0, MFC 4.0, and their in-sync successors.

Win32 Common Controls

Common controls are a category of Windows controls (to be distinguished from OLE controls) that are implemented a dynamic-link library (DLL) called the common-control DLL, or common-control library. The common-control library is supplied with Version 3.51 and later of Windows NT, as well as with Windows 95. You can't use common controls in programs that run under earlier versions of Windows.

To use common controls in an application, you must make sure that your application loads the common-control DLL. In a non-Visual C++ application, the way to do that is to call the Win32 function **InitCommonControls**. Then you can create a common control at any time you like by calling the Win32 function **CreateWindowEx**.

When you write a Visual C++ application using an AppWizard framework (see Chapter 6, "Windows 95 and Visual C++"), you don't have to worry about any of that; AppWizard makes sure that your application has all the functionality it needs to use common controls.

Varieties of Common Controls

Table 5.1 lists and describes the new and enhanced common control classes available in MFC 4.0. Notice that the controls listed in the table are divided into four categories:

- *List-related controls,* which can help you create and manage lists
- *Utility controls,* which provide user-interface functionalities that are often used in Windows 95 programs
- *Control-bar objects,* which you can use to create toolbars, status bars, and objects to support them
- *Property pages*—tabbed dialog boxes that can be used to display and set the properties of objects

Later in this chapter, each control listed in Table 5.1 is described in more detail.

Table 5.1 New and enhanced common controls in Windows 95

MFC Class	Description	Kind of Control
CToolbar	Base class for creating and managing toolbar controls.	Control bar
CToolbarCtrl	Displays a toolbar control.	Control bar
CToolTipCtrl	Displays tiny tool-tip windows when the mouse passes over toolbar buttons.	Control bar
CStatusBar	Base class for creating and managing status bars	Control bar
CStatusBar-Ctrl	Displays a status-bar control.	Control bar
CProper-tyPage	Creates and manages a property-page (tabbed) dialog box.	Property page
CProperty-Sheet	Creates and manages a tabbed panel in a property-page dialog box.	Property page
CTabCtrl	Displays a tab control like those used in property-page dialog boxes.	Property page
CProgressCtrl	Displays a progress control.	Utility

Table 5.1 New and enhanced common controls in Windows 95

MFC Class	Description	Kind of Control
CSpinButton-Ctrl	Displays a spin-button control.	Utility
CSliderCtrl	Displays a slider control.	Utility
CAnimate-Ctrl	Displays a control that can play AVI video files (without sound).	Utility
CHotKeyCtrl	Displays a dialog box that lets the user create hot keys (keystroke shortcuts).	Utility
CListCtrl	Encapsulates the functionality of a list view control, which displays a collection of items. Each item is represented by an icon (or a user-defined image) and a label.	List-related
CTreeCtrl	Displays a hierarchical list of items, such as headings in a document, entries in an index, or files and directories on a disk.	List-related
CImageList	A tool for storing and displaying graphics images (such as icons) that can be used alongside the names of items in lists.	List-related
CDragListBox	Constructs list boxes with items that can be dragged and dropped.	List-related
CHeaderCtrl	Displays windows that can be used as column headings in lists and tables.	List-related

How Common Controls Work

Common controls are implemented as windows—specifically, as child windows that are used with parent windows to perform input and output (I/O) tasks.

Because a common control is a child window, it sends its parent window a notification message when the user of your application takes an action that affects the control. Your application can then determine how it should respond to the user's action. Slider controls (also known as track bars; see "Slider Controls" on page 198) fire WM_HSCROLL messages. But all other common controls respond to user actions by dispatching WM_NOTIFY messages. When a common control sends a WM_NOTIFY message to its parent window, the common control identifies itself and provides its parent window with a notification code that specifies what kind of action the user has taken.

Each type of common control has a corresponding set of notification codes. The common control library also provides notification codes that can be sent by more than one type of common control.

Because common controls are windows, an application can send messages to common controls as well as receiving messages from them. For example, an application can find out what font a control is using by sending a WM_GETFONT message or can set a label or a caption used by a control by sending a WM_SETTEXT message. Also, there are many control-specific messages, functions, and macros that applications can use to manage various kinds of special features of individual controls.

Techniques for Creating Common Controls

One good example of a common control is the progress-bar control: a thermometer-style bar control that an application can use to indicate the progress of time-consuming operations.

A progress bar takes the form of a long horizontal or vertical rectangle that gradually fills with color as an operation progresses. However, progress bars can also appear in other kinds of locations—for example, inside a task bar, as shown in Figure 5.1.

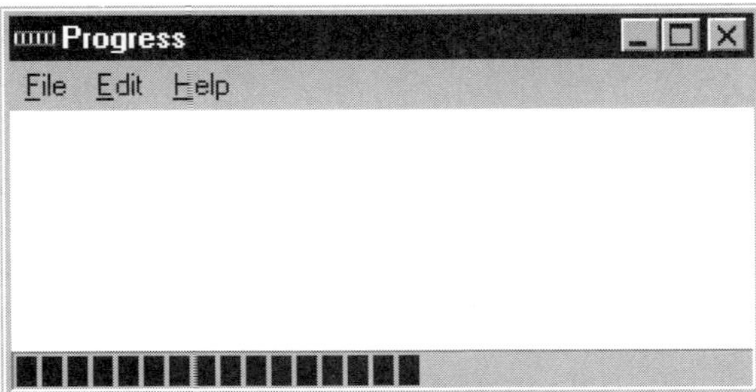

Figure 5.1 A progress-bar control inside a task bar

You can display text inside a progress bar. If text is shown in a progress bar, it typically is a number, expressed as a percentage, that decrements to zero as the operation being monitored progresses.

Common controls have various kinds of properties. For example, every progress bar control has a pair of properties called *range* and *current position*. The range property of a progress bar usually represents the entire duration of the operation that the progress bar is monitoring. A progress bar's current position property—along with the text displayed inside the progress bar, if their is any—give the user an idea of how much longer it will take to complete the operation being monitored.

A progress-bar control, like all common controls provided in MFC 4.0, can be created in two ways: interactively (using the Developer Studio's dialog-box editor) and programmatically (using MFC member functions.)

To create a common control programmatically, you must instantiate an object of the appropriate class—for example, to create a progress-bar control, you instantiate an object of the CProgressCtrl class. To instantiate a CProgressCtrl object, you must first call the CProgressBar constructor and then call the **`CProgressBar::Create`** member function.

Once you have created a common control, you can get and set its attributes and manipulate it in other ways by calling member functions of its MFC class. For example, progress-bar controls have the following attributes:

- **`SetRange`** sets the minimum and maximum ranges for a progress bar control; redraws the bar if necessary to reflect the bar's new ranges.
- **`SetPos`** sets a progress bar's current position for control and redraws the bar if necessary to reflect the new position.
- **`OffsetPos`** advances the current position of a progress bar control by a specified increment and redraws the bar to reflect the new position.
- **`SetStep`** specifies the step increment for a progress bar control.
- **`StepIt`** advances the position of a progress bar control by the bar's step increment and redraws the bar to reflect its new position.

Creating Common Controls with Visual C++ 4.0

In a Visual C++ program, the easiest way to implement a common control is to create it interactively using the Developer Studio dialog-box editor. You can then use the ClassWizard utility to create member variables that are associated with the control and to link those variables to the rest of your application.

The procedures for creating a control using the Visual C++ 4.0 Developer Studio are quite different from the techniques you may have used to create controls using earlier versions of Visual C++. Under the next heading, "Creating a Common Control Step by Step," you'll get an opportunity to use Developer Studio to create a dialog box containing a common control. The control you'll create will be a progress bar.

Creating a Common Control Step by Step

By following the steps listed in this section, you can create a progress bar like the one presented in "Example: Creating a Progress-Bar Control" on page 233. Before you start the following exercise, you may want to build the PROGBAR program and execute it. Then you'll have a clear understanding of exactly how a progress bar works. Figure 5.2 shows the dialog box displayed by the PROGBAR program. The program that implements a progress-bar control in a file named COMMCTRLDlg.cpp. The source code of the portion of the COMM-CTRLDlg.cpp file is presented in "Example: Creating a Progress-Bar Control" on page 233.

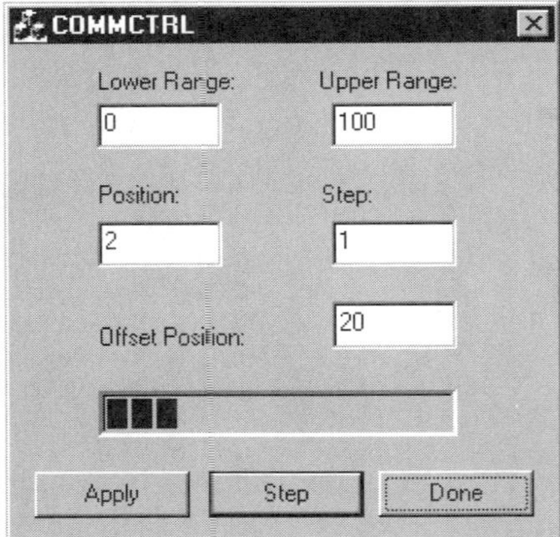

Figure 5.2 Output of the PROGBAR program

✔ To create a common control using the Visual C++ dialog-box editor, these are the general steps to follow:

1. Start Developer Studio if it isn't already started.
2. Use AppWizard to generate a dialog-based Visual C++ program. In this exercise, you'll be creating an ordinary control—not an OLE control—so you won't have to choose any of the OLE options that AppWizard offers when you generate the framework for your application. Just build an ordinary dialog-based program. (If

you need to refresh your memory on how to do that, see "Example Program: Exploring the Registry" on page 48.)

3. When AppWizard has generated an application framework, open the Visual C++ dialog-box editor by clicking the resource tab under the left-hand panel in Developer Studio's editor window, shown in Figure 5.3.

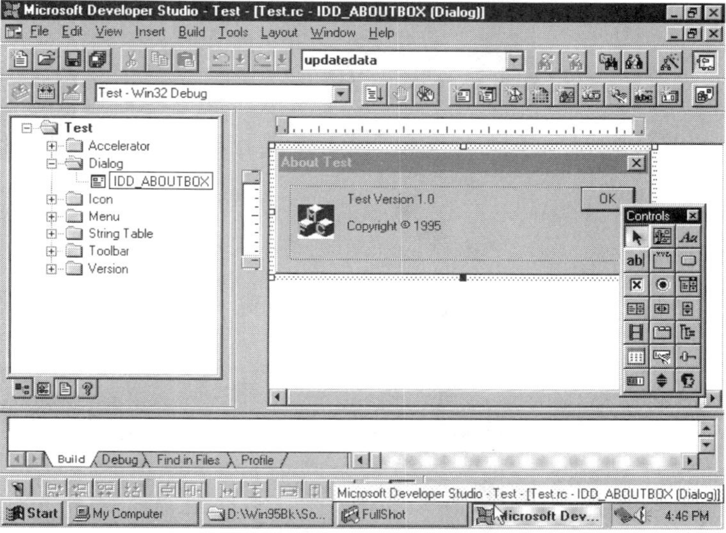

Figure 5.3 The Developer Studio dialog-box editor

Alternatively, you can open the dialog-box editor by executing the **Insert | Resource** menu command. Developer Studio responds by opening an **Insert Resource** dialog box like the one shown in Figure 5.4. You can then open the dialog-box editor by selecting the **Dialog** icon from the **Resource Type** list box and clicking the **OK** button.

Figure 5.4 The Insert Resource dialog box

4. When the dialog-box editor opens, check to see if a **Controls** toolbar like the one shown in Figure 5.5 is visible (it may have a different shape; the **Controls** toolbar is user-realizable). If you don't see a **Controls** toolbar, open one by choosing the **View | Toolbars** menu item and then checking the **Controls** check box.

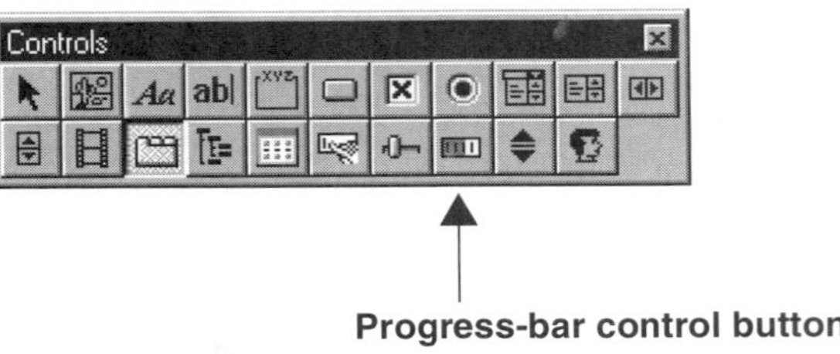

Figure 5.5 The Controls toolbar

5. When the **Controls** toolbar appears, select the button that represents the control you went to create. Then place the control inside the dialog-box template shown in the dialog-box editor by simply clicking the mouse inside the dialog box (see Figure 5.6). (To help you interpret the icons in the **Controls** toolbar, the dialog-box editor displays a tool-tip box each time you pause the mouse over a toolbar button.)

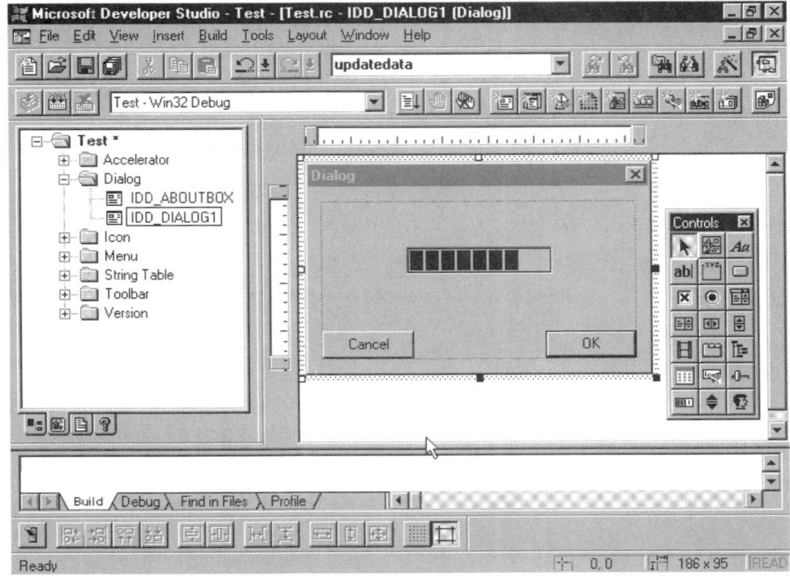

Figure 5.6 Editing a control

6. When you have placed a control inside your dialog-box template, you can drag the control around and resize it to suit the needs of your application. For example, to place a progress-bar control in the center of a dialog box, simply drag it there, as shown in Figure 5.6 on page 188.
7. When you have completed the preceding steps, test your application by executing Developer Studio's **Build | Execute** menu command. At this stage of development, the dialog box displayed by your PROGBAR program should resemble the one shown in Figure 5.7.

In the next section, "Creating a Class for a Common Control," you'll get a chance to complete the PROGBAR application and execute it in its finished form.

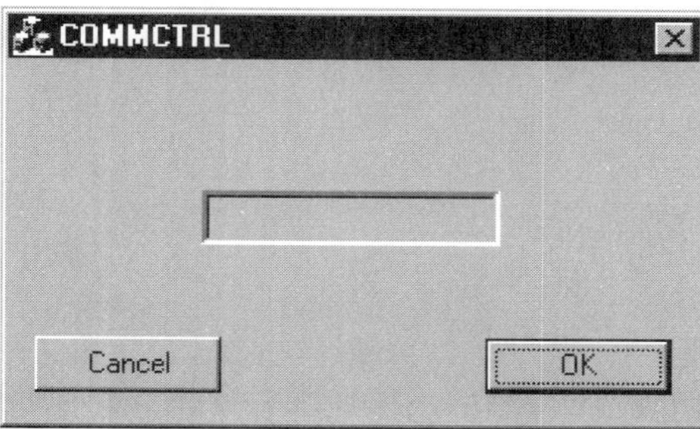

Figure 5.7 The PROGBAR application, Phase 1

Creating a Class for a Common Control

When you have created a common control with the Developer Studio dialog-box editor, you can open the Visual C++ ClassWizard utility and create a member variable that corresponds to your common control. Then, at runtime, you can use the Visual C++ DDX mechanism to move date back and forth between your common control and other parts of your application.

(For a brief review of how the DDX mechanism works, you may want to go back and reread "Retrieving Dialog-Box Data with the DDX Mechanism" on page 50.)

✔ To create a member variable that can be used to pass values back and forth between a common control and an application, follow these steps:

1. Open the Visual C++ dialog-box editor if it isn't already open, and display the PROGBAR dialog-box template shown earlier in Figure 5.3 on page 187.
2. Execute the **View | ClassWizard** menu item. The ClassWizard window then opens, as shown in Figure 5.8.

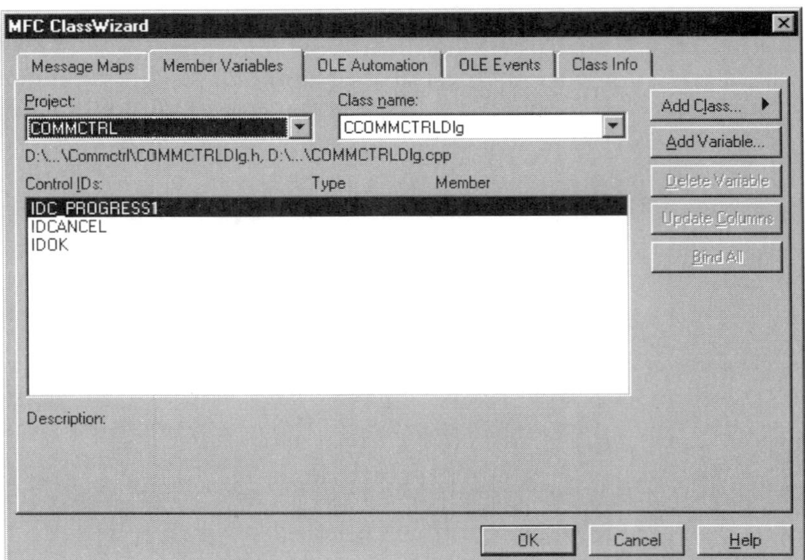

Figure 5.8 Creating a member variable with ClassWizard

3. Click the **Add Variable** button. A dialog box titled **Add Member Variable** then opens (see Figure 5.9 on page 191).
4. Add a member variable named **`m_progCtrl`** to your application by typing its named in the text box labeled **Member variable name**.
5. Close the **Add Member Variable** dialog box by clicking its **OK** button.
6. When the **ClassWizard** window becomes active again, close it by clicking its **OK** button.

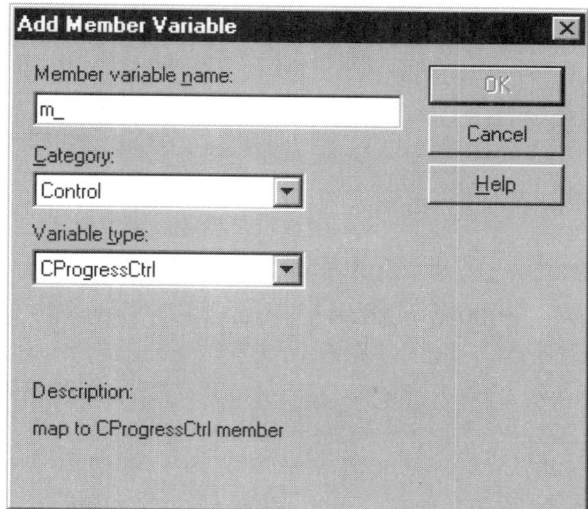

Figure 5.9 Adding a member variable to a dialog box

7. Open the source file that implements your application's dialog box. (In this chapter's PROGBAR program, that's a file named COMMCTRLDlg.cpp.) When the file that implements your dialog box opens, notice that ClassWizard has added an entry for your new **m_progCtrl** variable to your dialog box's data map:

```
void CCOMMCTRLDlg::DoDataExchange(CDataExchange* pDX)
{
   CDialog::DoDataExchange(pDX);
   //{{AFX_DATA_MAP(CCOMMCTRLDlg)
   DDX_Control(pDX, IDC_PROGRESS1, m_progCtrl);
   //}}AFX_DATA_MAP
}
```

Once a member variable associated with a control has been added to a dialog box's data map, the Visual C++ DDX mechanism can be used to move information back and forth between the member variable and its associated dialog-box control. For example, in this chapter's PROGBAR program, these four member functions in the COMMCTRLDlg.cpp file are used to initialize the values used by the program's progress-bar control:

```
m_progCtrl.SetRange(0, 100);
m_progCtrl.SetPos(2);
m_progCtrl.SetStep(1);
m_progCtrl.OffsetPos(20);
```

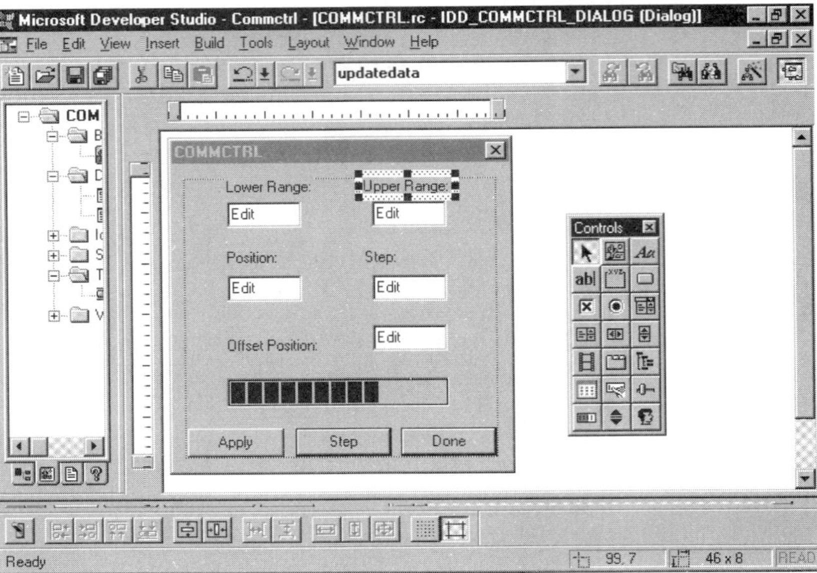

Figure 5.10 PROGBAR dialog-box controls

8. Once a common control has been placed in a dialog box and activated, it's easy to add more controls to the dialog box and to manipulate the state of the control with other DDX functions.

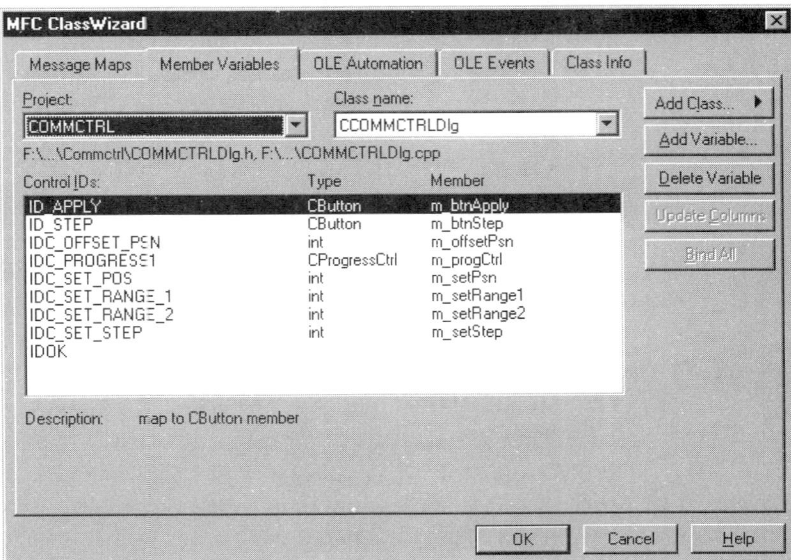

Figure 5.11 PROGBAR controls and member functions

In this chapter's PROGBAR program, a couple of button controls and several text-edit controls are used to change the state (and the looks) of the program's progress control interactively. To add the same collection of buttons and text boxes to the application you are developing, use the Visual C++ dialog-box editor to create the set of controls shown in Figure 5.10 on page 192.

9. Open ClassWizard and create a set of member variables for your dialog-box controls as shown in Figure 5.11 on page 192.
10. Close ClassWizard and execute your program. The dialog box it displays should resemble the one shown in Figure 5.12.

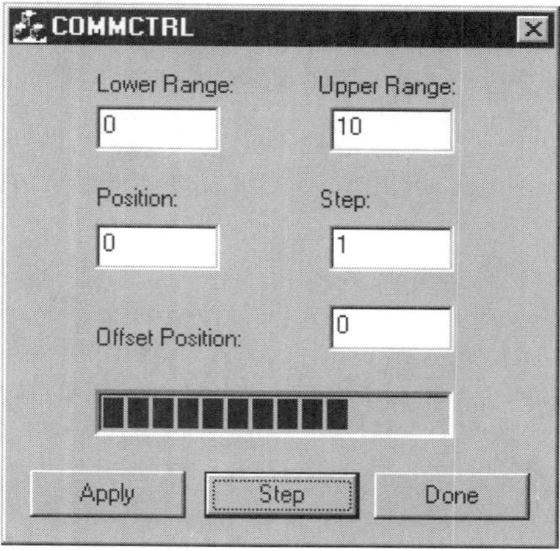

Figure 5.12 Executing the PROGBAR program

11. Experiment with your program by changing the values in its text boxes and then clicking the **Apply** and **Step** buttons. When you are finished, quit the program by clicking the **Done** button.

Connecting a Common Control to an Application

When you have created a common control with the Developer Studio's dialog-box editor, and have created a member function that is to be associated with your control, you must connect your new member variable to the code in your application if you want your control to have any useful functionality. In a Visual C++ program, you connect a common control to an application by creating the appropriate kinds of MFC objects and then calling the appropriate member functions.

In the previous exercise, you saw how you can use the Visual C++ dialog-box editor to implement common controls such as progress bars. In MFC 4.0, all the other common control described in this chapter can be created in the same fashion. For example, docking toolbars (like the dialog editor's **Controls** toolbar) are instantiated from the CToolbar class, animated controls are instantiated from the CAnimateCtrl class, and so on.

You can also create common controls in Visual C++ without using the Developer Studio's dialog-box editor. It isn't as easy to create a control programmatically as it is to create one interactively, but sometimes you need more control over a control than the interactive creation technique can give you. Back in Chapter 1, in "Example Program: Exploring the Registry" on page 48, you saw how a CButton object can be used to create a button control that can be activated and deactivated. That was one example of how you must sometimes create a control programmatically when you want it to have special capabilities or special features.

It generally takes two steps to instantiate and create a common control programmatically in an MFC application: First you call the constructor of the control's class, and then you call the control's **Create** member function—a virtual function of the CWnd class. All common controls override the **CWnd::Create** member function to provide control-specific features. For example, to instantiate a list-header control (control that displays a heading over a list), you call the **CHeaderCtrl::Create** member function:

```
BOOL Create( DWORD dwStyle, const RECT& rect, CWnd*
   pParentWnd, UINT nID );
```

When you call **CHeaderCtrl::Create**, you can set the control's style by passing a constant in the *dwStyle* parameter. You can apply multiple settings at the same time by connecting them with the logical-OR (|) operator.

As you'll see later, in "Image Lists" on page 218, the CHeaderControl class has a number of control-specific attributes that you can set using the *dwStyle* parameter. In addition, the CWnd class has a number of attributes that all common controls can use. To set any of these CWnd attributes in the *dwStyle* parameter, you can simple place the appropriate constant in the *dwStyle* parameter, along with any control-specific settings that you want your control to have.

Setting Attributes and Managing Controls

These are the window-style attributes you can place in the *dwStyle* parameter when you create any common control:

- WS_CHILD—Creates a child window. Set by default when you create a common control; all common controls are child windows.
- WS_VISIBLE—Creates a control that is initially visible.
- WS_DISABLED—Creates a control that is initially disabled.
- WS_GROUP —Specifies the first control of a group of controls in which the user can move from one control to the next with the arrow keys. All controls defined with the WS_GROUP style after the first control belong to the same group. The next control with the WS_GROUP style ends the style group and starts the next group (that is, one group ends where the next begins).
- WS_TABSTOP—Specifies one of any number of controls through which the user can move by using the TAB key. The TAB key moves the user to the next control specified by the WS_TABSTOP style.

Many common controls also have member functions for getting and setting various attributes and for manipulating the control in various ways. For example, when you have created a list control using the CListCtrl class, you can get and set items in the list by calling **`GetItem`** and **`SetItem`**; search for an item in the list by setting up a loop that calls **`GetNextItem`**; and get or replace the text of an item by calling **`GetItemText`** or **`SetItemText`**.

Other common controls have similar member functions for getting and setting attributes and for performing similar control-specific operations.

Utility Controls

Many of the new and enhanced controls in MFC 4.0 fall into a category I call *utility controls* (see Table 5.1 on page 182). Utility controls, according to this definition, are miscellaneous gadgets—such as spin buttons and thermometer-style progress bars—that you might useful when you create Windows 95 applications.

In a Visual C++ program, you can add any utility-style common control to a dialog box using the dialog-box editor. You'll learn how to do that in Chapter 6, "Windows 95 and Visual C++."

Controls that can be placed in the user-interface category are:

- The *spin-button control*—A pair of up-and-down or left-and-right arrows that the user can click or hold down to increment or decrement a value. As the user clicks or holds down the arrow, a text box displays the changing value.
- The *slider control* (sometimes called a track bar)—A control that takes the form of a slider, which looks much like a scroll bar. When the user moves the slider, the control dispatches messages notifying your application of changes in the value of a variable.
- The *progress-bar control*—A control that shows the progress of a time-consuming operation. A progress bar, as you saw in "Creating a Common Control Step by Step" on page 186, usually takes the form of a long, thermometer-like a rectangle that is gradually filled in as an operation progresses. Programs that install applications often make use of progress-bar controls. "Example: Creating a Progress-Bar Control" on page 233 shows how you can create and implement a progress-bar control in a Windows 95 program.
- The *hot-key control*—A control that lets the user to create a *hot key*, that is, a shortcut key combination that the user can press to perform an action quickly. A hot-key control displays a dialog box that the user can open to set up hot-key shortcuts.
- The *animation control*—A rectangular window that displays a video clip in AVI (Audio Video Interleaved) format. An AVI clip is a video clip that is stored as a series of bitmap frames and can be played back as a video movie.

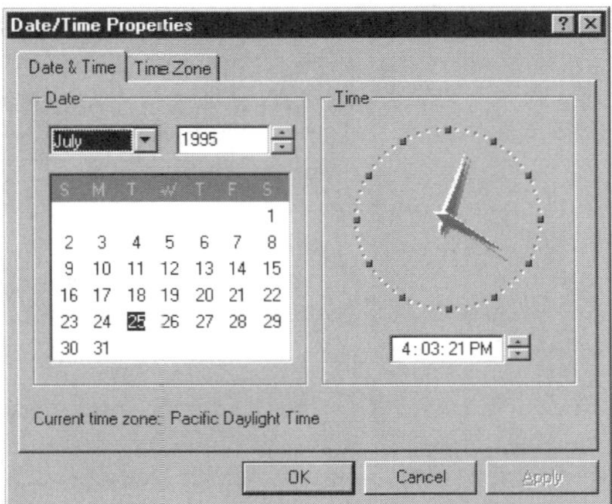

Figure 5.13 A spin-button control (under the clock)

Spin-Button Controls

A *spin-button control* is pair of up-and-down or left-and-right arrows that the user can click or hold down to increment or decrement a value. As the user clicks or holds down the arrow, a text box displays the changing value.

The value by which a spin button increments or decrements can represent various kinds of things, depending on the requirements of your application. The Date/Time applet, which you can access from the Windows 95 Control Panel, uses a spin-button to let the user set the time (Figure 5.13 on page 196).

You can use spin controls to perform many other kinds of operations, too. For example, spin controls can change the scrolling positions of screen objects and can change values displayed in other controls.

To display numbers incremented or decremented by a spin control, you can use a companion control called a *buddy window*. In Figure 5.13, the text box that displays the time is a buddy window.

A buddy window is often an edit control like the one shown in Figure 5.13. If you like, you can design a buddy window that gives the user a choice between typing in a number or changing the displayed number using the spin button.

You can create spin buttons that do not have buddy window. A spin button that doesn't have a buddy window can work like a simplified scroll bar. For example, tab controls sometimes use spin buttons that let the user to scroll hidden tabs into view.

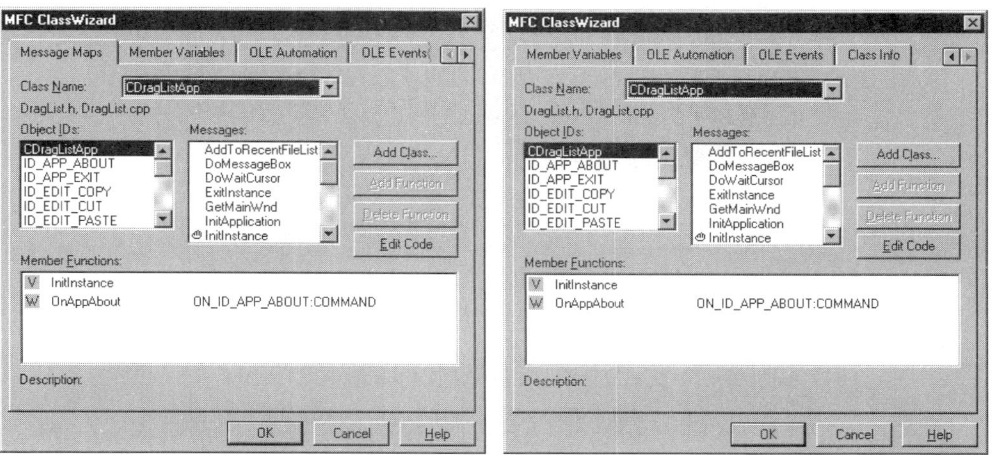

Figure 5.14 Using a spin-button control to move tab controls

Figure 5.14 on Page 197 shows how the Visual C++ ClassWizard tools uses a spin control to select tabs that let the user move from one property sheet to another. In case you can't find the spin control in the two dialog boxes shown in the illustration, it's the tiny pair of arrows just to the right of the property-sheet tabs at the top of the ClassWizard dialog box.

In the dialog box on the left, notice that the OLE Events tab next the spin control has a ragged right edge. When you click the right arrow in the spin control, all the tabs move one step to the left, and the **OLE Events** tab is replaced by a tab labeled ClassInfo, as shown in Figure 5.14.

Slider Controls

A *slider control* (there are two of them in Figure 5.15) contains a slider that can be moved back and forth like a volume control on a car-stereo equalizer. Optionally, you can place tick marks on a slider control to show a range of settings.

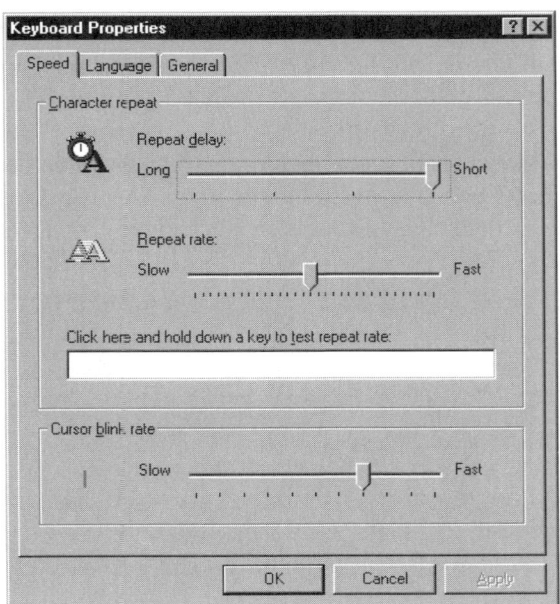

Figure 5.15 How the Keyboard applet uses slider controls

The user of an application can adjust a slider control using either the mouse or the arrow keys on the keyboard. As the user adjusts a slider control, the slider can change the value of a variable and can dispatch a message to your application, notifying your program of the change.

Slider controls can be handy when you want give the user a GUI-oriented mechanism for adjusting volume or adjusting other kinds of settings in a predetermined range. For example, the Windows 95 keyboard applet, which can be accessed from the Control Panel, has three slider controls. One adjusts the repeat delay of keys on the keyboard, another sets the repeat rate of keys, and still another sets the cursor's blinking rate.

You can use slider controls in many other ways in your Windows 95 applications. For example, the **Multimedia** applet—which the Windows 95 user can also access from the Control Panel—adjusts audio playback volume using a slider control.

A slider moves in increments that you specify at design time. For example, to create a slider control with nine settings—each one identified by a tick mark—you designate 10 discrete positions. Typically, the leftmost tick mark on the slider control represents a setting of zero—the "off" setting—and each tick mark to its right represents one incrementation level.

You can create a slider control programmatically by instantiating or deriving an object from the MFC CSliderCtrl class, and then calling **`CSliderCtrl::Create`**.

Animation Controls

An *animation control* is a rectangular window-based control that displays a video clip in AVI (Audio Video Interleaved) format — the standard Windows video/audio format. An AVI clip is a series of bitmap frames, like a movie.

An animation control can play clips stored as AVI resources or stored in separate AVI files. When an animation control plays a video clip, it does not play any sound.

One use for an animation control is to show an animated cartoon that performs some action while a time-consuming operation takes place. For example, the **Find** dialog box of the Windows 95 Explorer displays a moving magnifying glass while the system searches for a file (Figure 5.16).

Figure 5.16 Explorer's file-finding animation control

Restrictions on Using Animation Controls

There are several rules you must follow when you use animation controls in an application:

- An animation control can use only one video stream.
- The stream must contain at least one frame.
- An AVI file displayed by an animation control can contain no more than two streams. Typically, if there is a second stream, it is an audio stream—which an animation control ignores.
- The clip can be either compressed or uncompressed. If it is compress, it must be compressed using the RLE8 compression system.
- No palette changes are allowed in the video stream.

The CAnimateCtrl class

The CAnimateCtrl class provides the functionality of the Windows Common animation control. To create an animation control, you call the CAnimateCtrl constructor and then call the Create member function. Other member functions of the CAnimateCtrl class are:

- **`Open`**—Opens an AVI clip from a file or resource and displays the first frame.
- **`Play`**—Plays an AVI clip without sound.
- **`Seek`**—Displays a selected single frame of an AVI clip.
- **`Stop`**—Stops playing an AVI clip.
- **`Close`**—Closes an AVI clip that was previously opened.

Hot-Key Controls

A *hot-key control* displays a control box that lets the user create a *hot key*—that is, is a key combination that the user can press to perform an action quickly. For example, a user might create a hot key that activates a given window and brings it to the top of the Z order.

The hot-key control displays hot-key options set by the user and ensures that the user selects a valid key combination. Figure 5.17 is a dialog box that contains a hot-key control.

When the user of your application chooses a key combination using the hot-key dialog box, your program can retrieve the specified key combination from the control and use the WM_SETHOTKEY message to set up the hot key in the system.

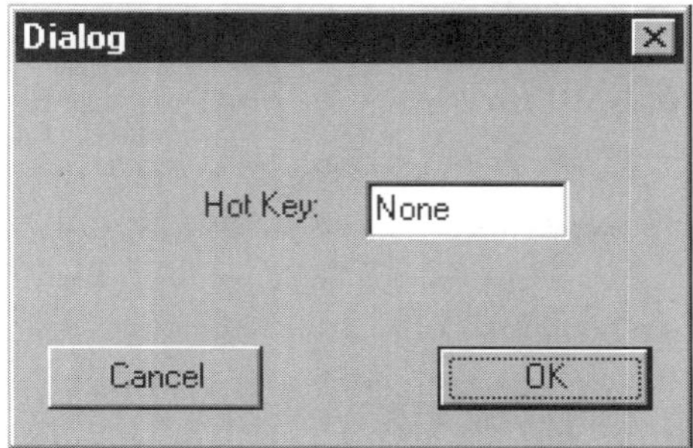

Figure 5.17 A hot-key control

Subsequently, whenever the user presses the hot key that has been set, the window specified in the WM_SETHOTKEY message receives a WM_SYSCOMMAND message that activates the window. The hot key remains valid until the application that called WM_SETHOTKEY exits.

To create a hot-key control using MFC, you construct an object of the CHotKeyCtrl class and then call the **`CHotKeyCtrl::Create`** member function. You can then call **`CHotKeyCtrl::SetHotKey`** to set up a hot-key control or call **`CHotKeyCtrl::GetHotKey`** to retrieve a hot-key setting entered by the user. The **`CHotKeyCtrl::SetRules`** member function defines invalid key combinations and the default modifier combination for a hot-key control.

Control Bars

A *control bar* is a common control that is usually aligned to the top or bottom of a frame window, or to one of the window's sides. MFC encapsulates three kinds of control bars: tool bars, status bars, and dialog bars.

Examples of CWnd-derived controls are buttons, list boxes, and edit controls. Examples of non-Cwnd-derived controls are status-bar panes and bitmap buttons.

Control-bar windows are usually child windows of parent frame windows. Also, they are usually siblings to the client view or MDI client of frame windows. A CControlBar object uses information about the parent window's client rectangle to position itself. It then informs the parent window as to how much space remains unallocated in the parent window's client area.

A control bar can contain child objects that are either CWnd-derived controls (Windows windows that generate and respond to Windows messages) or non-CWnd-derived objects (which are not windows and are managed by application code or framework code).

In MFC, the CControlBar class is the base class for all three kinds of control bars. The child classes of CControlBar that create toolbars, status bars, and dialog bars are CToolBar, CStatusBar, and CDialogBar.

CControlBar member functions include:

- **`GetBarStyle`**—Retrieves the control bar style settings.
- **`SetBarStyle`**—Modifies the control bar style settings.
- **`GetCount`**—Returns the number of non-HWND elements in the control bar.
- **`GetDockingFrame`**—Returns a pointer to the frame to which a control bar is docked.
- **`IsFloating`**—Returns a nonzero value if the control bar in question is a floating control bar.
- **`CalcFixedLayout`**—Returns the size of the control bar as a CSize object.

One virtual member function of CControlBar—**`EnableDocking`**—allows a toolbar to be docked or floating.

Toolbar Controls

Toolbar controls are one of the most useful categories of common controls available in MFC 4.0. As you probably know, a toolbar is a control bar equipped with at least one row of bitmapped buttons and optional separators. Clicking a toolbar button is a shortcut for choosing a menu item. In a well-behaved Windows 95 application, all the controls on a toolbar are supposed to have corresponding menu commands.

You can use toolbars for all sorts of things: color pickers, tool palettes, editing controls, and much more.

Figure 5.18—a picture of the Visual C++ resource editor with every available control activated—is a good example of how far you can go if you aren't careful in equipping a user interface with various kinds of toolbar controls.

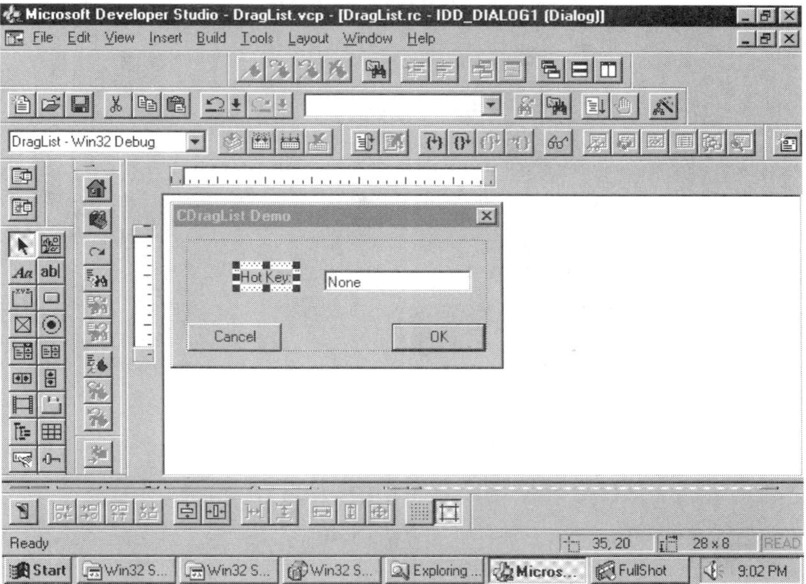

Figure 5.18 Visual C++ dialog editor: Too many toolbar controls?

When you create a CToolBarCtrl object, it draws its toolbar buttons by loading a single bitmap that contains one image for each button. A toolbar bitmap takes the form of a long horizontal rectangle, with button images placed on it side by side. All the images on a toolbar bitmap are the same size; the default is 16 pixels wide and 15 pixels high.

In Windows 95, a toolbar can be fixed or movable—but moveable, *dockable* toolbars are now so easy to create and implement that there are probably not many situations in which you'd want to use any other kind. A dockable toolbar is one that attaches itself to the top, bottom or side of a window when the user drags it to the edge of a window with the mouse.

When a dockable tool bar has been stuck to a window's edge, it doesn't stick very hard; the user can pull it away from its docking station with the mouse at any time, and it then floats inside the window like a tool palette.

Figure 5.19 shows what a toolbar looks like in two positions—when it is docked along a window's top edge and when it has been pulled away to float like a tool palette inside a window.

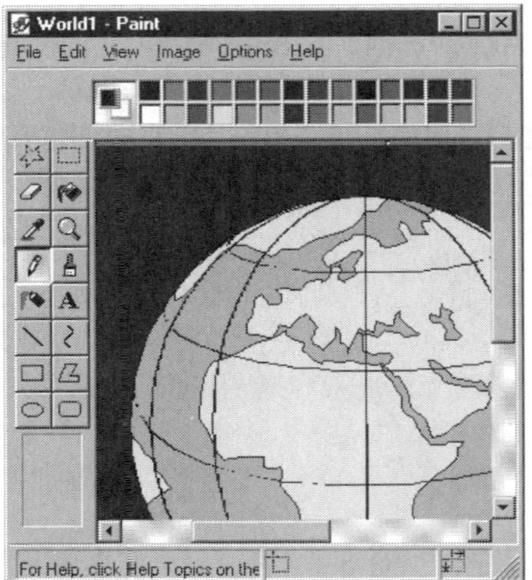

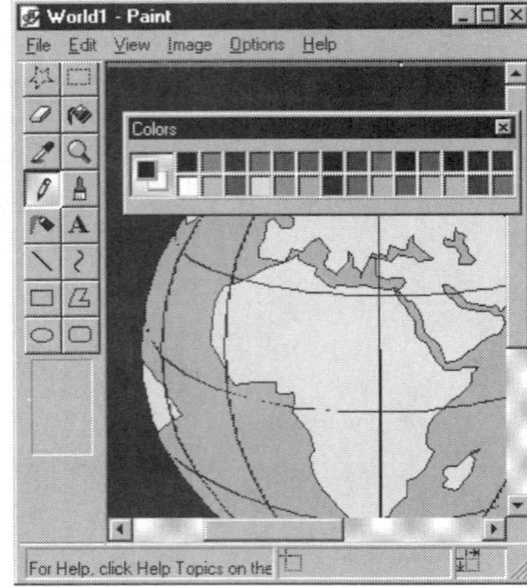

Figure 5.19 Using a dockable toolbar

Toolbar Improvements in MFC 4.0

Toolbar controls have been available in MFC for quite a while now, but in MFC 4.0 they have more features than ever, and they are easier to use than they have ever been.The most notable toolbar improvement is that it's now remarkably easy to create *dockable* toolbars—that is, toolbars that can be torn away from the edges of a window and made to float like tool palettes.

Microsoft has simplified the creation and implementation of dockable toolbars in two different ways. MFC now has some new classes and member functions for working with dockable toolbars, and the Visual C++ Developer Studio has a brand-new GUI editor designed especially to help you create dockable toolbars.

Thanks to these new tools, you can now create toolbars that can automatically separate from their docking stations, can reshape and resize themselves to snuggle into various parts of windows, and can automatically realign themselves along the edges of windows.

Creating a Toolbar Resource

Dockable toolbars are such an important feature in MFC 4.0 that the Visual C++ Developer Studio now has a special editor for creating toolbar resources. To open this new editor, start Developer Studio (if it isn't started already) and choose the **Insert | Resource** menu item. When the Insert Resource dialog box open, click the **Toolbar** icon and then click **OK**. Developer Studio then opens its toolbar editor (Figure 5.20).

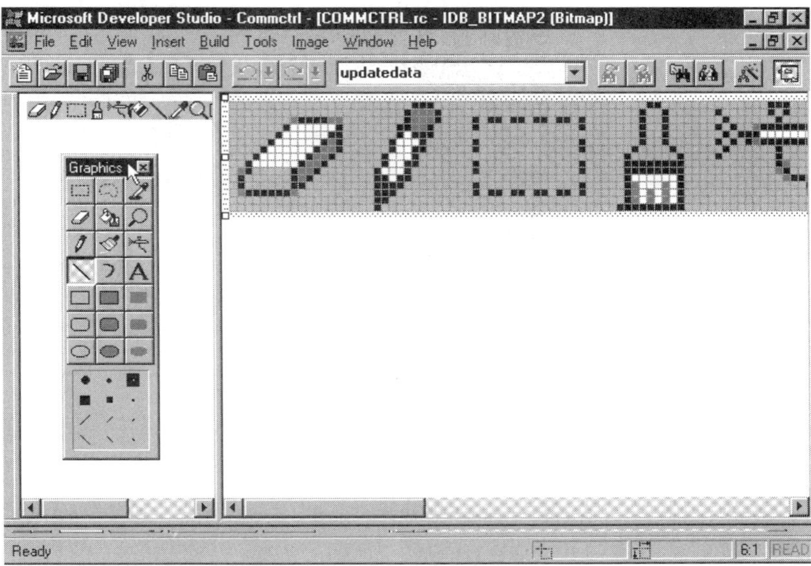

Figure 5.20 The Developer Studio toolbar editor

When the toolbar editor opens, you can create a dockable toolbar by following these steps:

1. Open your project's existing bitmap resource in the Developer Studio's graphics editor.
2. Select the **Image | Toolbar Editor** menu item. The **New Toolbar** dialog box is displayed. You can change the width and height of

the icon images to match the bitmap. Then the toolbar image is displayed in the Toolbar Editor.

3. To finish the conversion, change the command IDs on the buttons in the toolbar.
4. Open the property page on the toolbar button.
5. Type in the new ID or select an ID from the drop-down list.

Instantiating a Toolbar Control

When you have created a toolbar resource with the Developer Studio's toolbar editor, you can turn it into a functioning toolbar by instantiating an object of the CToolBarCtrl class and then calling the **`CToolBarCtrl::Create`** member function.

The **`CToolBarCtrl::Create`** member function returns a nonzero if is successful. Otherwise, it returns zero.

The syntax of the **`CToolBarCtrl::Create`** member function is:

```
BOOL Create( DWORD dwStyle, const RECT& rect,
    CWnd* pParentWnd, UINT nID );
```

`CToolBarCtrl::Create` accepts the following parameters:

- *dwStyle*—Specifies the toolbar control's style. Toolbars must always have the WS_CHILD style. In addition, you can specify any combination of toolbar styles and window styles as described under Remarks.
- *rect*—Optionally specifies the toolbar control's size and position. It can be either a CRect object or a RECT structure.
- *pParentWnd*—Specifies the toolbar control's parent window. It must not be NULL.
- *nID*—Specifies the toolbar control's ID.

You can apply the following window styles to a toolbar control when you call **`CToolBarCtrl::Create`**:

- WS_CHILD (always used with toolbar controls)
- WS_VISIBLE (usually used)
- WS_DISABLED (rarely used)

Optionally, you can apply one or more of the common control styles to a toolbar control:

- CCS_ADJUSTABLE—Allows toolbars to be customized by the user. If this style is used, the toolbar's owner window must handle the customization notification messages sent by the toolbar, as described in CToolBarCtrl: Handling Customization Notifications.

- CCS_BOTTOM—Causes the control to position itself at the bottom of the parent window's client area and sets the width to be the same as the parent window's width.
- CCS_NODIVIDER—Prevents a two-pixel highlight from being drawn at the top of the control.
- CCS_NOHILITE—Prevents a one-pixel highlight from being drawn at the top of the control.
- CCS_NOMOVEY—Causes the control to resize and move itself horizontally, but not vertically, in response to a WM_SIZE message. If the CCS_NORESIZE style is used, this style does not apply.
- CCS_NOPARENTALIGN—Prevents the control from automatically moving to the top or bottom of the parent window. Instead, the control keeps its position within the parent window despite changes to the size of the parent window. If the CCS_TOP or CCS_BOTTOM style is also used, the height is adjusted to the default, but the position and width remain unchanged.
- CCS_NORESIZE—Prevents the control from using the default width and height when setting its initial size or a new size. Instead, the control uses the width and height specified in the request for creation or sizing.
- CCS_TOP—Causes the control to position itself at the top of the parent window's client area and sets the width to be the same as the parent window's width. Toolbars have this style by default.

Finally, you can apply one or both of the following toolbar control styles to a toolbar control:

- TBSTYLE_TOOLTIPS—Causes the toolbar to create and manage a tool tip control. A tool tip is a small pop-up window that contains a line of text describing a toolbar button. It appears only when the user puts the cursor on a toolbar button and leaves it there for a second or less. The tool tip is displayed near the cursor. If you use this style, you must handle tool tip notifications as described in CToolBarCtrl: Handling Tool Tip Notifications.
- TBSTYLE_WRAPABLE—Creates a toolbar control that can have multiple lines of buttons. Toolbar buttons can "wrap" to the next line when the toolbar becomes too narrow to include all buttons on the same line.

When you create a toolbar control by calling **`CToolBarCtrl::Create`**, MFC automatically sets the size and position of the toolbar window. The height is based on the height of the buttons in the toolbar. The width is the same as the width of the parent window's client area. The CCS_TOP and CCS_BOTTOM styles determine whether the toolbar is positioned along the top or bottom of the client area. By default, a toolbar has the CCS_TOP style.

Tool-Tip Controls

One useful new feature of toolbars in MFC 4.0 is the ability to display small message windows called *tool tips*. A tool tip is a tiny window that pops up when the user moves a mouse over a toolbar button (Figure 5.21). By default, a tool tip associated with a toolbar button contains the name of the button's corresponding menu item. But you can modify any tool tip to provide any kind of information you like.

A tool tip is hidden most of the time, appearing only when the user puts the cursor on a tool and leaves it there for a moment. The tool tip appears near the cursor and disappears when the user clicks a mouse button or moves the cursor off of the tool.

Tool tip

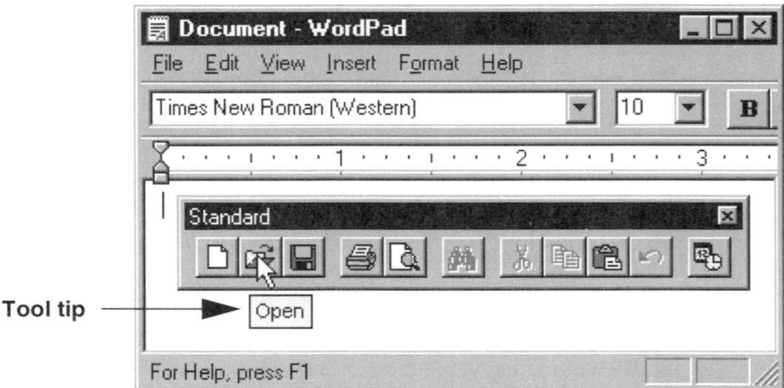

Figure 5.21 A tool-tip control

In a Visual C++ application, you don't have to do anything special to equip a toolbar with a set of tool-tip controls; tool-tip functionality is created automatically when you design a toolbar. In non-Visual C++ applications, you can derive tool-tip controls from the CToolTipCtrl class and create them by calling **`CToolTipCtrl::Create`**. Then you must manage them by calling CToolTipCtrl member functions.

Mini-Frame Windows

A mini-frame window is a frame window with a half-height title bar. When you pull a toolbar away from its docking station and let it float inside its parent window, the AppWizard framework automatically creates the mini-frame window that turns the toolbar into a tool palette.

Figure 5.22 shows what a toolbar looks like when it has been freed from its docking station and has been equipped with a mini-frame window.

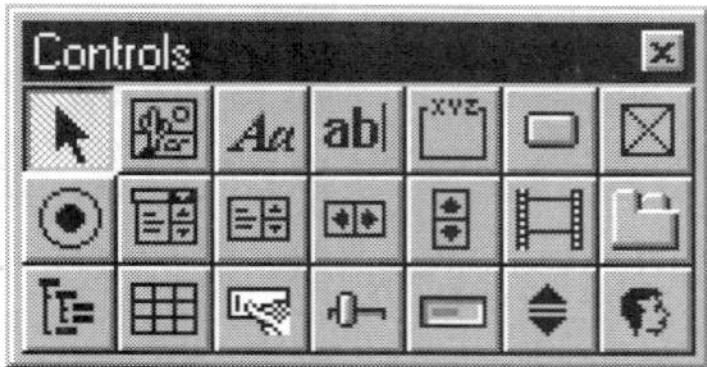

Figure 5.22 A mini-frame window

Characteristics of Mini-Frame Windows

In MFC 4.0, mini-frame windows are instantiated from the CMini-FrameWnd class. With a few exceptions, they behave like normal frame windows. The most important differences are:

- The title bars of mini-frame windows are not equipped with minimize or maximize buttons.
- Mini-frame windows cannot be equipped with menus.
- You can close a mini-frame window by single-clicking its go-away button.

Creating a Mini-Frame Window

In a Visual C++ program designed with AppWizard's help, you don't have to do anything special to create any mini-frame windows your application might need. Each time you create a toolbar for an AppWizard program (see "Hot-Key Controls" on page 200), AppWizard automatically generates all the code that's required to create a mini-frame window from the toolbar whenever the toolbar is torn away from its docking station and turns into a tool palette.

But not everyone uses AppWizard—or Visual C++, for that matter—and it's always possible that someone will have some unexpected use for a mini-frame window. So Microsoft has made it quite easy to create mini-frame windows without having to rely on AppWizard.

To create a mini-frame window without using AppWizard, it takes the usual two steps. First you instantiate a CMiniFrameWnd object by calling its constructor. Then you call the **`CMiniFrameWnd::Create`** member function to display the mini-frame window.

Status-Bar Controls

A *status bar*, or *status-bar control*, is a horizontal bar-shaped control that can appear along the bottom of a frame window. Status bars are designed to provide information about the object currently selected in a window. Figure 5.23 shows a typical status-bar control.

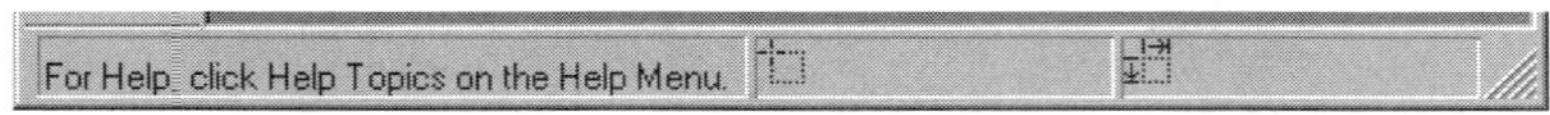

Figure 5.23 A status-bar control

A status bar can reveal any kind of information you like about an object, including the object's current state or operations that can be performed on the object. For example, a status bar often contains a line of text that explains the functionality of a selected menu command. A status bar can also show the current of the SCROLL LOCK key, the NUM LOCK key, and other keys.

How Status Bars Work

A status bar, like a toolbar, is embedded in its parent frame window and is generated automatically when its frame window is constructed. To have any useful functionality, a status bar must contain a set of controls.

Typically, the controls in a status bar are text output panes. These output panes are called *indicators*. The indicators in a status bar are designed to display information about the status or state of a pending operation.

Creating a Status Bar

At first glance, status bars may appear to be difficult to create because the **Controls** toolbar provided by the Visual C++'s dialog-box editor doesn't have a special button for creating status bars. But it's really quite easy to equip a Visual C++ application with a status bar.

To display a status bar, an application must contain an array of IDs for the bar's indicator panes. But when you create a program using AppWizard, those IDs are generated automatically. If you choose the **Initial Toolbar** option when you set up your program, AppWizard creates an ID array to display a status bar as well as the array for a toolbar in the source file for your main frame-window class.

The array looks like this:

```
static UINT BASED_CODE indicators[] =
{
    ID_SEPARATOR,           // message line indicator
    ID_INDICATOR_CAPS,
    ID_INDICATOR_NUM,
    ID_INDICATOR_SCRL,
};
```

When your application contains an array like the one shown in the preceding example, a status bar is constructed automatically when its frame window is constructed. The status bar contains an indicator for each ID in your application's indicator array. The indicators are arranged along the status bar from left to right, in the same order in which they appear in your application's indicator array.

In a Visual C++ application, it's very easy to set the indicators in the program's status bar to show information about menu items that the user selects. When you create a menu item using the Developer Studio menu editor, just right-click the mouse over the menu item you have created. When the menu editor displays your menu item's property sheet (Figure 5.24), place the message you like in the Prompt text box. Then, when the user of your application chooses the menu item you have created, your application automatically displays the menu item's message in its status bar.

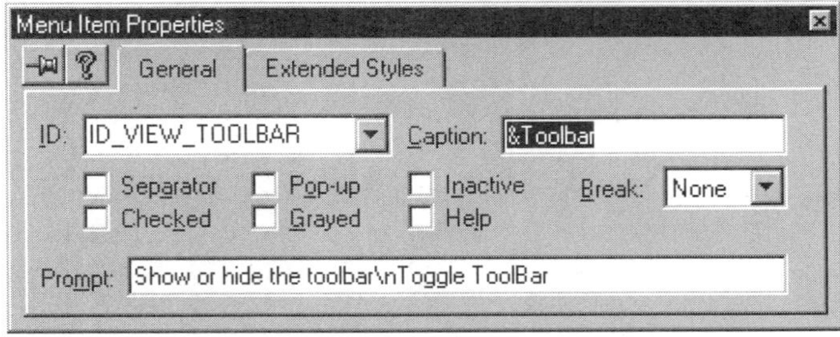

Figure 5.24 Creating a message for a status bar

Once your application contains a status bar, you can add more indicators by adding more IDs to your ID array. You can also place separators between a status bar's indicators by inserting ID_SEPARATOR lines in your application's status-indicator array.

The CStatusBarCtrl Class

Status-bar controls are instantiated from the CStatusBarCtrl class, which is derived from the CStatusBar class. CStatusBar is derived, in turn, from CControlBar.

When you execute an AppWizard application that implements a status bar, the AppWizard framework calls the **`CStatusBar::SetIndicators`** member function to associate each indicator in the stack bar with its corresponding ID in the application's status-bar array. When a frame window containing a status bar closes, the AppWizard framework destroys the window's status bar.

MFC 4.0 provides a number of member functions for managing status bars. For example, **`CStatusBar::GetStatusBarCtrl`** returns a reference to a CStatusBarCtrl object. You can then perform various kinds of operations on the control, such as setting the sizes of its indicators and specifying the messages it displays and when it displays them.

Dialog-Bar Controls

A *dialog-bar control* (Figure 5.25) is a user-interface control that works something like a toolbar but can be equipped with any kind of Windows control. A toolbar, in contrast, must derive its display from a special kind of bitmap (see "Toolbar Controls" on page 202).

Figure 5.25 A dialog-bar control

A dialog-bar control also has some features in common with a property-sheet dialog box (see "Property-Sheet Dialog Boxes" on page 224). A dialog-bar control, like a property-sheet dialog box, can be used to navigate from one property page to another. To move from one property page to another with a dialog bar, the user clicks buttons—in much the same way that index tabs are clicked to move from one page to another in a property-sheet dialog box.

A good example of a dialog bar is the one that appears in the Visual C++ AppWizard utility's main window (see "Customized Wizard Dialog Boxes" on page 228). Dialog bars are also used in many other kinds of system dialog boxes—such as the disk-properties property-sheet dialog box shown later in this chapter, in Figure 5.31 on page 223.

Typically, a dialog bar contains ordinary buttons identified by text labels. By clicking the buttons displayed on a dialog bar, the user can navigate from one property page to another or close the dialog box that displays the dialog bar.

The main difference between a dialog bar and a tool palette is the kinds of controls the two kinds of windows can contain. In MFC 4.0, a tool palette is usually derived from the CToolBarCtrl class, which can contain only glyph-style button controls that are generated by a special kind of bitmap. In contrast, a dialog bar—derived from the CDialogBar class—is created from a dialog template and can contain any kind of Windows control.

A dialog bar can be aligned to the top, bottom, left, or right side of its parent frame window.

You can create a dialog-bar control with the Visual C++ dialog editor, in much the same way you would create a CFormView object. First, use the dialog editor to define a dialog template with just one style: WS_CHILD. Make sure that the style WS_VISIBLE is not set.

When you have designed your dialog bar, instantiate it by calling its constructor. Then call **`CDialogBar::Create`** to create a dialog-bar window and attach it to your CDialogBar object.

List-Related Controls

MFC 4.0 provides five new C++ classes that can help you create and manage lists in Windows 95 applications:

- *CListCtrl*: Encapsulates the functionality of a list view control, which displays a collection of items. Each item is represented by an icon (or a user-defined image) and a label.
- *CTreeCtrl*: Displays a hierarchical list of items, such as headings in a document, entries in an index, or files and directories on a disk.
- *CDragListBox*: Used to create list boxes with items that can be dragged and dropped.
- *CHeaderCtrl*: Creates windows that can be used as column headings in lists and tables.
- *CImageList*: Not actually a control, but an MFC class that makes it easier to manage collections of bitmaps and other kinds of graphics images.

The classes in the preceding list are covered in more detail under the headings that follow.

List-View Controls

A *list-view control* can display a list of items, each represented by an icon (or a user-defined image) and a label. The Windows 95 Explorer application creates the display in its right-hand panel using a list-view control, as shown in Figure 5.26.

Items and Subitems

Each item in a list-view control has four parts: an icon, a label, a current state, and an application-defined value. One or more *subitems* can also be associated with each item in the list.

A subitem is a string that you can display in a column to the right of an item's icon and label. For example, when the user chooses Explorer's **View | Details** menu item, Explorer uses subitems to display the names, sizes, and types of displayed files and folders, along with information about the modification dates of files.

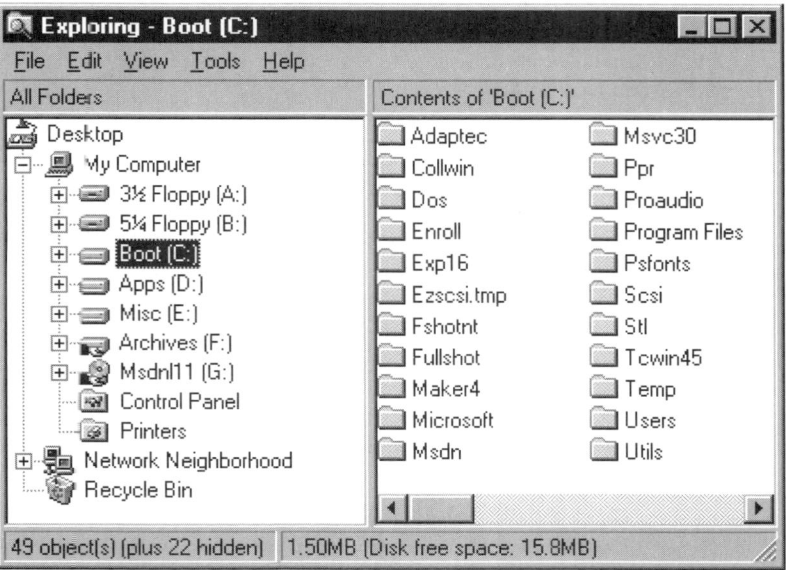

Figure 5.26 The panel on the right is a list-view control

Varieties of List Views

List-view controls can display their contents in four different ways, called *views*. List-view controls use four different window styles, and the window style used by the control determines the control's view.

The four kinds of list views, and their characteristics, are:

- *Icon view*—A view that uses the LVS_ICON window style. Each item appears as a full-sized icon with a label below it. The user can drag the items to any location in the list view window.
- *Small-icon view*—A view that uses the LVS_SMALLICON window style. Each item appears as a small icon with the label to the right of it. The user can drag the items to any location.
- *List view*—A view that uses the LVS_LIST window style.Each item appears as a small icon with a label to the right of it. Items are arranged in columns and cannot be dragged to any arbitrary location by the user.
- *Report view*—A view that uses the LVS_REPORT window style. Each item appears on its own line with information arranged in columns. The leftmost column contains the small icon and label, and subsequent columns contain subitems as specified by the application. Unless the LVS_NO-COLUMNHEADER window style is also specified, each column has a header.

When you use a list-view control to create an icon view or small-icon view, you can control the way items are arranged in the view by specifying one of four other window styles: LVS_ALIGNTOP (the default), LVS_ALIGN-BOTTOM, LVS_ALIGNLEFT, or LVS_ALIGNRIGHT. You can use other window styles to set other options. For example, you can use window styles to specify whether a user can edit labels in place, whether more than one item can be selected at a time.

Using Image Lists with List-View Controls

List-view controls create their displays using icons stored in *image lists*. An image list is an MFC object (an object of the CImageList class) that makes it easier to manage collections of graphics images. For example, if your application uses a collection of bitmaps, an image-list object provides member functions that can help you manage those bitmaps and draw them when they are needed. Image-lists objects are covered in more detail in "Image Lists" on page 218.

List views commonly use two kinds of image lists: one kind that holds full-sized icons for use in icon views, and a second kind that holds smaller versions of the same icons for use in other views.

You can create an image list that uses both these kinds of image lists, or you can create an image list that uses just one, depending on what kind of graphics you want your list view to display. If you create both kinds of lists, both lists must contain corresponding images arranged in the same order. That's because a single value is used to identify a list view item's icon in both image lists.

You can also specify a third image list that contains *state images*, which are displayed next to an item's icon to indicate an application-defined state. For example, your application could create a list view that displays controls such as check boxes instead of icons.

The CListCtrl Class

When you have created a resource and a class for a list-view control, you can instantiate your control by deriving an MFC object from the CListCtrl class. You can then create and display your control by calling the **CListCtrl::Create** member function.

After you have created a list control, there are various member functions you call to set get and set items in your list and to manipulate your list control in various ways. For example, you can obtain and replace items by calling **GetItem** and **SetItem**; search for an item in the list by calling **GetNextItem** in a loop; and get or replace the text of an item by calling **GetItemText** or **SetItemText**.

To assign an image list to a list-view control, you call the MFC member function **CListCtrl::SetImageList**. You can pass parameters to **SetImageList** specifying the kinds of images you want your list view list to display: large icons, small icons, or state images. To retrieve the handle of an image list currently assigned to a list-view control, you can call the **CListCtrl::GetImageList** function. For more details about image lists, see "Image Lists" on page 218.

Tree-View Controls

A *tree-view control* is a window that displays a hierarchical list of items, such as headings in a document, entries in an index, or files and directories on a disk. Each item listed in a tree-view control has a label and an optional bitmapped image. Each item can also be equipped a list of subitems.

Tree-view controls have many of the same characteristics as list-view controls, which are described in "List-View Controls" on page 214. The main difference between items listed in a tree-view control and items listed in a list-view control is that tree-view items are expandable. By clicking an item, the user can expand and collapse the item's list of subitems.

The Explorer application uses a tree-view control to create its left window pane, as shown in Figure 5.27.

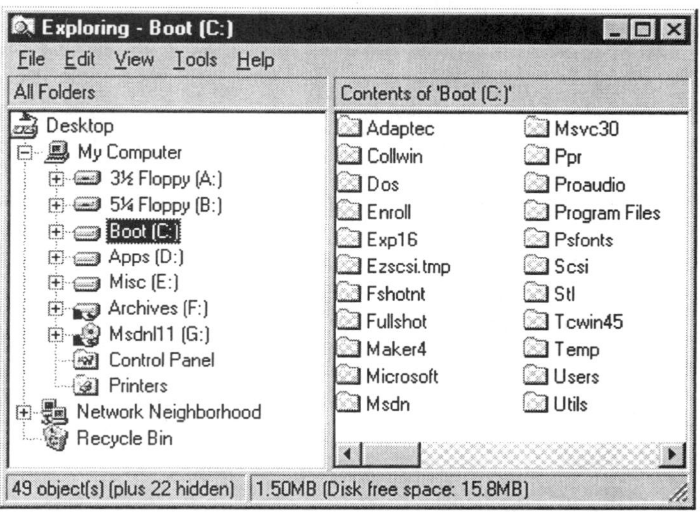

Figure 5.27 The panel on the left is a tree-view control

As Figure 5.27 shows, a tree-view control is a window that displays a hierarchical list of items—for example, headings in a document the entries in an index, or (as in Explorer window) files and directories on a disk. Tree-view controls, like list-view controls, create displays from images stored in image lists (see "Image Lists" on page 218).

The easiest way to start designing a tree-view control is to create a resource for it using the Visual C++ dialog editor. Open the Developer Studio's dialog-box editor and select the tree-view icon in the **Control** toolbar (Figure 5.28).

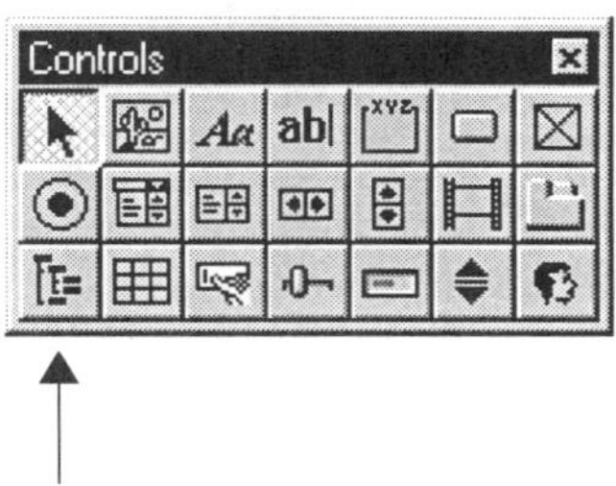

Tree-view control button

Figure 5.28 The Control toolbar's tree-view control button

Except for deciding which **Control** toolbar button to click, the steps you follow to create a tree-view resource are identical to those outlined in "List-View Controls" on page 214.

To instantiate a tree-view control, you call the constructor of the CTreeCtrl class and then call `CTreeCtrl::Create`. You can then get and set various attributes of your control, and manipulate your control in various ways, by calling member functions similar to those used by list-view controls.

You can obtain and replace items by calling `CTreeCtrl::GetItem` and `CTreeCtrl::SetItem`; search for an item in the list by calling `CTreeCtrl::GetNextItem` in a loop; and get or replace the text of an item by calling `CTreeCtrl::GetItemText` or `CTreeCtrl::-SetItemText`.

To assign an image list to a tree-view control, you call the MFC member function `CTreeCtrl::SetImageList`. You can pass parameters to `SetImageList` specifying the kinds of images you want your list view list to display: large icons, small icons, or state images. To retrieve the handle of an image list currently assigned to a list-view control, you can call the `CTreeCtrl::GetImageList` function. For more details about image lists, see the next section.

Image Lists

An *image list* is not really a control; rather, it is an MFC object that makes it easier to manage collections of graphics images. For example, if your application needs to manage a collection of bitmaps, the image list provides an easy way to manage those bitmaps and to draw them when they are needed.

In MFC 4.0, the CImageList class provides all the functionality you need to create image-list objects.

Image lists are easy to use because they don't require memory DCs or complicated bitmap operations. For example, they eliminate the need for `BitBlt` functions when you just want to display simple graphics. (If you don't know what DCs, bitmap handles, and `BitBlt` functions are, you need a refresher course in Windows graphics. For a crash course, consult the classic *Programming Windows 3.1* by Charles Petzold. Some other good texts are listed in the Bibliography.)

Image lists also eliminate the need for complex drawing operations such as drawing a transparent bitmaps through masks (an operation that is described in detail in my own *C++ Windows NT Programming*, which is listed in the Bibliography).

Finally, the CImageList class has built-in support for drag-and-drop operations. When you create an image using an image list, you can drag the image around the screen with the mouse and drop it into any container you like. All the code that's needed to manage drag-and-drop operations is built right into the CImageList class.

How Explorer Uses Image Lists

An image list is a very handy tool to use when you want to create a CListView control or a CTreeView control. When you couple a list-view or tree-view object with an image-list object, you can use the image list to draw the images next to the items in your list-view or tree-view control.

To see how image lists works, you need look no farther than the Windows 95 Explorer. Explorer uses image lists to display the graphics images shown earlier in this chapter, in Figure 5.26 on page 214 and Figure 5.27 on page 217.

If you wanted to create a list view like the one Explorer displays in its right panel, all you would have to do is place a collection of icons in an image list. Then you could assign the list you have created to the list view control.

How Image Lists Work

One way to view an image list is to see it as a series of frames on a reel of movie film. If you place an image in each frame, the whole reel becomes an image list, as illustrated in Figure 5.29.

Figure 5.29 Images in an image list.

The images in an image list are numbered from 0 to n - 1, with n being the number of images you specify when you create the list. Each image in an image list must be the same size.

Some Windows 95 controls, such as the CListView and CTreeView controls, can automatically draw images stored in image lists in just the right places; you don't have to write complicated user-draw code to get your images displayed in the list.

Internally, an MFC application stores an image list as a single bitmap. Each image in the list is a portion of that bitmap—in much the same way that each image on a reel of movie film is one small portion of the entire film. That's a good analogy because an image list always stores the individual images that it contains in one row—a long strip of images, just like the individual frames on a reel of film.

When you create a bitmap to store the images in an image list, your bitmap can be no larger than 32K pixels by 32K pixels. (That's about 32,000 by 32,000 pixels—a good deal of room for a set of images.) To calculate exactly how many images a particular image list can hold, just divide the width of one image into 32K.

When your application draws a nonmasked image, it simply copies the image into the target device context without regard to be background; the image is merely drawn over the existing background color of the device context. As a result, if the image's background color is different from the destination device's background color, the image appears against its own background, in a square rectangle placed on top of the destination device's original background color.

Creating an Image List

To create an image list, you call the `CImageList` constructor and then call the `CImageList::Create` function. There are four overridden versions of the `CImageList::Create` member function:

```
BOOL Create( int cx, int cy, BOOL bMask, int nInitial,
    int nGrow );
BOOL Create( UINT nBitmapID, int cx, int nGrow,
    COLORREF crMask );
BOOL Create( LPCTSTR lpszBitmapID, int cx, int nGrow,
    COLORREF crMask );
BOOL Create( CImageList& imagelist1, int nImage1,
    CImageList& imagelist2, int nImage2, int dx, int dy
    );
```

Setting an Image List's Attributes

As you can see, you can set the following CImageList attributes by calling the various forms of the `CImageList::Create` member function:

- *cx*—Dimensions of each image, in pixels.
- *cy*—Dimensions of each image, in pixels.
- *bMask*—TRUE if the image contains a mask; otherwise FALSE.
- *nInitial*—Number of images that the image list initially contains.
- *nGrow*—Number of images by which the image list can grow when the system needs to resize the list to make room for new

images. This parameter represents the number of new images the resized image list can contain.

- *nBitmapID*—The number of resource IDs associated with the image list.
- *crMask*—The color used to generate a mask, if one is used. Each pixel of this color in the specified bitmap is changed to black, and the corresponding bit in the mask is set to one.
- *lpszBitmapID*—A string containing the resource IDs of the images.
- *imagelist1*—A pointer to the first CImageList object used in an image list.
- *nImage1*—The number of images contained in *imagelist1*.
- *imagelist2*—A pointer to the second CImageList object used in an image list.
- *nImage2*—The number of images contained in *imagelist2*.
- *dx*—Dimensions of each image, in pixels.
- *dy*—Dimensions of each image, in pixels.

You can assign an image list to a list-view control by calling the `CListCtrl::SetImageList` member function. When you call `SetImageList`, you can pass parameters specifying whether you want your image list to contain large icons, small icons, or state images. You can retrieve the handle of an image list currently assigned to a list-view control by using the `CListCtrl::GetImageList` function.

Destroying an Image List

By default, a list-view or tree-view control destroys any image lists assigned to it when it is destroyed. But if you create a list-view or tree-view control that has the window style LVS_SHAREIMAGELISTS, you are responsible for destroying any image list associated with your list control when the control is no longer needed. If you don't take that precaution, more than one control might try to destroy the same image list.

Header Controls

A *header control* is an MFC class that can help you create column headings for lists or tables. A header control is implemented as a window that is usually placed above columns in a list or a table.

You can divide a header control into parts, with each part containing a title that serves as a column heading. You can place column dividers between each column in your a header control, and the user of your application can drag the dividers that separate the parts to set the width of each column.

Figure 5.30 shows how a header control can be used in a Windows 95 application.

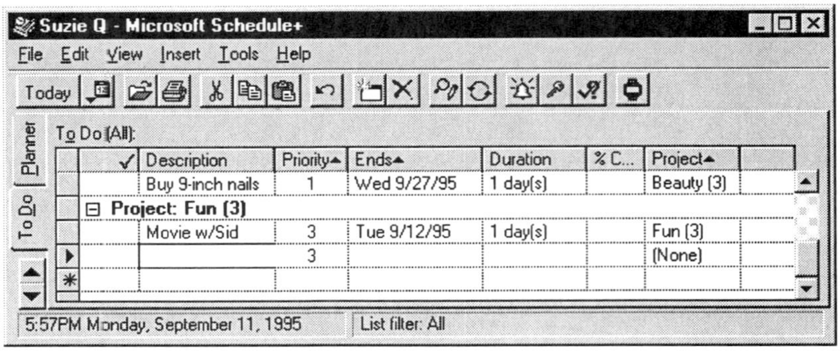

Figure 5.30 A list with a header control

To create a header control, you instantiate or derive an object from MFC's CHeaderCtrl class. Then you can create your control and set certain styles used to display it by calling the `CHeaderCtrl::Create` member function:

```
BOOL Create(DWORD dwStyle, const RECT& rect, CWnd*
    pParentWnd, UINT nID);
```

When you call `CHeaderCtrl::Create`, you can set many of its attributes by placing predefined constants in its *dwStyle* parameter. A header control, like any other common control, recognizes a number of style constants predefined for the CWnd class (see "Setting Attributes and Managing Controls" on page 195).

The CHeaderCtrl class also predefines several style constants of its own:

- HDS_BUTTONS —Makes header items behave like buttons.
- HDS_HORZ—Makes the header control horizontal.
- HDS_DIVIDERTRACK—Allows the user to set the width by dragging the item's divider.
- HDS_VERT—Makes the header control vertical (at the time this book was written, this style is not currently implemented).
- HDS_HIDDEN—Makes the header control invisible in *details* mode.

When you call can `CHeaderCtrl::Create`, you can set multiple styles from the preceding list by combining them using the logical OR (|) control.

Drag-and-Drop List Boxes

Drag-and-drop list boxes provide something that many Windows programmers have wanted for years: a mechanism that lets you drag items out of a list box and drop them into another list box or some other kind of container.

Drag-and-drop list boxes can also let the user resort the items in list boxes, or copy listed items from one place to another instead of moving them. When you create a sortable drag-and-drop list box, the user can re-sort listed items such as filenames and strings by using the mouse to move them from one spot inside a list box to another.

In a Visual C++ program, it's easy to add a drag list box to an existing dialog box. Just add a list-box control to your dialog template using the dialog-box editor, and then assign a member variable (of Category Control and Variable Type CDragListBox) corresponding to the list box control in your dialog template.

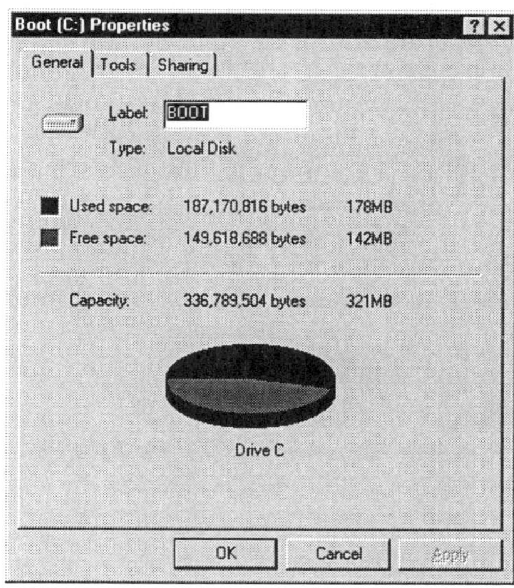

Figure 5.31 A Windows 95 property-sheet dialog box

Property-Sheet Dialog Boxes

If you don't know what a property sheet is, visualize a tabbed dialog box. For some reason, Microsoft calls tabbed dialog boxes *property sheets* and refers to the tabbed panels inside a property sheet as *property pages*.

Figure 5.31 on page 223 is a typical Windows 95 property-sheet dialog box. It's the **Properties** dialog box that you can open by right-clicking a disk icon on the desktop. Notice the index tabs at the top of the dialog box.

When you create a property sheet, the user of your application can click its index tabs to move from one of your property sheet's property pages to another.

Using Property-Sheet Dialog Boxes

The Windows 95 system uses property sheets in many ways, and so can you. Figure 5.32 is a property sheet you can display by clicking the right mouse button over the **Network Neighborhood** icon on the Windows 95 desktop (provided your computer is connected to a network). It displays the properties of your system's networking configuration.

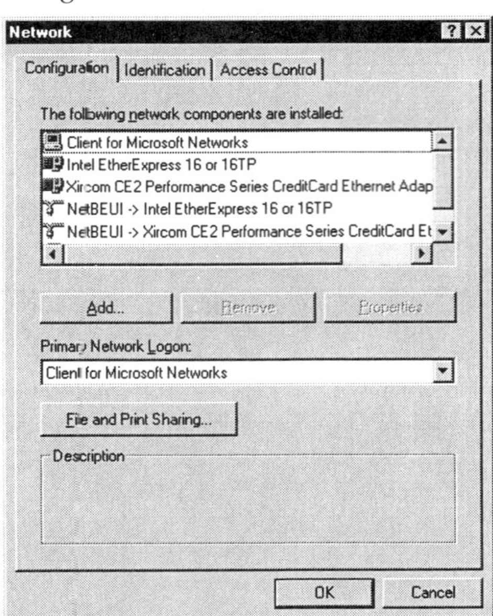

Figure 5.32 A property-sheet dialog box

Creating a Property-Sheet Resource Step by Step

In a Visual C++ program created with AppWizard, you can create a property-sheet resource using the dialog-box editor. Then you can create a class for your property sheet using ClassWizard. When you have finished doing that, you must write a little code to instantiate and display your property sheet in your application.

✔ To create a property-sheet resource and a property-sheet class, these are the steps to follow:

1. From the Developer Studio menu bar, choose **Insert | Resource**.
2. When the Insert **Resource** dialog box opens, select the **Dialog** icon and then click the **OK** button.
3. When the Visual C++ dialog-box editor opens, displaying a dialog-box template, choose the **View | Toolbars** menu item.
4. When the **Toolbars** dialog box opens, check the **Controls** check box and click the **OK** button.
5. When the **Controls** toolbar opens, click the property-sheet button (Figure 5.33).

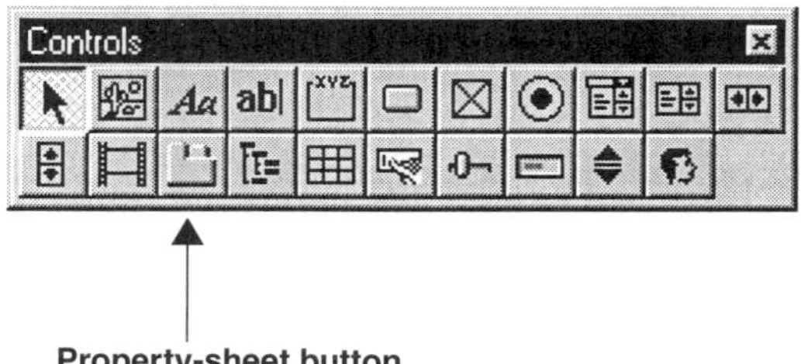

Figure 5.33 The property-sheet toolbar button

6. To place a property-sheet control in a dialog box, click the mouse over the dialog-box template that Developer Studio has created.

Developer Studio then places a set of property sheets inside your dialog-box template, as shown in Figure 5.34.

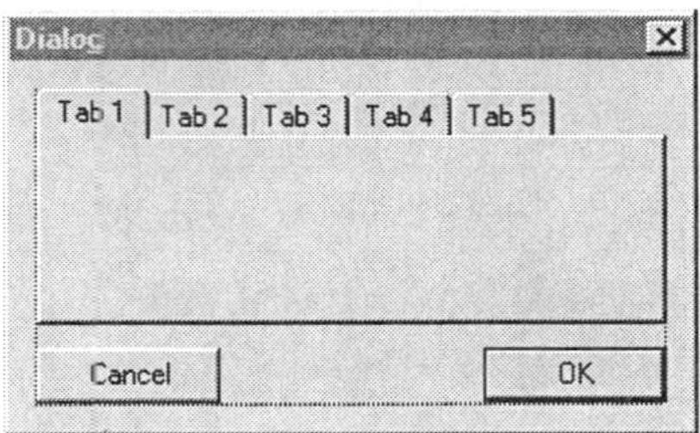

Figure 5.34 Creating a property-sheet dialog box

7. Use ClassWizard to add member functions to your property sheet and to integrate it into your application.

Creating and Displaying a Property Sheet

Property-sheet dialog boxes are not instantiated from the CDialog class as ordinary MFC dialog boxes are. Instead, property-sheet dialog boxes are derived from another MFC class named CPropertySheet. The pages in a property sheet are derived from another class named CPropertyPage.

You can instantiate a property-sheet object directly from the CPropertySheet class. But you must derive a separate class from the CPropertyPage class for each property page in your property-sheet dialog box.

When you have created a property-sheet resource using the dialog-box editor and have created a property-sheet class using ClassWizard, you must write the code that it takes to instantiate and display your property sheet.

Creating and displaying a property sheet is very similar to creating and displaying a conventional dialog box. But because a property sheet has to be supplied with property pages, a few more steps are involved.

First you instantiate a CPropertySheet object by calling the CPropertySheet constructor. Then you can display your property sheet by calling the `CPropertySheet::DoModal` function (for a modal property sheet) or the `CPropertySheet::Create` function (for a modeless property sheet).

When you have created and displayed a property sheet, you must create a CPropertyPage object for each its pages. You must call

`CPropertySheet::AddPage` for each property page in your property sheet, and then display the property sheet by calling `CPropertySheet::DoModal` for a modal property sheet, or `CPropertySheet::Create` for a modeless property sheet.

Exchanging data between a CPropertySheet object and some external object is similar to exchanging data with a CDialog object. The important difference is that the settings of a property sheet are normally member variables of the CPropertyPage objects rather than of the CPropertySheet object itself.

Tab Controls

A *tab control* is analogous to the dividers in a notebook or the labels in a file cabinet. By using a tab control, an application can define multiple pages for the same area of a window or dialog box. Each page consists of a set of information or a group of controls that the application displays when the user selects the corresponding tab. A special type of tab control displays tabs that look like buttons. Clicking a button should immediately perform a command instead of displaying a page.

The CTabCtrl class provides the functionality of the Windows common tab control. This control (and therefore the CTabCtrl class) is available only to programs running under Windows 95 and Windows NT version 3.51 and later.

Customized Wizard Dialog Boxes

In Visual C++ 4.0, you can create a special kind of tabbed dialog box called a *wizard*—the same kind of wizard that the Visual C++ development environment uses to set up applications (Figure 5.35).

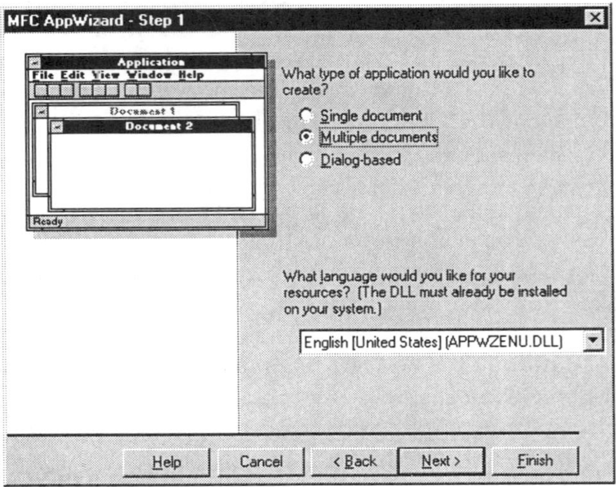

Figure 5.35 A wizard-style dialog box

A wizard is a property sheet with a sequence of property pages that guide the user through the steps of an operation, such as setting up a device or creating a newsletter. In a wizard-type tab dialog box, the property pages do not have tabs, and only one property page is visible at a time. Also, instead of having OK and Apply Now buttons, a wizard-type tab dialog box has a Back button, a Next or Finish button, and a Cancel button.

To create a wizard-type dialog box, follow the same steps you would follow to create a standard property sheet, but call the `SetWizardMode` function before you call `DoModal`. To enable the wizard buttons, call `SetWizardButtons`, using flags to customize their function and appearance. (See the SETWIZBUTTONS structure in the Win32 SDK documentation for more information about SetWizardButtons flags.) To enable the Finish button, call `SetFinishText` after the user has taken action on the last page of the wizard.

Common Dialog Boxes

Of all the new user-interface features of Windows 95, the easiest ones to create are the new MFC common dialog boxes. When you write a Visual C++ application using AppWizard, the AppWizard framework automatically equips your program with a set of new-style common dialog boxes if the user runs it under Windows 95 or under Version 3.51 or later of Windows NT. Otherwise, your application displays an ordinary, old-style dialog box of the Windows 3.1 variety.

Varieties of Common Dialog Boxes

MFC 4.0 provides several newly designed common dialog boxes, including **Open**, **Save/Save As**, **Page Setup**, **Find/Replace**, and **Fonts**. These new common dialogs are very different in both appearance and operation from their Windows 3.1 predecessors, as you can easily see by examining the new **File | Open** dialog box shown in Figure 5.36.

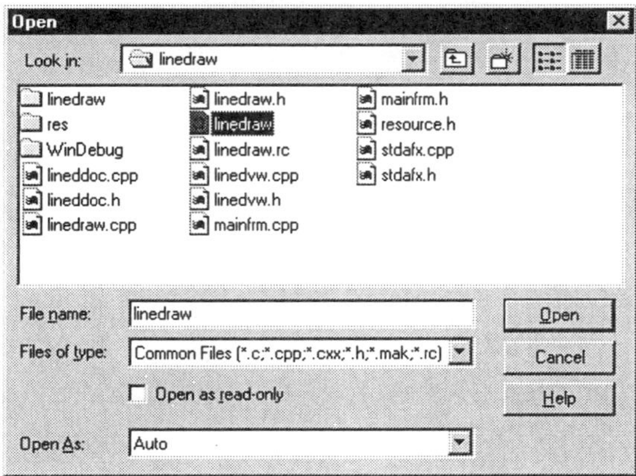

Figure 5.36 The new File|Open dialog box

Common dialog boxes, as you may know, offer application developers an easy way to implement commonly used Windows dialog boxes such as **File | Open**, **File | Save As**, **Page Setup**, and **Find/Replace**. Common dialog boxes are not only easy to use, but also can improve your application because they comply with recognized Windows design standards.

All common dialog boxes are derived from the CCommonDialog class, which sets the standards for common dialog boxes.

You can use the common dialogs derived from CCommonDialog right out of the box, instantiating them with the constructors that MFC provides, or you can derive your own dialog classes from the CFileDialog or from other classes derived from CCommonDialog. Then you can write customized constructors that suit your needs.

Either way, you can be confident that your dialog boxes will behave like standard Microsoft Foundation class dialog boxes. That's because the CFileDialog class is derived from the CCommonDialog class, which sets the standards for all common dialog boxes.

The Open, Save, and Save As Dialog Boxes

The new MFC **File | Open** dialog box shown earlier in Figure 5.36 is derived from the CFileDialog class, which encapsulates the Windows common file dialog box.

In an application written using Visual C++ and the AppWizard utility, the common **File | Open** dialog box opens automatically when the user chooses the **Open** item from the **File** menu. The user can then navigate to any available file on any available disk and open it by double-clicking its icon or clicking the **Open** button.

When the user chooses **File | Save** or **File | Save As**, an AppWizard application opens a similar dialog box that lets the user save the currently active file under its own name or a different name.

When you write an MFC application without using Visual C++, you can instantiate a Win95-style **Open**, **Save**, or **Save As** dialog box by calling the appropriate constructor and then calling the appropriate `Create` command. For more details, see the MFC Books Online documentation or your compiler's online help files.

The CFindReplaceDialog Class

MFC 4.0 supplies common **Find** and **Find-and-Replace** dialog boxes that you can incorporate into an application by instantiating objects of the CFindReplaceDialog class. Unlike the other Windows common dialog boxes, CFindReplaceDialog objects are modeless. That prevents them from annoyingly disappearing during sequences of search-and-replace operations. Figure 5.37 is an example of a common **Find/Replace** dialog box used by Word 95.

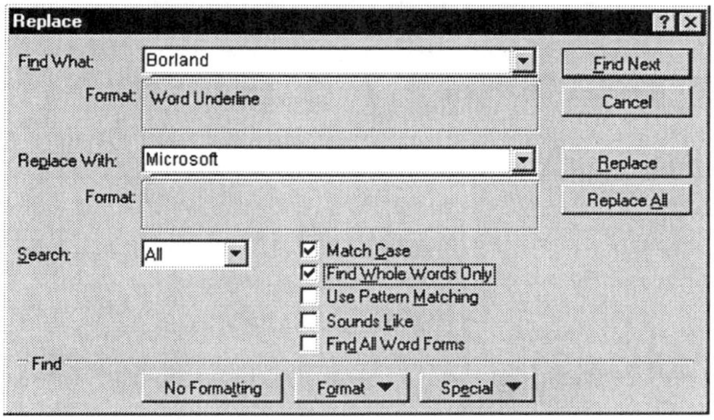

Figure 5.37 The common Replace dialog box

You can create two kinds of dialog boxes using the CFindReplaceDialog class: **Find** dialog boxes and **Find/Replace** dialog boxes. Although these two kinds of common dialog boxes let the user input strings to search for, they do not (alas!) supply the functionality that is needed to actually perform searching or replacing functions. If you want to equip a search or a search-and-replace dialog box with any useful functionality, you must add that functionality to your application yourself.

To construct a CFindReplaceDialog object, you call the CFindReplaceDialog constructor, which takes no arguments. Because a search or a search-and replace dialog box is modeless, you should allocate the object on the heap—that is, using the `new` operator—rather than instantiating the object on the stack.

When you have constructed a CFindReplaceDialog object, you must call the `CFindReplaceDialog::Create` member function to create and display the dialog box.

For more information on creating and implementing a CFindReplaceDialog object, consult your MFC Books Online files or your compiler's online help files.

The Page Setup Dialog Box

MFC 4.0 provides a new **Page Setup** dialog box that is implemented by a class named CPageSetup (Figure 5.38).

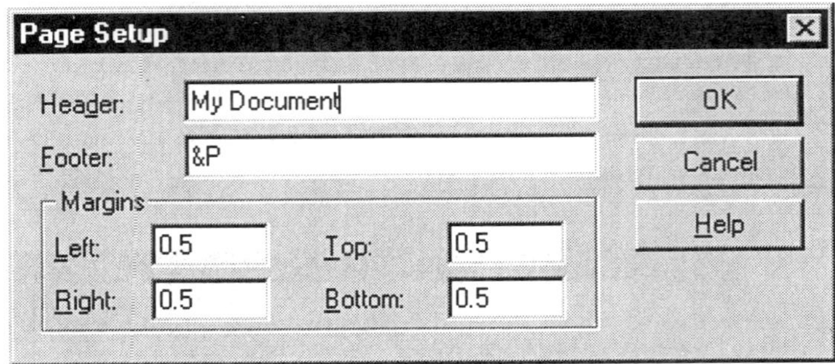

Figure 5.38 The common Page Setup dialog box

The CPageSetup class is designed to be a replacement for the old **Print Setup** dialog box that is familiar to users of Windows 3.*x*. Microsoft encourages Windows 95 developers to use the **Page Setup** dialog box instead of the **Print Setup** dialog box, and to stop using **Print Setup** in their applications.

The reason is that **Page Setup** is device-independent; it lets the user set properties such as margins, scaling, and page orientation for all output devices at the same time, instead of setting them for just one printer.

For program developers, there is a down side to using the common **Page Setup** dialog box; it takes more effort to use **Page Setup** than it did to use **Print Setup**, even to the extent of requiring some (shudder) coding. But the effort you spend on implementing **Page Setup** in your applications has a payoff; it results in easier-to-use programs. And the CPageSetupDialog class does do a lot of the extra work that is required to implement the **Page Setup** dialog box in your applications.

To create a CPageSetupDialog object programmatically, call the CPageSetupDialog constructor and then call `CPageSetupDialog::Create`. Your application then call the `DoModal` member function to display your **Page Setup** dialog box and allow the user to select print options. `DoModal` returns a binary value that reveals whether the user selected the OK (IDOK) or Cancel (IDCANCEL) button to close the **Page Setup** dialog box.

The Fonts Dialog Box

The CFontDialog class allows you to incorporate a **Fonts** dialog box into your application. A **Fonts** dialog box displays a list of fonts that are currently installed in the user's system.

When the user selects a particular font from the list, the selected font is reported back to the application. The application can then take whatever action is needed to switch to the font selected by the user.

Figure 5.39 is a picture of the MFC 4.0 common font dialog box.

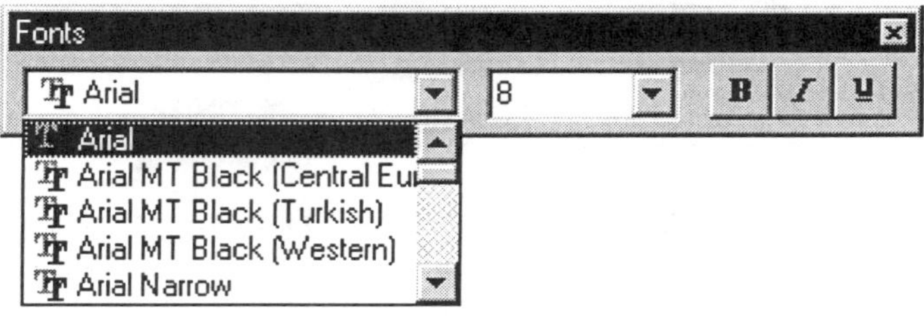

Figure 5.39 The common Font dialog box

To construct a CFontDialog object, you can either call the CFontDialog constructor or derive your own class from the CFontDialog class and then call your own custom constructor.

When you have constructed a Fonts dialog box, you can call the `DoModal` member function to display the dialog box and allow the user to select a font. DoModal returns a binary value specifying whether the user selected the OK (IDOK) or Cancel (IDCANCEL) button. Your application can then take whatever action is appropriate.

Example: Creating a Progress-Bar Control

Earlier in this chapter, in the section titled "Creating a Common Control Step by Step" on page 186, you had an opportunity to write and execute an application that displays a progress-bar control. The application you created was patterned after a sample program, named PROGBAR which you can find in this chapter's folder on your bonus disk.

The PROGBAR program creates and implements a progress-bar control in a file named COMMCTRLDlg.cpp. The source code of the COMMCTRLDlg.cpp file is presented in Listing 5.1.

Listing 5.1 The COMMCTRLDlg.cpp file

```
// COMMCTRLDlg.cpp : implementation file
//
#include "stdafx.h"
#include "COMMCTRL.h"
#include "COMMCTRLDlg.h"
#ifdef _DEBUG
#define new DEBUG_NEW
#undef THIS_FILE
static char THIS_FILE[] = __FILE__;
#endif
/////////////////////////////////////////////////////////////////////
///////
// CAboutDlg dialog used for App About
class CAboutDlg : public CDialog
{
public:
  CAboutDlg();

// Dialog Data
  //{{AFX_DATA(CAboutDlg)
  enum { IDD = IDD_ABOUTBOX };
  //}}AFX_DATA
  // ClassWizard generated virtual function overrides
  //{{AFX_VIRTUAL(CAboutDlg)

  protected:
  virtual void DoDataExchange(CDataExchange* pDX); // DDX/DDV support

  //}}AFX_VIRTUAL
// Implementation
protected:
  //{{AFX_MSG(CAboutDlg)
  //}}AFX_MSG
  DECLARE_MESSAGE_MAP()
};
CAboutDlg::CAboutDlg() : CDialog(CAboutDlg::IDD)
{
  //{{AFX_DATA_INIT(CAboutDlg)
  //}}AFX_DATA_INIT
}
void CAboutDlg::DoDataExchange(CDataExchange* pDX)
{
```

```
    CDialog::DoDataExchange(pDX);
    //{{AFX_DATA_MAP(CAboutDlg)
    //}}AFX_DATA_MAP
}
BEGIN_MESSAGE_MAP(CAboutDlg, CDialog)
    //{{AFX_MSG_MAP(CAboutDlg)
        // No message handlers
    //}}AFX_MSG_MAP
END_MESSAGE_MAP()
////////////////////////////////////////////////////////////////////
///////
// CCOMMCTRLDlg dialog
CCOMMCTRLDlg::CCOMMCTRLDlg(CWnd* pParent /*=NULL*/)
    : CDialog(CCOMMCTRLDlg::IDD, pParent)
{
    //{{AFX_DATA_INIT(CCOMMCTRLDlg)
    m_offsetPsn = 20;
    m_setPsn = 2;
    m_setRange1 = 0;
    m_setRange2 = 100;
    m_setStep = 1;
    //}}AFX_DATA_INIT

    // Note that LoadIcon does not require a subsequent DestroyIcon in
    // Win32

    m_hIcon = AfxGetApp()->LoadIcon(IDR_MAINFRAME);
}
void CCOMMCTRLDlg::DoDataExchange(CDataExchange* pDX)
{
    CDialog::DoDataExchange(pDX);

    //{{AFX_DATA_MAP(CCOMMCTRLDlg)
    DDX_Control(pDX, ID_STEP, m_btnStep);
    DDX_Control(pDX, ID_APPLY, m_btnApply);
    DDX_Control(pDX, IDC_PROGRESS1, m_progCtrl);
    DDX_Text(pDX, IDC_OFFSET_PSN, m_offsetPsn);
    DDX_Text(pDX, IDC_SET_POS, m_setPsn);
    DDX_Text(pDX, IDC_SET_RANGE_1, m_setRange1);
    DDX_Text(pDX, IDC_SET_RANGE_2, m_setRange2);
    DDX_Text(pDX, IDC_SET_STEP, m_setStep);
    //}}AFX_DATA_MAP
}
BEGIN_MESSAGE_MAP(CCOMMCTRLDlg, CDialog)
    //{{AFX_MSG_MAP(CCOMMCTRLDlg)
    ON_WM_SYSCOMMAND()
    ON_WM_PAINT()
    ON_WM_QUERYDRAGICON()
```

```
  ON_BN_CLICKED(ID_APPLY, OnApply)
  ON_BN_CLICKED(ID_STEP, OnStep)
  //}}AFX_MSG_MAP
END_MESSAGE_MAP()
////////////////////////////////////////////////////////////////////
///////
// CCOMMCTRLDlg message handlers
BOOL CCOMMCTRLDlg::OnInitDialog()
{
  CDialog::OnInitDialog();

  // Add "About..." menu item to system menu.
  // IDM_ABOUTBOX must be in the system command range.
  ASSERT((IDM_ABOUTBOX & 0xFFF0) == IDM_ABOUTBOX);
  ASSERT(IDM_ABOUTBOX < 0xF000);

  CMenu* pSysMenu = GetSystemMenu(FALSE);
  CString strAboutMenu;
  strAboutMenu.LoadString(IDS_ABOUTBOX);
  if (!strAboutMenu.IsEmpty())
  {
    pSysMenu->AppendMenu(MF_SEPARATOR);
    pSysMenu->AppendMenu(MF_STRING, IDM_ABOUTBOX, strAboutMenu);
  }

  // Set the icon for this dialog.  The framework does this
  // automatically
  //  when the application's main window is not a dialog
  SetIcon(m_hIcon, TRUE);// Set big icon
  SetIcon(m_hIcon, FALSE);// Set small icon

  // TODO: Add extra initialization here

  m_progCtrl.SetRange(0, 100);
  m_progCtrl.SetPcs(2);
  m_progCtrl.SetStep(1);
  m_progCtrl.OffsetPos(20);
  return TRUE;  // return TRUE  unless you set the focus to a control
}
void CCOMMCTRLDlg::OnSysCommand(UINT nID, LPARAM lParam)
{
  if ((nID & 0xFFF0) == IDM_ABOUTBOX)
  {
    CAboutDlg dlgAbout;
    dlgAbout.DoModal();
  }
  else
  {
```

```
        CDialog::OnSysCommand(nID, lParam);
    }
}
// If you add a minimize button to your dialog, you will need the
code below
//  to draw the icon. For MFC applications using the document/view
// model,this is automatically done for you by the framework.
void CCOMMCTRLDlg::OnPaint()
{
    if (IsIconic())
    {
        CPaintDC dc(this); // device context for painting
        SendMessage(WM_ICONERASEBKGND, (WPARAM) dc.GetSafeHdc(), 0);
        // Center icon in client rectangle
        int cxIcon = GetSystemMetrics(SM_CXICON);
        int cyIcon = GetSystemMetrics(SM_CYICON);
        CRect rect;
        GetClientRect(&rect);
        int x = (rect.Width() - cxIcon + 1) / 2;
        int y = (rect.Height() - cyIcon + 1) / 2;
        // Draw the icon
        dc.DrawIcon(x, y, m_hIcon);
    }
    else
    {
        CDialog::OnPaint();
    }
}
// The system calls this to obtain the cursor to display while the
// user drags the minimized window.
HCURSOR CCOMMCTRLDlg::OnQueryDragIcon()
{
    return (HCURSOR) m_hIcon;
}
void CCOMMCTRLDlg::OnApply()
{
    // TODO: Add your control notification handler code here
    UpdateData(CTRL2VAR);
    m_progCtrl.SetRange(m_setRange1, m_setRange2);
    m_progCtrl.SetPos(m_setPsn);
    m_progCtrl.SetStep(m_setStep);
    m_progCtrl.OffsetPos(m_offsetPsn);
}
void CCOMMCTRLDlg::OnStep()
{
    // TODO: Add your control notification handler code here
    m_progCtrl.StepIt();
}
```

Summary

This chapter examined a host of new or enhanced MFC classes that you can use to incorporate the new look and feel of the Windows 95 interface into your own applications. Topics covered in this chapter included:

- The Win32 common controls, including progress controls, spin-button controls, animation controls, slider controls and many more
- MFC classes you can use to create and implement control bars such as dockable toolbars, status bars, task bars, and dialog bars
- MFC classes you can use to create property sheets (tabbed dialog boxes) and tabbed property pages
- The common dialog-box classes that are used to create commonly used Win95-style dialog boxes such as **File | Open**, **File | Save**, **File | Save As**, **Find/Replace**, **Page Setup**, and more.

In this chapter, you had an opportunity to write and execute an application that makes use of a progress-bar control—one of the new common controls encapsulated into classes in Version 4.0 of the Microsoft Foundation Class library. In the next chapter, "Windows 95 and Visual C++," you'll learn about many more new features of MFC 4.0 and Visual C++ 4.0.

6

Windows 95 and Visual C++

The first thing you may notice about Visual C++ 4.0 that the old Visual C++ user-interface package, which was called the Programmer's Workbench, is gone. It has been replaced with a new, better-looking, more programmer-friendly environment named Developer Studio.

As soon as you start Microsoft Visual C++ 4.0, you can see that it's very different from earlier versions of the Visual C++ development package.

The first thing you may notice about Visual C++ 4.0 that the old Visual C++ user-interface package, which was called the Programmer's Workbench, is gone. It has been replaced with a new, better-looking, more programmer-friendly development environment named Developer Studio (shown in Figure 6.1 on page 240).

But the most important new features of Visual C++ 4.0 are those you can't see: powerful new features such as Component Gallery, which makes code reuse easy, and OLE controls, the long-awaited 32-bit successors to Microsoft's popular 16-bit VBX controls.

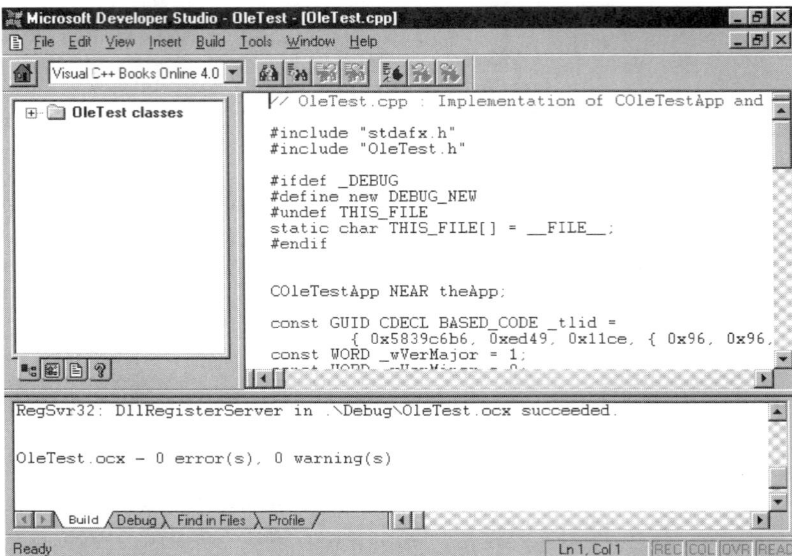

Figure 6.1 The Developer Studio programming environment

This chapter introduces many of the new Visual C++ features that you can see, but focuses mostly on those you can't. Some of the topics discussed in this chapter are:

- The new and improved features of the Visual C++ user interface. You'll also receive some tips on where you can find some familiar Visual C++ features that have been moved around.
- A new Visual C++ tool named *Component Gallery*. In Visual C++ 4.0, *components* are reusable controls, classes, and other objects that you can drop into any Visual C++ program. Component Gallery is an interactive tool you can use to manage components in your Visual C++ applications. With Component Gallery, you can insert any component into a Visual C++ application at the click of a menu item.
- *OLE controls*. OLE controls are Microsoft's long-awaited 32-bit successors to VXB controls. OLE controls are much more powerful than VBX controls and are actually quite easy to use, as you will learn in this chapter.

The major topics covered in this chapter are:

The chapter concludes by presenting a sample application, named COMPGAL, that shows how you can add an OLE control to a dialog box and then use it in a Visual C++ program.

Figure 6.2 shows the dialog box displayed by the COMPGAL program. The yellow face in the dialog box is an OLE control. You can make the face sad or happy by clicking the **Demeanor** button. The **Demeanor** button executes an OLE-control method that toggles the face back and forth between a smile and a frown.

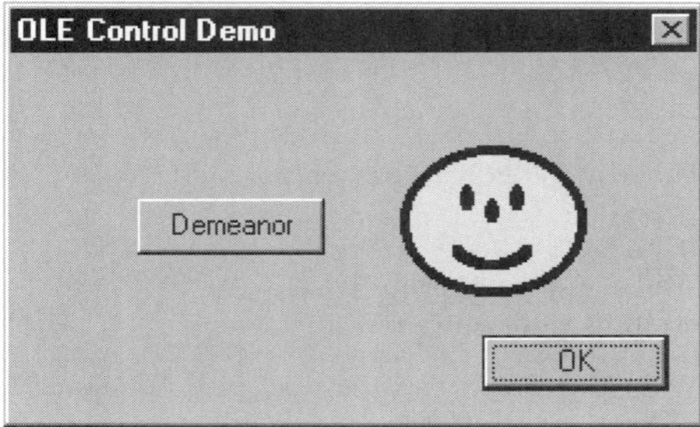

Figure 6.2 Using an OLE control in a Visual C++ program

The Visual C++ 4.0 User Interface

Along with its new look, Visual C++ 4.0 has an impressive set of new features. Here are descriptions of several of the most important ones:

- *Developer Studio*, as noted earlier, is the successor to the Programmer's Workbench interface. The tools built into Developer Studio are more tightly integrated into the Visual C++ programming environment than were provided with earlier versions of Visual C++. For example, both the App Studio resource-management tool and the OLE Control Developer's Kit (CDK) have disappeared from Visual C++. They are now built right into Developer Studio, the Visual C++ user interface.
- *Component Gallery* is a new tool that lets you drop predesigned custom components into a project in much the same way that you

can drop event-handling member functions into your applications with the ClassWizard tool.

- *Support for OLE controls* is a long-awaited new feature of Visual C++ that lets you turn practically any object in an application into an OLE-control container. In previous versions of Visual C++, you could create OLE controls, but there was no way to use them in your applications because you couldn't create OLE containers. In Visual C++ 4.0, you can create both controls and containers very easily, so you can finally use OLE controls in your applications.
- *MFC extensions* let you add your own extensions to the Microsoft Foundation Class library. The MFC extensions that support OLE controls include the COleControl class (described under the previous heading) and a host of new tools for developing OLE controls.
- *Custom AppWizards*—This is another powerful new feature that lets you design customized AppWizards that work just like the Microsoft AppWizard that comes with Visual C++.

You'll learn more about all these new features of Visual C++ under separate headings later in this chapter.

Visual C++ and Its Competitors

Microsoft Visual C++ is not the only programming package available for Windows 95. You can also program for Windows 95 using competitive compilers such as Borland C++, Symantec C++, Watcom C++, and MetaWare C++. Furthermore, three of those four companies—Symantec, Watcom, and MetaWare—have licensed the Microsoft Foundation Class (MFC) library from Microsoft. So you don't have to write MFC programs for Windows 95 using the Visual C++ compiler.

However, with the twin introductions of Visual C++ 4.0 and Version 4.0 of the MFC library, Visual C++ and the MFC library now seem to be so tightly integrated that it's worthwhile learning to use the Visual C++ compiler, even though you might eventually wind up doing your programming using some other development environment. Version 4.0 of the MFC library contains many classes and member functions that seem to have been designed solely to support features of Visual C++.

Familiar Features of Visual C++

Although many new features have been added to Visual C++, there are also a lot of features that haven't changed. You can still use the AppWizard program-framework generator to create a working application at the click of a menu item, and you can still create and manage C++ classes for your application using ClassWizard.

To develop a Visual C++ application, you still create a project—a group of source files and other files needed to build your program—and AppWizard still creates framework applications that use a document-and-view architecture: that is, a structure in which data is stored in documents and screen displays are managed by views.

Finally, AppWizard still creates message maps for your applications, and ClassWizard still maintains those message maps when it creates classes and member functions.

Along with these old familiar features, Visual C++ has a number of new features that are described under the headings that follow.

Developer Studio's Property Sheets

One feature of Visual C++ 4.0 that may not look familiar is Developer Studio's use of *property sheets* (Microsoft's term for tabbed dialog boxes). For example, the upper left-hand pane of the Developer Studio window is a property sheet containing three property pages:

- A **Build** page, which contains a tree-list view of your project's files and folders
- A **Classes** page, which displays the C++ classes used in your project
- A **Help** page, which you can use to navigate to Books Online or other **Help** files without leaving Developer Studio.

The bottom pane in the Developer Studio window is a property sheet that allows you to tab to four more property pages:

- The **Build** property page, which displays messages generated by the compiler and the linker when your program is being built.
- The **Debug** page, which displays debugging information.
- The **Find in Files** page, which displays the output of **File | Find in Files** menu command. (Incidentally, the Visual C++ 4.0 **Find in Files** feature is much more powerful than the **Find in Files** feature in earlier versions of Visual C++.)
- The **Profile** page (a new feature of Visual C++ 4.0), which displays important information about your application's performance if you compile it with *profiling* enabled. To enable profiling, you must set the **Enable Profiling** linker option on the **Link** page of the **Project Settings** property sheet. To display the **Project Settings** property sheet, choose the **Build | Settings** menu item.

Where Have All the Menus Gone?

If you've used earlier versions of Visual C++, you may have a hard time tracking down some of features you need the first time you use Visual C++ 4.0. In the interest of user friendliness and a more intuitive design, the developers of Visual C++ 4.0 moved a few menu items around and changed a few other familiar user-interface features when they dumped the old Programmer's Workbench and replaced it with Developer Studio.

These changes resulted in a much more smoothly working user interface, but Visual C++ old-timers may find themselves a little disoriented when they start trying to track down familiar features using the new interface. In the paragraphs that follow, I'll help you track down some of the Visual C++ menu items that have been moved around.

Creating a New Project with Visual C++ 4.0

One significant change in Visual C++ 4.0 is the way you create a new project with Developer Studio. First you choose the **File | New** menu item, just as you did in Visual C++ 2.*x*. Developer Studio then displays a dialog box labeled **New** (Figure 6.3). To start a new project, you select **Project Workspace** from the **New** list box, as shown in the illustration.

Notice that there are also a number of other options to choose from. For example, you can use the same dialog box to open code or text files, resource scripts, or even graphics files such as bitmaps, icons, and cursors.

When you select **Project Workspace** from the **New** dialog box and click the **OK** button, Developer Studio opens another dialog box named **New Workspace** (Figure 6.4 on page 245).

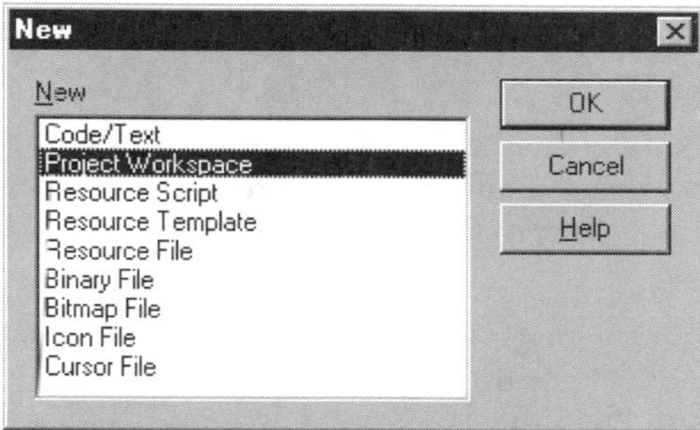

Figure 6.3 The New dialog box

You can then browse to the folder of your choice by clicking the **Browse** button, type a name for your new project in the **Name** text box, and select the kind of project you want to create (AppWizard application, dynamic-link library, or whatever) from the **Type** list box. Then you can create your new project by clicking the **Create** button. If the AppWizard item is selected when you click Create, Developer Studio opens a series of AppWizard dialog boxes (Figure 6.5) that you can use to set up and create your application.

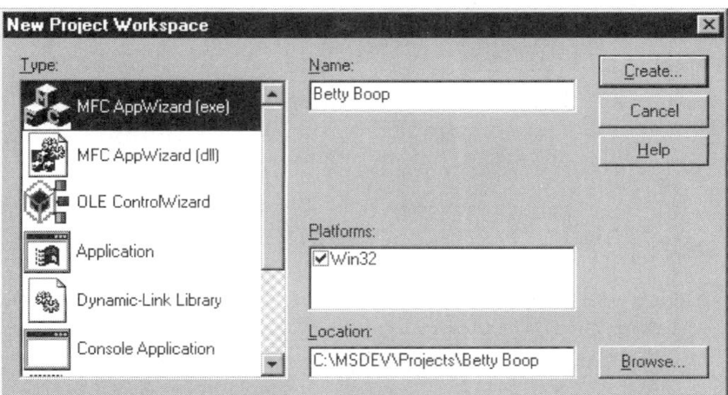

Figure 6.4 The New Project Workspace dialog box

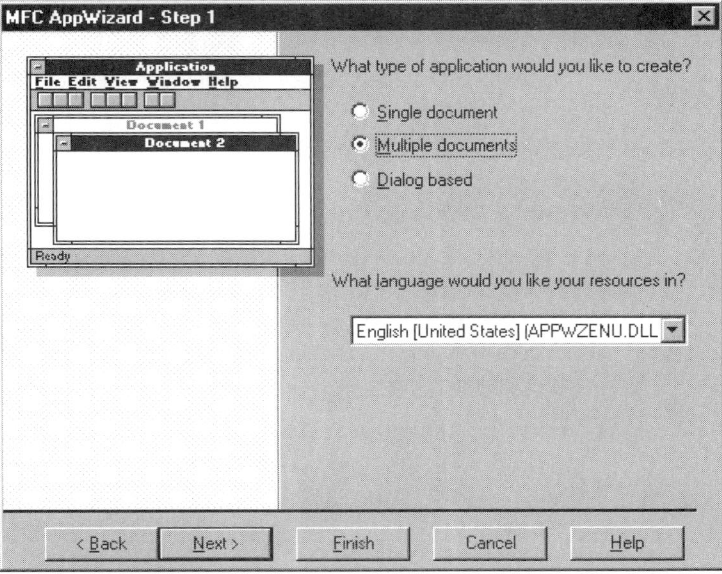

Figure 6.5 The first AppWizard dialog box

Creating and Managing Resources

App Studio, the Visual C++ resource-management tool, has faded away in Visual C++ 4.0. But don't worry—it's been replaced by something better.

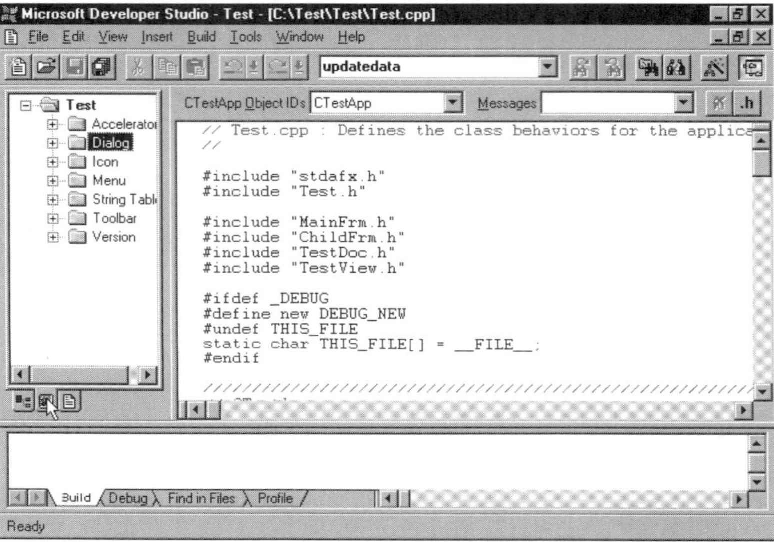

Figure 6.6 Selecting resources to edit with Visual C++ 4.0

App Studio was a standalone application in Visual C++ 1.0, became an integrated part of the Programmer's Workbench in Visual C++ 1.5 and 2.*x*, and has completely gone away in Visual C++ 4.0.

Opening an Existing Resource

In Visual C++ 4.0, App Studio has been completely replaced by a set of graphics editors that you can open by tabbing to Developer Studio's **Build** page (described earlier) and double-clicking your application's .RC (resource) icon. Developer Studio then displays a set of panes like those shown in Figure 6.6.

When your Developer Studio display takes on the form shown in Figure 6.6, you can open an editor for any kind of resource shown in the upper right-hand pane by double-clicking the resource file's icon. When you double-click on a resource-file icon, Developer Studio opens the appropriate resource editor. For example, if you double-click on an icon that represents a dialog-box resource, Developer Studio opens its dialog-box editor (see Figure 6.7 on page 247).

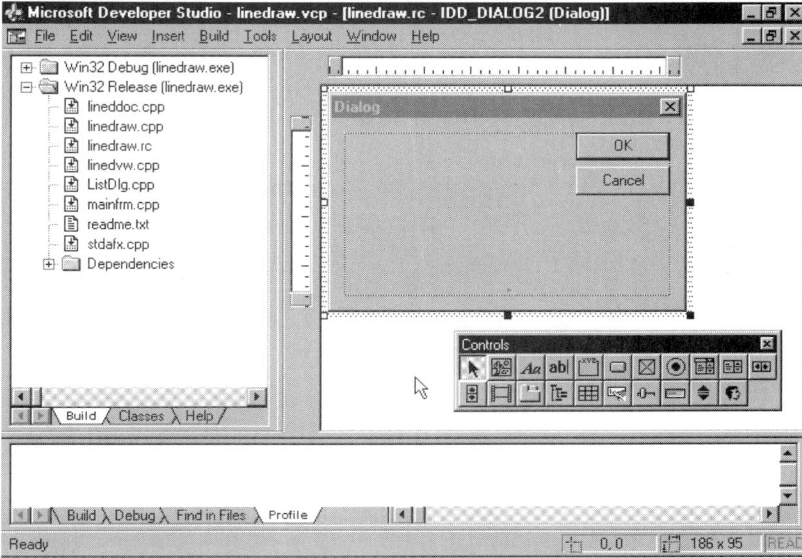

Figure 6.7 The Developer Studio dialog-box editor

Creating a New Resource

To create a new resource for a Visual C++ 4.0 project, choose the **Insert | Resource** menu item. Developer Studio then opens an **Insert Resource** dialog box like the one shown in Figure 6.8.

When the **Insert Resource** dialog box appears, you can select the kind of resource you want to create and click the OK button. Developer Studio then opens the appropriate resource editor.

Figure 6.8 The Insert Resource dialog box

Displaying Toolbars and Tool Palettes

In MFC 4.0, a tool palette is just a dockable toolbar that has been pulled away from its docking station (see "Toolbar Controls" on page 202). And Developer Studio creates toolbars using MFC 4.0.

So, in Visual C++ 4.0, the way to display a tool palette like the one shown in Figure 6.7 on page 247 is to select the **View | Toolbars** menu item. Developer Studio then opens a **Toolbars** dialog box like the one shown in Figure 6.9, and you can check or uncheck any toolbars that you want to display or remove from the screen.

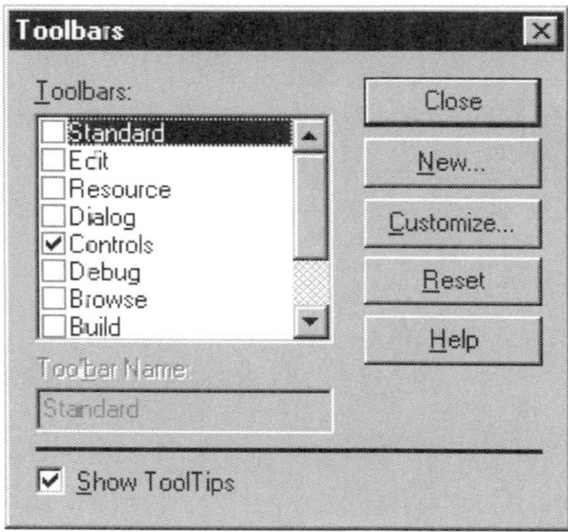

Figure 6.9 The Toolbars dialog box

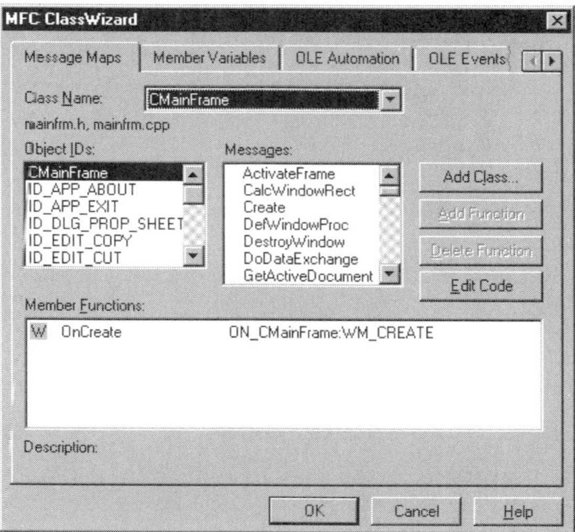

Figure 6.10 The ClassWizard property page

Using ClassWizard in Visual C++ 4.0

To open ClassWizard, you choose the **View | ClassWizard** menu item. Developer Studio may respond by displaying a message box or two to get some input from you about the classes in your application.

When it has all its facts straight, Developer Studio opens a property page like the one shown in Figure 6.10 on page 248. You can then operate ClassWizard in just about the same way you did under earlier versions of Visual C++—except for the fact that you now access its various options by tabbing to property pages.

Debugging Applications with Visual C++ 4.0

To debug an application with the Visual C++ 4.0 debugger, you choose the **Build | Debug** menu item. To set and clear breakpoints, you have to move to the **Edit** menu and choose the **Breakpoints** menu item.

Obtaining Online Help

Online **Help** has changed a lot in Visual C++ 4.0. When you choose the **Help | Contents** menu item, a **Help** page opens in the upper left-hand pane of the Developer Studio window. Then the contents of whatever help file you're using are displayed there, as shown in Figure 6.11.

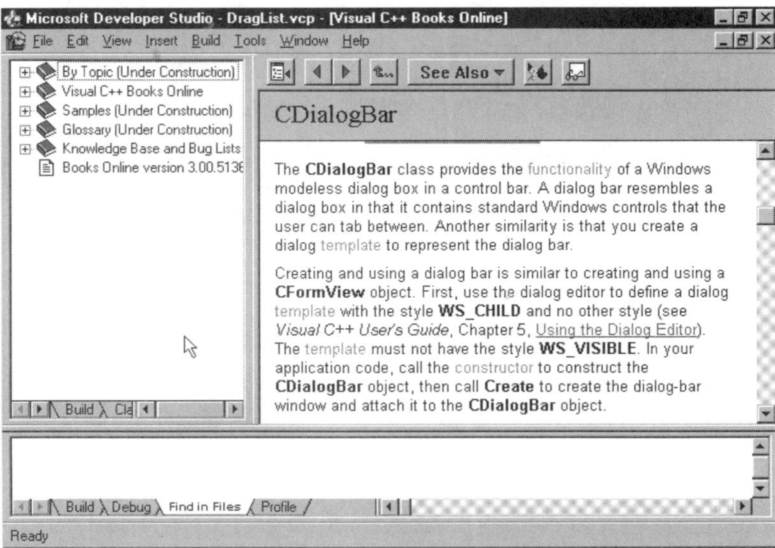

Figure 6.11 Using online Help in Visual C++ 4.0

The **Help** page, as mentioned earlier, is one of the tabbed pages in the upper left-hand pane of the Developer Studio window. When **Help** information is displayed in that pane and you want to see something else there—for example, the files and folders in your project—don't try to replace the **Help** panel with project information by searching for a menu item.

Instead, just click the **Build** tab at the bottom of the pane in which your **Help** files and folders appear, and that will replace those **Help** files and folders with your project's file and folder icons.

To search for a keyword or a key phrase in online help, choose the **Help | Search** menu item. Developer Studio then displays a very powerful two-page property sheet for file-searching. The Index page displays a list of available Help topics and lets you pick one. Clicking the `Query` tab brings up a property page that lets you narrow your search or choose from many different kinds of searching options.

Other Menu Items

The preceding paragraphs have only hit the highlights of the facelift Microsoft has given Visual C++ with the premiere of Visual C++ 4.0 and the Developer Studio. There are also menu items for incorporating predesigned components into Visual C++ programs, for configuring projects, for setting properties of window panes, and for doing all sorts of things with OLE objects and OLE controls.

Component Gallery

One of the most important new features of Visual C++ is *Component Gallery*, a new tool that lets you use predesigned custom *components* in a project. With Component Gallery, you can drop components into an application in much the same way that ClassWizard lets you drop event-handling member functions into your programs. Component Gallery is an important new utility in Visual C++ because it can bring you one step closer to that elusive goal of object-oriented programming, real code reusability.

Component Gallery is a storehouse where you can store prewritten, pre-debugged components that are always ready for use in any application. You can use components in much the same way that Windows 3.*x* programmers used VXB controls—although, as you will soon see, components are much more powerful than VXB controls ever were.

A component can be almost anything—for example, a dialog-box control, a C++ class created with AppWizard, or custom-tailored code objects that you design yourself.

When you have an object that you want to tuck away in Component Gallery for future use, the Component Gallery utility stores your object in the form of source-code (.CPP) files, header (.H) files, and associated resources. Once you have exported a component into Component Gallery, you can use the component whenever you like, in whatever application you like, and for any purpose you choose.

There are three main reasons you might want to use Component Gallery during the development of a project:

- To add OLE controls or other components to a project.
- To remove OLE controls or other components from Component Gallery. In this case, you need not open a project.
- To make OLE controls or other components available to other developers.

As you increase the number of components stored in your computer's Component Gallery, the amount of reusable C++ code at your disposal will start to grow. Eventually, a virtually unlimited number of components could be at your disposal—instantly available to you and every developer on your team at the click of a button or a menu item.

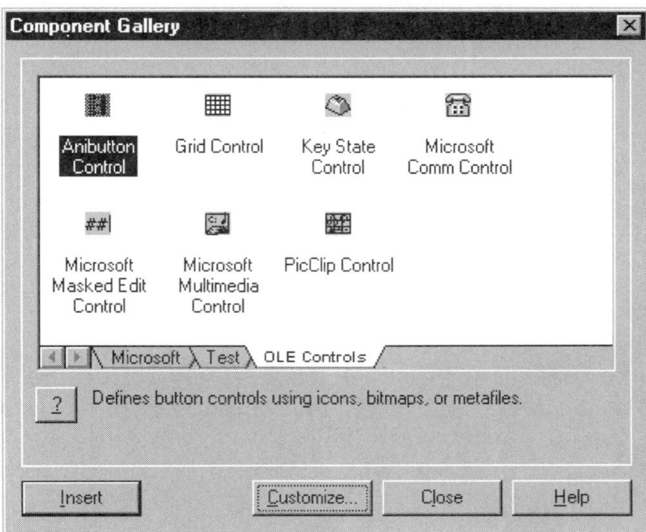

Figure 6.12 The Component Gallery dialog box

How Component Gallery Works

Component Gallery is built right into Developer Studio, just like other familiar Visual C++ tools such as ClassWizard and AppWizard. With Component Gallery, you can insert components into your application's source code in much the same way that you insert event-driven member functions into your source code using ClassWizard.

When you import a component into an application using Component Gallery, Visual C++ also adds any resources owned by the component to your application's resource script (.RC file).

The sections that follow describe some of the most important features of Component Gallery and show how you can use Component Gallery to insert components into your programs.

Using Component Gallery Step by Step

✔ To start adding components to a project using Component Gallery, only three steps are required:

1. Start Developer Studio if it isn't started already.
2. Choose the **Insert | Component** menu item. Component Gallery then opens its main property sheet (see Figure 6.12 on page 251). Notice that Visual C++ comes with a number of prebuilt components that you can examine by tabbing to different property pages. One property page—the one shown in Figure 6.12—offers a set of predesigned OLE controls that you can use as components in your applications
3. When the **Component Gallery** property sheet opens, click the **Customize** button. Developer Studio opens a dialog box titled **Customize Component Gallery** (Figure 6.13 on page 253). When the **Customize Component Gallery** dialog box appears, you can click the **Categories** and **Component** list boxes to add, delete, and move components managed by Component Gallery. You can also import components, move components from one category to another, and set the properties of components.

Customizing Components

You can use the **Customize Component Gallery** dialog box to create new categories of components, to move components between categories, add components to a category, and delete components or categories.

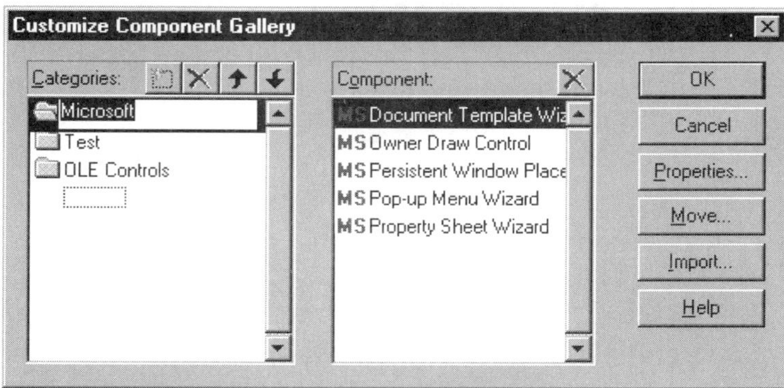

Figure 6.13 The Customize Component Gallery dialog box

The Categories List Box

The **Categories** list box, on the left side of the **Customize Component Gallery** dialog box, lists categories of components in the Component Gallery. Categories of components are displayed as folders in the **Categories** panel.

You can select any component category that is listed in the **Categories** list box and then do any of the following:

- Move the focus to the category's components by pressing the TAB key.
- Move the category to a new position in the **Categories** list box by clicking the up arrow or the down arrow in the toolbar just above the list box. Alternatively, you can drag the category with the mouse while holding down the left mouse button or by selecting the category and pressing **Alt+Up Arrow** or **Alt+Down Arrow**.
- Rename a category by selecting it and typing a new name.
- Add a new category by typing a new name.
- Remove a category by selecting it and clicking the **X** toolbar button or pressing **Del**.

The Component List Box

The **Component** list box, on the right side of the **Customize Component Gallery** dialog box, lists the components in the currently open component category.

You can perform any of the following actions on components listed in the **Component** list box:

- Select one or more components and click the **Move** button to move the selected components to a new category in the **Categories** list box. To select multiple components, press **Ctrl+Up** or **Ctrl+Down**.
- Remove a component by selecting it and clicking the **X** toolbar button or pressing the **Del** key.
- Move the focus to the Categories list box by pressing **Ctrl+Shift+Tab**.

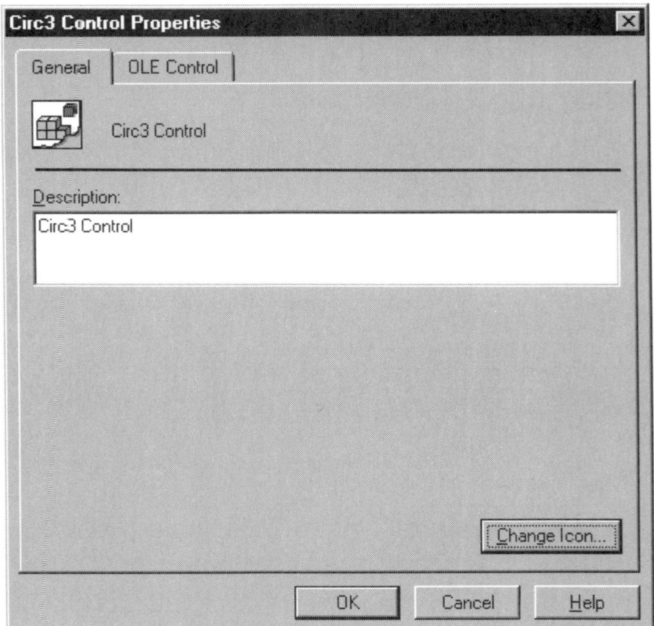

Figure 6.14 The Control Properties dialog box

The Properties Button

The **Properties** button displays the **Properties** dialog box, which allows you to view and modify component properties.

When you click the **Properties,** Component Gallery opens a dialog box titled **Control Properties** (Figure 6.14). The **Control Properties** dialog box lets you view and change the properties of components.

For example, you can click the **Icon** button in the **Control Properties** dialog box to change a component's icon. You can also change the description that a component displays on the main Component Gallery dialog box, and you can change the component's icon.

The Move Button

The **Move** button displays the **Move** dialog box, which allows you to use the keyboard to move components to one category to another.

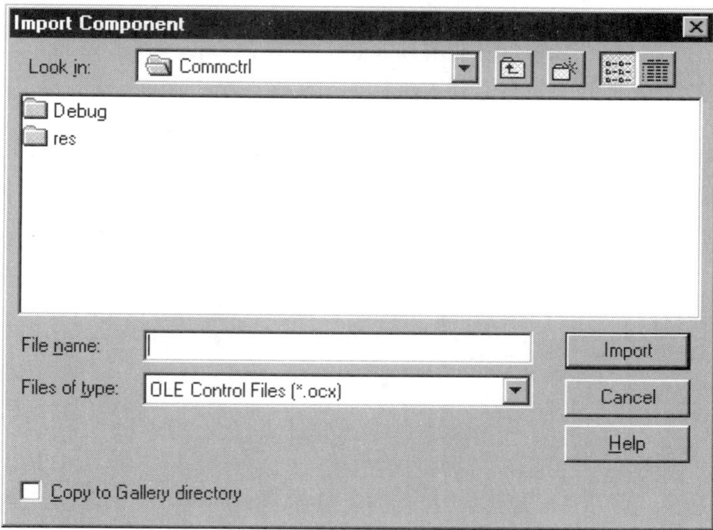

Figure 6.15 The Import Component dialog box

The Import Button

When you click the **Import** button in the **Customize Component Gallery** dialog box, Component Gallery opens a dialog box titled **Import Component** (Figure 6.15). You can use the **Import Component** dialog box to import components into a category from an external source. That's how you add OLE controls and other components to the Component Gallery.

When you import an OLE control, Component Gallery automatically carries out some important procedures that are needed to make the control work properly.

For example, Component Gallery creates an *OLE wrapper*, which allows the imported OLE control to communicate with your application. Component Gallery also *registers* the OLE control with your project, making the control accessible from the Developer Studio dialog-box editor's toolbar. (For more information about OLE-control registration, see "The Component Object Model and OLE Interfaces" on page 258.)

Completing the Installation Process

By clicking the **Insert** button in the **Component Gallery** dialog box, you can add files to your Visual C++ projects to define and implement components. The **Insert** button adds the header and implementation files associated with a component to your project and updates Developer Studio's **Classes** and **Build** panes.

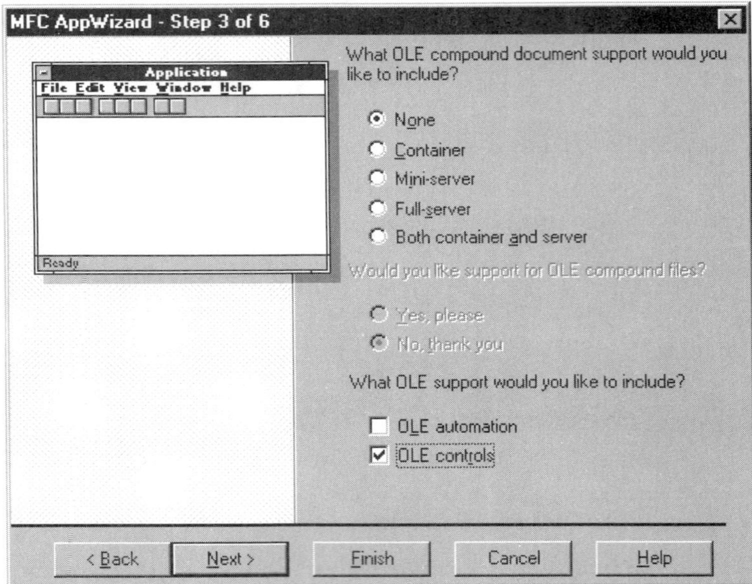

Figure 6.16 Building an application that supports OLE controls

Example: Importing a Component

✔ It's very easy to import an existing component into Component Gallery. To import an existing component into your Visual C++ Component Gallery, follow these steps:

1. Use AppWizard to create an SDI (single-document interface) application that supports OLE controls. To build OLE-control support into your application, just check the OLE controls check box when AppWizard displays the dialog box shown in Figure 6.16.
2. Build your application.

3. Choose the Developer Studio's **Insert | Component** menu item.
4. When the **Component Gallery** dialog box appears, click the **Customize** button. Component Gallery then opens the **Customize Component Gallery** dialog box (previously shown in Figure 6.13 on page 253).
5. When the **Customize Component Gallery** dialog box opens, click the **Import** button. Component Gallery then opens the **Import Component** dialog box (previously shown in Figure 6.15 on page 255).
6. When the **Import Component** dialog box appears, navigate to the folder in which you have installed the files from your bonus disk. Then navigate this chapter's folder and open the SMILECTL folder that's inside it.
7. Notice that a file named SMILE.OCX appears inside the large list box in the **Import Component** dialog box. Select the SMILE.OCX icon and click the **Import** button.
8. When the **Import Component** dialog box closes and the **Customize Component Gallery** dialog box again becomes the active window, notice that an icon labeled **Smile Control** now appears in the **Customize Component Gallery** dialog's **Component** list box.

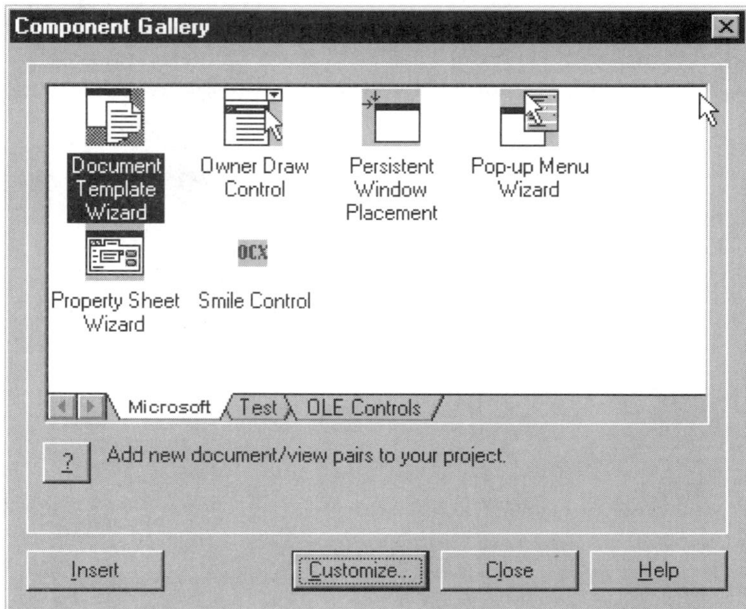

Figure 6.17 Adding a component to Component Gallery

9. Click the **Customize Component Gallery** dialog box's **OK** button.
10. When the **Component Gallery** property sheet becomes the active window, notice that an icon labeled **Smile Control** now appears on the property page that is currently active (see Figure 6.17 on page 257). That shows that you have now completed the process of importing a component into Component Gallery. When you have added a component to Component Gallery, you can use the component in any application you build with your copy of Visual C++.

The Component Object Model and OLE Interfaces

The *component object model (COM)* is the cornerstone of all OLE operations. It is partly a specification and partly an implementation. The specification half of the component object model is a binary standard for implementing Windows objects in a way that is independent of any particular programming language.

That means that by adhering to the COM standard, applications can communicate with each other through object-oriented interfaces, even if neither program knows how the other application implements functionalities that the two applications are exchanging information about.

OLE controls work by using OLE *interfaces*. An interface is a mechanism for accessing OLE objects indirectly. In OLE, the names of interfaces always begin with I, just as the names of classes begin with C in the Microsoft Foundation Class (MFC) library.

When an application communicates with an OLE object through an OLE interface, the interface isolates the application from much of the code that implements the object. That makes it possible for an application written in one language to communicate with an OLE object written in a different language.

OLE interfaces also make it possible for 16-bit and 32-bit objects and applications to communicate with each other. Finally, they make it possible for users of your application to drag a document created with one application into a document created by another application, and to edit the document on the spot, without starting the application that created it.

More details about how this all works are provided in Chapter 7, "OLE 95."

OLE Controls

One of the most important new features of Visual C++ 4.0 is its support of OLE controls. Ever since the move to a 32-bit world of PC programming began, would-be Windows 95 programmers have been universally disheartened by the fact that VBX controls—which are immensely popular in 16-bit Windows programming—cannot be easily incorporated into 32-bit applications.

Visual C++ 4.0, with its support of both OLE controls and OLE control containers, now stands ready to solve that problem. Briefly, OLE controls are Microsoft's 32-bit successors to VBX controls. In fact, they are much more powerful than VBX controls and are much better suited for use in C++ programs.

An OLE control, like a VBX control, is a small, powerful custom control that is also very portable. An OLE control is usually—but not always—a visual element such as a button or a list box. When an OLE control is visible, it often resembles an ordinary Windows custom control such as a list box or a group of radio buttons.

It is possible to implement an entire application, such as Microsoft Excel, as an OLE control. That would be a pretty hefty OLE control, but there is no law against doing such a thing.

More often, an OLE control is a visible object that can interact with the user and can also display values in specific ways—for example, in the form of a pie chart.

Creating an OLE Control

When you want to place an OLE control in a dialog box or in a window that behaves like a dialog box—for example, a CFormView object—you can create your OLE interactively using two Visual C++ utilities: ControlWizard, which is designed specifically for creating OLE controls, and the ClassWizard class-management utility that you've used in earlier chapters.

In some situations—for example, when you need to create an OLE control in a window that is not derived from the CDialog class—ControlWizard may lack some of the functionality to you might need to design an OLE control that meets your requirements. For example, you may need to implement in-place activation—that is, in-place editing of your control inside its container. In a case like that, you might have to create the control dynamically—by calling its constructor and then calling the **`Create`** member function—instead of implementing it interactively using ControlWizard, ClassWizard, and the Developer Studio dialog-box editor.

In this chapter, in the section headed "Implementing OLE Controls" on page 283, you'll learn how to implement an existing OLE control in a Visual C++ application. Chapter 7, "OLE 95," explains how to create and implement your own OLE controls. You'll learn how to do that in the section headed "Adding Properties and Methods to OLE Controls" on page 316.

OLE Controls and VBX Controls

OLE controls are reminiscent of the VBX controls you may have used in 16-bit Windows programs, but they are easier to use and much more powerful.

OLE controls, like VBX controls, are portable from application to application. Another similarity between VBX controls and OLE controls is that OLE controls can be stored in a central location (such as Component Gallery) and can be used by any application that has access to them.

There are also significant differences between OLE controls and VBX components. These are some of the most important:

- OLE controls are implemented using Visual C++ source files and are compiled into Visual C++ applications at link time. That means that when you add an OLE control to an application, the component becomes an integral part of the application. So the application that contains the component runs fast and efficiently.
- OLE controls are 32-bit objects that are compiled and linked by the Visual C++ 4.0 compiler.
- OLE controls fully support OLE—as you would expect, since they're OLE controls.

The Evolution of OLE Controls

Long ago, as far back as the age of Windows 1, Windows was equipped with user-interface objects called *Windows custom controls*. A Windows custom control was an actual window with some added functionality that enabled it to perform certain tricks, such as drawing itself.

Viewed in today's terms, Windows custom controls were simple little creatures. They didn't have properties, they didn't have methods, and all they had in the way of events were Windows notification messages. So they were quite limited in what they could do.

The Death of the VBX Control

That began to change in 1991 and 1992 when Microsoft introduced a new programming language called Visual Basic. With the introduction of Visual Basic, a new kind of control was born: the Visual Basic control, or VBX control. A VBX control was a little more complex than an ordinary Windows custom control. When you had created a VBX control in a Visual Basic application, you could add it to a tool palette and then import it into other applications.

VBX controls quickly became so popular that they sparked the creation of an industry. Within a year or two, dozens of software vendors were creating and selling VBX controls: ready-made controls that you could drop into your Visual Basic—or even Visual C++—applications.

Unfortunately, VBX controls had a few limitations. Their most serious shortcoming was that they were designed to work only in 16-bit programming environments—in fact, they were limited to working in *Intel* 16-bit environments. When 32-bit operating systems such as Windows NT and Windows 95 appeared on the horizon, it became clear that the future lifespan of VBX controls was limited. Something much more robust was needed.

The Birth of the OLE Control

And then—OLE!

OLE controls are much more than just the 32-bit successors to VBX controls. An OLE control has all the functionality of a VBX control, and a whole lot more. OLE controls can be used a wide variety of 16-bit and 32-bit platforms. They can be used on RISC systems, Power PC systems, MIPS systems, and Intel systems, and the list keeps growing. So you can create an OLE control using one operating systems, and then just recompile it for use in other systems.

Unfortunately, though, it has been quite difficult up to now to make use of OLE controls in ordinary applications. Until the advent of MFC 4.0 and Visual C++ 4.0, Microsoft provided a toolkit for writing OLE controls (the Control Developer's Kit, or CDK), but didn't provide any mechanism for making them work in Visual C++ applications. Until Visual C++ 4.0 came along, the only containers in which you could embed OLE controls were Microsoft applications such as Excel and Word, and a special "testing" application that came with the CDK.

Now, with the unveiling of Visual C++ 4.0, that has all changed—and things are definitely looking up for OLE controls. In Visual C++ 4.0, Microsoft designers have made it so easy to create control containers that it makes you wonder why it took them so long.

To design an AppWizard program that makes use of OLE controls and control containers, all you have to do is choose the appropriate AppWizard options. Then AppWizard automatically equips your application with all the functionality it needs to support OLE controls and OLE control containers.

Now that designing OLE controls and containers has become so easy, Microsoft now predicts that the creating and marketing of OLE controls will soon become an industry, just as the creating and marketing of VBX controls did a couple of years ago. In fact, OLE controls can do so much more than VBX controls could ever do that the OLE-control market may become much larger than the VBX-control market ever was.

Don't Call Them OCX Controls

Some people call OLE controls OCX controls. Microsoft frowns on the use of that name, even though you sometimes hear Microsoft engineers use it. The term .OCX (with a period in front of it) is the name of a file type, not the name of a control. And the file type of an OLE control doesn't even have to be .OCX.

So please don't call them .OCX controls. Call them by their real name—OLE controls.

Features of OLE Controls

OLE controls have several important features that you'll hear over and over again as you learn more and more about OLE. Important features of OLE controls include methods, properties, event firing, persistence, and portability.

OLE-Control Properties

All OLE controls have attributes called *properties*. To get and set the properties of an OLE control, you can create tabbed dialog pages called property pages. But property pages are optional. You'll learn more about property pages in Chapter 7, in the section headed "Property Pages" on page 316.

An OLE control can have four kinds of properties, which are described in the following list:

- A *custom property* is one that you write and define. You determine the name, the parameter types, and the return value of a custom property—as well as determining what it actually does.
- A *stock property* is one that ControlWizard implements when it creates an OLE control. A stock property is a standard property whose semantics are predefined. When you implement a stock property, what you get is its predefined implementation, which is built in.
- An *ambient property* is a property that belongs not to an OLE control, but to the client site in which the control is embedded (see "Container Sites" on page 266). A client site, like a control can have properties—such as a font or a color, for example. When you embed an OLE control in a client site that has properties, those properties become ambient properties of the control, and the control can obtain access to those properties.
- An *extended property* is a property that appears to the user to be owned by an OLE control, but is actually a property of the container. Properties of a control such as left, right, and tab position—which determine the position of a control in a window—are often maintained by a container rather than a control. So it is sometimes convenient to implement them as extended properties owned by the container but used by the control.

You'll learn more about properties of OLE controls in Chapter 7, "OLE 95."

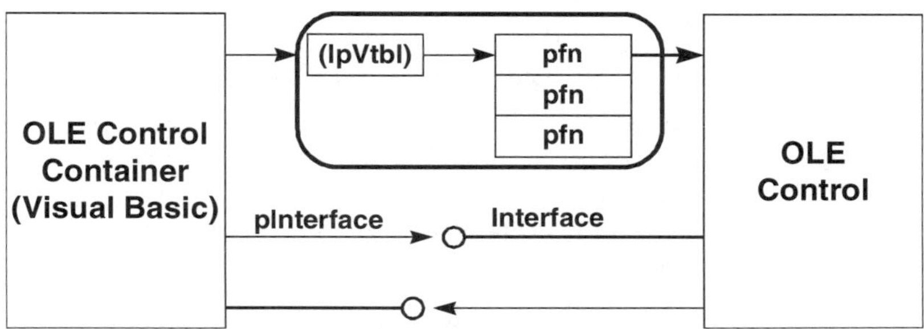

Figure 6.18 How OLE controls expose interfaces

OLE-Control Methods

In OLE, functions pointed to by table entries are often referred to as *methods*. (Once again, in diagrams that depict OLE objects and relationships, OLE interfaces are represented by small circles, as they are in Figure 6.18 on page 263.)

The reason an application can access an OLE control is that an OLE control *exposes* certain interfaces by providing tables of pointers to functions that your application can call. Figure 6.18 shows how an OLE control can expose interfaces, making communication with applications possible.

In Figure 6.18, the two small circles near the bottom of the diagram represent OLE interfaces. You'll learn much more about how all this works in Chapter 7, "OLE 95."

OLE-Object Events

Events are still another feature of OLE controls. An OLE control has the ability to detect important actions such as mouse clicks and data input. When a control detects such an event, it can *fire* the event by notifying its control container that the event has occurred. Your application can then respond to the event in whatever way you consider appropriate.

You'll see how an OLE control fires events in Chapter 7, in "Example: Creating Event Handlers for OLE Controls" on page 336.

OLE Controls and the MFC Library

OLE controls are implemented in a special set of classes that were added to the Microsoft Foundation Class (MFC) library with the release of MFC 4.0. You can create and manage OLE controls with a special set of graphically based tools that were added to Visual C++ with the release of Visual C++ 4.0.

The MFC OLE classes support many of the functionalities provided in the OLE API, including in-place activation, OLE automation, and drag-and-drop capabilities. You'll learn more about all those features of OLE controls in Chapter 7, "OLE 95."

In the OLE examples that appear in this book—and in most of the applications in which you will use OLE objects—you won't deal directly with OLE interfaces very much. Instead, you will access them through MFC classes. If you've dealt directly with OLE interfaces in the past, switching to MFC will be a welcome change. You'll find that it's much easier and much more efficient, and results in code that is leaner, simpler, more efficient, and much less subject to programming snafus.

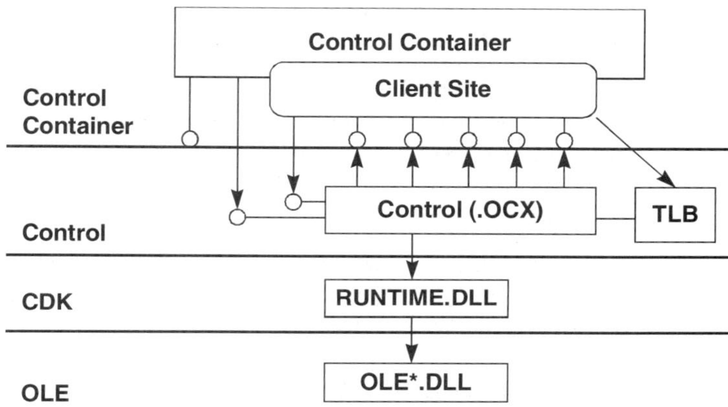

Figure 6.19 The world of OLE controls

Communications between OLE Controls and Containers

In the world of OLE, communications move in two directions. An OLE control container must provide a set of interfaces to which an OLE control can speak. Then there can be two-way communication between the OLE control and its container.

Figure 6.19 is a simplified diagram of the world of OLE controls. At the top of the diagram you can see an OLE control container. As you can see from the small circles on the diagram, the control container in the illustration implements several OLE interfaces.

Although a container site lives in an OLE container, it is really a separate OLE object. In fact, every OLE control is actually owned by a container site. A container site provides a number of interfaces to which an OLE control can connect.

Below the first horizontal line from the top in Figure 6.19, there is a rectangle that represents an OLE control. As you can see, the control whose world is illustrated in the diagram is implemented in an .OCX file (basically, a DLL). The control calls a number of the interfaces provided by its container and by its control site. It is also called by various interfaces provided by both its client site and its container.

Type Libraries

On the right-hand side of Figure 6.19, notice the rectangle labeled *type library*. A type library is a description of a set of interfaces presented by an OLE control. It describes the properties, the methods, and the events that the OLE control implements.

An OLE control container can read an OLE control's type library and determine which properties and methods it should call—and which events it will implement when it is called upon to do so.

Container Sites

Within an OLE container, at each point where an OLE control is embedded, there is an object called a *client site*, or *container site* (OLE containers used to be called OLE clients, and you still run across the term now and then). In Figure 6.19, the client site is represented as a rectangle just below the rectangle that represents the OLE control container.

Runtime DLLs

Just below the rectangle labeled **OLE Control** in Figure 6.19, notice that there is a smaller rectangle labeled **Runtime DLL**. Every OLE control relies on a runtime DLL (dynamic-link library). This DLL is generated automatically when you create an OLE control using the Visual C++ ControlWizard utility.

The runtime DLL associated with an OLE control provides a set of MFC classes that offer all the basic functionality that an OLE control requires. The runtime DLL that an OLE control relies on services provided by OLE, so it makes calls to OLE DLLs within the system. Those DLLs are represented by the rectangle at the bottom of Figure 6.19.

Figure 6.20 on page 267 shows the internal structure of an OLE control's runtime DLL. As you can see, an OLE control runtime DLL provides a number of MFC-derived classes that support OLE controls. There are classes to do the following:

- Maintain the *.OCX file* (the DLL) in which the OLE control resides.
- Supply *methods* that implement stock properties, stock events, and stock methods.
- Provide *stock property pages* that you can use in your applications. OLE provides three stock properties you can use to assign proper-

ties to OLE controls: one for fonts, one for colors, and one for pictures.

- Provide a *stock property-sheet frame* in which the three stock property pages can be embedded. This stock frame takes the form of a property sheet—a tabbed dialog box—and the stock pages provided by the runtime DLL take the form of tabbed property pages. (Containers can also provide their own property-sheet frames if they so choose.)

Figure 6.20 Architecture of an OLE runtime DLL

Packaging OLE Controls

The code that implements an OLE control resides in a dynamic-link library, or DLL (to learn more about DLLs, read Chapter 10, "Windows 95 DLLs"). By convention, an OLE-control file has the filename extension .OCX. Typically, an OLE control container uses as many .OCX files as it needs to communicate with its OLE controls, and each OLE control uses the OLE runtime DLL (see "Runtime DLLs" on page 266).

Figure 6.21 on page 268 is a simplified diagram that shows something about how OLE controls are packaged.

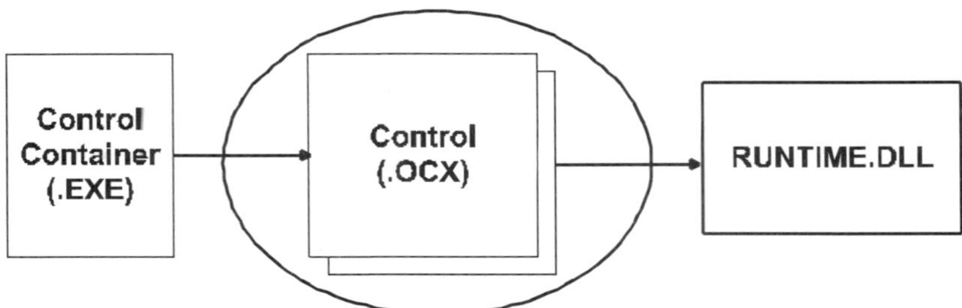

Figure 6.21 The packaging of an OLE control

In-Process Servers

The mechanism that implements an OLE control is sometimes referred to as an *in-process server*. "In-process server" is really nothing more than a fancy word meaning "DLL." An OLE control is sometimes called an in-process server because an OLE control and the application using it reside within the same process (for more about processes, see Chapter 8, "Programs and Processes").

Figure 6.22 is a diagram of an OLE control represented as a classic in-process server. The interfaces you see in the diagram are those that are typically implemented by both an OLE control and its server.

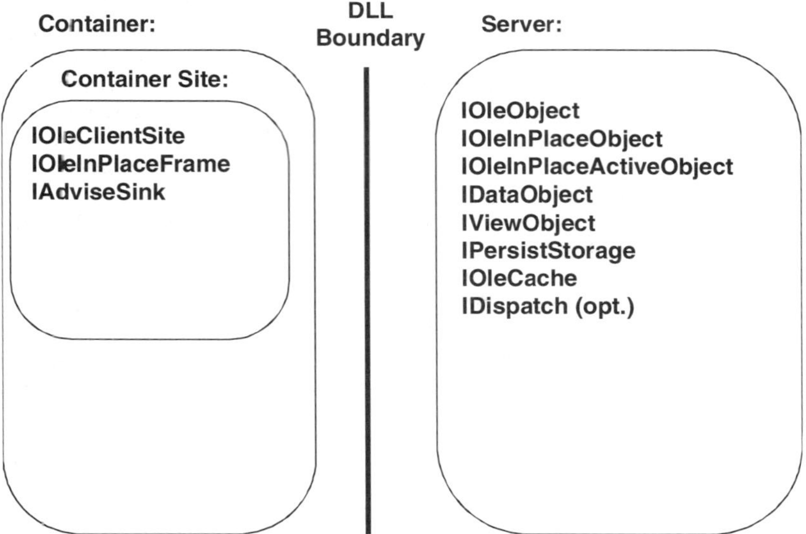

Figure 6.22 An OLE control as an in-process server

As Figure 6.22 illustrates, an OLE container is really a container for a container site (described in "Container Sites" on page 266). The container site in an OLE container implements interfaces such as IOle-ClientSite, IOleInPlaceFrame (if it supports in-place editing), and IAdviseSink.

A server implements interfaces such as IOleObject, IOleInPlaceActive object, and all the other "I" objects you see in the right-hand rectangle in Figure 6.22.

Interfaces Implemented by OLE Controls

OLE controls implement various kinds of OLE interfaces, just as in-process servers do. Figure 6.23 shows the kinds of interfaces that a typical OLE control can implement. As the illustration shows, an OLE control can implement an even wider variety of OLE interfaces than an in-process server can

One important interface that an OLE control implements is the *IDispatch interface*. The IDispatch interface is an OLE interface that implements an OLE control's properties and methods.

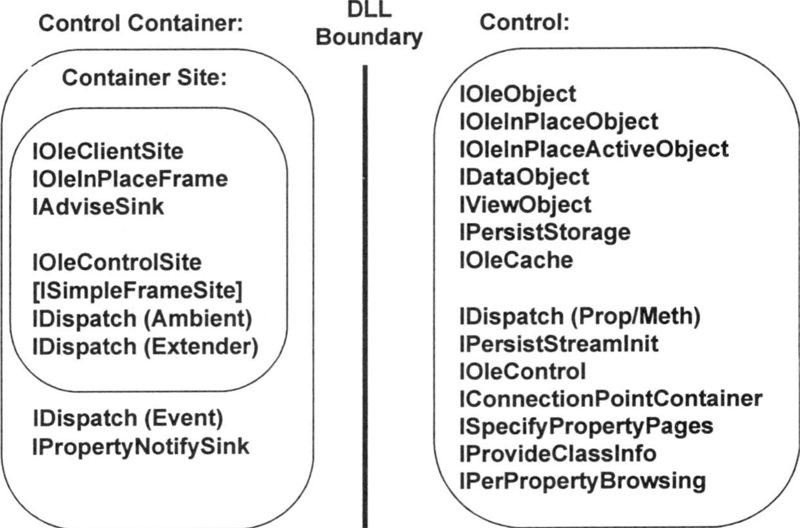

Figure 6.23 How an OLE control implements interfaces

Broadly speaking, the IDispatch interface is what implements *OLE automation* (OLE automation is a form of OLE that makes it possible for OLE objects written in different languages to communicate with each other; details are spelled out in Chapter 7, "OLE 95.") The easiest way to use OLE automation is to use the IDispatch interface.

Another noteworthy interface that an OLE control can implement is IPersistStreamInit, an interface for *persistent storage*. When an OLE control has a persistent-storage property, it can automatically store its current state to a disk and load its last known state from a disk, without any extra effort on the part of the application that implements it.

The IConnectionPointContainer interface, shown in the right-hand rectangle in Figure 6.23, provides *connection points*: the mechanism that makes events work.

OLE Automation: A Cinderella Story

Until the advent of MFC 4.0, OLE automation was the scruffy stepsister in the OLE family—the one nobody wants to take to dinner. It was a script-based technology, and its design principles were based on Visual Basic. In Visual C++ implementations it was unwieldy, slow, and notoriously type-unsafe, so Visual C++ purists avoided it like the plague.

Well, with the unveiling of C++, Cinderella has tried on the glass slipper and is off to the ball. It turns out that OLE controls, which now wear the crown jewels at Microsoft, are based on—would you believe this?—OLE automation. So, if you've turned up your nose at OLE automation in the past, you'd better give it another look. It's blossomed out, and it seems to be here to stay.

Interfaces Implemented by OLE Containers

If in-process servers can implement interfaces, and if OLE controls can implement interfaces, you might conclude that OLE containers can implement interfaces, too. And that is true.

In the left-hand rectangle in Figure 6.23, notice that an OLE control container has an IOleClientSite interface. (OLE in-process servers also have IOleClientSites, as you saw back in Figure 6.22 on page 268).

Also notice the IOleControlSite interface (inside the inner left-hand rectangle). That interface provides extra functionality required by OLE controls.

The ISimpleFrameSite interface, which you can also find inside the inner left-hand rectangle, is an interface that lets one OLE control contain a group of other controls, such as a group of radio buttons or check boxes.

An OLE control container can implement several kinds of IDispatch interfaces. In the left-hand rectangle in Figure 6.23, you can see three different kinds of IDispatch interfaces. One IDispatch interface implements ambient properties, which are seen by the OLE control as well as by the control's container sites.

There is also an IDispatch interface for extended properties, through which an application can communicate with a property of the control or its container without having to know whether the property is owned by the control or its container.

Finally, there is an IDispatch interface for events. When an OLE control implements an event, it tells the container what interface it wants the container to implement. That interface is based on IDispatch, so the container builds an IDispatch interface based on a description in your application's type library.

IPropertyNotifySink is an interface that can tell an OLE container that a property value has changed without the container's knowledge. The container can then do whatever it should do when the specified property has changed.

OLE Controls and the MFC Library

As you may know, a class named CObject is the mother of (almost) all the classes in the Microsoft Foundation Class (MFC) library. The CObject class is the class that implements the basic MFC runtime object. CObject provides MFC applications with important functionalities, including the ability to obtain runtime type information about classes and support for serialization (automatically loading and storing data used by applications).

Control Extensions in the MFC Library

MFC 4.0 contains a new set of *control extensions* that were designed specifically to support OLE controls. These extensions include a new base class named COleControl. In MFC, all OLE controls are derived from the COleControl class.

To support OLE controls, the MFC control extensions do the following:

- They implement a standard set of OLE interfaces required by embedded objects.
- They implement an interface named IDispatch to handle the properties and methods of OLE controls.

- They expose a set of APIs that make it possible for OLE controls and the container sites to communicate.

Figure 6.24 is a diagram of the MFC 4.0 hierarchy. Figure 6.25 shows how the MFC 4.0 class hierarchy is related to the world of OLE.

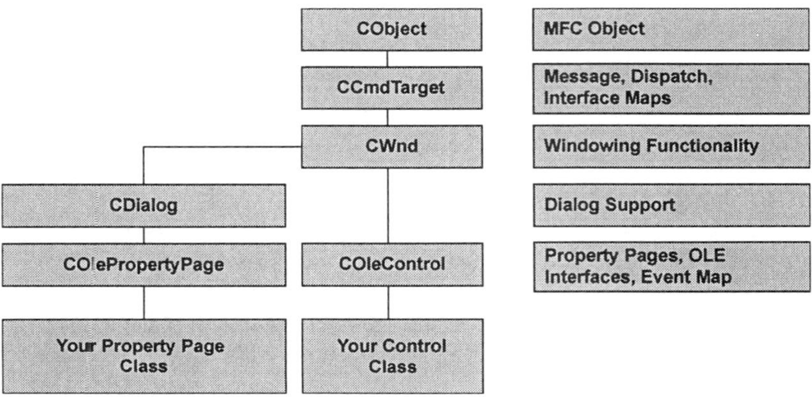

Figure 6.24 The MFC class hierarchy

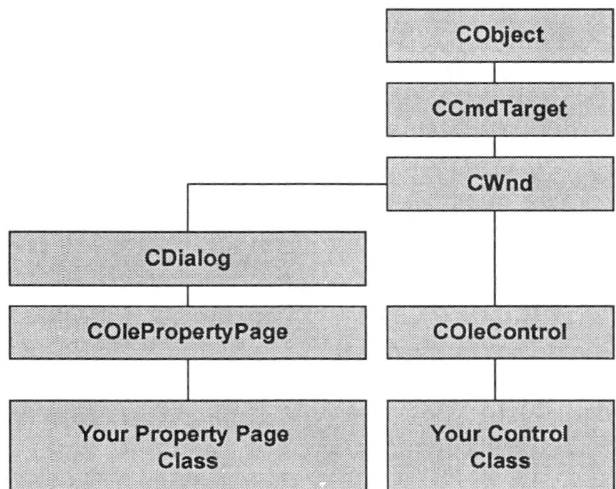

Figure 6.25 The MFC class hierarchy in the world of OLE

The COleControl Class

When you want to create an OLE control, you must derive a class from the COleControl class—which, as noted in the previous section, is derived from CWnd.

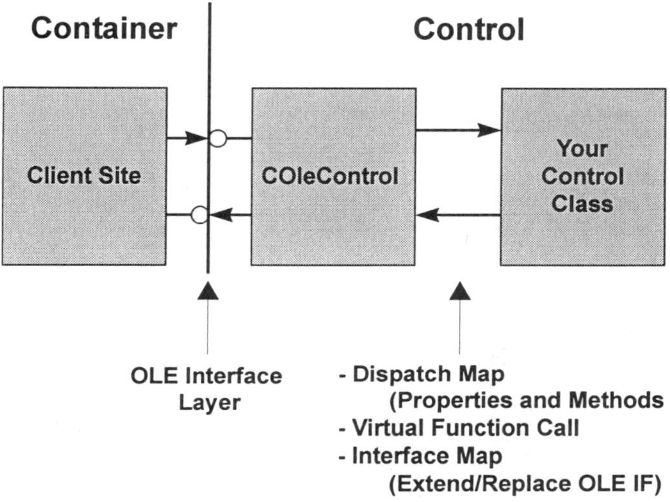

Figure 6.26 Developing an OLE control

The COleControl class implements the standard functionalities required by embedded objects. An embedded object is an OLE object that is created by one application but can be dragged into a document created by another object and edited there. For example, because Microsoft Excel and Microsoft Word have built-in embedded-object capabilities, you can create a chart in Excel and embed it in a document created by Word. OLE controls require this same kind of support because they are visual editable objects.

Figure 6.26 illustrates the process of developing an OLE control.

When you derive a class from COleControl, your class makes use of standard OLE-control mechanisms such as a *dispatch map* (described in "The CCmdTarget Class" on page 274). The COleControl supplies virtual function calls for many of its functionalities so you can override those functionalities and change them if you need to. Specifically, some of the important functionalities supplied by the COleControl class are:

- Implementation of any standard OLE interfaces that an OLE control might require. The COleControl class supports *interface maps* supplied by the Microsoft Foundation Class library, which make it easy to add your own interfaces or other OLE interfaces to your controls. OLE interfaces are described in Chapter 7, "OLE 95."

- Implementation of a *dispatch interface* that can be used to keep track of the properties and methods of available OLE objects so their functionalities can be used as needed. Dispatch interfaces are also described in Chapter 7.
- Exposure of a set of APIs to control container-to-site and site-to-container communication.

The CCmdTarget Class

One class that's important in the world of OLE controls is the CCmd-Target class. CCmdTarget, as you may know, is the base MFC class for all classes of objects that can receive and respond to messages. In MFC, the CCmdTarget class implements *message maps*—the mechanisms through which functions in Visual C++ applications communicate with each other by sending and receiving messages. OLE controls make use of a similar kind of map, called a *dispatch map*.

Dispatch Maps

In a Visual C++ program, when an event takes place in an ordinary Windows custom control) the application receives a WM_COMMAND or WM_NOTIFY message. The application then dispatches that message to an appropriate member function of the control's container through a message map. The function to which a message is mapped in this way is often referred to as a *handler* function. By mapping messages to message handlers, a Visual C++ application calls the appropriate member function each time a WM_COMMAND or WM_NOTIFY message is received.

In OLE-aware applications, objects of the CCmdTarget class also provide *dispatch maps*, which OLE-automation objects (including OLE controls) use in a similar fashion.

In the world of OLE, a dispatch map works much like a message map. When ControlWizard creates an OLE control, or adds an existing control to a project, it automatically creates a dispatch map and inserts it into the application's source code. A dispatch map resembles a message map. It looks like this:

```
BEGIN_DISPATCH_MAP(COleCtrlCtrl, COleControl)
   //{{AFX_DISPATCH_MAP(COleCtrlCtrl)
   // NOTE - ClassWizard will add and remove
    dispatch
   // map entries
   // DO NOT EDIT what you see in these blocks of
   // generated code !
```

```
    //}}AFX_DISPATCH_MAP
    DISP_FUNCTION_ID(COleCtrlCtrl, "AboutBox",
      DISPID_ABOUTBOX, AboutBox, VT_EMPTY, VTS_NONE)
END_DISPATCH_MAP()
```

Using Dispatch Maps

When ControlWizard has inserted a message map into a control's source file, the application using the control can track down the properties and methods of an OLE control when needed.

Once a dispatch map has been created, ControlWizard uses it to define the properties and methods for the OLE objects Each time a new property or method is defined for an OLE object, ControlWizard inserts a macro defining that property or method into your application's dispatch map. Subsequently, when an OLE object with a particular property is needed, your application can use ControlWizard's dispatch maps to track down a CCmdTarget object that implements that property.

The CWnd class, the main window class in MFC, is derived from the CCmdTarget class. And COleControl class, which supplies most of the functionality used by OLE controls, is derived from the CWnd class.

Exploring ControlWizard

The easiest way (and the recommended way) to create an OLE control is to use Visual C++'s GUI (graphical user interface) programming tools: ControlWizard, ClassWizard, and the Developer Studio dialog-box editor.

ControlWizard is a Visual C++ utility for creating the skeleton of an OLE-control DLL. (All OLE controls are implemented in DLLs, or dynamic-link libraries. An OLE-control DLL, you may recall, is by convention a DLL with a file-name extension .OCX.)

ControlWizard is similar to the Visual C++ AppWizard utility—but, instead of generating application frameworks, ControlWizard generates OLE controls.

In this section, you'll get a chance to open ControlWizard and take a look at how its various features work. In Chapter 7, "OLE 95," you'll get an opportunity to create and implement an OLE control using the ControlWizard utility.

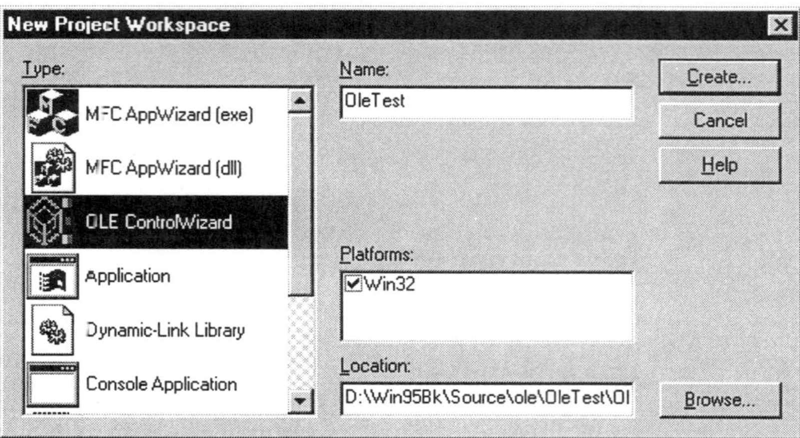

Figure 6.27 Starting ControlWizard

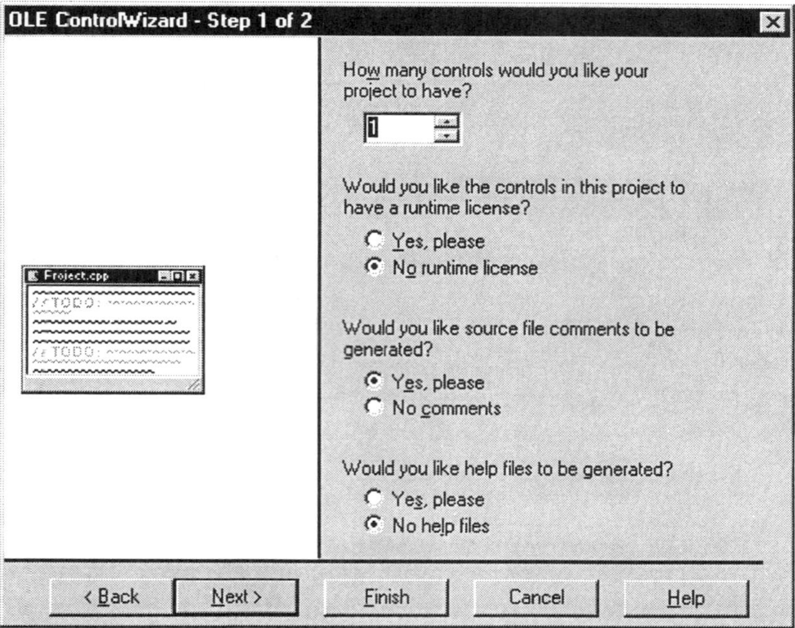

Figure 6.28 The first ControlWizard dialog box

Exploring ControlWizard Step by Step

✔ To open ControlWizard and examine its features, follow these steps:

1. Start Developer Studio if it isn't already running
2. Open the Developer Studio's **File | New** menu item.
3. When the **New** dialog box opens, select the **Project Workspace** item from the **New** list box and click **OK**. Developer Studio then opens a dialog box titled **New Project Workspace** (see Figure 6.27 on page 276).
4. When the **New Project Workspace** dialog box appears, use the **Browse** button to navigate to a folder in which you might want to place an OLE control. Then select the **OLE ControlWizard** icon in the **Type** list box and click **Create**. Developer studio opens the first of two ControlWizard dialog boxes (see Figure 6.28 on page 276).
5. When the ControlWizard dialog box shown in Figure 6.28 on page 276 opens, notice that you can specify how many OLE controls you want to incorporate into your application. You can also click buttons to answer the three other questions in the dialog box. When you click the **Next** button, Developer Studio displays a second ControlWizard dialog box (Figure 6.29).

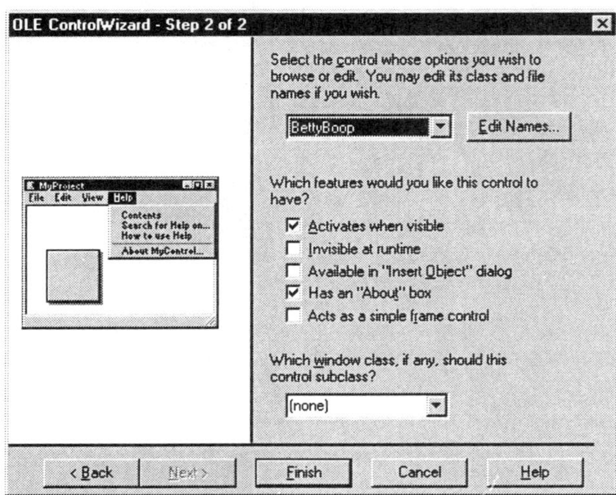

Figure 6.29 The second ControlWizard dialog box

6. When you answer the questions presented in the second Control-Wizard dialog box, you can finish setting up the attributes of your control by clicking the **Finish** button. Developer Studio then

displays an information dialog box. When you click the **OK** button in that dialog box, ControlWizard creates your OLE control. ControlWizard also adds your new control to your Visual C++ Component Gallery automatically.

Putting VBX Wine into OLE Bottles

ControlWizard can construct a shell for an OLE control by reading a Visual Basic (VBX) control and constructing an OLE control skeleton that has the same properties as the VBX control. ControlWizard doesn't copy the VBX control's code—just its properties and signatures. After the new OLE control skeleton is constructed, you have the responsibility of translating the VBX's code into C++ so it can operate as an OLE control.

How ControlWizard Works

Figure 6.26 on page 273 shows what happens when you use Control Wizard to create an OLE control. As you can see, the illustration is divided into two parts—a 16-bit part and a 32-bit part—because Microsoft still supports (for the moment, anyway) the development of 16-bit OLE controls.

Version 1.5 of Visual C++, shown in the left half of the diagram, was the last surviving member of Microsoft's 16-bit compilers when this was written. The right half of the diagram shows what happens when you use Version 2.*x* through Version 4.0 of Visual C++ to develop OLE controls.

Goodbye, CDK; Long Live ControlWizard

In pre-4.0 versions of Visual C++, you had to install a special software package called the Control Development Kit (CDK) before you could create an OLE control. Furthermore, to put it kindly, once you created your control, there was no way to create an application that could use it; that was one minor shortcoming of developing controls with the CDK.

Now that we have Visual C++ 4.0, there is no longer a need for an OLE CDK. Visual C++ has a built-in utility called ControlWizard that can create OLE controls without using any external tools. And that makes the OLE CDK obsolete. You can now create OLE controls—and use them in your applications—without worrying about installing or using the old OLE CDK.

Functionalities Provided by ControlWizard

These are the functionalities that ControlWizard provides for your OLE control:

- An MFC class for your control. When you start ClassWizard, the ClassWizard tool prompts you for a name for your class. ClassWizard then derives your class from COleControl. Your control comes equipped with a set of default methods that you can change to suit your application's requirements.
- A set of message maps, dispatch maps, and event maps for your OLE-control class. Generally, these maps are empty when ClassWizard first creates your control—although you can have ClassWizard set up a dispatch-map entry for a default About box if you want your control to have one.
- A set of stubs that you can fill in with member functions that take care of property access, method access, and other common functionalities. Once your OLE-control class is created, you can fill in these empty member functions with executable code. The code you add will give your control's member functions whatever functionality your application requires.
- Code to register your OLE control in the system registry. The act of registering a control tells the Windows 95 system that the control exists and where it exists. That's what makes it possible for any OLE-aware applications that may be running on the system to find and use your control.
- An object-description-language (ODL) file for your control (ODL is a language that Visual C++ uses internally for dealing with OLE controls. If you're interested in learning more about it, refer to *Inside OLE*, which is listed in the Bibliography).
- A *property page*—that is, a dialog box that you can use to get and set the properties of your OLE control, and to set up the code that is called when your control fires events. As you'll see in Chapter 7, in "Property Pages" on page 316, you can modify this default property page to suit your application's particular requirements.

Files Created by ControlWizard

ControlWizard generates quite a few files when it creates an .OCX DLL. It also generates a README file that lists each file and explains what it does, so there's no need to provide that information here.

It might be helpful, though, to list some of the most important files and to say a little about them:

- YOURCTL.CPP—This is the file that implements the class for your OLE control class, which is derived from COleControl.
- YOURCTL.H and YOURCTL.CPP—These are your DLL's main source files; they are the files that would be the main application files if you were writing an application instead of a DLL. They implement a class which is derived in turn from CWinApp. The SAMPLE.CPP files handles such tasks as self-registration and initialization.
- YOURCTL.H and YOURCTL.PPG—These files define and implement a default property page that ControlWizard generates for your control.
- YOURCTL.ODL—Your control's object-description-language (ODL) file.

Testing and Registering OLE Controls

When you have created an OLE control, you can test it by running the Test Container application supplied with Visual C++ (Figure 6.30). To use the Test Container program, just double-click on the Test Container icon on the Windows 95 desktop or run the Test Container application by executing the **Start | Run** task-bar command.

When the Test Container application starts, you can load any OLE control into the Test Container window by choosing the **Edit | Insert Ole Control** menu command. The specified control then appears in the Test Container window, as shown in Figure 6.30.

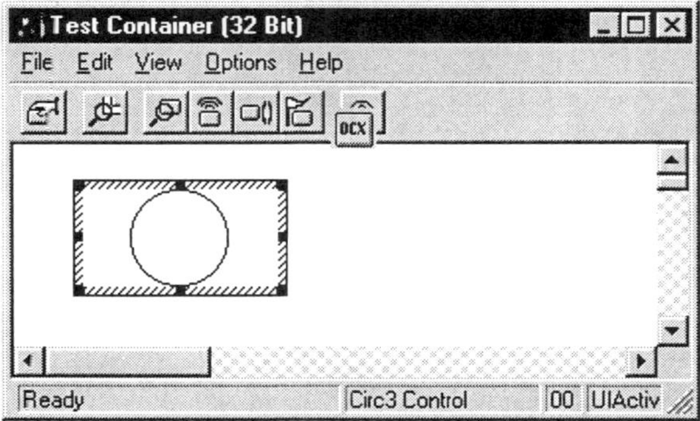

Figure 6.30 Testing an OLE control

The Test Container Application

When you open an control in the Test Container window, you can experiment with the control to see whether it does what you want it to do. You can also drag it around the screen by clicking the mouse button in its hatched border and dragging the mouse. You can size it by dragging its sizing handles, and you can flash its color by clicking the mouse in the circle inside the control.

You can examine the control's properties by choosing the **View | Properties** menu item, and you can view other information about the control and perform other tests on it by choosing other menu commands.

Registering OLE Controls

One of the most important features of the Test Container application is its ability to register OLE controls. Before you can use an OLE control on a particular computer system, you must register it in the system registry (see "The Windows 95 Registry" on page 35).

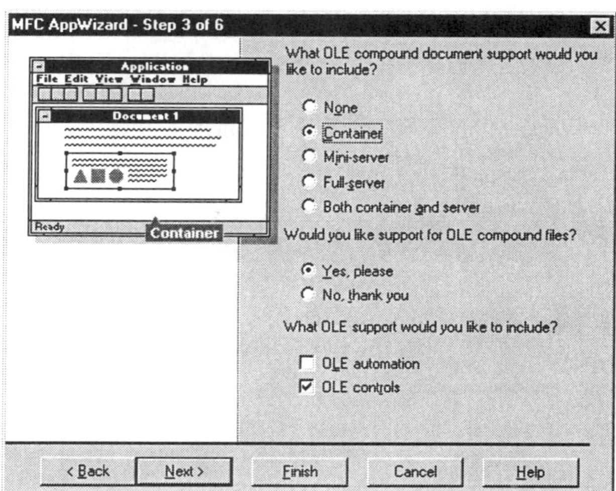

Figure 6.31 Creating an application that supports OLE controls

When you use an OLE control on the same computer system that was used to create it, registration generally is not a problem. That's because ControlWizard takes care of registering new OLE controls automatically. But before you can use an OLE control that has been created on someone else's computer, it must be registered on your computer system.

If an OLE control is not registered on your system automatically—for example, by an installation program—you can use the Test Container application to register the control manually.

Registering a Control Step by Step

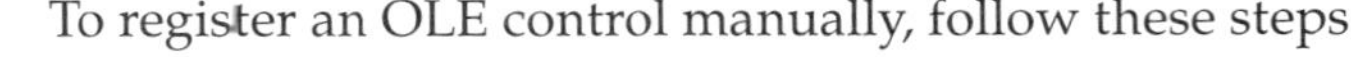

✔ To register an OLE control manually, follow these steps:

1. Open Developer Studio if it isn't already open.
2. Use AppWizard to create an application that is an OLE container and supports OLE controls. To generate an application that meets those specifications, select the **Container** and **OLE controls** buttons when AppWizard displays the dialog box shown in Figure 6.31 on page 281.
3. When AppWizard finishes creating your application, build it by choosing Developer Studio's **Build | Build** menu item.
4. Create a new OLE control for your application (for a review of how to do that, see "Creating an OLE Control" on page 259).
5. From Developer Studio's **Tools** menu, choose **Test Container**. Developer Studio then starts the Test Container application.
6. From the Test Container application's **File** menu, choose **Register Controls.** The **Controls Registry** dialog box then opens (Figure 6.32)

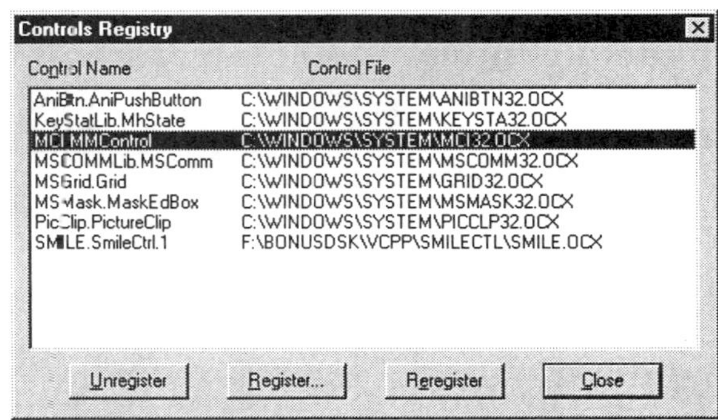

Figure 6.32 Registering an OLE control

7. When the **Controls Registry** dialog box appears, click the **Register** button. The **Register Controls** dialog box then opens (Figure 6.33 on page 283).

8. Navigate to the directory where you have installed an OLE control and select your OLE control.

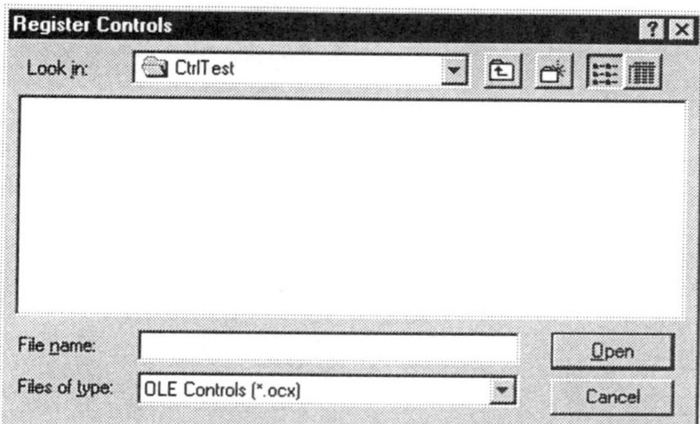

Figure 6.33 The Register Controls dialog box

9. In the filename list box, double-click your OLE control's .OCX filename. Test Container then registers your control and adds it to the list in the Controls Registry dialog box.
10. Close the **Controls Registry** dialog box by clicking the Close button.

You can now use your OLE-control component in any dialog box that supports the use of OLE controls, or in any other control container.

Implementing OLE Controls

One of the most common ways to use OLE controls is in dialog boxes and windows that resemble dialog boxes—that is, windows derived from MFC classes CFormView, CDialogBar, and CPropertyPage. As you will see in this section, implementing an OLE control in a dialog box using the dialog-box editor is not very different from creating any other kind of control interactively.

Adding an OLE Control to Component Gallery

Before you can add an OLE control to a dialog box using the dialog-box editor, you must make the control available to the dialog-box editor's **Controls** toolbar.

The best way to add an OLE control to the dialog-box editor's **Controls** toolbar is to import it from the Visual C++ Component Gallery. Of course, before you can import an OLE component from Component Gallery, you must add it to the Component Gallery. You can do that by following the steps outlined under the heading "Example: Importing a Component" on page 256.

When you add an OLE control to Component Gallery, Developer Studio automatically places an icon representing the control on your the dialog-box editor's **Controls** toolbar. Then you can select the control's icon and place it on a dialog-box template in exactly the same way you would add an ordinary common control to a dialog box using the dialog-box editor.

Adding an OLE Control to a Project Step by Step

✔ To add an OLE-control component to a dialog box, these are the general steps to follow:

1. Start Developer Studio if it isn't already started.
2. Open the Visual C++ dialog-box editor and create a new dialog-box template by.
3. Choose the **Component | Import** item. Developer Studio then opens the **Component Gallery** dialog box.

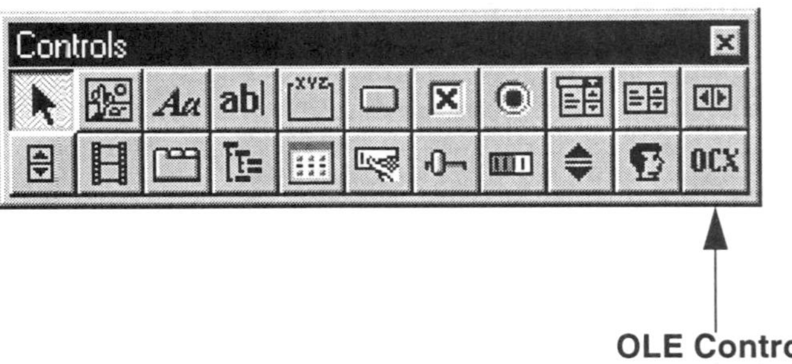

Figure 6.34 Placing an OLE control on the Controls toolbar

4. When the **Component Gallery** dialog box opens, select the control you want to use and click the **Insert** button (or just double-click the desired OLE control). An icon representing the control you have selected then appears on the dialog-box editor's **Controls** toolbar, as shown in Figure 6.34.
5. When you have completed Step 4, you can select the OLE control you have added to the **Controls** toolbar and place it in your dialog-box template in the same way you would implement any dialog-box control.

Example: The COMPGAL Program

The COMPGAL example program, in this chapter's folder on your bonus disk, shows how you can implement an existing OLE control in a Visual C++ application. The COMPGAL application is an SDI (single-document interface) application that was created with AppWizard. When you execute the COMPGAL program and choose the **Smile Dialog** item from the **View** menu, the application displays the dialog box shown in Figure 6.35.

The dialog box in Figure 6.35 face was designed using the Developer Studio dialog-box editor. The yellow face in the dialog box is an OLE control. You can toggle back and forth between a smiling face and a frowning face by clicking the button labeled **Demeanor**. Clicking the **OK** button closes the dialog.

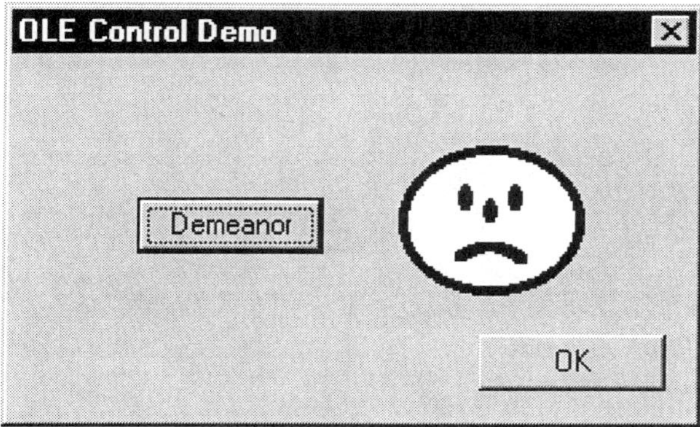

Figure 6.35 The COMPGAL dialog box, featuring an OLE control

Creating an OLE-Control Application

✔ To create a program similar to the COMPGAL application, these are the steps to follow:

1. Open Developer Studio if it isn't already open.
2. Create an AppWizard application that is a control container and supports OLE controls. For details on how to create such an application, see "Registering a Control Step by Step" on page 282. Name your application COMPGAL, and accept AppWizard's defaults for the names of all the program's files.
3. If you haven't done so already, import the smiling-face component named SMILE.OCX into your Component Gallery by

following the steps outlined in "Example: Importing a Component" on page 256.

4. Open the **Component Gallery** dialog box and click the **Import** button.
5. Find the SMILE.OCX control's icon and click the **Insert** button.
6. When the **Confirm Classes** dialog box (Figure 6.36) opens, make sure that only the **CSmile** check box is checked and click the **OK** button.

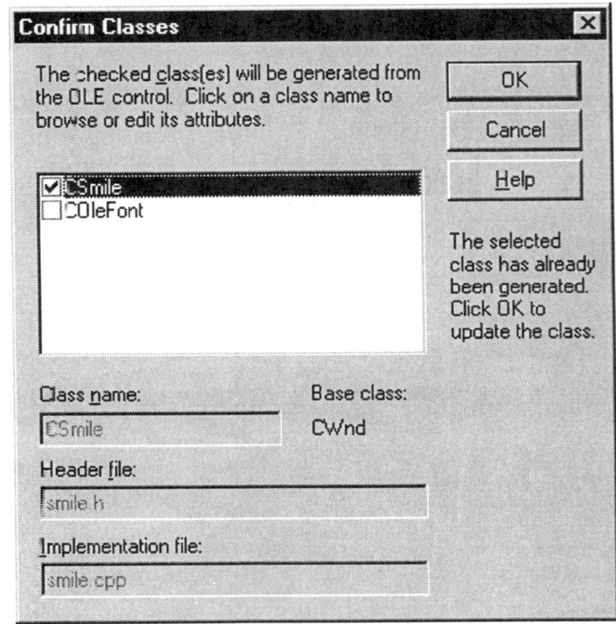

Figure 6.36 The Confirm Classes dialog box

7. When the **Component Gallery** dialog box reappears, close it by clicking its **Close** button.
8. When the Developer Studio windows reclaims the focus, choose the **Insert | Files** into project menu item and add the SMILE.CPP and SMILE.H files to your project. (They're in the SMILECTL folder inside this chapter's folder on your bonus disk.)
9. Open the Test Container application and register the SMILE.OCX component by following the steps presented in "Registering OLE Controls" on page 281.

10. Using the dialog-box editor, add a dialog box to your application.
11. Using ClassWizard, create a class for your dialog box. Name the dialog-box class CSmileDlg, and name the files that define and implement the class SMILEDLG.CPP and SMILEDLG.H.
12. Following the steps outlined in "Adding an OLE Control to Component Gallery" on page 283, add a SMILE.OCX control to your dialog-box template and arrange the controls in your dialog box to resemble those shown in Figure 6.35 on page 285. Notice that the default **Cancel** button has been removed from the template shown in Figure 6.35, and that a button labeled **Demeanor** has been added.
13. Open ClassWizard and assign a pair of member variables named `m_btnSad` and `m_ctrlSmile` to the CButton and CSmile classes, as shown in Figure 6.37.

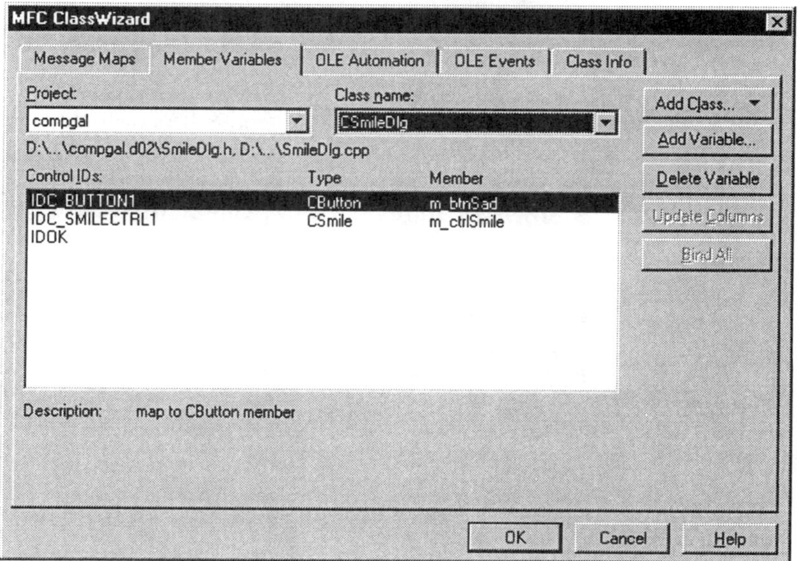

Figure 6.37 Adding member variables to the CSmileDlg class

14. Open the COMPGALVIEW.CPP file and insert the following `#include` directive into the appropriate spot in the file (where all the other `#include` directives are):

```
#include "smiledlg.h"
```

15. Using the Visual C++ menu editor, add an item named **Smile Dialog** to your application's main menu.

16. Using ClassWizard, create the following message-handler function for the **Smile Dialog** menu item in the COMPGALVIEW.CPP file:

```
void CCompgalView::OnViewSmiledialog()
{
   // TODO: Add your command handler code here
   CSmileDlg smileDlg;
   smileDlg.DoModal();
}
```

17. Using ClassWizard, create the following `BN_CLICKED` message handler for the **Demeanor** button in the CSmileDlg dialog box.

```
void CSmileDlg::OnButton1()
{
   if (m_ctrlSmile.GetSad() == TRUE)
      m_ctrlSmile.SetSad(FALSE);
   else m_ctrlSmile.SetSad(TRUE);
}
```

    The preceding procedure is the function that toggles the face in the dialog box between a smile and a frown. The `GetSad` and `SetSad` functions are methods provided in the SMILE.H and SMILE.CPP files, which implement the SMILE.OCX OLE control.

18. When you have completed all the preceding steps, you're ready to try out your application. If you have problems with it, open the COMPGAL application in this chapter's folder on your bonus disk and compare your own work with the example application to find out what went wrong.

Summary

This chapter introduced the Visual C++ 4.0 Component Gallery and showed how Visual C++ 4.0 supports OLE controls. The chapter concluded with a step-by-step tutorial that showed you how you can create and use OLE controls in your own Visual C++ applications.

Chapter 7, "OLE 95," covers OLE controls and control containers in more detail. In Chapter 7, you'll learn how to design your own OLE controls using ControlWizard—a new automated tool designed specifically for creating OLE controls.

Chapter

7

OLE 95

What OLE gives you is something every software manufacturer has been looking for—a way to write programs that don't just contain reusable code, but are actually made up of reusable, mass-producible, interchangeable components

OLE is such an important topic in MFC 4.0 that two chapters of this book have focused almost exclusively on OLE. In Chapter 6, "Windows 95 and Visual C++," you learned how to add existing OLE controls to Component Gallery, how to import existing OLE controls from Component Gallery, and how to implement existing OLE controls into your Visual C++ applications.

In this chapter, you'll learn how to create and implement your own OLE controls, and how to customize them by adding your own properties, methods, and event handlers. You'll also learn how to create and implement property pages that let users retrieve and set the properties of your controls.

OLE, as mentioned once or twice already in this volume, stands for *object linking and embedding*. But people rarely refer to OLE by its full name any more. Instead, the OLE acronym is now used generically to refer to what Microsoft likes to call *system-object technology*.

What that means is that OLE is a technology for creating and managing objects running together in a system. In the future, objects running at the same time on multiple systems will also be able to communicate with each other using OLE. At least that's Microsoft's plan.

And why did Microsoft invent OLE? Because ordinary dynamic-link libraries—which have been the communications links between objects running in systems up to now—have too many limitations in today's world of 32-bit multithreaded programs, network-linked communications, and multiprocessor systems.

Dynamic-link libraries, or DLLs, have been widely used for years in Windows. In fact, Windows itself is implemented as a very large collection of DLLs. And now that the age of OLE has arrived, DLLs will continue to be important. In fact, the mechanism that implements OLE objects is really an enhanced, expanded, and considerably glorified DLL. (In case you need to refresh your memory about DLLs, they're the topic of Chapter 10, "Windows 95 DLLs.")

When you deal with OLE objects, then, what you're really dealing with is objects that reside in turbocharged DLLs. If you're accustomed to working with DLLs, and understand how they work, that news might make you feel a little more comfortable about learning how to work with OLE objects.

About This Chapter

In Chapter 6, "Windows 95 and Visual C++," you learned some fundamental facts about OLE and got a chance to see how OLE automation works by creating and experimenting with an OLE control. In this chapter, you'll learn more about OLE so you'll be better equipped to use it in your Windows 95 applications. In Chapter 6, you learned how to create an OLE control with Developer Studio's ControlWizard tool, and how to implement an OLE control as a component in a Visual C++ application.

This chapter covers OLE controls in a little more detail, and explains how they work together with their containers.

In this chapter, you'll get answers to these questions:

- How does an application create an OLE control? (In this section, "creating" a control will mean instantiating an existing control rather than creating a brand-new one from scratch.)

- When an application has instantiated a control, how can the application use the control? (Hint: It must be treated as a CWnd-derived class; then you can use the same MFC member functions you would use to access and manage any CWnd-derived window.)
- How do OLE controls implement properties and methods?
- How do OLE controls handle events?
- What are ambient properties and how do you use them?
- How can get under the hood and manage an OLE interface directly, without having to use the tools provided by MFC and Visual C++?

The following main topics are covered in this chapter:

About OLE

Welcome back. I'll start where we left off. It's important to remember that OLE is not a technology for writing source code. It's a binary mechanism, not a programming mechanism. To create and implement OLE objects, you don't mess with the underlying binary mechanism. Instead, you communicate with it through OLE *interfaces* (see "OLE Interfaces" on page 298).

In a Visual C++ program, the easiest way to create OLE objects is to use special graphics-based tools provided by Developer Studio—tools such as ControlWizard and ClassWizard. Then you can manipulate the OLE objects you have designed through member functions and message handlers created by AppWizard.

If you don't write your programs with Visual C++ but do use the MFC library, you won't have the benefit of tools such as ControlWizard or ClassWizard, but you can still call MFC member functions to do almost anything you'll ever need to do with OLE objects.

If you develop your programs without using either Visual C++ or AppWizard, life will be much more difficult. Then you'll have to deal with OLE's component objects more directly: by using OLE interfaces to make C-style calls to the OLE API. Things can get pretty hairy if that's what you choose to do, but it is possible.

A Brief History of OLE

When Microsoft first started working on OLE—that would be back around 1989 or so—about the only thing you could do with OLE was create and manage what we now call compound documents. A compound document is a document that can store information from a variety of sources, as illustrated in Figure 7.1.

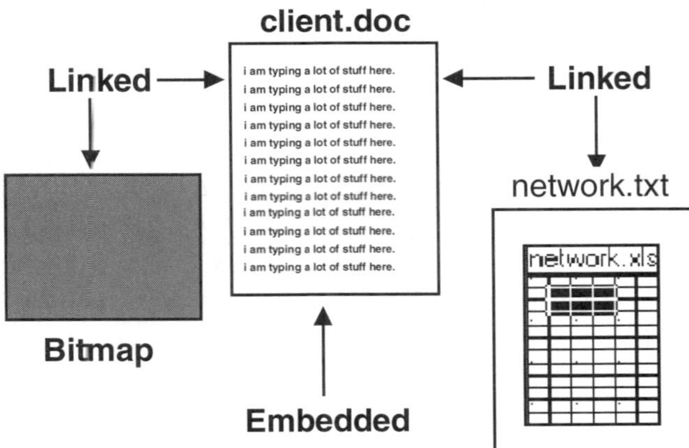

Figure 7.1 How a compound document works

The first big revision of OLE took place in April 1993 with the release of OLE 2. OLE 2 was released to enhance what was already available in OLE 1. But OLE 2 had many new features.

Compound documents—now more widely referred to simply as *OLE documents*—were enhanced to include a feature called *in-place activation*.

When an OLE compound document supports in-place activation, the user can:

1. create an object using any OLE application
2. drag the objects into the OLE compound document
3. edit them inside the OLE compound document, in exactly the way the object would be edited when opened in its native application.

Compound-Document Technology and How It Grew

When Microsoft engineers started working on compound-document technology, they discovered that there were many other features they could create to make compound-document technology work well. So they created a large collection of other supporting technology, such as:

- The *component object model*, or COM—which is now the underlying structure of everything else in OLE. You'll learn more about the component object model in "The Component Object Model" on page 297.
- *Structured storage*—ways to share individual files between different pieces of component software instead of requiring one application manage the entire file itself.
- *Persistence of objects*—In OLE, *persistent* objects are objects that can save and load themselves from disk automatically, without any particular effort on the part of the user. OLE objects can also have persistent *properties*, which are also saved and loaded automatically, along with the objects they belong to.
- *Dragging and dropping*—All the new drag-and-drop capabilities built into Windows 95 are based on OLE. In OLE, dragging and dropping is implemented using a new kind of technology. With this technology, you can very graphically and very directly move information from one place to another using the mouse—instead of using more indirect mechanisms such as the clipboard.
- *Caching of information*—Information caching is an OLE feature that lets you create a compound document, take it to another machine, and view and print it there, even though the application that created the document may not be available on the destination machine.
- New standards for dealing with *data transfers*. With these new standards, you can transfer data quickly and efficiently. With

OLE, applications can make use of information stored on disk and in memory in a very direct way, without using the clipboard. This capability makes it possible to transfer data with better performance and more flexibility than Windows 3.*x* could provide.

- *Monikers*—a uniform naming technology that makes it easier for OLE-aware applications to access objects.
- *OLE automation*—a technology that makes it possible for applications to communicate with each other and to use each other's data, even if the applications are written in different languages. OLE controls are based on *OLE automation*. OLE controls were introduced in Chapter 6, "Windows 95 and Visual C++," and are covered in more detail in this chapter.

What OLE Can Do for You

With OLE, you can develop and implement OLE controls—one of the most important new capabilities built into Visual C++ and the MFC library. When you have created an OLE component, you can stow it away in Component Gallery so you can later reuse it in other applications. You can even protect your components through licensing and can distribute them to other developers for use in their own applications.

What Hath OLE Wrought

Microsoft expects OLE controls to bring about some big changes in the way applications are created, designed, and marketed. With the help of OLE, your company can take two different components that two different people developed at two different times, and put them together at runtime in such a way that they can work together conveniently and efficiently. You can repeat that scenario with as many different components as you like and as many times as you like, confident in the assurance that everything you're putting together will work together properly.

What OLE gives you, in other words, is something that just about every software manufacturer has been looking for—a way to write programs that don't just contain reusable code, but are actually made up of reusable, mass-producible, interchangeable components.

It's Great for Users, Too

OLE also gives the users of your applications some things they may really like. According to customer surveys that Microsoft has conducted, there are three things that users want in the programs they buy:

- They want different programs to be well integrated. They want their word processors, their spreadsheets, and their other programs (such as e-mail) to come together in a meaningful way so they can create more interesting solutions than just working on documents, working on spreadsheets, or sending e-mail.
- They want consistency—not just between the applications they use, but also between the elements that they create using those applications. Consistency in applications saves training costs, providing developers with new ways not only to reuse code, but also to reuse knowledge.
- Finally, according to the results of Microsoft's studies, software users want new features—for example, they want (what a coincidence!) drag-and-drop capabilities, shell extensions, and the ability to view documents without having to open the applications that created the documents.

OLE Today—and Tomorrow

One of the most important characteristics of OLE is that it is an *extensible technology*. Because of its extensibility, OLE offers you is a way to customize your components in any way you like by designing reusable components. OLE also lets you define new interfaces and new component types.

One interesting fact related to all this is that Microsoft does not have to be involved at all in the way you distribute, or even market, your OLE controls. When you develop a new OLE control, you don't have to go to Microsoft and request that a new API to manage your control be added to the system. Instead, you can extend the system yourself by creating new interface and new components as the need for them arises.

As one Microsoft marketer modestly put it in a conference address, a "dream of the computer industry" has finally been realized with the development of OLE. This dream, Microsoft says, is the dream of *component software*.

With OLE, this spokesperson explained, you can take a collection of binary components, put them together, link them up, and wind up with an instant application customized to your exact specifications.

This may not happen for another five or ten years, the engineer said, but he said he is convinced that it will happen, and that "OLE is going to be there to make it work."

Demystifying OLE

Because OLE is such a large and complex technology—and because the only way to make use of it up to now was with some very low-level programming—Microsoft engineers and evangelists have had some difficulty explaining to software developers just what OLE is all about. Consequently, OLE has developed a reputation of being a technology that's difficult to use and even more difficult to understand.

Fortunately, with the new features built into MFC 4.0 and Visual C++ 4.0, it has become much easier to use OLE in your applications. Now, when you build a Visual C++ program using AppWizard, you are provided with many new tools for incorporating various OLE features into your application.

Consequently, you don't have to a thorough understanding of OLE to start using it in your programs. The more you do know about OLE, the better off you are, of course—but thanks to the tools now built into Visual C++ to support OLE programming, the most important thing to know is what OLE can do, not how to write the code that it takes to do it. Now, with the help of MFC 4.0 and Visual C++ 4.0, you can immediately start taking advantage of the OLE features you're interested in, and learn more about the many other capabilities as you go along.

How OLE Works

As mentioned in Chapter 6, "Windows 95 and Visual C++," OLE provides you with a way to write programs that don't just contain reusable code, but are actually made up of reusable, mass-producible, interchangeable components.

To accomplish this kind of intra-process and intra-application communication, OLE has a rich set of technology for dealing with the kinds of information that can be passed between components and how the components can communicate.

Everything in OLE depends on the *component object model*, often abbreviated *COM*. In OLE, the component object model provides the basic plumbing that makes communication between components possible.

The Component Object Model

The *component object model (COM)* is the cornerstone of all OLE operations. The component object model has always been a little difficult to describe because it can be viewed in two ways: as a specification and also as an implementation.

The COM Specification

The specification half of the component object model is a binary standard for implementing Windows objects in a way that is independent of any particular programming language. That means that by adhering to the COM standard, applications can communicate with each other through object-oriented interfaces, even if neither program knows how the other application implements functionalities that the two applications are exchanging information about.

As a specification, the component object model ensures that applications written in different languages can use access and execute the same binary code. As it turns out, this system works so well that 32-bit applications and 16-bit applications really can share binary code if both applications are OLE-aware.

The COM Implementation

In its implementation role, the COM standard defines a component object—that is, an object that complies with the COM standard. Component objects are defined in a special library called the *component object library*.

In an application, a component object is always identified with a unique *class identifier*. When you use a COM object's class identifier in your application, you are provided with a pointer to a table of functions (called an *interface*) that the object implements. Through the pointer you are given, you can call the functions that are accessible through the table. (For more about OLE interfaces, see "OLE Interfaces" on page 298.)

The COM standard, in its implementation role, provides a standard object-creation technique within OLE that is independent of the programming language you are using. With the help of the COM mechanism, your application can access any component object without having to know what executable implements the object (COM objects can be implemented in dynamic link libraries or in .EXE files). Your application is not required to know the location of the component objects it accesses because the component object library handles all communication between COM modules.

Marshaling

When your application implements an OLE control, the component object model makes the control accessible to other applications using a process called *marshaling*—a term used to describe the passing of function calls and parameters across process boundaries.

Because a COM object's code can execute in a process space that is not the one in which it resides, the COM library handles the translation of calling conventions when the object and the routine using the object are written in different languages. The COM library also handles the conversion that's needed to convert back and forth between 16-bit and 32-bit parameters when the object and the routine using the object are running in different process spaces.

For example, if a COM object is executing in a 32-bit process space, it might treat data types such as UINT as 32-bit values. The user of the object might be running in a 16-bit process space and might attempt to call a function in the object by passing a 16-bit UINT as a parameter. The COM library, which sits between the two processes, has the responsibility of marshaling the 16-bit UINT passed as a parameter into a 32-bit UINT that can be processed by the function that receives the parameter.

Other types, such as pointers and memory handles, are handled in a similar fashion by the COM library. The library makes sure that when an OLE object and the user of an object communicate, each sees the other in terms of its own process space.

OLE Interfaces

OLE controls work by using OLE *interfaces*. In the world of OLE, an interface is a mechanism for accessing an OLE object indirectly. Interfaces are important in OLE because when you want to access an OLE object, the only way you can do it is indirectly. That isn't surprising, since the whole reason for using OLE is to let multiple functions and multiple applications access OLE objects at the same time. OLE interfaces are the mechanisms that make that possible.

When an application communicates with an OLE object through an OLE interface, the interface isolates the application from much of the code that implements the object. That is what makes it possible for an application written in one language to communicate with OLE object written in a different language.

OLE interfaces also make it possible for 16-bit and 32-bit objects and applications to communicate with each other. Finally, they make it possible for users of your application to drag a document created with one application into a document created by another application, and to edit the document on the spot, without starting the application that created the document.

The 'I' Word

In OLE, the names of interfaces always begin with I, just as the names of classes begin with C in the Microsoft Foundation Class (MFC) library. For example, there is an IOleObject interface that roughly corresponds to the MFC CObject class. Just as the CObject class is the base class for almost all MFC classes, IOleObject is the base interface for almost all OLE interfaces.

There are many other OLE interfaces, such as IOleDispatch, IOleControl, IOleInPlaceObject, and IOlePersistStorage. You'll learn more about these and other OLE interfaces later in this chapter.

OLE interfaces have many other things in common with MFC classes besides the way they are named. For example, you can instantiate an OLE object using an OLE interface, in much the same way that you instantiate a C++ object from a class. And objects instantiated from OLE interfaces have attributes very similar to member variables, which are called *properties*. They also have attributes that work much like member functions and are called *methods*.

When you have instantiated an OLE object, you can set its properties using member functions—which are called *methods* in OLE. You can also use OLE methods to manipulate OLE objects in many ways—in much the same way that you use member functions to manipulate objects instantiated from C++ classes.

Although you can do all those things by using OLE interfaces—those words that begin with I—the need to access OLE interfaces directly is now slowly fading away. That's because more and more OLE functionalities are being encapsulated into OLE-related classes in the MFC library.

Instantiating OLE Interfaces

To *instantiate* an interface implementation, you use an array of pointers to OLE member functions (or methods). Any application that has access to such an array—generally through a pointer that lets the application access the top of the array—can call the methods in the corresponding interface, as shown in Figure 7.2.

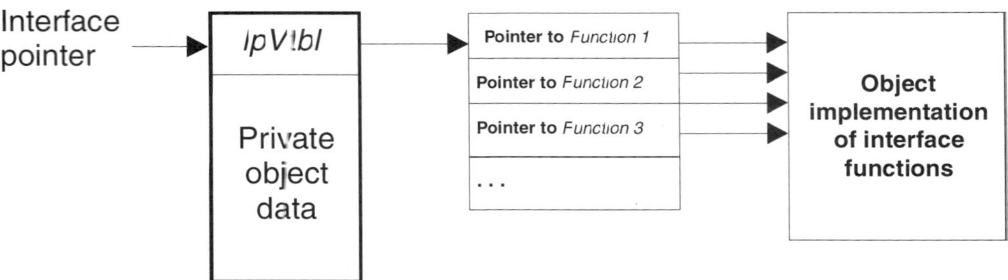

Figure 7.2 How OLE interfaces work

Figure 7.2 illustrates shows how an OLE interface is instantiated as a table of pointers to functions. In OLE, the tables of pointers that instantiate interfaces work much like the V-tables used to access virtual functions in C++.

OLE Controls Revisited

To many software developers, one of the most welcome new features of both MFC 4.0 and Visual C++ 4.0 is their full support for OLE controls and OLE control containers.

OLE controls, as noted back in Chapter 6, are Microsoft's 32-bit successors to VBX controls. OLE controls, like VBX controls, are predesigned objects that you can easily incorporate into any application. But OLE objects have many more built-in features than VBX controls ever had.

One reason OLE controls are a considerable improvement over VBX controls is that OLE controls are based on MFC classes instead of on mechanisms provided by Visual Basic. Consequently, OLE controls enjoy all the functionality of C++ classes in general and MFC classes in particular. And, being OLE objects, they also have all the functionality supplied by the underlying OLE API, such as support for dragging and dropping, support for in-place activation, and a number of other capabilities you were introduced to back in Chapter 6.

In previous versions of MFC, you could create all the OLE controls you wanted, but there was no documented way to use them in your MFC applications. Until MFC 4.0 was introduced, only a few real-world applications, such as Microsoft Excel, supported OLD controls. To put it as kindly as possible, that was something of a limitation to the usefulness of OLE controls.

Now, with the release of MFC 4.0, there is finally a way to use OLE controls in your applications. In fact, as you saw in Chapter 6, implementing OLE controls is now downright easy. With Visual C++ 4.0, you just open ControlWizard and click a few buttons, and presto! ControlWizard creates an OLE control.

What Is an OLE Control?

One reason OLE controls have gained a reputation of being hard to understand is that they can be described in so many different ways. You could say that an OLE control is any of these things:

- A custom control that is based on the OLE model.
- The 32-bit replacement for the old 16-bit VBX custom control model.
- An in-place active, or "visual editing" server. That means an OLE control can be edited in any container, without the need for a separate top-level window that is activated when the user activates the control.
- An in-process server—that is, a control that is implemented as a DLL and runs in the same address space as the containing process. (There are some OLE controls that don't fit this description, but they are rare and won't be covered in this chapter.)
- An OLE object that supports OLE automation. This means that an OLE control can have properties and methods that an external entity like a container can invoke to examine property values, set property values, and cause methods to be executed.
- A control that uses the standard OLE automation dispatcher—the IDispatch interface—and follows all the other rules for any OLE automation server.

OLE and the CWnd Class

To make all this magic possible, the developers of MFC 4.0 have built a lot of new functionality into the CWnd class, the main MFC class for creating and managing windows and other CWnd-derived objects. This new code can almost magically turn CWnd objects into containers for OLE controls. And, because MFC now does most OLE-related work automatically, you OLE controls have become remarkably easy to create and implement.

When you want a window (or some other Windows object) to serve as a container for an OLE control, all you have to do is instantiate or derive an object from the CWnd class. That object can then serve as a container for OLE control, and no more work on your part is necessary.

A Word about Objects

In the preceding paragraph, you may notice that two different kinds of objects are mentioned: Windows objects and C++ objects. These two kinds of objects are very different Windows objects are programming entities that Windows developers have been working with since the dawn cf the Windows era. C++ objects have only been around since the invention of C++. If you're uncertain what the differences are between Windows objects and C++ objects, you may need the assistnace of a basic book on Windows programming (*Programming Windows 3.1* by Charles Petzold is the recognized classic) or a good book cn C++. Several of those are listed in the Bibliography.

Because a CWnd object can serve as a container for OLE controls, MFC objects derived from the CWnd class can serve as OLE containers, too. Objects derived from CWnd include views (CView objects), form views (CFormView objects), dialog bars, control bars, and many other kinds of CWnd objects. That means that any kind of window or CWnd-derived object used in Windows 95 now has all the functionality it needs to serve as an OLE control container.

OLE Objects and the CWnd Class

It's important to remember that there is no special MFC class for OLE controls. You won't find a COleControl class, or anything similar, in the MFC library. That's because OLE controls are derived from CWnd or from CWnd-derived classes, not from any special OLE-control class. Any CWnd or CWnd-derived object can serve as an OLE control, as well as an OLE control container.

There is a difference, however, in the way a CWnd object is used as a control and the way a CWnd object is used as a control container. The difference is that every CWnd object has all the built-in functionality it needs to serve as an OLE control container. But if you want a CWnd object to serve as an OLE control, you must add OLE control support to the object yourself. You do that by calling the MFC library's OLE-related member functions, which are described later in this chapter.

If you write your Windows programs using Visual C++, creating OLE object containers gets even easier: Just generate your application using AppWizard, and support for OLE controls and control containers is automatically built in. You saw how that works back in Chapter 6, and you'll read more about it later in this chapter.

Windows Styles Used by OLE Controls

OLE controls rely on only a small subset of the predefined constants that are used to set CWnd styles. The style constants used by OLE controls are:

- WS_VISIBLE—Makes a control visible when its containing window becomes visible.
- WS_GROUP—Specifies that an OLE control in a dialog box is a member of a group of controls, such as a group of radio buttons.
- WS_TABSTOP—Specifies what should happen when the user selects an OLE control inside a dialog box and presses the tab key or an arrow key.
- WS_DEFPUSHBUTTON—Applies to a OLE-control button inside a dialog box; identifies the dialog-box button that corresponds to the **Return** key.
- WS_DISABLED—Specifies that a control is disabled.
- WS_BORDER—Sets an OLE control's border-style property, if there is one.

Creating OLE Controls Dynamically

MFC 4.0 offers two methods for creating OLE controls: dynamic creation and design-time creation. In Chapter 6, "Windows 95 and Visual C++," you learned how to create an OLE at design time by using ControlWizard. In the hands-on exercises at the end of this chapter, you'll learn more about creating and customizing OLE controls using ClassWizard.

The easiest way to create and design OLE controls is with AppWizard. But there is no law that says you have to use ClassWizard to create and implement OLE controls. You can also create OLE controls dynamically—that is, at runtime.

Creating an OLE control at runtime is not very different from creating any other CWnd-derived object. All you have to do is instantiate your control by calling its constructor, and then calling an MFC member function named **`CWnd::CreateControl`**.

The **`CWnd::CreateControl`** function works much like the **`CWnd::-Create`** member function that creates ordinary windows. The only difference between calling **`CWnd::CreateControl`** and calling

CWnd::Create is that **CWnd::CreateControl** expects a slightly different set of parameters. **CWnd::CreateControl** takes a class ID (expressed as a string or a number) as its first parameter, while **CWnd::Create** takes a string called a *ProcID*. **CWnd::CreateControl** also takes some optional additional parameters.

How the *CreateControl* Member Function Works

The **CWnd::CreateControl** member function creates an OLE control that your MFC application sees as a CWnd object. **CreateControl** is a direct analogue of the **CWnd::Create** member function; it just creates an OLE control instead of an ordinary window.

Listing 7.1 is an example of a call to **CWnd::CreateControl.**

Listing 7.1 Creating an OLE Control

```
int CMyContainer::OnCreate(LPCREATESTRUCT
    lpCreateStruct)
{
   if (CWnd::OnCreate(lpCreateStruct) == -1)
      return -1;

   m_wndMyControl.CreateControl(
      _T("SAMPLE.Sampl trl.1"),
      _T("Option 1"),
      WS_VISIBLE,
      CRect(50, 50, 200, 100),
      this,
      IDC_MYCONTROL);

   return 0;
}
```

The first parameter of the **CWnd::CreateControl** member function shown in Listing 7.1 is a *class ID*—that is, a string representing the class of the control to be created.

_T("SAMPLE.SampleCtrl.1")

In a call to **CWnd::CreateControl**, this class ID parameter can take three forms:

- a string that identifies an OLE control (called a ProgID)
- a formatted 128-bit numeric OLE ID called a GUID
- 128-bit OLE identifier used in its raw form.

When you pass **CreateControl** a string representing the class of the control to be created, the string may be either an OLE *ProgID*—that is, a string with the form **"SAMPLE.SampleCtrl.1"**—or a GUID, which is the string form of a 128-bit OLE class ID formatted and enclosed in braces—for example, "**{01234567-0123-0123-0123-0123456789ab}**".

A Non-Technical Note

The 128-bit number used to identify an OLE control is a number that is guaranteed to be unique. An explanation of how it is generated would take up too much space and would be too boring to discuss any further here. For more information about GUIDs and unique OLE ID numbers, see Books Online.

The rest of the **CWnd::CreateControl** parameters shown in Listing 7.1 are just like those passed to the **CWnd::Create** member function. In addition, there are some optional **CWnd::-CreateControl** parameters that are not shown. These optional parameters are related to the licensing of OLE controls and to *object persistence.* Object persistence is a feature that allows an OLE control to save its current state to disk, and to retrieve its last saved state the next time it is loaded.

Figure 7.3 shows what happens when an application executes **CWnd::CreateControl**.

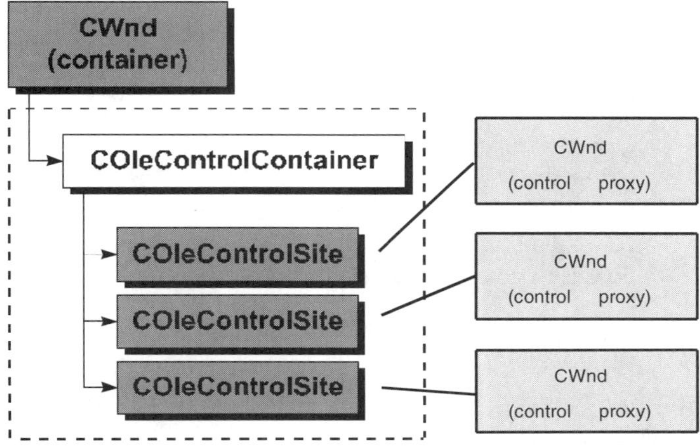

Figure 7.3 An inside view of the CreateControl function

Control Proxies

One important characteristic of the arrangement shown in Figure 7.3 is that the rectangle labeled CWnd at the top of the diagram is not exactly what it appears to be. It is not a real window, but is what is sometimes called a *control proxy*.

Although you might conclude from the diagram that the COleControlContainer object shown in the picture is derived from the CWnd class, that is really not the case. Actually, the COleControlContainer object shown in the illustration is derived from a kind of phony, or *proxy*, CWnd object.

A proxy CWnd object looks just like a real CWnd object to most of your application, but it is actually a stand-in for a real CWnd object. The OLE API supplies this imitation CWnd object and actually derives OLE objects from it.

From an OLE control's point of view, this proxy CWnd object acts like a real CWnd object, and can do anything that a real CWnd object can do. Nonetheless, it's really a proxy CWnd object that's available only to—and used only by—OLE controls.

The proxy CWnd class is designed to provide OLE controls with special functionalities that are different from those of an ordinary CWnd object. That's because OLE objects sometimes work better if they do certain things different from the way they're done by other kinds of CWnd objects.

So, during the development of the OLE-related classes and member functions provided by MFC 4.0, many CWnd-related functions that worked just fine with ordinary CWnd-derived objects were rewritten for OLE.

One reason this is true is that not all OLE objects are implemented using the MFC library. If a developer creates an OLE control without the aid of the MFC library, the MFC library is not available to the control—so the control has no way to access a real MFC CWnd object. So OLE provides a proxy CWnd object of its own.

Overloading *CreateControl*

Because the first parameter passed to **CWnd::CreateControl** can be either a string or a number, there are two versions of the **CWnd::CreateControl** function:

```
BOOL CreateControl( REFCLSID clsid, LPCTSTR
   pszWindowName, DWORD dwStyle, const RECT& rect,
   CWnd* pParentWnd, UINT nID, CFile* pPersist =
   NULL );
BOOL CreateControl( LPCTSTR pszClass, LPCTSTR
   pszWindowName, DWORD dwStyle, const RECT& rect,
   CWnd* pParentWnd, UINT nID, CFile* pPersist =
   NULL );
```

The rest of the parameters you can pass to **CWnd::CreateControl** are:

- *clsid*—A reference to the class ID of the control
- *pszWindowName*—A pointer to a string containing the window name.
- *dwStyle*—Specifies the control's style. You can apply any combination of window styles to the control.
- *rect* —Specifies the control's size and position. The *rect* parameter can be either a CRect object or a RECT structure.
- *pParentWnd*—Specifies the control's parent window, usually a CDialog. This parameter must not be **NULL**.
- *nID*—Specifies the control's ID.
- *pPersist* —A pointer to a CFile containing the persistent state for the control.

Implementing and Instantiating OLE Controls

Referring back to Figure 7.3 on Page 305, notice that one COleControl-Container object is derived from the proxy CWnd object shown at the top of the diagram, and that the COleControlContainer object is the parent of three COleControlSite objects.

Why are there three COleControlSite objects? Because the diagram illustrates the implementation of three OLE controls. And there is one COleControlSite object for each control.

Instantiating OLE Controls

In Figure 7.3, those three objects are surrounded by a dotted line. If you work with OLE objects using MFC and Visual C++, you'll rarely, if ever, have to be concerned with the details of how the objects inside that dotted line are implemented in the OLE API. But they are where everything actually happens when you create an OLE control using MFC, so we'll take a closer look at them now.

Instantiating a Control Site

Assume that an application implementing the architecture shown in Figure 7.4 has started executing. As soon as there is a request to create a control, a COleControlSite object is instantiated, along with its OLE-control sites.

As soon as an instance of the next the next OLE control is created, the second control's COleControlSite object is instantiated. Finally, when a third control is created, the third COleControlSite is instantiated.

At that point, the architecture that implements the application's OLE controls looks like the architecture shown earlier in Figure 7.4.

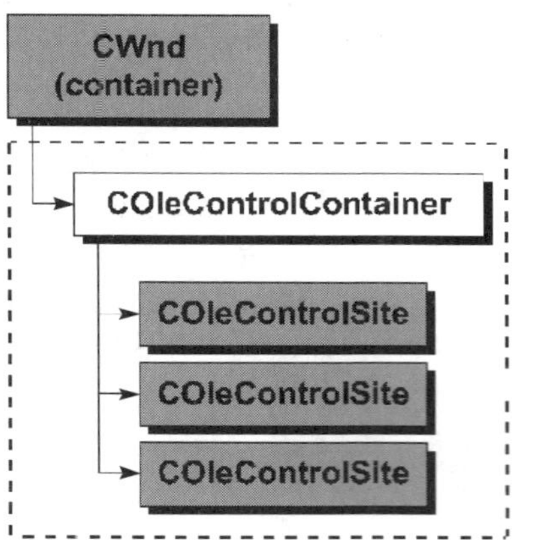

Figure 7.4 Instantiating an OLE control

New CWnd Member Functions

Along with changing some CWnd member functions to make them get along better with OLE, the OLE designers created a number of completely new CWnd member functions designed specifically for use with OLE..

Three of these new member functions are **`CWnd::SetProperty`**, **`CWnd::GetProperty`**, and **`CWnd::InvokeHelper`**. As you might expect, **`SetProperty`** and **`GetProperty`** are member functions for setting and getting properties of OLE controls. **`InvokeHelper`** is a helper function for invoking methods.

Two CWnd member functions that have been rewritten for OLE are **`CWnd::MoveWindow`** and **`CWnd::ShowWindow`**. Both those functions are typically performed on child windows, and the OLE team had to rewrite both of them so they'd work well with OLE controls.

Why? To answer that question, consider the **`MoveWindow`** member function. When the user of an application drags an OLE control with a mouse, the application can't just grab the control's HWND handle and move it. That's because the code that implements an OLE control expects to receive certain kinds of OLE requests from the control that is about to be moved.

If the code that implements an OLE control doesn't receive the kinds of OLE requests it requires, it may not be aware of the fact that the control has been moved. At that point, some parts of the application may have received notifications that a control has moved, while other parts of the program may not have received such notifications. And that could a recipe for disaster.

OLE-Control Events

You learned in Chapter 6 that OLE controls have properties and methods. Later in this chapter (in "OLE-Control Events" on page 309), you'll learn about another important attribute of OLE controls: the ability to *fire events*.

In OLE-control terminology, an *event* is a message that a control sends back to its container when something it considers significant has happened; for example, when a mouse button has been clicked over the control.

An OLE control is capable of firing evens that go back from the control to its container to inform the container when things have happened. This capability closes a communication loop that would otherwise exist; it gives you full two-way communication between the control and its container.

For example, a control might fire an event when:

- The user clicks on the control with a mouse
- A timer expires, meaning it's time for your application to take some action
- The control's container needs to be informed that some property of the control has changed its value.

The ability to fire events is one of the most important capabilities of an OLE control. Events are what make user control over OLE controls.

How OLE Controls Handle Events

When you need to send messages to controls, MFC provides many member functions to help you out. A trickier problem is how to get messages back from a control. In a Windows 95 application that implements OLE controls, the way you do that is with something called an *event sink map*.

Where did that name come from? Microsoft soothsayers explain that some anonymous physics major thought it up. If controls are sources for events, this engineer reason, then containers must be *sinks* for events. You can accept that or look it up—your call.

Event Sink Maps

An *event sink map* is similar to a dispatch map—which is, in turn, similar to a message map (as mentioned in "The CCmdTarget Class" back on page 274).

In case you need a short refresher course on message maps, here's a brief review: In a Visual C++ application, when events take place in an ordinary Windows custom control (to be distinguished from a Windows OLE control), the application receives a WM_COMMAND or WM_NOTIFY message and maps that message through a table to some member function of the control's container.

In that way, the appropriate member function is called each time a WM_COMMAND or WM_NOTIFY message is received. The function to which a message is mapped in this way is often referred to as a *handler* function.

How Event Sink Maps Work

An event sink map works in a similar way. It contains one entry for each handled event. If a container contains multiple controls, one event sink map can handle all of them. This is what an event sink map looks like in a Visual C++ program:

```
BEGIN_EVENTSINK_MAP(CMyContainer, CWnd)
   EVENTSINK_EVENT(
   CMyContainer, // container class
   IDC_SOMECONTROL,// control ID
   DISPID_CLICK, // event ID
   OnSomeControlClick,// handler
   function
   VTS_NONE)     // parameter types
END EVENTSINKMAP()
```

As you can see, the first entry in an event sink map is the name of the container class that contains the appropriate OLE control. The second parameter is the control's ID.

Handling Property Notifications

When an OLE control needs to notify its container (or your application) that the value of one of its properties has changed, it send out a *property notification*. Property notifications are handled using the same mechanism that events use—the event sink map. When you create an OLE control, you can set up its properties to notify their control's container whenever their value changes—or even before their value changes, if that is what your application requires.

When you use an event sink map to handle property notifications, you have to use a few event-map entries that are different from those used for events. Event-map entries for property notifications process the notifications and map them into additional handler functions in your container class.

Handling Ranges of Controls

Event sink maps support *ranges* of controls. To illustrate, suppose your application uses a dialog box that contains a group of radio buttons. Also suppose you want the same function invoked when any button in the group is clicked. That could be the case if you want to handle the buttons using, for example, a case statement.

In a situation such as this, you can set up an entry in an event sink map that is sensitive to control IDs within a certain range. In this way, any button with an ID in the specified range is clicked, the same member function can be called. That can save you from having to write redundant code in your applications.

How Event Sink Maps Route Events

In an event sink map, events are routed just as commands are in an ordinary message map. In a Visual C++ program, if a message dispatched by a control is not handled by its first recipient—typically the direct container of the control—the message is routed to various other objects in the application so they can get a chance to determine whether they can handle the message or not.

Events are routed in exactly the same way in an event sink map. That means you can put the handler for an event where it makes the most sense in your application's structure. If you are accustomed to using message maps in Visual C++ applications, there is nothing new to learn here. In fact, event sink maps use the same code that message maps have used all along in Visual C++ applications.

Properties of OLE Controls

As noted in "OLE-Control Properties" on page 262, OLE controls can have four kinds of properties: stock properties, ambient properties, extended properties, and custom properties.

Stock Properties

A *stock property* is one that ControlWizard implements when it creates an OLE control. A stock property is a standard property whose semantics are predefined. When you implement a stock property, what you get is its predefined implementation, which is built in.

Ambient Properties

Ambient properties are values that an OLE control can obtain from its container. They enable the control to fit in with its ambient surroundings. For example, when an OLE control is implemented inside a dialog box, it might be desirable for the control use the same font that's being used by other controls in the dialog box.

The easiest way to handle such a situation is to make the font being used in the dialog box a property of the control's container—which is the dialog box—instead of making the font a property of the control. When an OLE control uses a property of its container, rather than a property of its own, the control is said to be using an *ambient property*.

Colors, locale information, and language information are other examples of properties that often work best when they are implemented as ambient properties.

In an MFC application, most common ambient properties are automatically handled by the COleControlContainer class—which, as you may recall, is instantiated when the programplaces the first OLE control in a control container.

The OLE API provides default values for all ambient properties that an OLE control typically requires. Those properties are initialized with values that the OLE API considers appropriate in most situations. For example, the font that an OLE control uses is an ambient property that is retrieved from its container object with a WM_GETFONT message. Similarly, an OLE control's foreground and background colors are retrieved from its container object with the appropriate Windows messages.

When you need to override a default ambient property of an OLE control, you can call the **OnAmbientProperty** member function, which lets you define an ambient property in whatever way you like. A typical **OnAmbientProperty** member function looks like this:

```
BOOL CMyContainer::OnAmbientProperty(COleControlSite*
   pSite, DISPID dispid, VARIANT *pvar)
{
   switch(dispid) {
      // Handle overridden ambient properties here.
      default:
         return Cwnd::OnAmbientProperty(pSite, dispid,
            pvar);
   }
}
```

By calling the **OnAmbientProperty** member function, you can override an ambient property of an OLE control in whatever way you want. **OnAmbientProperty** can accept a request to override any ambient property. It returns a Boolean value that you can use in any way that's appropriate in your application.

Extended Properties

An *extended property* is a property that appears to the user to be owned by an OLE control, but is actually a property of the control's container. Properties of a control such as left, right, and tab position—which determine the position of a control in a window—are often maintained by a container rather than a control. So it is sometimes convenient to implement such properties as extended properties owned by the container but used by the control.

Custom Properties

A *custom property* is one that you write and define. You determine the name, the parameter types, and the return value of a custom property—as well as determining what it actually does.

OLE-Control Methods

OLE controls, unlike ordinary dialog-box controls, can be equipped with member functions called *methods*. These are some of the methods you typically must modify to add useful functionality to an OLE control:

- An **OnDraw** method that draws your control on the screen. When you create an OLE control, it has a default **OnDraw** function that draws an ellipse. Your mission, if you choose to accept it, is to delete the line in ControlWizard's source code that says **`Ellipse`**, and to substitute whatever **`OnDraw`** function you want your control to use.

- A **`DoPropExchange`** method that moves move your control's properties and methods between the control and its container in a persistent fashion. A property is said to be persistent when it can save its state when the user quits your application and can restore its state when your application starts up again. To make a proprety persistent, you must place some code that makes that possible in the **`DoPropExchange`** function.
- A set of Get and Set (or Notify) method for properties.
- Implementations of any methods that your control will execute.
- Any Windows message handlers that your control requires (you use ClassWizard for this).
- Code to fire any events that you want your code to fire.

Properties, Methods, and Events

In OLE, as in the real world, properties are *attributes*—something that all objects have. In the real world, if your car is blue, you could say that your car has a property that defines its color, and you could call that property *color*.

To change your car's color property from blue to yellow, you could paint your car. But changing a property of an OLE control is usually a little easier. To change a blue control to a yellow control, all you have to do is change its color property.

OLE-Control Properties

Properties of OLE controls can be implemented in two different ways:

- A default property of an OLE control is called a *stock property*. When you equip an OLE control with a stock property, MFC takes care of setting the value of the property to a commonly used value.
- A property that you implement for a control you create is called a *custom property*.

Implementing Custom and Stock Properties

When you have created an OLE control, you can use ClassWizard to provide it with both stock properties and custom properties. In the implementation of an OLE control, a custom property works much like a member variable of a C++ class; it's simply a variable that holds a value that represents a particular property.

When you equip an OLE control with a custom property, you can change the property's value by setting the value of its corresponding member variable. Similarly, you can retrieve the property's value by getting the value of its corresponding member variable.

A custom property in an OLE control has one annoying shortcoming: It can be difficult to determine out when its value has been changed. So MFC provides a *notification function* called **OnPropertyChanged** that can tell you when a property of an OLE control has changed. The **OnPropertyChanged** function is called whenever the property of an OLE control has changed.

Adding Parameters to Properties

You can also add parameters to properties. If you want a property to behave like an array—which might be the case if there is an array of radio buttons inside a control—you can create a single property that behaves like an array, returning a value that can uniquely identify any object in the array.

OLE-Control Events

An *event* is a notification that a control sends to its container to notify the container that something has happened. Some events are predefined for all OLE controls, but others are completely arbitrary—you and your application are free to determine what they are. To the built-in events that are provided to all OLE controls, you can add events of your own as you see fit.

You can use ClassWizard to provide OLE controls with *event handlers,* in much the same way you use ClassWizard to create message handlers for class member functions. You'll learn how to provide OLE controls with event handlers using ClassWizard in "Example: Creating Event Handlers for OLE Controls" on page 336.

OLE-Control Methods

A *method* is a request that is sent to an OLE control when the control is to perform a specific action. For example, an application can use a method to ask a control to save its state in a database, to close down a program, or to perform other kinds of actions.

MFC also provides Get and Set methods that an application can use to retrieve and set properties of OLE objects. When you use ClassWizard to set up a control's properties, the ClassWizard utility provides you with two functions: one to get the value of the property and one to set the value of the property. You can fill in these Get and Set methods with the code that is required to provide access to the values of your control's properties.

If you like, you can write a Set method in such a way that it validates your control's Set method, allowing the user to input only values that fall within a particular range.

Property Pages

A *property page* is a GUI (graphical user interface) tool you can use to change a control's properties. An OLE control is not required to have a property page. But if a control does have a property page, the property page should adhere to certain standards. The most important standard is to implement your control's property page as a tabbed page inside a *property sheet*, or tabbed dialog box.

MFC 4.0 provides considerable support for writing property pages for OLE controls. This support includes blank property pages that you can customize to suit your own needs and stock property pages that require you only to fill in some blanks.

There are three stock property pages: one to set a control's colors, one to set its fonts, and one to select pictures that will be used to draw the control.

You'll learn how to create property pages for OLE controls in "Property Sheets and Property Pages" on page 323.

Adding Properties and Methods to OLE Controls

In Chapter 6, in the section headed "Example: The COMPGAL Program" on page 285, you learned how to create and implement an OLE control. In this section, you'll learn how to customize your OLE controls by adding properties, methods, and events.

When you have created a control, there are two ways to customize it. One way to provide this kind of extra functionality is to equip your control with methods and properties interactively, using ClassWizard. The other way is to add properties and methods programmatically—that is, to write any special code that may be needed to customize your control in ways that ClassWizard is not able to handle.

The easiest way to customize an OLE control is to start off by using ClassWizard. Then, if it becomes necessary, you can add customized code to provide functionalities that are beyond the reach of ClassWizard.

Customizing OLE Controls with ClassWizard

In Visual C++ 4.0, ClassWizard has been equipped with a number of extensions that are designed especially for use with OLE controls. These special ClassWizard extensions make it as easy to create methods and properties for OLE controls as it is to equip ordinary controls with message handlers and member variables.

This chapter's sample program, named OLEPROG, shows how to create an OLE control, place it in a dialog box, and customize it using ClassWizard.

The OLE control that the program creates is implemented its own separate project, which is named OLETEST.

You can use ClassWizard to connect the OLEPROG application with OLE control implemented in the OLETEST project.

Figure 7.5 The OLEPROG application's dialog box

Using OLE Controls

When you have created an OLE control, how do you use it?

Before the introduction of Version 4.0 of the Microsoft Foundation Class library, that was a real problem. Now, finally, that problem is solved. At last, thanks to some new capabilities built into MFC 4.0, when you implement an OLE control in a Visual C++ application, it just works.

One reason it just works is that Visual C++ is equipped the proxy CWnd class described in "Control Proxies" on page 306. This proxy class is equipped with enough features to meet the needs of just about any kind of OLE control.

Example: The OLEPROG Application

Like the COMPGAL application presented in Chapter 6, OLEPROG is a single-document interface (SDI) program that displays a dialog box when you choose a special View menu item. When you run the OLEPROG application, you can open the program's dialog box by choosing the **View | OLE** Dialog menu item. The program then displays the dialog box shown in Figure 7.5 on Page 317.

Running a the OLEPROG Application

✔ Before you start examining the source code of this chapter's example programs, you might want to run the finished version of the OLEPROG program to see how it works. To execute the program, follow these steps:

1. Open Developer Studio if it isn't already open.
2. Open the OLE_02\OLETEST folder inside this chapter's folder on your bonus disk and build the OLETEST project.
3. Open the OLE_02\OLEPROG folder and build the OLEPROG project.
4. Run the OLEPROG application and choose the View | OLE Dialog menu item. The program then displays the dialog box shown in Figure 7.5.

How the OLEPROG Program Works

✔ To examine the OLEPROG and OLETEST projects and see how they work, follow these steps:

1. Open the OLE_02\OLETEST folder again and start ClassWizard. When the ClassWizard property sheet opens, notice that it contains two OLE-related tabbed property pages: one labeled **OLE Automation** and one labeled **OLE Events** (see Figure 7.6 on Page 319).

2. Tab to the **OLE Automation** property sheet, as shown in Figure 7.6. Notice that it is equipped with two OLE-related buttons: one labeled **Add Method** and the other labeled **Add Property**.

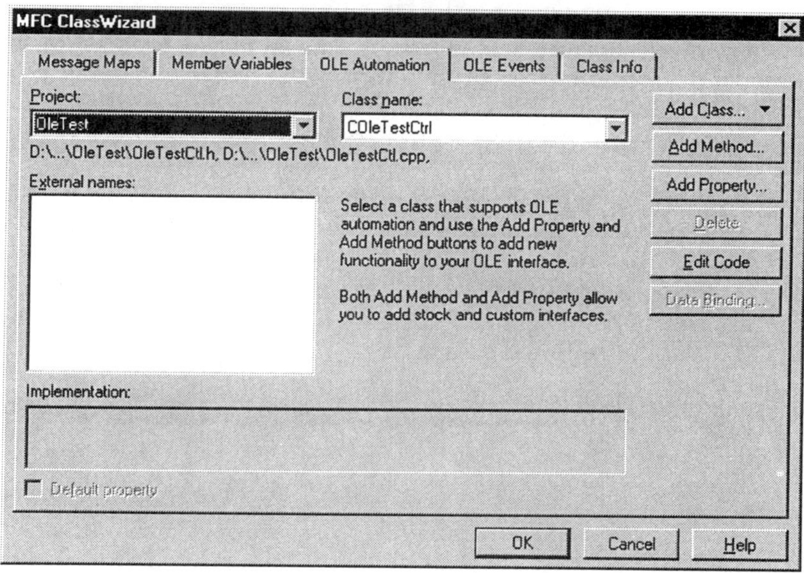

Figure 7.6 The OLE Automation property sheet

3. Click the **Add Method** button. ClassWizard opens another dialog box titled **Add Method** (Figure 7.7 on Page 320). With the controls in the **Add Method** dialog box, you can equip an OLE control with methods in much the same way that you add message handlers to an application using ClassWizard.

   When you create a custom method with the **Add Method** dialog box, you can specify two different names for it: one used externally (on your OLE control's property sheet, for example), and one used internally. When you implement a custom method, you can also specify the method's parameters in the **Parameter** list box at the bottom of the dialog box.

   With the two radio buttons in the **Add Method** dialog box's **Implementation** panel, you can create two kinds of methods: stock methods and custom methods. Stock methods are methods with default implementations that you don't have to write your; for example, the stock version of the **Refresh** method (specified in the **External Name** text box in Figure 7.7) is a method that executes whenever an OLE control needs to be redrawn.

To implement a stock method, all you have to do is create it; ClassWizard writes the code required to implement the method.

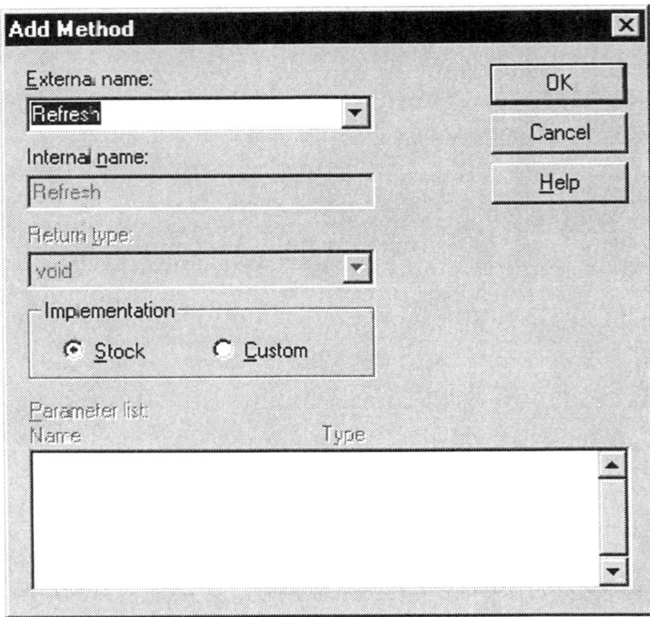

Figure 7.7 The Add Method dialog box

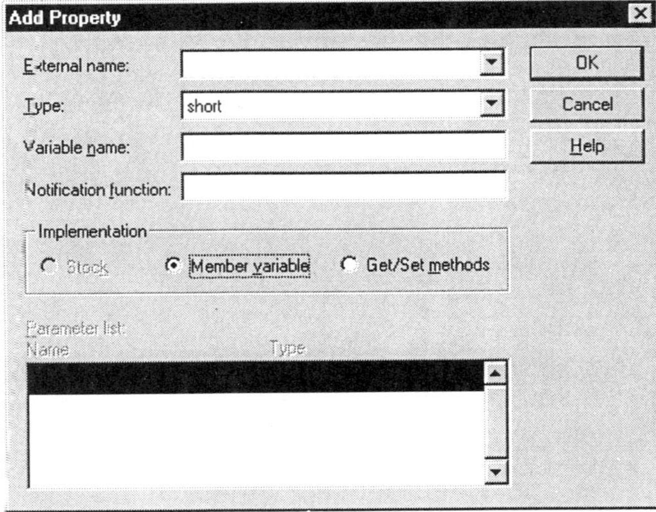

Figure 7.8 The Add Property dialog box

However, when you use the Add Method dialog box to add a custom method to an OLE control, it is up to you to write the code that implements the method.

4. When you have finished examining the **Add Method** dialog box, close it by clicking its **Cancel** button.
5. When focus shifts back to the **ClassWizard** property page, click the **Property** button. ClassWizard then opens a dialog box named **Add Property** (see Figure 7.8 on Page 320). With the controls in the **Add Property** dialog box, you can add stock properties and custom properties to your OLE control, in much the same way that you add member variables to ordinary controls using ClassWizard. When you create a custom property, you can specify its name, its data type, and its parameter list.

   You can also use the **Add Property** dialog box to add Get and Set methods to your OLE control.
6. Try out some of the controls provided by the **Add Property** dialog box. Then close it by clicking its **Close** button.
7. Tab the ClassWizard property page to the property sheet labeled **OLE Events**.

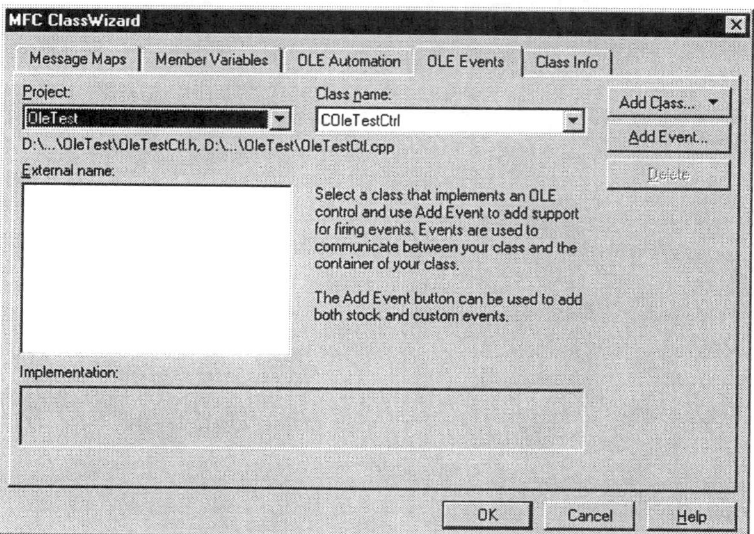

Figure 7.9 The OLE Events property sheet

8. When you have completed your examination of the **Add Method** dialog box, close it by clicking its **Cancel** button and tab the ClassWizard property page to the property sheet labeled **OLE Events** (Figure 7.9).

9. With the controls provided by the **OLE Events** property sheet, you can create event handlers for OLE controls. Most of the event handlers that you add to controls with ClassWizard are member functions that are called when stock events or custom events are detected. But you can also use the OLE Events property sheet to create custom event handlers for OLE controls.

   When you add a custom event handler to a control using ClassWizard, the ClassWizard utility adds an appropriate entry to your control's event sink map and then creates an empty member function that is called when the event is detected. When you create a custom OLE-control event, is up to you to add the code that the memory function will execute to *fire* the event—that is, to make something happen when the event is detected.

10. To add a stock event handler to a control, all you have to do is click the **OLE Events** property sheet's **Add Event** button. ClassWizard then opens a dialog box titled **Add Event** (Figure 7.10).

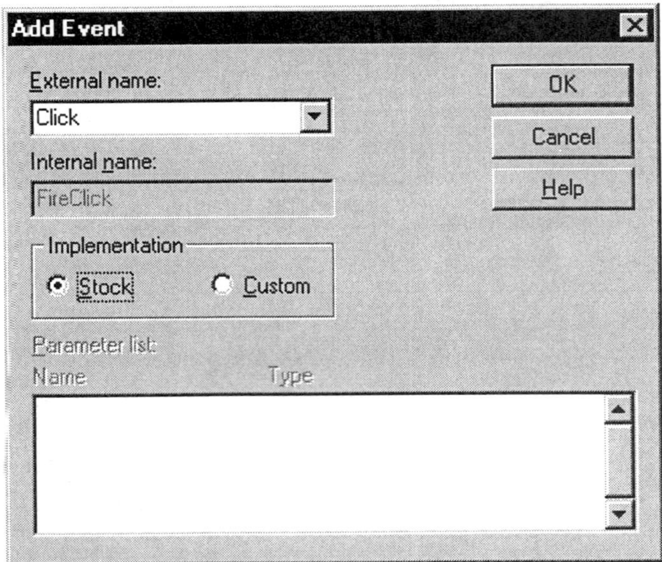

Figure 7.10 The Add Event dialog box

With the controls in the **Add Event** dialog box, you can create stock event handlers or custom event handlers for your OLE control. When you create an event handler, ClassWizard adds the appropriate entry to your control's event sink map and adds the appropriate member function to your control's class.

Stock events have default behaviors, so when you create a stock event, all that all happens automatically. When you create a custom event, you are responsible for writing your own code, but ClassWizard still creates all the functionality that makes firing your event possible.

Property Sheets and Property Pages

Properties are one of the most important characteristics of OLE controls. To help you get, set, and manipulate the properties of OLE controls, MFC 4.0 provides a property sheet to which you can add your own property pages. You can then use your property pages to get, set, and control whatever kinds of properties your OLE controls have.

An OLE control's property sheet is the dialog box that pops up when you open Developer Studio's dialog-box editor, display a popup menu by right-clicking an OLE control, and then choose the **Properties** menu item.

Figure 7.11 shows a typical OLE-control property page.

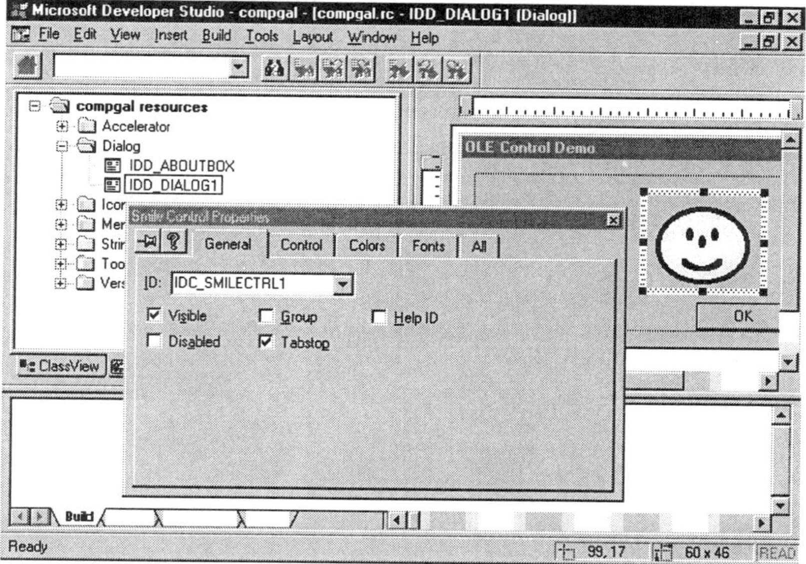

Figure 7.11 An OLE control's property page

To manage an OLE control's properties, you can add whatever kinds of property pages you need to your control's property sheet. Then you can create dialog-box items on the property page you have set up to manage your control's properties.

The easiest way to set up property pages for an OLE control is to use the Developer Studio's dialog-box editor. Then you can use Class-Wizard to connect the dialog-box items inside your control's property page to their corresponding properties.

Setting and Getting OLE-Control Properties

When you have created an OLE control, you can set and get its properties by using a function named `DoDataExchange`. The `DoDataExchange` function is used in association with a property-page mechanism called DDP. The DDP mechanism is similar to the dialog data exchange (DDX) mechanism that is used to pass data back and forth between member functions in an application and ordinary (non-OLE) dialog-box controls.

Varieties of Property Pages

There are two kinds of property pages that you can add to an OLE control's property sheet: *stock property pages* and *custom property pages*. Stock property pages are property pages that the dialog-box editor displays by default when you don't do anything special to change them. Custom property pages are property pages you design yourself.

There are three kinds of stock property pages: *font property pages*, *color property pages*, and *picture property pages*. You can use these three kinds of stock property pages to set:

- The font in which your OLE control's caption is displayed.
- Your control's foreground and background colors.
- Any bitmaps or other kinds of graphics you want to use to display your OLE control.

To supply an OLE control with a a stock property page, all you have to do is choose the kind of property page you want and add an entry for the kind of pages you have chosen to a block of code in the control's implementation file called a *property-page ID map*. A property-page ID map, as you might guess, is a map of all the property pages assigned to a control. You'll learn how to equip an OLE control with a property page in the section headed "Example: Adding a Property Page to an OLE Control" on page 332.

Example: A Program that Implements an OLE Control

To create an OLE control that has any useful functionality, you must also have an application that implements the control. To create and implement the control itself, these are the general steps to follow:

1. Use ControlWizard to generate and build an SDI application that supports OLE control.
2. Use ControlWizard to generate a project that creates and implements an OLE control (or multiple OLE controls).
3. Use ClassWizard to add properties and events to your control (or controls).
4. Use the Developer Studio dialog-box editor to lay out a property page for your control (or controls).
5. Test your control with the Test Container application.
6. Register your control, if necessary.

Creating an OLE Control Step by Step

Now that you know the general steps for creating an OLE control, you have all the knowledge you need to create a real OLE control that works in a Visual C++ program.

To create control and an application that implements it, follow these steps:

1. Start Developer Studio if it isn't already started.
2. Navigate to the directory in which you have installed your bonus-disk files.
3. Open the OLEPROG folder inside the OLE_1 folder.
4. Inside the OLEPROG folder, create an SDI project that supports OLE controls. (For a review of how to do that, see "Registering a Control Step by Step" on page 282.) Call your SDI-application project OLEPROG.
5. Choose **New** from the **File** menu.
6. When the **New** dialog box opens, select **Project Workspace** from the New Dialog box and click the **OK** button.

7. When the **New Workspace** dialog box opens, select **OLE Control-Wizard** from the **Type** list box, as shown in Figure 7.12.

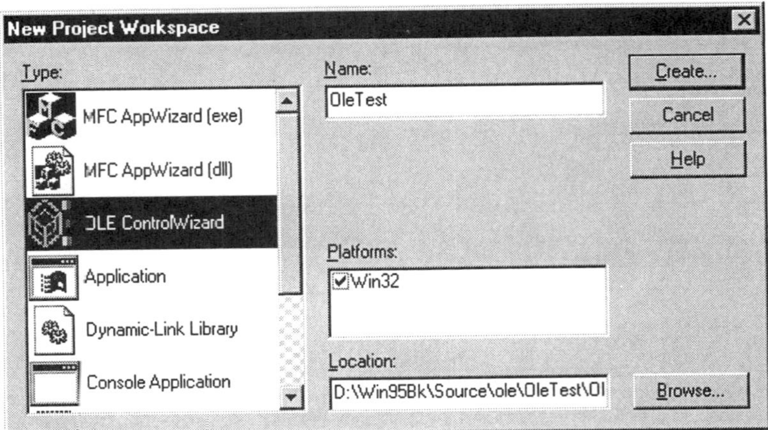

Figure 7.12 Creating an OLE Control

8. Using the **Browse** button, navigate to the OLETEST folder inside the OLE_1 folder.
9. Type `OleTest` in the **Name** text box.
10. Click the **Create** button. ControlWizard responds by opening a dialog box labeled **OLE ControlWizard—Step 1 of 2** (Figure 7.13).

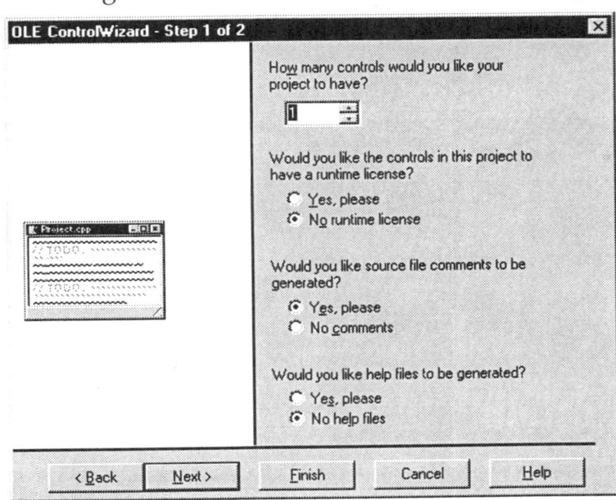

Figure 7.13 Creating a control: Step 1

11. Leaving all defaults as they are for this exercise, click **Next**. ControlWizard then displays a dialog box titled **OLE Control-Wizard—Step 2 of 2** (Figure 7.14).

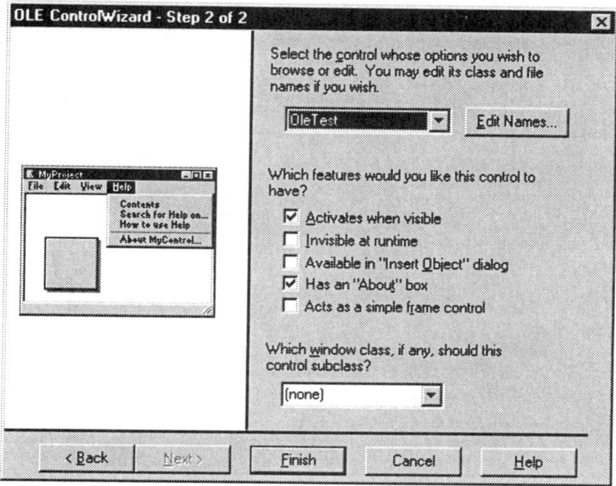

Figure 7.14 Creating a control: Step 2

12. Again leaving all defaults as they are, click **Finish**. ControlWizard then creates your OLE control.
13. Compile the code for your new control by choosing the **Build OleCtrl.ocx** item from the **Build** menu.
14. To register and test your new control, choose **Test Container** from the **Tools** menu.
15. When the Test Container application opens, choose the **File | Register Controls** menu item.
16. When the **Controls Registry** dialog box appears, select the OLETEST list-box item and click the **Register** button.
17. When the Test Container window reopens, choose the **Edit | Insert** menu item. Your control then appears inside the Test Container window, and a button labeled OCX appears on the Test Container application's toolbar, as shown in Figure 7.15 on Page 328.
18. Close the Test Container application.
19. From Developer Studio, execute the OLEPROG application.
20. Select the **View | OLE Dialog** menu item. The OLEPROG program then displays your OLETEST control (Figure 7.16 on Page 328).

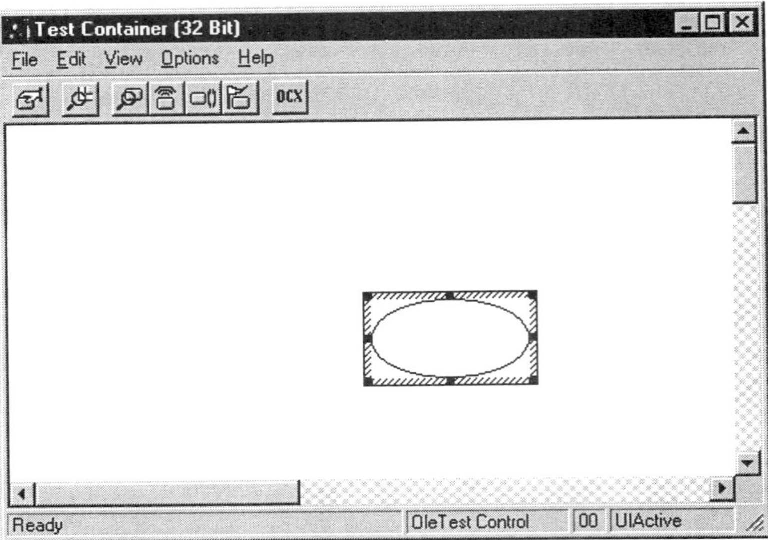

Figure 7.15 testing your OLE control

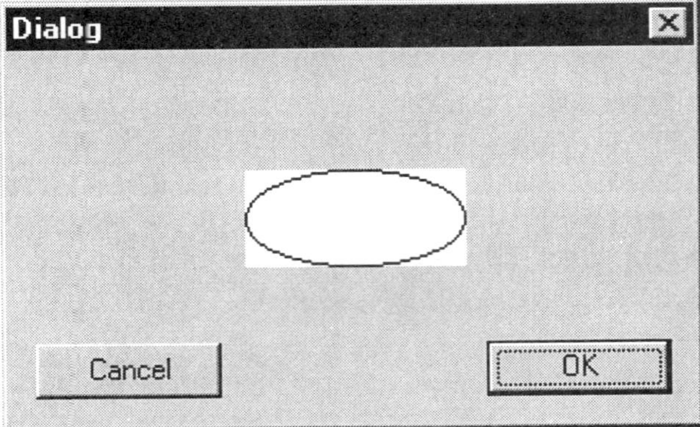

Figure 7.16 Implementing your OLE control

Congratulations! You have now created and implemented your first OLE control.

In the next sections, you'll learn how to personalize your control by adding your own properties, methods, and event handlers, and how to create property pages for your controls.

Example: Adding a Property to an OLE Control

When you execute the OLEPROG application, you may notice that your control's background color doesn't quite match the default background color of Windows 95 dialog boxes, which is a silver gray. In this section, you'll get a chance to make the background color of your control match the background of the dialog box in which it's implemented.

Adding a Property Step by Step

✔ To correct the background-color property of your OLE control, follow these steps:

1. Start Developer Studio if it isn't already started.
2. Open the OLETEST project that you created in the previous exercise.
3. Choose the **ClassWizard | View** menu item.
4. Select the **OLE Automation** tab.
5. Select the **COleTestCtrl** from the **Class Name** drop-down list box.

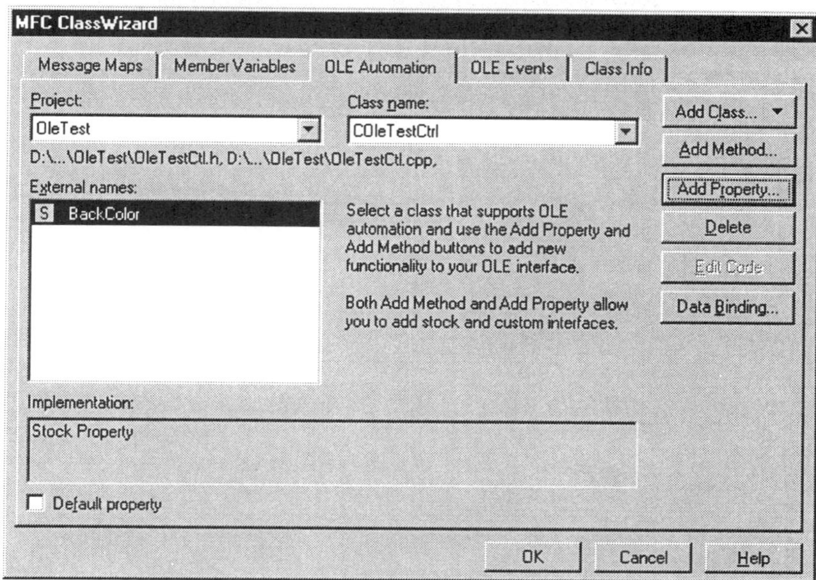

Figure 7.17 Adding a property to an OLE control

6. Click the **Add Property** button.
7. When the **Add Property** dialog box opens, select the **BackColor** item from the **External Name** drop-down combo box.
8. Make sure that the **Stock** option is selected in the **Implementation** panel.
9. Close the **Add Property** dialog box by clicking **OK**.
10. When the ClassWizard property sheet reclaims the focus, notice that ClassWizard has added a **BackColor** item to the **External names** list box, as shown in Figure 7.17 on Page 329.
11. Close ClassWizard by clicking the **OK** button. ClassWizard then creates the code needed to add the **BackColor** property to the COleTestCtrl class and to the OLETEST control's type-library file, OLETEST.ODL.
12. From Developer Studio, open the OLEPROG application (the program that implements the OLETEST control.)
13. Open Developer Studio dialog-box editor.
14. Open the dialog box that implements your OLE control.
15. Right-click the mouse over your OLE control's in the dialog-box template. A popup menu appears, as shown in Figure 7.18.

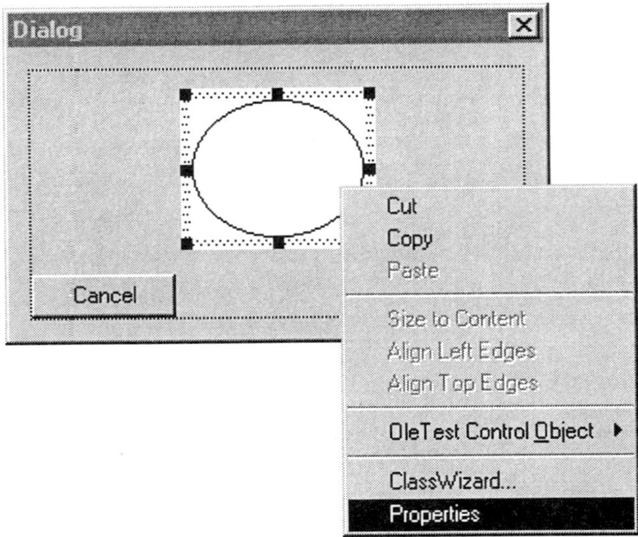

Figure 7.18 Displaying an OLE control's popup menu

16. Chose the **Properties** menu item. Developer Studio then displays a property sheet titled OleTestControl Properties (Figure 7.19).

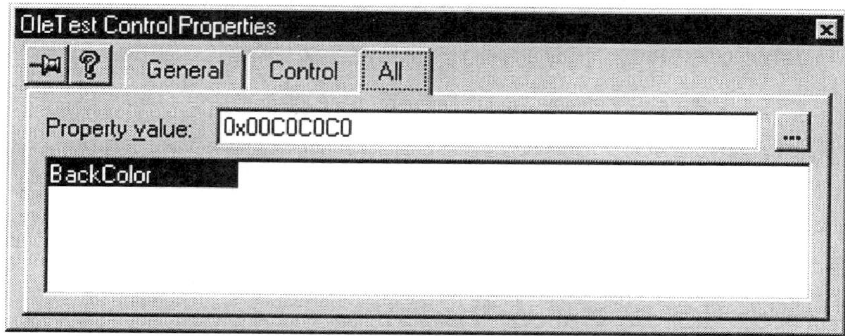

Figure 7.19 An OLE control's property page

17. Tab to the **All** property page. The **BackColor** entry shows you that your OLE control now has a **BackColor** property.

In the next exercise—"Example: Adding a Property Page to an OLE Control" on page 332—you'll get an opportunity to add another property page to the OLETEST property sheet. This new page will be a stock color property page. It will let the user interactively change the control's background property.

How ClassWizard Adds a Property to an OLE Control

When ControlWizard creates an OLE control, or adds an existing control to a project, it automatically creates a *dispatch map* and inserts it into the source code of the application that implements the control. As noted in "The CCmdTarget Class" on page 274, a dispatch map resembles an ordinary Visual C++ message map. (A message map, you may recall, is a block of code that ClassWizard creates to connect events with event handlers in Visual C++ programs.)

In a program that supports OLE controls, dispatch maps are automatically created to handle properties, methods, and events. When you add a property to an OLE control using ClassWizard, the ClassWizard utility automatically modifies the COleCtrl class's dispatch map in CIRCCTL.CPP by adding a macro named `DISP_STOCKPROP_BACKCOLOR`. The resulting dispatch map looks like this:

```
BEGIN_DISPATCH_MAP(COleTestCtrl, COleControl)
    //{{AFX_DISPATCH_MAP(CCircCtrl)
    DISP_STOCKPROP_BACKCOLOR()
    //}}AFX_DISPATCH_MAP
```

```
    DISP_FUNCTION_ID(COleTestCtrl, "AboutBox",
   DISPID_ABOUTBOX, AboutBox, VT_EMPTY, VTS_NONE)
END_DISPATCH_MAP()
```

In the preceding example, notice that the entry DISP_STOCK-PROP_BACKCOLOR has been added to the OLETEST control's dispatch map. That entry means that DISP_STOCKPROP_BACKCOLOR is the value of the **BackColor** property. DISP_STOCKPROP_BACKCOLOR os the value of the stock background color property of an OLE control. The **BackColor** property has a data type named DISP_STOCKPROP_-BACKCOLOR, which means that the value of the BackColor property can be modified only through its Get and Set methods.

ClassWizard also modifies the OLETEST control's type-library file, OLETEST.ODL, to add the **BackColor** property to the control's list of properties.

The Set method of the **BackColor** property is a member function named SetBackColor. When your application calls SetBack-Color, the SetBackColor member function sets the value of the **BackColor** property and then automatically calls a member function named OnBackColorChanged, invalidating the control. When the control is invalidated, the Visual C++ framework calls the MFC member function OnDraw. The control is redrawn, using its new background color.

Example: Adding a Property Page to an OLE Control

MFC 4.0 provides several predesigned property pages for OLE controls. These include a color property page, a font property page, and a bitmap property page. In this exercise, you'll add a color property page to the OLETEST control's property sheet. This new property page will let the user interactively change the background color of the OLETEST control.

✔ To add a color property page to your control's property sheet, follow these steps:

1. From Developer Studio, open the OLETEST project if it isn't already open.
2. In the OLETESTCTL.CPP file, find these three lines of code:

```
BEGIN_PROPPAGEIDS(COleTestCtrl, 1)
   PROPPAGEID(COleTestPropPage::guid)
END_PROPPAGEIDS(COleTestCtrl)
```

3. Insert an additional line of code and change the number 1 in the first line of code to a 2:

```
BEGIN_PROPPAGEIDS(COleTestCtrl, 2)
   PROPPAGEID(COleTestPropPage::guid)

   PROPPAGEIED(CLSID_CColorPropPage)
END_PROPPAGEIDS(COleTestCtrl)
```

   The new line in the preceding code fragment adds a stock color property page to the OLETEST control. The incrementation of the number 1 to 2 in the first line of the example specifies that there is now an addition property page in the OLETEST control's property sheet.
4. Rebuild the OLETEST control.
5. Open the OLEPROG project.
6. Open the Developer Studio's dialog-box editor to the OLETEST control template.
7. Right-click over the OLE-control icon and choose the **Properties** item from the icon's popup menu.
8. Notice that the OLETEST control's property sheet now contains a stock color property page (Figure 7.20).

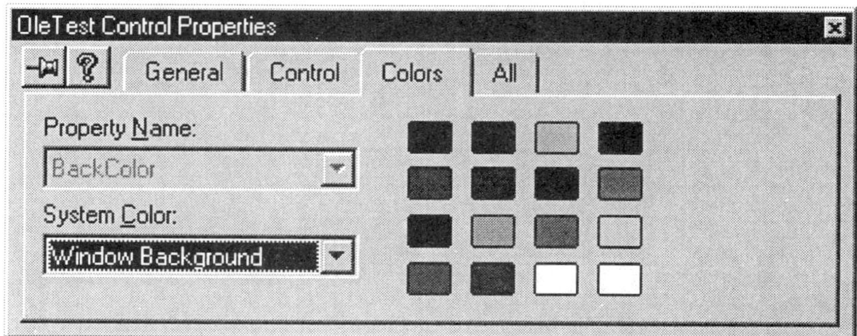

Figure 7.20 A stock color property page

Although you have now equipped your OLE control with a color property page, you have not yet activated your new property page. You'll do that in the next exercise.

Example: Drawing a Control

When you create a property that affects the appearance of an OLE control, you must modify the control's `OnDraw` member function to modify its looks. (In a Visual C++ program, `OnDraw` is a member function that redraws objects when needed; for details, see your Visual C++ documentation.)

When you create an OLE control with ControlWizard, the Control-Wizard utility generates a default `OnDraw` function that draws a plain white ellipse with a black outline, as shown earlier in Figure 7.16 on Page 328.

A default `OnDraw` function that produces this control is in the OLETESTCT.CPP file. It looks like this:

```
void COleTestCtrl::OnDraw(CDC* pdc, const CRect&
    rcBounds, const CRect& rcInvalid)
{
   // TODO: Replace the following code with your own
   //drawing code.
   pdc->FillRect(rcBounds, CBrush::FromHandle
      ((HBRUSH)GetStockObject(WHITE_BRUSH)));
   pdc->Ellipse(rcBounds);
}
```

With a little editing, you can modify your control's default `OnDraw` function to produce a different result. For example, the following `OnDraw` function produces a yellow ellipse-shaped control with a user-definable background color:

```
void COleTestCtrl::OnDraw(CDC* pdc, const CRect&
    rcBounds, const CRect& rcInvalid)
{
   CBrush brushYellow, *pOldBrush;
   CPen *pOldPen;
   CBrush bkBrush (TranslateColor(GetBackColor()));

   // Paint the background
   pdc->FillRect(rcBounds, &bkBrush);

   // Prepare the ellipse.
   pOldPen = (CPen*)pdc->SelectStockObject(BLACK_PEN);
   brushRed.CreateSolidBrush(RGB(0Xff, 0xff, 0x00));
   pOldBrush = pdc->SelectObject(&brushYellow);

   // Draw the ellipse.
   pdc->Ellipse(rcBounds);
```

```
    // Release CPen and CBrush objects.
    pdc->SelectObject(pOldPen);
    pdc->SelectObject(pOldBrush);
}
```

To modify your OLE-control code in such a way that it draws a yellow ellipse, follow these steps:

1. Using the Developer Studio editor, modify the `OnDraw` function in the OLETEST.CPP file to match the preceding example.
2. Rebuild the OLETEST project.
3. Open the OLEPROG project.
4. Open Developer Studio's dialog-box editor.
5. Right-click the mouse over your control's image and choose the **Properties** item from the control's popup menu.
6. When the **Control Properties** dialog box opens, tab to the **Colors** page.
7. Select various colors and notice that you can change the background color of your control. Before you close the **Control Properties** dialog box, select the gray background color—the same color as the default background color used by Windows 95 dialog boxes.
8. Close the **Control Properties** dialog box.
9. Execute the OLEPROG project.
10. Choose the **View | OLE Dialog** menu item. Your application now displays a dialog box that resembles the one shown in Figure 7.21.

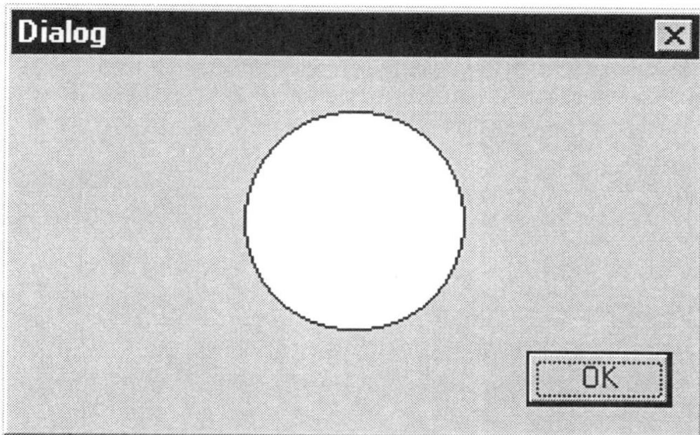

Figure 7.21 A modified OLE control

Example: Creating Event Handlers for OLE Controls

In this section, you'll learn how to implement event-firing mechanisms for OLE controls. Specifically, you'll learn how to fire an event when the user of your application clicks the mouse inside an OLE control

The example program presented in this section is similar to the OLE-control program presented back in Chapter 6, "Windows 95 and Visual C++" on page 239. This chapter's sample program, like the one in Chapter 5, implements an OLE control that has the form of a smiling face. But there's an important difference between the two programs.

In the example program presented in Chapter 5, you could click a button to toggle the expression on the face back and forth between a toggle and a frown. In this chapter's example program, you can also change the expression on the face, but you don't need a special button to do it. The OLE control you'll be creating in this section is equipped with an event-firing mechanism that detects when the user has clicked the mouse inside the control. So no second button is needed.

When this chapter's sample program detects a mouse inside an OLE control's rectangular boundary, the control conducts a simple check called a *hit test*. If the control determines that the mouse has been clicked inside circular border, the expression on the OLE-control face changes. If the mouse has been clicked outside the control's border, the application does nothing.

Creating an Event-Firing Mechanism Step by Step

Events, like properties, can added to OLE custom controls using ClassWizard. When you add a custom event to a control, ClassWizard creates the code necessary to declare the even. But it is your responsibility to write the code that fires the event.

✔ To implement this hit-testing operation and the resulting actions, these are the steps to follow:

1. Using Developer Studio, open the OLETEST project.
2. Open ClassWizard.
3. Tab to the **OLE Events** property page.
4. Choose the **COleTestCtrl** item from the **Class** name drop-down list box.
5. Click the **Add Event** button.

6. When the **Add Event** dialog box opens, type `ClickIn` in the drop-down combo box labeled **External name**.
7. Close the **Add Event** dialog box by clicking **OK**.
8. Close ClassWizard by clicking its **OK** button.
9. Open the OLETESTCTL.CPP file and find your control's event map. ClassWizard has modified it to look like this:

```
BEGIN_EVENT_MAP(COleTestCtrl, COleControl)
   //{{AFX_EVENT_MAP(COleTestCtrl)
   EVENT_CUSTOM("ClickIn", FireClickIn, VTS_I2
      VTS_I2)
   EVENT_CUSTOM("ClickOut", FireClickOut,
      VTS_NONE)
   //}}AFX_EVENT_MAP
END_EVENT_MAP()
```

10. Close ClassWizard by clicking its **OK** button.

    Once you implement an `ClickIn` event for an OLE control, the control can be fired. An OLE control is smart enough to determine by itself when a custom event should be fired. In this exercise, the `ClickIn` event fires whenever the user clicks the left mouse button with the cursor inside the control's circular border.

11. In this exercise, the code that fires your control's `ClickIn` event is triggered when a `WM_LBUTTONDOWN` message is received from the Windows 95 operating system. The COleTest control's handler for the `WM_LBUTTONDOWN` message is the `OnLButtonDown` function in your application's OLETESTCTL.CPP file. You must add some code to the `OnLButtonDown` function to fire your control's `ClickIn` event. Modify your control's OnButtonDown function to read as follows:

```
void COleTestCtrl::OnLButtonDown(UINT nFlags, CPoint
   point)
{
   CRect rcBounds;
   GetClientRect(&rcBounds);
   long xLeft = rcBounds.left;
long yTop = rcBounds.top;
long xScale = rcBounds.Width();
long yScale = rcBounds.Height();
if (InEllipse(point, X(10), Y(15), X(90), Y(95))) {
   FireClickIn((short)point.x, (short)point.y);
   if (GetSmile()) {
      SetSmile(FALSE);
   } else {
      SetSmile(TRUE);
```

```
      }
   }
   else
      FireClickOut();

   COleControl::OnLButtonDown(nFlags, point);
}
   //Simple Ellipse Hit-Testing
   BOOL COleTestCtrl::InEllipse(const CPoint& pt,
      int x1, int y1, int x2, int y2)
   {
   // Determine radii
      double a = (x2 - x1) / 2;
      double b = (y2 - y1) / 2;

      // Determine x, y
      double x = pt.x - (x1 + x2) / 2;
      double y = pt.y - (y1 + y2) / 2;

      // Apply ellipse formula
      return ((x * x) / (a * a) + (y * y) / (b * b)
         <= 1);
```

Firing a 'Click-In' Event

When the user of your application clicks the mouse inside an OLE control's bounding rectangle, OLEPROG program uses a simple algorithm to determine whether the click occurred inside or outside the control's circular border.

When the user clicks the left mouse button and the insertion point is outside the control circle, the `ClickOut` event fires, as you saw under the pre. A `ClickOut` event defines no arguments because it doesn't do anything when it is fired. So it is easier to implement than a `ClickIn` event.

✔ To implement the firing of a ClickOut event, follow these steps:

1. Repeat Steps 1 through 5 of the previous exercise.
2. When the **Add Event** dialog box opens, type `ClickOut` in the **External Name** drop-down combo box.
3. Close the **`Add Event`** dialog box by clicking `OK`.
4. When ClassWizard reclaims the focus, close ClassWizard by clicking **OK**.

Modifying the *OnDraw* Method

When you have used ClassWizard to activate the event-firing mechanisms for an OLE control, you must write the code to implement the specific actions you want your application to perform when each event is fired.

In this chapter's example program, a Boolean member function named `m_bSmile` is provided to keep track of whether the face inside the dialog box is smiling or frowning. When the face is smiling, the value of the `m_bSmile` variable is `TRUE`. When the face is frowning, the value of `m_bSmile` is `FALSE`.

If there is a hit inside the face while it is frowning, a Set method named `SetSmile` is called to change the value of `m_bSmile` from `TRUE` to `FALSE`. If the hit occurs while the face is smiling, the `SetSmile` method is called to change the value of `m_bSmile` from `FALSE` to `TRUE`.

The OLE control's `OnDraw` method is constantly on guard to keep track of whether the value of change the value of `m_bSmile` is `TRUE` or `FALSE`. The `OnDraw` function automatically takes care of redrawing face when its expression changes. So you don't have to worry about calling `OnDraw` when there is a change in the appearance of the face. But you do have to write the code that changes the face's expression back and forth between a frown and a smile.

To set up the `m_bSmile` variable and the functions that set and get its value, follow these steps:

1. Open the OLETESTCTL.H file.
2. Define a Boolean variable named `m_bSmile`, as follows:

```
Boolean m_bSmile;
```

3. Open ClassWizard.
4. Tab to the **OLE Automation** page.
5. Click the **Add Property** button.
6. When the **Add Property** dialog box opens, select the **Get/Set methods** radio button in the **Implementation** panel.Notice that ClassWizard automatically echoes your typing by placing the names **GetSmile** and **SetSmile** in the **Get function** and **Set function** text boxes.
7. type **Smile** in the **External Name** list box.
8. Close the **Add Property** dialog box clicking the **OK** button.
9. Close ClassWizard by clicking its **OK** button.

10. Open the OLETESTCTL.CPP file and modify your OLE control's `OnDraw` method to read as follows:

```
void COleTestCtrl::OnDraw(
        CDC* pdc, const CRect& rcBounds, const CRect&
    rcInvalid)
{
   long xLeft = rcBounds.left;// Use with scaling macros
   long yTop = rcBounds.top;
   long xScale = rcBounds.Width();
   long yScale = rcBounds.Height();
   int iPenWidth = max(CX(5), CY(5)); // Pen width based
    on control size
   CBrush brushBack;    // Background brush
   CBrush brushBlack;
   CBrush brushYellow;
   CPen penBlack(PS_SOLID, iPenWidth,
    RGB(0x00,0x00,0x00));
   CPen penNull(PS_NULL, 0, (COLORREF)0);// Null pen for
    drawing filled ellipses
   COLORREF crBack = TranslateColor(GetBackColor());
    //Use BackColor
   brushBack.CreateSolidBrush(crBack);
    //Stock Property
   brushBlack.CreateSolidBrush(RGB(0x00,0x00,0x00));
   brushYellow.CreateSolidBrush(RGB(0xff,0xff,0x00));
   pdc->FillRect(rcBounds, &brushBack);// Clear
    background
   CPen* pPenSave = pdc->SelectObject(&penBlack);
   CBrush* pBrushSave = pdc->SelectObject(&brushYellow);
   pdc->Ellipse(X(10), Y(15), X(90), Y(95));// Head
   if (m_bSmile)// Use Smile

   // Custom Property
   pdc->Arc(X(25), Y(10), X(75), Y(80),// Smile mouth
      X(35), Y(70), X(65), Y(70));
    }
   else
   {
      pdc->Arc(X(25), Y(70), X(75), Y(140),// Frown
            X(65), Y(75), X(35), Y(75));
   }
   pdc->SelectObject(&penNull);     // No draw width
   pdc->SelectObject(&brushBlack);
   pdc->Ellipse(X(57), Y(35), X(65), Y(50));

   pdc->Ellipse(X(35), Y(35), X(43), Y(50));// Right eye
   pdc->Ellipse(X(46), Y(43), X(54), Y(58));// Nose
```

```
    pdc->SetBkMode(TRANSPARENT);// Use ForeColor
    pdc->SetTextColor(TranslateColor(GetForeColor()));//
     Stock Property
    SelectStockFont(pdc);// Use Font
                // Stock Property
    CRect rect = rcBounds;
    pdc->DrawText(InternalGetText(), -1, rect,
      DT_SINGLELINE | DT_CENTER | DT_TOP);
    pdc->SelectObject(pBrushSave);
    pdc->SelectObject(pPenSave);
}
```

11. Close ClassWizard.

Writing Methods for a Control

When you use ClassWizard's **Get/Set methods** options to create a property for an OLE control, ClassWizard automatically creates the appropriate Get and Set methods for the control and places handlers for both functions in the control's dispatch map. All you have to do is fill in the code that gives each method the proper functionality.

✔ To do that, follow these steps:

1. Open the OLETESTCTL.H file.
2. Modify the `GetSmile` and `SetSmile` methods that ClassWizard created to read as follows:

```
BOOL COleTestCtrl::GetSmile()
{
    // TODO: Add your property handler here
    return m_bSmile;
}
void COleTestCtrl::SetSmile(BOOL bNewValue)
{
    // TODO: Add your property handler here
    m_bSmile = bNewValue;
    InvalidateControl();
    SetModifiedFlag();
}
```

3. Rebuild the OLETEST project.
4. Open the OLEPROG project.
5. Execute it.
6. Choose the `View|OLE Dialog` menu item.

7. The dialog box that the program displays looks just like it did before, but now you can change the expression on the face in the OLE control by simply left-clicking the mouse over the control.

Summary

Chapter 6, "Windows 95 and Visual C++," showed how to import existing OLE controls using Component Gallery, and how to implement existing controls in Visual C++ applications.

In this chapter, you learned how to create your own OLE controls, and how to customize them by adding properties, property page, methods, and event handlers.

To demonstrate what you have learned, you had a chance to build an OLE control from scratch and to write a Visual C++ application that creates and implements the control. The OLE control that you created has a stock color property page that can be used to set its background color. It also has an event-firing mechanism that detects mouse hits inside the control and executes specific methods when hits are detected.

Best of all, if you ever write another application that needs such a control—or even a control that is similar—you can reuse and modify the control you have written. You can place your control in your computer's Component Gallery, and it will be there whenever you need it, all prewritten, debugged, and ready to go at the touch of a toolbar button.

Now that you know the fundamental principles of creating and implementing OLE controls, you are ready to start designing and using OLE controls in your Visual C++ applications. Although OLE controls are a little more complicated to design and implement than ordinary controls, many useful new tools for creating and using OLE controls have been built into Visual C++—and, once you have written an OLE control, Component Gallery makes it extremely easy to reuse the control in other applications.

All in all, once you get the hang of creating and implementing OLE controls, you'll probably agree that they're well worth the extra effort. Now that you know how to design and implement OLE controls, you'll probably be finding many different ways to use them from now on.

Chapter

8

Programs and Processes

Under Windows 95, multiple processes (a new name for what used to be called tasks under Windows 3.x) can share CPU time using an advanced technology called preemptive multitasking.

As you know if you're a DOS programmer, MS-DOS was originally designed to do just one thing at a time. In the earliest implementations of MS-DOS, one application was loaded into memory at a time. The computer ran that one application, and that was about all the CPU could handle.

Because MS-DOS could run only one thread at a time, it was what is now sometimes called a *single-threaded* operating system. In the era of MS-DOS, every application had a single thread, and only one thread could run at a time.

Windows 3.*x* was a little smarter. In the non-preemptive multitasking environment introduced by Windows 3.*x*, several applications could reside in memory at the same time, but only one application could be running at any given time. When an application was executed under Windows 3.*x*, the program still used all the time the CPU had available; although other applications might be memory-resident and might be waiting for a chance to run, they had to sit and wait until the currently executing application terminated.

When Windows 3.*x* performed a background task, such as file I/O or background program, it managed to present the illusion that the background task was being carried out at the same time other operations were being performed. But what was really happening was that the foreground task was briefly interrupted many times each second so the background task could be performed. This kind of CPU time-sharing is called *non-preemptive multitasking* because the CPU has no direct control over the amount of time allocated to each task.

There were some exceptions to this rule. Windows 3.*x* did have mechanisms for handling interrupts that switched from one task to another temporarily. And a task could—theoretically, at least—run in the background while a higher-priority task was executing. But as you may know, especially if you've tried to do some background printing, Windows 3.*x* never was really much good at background processing.

Today, under Windows 95, it is no exaggeration to say that Windows programs have entered a whole new era in CPU time-sharing. Now, thanks to multithreading and preemptive multitasking, the Windows operating system can run multiple processes (the Windows 95 equivalent of tasks) on the same computer at the same time, allocating each process a share of CPU time in accordance with predetermined priorities.

Under Windows 95, multiple *processes* (a new name for what used to be call *tasks* under Windows 3.*x*) can share CPU time using a more advanced technology called *preemptive multitasking*. Under preemptive multitasking, an operating system divides processes into threads and allocates each thread an individual share of CPU time, depending upon preallocated thread priorities.

With preemptive multitasking, Windows 95 can give each individual process its own slice of CPU time, and each process can use its slice of CPU in whatever way it wants, without directly affecting other processes. *Multithreading* is a term used to describe the allocation of CPU time using to multiple processes using multiple threads.

About This Chapter

In this chapter, you'll see how Windows 95 creates and manages processes. Chapter 9, "Multithreading and Multitasking," explains how Windows 95 uses multithreading to implement preemptive multitasking.

The following major topics are covered in this chapter:

To demonstrate how processes are created and used in Windows 95, this chapter presents two sample programs: one named SLIMMDI and one named MYCONSOL. Both these sample programs demonstrate the use of console windows: text windows created using functions in the Win32 API.

The MYCONSOL program is a simple console application that shows how you can display a console window in Windows 95. The SLIMMDI program is a little more complicated; it demonstrates how you can start and execute a console process from a standard Windows 95 window.

Figure 8.1 shows the output of the MYCONSOL program.

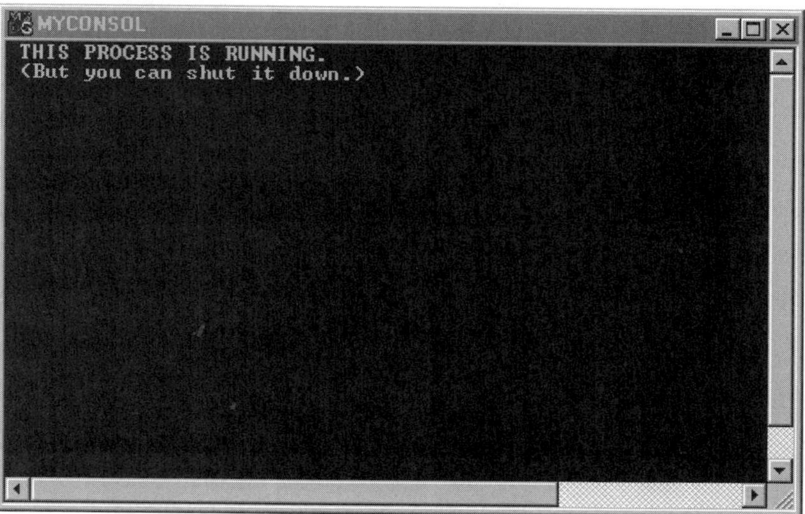

Figure 8.1 Output of the MYCONSOL program

Processes and Threads

To understand how multiprocessing works, it helps to have an understanding of *tasks* and *processes*. Under Windows 3.*x*, the smallest entity that was allocated CPU time was often called a *task*. Under Windows 95, what used to be called a task is known as a *process*.

When Windows 95 is executing an instance of an application, that instance is a *process*. For example, when you double-click an icon in the Windows 95 desktop, you start a process that runs the application associated with the icon you clicked.

A Windows 95 process consists of the code, data, and other resources of whatever program is being executed. Every process has at least one *thread*, and can start up other threads at any time.

One of the most important features of the Windows 95 operating sytem is its ability to execute more than one thread at a time, using a mechanism called *preemptive multitasking*. When an operating system uses preemptive multitasking to manage threads, it sets the priority of each thread and automatically allocates each thread a specific slice of CPU time, based on the relative priorities of the threads that are running. Under earlier 16-bit versions of Windows, preemptive multitiasking was not supported.

When a process creates a thread in Windows 95, the process can set that thread's priority in relation to other threads running on the system. Each thread creatred by a process shares all the *resources* of the process under which it runs. From the standpoint of process management, the resources of a process include code, data, semaphores (see "Semaphore Objects" on page 443), and dynamically allocated memory. (For more information on dynamically allocated memory, see "Closing Handles" on page 359.)

A *thread* is a path of execution within a process. When you start an application under Windows 95, the operating system creates a process and begins executing the primary thread of that process. When this primary terminates, so does the process.

Every thread runs under the control of a process. A Windows 95 process consists of the code, data, and other resources of whatever program is being executed. Every process has at least one thread, and any process can start up other threads at any time.

The next section, "Creating and Using Windows 95 Processes," explains how processes work in Windows 95. Threads are the topic of Chapter 9, "Multithreading and Multitasking."

Creating and Using Windows 95 Processes

Console-related functions provided by the Win32 API can be divided into the following categories:

- Functions that create console windows
- Functions that release console windows
- Console I/O
- Functions that manage I/O handles
- Functions that manage I/O buffers
- Console mode functions.

Functions that fall into each of these categories are described in this section.

Creating a Process with the CreateProcess Function

In Windows 95, an application can create a new process by calling the Win32 function **CreateProcess**. When a process creates a child process, the child process runs independently of the creating process.

When the **CreateProcess** function creates a new process, it also creates the new process's primary thread. The new process then executes a specified file.

CreateProcess can create and start up any kind of Windows 95 process. For example, if an application creates a console process, it can open a console for that process by calling the **AllocConsole** function or by simply jumping to a **main** function that is used as an entry point by a console associated with the process. **AllocConsole** opens a console window that is attached to the calling process.

A process can also create a consoleprocess by calling the **CreateProcess** function with the **CREATE_NEW_CONSOLE** flag set. **CreateProcess** starts a new process and attaches it to a console—either a new console or a console that is attached to the calling process, depending on the parameters passed to **CreateProcess**.

In the SLIMMDI program on your bonus disk, the **CreateProcess** function is called to create a console window. **CreateProcess** is called from this statement in the SLIMMDI.CPP file:

```
// Create a new console process.
CreateProcess("MYCONSOL.EXE", NULL, NULL, NULL, TRUE,
   DETACHED_PROCESS, NULL, NULL, &sui, &pi);
```

Syntax of the CreateProcess Function

This is the syntax of the **CreateProcess** function:

```
BOOL CreateProcess(LPCTSTR lpszImageName,
   LPCTSTR lpszCommandLine,
   LPSECURITY_ATTRIBUTES lpsaProcess,
   LPSECURITY_ATTRIBUTES lpsaThread,
   BOOL fInheritHandles,
   DWORD fdwCreate,
   LPVOID lpvEnvironment,
   LPCSTR lpszCurDir,
   LPSTARTUPINFO lpsiStartInfo,
   LPPROCESS_INFORMATION lppiProcInfo)
```

If the **CreateProcess** function succeeds, it returns a value of **TRUE**; if not, it returns a value of **FALSE**.

As you will see later, in "Windows 95 Console Processes" on page 366, several of the **CreateProcess** parameters are particularly applicable to console processes. For example, the *lpsiStartInfo* parameter is a pointer to a **STARTUPINFO** structure that defines the characteristics of a console window. The *lppiProcInfo* parameter is also a pointer to a structure: a **PROCESS_INFORMATION** structure, which contains information about the console process being created.

The following parameters can be passed to the **CreateProcess** function:

- *lpszImageName*: The pathname and filename of the object-code module to execute as a new process.If a partial name is specified, the current drive and current directory are used by default. If the *lpszImageName* parameter is **NULL**, the module name must be entered in the *lpszCommandLine* string. The specified module can be a Win32 application, or it can be some other type of module (for example, an MS-DOS or OS/2 module) if the appropriate subsystem is available on the local computer.
- *lpszCommandLine*: The address of any command line that must be executed to run the new process. If this parameter is **NULL**, the *lpszImageName* string is recognized as the command line. If neither *lpszImageName* nor *lpszCommandLine* is **NULL**, *lpszImageName* specifies the module to execute and *lpszCommandLine* is recognized as the command line.
- *lpsaProcess*: Points to a **SECURITY_ATTRIBUTES** structure that specifies the security attributes for the created process. If *lpsaProcess* is **NULL**, the process is created with a default security

descriptor. For more about security attributes, see "The SECURITY_ATTRIBUTES Structure" on page 353.

- *lpsaThread*: Points to a **SECURITY_ATTRIBUTES** structure that specifies the security attributes for the primary thread of the new process. If *lpsaThread* is **NULL**, the process is created with a default security descriptor. Security attributes are described in more detail in "The SECURITY_ATTRIBUTES Structure" on page 353.
- *fInheritHandles*: Specifies whether the new process inherits handles from the calling process. If *fInheritHandles* is **TRUE**, each inheritable open handle in the calling process is inherited by the new process. Inherited handles have the same value and access privileges as the original handles. For more details about the inheritance of handles by processes, see "Objects and Handles" later in this chapter.
- *fdwCreate*: This parameter is used with a set of flags that control the priority of the process and specify certain facts about how the new process is to be created. The following flags can be used with the *fdwCreate* parameter are:
  - **CREATE_SUSPENDED**: If this flag is set, the primary thread of the new process is created in a suspended state and does not run until the Win32 function **ResumeThread** is called.
  - **DETACHED_PROCESS**: This flag applies specifically to console processes (Chapter 6). If the flag is set, the new process does not have access to the console of the calling process.The new process can create a new console by calling the **AllocConsole** function, or by simply jumping to the beginning of a **main** function that the console uses as an entry point. The **DETACHED_PROCESS** flag cannot be used with the **CREATE_NEW_CONSOLE** flag.
  - **CREATE_NEW_PROCESS_GROUP**: If this flag is set, the new process is the root process of a new process group. A process group, identified by an ID number, includes all processes that are descendants of this root process. The process group ID of the new process group is the same as the process ID, which is returned in the *lppiProcInfo* structure. Process groups enable the Win32 function **GenerateConsoleCtrlEvent** to send the special character signals CTRL+C and CTRL+BREAK to groups of console processes.
  - **DEBUG_PROCESS**: If this flag is set, the calling process is treated as a debugger, and the new process is a process being debugged. This means that the system notifies the debugger

(the calling process) of all debug events that occur in the process being debugged (the new process).

- **DEBUG_ONLY_THIS_PROCESS**: If this flag is set, the calling process is treated as a debugger, and the new process is a process being debugged.

  Another set of flags used with *fdwCreate* parameter control the new process's *priority class*, which is used in determining the scheduling priorities of the process's threads. If no priority class is specified, the priority class defaults to **NORMAL_PRIORITY_CLASS**, unless the priority class of the creating process is **IDLE_PRIORITY_CLASS**. In this case the default priority class of the child process is also **IDLE_PRIORITY_CLASS**.

The following priority flags can be used with the *fdwCreate* parameter:

- **REALTIME_PRIORITY_CLASS**: The highest possible priority. Preempts the threads of all other processes, including operating-system processes that may be performing important tasks: for example, flushing information cached to a disk. If you ever think you need to use a real-time process, think twice and then make it active only for the shortest possible period of time. Otherwise, the results may be unfortunate. For example, disk caches may not flush and mouse operations may hang.
- **HIGH_PRIORITY_CLASS**: A process that performs a time-critical task and must therefore be executed immediately. The threads of a high-priority class process preempt the threads of normal or idle priority class processes. An example of a process that might be given a high priority is Windows Task List, which must respond quickly when called by the user, regardless of the load on the operating system. Do not be tempted to use high-priority tasks indiscriminately. In fact, use extreme care in assigning this priority, because a high-priority class CPU-bound application can use nearly all available cycles.
- **NORMAL_PRIORITY_CLASS**: An ordinary process with no special scheduling needs.
- **IDLE_PRIORITY_CLASS**: A process whose threads run only when the system is idle and are preempted by the threads of any process running in a higher priority class. An example of a process that might have an idle priority class is a screen-saver program.

- *lpvEnvironment*: Points to an environment block for the new process. If this parameter is **NULL**, the new process uses the environment of the calling process. The environment block consists of a null-terminated block of null-terminated strings (that is, two null bytes at the end of the block).

- *lpszCurDir*: Points to a null-terminated string that specifies the current drive and directory for the new process. The string must be a full path and filename that includes a drive letter. If this parameter is **NULL**, the new process is created with the same current drive and directory as the calling process. This option is provided primarily for shells that start applications.
- *lpsiStartInfo*: A pointer to a **STARTUPINFO** structure that defines the characteristics of a window. By passing a pointer to a **STARTUPINFO** structure when it calls **CreateProcess**, a parent process can specify the properties of with the main window of its child process (see "The STARTUPINFO Structure" on page 355).

  If the calling process supplies **CreateProcess** with a customized **STARTUPINFO** structure, the calling process must either set the **CREATE_NEW_CONSOLE** flag (described earlier) or call **the AllocConsole** function to create a new console window. A **STARTUPINFO** structure can set the following characteristics of a console window:

  - The size (expressed in character cells) and the location (expressed in screen pixel coordinates) of the new console window
  - The size (expressed in character cells) of the new console's screen buffer
  - The text and background color attributes of the new console's screen buffer.
  - The name that appears in the title bar of the new console's window.

  A child process can call the **GetStartupInfo** function to determine the values assigned to the member variables of its **STARTUPINFO struct**. A process cannot change the location of its console window on the screen, but several console functions are available to set or query the other properties specified in the **STARTUPINFO** structure.
- *lppiProcInfo*: The address of **PROCESS_INFORMATION** structure that receives identification information about a new process (see "The SECURITY_ATTRIBUTES Structure" on page 353).

For an example of how the **CreateProcess** function can be used in a Windows 95 program, see "This Chapter's Example Programs" on page 401.

Calling *CreateProcess* in the SLIMMDI Program

One of this chapter's sample programs—the one named SLIMMDI—calls the **CreateProcess** function to create a new console process. The call is made is called in the SLIMMDI.CPP file from a function named **ShowConsole**, which looks like this:

```
void ShowConsole()
{

    sui.cb                  = sizeof (STARTUPINFO);
    sui.lpReserved          = 0;
    sui.lpDesktop           = NULL;
    sui.lpTitle             = NULL;
    sui.dwX                 = 10;
    sui.dwY                 = 10;
    sui.dwXSize             = 400;
    sui.dwYSize             = 200;
    sui.dwXCountChars       = 80;
    sui.dwYCountChars       = 42;
    sui.dwFillAttribute     = 0;
    sui.dwFlags             =
        STARTF_USEPOSITION|STARTF_USESIZE|
        STARTF_USECOUNTCHARS|
        STARTF_USESHOWWINDOW;
    sui.wShowWindow         = SW_SHOWNORMAL;
    sui.cbReserved2         = 0;
    sui.lpReserved2         = 0;

   // Create a new console process.
   CreateProcess("MYCONSOL\\MYCONSOL.EXE", NULL, NULL,
NULL,
   TRUE, DETACHED_PROCESS, NULL, NULL, &sui, &pi);

}
```

When **CreateProcess** is called in the preceding code fragment, it is passed the address of a **STARTUPINFO** structure named **sui**. That structure determines the size, the colors, and a few other characteristics of the console window that the **ShowConsole** function displays.

The process that is opened by the **CreateProcess** function is an executable file named MYCONSOL.EXE. This file resides in a subdirectory named MYCONSOL.

The SLMMDI program creates a new console process when you choose the **Console | Process** menu item. The console process displays a console window that looks like the one shown in Figure 8.2 on Page 353.

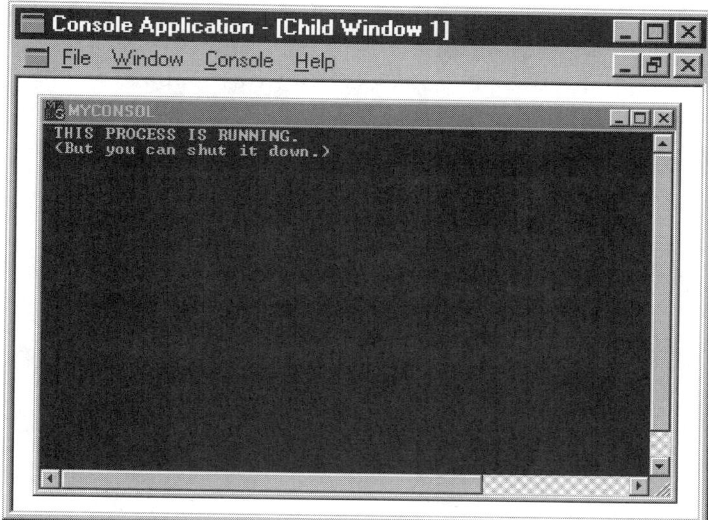

Figure 8.2 The SLIMMDI program's console process

The SECURITY_ATTRIBUTES Structure

The *lpsaProcess* and *lpsaThread*: parameters of the **CreateProcess** call point to a **SECURITY_ATTRIBUTES** structure. The structure pointed to by *lpsaProcess* specifies the security attributes for the created process, and the structure referenced by *lpsaThread*: specifies the security attributes for the primary thread of the new process. If either of these parameters is **NULL**, a default security descriptor is used.

This is the architecture of a **SECURITY_ATTRIBUTES** structure:

```
typedef struct _SECURITY_ATTRIBUTES ( /* sa */
   DWORD nLength;
   LPVOID lpSecurityDescriptor;
   BOOL bInheritHandle;
} SECURITY_ATTRIBUTES;
```

In a SECURITY_ATTRIBUTE structure:

- The *nLength* element specifies the length of the structure.
- The *bInheritHandle* is a Boolean value that specifies whether the handles associated with the process being created can be inherited. For more on this topic, see "Objects and Handles" on page 357.

- The *lpSecurityDescriptor* element points to a **SECURITY_DESCRIPTOR** structure that contains security information associated with the process being created. A **SECURITY_DESCRIPTOR** structure includes the following:
    - A pair of security identifier (SID) structures that identify the owner of a process and a primary group to which the process belongs
    - A pair of access-control-list (ACL) structures that provide access information about the new process.

For each kind of object associated with a process, there is a creation function (such as **CreateProcess** or **CreateFile**) that takes a security-attributes argument. This argument always points to a **SECURITY_ATTRIBUTES** function whose inherit flag determines whether the handle can be inherited.

The PROCESS_INFORMATION Structure

The *lppiProcInfo* parameter of the **CreateProcess** function is a pointer to a **PROCESS_INFORMATION** structure, which **CreateProcess** fills in with information about the console process being created. This is the definition of the **PROCESS_INFORMATION** structure:

```
typedef struct _PROCESS_INFORMATION { /* pi */
   HANDLE hProcess;
   HANDLE hThread;
   DWORD dwProcessID;
   DWORD dwThreadID;
} PROCESS_INFORMATION;
```

The *hProcess* member variable of the **PROCESS_INFORMATION** structure is the handle of the process that has been created. The *hThread* variable is the handle of the new process's main thread. By default, these handles are created with full access rights to the calling process. However, access can be restricted if a security descriptor is specified.

The *dwProcessID* variable is a global identifier that identifies the process that has been created. The *dwThreadID* variable is a global identifier that identifies the new process's main thread.

For an example of how **a PROCESS_INFORMATION** structure can be used with the **CreateProcess** function, see "This Chapter's Example Programs" on page 401.

The STARTUPINFO Structure

As mentioned earlier, in "Creating a Process with the CreateProcess Function" on page 347, the **CreateProcess** function takes a pointer to a **STARTUPINFO** structure as one of its parameters. Subsequently, a process can call the Win32 function **GetStartupInfo** function to retrieve the **STARTUPINFO** structure that was specified when the process was created.

When an application calls the **CreateProcess** function to create a new process, the application can create a **STARTUPINFO** structure to specify important properties of the new console window. The console can then pass the address of that structure to the **CreateProcess** call in the *lpsiStartInfo* parameter.

If an application supplies **NULL** value for the *lpsiStartInfo* parameter, **CreateProcess** creates a standard **STARTUPINFO** structure with default values.

This is the definition of the **STARTUPINFO** structure:

```
typedef struct _STARTUPINFO { /* si */
    DWORD cb;
    LPTSTR lpReserved;
    LPTSTR lpDesktop;
    LPTSTR lpTitle;
    DWORD dwX;
    DWORD dwY;
    DWORD dwXSize;
    DWORD dwYSize;
    DWORD dwXCountChars;
    DWORD dwYCountChars;
    DWORD dwFillAttribute;
    DWORD dwFlags;
    WORD wShowWindow;
    WORD cbReserved2;
    LPBYTE lpReserved2;
    HANDLE hStdInput;
    HANDLE hStdOutput;
    HANDLE hStdError;
} STARTUPINFO, *LPSTARTUPINFO;
```

When the **CreateProcess** function creates a process with a main window, the members of the **STARTUPINFO** structure passed to **CreateProcess** specify the window's properties.

When a graphical user interface (GUI) process is created, the **START-UPINFO** parameter affects the first window created by the **CreateWindow** function. When a console process is created, **START-**

UPINFO sets the properties of the process's console window. Subsequently, the new process can call the Win32 function **GetStartupInfo** function to retrieve the **STARTUPINFO** structure that was specified when it was created.

These are the members of the **STARTUPINFO** structure:

- *cb*: This member specifies the size, in bytes, of the **STARTUPINFO** structure.
- *lpReserved*: Set this element to **NULL** before passing the structure to **CreateProcess**.
- *lpDesktop*: This field specifies the name of a desktop to start the process in. If the desktop exists, the new process is associated with this desktop. If the desktop does not exist, a desktop with default attributes is created by this name for the new process.
- *lpTitle*: If the new process that is being creates a new console window, this element is a pointer to a string to be displayed as a title in the console window's title bar . If the *lpTitle* parameter is **NULL**, the name of the process's executable file is used as the window title. This member must be **NULL** for GUI or console processes that do not create a new console window.
- *dwX, dwY*: These members are ignored unless *dwFlags* specifies **STARTF_USEPOSITION**. If the new process creates a window and the *dwX* and *dwY* parameters are used, they specify the vertical (*x*) and horizontal (*y*) offsets, in pixels, of the upper left-hand corner of the window. The offsets are calculated beginning at the upper left-hand corner of the screen. For GUI processes, if the *x* parameter of **CreateWindow** is **CW_USEDEFAULT**, the specified position is used the first time **CreateWindow** is called to create an overlapped window.
- *dwXSize, dwYSize*: These members are ignored unless *dwFlags* specifies **STARTF_USESIZE**. If the new process creates a window, these elements specify the width (*dwXSize*) and height (*dwYSize*), in pixels, of the new window. For GUI processes, if the *nWidth* parameter of **CreateWindow** is **CW_USEDEFAULT**, these members apply only the first time **CreateWindow** is called to create an overlapped window .
- *dwXCountChars, dwYCountChars*: These elements are ignored unless *dwFlags* specifies **STARTF_USECOUNTCHARS**. For console processes that create a new console window, *the dwXCountChars and dYCountChars* elements specify the screen buffer width (*dwXCountChars*) and height (*dwYCountChars*), in character columns and rows. These values are ignored in GUI processes.

- *dwFillAttribute*: This member is ignored unless the value of *dwFlags* is **STARTF_USEFILLATTRIBUTE**. When **CreateProcess** is used to create a console process, *dwFillAttribute* specifies the initial text and background colors used by the window.

For an example of a **STARTUPINFO** structure used with the **CreateProcess** function, see "This Chapter's Example Programs" on page 401.

Creating GUI Processes and Console Processes

When **CreateProcess** is called to start a GUI process, the **STARTUPINFO** structure specifies the default values that are to be used the first time the new process calls the **CreateWindow** and **ShowWindow** functions to create and display an overlapped window.

When **CreateProcess** is called to start a console process, the values specified in the **STARTUPINFO** structure are used only when a new console process is created.

When an application calls **CreateProcess** is called to start a GUI process, the calling process can specify the width and height (in pixels) of the window created by **CreateWindow**, the location (in screen coordinates) of the window created by **CreateWindow**, and the *nCmdShow* parameter of **ShowWindow**.

Environment Variables

Every process has an environment block that contains a set of environment variables and their values. By default, a child process inherits its parent process's environment variables. However, an application can specify a different environment for the child process by creating a new environment block and passing a pointer to it as a parameter to the **CreateProcess** function.

You can obtain a pointer to a process's environment block by calling the Win32 function **GetEnvironmentString**. To change an environment variable, call the Win32 function **SetEnvironmentVariable**. To determine whether a specified variable is defined in the environment of the calling process, and, if so, what its value is, call the **GetEnvironmentVariable** function.

Objects and Handles

When a process creates a child process, the child process inherits a number of properties and resources from its parents by default. But an application, by overriding certain default settings, can prevent the inheritance of specified properties and resources—or of any properties and resources at all.

To understand how the inheritance of properties and resources works, it helps to understand how *objects*—Windows SDK objects, not C++ objects—are used in Windows 95 programs.

In the Win32 SDK, an *object* is an internal structure that represents a system resource, such as a file, a thread, or a graphic image. Applications cannot access SDK objects directly, but must address them through *handles*. A handle is usually (but not always) implemented as a pointer to a pointer. Handles are often used to access objects in Windows programs because a handle is sometimes the only way to keep track of an object as it is moved around in memory by the Windows memory manager.

Using Handles and Pointers in Windows 95 Programs

In SDK (non-Visual C++) applications, it is usually safer to reference a Windows object using a handle than it is to reference the object using a pointer. That's because the operating system manages handles, making sure that an object can always be accessed through its handle, even when the object is moved from one location to another in physical memory.

In Visual C++ applications, it is perfectly safe to use the **this** pointer and other pointers supported by the Microsoft Foundation Class library. So you'll often see both handles and pointers being used quite liberally in Visual C++ programs written for Windows 95.

The Win32 API provides a number functions for manipulating the handles that are used to access most kinds of objects. These functions can be used to create object handles, close object handles, and destroy objects.

Handles to some Windows objects can be inherited by threads and child processes, while other objects have handles that cannot be inherited. Also, some objects have handles that can be used only by the processes that create the objects, while other objects have handles that can be used by other processes.

When you create a new process by calling **CreateProcess**, the *fInheritHandles* parameter determines whether the child process inherits the parent process's inheritable handles. For more details about how handles are inherited, see "Handles to Processes" on page 362.

Duplicating Handles

Handles of objects associated with a process can sometimes be duplicated by another process. This is how the duplication of a handle works:

Suppose that an application creates an event object by calling the Win32 function **`CreateEvent`**. The **`CreateEvent`** function returns a handle to the event object that it creates, and event objects that are created by **`CreateEvent`** can have multiple handles.

Subsequently, if another application needs to open the event that has been created, it can call the Win32 function **`OpenEvent`** to obtain its own unique handle to the event object. Alternatively, the second application can call **`DuplicateHandle`** to obtain a handle to the event.

When a process makes a copy of a handle by calling **`DuplicateHandle`**, the duplicate handle can be used only by the process that created it. The **`DuplicateHandle`** function can be called either by a process that owns a handle or by a child process or a thread of the process that owns the handle.

The **`DuplicateHandle`** function has several uses, including these:

- It can create a non-inheritable copy of an original handle.
- It can make a duplicate handle with access rights that are different from those of the original handle.

If a process that owns an original handle makes a copy of the handle by calling **`DuplicateHandle`**, the handle that is returned by **`DuplicateHandle`** is a non-inheritable copy of the original handle.

If a thread or a child process calls **`DuplicateHandle`** to obtain a handle created by a parent process, the handle returned by **`DuplicateHandle`** is a non-inheritable handle that can be used only by the child process.

If more than one application has a handle to the same event object, each application is responsible for deleting its handle to the object when it finishes using the object. When all handles to an object are closed, the operating system removes the handle from memory.

Closing Handles

When a process terminates, the operating system automatically closes all handles used by the process and deletes all objects created by the process. However, when a thread terminates, the operating system—

with some exceptions—does not automatically close handles that are owned by the thread, or delete their associated objects. The objects to which these exceptions apply are *window objects, hook objects, window position objects*, and *dynamic data exchange (DDE) objects*. (For details, see Volume 2 of the *Microsoft Win32 Programmer's Reference*.)

For more information about object handles, see "Functions That Manage I/O Handles" on page 389.

Varieties of Windows Objects

There are three kinds of Windows objects (not to be confused with C++ objects): user objects, graphics device interface (GDI) objects, and kernel objects. These three kinds of objects are implemented in the six core dynamic-link libraries that are supplied with the Windows 95: specifically, the 16-bit and 32-bit versions of the USER32, GDI32, and KERNEL32 DLLs (see "The Windows Subsystem DLLs" on page 124).

User objects include windows, menus, icons, cursors, the desktop, and other kinds of user-interface and windows-related objects. GDI objects include brushes, bitmaps, fonts, devices contexts, regions, palettes, pens, and other kinds of graphics-related objects. Kernel objects include processes, threads, files, events, and other kinds of objects related to memory management.

User objects support window management, GDI objects support graphics, and kernel objects support memory management.

User Objects

User objects include windows, menus, icons, cursors, the desktop, and other kinds of user-interface and windows-related objects.

As mentioned earlier, handles to some kinds of objects can be duplicated, while handles to other kinds of objects are private to the process that created them. Also, some kinds of objects have handles that can be inherited by threads and child processes, while other kinds of objects have non-inheritable handles.

Handles to user objects are public; when a process creates a user object, it can share the object's handle with other processes.

GDI Objects

Handles to *GDI objects* are private; only the process that creates a GDI object can use the object's handle. If another process needs to access the same kind of GDI object, it must create a GDI object of its own.

A kernel (memory-management) object can have multiple handles. That means that when a process creates a kernel object, other processes can obtain their own individual handles to the object. Other characteristics of kernel objects vary, as explained under the next heading, "Kernel Objects."

Table 8.1 lists the three kinds of object handles and shows whether each type of handle can be duplicated or inherited.

Table 8.1 Characteristics of Object Handles

	User Objects	**GDI Objects**	**Kernel Objects**
Maximum handles per object	1	1	Multiple
Handles duplicatable?	No	No	Yes
Handles private?	No	Yes	Varies
Handles inheritable?	Yes	No	Varies

As Table 8.1 shows, user objects (window-related objects) and GDI objects (graphics-related objects) support only one handle per object. That means that handles to user objects and GDI objects cannot be duplicated by other processes.

Kernel Objects

To access a handle to a *kernel object*, a process must either create a new kernel object or open an existing kernel object. Any process can create a new handle to any existing kernel object, provided the process is aware of the name of the object and has security access to the object (for details on the security restrictions on access to Windows objects, see "The SECURITY_ATTRIBUTES Structure" on page 353).

Processes can inherit or duplicate handles to the following kinds of kernel objects:

- Processes
- Threads
- Event objects
- Semaphore objects
- Mutex objects
- Named and anonymous pipes
- Mailslots (pseudo-files used for one-way interprocess communications; see your Windows 95, Win32, and Visual C++ documentation)

- Files
- Communications devices.

All kernel objects except those listed are private to the process that created them and cannot be duplicated or inherited.

Handles to Processes

As explained in "Creating and Using Threads" on page 421, the **CreateProcess** function fills in the fields of a structure named **PROCESS_INFORMATION** when it is called. The **PROCESS_INFORMATION** structure call contains handles to both the newly created process and its primary thread.

These handles can be used as parameters to any function that accepts a thread or process handle. And they can be inherited by child processes, provided inheritance is granted by the flag that is specified when they are created. The handles are valid until closed, even after the process or thread they represent is terminated.

When an application has created a new process, the Win32 function **OpenProcess** can be called to obtain a handle to the process. **OpenProcess** can also be called to obtain a process handle's access rights and inheritability properties.

The Win32 function **GetCurrentProcess** returns a "pseudohandle" to the current process, and the **GetCurrentThread** function returns a pseudohandle to the current thread. Pseudohandles can be used just like ordinary handles by the calling process, but they cannot be inherited or duplicated for use by other processes.

Each of the three functions that creates a process or a thread (**CreateProcess**, **CreateThread**, and **CreateRemoteThread**) returns an identifier that uniquely identifies the process or thread being created. A process can obtain its own process identifier by calling the **GetCurrentProcessId** function.A thread can obtain its own thread identifier by calling **GetCurrentThreadId**. A thread or process identifier is valid from the time the thread or process is created until the thread or process terminates.

Inheritance of Handles and Other Resources

Processes can inherit handles and other resources—as well as processes—from a parent process. The following handles and resources can be inherited by processes:

- Any inheritable open handle returned by the **CreateFile** function. This category includes handles to files, console input buffers, console screen buffers, named pipes, serial communication devices, and mailslots. the console of parent process, unless the process is detached or a new console is created. A child console process also inherits the parent's standard handles, as well as access to the input buffer and the active screen buffer.
- Inheritable open handles to process, thread, mutex, event, semaphore, named pipe, anonymous pipe, and file mapping objects.
- Environment variables.
- The current directory.

How Handles Are Inherited

You can tell whether a handle is inheritable by examining the function that is used to open, create, or duplicate the handle. For each kind of object associated with a process, there is a creation function (such as **CreateProcess** or **CreateFile**) that takes a security-attributes argument. This argument points to a **SECURITY_ATTRIBUTES** structure with a flag that determines whether the handle can be inherited. If the security-attributes argument is **NULL**, the handle is not inherited. (For a description of the **SECURITY_ATTRIBUTES** structure, see "The SECURITY_ATTRIBUTES Structure" on page 353.)

A handle that is inherited by a child process refers to the same object as the parent process's handle does. Furthermore, it has the same value and the same access privileges as the corresponding handle of the parent process.

To use a handle, however, a child process must retrieve the handle and must have the information that it needs to access the object to which the handle refers. In most cases, the parent process must communicate this information to the child process. This communication can be carried out using various methods, including command lines, pipes, and shared memory).

When a process changes the state of an object whose handle is inherited, the change affects both processes. For example, if process uses a handle to read from a file whose handle it has inherited, the current file position is moved for all processes using the same handle.

A child process inherits the environment variables and current directory of its parent process by default. However, **CreateProcess** enables the parent process to specify a different current directory or a different block of environment variables. (Environment variables are symbolic variables that represent elements of the operating system. For example, paths and filenames are environment variables.)

Pseudohandles and Identifiers

A thread can obtain a *pseudohandle* to its own thread object by calling the Win32 function **GetCurrentThread**. A pseudohandle works like any other handle when it is used by the calling process; however, it cannot be inherited or duplicated for use by other processes.

Every thread has a 32-bit identifier as well as a handle. A thread can obtain its own thread identifier by calling the Win32 function **GetCurrentThreadId**. A thread's identifier is valid from the time the thread is created until the time it terminates.

Terminating a Process

A process terminates when any of the following conditions occurs:

- The last thread of the process terminates
- Any thread of the process calls the Win32 function **ExitProcess**
- The primary thread of the process returns (this results in an implicit call to **ExitProcess)**
- The Win32 function **TerminateProcess** is called, with a handle to the process.

What Happens when Processes Terminate

When a process terminates, the following events occur:

- Open handles to files or other resources associated with the process are closed automatically. (Note that the objects referenced by these handles exist until all open handles are closed. This means that an object remains valid after a process closes, if another process has a handle to it.)
- The state of the process object becomes signaled, satisfying any threads that are waiting for the process to terminate. (For more about synchronization and signaled and unsignaled states, see "Signaled and Unsignaled States" on page 425.)
- The termination status of the process changes from **STILL_-ACTIVE** to the process's exit code. (The termination status of processes is covered under the next heading, "The ExitProcess Function."

The ExitProcess Function

The safest way to terminate a process is to call the Win32 function **ExitProcess**. **ExitProcess** notifies all DLLs attached to the process that the process is being terminated. (For more information about DLLs, see Chapter 4, "Dynamic-Link Libraries.") **ExitProcess** also ensures that all threads of the process are terminated. This is important because child processes are not automatically terminated when a parent process terminates.

The TerminateProcess Function

An application can also terminate a process by calling the Win32 function **TerminateProcess**—but calling **TerminateProcess** is not recommended except in emergency situations, and Microsoft does not spell out what those situations are. It is clear that we should use **TerminateProcess** rarely, if at all.

The main shortcoming of **TerminateProcess** is that it does not notify DLLs that may be attached to the process that the process is being terminated. In contrast, when a function terminates with a call to **ExitProcess**, the news is passed to each attached DLL.

When a process is running, it has a 32-bit termination status that an application can obtain by calling the Win32 function **GetExitCodeProcess**. When a process terminates, its termination status becomes an exit code that can vary, depending on what caused the process to terminate. Therefore, an application can check to see if a process has terminated by calling **GetExitCodeProcess**.

While a process is running, its termination status is **STILL_ACTIVE**. When the process terminates, its termination status becomes an exit code that can be one of the following:

- The exit code specified by a call to **ExitProcess** or **TerminateProcess**
- The return value from a process's **main** or **WinMain** function
- An exception code for an unhandled exception that caused the process to terminate.

The fact that an exit code can have any of these values may seem confusing. Fortunately, however, the only process termination status that you'll usually have to be concerned with is the status **STILL_ACTIVE**. If a call to **GetExitCodeProcess** reveals that the termination status of a process is **STILL_ACTIVE**, you'll know that the process is still active. If **GetExitCodeProcess** returns any other value, that means that the process has terminated.

You can terminate a process by passing its exit code to **`ExitProcess`** or **`TerminateProcess`**. If a process is terminated in some other way (for example, by a fatal unhandled exception or a CTRL+C signal), the process's termination code is the exception code that caused the termination. The process's exit code is also used as the exit code of any threads of the process that have not yet terminated.

Windows 95 Console Processes

To show how Windows 95 creates and uses processes, this chapter presents a two example programs: a windows application named SLIMMDI and a console application named MYCONSOL. (In Windows 95, a console window is a plain-vanilla text window that lacks most of the fancy graphics features of full-fledged GUI windows. A console window cannot be equipped, for example, with dialog boxes, icons, Windows-style pull-down menus, or other GUI-style interface objects.)

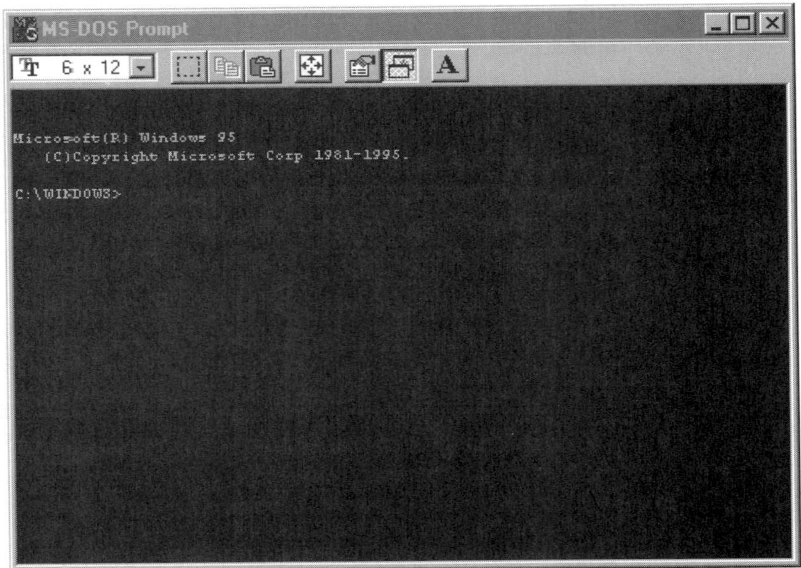

Figure 8.3 A console window

Both the sample programs presented in this chapter display interactive console windows like the one shown in Figure 8.3. Along with showing how Windows 95 processes work, the SLIMMDI and MYCONSOL programs demonstrate the use of the *Windows 95 console*:

a powerful API for developing and running text-based applications. With the Windows 95 console, you can create text-based windows for Windows 95 programs.

Building Console Applications

The Visual C++ AppWizard utility makes it easy to build a console application. When you choose the **File | New** menu item and the choose the **Project Workspace** item from the **New** dialog box, AppWizard displays a dialog box titled **New Project Workspace**. You can then build a console application by selecting the the **Console Application** item from the **Type** list box, as shown in Figure 8.4

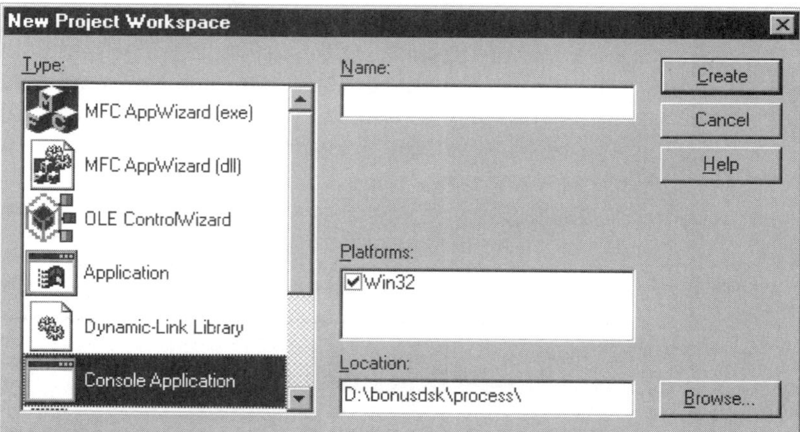

Figure 8.4 Creating a console application

Uses for Console Windows

Because Windows 95 does not have the kind of text mode as old-fashioned computers used to have, console windows are quite important in Windows 95 programs. Not only can they display text output when the need arises; they can come in handy when you want to port a text-based application to Windows 95 or when you want to do some special job, such as testing a snippet of code, porting an application from MS-DOS to Windows 95, or communicating with UNIX computers over a net.

You'll find console windows particularly useful if you ever have to port a DOS or UNIX application to Windows 95—especially if you're a DOS or UNIX programmer without much experience writing Windows-style applications. If that's your background, you can simply go through your DOS or UNIX code and convert its I/O functions—such as **`printf`** and **`scanf`**—to corresponding functions provided by the console API. Then you can simply compile and execute your Windows 95 console application.

These are other potential uses for console windows:

- They can be useful in networking and communications programs. Communications programs are often designed around text windows that accept keyboard input and display characters line by line on the screen. A console window can be an ideal way to manage that kind of I/O.
- A console window can also be a useful device for displaying error messages—particularly when GUI operations are disabled by errors that affect screen graphics.
- You can use console windows to create text-based programming tools such as interpreters, compilers, and debuggers. Windows 95 can display graphical windows and console windows on the screen simultaneously. You can use one console window to monitor code that is generating debugging information, while using others to observe such things as memory dumps, error notifications, and event logs.

Figure 8.5 on Page 369 shows how you can display multiple console windows on the same monitor screen.

The Win32 Console API

The tool used to display console windows is the *console API*, a set of functions provided in the Win32 SDK. Specifically, the functions and data structures that are used to create, display, and manipulate console windows are defined in a Win32 header file named WINCON.H.

Console windows are supported not only by Windows 95, but also by Windows NT, which also makes use of the Win32 API. They are not available in the Windows 3.*x* environment; to create text-only windows for 16-bit versions of Windows, you can use the QuickWin utility that is supplied with Visual C++. For more information about QuickWin, see the documentation that comes with 16-bit Visual C++.

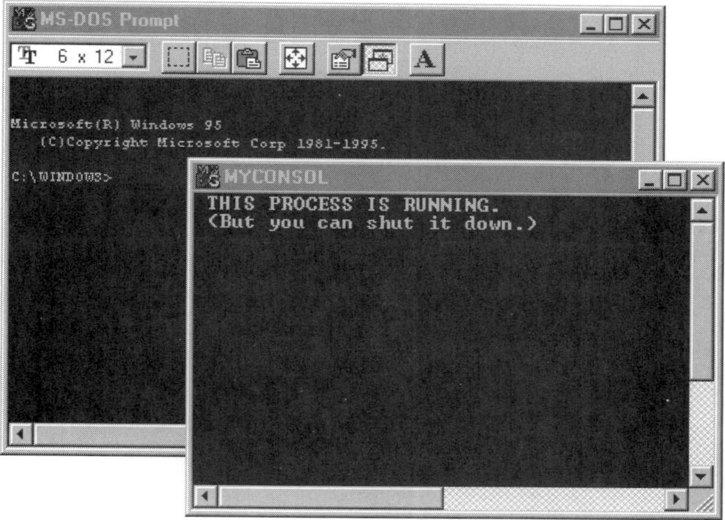

Figure 8.5 Displaying multiple console windows simultaneously

Using Console Windows

When you create a console window in a Windows 95 application, you do not have to worry about the intricacies of managing windows, dialog boxes, or other Windows-related I/O operations associated with your console window. Console windows do not support them. A console window cannot be equipped with most kinds of GUI-style I/O features, such as icons, full-featured pull-down menus, or dialog boxes.

But console windows do have a few of the same characteristics as full-fledged GUI-style windows. For example, you can size a console window, you can close it by selecting the **Close** item from a close-box menu, and you can scroll the text inside a console window with standard scroll bars.

The bottom line is that console windows are designed to handle purely text-based input and output; they manage I/O operations using a set of text-based API functions that have capabilities similar to those of the **`printf`** and **`scanf`** family of functions that are familiar to C-language programmers.

That is not always a handicap. Because of its limitations, as well as its features, a console window can be a useful alternative to a full-fledged GUI window when you want to perform a simple job quickly—for example, when you want to test a section of code for a process or a program.

Console Windows and GUI Windows

Although a console window works only with text-based operations, it does not have to be the only window that is visible on the Windows 95 screen. As Figure 8.5 shows, an application can display multiple console windows, and multiple GUI windows, on the same screen simultaneously.

When a console window is open, it works just like a UNIX or MS-DOS text screen. In fact, one example of a console application is the DOS window application that comes with Windows 95.

When you double-click the icon labeled **Command Prompt** in the main icon group of the Windows 95 desktop, a console window opens, as shown in Figure 8.5. From that window, you can execute any MS-DOS command in the same way you would from any DOS window: by typing the command and then pressing the **`Return`** key.

Creating Console Windows

When Windows 95 starts a GUI (graphical user interface) process—that is, an ordinary Windows 95 process—the process is not automatically supplied with a console window. But a GUI process can open a console window by calling a Win32 SDK function named **`AllocFunction`**.

When an application opens a console window by calling **`AllocFunction`**, the console window is attached to the currently executing process. An application can detach a console window from the current process by calling the Win32 procedure **`FreeFunction`**.

An application can also create a console window by starting a new process that is specifically identified as a console process. To start a new console process, you call theWin32 function **`CreateProcess`** function with a special flag set. That flag is known as the **`CREATE_NEW_CONSOLE`** flag. To learn how to set and use the **`CREATE_NEW_CONSOLE`** flag, see "Creating and Using Windows 95 Processes" on page 347. For more information about threads, see Chapter 9, "Multithreading and Multitasking."

When **`CreateProcess`** is called with the **`CREATE_NEW_CONSOLE`** flag set, a new console window is created and is attached to the newly created process. If a flag named **`DETACHED_PROCESS`** is set when

CreateProcess is called to create a console process, the new process inherits its console from the calling process.

The STDIN, STDOUT, and STDERR Handles

When Windows 95 creates a console, three handles for controlling the console's I/O operations are also created:

- The STDIN handle, which can be used to access the console's input buffer
- The STDOUT handle, which can access the standard output associated with a process
- The STDERR handle, which can access the standard diagnostic (error) handle associated with a process.

A process can obtain these three handles by calling the **GetStdHandle** function, and can set them by calling the **SetStdHandle** function. With the **SetStdHandle** function, a process can also redirect any or all of these three handles to locations other than a console's I/O functions. That makes it possible to pipe data back and forth between a console's I/O functions and other sources and destinations using named and anonymous pipes (programming mechanisms that can move information from one process to another).

Named pipes are pipes that are assigned names and can be accessed locally or across a network using their names. Anonymous pipes are not named and can be accessed only from within the same program in which they are created.

When a process has obtained a standard I/O handle from a console process by calling **GetStdHandle**, the calling process can access the handle by calling any of four console I/O functions provided by the Win32 SDK. To read from a console's standard output handle, the process can call **ReadFile** or **ReadConsole**. To write to a console's standard input handle, a process can call **WriteFile** or **WriteConsole**.

For more details about these four functions, see "Functions That Access Console I/O Buffers" on page 393.

Creating a Console Window with *AllocConsole*

The **AllocConsole** function allocates a new console for the calling process. **AllocConsole** does not create a new console process; it merely creates a new console and attaches it to the calling process. To create a new console process, an application must call **CreateProcess**, the next call listed in this section.

Syntax of the AllocConsole Function

This is the syntax of the **AllocConsole** function:

```
BOOL AllocConsole()
```

If **AllocConsole** succeeds, it returns a value of **TRUE**; otherwise, it returns a value of **FALSE**.

A process can be associated with only one console, so **AllocConsole** fails if the calling process already has a console.

When an application allocates a console by calling **AllocConsole**, Windows 95 equips the new console with a set of handles for standard input, standard output, and standard diagnostic output. The new console can then use those handles to manage input, output, and the handling of error messages. A console can obtain its standard I/O handles by calling the Win32 function **GetStdHandle**.

Using the AllocConsole Function

In the SLIMMDI program on your bonus disk, this code fragment in the SLIMMDI.CPP file creates a new console by calling the **AllocConsole** function:

```
void ConsoleAlloc()
{
   AllocConsole();
   while (TRUE);
   FreeConsole();
        }
```

This code fragment does the absolute minimum that is required to display a console window; it merely opens a console window by calling **AllocConsole**, loops until the user closes the console window, and then frees the console when the window closes. As you can observe by executing the SLIMMDI program and selecting the **Alloc** item under the **Console** menu, this minimum programming effort yields minimum results; the console window that is created doesn't display any text on the screen or respond to typed input from the user, and when the user closes the window by selecting the close item from the window's close-box menu, the whole application shuts down.

Creating a Console with the *CreateProcess* Function

Another way to create a and manage a console window is to open a new process with its own console window by calling **Create-**

Process. The new process can then open a console window by making its own AllocConsole call.

As noted in "Syntax of the CreateProcess Function" on page 348, one of the parameters passed to the CreateProcess is a pointer to a STARTUPINFO structure. A process can obtain information about the STARTUPINFO structure currently in use by calling the GetStartupInfo function.

Console processes can use the following functions to get and set the values of individual member variables of STARTUPINFO structure:

- GetConsoleScreenBufferInfo can obtain the window size, the screen buffer size, and the color attributes of a console from a STARTUPINFO structure.
- GetConsoleTitle obtains the title currently displayed in a console window's title bar.
- SetConsoleScreenBufferSize can change the size of a console window's screen buffer.
- SetConsoleTextAttribute sets the color attributes of a console window.
- SetConsoleTitle specifies the title to be displayed in a console window's title bar.
- SetConsoleWindowInfo can change the size of a console window.

Each member variable of the STARTUPINFO struct is described in Chapter 9, "Multithreading and Multitasking."

Input Buffers and Screen Buffers

A *console* (the Win32 mechanism that displays console windows) has two components: an *input buffer* and a *screen buffer*. When the user of an application types information that is to be displayed in a console window, the data is stored in the console's input buffer.

The input buffer stores information that is input by the user in a queue of input records. Each input record contains information about an input event.

When information has been placed in a console's input buffer, it can be transferred to a screen buffer. Then it can be displayed on the screen.

A screen buffer is a two-dimensional array of character and color data that can be displayed in a console window. In a console screen buffer, the data for each character to be shown on the screen is stored in a `CHAR_INFO` structure. A `CHAR_INFO` structure contains a code that represents specifies the ANSI or Unicode character to be displayed (see box, below), along with the foreground and background colors that are used to display the character. For more details about the `CHAR_INFO` structure, see "Functions for Managing Screen Buffers" on page 394.

A console can be equipped with multiple screen buffers, but only one screen buffer can be displayed at a time.

Screen Buffers and Console Windows

There is a difference between a screen buffer and a console window. A console window is the rectangular region of a console screen buffer that is displayed on the screen.

When an application creates a new console, a new input buffer and a new screen buffer for the console are automatically created. A process can call the Win32 function `CreateConsoleScreenBuffer` to create additional screen buffers for its console. (The `CreateConsoleScreenBuffer` function is examined more closely in "Creating and Using Windows 95 Processes" on page 347. Processes are covered in Chapter 9, "Multithreading and Multitasking.")

The process associated with the new console can obtain the handles of the new console's input and screen buffers by making a Win32 call named `GetStdHandle`. The new process can then use those handles to access its console.

When a console window is accepting keyboard input, or has what is known as the *keyboard focus*, the console API formats each input event—such as a single keystroke, a movement of the mouse, or a mouse-button click—as an input record. That record is kept in the console's input buffer until it is transferred to the screen buffer. Thus, when a console process is running, the console's input buffer contains a queue of input event records.

The screen buffer that is displayed in the console window is considered the active screen buffer. A new screen buffer becomes active when its handle is specified in a call to the `SetConsoleActiveScreenBuffer` function (for more information, see "Creating and Using Windows 95 Processes" on page 347). Even when a screen buffer is inactive, a console process can access it for both reading and writing.

The Unicode Character Set

Unicode is an international 16-bit standard for encoding characters. Unicode is preferred over the ANSI-code standard in international circles because it can encode the complete character sets of languages such as Chinese and Japanese, which have thousands of character symbols. Windows 95 supports the use of both ANSI and Unicode characters.

The Win32 SDK is equipped with a set of macros and naming conventions that make it comparatively easy to edit and recompile existing ANSI-compliant applications using the Unicode character set. ANSI and Unicode characters can be intermixed in the same application.

To use Unicode in an application, you must substitute certain Windows functions for common C-language functions. For example, Unicode applications use the `lstrcmp` function in place of the `strcmp` function, and `lstrlen` in place of `strlen`. Also, applications that use Unicode must define the precompiler variable _UNICODE, and must include the header files TCHAR.H and WCHAR.H.

Setting Screen Buffer Properties

The Win32 SDK provides a large assortment of functions for changing the size, shape, and appearance of console windows. If a console has multiple screen buffers, the properties of each console screen can be set independently. The properties associated with a screen buffer include the following:

- Screen buffer size, usually expressed in character rows and columns
- Text attributes, including the foreground and background colors used for displaying text in console windows
- The size and location of console windows
- The position, appearance, and visibility of the cursor used in a console window.

The Win32 functions that are used to set screen buffer properties are listed and described in "Creating and Using Windows 95 Processes" on page 347.

Input Buffer and Screen Buffer Handles

When an application creates a new console process by calling `CreateProcess` with the `CREATE_NEW_CONSOLE` flag set, Windows 95 creates a new console window, a new input buffer, and a new screen buffer. (For more about calling `CreateProcess` to start new processes, see Chapter 9, "Multithreading and Multitasking.")

A console's input buffer and screen buffer can be accessed through a handle. To write to an input buffer, or to set the attributes of text displayed in a screen buffer, an application must obtain the buffer's handle.

An application can obtain handles to access a console's input buffer and screen buffer by calling the Win32 function `GetStdHandle`. The application can then use those handles to access its console buffers.

High-Level and Low-Level Functions

The Win32 SDK provides two kinds of functions for retrieving information that has been input by a user and has been stored in a console's input buffer. These two kinds of functions are called high-level functions and low-level functions.

When low-level functions are used for input-buffer and screen-buffer I/O, the event records stored in a console's input buffer can contain information about keyboard events, mouse events, buffer-resizing events, and menu events. When an application uses high-level console I/O functions, the event records stored in the input record contain only character data.

How High-Level and Low-Level Functions Work

When information that is input by the user has been stored in a console's input buffer, high-level functions filter and process the information before it is displayed on the screen. This ensures that nonprinting characters behave as expected when they are typed in by the user and sent to the screen.

When data stored in a console input buffer is processed using high-level functions, nonprinting characters behave in the standard ways that most applications expect when they are input and output using high-level functions.

Although high-level functions recognize keyboard information that is input by the user, they do not recognize most mouse operations.

Low-level functions provide direct access to a console's input buffer. They do not filter or process information that is input by the user before it is displayed on the screen.

Low-level functions track mouse events as well as keyboard events received from the user.

High-Level and Low-Level I/O

As noted in the preceding paragraphs, the two kinds of functions offered by the Win32 console API—high-level functions and low-level functions—can be used to place information in a console's input buffer and to write information to the console's screen buffer.

The I/O functions provided by the console API can also be divided into two other categories: *input functions* and *output functions*. Input functions read information from a console's input buffer, and output functions write that information to the screen.

High-level input functions filter and process the data in a console's input buffer and return input as a stream of characters, discarding mouse and buffer-resizing events before the data is written to the screen. *High-level output functions* write streams of characters to the screen, starting at the current cursor location in the screen buffer. The high-level console I/O functions provided by the Win32 API are `ReadFile`, `WriteFile`, `ReadConsole`, and `WriteConsole`. All these functions are described in this section.

Low-level input functions and *low-level output functions* provide direct access to a console's input buffer and output buffer, but require more programming attention from the software developer. The low-level console I/O functions are `ReadConsoleInput`, `WriteConsoleInput`, `PeekConsoleInput`, `GetNumberOfConsoleInputEvents`, and `FlushConsoleInputBuffer`.

For more about high-level and low-level I/O functions, see "High-Level Console I/O Functions" on page 386 and "Low-Level Console I/O Functions" on page 388.

High-Level and Low-Level Functions Compared

High-level I/O functions provide the easiest way to read a stream of characters from console input or to write a stream of characters to console output. So high-level functions are often used in applications that make use of line-by-line input and output, such as networking and communications programs.

Low-level console functions can give an application more precise control over a console's operation than high-level functions can. For example, low-level functions can respond to mouse movements and mouse clicks, and they can handle cut-and-paste operations that involve odd-sized rectangles of text. But low-level functions are more difficult to handle than high-level functions, and they tend to make a programmer's life more complicated.

An application does note have to use high-level console functions or low-level console functions exclusively; it can use any combination of high-level and low-level functions.

How High-Level I/O Functions Work

When a console window is managed using high-level functions, it retrieves data from its input buffer by reading from standard input and writes data to its screen buffer by writing to standard output. A console can also write error messages to standard diagnostic output.

High-level console functions also support redirection of information via pipes (software constructs that can pass information from one process to another). That capability makes high-level functions useful in networking and communications programs, as well as in other kinds of client-server applications.

How Low-Level I/O Functions Work

If a console application requires the use of a mouse as well as the use of a keyboard, low-level functions can be used to track mouse events—that is, events triggered by mouse movements, by the pressing and releasing of mouse buttons, and by mouse actions that affect the size of the active screen buffer. Low-level console functions can be useful when you want to port a character-based application from a text-based environment, such as DOS or UNIX, to Windows 95.

Low-level console calls can also be used by applications that rely on mouse input as well as character input from the keyboard.

The ReadFile and ReadConsole Functions

When an application manages console I/O using high-level console functions, the application reads data from the console's input buffer by executing either the `ReadFile` function or the `ReadConsole` function. The `ReadFile` function supports only the ANSI character set, while the `ReadConsole` function supports both ANSI characters and Unicode, an expanded character set that can handle multibyte characters (for more about Unicode, see the box titled "The Unicode Character Set" on page 375).

Another difference between `ReadFile` and `ReadConsole` is that `ReadFile` can be used to access files, pipes, and serial communications devices, while `ReadConsole` can be used only with console handles. This distinction is important if an application relies on standard handles that may have been redirected.

The WriteFile and WriteConsole Functions

To write data to a console's screen buffer using high-level functions, you can execute the `WriteFile` function or the `WriteConsole` function. The `WriteFile` function supports only the ANSI character set, while the `WriteConsole` function supports both ANSI characters and Unicode characters (see box, "The Unicode Character Set" on page 375). Also, `WriteFile` can be used to access files, pipes, and serial communications devices, while `WriteConsole` can be used only with console handles.

For more information about the syntax and use of the `ReadFile`, `ReadConsole`, `WriteFile`, and `WriteConsole` functions, see "Console Control Handlers" on page 381.

Other Low-Level I/O Functions

When you manage console I/O using low-level functions, you can read from a console's input buffer by executing the `ReadConsoleInput` function. To write to a console's screen buffer, you execute the `WriteConsoleInput` function. Other Win32 functions that are used in low-level console I/O:

- `PeekConsoleInput`, which reads data from a console input buffer without removing any pending input records that the buffer might contain
- `GetNumberOfConsoleInputEvents`, which obtains the number of unread records in a console input buffer
- `FlushNumberOfConsoleInputEvents`, which discards all unread events in a console input buffer.

Refer to the *Microsoft Win32 Programmer's Reference* for more details about the functions `PeekConsoleInput`, `GetNumberOfConsoleInputEvents`, and `FluxhNumberOfConsoleInputEvents`. For more information about the `ReadConsoleInput` and `WriteConsoleInput` functions, see "Console Control Handlers" on page 381.

Console Input and Output Modes

Every console input buffer is associated with a set of *input modes* that affects input operations. Similarly, every console screen buffer has a set of *output modes* that affects output operations.

The input modes provided by the console API can be divided into two groups: modes that affect high-level input functions, and modes that affect low-level input functions. The output modes provided by the console API affect only applications that use the high-level output functions.

By setting a console's input and output modes, an application can determine how information from the keyboard is filtered and processed.

By default, high-level console functions filter and process keyboard information to make nonprinting characters behave in ways that many applications expect; for example, the tab character moves the cursor forward (12 spaces by default), and a beep sounds when the bell key is pressed.

When the console is in its default low-level mode, mouse input and buffer-resizing events are recognized, and nonprinting characters behave in ways that most applications expect.

You can obtain and set a console's input and output modes by calling the Win32 functions `GetConsoleMode` and `SetConsoleMode`, which are described in "Creating and Using Windows 95 Processes" on page 347.

High-Level Input Modes

The following are high-level input modes available to console processes:

- *Line input mode*, which determines whether line-by-line input from the user is supported. When line input mode is enabled, the `ReadFile` and `ReadConsole` functions return when the Enter key is pressed. When line input mode is disabled, `ReadFile` and `ReadConsole` return each time a character becomes available in the console's input buffer.
- *Processed input mode*, which controls the processing of information received from the backspace, tab, bell, carriage return, and linefeed characters. When processed input mode is enabled, all those characters behave in the same way they behave when text is being typed on a typewriter.
- *Echo input mode*, which determines whether keyboard input that is received from the input buffer is echoed to the active screen buffer. The effects of echo input mode depend upon the output mode of the active screen buffer.

By default, all three of these high-level input modes are enabled. When that is the case, the console is said to be running in "cooked" mode. If you decide to deactivate one of these modes, it is recommended that you deactivate all three of them, because all three are designed to work together. When all three high-level input modes are deactivated, the console is said to be running in "raw" mode.

High-Level Output Modes

The following are the console API's high-level output modes:

- *Processed output mode,* which determines whether information in the input buffer is filtered and processed before it is displayed on the screen
- *Wrapping at EOL (end of line) output mode,* which determines whether the cursor moves to the first column in the next screen row when it reaches the end of the current row in the console window.

By default, both of the high-level output modes are enabled, along with the three high-level input modes described under the previous subheading. All five high-level console modes should generally be turned on or off in a group, not individually, because all five modes are designed to work together.

Low-Level Input Modes

The low-level input modes supported by the Win32 API are:

- *Mouse input mode,* which determines whether mouse events sent to the input buffer are recognized
- *Window input mode,* which determines whether buffer-resizing events are recognized
- *Processed input mode,* which controls the filtering and processing of nonprinting characters.

You can obtain information about the current console mode by calling the Win32 function `GetConsoleMode`. To set the current console mode, you can call the function `SetConsoleMode`. You can specify which low-level or high-level mode (or combination of modes) you want to set by setting flag constants that are recognized by the `GetConsoleMode` and `SetConsoleMode` functions. These flags are listed and described in "Creating and Using Windows 95 Processes" on page 347.

Console Control Handlers

As DOS and UNIX programmers know, certain key combinations are often treated in special ways in text-based applications. For example, the CTRL+C key combination is often treated as an interrupt signal, and the CTRL+BREAK combination is often treated as a break signal.

When a Win32 console process is running, it handles certain key combinations and mouse events with a special kind of function called a *control handler*. Besides handling the key combinations such as CTRL+C and CTRL+BREAK, control handlers provide responses to certain mouse events, such as selection of the **Close** menu. Each console process has a set of control handler functions that are called by the system when the process receives a CTRL+C, CTRL+BREAK, or CTRL+CLOSE signal.

Initially, the list of control handlers owned by each process contains only a default handler function that calls the Win32 function `ExitProcess`. An application can provide a console process with additional handler functions—or it can remove existing handler functions from a console process—by calling Win32 procedure `SetConsoleCtrlHandler`.

Using a Console Control Handler

In the SLIMMDI example program on your bonus disk, this control handler appears in the MYCONSOL.CPP file:

```
BOOL CtrlHandler(DWORD fdwCtrlType) {
   DWORD exitCode;
   HANDLE hThisProcess = GetCurrentProcess();
   GetExitCodeProcess(hThisProcess, &exitCode);

   switch (fdwCtrlType) {
   case CTRL_C_EVENT:
      ExitProcess(exitCode);
      return TRUE;
   case CTRL_CLOSE_EVENT:
      ExitProcess(exitCode);
      return TRUE;
   case CTRL_BREAK_EVENT:
   case CTRL_LOGOFF_EVENT:
   case CTRL_SHUTDOWN_EVENT:
   default:
      return FALSE;
   }
}
```

In this code fragment, a `switch` statement controls what happens to keyboard and mouse events that are sent to the control handler. If the user presses CTRL+C (a `CTRL_C_EVENT`), `ExitProcess` is called and the control handler returns a value of `TRUE`. The same thing happens when the user activates a `CTRL_CLOSE_EVENT` by selecting Close from the console window's close-box menu. All other events tracked by the control handler return `FALSE`.

Registering a Control Handler

An application invokes a control handler by calling the Win32 function `SetConsoleCtrlHandler`, passing the function a pointer to the control handler that is to be used.

The `SetConsoleCtrlHandler` function always affects just one process; it does not affect the lists of control handlers for other processes. When a console process receives any of the control signals, it calls the handler functions on a last-registered, first-called basis until it encounters a control handler that returns `TRUE`. If no handler that returns `TRUE` is found, the process's default handler is called.

This code fragment, which also appears in the MYCONSOL.CPP file, registers a control handler:

```
// Set console's control handler.
BOOL bRetVal =
 SetConsoleCtrlHandler((PHANDLER_ROUTINE)CtrlHandler,
   TRUE);
if (!bRetVal)
   MyErrMsg("Could not set up control handler.",
      myConsole);
```

For more information on control handler functions, see Volume 2 of the *Microsoft Win32 Programmer's Reference* .

Functions That Release Console Windows

The following functions release console windows:

- `FreeConsole`
- `ExitProcess`
- `TerminateProcess`

The `FreeConsole` function detaches the calling process from its console window (provided the calling process has a console window), and destroys the console unless it is shared by other processes. If other processes share the console, it is not destroyed until it is released by all processes that share it.

The `ExitProcess` function detaches the calling function from its console window (if it has a console window), and then terminates the function. ExitProcess performs all necessary housekeeping before it terminates a process, and is therefore the recommended call for exiting a process.

`TerminateProcess`, like `ExitProcess`, detaches the calling console from its console window (if there is one) and then closes all threads of the calling function. Then, unlike `ExitProcess`, it performs a quick-and-dirty exit from the function. When you end a process by calling `TerminateProcess`, there is no guarantee that the integrity of all data associated with the process will be maintained; specifically, the state of any global data that is being used by any DLLs that are attached to the process may be compromised. So, if possible, you should avoid shutting down processes by calling `TerminateProcess`; call `ExitProcess` instead.

A console process, like any other process (see Chapter 9, "Multithreading and Multitasking."), remains in the system until all its threads have terminated and all handles to the process and any of its threads are closed. You can call the `CloseHandle` function to close any handle associated with a process. Alternatively, you can call `ExitProcess` to perform a clean shutdown of a process, all its threads, and all its handles.

When the last process that is attached to a console terminates or frees the console by calling `FreeConsole`, the console window is destroyed. When the last thread associated with a process terminates, Windows 95 services perform the following steps:

1. All objects opened by the process are implicitly closed.
2. The process's termination status (a value that can be obtained by calling `GetExitCodeProcess`) changes from its initial value (`STILL_ACTIVE`) to the termination status of the last thread that terminates.
3. The thread object of the main thread is set to the signaled state, satisfying the needs any threads that may have been waiting for the object.
4. The process object is set to the signaled state, satisfying the needs of any threads that may have been waiting for the object.

For more information about terminating processes, see Chapter 9, "Multithreading and Multitasking."

The FreeConsole Function

If a process is attached to a console, it can detach itself from its console by calling `FreeConsole`. This is the syntax of the `FreeConsole` function:

```
BOOL FreeConsole()
```

If the `FreeConsole` function succeeds, it returns a value of `TRUE`. If not, it returns a value of `FALSE`.

The ExitProcess Function

The best way to terminate a process is to call the `ExitProcess` function. That's because `ExitProcess` performs all necessary housekeeping before it terminates a function, so the function can shut down gracefully. Before `ExitProcess` shuts down a process, it informs all DLLs attached to the process that the process is terminating. The DLLs thus have a chance to protect the integrity of their global data before the process ends.

Because `ExitProcess` takes these steps, it is the function that your applications should call to shut down functions. An alternative function, `TerminateProcess` (next item) is much more dangerous. It does not protect the integrity of global data used by DLLs when the process ends, and should therefore be not be used to end a process except in the rare event of an emergency shutdown.

Syntax for Calling ExitProcess

This is the syntax used for calling the `ExitProcess` function:

```
VOID ExitProcess(UINT uExitCode)
```

The `ExitProcess` function does not return a value.

The *uExit* parameter shown in the preceding example is an exit code that applies to the process being terminated. This exit code also applies to all threads that are terminated as a result of the call.

An application can obtain the correct exit code for a function by calling a console API function named `GetExitCodeProcess`to retrieve the process's exit code. (As noted in Chapter 9, "Multithreading and Multitasking," a similar function—`GetExitCodeThread`—can be used to retrieve a thread's exit code.)

Calling the ExitProcess Function

In the SLIMMDI example program provided on your bonus disk, the `ExitProcess` function is executed inside a control handler. That takes place in a source-code segment that appears under the heading "Console Control Handlers" on page 381.

High-Level Console I/O Functions

As noted in the box titled "High-Level and Low-Level I/O" on page 377, the Win32 API provides two kinds of console I/O functions: high-level functions and low-level functions. The high-level I/O functions are `ReadFile`, `WriteFile`, `ReadConsole`, and `WriteConsole`. The low-level console I/O functions are `ReadConsoleInput`, `WriteConsoleInput`, `PeekConsoleInput`, `GetNumberOfConsoleInputEvents`, and `FlushConsoleInputBuffer`.

With the high-level console I/O functions—`ReadFile`, `WriteFile`, `ReadConsole`, and `WriteConsole`—an application can read console input and write console output as a stream of characters. The `ReadConsole` and `WriteConsole` functions behave just like the `ReadFile` and `WriteFile` functions, except that they can be used either as wide-character functions (in which text arguments must use Unicode characters) or as ANSI functions (in which text arguments must use characters from the Windows 3.*x* character set).

Applications that must maintain a single set of sources to support either Unicode or the ANSI character set should use the `ReadConsole` and `WriteConsole` functions. For more about Unicode characters, see the box titled "The Unicode Character Set" on page 375.

The ReadConsole Function

The `ReadConsole` function reads character input from the console input buffer and removes it from the buffer. The syntax of this function is:

```
BOOL ReadConsole(HANDLE hConsoleInput, LPVOID
lpvBuffer, DWORD
   cchToRead, LPDWORD lpcchRead, LPVOID lpvReserved)
```

`ReadConsole` returns a value of `TRUE` if it succeeds, and a value of `FALSE` if it does not.

When you call ReadConsole, you must provide the function with a handle to a console input buffer (*hConsoleInput*), a pointer to a buffer that receives data from the console input buffer (*lpvBuffer*), and the number of characters that you want the function to read (*cchToRead*). When the call returns, it reports the number of characters that have actually been read in the *lpcchReac* parameter. The *lpvReserved* parameter is reserved for future use and currently should not be used.

The ReadFile Function

The `ReadFile` function reads data from a file or from a console buffer, starting at the position specified by a file pointer. When the read operation is complete. `ReadFile` adjusts the file pointer by the number of bytes actually read, unless the file handle is created with a special attribute called the overlapped attribute. If the file handle is created with the overlapped attribute enabled, the `ReadFile` function must be provided with certain information that is used in asynchronous output. This information is used to adjust the position of the file pointer after the read takes place.

The syntax of the `ReadFile` function is identical to the syntax of the `ReadConsole` function, with two exceptions: The first parameter of a call to `ReadFile` can be either a file handle or the handle of an input buffer, and the fifth parameter of the function is the address of an `OVERLAPPED` structure, which contains information used in asynchronous I/O.

I/O Functions, Console Handles, and File Handles

`ReadConsole` and `WriteConsole` can be used only with console handles. In contrast, `ReadFile` and `WriteFile` can be used with other kinds of handles, such as handles that access files or pipes. `ReadConsole` and `WriteConsole` fail, however, if an application attempts to use them with a standard handle that has been redirected and is no longer a console handle.

If `ReadFile` or `ReadConsole` is called with line input mode enabled (the default), there is no return to the calling application until the ENTER key is pressed. If line input mode is disabled, `ReadFile` and `ReadConsole` do not return until at least one character is available. In either mode, all available characters are read until either no more keys are available or the specified number of characters has been read. Unread characters are buffered until the next read operation.

When `ReadFile` and `ReadConsole` return, they report the total number of characters that have been read. If echo input mode is enabled, characters read by `ReadFile` and `ReadConsole` are written to the active screen buffer at the current cursor position.

Using the WriteConsole and WriteFile Functions

The `WriteFile` and `WriteConsole` functions can write to either an active or an inactive screen buffer. `WriteFile` can also write to a file or a pipe if the `STDOUT` handle of the console is redirected.

When processed output mode or "wrap at EOL" output mode is enabled, the output mode determines the way in which characters are written or echoed to a screen buffer. Characters written by `WriteFile` or `WriteConsole`, or echoed by `ReadFile` or `ReadConsole`, are inserted in a screen buffer at the current cursor position.

As each character is written, the cursor position advances to the next character cell, except that the behavior at the end of a line depends on the screen buffer's wrap at EOL output mode. An application can use the `GetConsoleScreenBufferInfo` function to determine the current cursor position and the `SetConsoleCursorPosition` function to set the cursor position. More more details about these functions, see "Functions for Managing Screen Buffers" on page 394.

Low-Level Console I/O Functions

The low-level console I/O functions, as noted under the preceding headings, provide an application with direct access to a console's input and screen buffers. Thus, they provide the software developer with extensive control over console I/O.

With the low-level console I/O functions, an application can do the following:

- Obtain information about mouse and buffer-resizing events
- Obtain extended information about keyboard input events
- Write input records to the input buffer
- Read input records without removing them from the input buffer
- Determine the number of pending events in the input buffer
- Flush the input buffer
- Read and write strings of Unicode (16-bit) characters or ANSI characters at a specified location in a screen buffer
- Read and write strings of text and background color attributes at specified screen buffer locations
- Read and write rectangular blocks of character and color data at a specified screen buffer location
- Write single Unicode (16-bit) characters or ANSI characters, or text and background color attribute combinations, to a specified number of consecutive cells beginning at a specified screen buffer location

This is a powerful set of capabilities. However, as noted in the box titled "The ReadFile and ReadConsole Functions" on page 378, the usefulness of most of these functions in real-world applications seems limited. If you're interested in making a more detailed investigation of the low-level console I/O functions, see the *Microsoft Win32 Programmer's Reference* .

Functions That Manage I/O Handles

As explained in "Objects and Handles" on page 357, console processes use *object handles* to access the input and screen buffers of their consoles. To help applications manage these handles, the console API provides four functions: `GetStdHandle`, `SetStdHandle`, `CreateFile`, and `CreateConsoleScreenBuffer`.

Console handles returned by `CreateFile` and `CreateConsoleScreenBuffer` can be used in any console functions that require a handle of a console's input buffer or of a console screen buffer. Handles returned by `GetStdHandle` can be used by the console functions if they have not been redirected to refer to something other than console I/O.

If a standard handle has been redirected to refer to a file or a pipe, however, the handle can only be used by the `ReadFile` and `WriteFile` functions (for more about `ReadFile` and `WriteFile`, see "Functions That Access Console I/O Buffers" on page 393).

When a console process is running, an application can read from the console's standard output handle by calling the `ReadFile` function or the `ReadConsole` function. To write to a console's standard input handle, a process can call `WriteFile` or `WriteConsole`. These four functions are described under the headings that follow.

The GetStdHandle Function

When an application needs to read from or write to a console window, it can obtain the console's I/O handles by calling `GetStdHandle`. It can then obtain data from the console's input buffer by reading the data from the input handle obtained from `GetStdHandle`. Conversely, it can send data to the console's screen buffer by writing to the output handle provided by the `GetStdHandle` function. `GetStdHandle` also provides a diagnostic handle that can be used as a destination for error messages.

Syntax of the GetStdHandle Function

An application can call `GetStdHandle` using this syntax:

```
HANDLE GetStdHandle(DWORD fdwDevice)
```

If GetStdHandle is successful, it returns the handle it has obtained. If the call is not successful, it returns a NULL value.

The *fdwDevice* parameter shown in the preceding example is a constant that specifies the kind of handle that the function is being used to obtain. The *fdwDevice* parameter can have one of three values:

- STD_INPUT_HANDLE instructs the GetStdHandle function to return a standard input handle.
- STD_OUTPUT_HANDLE requests a standard output handle.
- STD_ERROR_HANDLE places an order for a standard error handle.

If the GetStdHandle function succeeds, it returns the requested handle. If it fails, it returns an INVALID_HANDLE_FLAG. To obtain more information about a failure of the function, an application can call the Win32 SDK's GetLastError Function.

Using the GetStdHandle Function

In the SLIMMDI example program, before GetStdHandle is called, a function named MConsole::Open runs a test to see whether the current process has an open console. If there is an open console, the function calls FreeConsole to close it down. Then AllocConsole is called to open a new console.

That done, the MConsole::Open function calls GetStdHandle.

In the SLIMMDI example program, the MConsole::Open member function appears in the MYCONSOL.H file. This is the definition of the function:

```
// Open the console.
BOOL MConsole::Open(BOOL addcrlf)
{
     if(isopen)
          return TRUE;

   if(!::AllocConsole()) {
      ::FreeConsole();
      if(!::AllocConsole())
         return FALSE;
   }

   hConsoleOutput = ::GetStdHandle(STD_OUTPUT_HANDLE);
   hConsoleInput = ::GetStdHandle(STD_INPUT_HANDLE);
   if(addcrlf)
      AddCRLF();
    isopen = TRUE;
```

```
    return TRUE;
}
```

Notice that the preceding code fragment calls `GetStdHandle` twice: once to obtain the current console's output handle, and again to obtain its input handle. Those two handles are then stowed away for safe-keeping in a pair of variables named `hConsoleOutput` nad `hConsoleInput`. Subsequently, the `hConsoleOutput` and `hConsoleInput` variables can be accessed at any time to retrieve the current console process's output and input handles.

The CloseHandle Function

An application can close a console handle by calling the `CloseHandle` function. The syntax of the `CloseHandle` function is:

```
BOOL CloseHandle(hObject)
```

When an application calls `CloseHandle`, the value of the *hHandle* parameter should be the handle to be closed. The `CloseHandle` function returns a value of `TRUE` if it succeeds, and a value of `FALSE` if it does not.

The DuplicateHandle Function

With the `DuplicateHandle` function, an application can create a duplicate console handle that has different access or inheritability characteristics from the original handle from which it is derived.

The CreateFile Function

The `CreateFile` function creates, opens, or truncates a file, pipe, communications resource, disk device, or console. `CreateFile` returns a handle that can be used to access the object.

`CreateFile` is not solely a console call; it can create any kind of file or file-like object. However, the function has certain parameters and behaviors that apply specifically to consoles.

Syntax of the CreateFile Call

This is the syntax of a call to `CreateFile`:

```
HANDLE CreateFile(LPCSTR lpszName,
   DWORD fdwAccess,
   DWORD fdwShareMode,
   LPSECURITY_ATTRIBUTES lpsa,
   DWORD fdwCreate,
   DWORD fdwAttrsAndFlags,
   HANDLE hTemplateFile;
```

If the `CreateFile` function succeeds, the return value is an open handle that accesses the specified file. If the specified file already exists when `CreateFile` is called, and the value of *fdwCreate* is `CREATE_ALWAYS` or `OPEN_ALWAYS`, a subsequent call to `GetLast-Error` always returns the constant `ERROR_ALREADY_EXISTS`—even if the function succeeds. If the file does not already exist when `CreateFile` is called, a subsequent call to `GetLastError` returns 0.

If the `CreateFile` function fails, its return value is `INVALID_-HANDLE_VALUE`.

CreateFile Parameters

In the syntax example shown above, the *lpszName* parameter points to a null-terminated string that specifies the name of the file, pipe, communications resource, disk device, or console that is being created, opened, or truncated. The *fdwAccess* parameter specifies the kind of access that is granted to the specified file.

The lpszName Parameter: When you call CreateFile to create, open, or truncate input or output to a console, you must set the *lpszName* to the value `CONIN$` or the value `CONOUT$`. `CONIN$` specifies console input, and `CONOUT$` specifies console output.

If the value of *lpszName* is set to `CONIN$` when the `CreateFile` function is called, `CreateFile` can create a handle to console input. If a handle to the process is open as a result of inheritance or duplication, `CreateFile` can create a handle to the active screen buffer if the *lpszName* parameter is set to `CONOUT$`. In the latter case, the calling process must be attached to an inherited console or one allocated by the `AllocConsole` function. For console handles, the `CreateFile` parameters should be set as follows:

- If *lpszName* is set to a value of `CONIN$` when `CreateFile` is called, the `CreateFile` function obtains a handle that accesses the specified console's input buffer, even if the `SetStdHandle` function has been used to redirect the standard input handle. You can call the `GetStdHandle` function to obtain the console's standard input handle.

- If *lpszName* is set to a value of CONOUT$ when CreateFile is called, the CreateFile function obtains a handle that accesses the specified console's active screen buffer, even if SetStdHandle has been used to redirected the consoles's standard output handle. In this case also, you can call GetStdHandle to obtain the console's standard output handle.

The fdwAccess Parameter: The value of the *fdwAccess* parameter can be set to zero, or it can be set to either one or both of two constants: GENERIC_READ and GENERIC_WRITE. When *fdwAccess* is set to zero, the application being executed can obtain attributes of a device without actually accessing the device. GENERIC_READ grants read access to the specified file or device, and GENERIC_WRITE grants write access. If both GENERIC_READ and GENERIC_WRITE are set, both read and write access to the file is granted.

If an application calls CreateFile with the *lpszName* parameter set to "CON" and the *fwdAccess* parameter set to GENERIC_READ, the CreateFile function opens a console for input. If CreateFile is called with *lpszName* set to "CON" and *fwdAccess* set to GENERIC_WRITE, CreateFile opens a console for output.

If CreateFile is called with *lpszName* set to "CON" and *fwdAccess* set to GENERIC_READ | GENERIC_WRITE, the CreateFile fails and returns an ERROR_PATH_NOT_FOUND error.

These are other parameters of the CreateFile function:

- *fdwShareMode*, which specifies how the specified file can be shared.
- *lpsa*, which points to a SECURITY_ATTRIBUTES structure that specifies the security attributes for the file.
- *fdwAttrsAndFiles*, which specifies the file's attributes and flags. Any combination of the following flags and attributes is acceptable, except that all other file attributes override FILE_ATTRIBUTE_NORMAL.

Functions That Access Console I/O Buffers

Every console process has one input buffer and at least one screen buffer. The Win32 console API provides many functions for accessing, manipulating, and setting the attributes of console screen buffers and input buffers. Those functions are described in this section. For more details, see Volumes 2, 4, and 5 of the *Microsoft Win32 Programmer's Reference* .

Functions for Managing Screen Buffers

The Win32 console API provides a number of functions for accessing, managing, and setting the attributes of screen buffers. These functions, and their most important characteristics, are as follows:

- `CreateConsoleScreenBuffer` can create additional screen buffers for a console process. (The first screen buffer that is attached to the process is created automatically when the process begins.)
- `SetConsoleActiveScreenBuffer` sets the active screen buffer for a console process. This function is useful only if a console has more than one screen buffer.
- `GetConsoleScreenBufferInfo` can obtain the size of a console window and the size of the screen buffer. This information can then be used to determine how data is displayed on the screen.
- `GetLargestConsoleWindowSize` returns the maximum possible size of a console's window based on the current font and screen sizes. This function, unlike the `GetConsoleScreenBufferInfo` function, ignores the screen buffer's size.
- `SetConsoleWindowInfo` can be used to set the size or location of a screen buffer's window. (Changing the active screen buffer's window size changes the size of the console window displayed on the screen.)
- `SetConsoleScreenBufferSize` can change the size of a screen buffer.
- `GetConsoleCursorInfo` returns the size of a console's cursor and tells whether the cursor is visible.
- `SetConsoleCursorInfo` sets the appearance and visibility of the cursor.
- `GetConsoleMode` returns the current I/O mode of a console. Console I/O modes are described in "Console Input and Output Modes" on page 379.
- `SetConsoleCursorPosition` sets a new cursor position. If that position is outside the boundaries of the current window rectangle, the window rectangle shifts automatically to display the cursor.
- `ScrollConsoleScreenBuffer` scrolls the text displayed in the console window by copying a rectangular block of characters from one screen buffer to another.

Some of the most frequently used functions in the preceding list are described under the headings that follow. For more information on the others, see Volumes 2, 4, and 5 of *Microsoft Win32 Programmer's Reference*

Calling the CreateConsoleScreenBuffer Function

The `CreateConsoleScreenBuffer` function creates a new screen buffer for a console and returns a handle to the buffer. That handle can then be used in any function that needs to access the console's screen buffer. The new screen buffer does not become active, however, until a function named `SetConsoleActiveScreenBuffer` is called.

When an application changes the active screen buffer by calling `SetConsoleActiveScreenBuffer` and `CreateConsole-ScreenBuffer`, the handle returned by the `GetStdHandle` call is not affected (see "The GetStdHandle Function" on page 389). Similarly, using `GetStdHandle` to change the STDOUT handle does not affect the active screen buffer.

How Text Is Stored in a Console Screen Buffer

Every character in a console screen buffer is stored in a `CHAR_INFO` structure, which is defined as follows:

```
typedef struct _CHAR_INFO {
   union {  /* Unicode or ANSI character */
      WCHAR UnicodeChar;
      CHAR AsciiChar;
   } Char;
   WORD Attributes;/* text and background colors */
} CHAR_INFO, *PCHAR_INFO;
```

The `CHAR_INFO` data structure contains a `union` named `Char` that allows an application to store either Unicode (16-bit) characters or ANSI characters in a console screen buffer. If Unicode characters are used, the application must be compiled as a Unicode-compatible application, as explained in the box "The Unicode Character Set" on page 375.

The `CHAR_INFO` structure also has a WORD member named `Attributes`, which can be used to set both the foreground color and the background color of each individual character stored in a console screen buffer. When each character in the console's window is displayed, it obtains its foreground (text) color and its background color from its own `CHAR_INFO` structure.

The SetConsoleTextAttribute Function

An application can set the foreground and background colors of all the characters in a screen buffer by calling the Win32 function `SetConsoleTextAttribute`. The syntax of the `SetConsoleTextAttribute` function is:

```
BOOL SetConsoleTextAttribute(HANDLE hConsoleOutput,
   WORD wAttr
```

`SetConsoleTextAttribute` returns a value of `TRUE` if it succeeds, and a value of `FALSE` if it does not.

When an application calls `SetConsoleTextAttribute`, the *hConsoleOutput* parameter is the handle of the console screen buffer being addressed. The *wAttr* parameter can be any combination of the following constants, which are defined in the WINCON.H header file:

- `FOREGROUND_BLUE`
- `FOREGROUND_GREEN`
- `FOREGROUND_RED`
- `FOREGROUND_INTENSITY`
- `BACKGROUND_BLUE`
- `BACKGROUND_GREEN`
- `BACKGROUND_RED`
- `BACKGROUND_INTENSITY`

By the Way

Changing a screen buffer's text attributes by calling `SetConsoleTextAttribute` does not affect the display of characters that have already been written to the screen. Also, the text attributes that are passed to `SetConsoleTextAttribute` do not affect characters written by low-level console I/O functions such as `WriteConsoleOutput` or `WriteConsoleOutputCharacter`.

When a console process calls `SetConsoleTextAttribute`, the C-language operator | can be used to combine any number of the preceding constants in any order. But sometimes the result of a *wAttr* setting might not be what one might expect, so some experimenting might be necessary. For example, if the *wAttr* parameter is set as follows, the result is bright cyan text on a blue background:

```
FOREGROUND_BLUE | FOREGROUND_GREEN | FOREGROUND_-
INTENSITY | BACKGROUND_BLUE
```

If no background constant is specified in the *wAttr* attribute parameter passed to `SetConsoleTextAttribute`, the background of the console window is black. If no foreground constant is specified, the text is black. For example, the following *wAttr* setting produces black text on a white background:

```
BACKGROUND_BLUE | BACKGROUND_GREEN | BACKGROUND_RED
```

Text Attributes in the Example Program

In the SLIMMDI example application, the MYCONSOL.H file contains three calls to the `SetConsoleTextAttribute` function. The SLIMMDI program calls just one of these functions: the one named `WhiteOnBlack`:

```
// Set screen colors (three choices).
void WhiteOnBlack(void) {
      SetConsoleTextAttribute(hConsoleOutput,
         FOREGROUND_RED | FOREGROUND_GREEN |
         FOREGROUND_BLUE);
   }
void BlackOnWhite(void) {
   SetConsoleTextAttribute(hConsoleOutput,
         BACKGROUND_RED | BACKGROUND_GREEN |
         BACKGROUND_BLUE | BACKGROUND_INTENSITY);
   }
void RedOnWhite(void) {
   SetConsoleTextAttribute(hConsoleOutput,
      FOREGROUND_RED | FOREGROUND_INTENSITY |
      BACKGROUND_RED | BACKGROUND_GREEN |
      BACKGROUND_BLUE | BACKGROUND_INTENSITY);
}
```

The `WhiteOnBlack` function in the above code fragment is called from the MCONSOL.CPP file, as follows::

```
// Set console attributes.
   myConsole.WhiteOnBlack();
```

By changing the `WhiteOnBlack` call in the MYCONSOL.CPP file to a call to `BlackOnWhite` or `RedOnWhite`, you can edit the SLIMMDI program's source code to call either of the other two functions—or you can write your own text-color and screen-color function.

The GetConsoleScreenBufferInfo Function

An application can call the `GetConsoleScreenBufferInfo` function to obtain the current text attributes of a screen buffer. The syntax of the `GetConsoleScreenBufferInfo` function is:

```
BOOL GetConsoleScreenBufferInfo(HANDLE hConsoleOutput,
   PCONSOLE_SCREEN_BUFFER_INFO pcsbi
```

The `GetConsoleScreenBufferInfo` returns a value of `TRUE` if it succeeds. If not, it returns a value of `FALSE`.

In the preceding syntax illustration, the *hConsoleOutput* parameter is the handle of the console screen buffer being accessed. The *pcsbi* parameter is a pointer to a `PCONSOLE_SCREEN_BUFFER_INFO` structure, which is defined as follows:

```
typedef struct _CONSOLE_SCREEN_BUFFER_INFO {
   COORD dwSize;
   COORD dwCursorPosition;
   WORD wAttributes;
   SMALL_RECT srWindow;
   COORD dwMaximumWindowSize;
} CONSOLE_SCREEN_BUFFER_INFO;
```

The *dwSize* member variable of the `CONSOLE_SCREEN_BUFFER-_INFO` structure specifies the size, of the specified screen buffer, expressed in character columns and rows. The *dwCursorPosition* variable specifies the column and row coordinates occupied by the cursor in the screen buffer. The *wAttributes* variable specifies the foreground and background color attributes that are currently set for the screen buffer. Color constants that can be used to set this variable are listed under the heading "The SetConsoleTextAttribute Function" on page 396.

The *srWindow* variable of the `CONSOLE_SCREEN_BUFFER_INFO` structure is a `SMALL_RECT` structure that contains the screen buffer coordinates of the upper left and lower right corners of the display window. (The architecture of the `SMALL_RECT` structure is described in the *Microsoft Win32 Programmer's Reference* .) The *dwMaximumWindowSize* variable specifies the maximum possible size of the console window, based on the size of the current screen and the size of the current screen buffer.

Console Mode Functions

As explained in "Console Input and Output Modes" on page 379, each console input buffer has an *input mode* and an *output mode*. A console's input mode determines the kinds of input events that are stored in the console's input buffer. The console's output mode determines how character data is displayed on the screen.

An application can set the input mode of a console by calling the Win32 function `SetConsoleMode`. By calling the `GetConsoleMode` function, an application can obtain information about a console's current mode. The `GetConsoleMode` function can report either the current input mode of a console's input buffer or the current output mode of a screen buffer, depending on the parameters passed to it when it is called.

The SetConsoleMode Function

The `SetConsoleMode` function sets the current mode of either a console input buffer or a screen buffer, depending on the parameters that are passed to it when it is called. This is the syntax of a call to `SetConsoleMode`:

```
BOOL SetConsoleMode(HANDLE hConsole, DWORD fdwMode)
```

When an application calls `SetConsoleMode`, the value of the *hConsole* parameter should be the handle of a console input buffer or the handle of a console output buffer. The *fdwMode* parameter is a constant that specifies the input or output mode to set.

Constants for Setting Console Modes

The constants listed under the following headings can be passed to the `SetConsoleMode` function in the *fdwMode* parameter, in any combination, and in any order. For more details about how they work, see "Console Input and Output Modes" on page 379.

Constants for Setting High-Level Console Input Functions

The constants in the following list can be passed to the `SetConsoleMode` call to enable high-level console input functions:

- `ENABLE_PROCESSED_INPUT`: If this constant is passed to the `SetConsoleMode` function in the *fdwMode* parameter and a console input handle is passed in the `hConsole` parameter, the specified console's input buffer is set to *processed input mode*, which supports line-by-line text entry. If line input is also enabled—which should be the case, since processed input mode and line input mode are designed to work together—backspaces and carriage returns are handled in accordance with most typists' expectations; a backspace causes the cursor to move back one space without affecting the character at the cursor position, and carriage return is converted to a carriage return-linefeed character combination.

  When both line input and processed input are enabled, the CTRL+C key combination is passed on to the appropriate control handler whether or not line input is enabled. For more information about control handlers, see "Console Control Handlers" on page 381.

- ENABLE_LINE_INPUT: When this constant is passed to SetConsoleMode along with a console input handle, the ReadFile and ReadConsole functions return when the **Enter** key is pressed. When line input mode is disabled, both those functions return when one or more characters are available in the input buffer.
- ENABLE_ECHO_INPUT: When this constant is passed to SetConsoleMode along with a console input handle, keyboard input that is read by the ReadFile or ReadConsole function is echoed to the active screen buffer, provided the process that calls ReadFile or ReadConsole has an open handle of the active screen buffer. Echo mode cannot be enabled unless line input is also enabled. The output mode of the active screen buffer affects the way echoed input is displayed.
- ENABLE_PROCESSED_OUTPUT: When this constant is used with a console screen buffer handle, the console API performs what are generally considered appropriate actions when nonprinting ANSI control characters that are written to a screen buffer. The **Backspace**, Tab, bell, Return, and linefeed characters are processed; a **Tab** character moves the cursor to the next tab stop (tab stops are set by default in eight- character increments); and a bell character produces a beep or some other sound, depending upon your system.
- ENABLE_WRAP_AT_EOL_OUTPUT: When this constant is passed to SetConsoleMode along with a console screen buffer handle, "wrap at EOL (end-of-line)" mode is enabled. When this mode is enabled, the cursor advances to the first column in the next row when it reaches the end of its current row. When the cursor reaches the bottom of the window region, the window's origin is moved down one row, scrolling the contents of the window up one row and keeping the cursor visible on the bottom line of the window. When the cursor reaches the bottom of the screen buffer, the contents of the screen buffer are scrolled up one row, and the top row of the screen buffer is discarded. When "wrap at EOL output mode" is disabled, the last character in the row is overwritten with any subsequent characters.

Constants for Setting Low-Level Console Input Functions

The constants in the following list can be passed to the SetConsoleMode call to enable low-level console input functions (for more details, see "Console Input and Output Modes" on page 379):

- `ENABLE_MOUSE_INPUT`: This constant controls whether mouse events are reported in the input buffer. By default, mouse input is enabled and window input is disabled. Changing either of these modes affects only input that occurs after the mode is set; pending mouse or window events in the input buffer are not flushed, and the mouse pointer is displayed regardless of the mouse mode.
- `ENABLE_WINDOW_INPUT`: Controls whether buffer-resizing events are reported in the input buffer. By default, mouse input is enabled and window input is disabled. Changing either of these modes affects only input that occurs after the mode is set; pending mouse or window events in the input buffer are not flushed. The mouse pointer is displayed regardless of the mouse mode.
- `ENABLE_PROCESSED_INPUT`: Controls the processing of input for applications using the high-level console I/O functions. However, if processed input mode is enabled, the CTRL+C key combination is not reported in the console's input buffer. Instead, it is passed on to the appropriate control handler function.

Noted in Passing

If a console has multiple screen buffers, the output modes of each can be different. An application can change I/O modes at any time.

The output modes of a screen buffer do not affect the behavior of the low-level output functions.

This Chapter's Example Programs

Two example programs are provided on your bonus disk show how to create and destroy processes. One of the programs, named MYCONSOL, shows how to build and run an application that is not equipped with a GUI window; the user interface of the MYCONSOL program consists solely of a console window.

The other program, named SLIMMDI, shows how to build and run a Windows-based application that displays both a GUI window and a console window.

Instructions for building and running the MYCONSOL and SLIMMDI programs are provided in "Building the Example Applications" on page 405.

The MYCONSOL and SLIMMDI Programs

No matter which method you choose to you launch the MYCONSOL process, the results are the same. The program opens a console window that displays a message on your computer monitor.

The SLIMMDI example program demonstrates how a console window can be incorporated into a Windows 95 program. SLIMMDI is an MDI (multi-document interface) application, so it can create multiple child windows. In turn, each child window can create multiple MYCONSOL processes. In this way, the SLIMMDI application implements multiple console windows.

When you execute the SLIMMDI program, you can select a menu item that displays a console window. To display its console window, the SLIMMDI application simply opens the console application named MYCONSOL and runs it as a process.

The SLIMMDI application was written using the Developer Studio development system, but it does not rely on the document-and-view structure that the AppWizard utility creates when it generates the framework for a Visual C++ program. That architecture makes the SLIMMDI program easier to port to Borland C++ or to other development environments that do not rely on the Microsoft Visual C++ document-and-view framework.

Executing the SLIMMDI Program

When you launch the SLIMMDI program, it displays a GUI window titled **Console Demo** (see Figure 8.6 on Page 403). The **Console Demo** window has two menu items that display console windows: **Process** and **Alloc**.

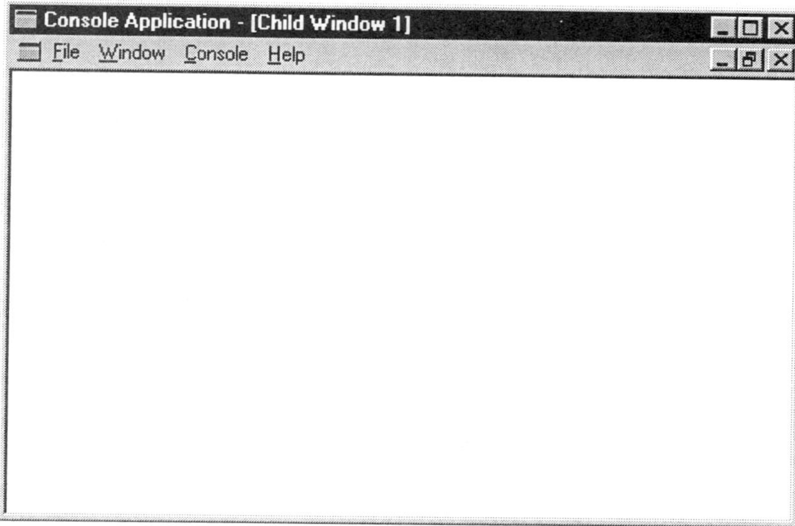

Figure 8.6 The SLIMMDI program's main window

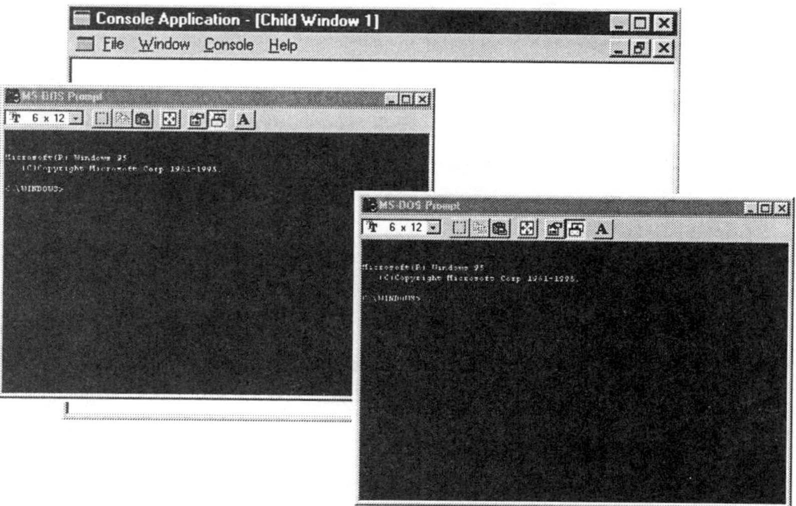

Figure 8.7 Running a console process

When you choose the **Process** item from the **Console** menu, the program displays a console window by starting a new process. This process starts this chapter's other example program, the console application named MYCONSOL program. You can run multiple instances of the MYCONSOL program from the SLIMMDI application. All the processes run independently of each other, and they also run independently of their of the application that created them, as shown in Figure 8.7 on Page 403.

How the SLIMMDI Program Creates Processes

The SLIMMDI program creates and manages multiple processes to displays multiple console windows on the screen. The application is equipped with a main frame window, multiple MDI windows, and a standard menu bar.

SLIMMDI creates console windows that interact with the user in an independent fashion, accepting typed input and displaying messages on the screen.

The main module of the SLIMMDI program is named SLIMMDI.CPP. The SLIMMDI.CPP file contains the program's `WinMain` function and its supporting functions.

When you choose a menu item labeled **Process** from a menu labeled **Console**, the SLIMMDI program creates a console window by calling the Win32 function `CreateProcess`. The address of the MYCONSOL.EXE process is passed to the `CreateProcess` call, as follows:

```
// Create a new console process.
CreateProcess("MYCONSOL.EXE", NULL, NULL, NULL, TRUE,
    DETACHED_PROCESS, NULL, NULL, &sui, &pi);
```

The `CreateProcess` function is called from the `ShowConsole` function in the SLIMMDI.CPP file.

When the SLIMMDI.CPP module executes the function shown above, the MYCONSOL.EXE module is launched as a new process, displaying a console window.

When you chose a different menu item labeled **Alloc**, the SLIMMDI application displays a console window not by creating a new process, but by calling the Windows function `AllocConsole`, as follows:

```
void ConsoleAlloc()
{
   AllocConsole();
   while (TRUE);
   FreeConsole();
}
```

The console window that appears when the user selects **Alloc** is a simple window that does nothing but close. When it closes, the application ends.

The **Process** menu item displays a console window in a more elegant—and more useful— manner. Each time the user chooses the **Process** menu item, the program starts a new process that creates a new console window. So multiple console windows—each created by a separate process—can appear at the same time on the screen.

Starting MYCONSOL from the SLIMMDI Program

When you launch the SLIMMDI program and choose **Process** from the **Console** menu, the SLIMMDI program starts a new process that executes the MYCONSOL application. The MYCONSOL application is a console application that can also be executed as a separate program.

To build the MYCONSOL program, you compile a pair of C++ source files named MYCONSOL.CPP and MYSTRING.CPP. The building of the MYCONSOL program is described in more detail in "Building the Example Applications" later in this section.

The SLIMMDI application launches the MYCONSOL application by calling the Windows function `CreateProcess` when the user chooses the Process command from the Console menu.

The MYCONSOL.CPP file contains the source code that displays a console window when the user selects Process from the Console menu. When MYCONSOL.CPP and its header file (named MYCONSOL.H) are compiled, they produce the console application named MYCONSOL.EXE.

Building the Example Applications

Because the SLIMMDI Windows application and the MYCONSOL console application are built from separate executables, you must build them separately. To build the MYCONSOL application using Visual C++, simply open the MYCONSOL project and execute the MYCONSOL makefile by choosing the **Build** command from the **Project** menu. To build the SLIMMDI application, open the SLIMMDI project and build it by selecting the **Build** command from the **Project** menu.

When you have built both projects, you can execute either of them from the Windows 95 desktop or from the Developer Studio menu.

Summary

One of the most important features of Windows 95 is preemptive multitasking—that is, the capability of running multiple processes (the Windows 95 equivalent of tasks) on the same computer at the same time by allocating each process a specified share of CPU time in accordance with a predetermined priority.

By using preemptive multitasking, the Windows 95 operating system can allocate each process a share of CPU time in accordance with predetermined priorities.

Because processes create and manage threads, you must understand how processes work before you can understand multithreading and preemptive multitasking. This chapter described and demonstrated how processes work in Windows 95 programs. Chapter 9, "Multithreading and Multitasking," explains the use of threads in Windows 95 programs.

To show how Windows 95 applications create and manage processes, this chapter presented two sample applications: one demonstrating how Windows 95 can create a process that displays a console window directly, and one showing how a console-window process can be created and managed from inside a Windows-base (GUI) program.

Console windows have a number of different uses in Windows 95 applications; for example, they can be useful in networking and communications programs that require terminal-emulation modes, and as windows for displaying error message that affect an application's GUI interface.

Console windows might also come in handy if you ever need to port a text-only program to Windows 95, or when you want to test a code module or prototype an application without bothering to write a full-fledged Windows interface.

Once you have a console process up and running, there are two ways to manage console I/O: with high-level functions, which support line-by-line input and output and with low-level functions, which support character-by-character input and output, plus many kinds of mouse operations.

Low-level console I/O functions can be convenient when you want to port a robust text-only application to Windows 95 because you can often convert character-based programs to Windows 95 from UNIX, DOS, and other platforms on a call-by-call basis.

That's because many I/O functions that are common in UNIX, DOS, and other text-based platforms work much like the I/O functions that are provided in the Windows console API.

All these techniques were described and demonstrated in this chapter.

Chapter

9

Multithreading and Multitasking

When an operating system uses preemptive multitasking, each individual process that is executed receives its own slice of CPU time and can use its time in whatever way it wants, without directly affecting other processes.

One of the most important features of Windows 95 is its ability to run applications using *preemptive multitasking*. As you may recall from Chapter 8, "Programs and Processes," preemptive multitasking is a mechanism that give each individual process its own slice of CPU time, in accordance with predetermined task priorities.

When an operating system executes programs using preemptive multitasking, each process can use its slice of CPU in whatever way it wants, without directly affecting other processes.

Multithreading, another important term in Windows 95, is a word used to describe the allocation of CPU time to multiple processes using multiple threads.

Earlier 16-bit versions of Windows supported multitasking—but not preemptive multitasking. When Windows 3.1 performed a background task, such as file I/O or a background program, it presented the illusion that the background task was being carried out at the same time other operations were being performed. But that wasn't really happening. Actually, the foreground task was briefly interrupted many times each second so the background task could be carried out. This kind of CPU time-sharing is called *non-preemptive multitasking*, or *cooperative multitasking*, because the CPU has no direct control over the amount of time allocated to each task.

Under Windows 95, multiple *processes* (a new name for what used to be call *tasks* under Windows 3.*x*) can share CPU time using preemptive multitasking. Under preeemptive multitasking, an operating system divides processes into *threads* and allocates each thread an individual share of CPU time, depending upon preallocated thread priorities.

When an operating system uses preemptive multitasking, each individual process that is executed receives its own slice of CPU time and can use its time in whatever way it wants, without directly affecting other processes.

Multithreading is a term used to describe the allocation of CPU time to multiple processes using multiple threads. This chapter explains how Windows 95 uses multithreading to implement preemptive multitasking, and presents some example applications that show how you can use multithreading in your own Windows 95 applications.

Figure 9.1 shows the output of one of these example programs, named THRDDEMO.

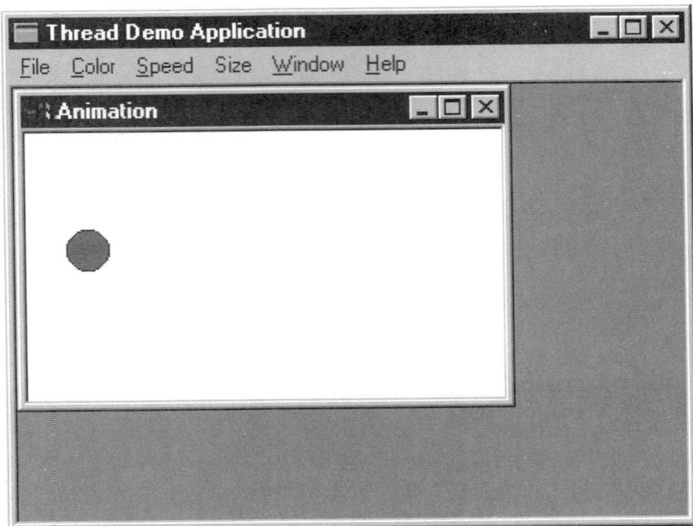

Figure 9.1 Output of the HRDDEMO program

The following topics are covered in this chapter:

Preemptive and Non-Preemptive Multitasking

As you know if you're a DOS programmer, MS-DOS was originally designed to run just one application at a time. Therefore, in the earliest implementations of MS-DOS, only one program was loaded into memory at a time. To run another application, you had to close the currently executing application and load another one into memory.

Another way of say that MS-DOS could run only one application at a time is to say that it could run only one *thread* at a time. So MS-DOS was what is now sometimes referred to a *single-threaded* operating system. In the era of MS-DOS, every application had a single thread, and only one thread could run at a time.

When Windows 3.*x* introduced, the single-threaded processing capability of MS-DOS gave way to what is now called a *non-preemptive multitasking* environment. In a non-preemptive multitasking environment—sometimes referred to as a *cooperative multitasking* environment—multiple applications can reside in memory at the same time, but only one application can be running at any given time.

When an application was executed under the Windows 3.*x*, non-preemptive multitasking environment, the application still used all the time the CPU had available. Other applications might be loaded into memory and might be waiting for a chance to run, but they they had to sit and wait until the currently executing application terminated.

In later versions of Windows 3.*x*, various mechanisms were devised for getting around the limitations of non-preemptive multitasking. For example, there were mechanisms for handling interrupts that switched from one task to another temporarily. And certain tasks were given limited abilities to run in the background while higher-priority tasks were executing. But as you may know, especially if you've tried to do some background printing under Windows 3.*x*, the non-preemptive multitasking environment never was very well suited to carrying out tasks that required background processing.

Even within an individual application, Windows 3.*x* could perform only one task at a time. Although Windows 3.*x* supported MDI (multi-document interface) applications, it was difficult to coerce Windows 3.*x* into performing different tasks in different windows at the same time.

Today, under Windows 95, a whole new technology is available to improve CPU time-sharing. Now, thanks to multithreading and preemptive multitasking, the Windows 95 operating system can run multiple *processes* (processes are the Windows 95 equivalent of tasks) on the same computer at the same time, allocating each process a share of CPU time in accordance with predetermined priorities.

Preemptive Multitasking and Windows 95

Just as Windows 3.*x* supported a form of multitasking—specifically, non-preemptive multitasking—it also supported a form of threading. But the kind of threading that Windows 3.*x* supported was *single-thread processing*—which is just another way of saying that Windows 3.x supported the running of just one thread at a time.

In contrast, Windows 95 supports *multithreading*—a mechanism that makes a more robust kind of multitasking possible.

In the world of data processing, threads are nothing new. Actually, threads have been around for a long time. A thread, at its most basic level, is simply a path of execution through a program. What's new about Windows 95 is that it permits an application to support more than one thread of operation and to execute multiple threads at the same time. In Windows 95, a thread can be defined as the smallest unit of execution that the operating system can be called upon to manage.

How Preemptive Multitasking Works

Under Windows 95, a thread has three ingredients:

- A *stack*
- Amechanism for storing the state of the CPU registers when the thread starts processing

- An entry in an *execution list* maintained by a thread manager called the *system scheduler*.

These three ingredients of a thread are described in more detail later in this chapter.

Tasks and Processes

To understand how multiprocessing works, it helps to have an understanding of *tasks* and *processes*. Under Windows 3.*x*, the smallest entity that was allocated CPU time was often called a *task*. Under Windows 95, what used to be called a task is known as a *process*.

When Windows 95 is executing an instance of an application, that instance is known as a *process*. For example, when you double-click an icon on the Windows 95 desktop, you start a process that runs the application associated with the icon you have clicked. Processes are the topic of Chapter 8, "Programs and Processes."

A Windows 95 process consists of the code, data, and other resources of whatever program is being executed. Every process has at least one *thread* and can start up other threads at any time. Threads are described in more detail under the next heading.

When a process creates a thread, it can set the priority that the thread has in relation to other threads. Each thread shares all the *resources* of the process under which it runs.

From the standpoint of thread management, the resources of a process fall into three categories: open files, semaphores (mechanisms that limit the number of threads that a process can run at the same time), and dynamically allocated memory. For more information on semaphores, see "Semaphore Objects" on page 443. For more about dynamically allocated memory, see "Memory Management in a Multithreading Environment" on page 414.

Threads

A *thread* is a path of execution within a process. When you start an application under Windows 95, the operating system creates a process and begins executing the primary thread of that process. When this primary thread terminates, so does the process.

Every thread runs under the control of a process. A Windows 95 process consists of the code, data, and other resources of whatever program is being executed. Every process has at least one thread, and can start up other threads at any time. Every thread runs under the control of a process.

When an application creates a primary thread, the application provides the operating system with a pointer to the thread's startup code. Usually, this pointer points either to the address of the thread's **`main`** function or to the thread's **`WinMain`** function, if it has one.

Multithreading and Multiprocessing

A *multithreaded* application is a program that has more than one thread. One use for multithreading is to handle background processes or maintenance processes while other processes are being executed.

In the Windows 95 environment, thread management is what makes it possible for multiple processes to run simultaneously. Under Windows 95, when more than one thread is running, your computer's microprocessor allocates a share of its processing time to each active thread in accordance with pre-established thread priorities. The Win32 operating system can automatically allocate different amounts of CPU time to different threads, depending on priorities specified both by the system and by applications that make use of multi-threading.

The System Scheduler

Windows 95 manages the execution of programs using a mechanism called the *system scheduler*. A program cannot execute until the system scheduler gives authorization to one of the program's threads.

The system scheduler determines which threads should run and when they should run. Lower-priority threads have to wait while higher-priority threads complete their tasks. On multiprocessor machines, the system scheduler can move individual threads to different processors to balance the CPU load.

Each thread in a process operates independently. Unless you make threads visible to each other, the threads in your application execute individually and are unaware of other threads—even threads controlled by the same process. Threads that share common resources, however, must coordinate their work by using semaphores or another objects called synchronization objects. See "Synchronization Objects" on page 439 for more information about thread synchronization.

Memory Management in a Multithreading Environment

One important feature of a thread is that it shares memory with the process that creates it. That means it has access to all its creating process's code and data. Every thread also has its own private stack, as well as a private *execution contex*—that is, a small area of memory for storing the state of the CPU's processor registers and certain other important data about the thread's execution environment.

As explained in Chapter 3, "Windows 95 Architecture," Windows 95 assigns every application loaded into memory its own private block of virtual RAM. That precaution provides a certain amount of protection against applications corrupting each other's code or data, causing programs to crash or bringing down the system.

Furthermore, because threads share the code and data of their parent processes, they don't usually consume much additional memory, and are (despite what you may have heardk) relatively easy to create. Later in this chapter, you'll get a chance to create some multithreaded applications. Then see if you don't agree with me that multithreaded applications aren't as difficult to write as many people make them out to be.

Preemptive and Non-Preemptive Multitasking

Under both DOS and Windows 3.*x*, with only one exception, the application that was currently being executed controlled the only available thread. The only time this was not true was when an interrupt occurred. For example, when an interrupt serviced the keyboard or activated a TSR, the application's single thread was suspended until the interrupt returned. When the interrupt finished whatever it had to do, control of the thread returned to the application.

Under Windows 3.*x*, even though every application had just one thread, multiple applications could be present in memory at the same time. When the Windows 3.*x* user switched from one application to another, Windows allocated a higher priority to the newly activated application window and a lower priority to the application that had been shuffled off into the background.

Although Windows 3.*x* could allocate some CPU time to background tasks, the system spent most of its time sending messages to the foreground application. Furthermore, a Windows 3.*x* thread could process only one message at a time. If an application had more than one window, Windows 3.*x* decided which window was to receive each message, and when. Not until an application's single thread returned from processing a message for one window could Windows 3.*x* instruct the thread to process a message for another window.

Windows 95 works very differently. Under Windows 95, an application always starts with a single thread whose lifespan is encapsulated in a **WinMain** function. This thread is known as the *main thread*. Additional threads can be created at any time and can share CPU with the main thread. Windows 95 has a built-in scheduling system that an application can use to determine how much CPU time is allocated to each active thread.

Here is another important difference between Windows 95 and Windows 3.*x*: In Windows 3.1 and its predecessors, if multiple applications were running at the same time, all active applications shared the same address space. In Windows 95, each application has its own private address space. Therefore, under Windows 95, unless two applications are explicitly sharing memory, they are never aware of each other, and therefore cannot interfere with each other.

Using Threads in Windows 95 Applications

The hallmark of Windows 95 multithreading is that it allows processes to perform multiple tasks at the same time. For example, an application might use one thread to handle real-time I/O, such as keyboard and mouse input from the user, while other threads with lower priorities handle tasks that don't have to be carried out in real time—for example, spreadsheet calculations or background printing.

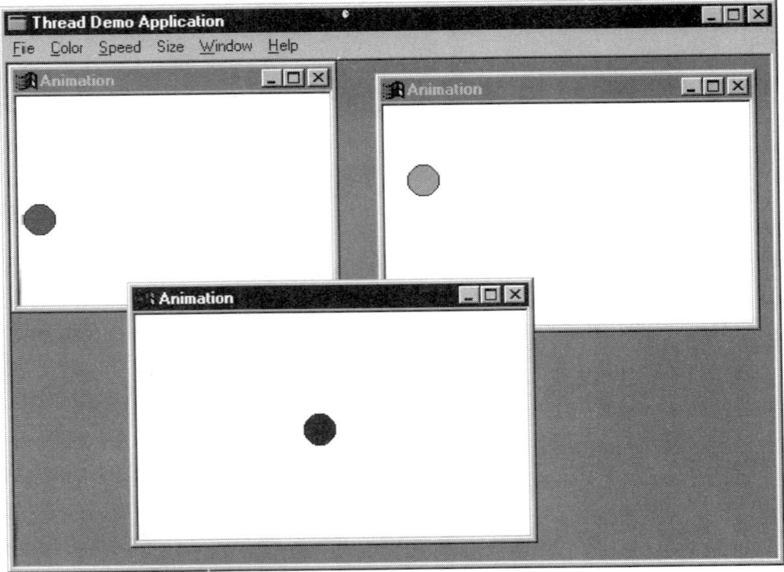

Figure 9.2 Bouncing balls

Multiple threads can also be useful in MDI (mutliple-document interface) applications. When a multi-window program has more than one window open, a separate thread can be assigned to handle the action that takes place in each window. You can see how that works by compiling and executing the example programs presented in this chapter.

Multithreading can be especially useful in networking and communications programs. For example, a named-pipe server might create a thread to handle communications with each client process that attaches to the pipe. Threads can also help an application manage input from multiple communications devices.

The Thread Is Quicker Than the Eye

Because multithreading divides CPU time into very small slices—typically on the order of 20 milliseconds or so—multithreading creates the illusion that all the activities of all currently active threads are taking place at the same time.

When you build and execute the example programs in this chapter, you'll be able to use threads to create as many bouncing balls as you like, of varying sizes and colors, and all the balls will seem to be bouncing around completely independently in their individual windows (Figure 9.2 on page 416).

Multithreading Under Windows NT

Windows NT, like Windows 95, supports multithreading. In fact, the Win32 API—which makes Windows multithreading in Windows 95 possible—is the same bit Windows API that is used by Windows NT.

Furthermore, you can run Windows NT on a multiprocessor system—and then multithreading works even better than it does on a single-processor system. The CPU can assign separate threads to separate CPUs, and time-slicing is not even necessary; all activities of all active threads really do take place at the same time. This capability speeds up processing even more because each thread has its own private microprocessor.

Uses for Multithreading

There is no requirement to use multithreading in Windows 95 programs. In fact, most Windows 95 applications written to date have not made much use of multithreading. For simple CPU time-sharing, it's often sufficient to allocate CPU time using the software timers supplied by Visual C++ and the Win32 API (for an example of a

Windows 95 program that uses timers, see "The TIMER Program" on page 449). But multithreading can come in handy when you want an application to perform multiple tasks simultaneously.

For example, multithreading is often used for purposes such as these:

- *To apportion tasks efficiently*: When a program must perform different tasks simultaneously, it's usually more efficient to implement a thread for each task than it is to launch a separate process for each task.
- *To assign different priorities to different tasks*: When a process has multiple threads, each thread can be assigned a different priority, depending on the needs of your application.
- *For background processing*: Threads can be ideal mechanisms for the management of background processes, such as background printing. In a well-designed multithreaded program, important time-critical tasks—such as interactive keyboard and mouse I/O—can proceed uninterrupted, in a peppy and responsive manner, while less time-critical processes grind away unnoticed in the background.
- *To apportion the execution of parallel tasks*: Sometimes an application creates several instances that do exactly the same thing. For example, a named pipe server can allocate an identical thread to manage each instance of a pipe (a programming mechanism that can move information from one process to another).
- *For the sake of efficiency*: Threads can use processing time and memory more efficiently than full-fledged processes because they don't need the startup code that processes require. Moreover, all threads of a process share the same address space and can access the process's global variables. This feature can simplify communications between threads.

You may be able to think of other situations in which threads can be useful, but these are a start.

Shortcomings of Multithreading

On a single-processor system, multiple threads do not improve execution speed. In fact, a single-CPU computer can slow down if it is forced to keep track of too many threads. You can confirm that for yourself by running this chapter's thread-demonstration programs on a single-processor PC; just watch the bouncing ball slow down as you add more threads.

Multithreading can have other drawbacks, too. For example, if your application needs to synchronize its threads so they don't conflict with each other, it must create structures and routines that consume memory. You must create those structures and routines, and that requires extra development time. Moreover, keeping track of large numbers of threads consumes CPU time. And deadlocks can occur, bringing everything to a screeching halt, when competing threads scramble for CPU time in poorly designed multithreaded programs.

All these factors should be considered carefully before you commit yourself to using multithreading in an application.

Alternatives to Multithreading

When you want to execute multiple tasks simultaneously, multithreading isn't always the best solution. Alternatives to multithreading include overlapped I/O, multiple processes, and mechanisms that make it possible for the system to wait for multiple events.

Overlapped I/O

Overlapped I/O, sometimes referred to as *asynchronous I/O,* is a mechanism that lets an application perform separate input-output operations without using threads. Overlapped I/O enables a single thread to initiate multiple time consuming I/O requests that can run concurrently.

Overlapped I/O is often used by *pipes* (programming mechanisms that can move data from one thread, process, or application to another). In an application that uses overlapped I/O, a single pipe can read and write data simultaneously, or a single thread can perform simultaneous I/O operations on multiple pipe handles.

Multiple Processes

When a Windows 95 application needs to carry out multiple tasks simultaneously, it can often use multiple processes instead of multithreading. To use multiple processes, an application simply creates a separate process rather than a separate thread for each task to be performed. This technique is widely used as an alternative to threads in 16-bit Windows applications (although, under Windows 3.*x*, processes are more commonly referred to as tasks).

Under Windows 95, an application can call the Win32 function **`CreateProcess`** to start a child process. (For an example of how

`CreateProcess` works, see the SLIMMDI program presented in Chapter 8, "Programs and Processes." When you run the SLIMMDI program, separate processes display a GUI window and a console window at the same time; the GUI window launches a separate process to display the console window.)

In some cases, it's better to split up an application's tasks by using multiple processes that it is to write a separate thread for each task. For example, an application might use multiple processes for functions that require private address spaces and private resources that protect them from the activities of other threads.

Generally speaking, though, the multiple-process approach is not the most efficient architecture for applications that carry out multiple tasks simultaneously. It's usually more efficient to use threads because Windows 95 can create and execute a thread more quickly than it can create and launch a process. The main reason this is true is that when a thread is created, the code for the thread has already been mapped into the address space of the process from which it is called, while the code for a new process must be loaded before the process can execute.

Multithreading with the Win32 API and with the MFC Library

There are two ways to implement multithreading in a Windows 95 application. One way is to use the functions provided in the Win32 API. The other method is to instantiate a thread object from the MFC CWinThread class and to use that object to implement multithreading.

To learn how to implement multithreading in MFC programs using the CWinThread class, see "Multithreading and the MFC Library" on page 425.

Creating and Using Processes

As you have seen, a *process* consists of the code, data, and other resources of whatever program is being executed. Every process has at least one *thread* and can start up other threads at any time. When a process creates a thread, it can set the priority that the thread has in relation to other threads.

In Windows 95, each thread shares all the *resources* of the process under which it runs. Resources can include files, pipes, and thread synchronization objects that are accessible to a process's threads.

A process, unlike a thread, has a private virtual address space. When a process starts, it has a single thread, known as a *primary thread.* At any time during the execution of an application, more threads can be created.

When a process starts more than one thread, each thread shares the virtual address space of the process and can access the process's global variables and system resources. A thread can execute any part of a program's code and can create more threads.

Creating Processes

In Windows 95, an application can create a new process by calling the Win32 function **CreateProcess**. When a process creates a child process, the child process runs independently of the creating process.

For more about calling **CreateProcess** to start new processes, see Chapter 8, "Programs and Processes."

Creating and Using Threads

The Win32 SDK contains two functions that you can call to create new threads. The Win32 function **CreateThread** starts a thread that runs in the address space of the calling process. The Win32 function **CreateRemoteThread** starts a new thread that runs in the address space of a different process.

The Win32 function **CreateThread** creates a thread that executes within the address space of the calling function. This is the syntax of the **CreateThread** function:

```
HANDLE CreateThread(LPSECURITY_ATTRIBUTES lpsa,
   DWORD cbStack,
   LPTHREAD_START_ROUTINE lpStartAddr,
   LPVOID lpvThreadParm, DWORD fdwCreate,
   LPDWORD lpIDTthread);
```

If a call to **CreateThread** succeeds, the **CreateThread** function creates a thread and returns handle to the new thread. If a call to **CreateThread** does not succeed, **CreateThread** returns a **NULL** value. (Similarly, when **CreateProcess** is called to create a new process, handles to the new process and its primary thread are returned.)

In the THRDDEMO program described under the heading "The THRDDEMO Program" on page 450, this call to the **CreateThread** creates a new thread:

```
// Call CreateThread
m_hThread = CreateThread(NULL, 0,
   (LPTHREAD_START_ROUTINE)ThreadFunc,
   this, CREATE_SUSPENDED,
   (LPDWORD) &m_IDThread);
```

The CreateRemoteThread Function

The **CreateRemoteThread** function is identical to the **CreateThread** function, except that **CreateRemoteThread** has one additional parameter: a handle to the process in which the new thread is to created. This is the syntax of the **CreateThread** function:

```
HANDLE CreateRemoteThread(HANDLE hProcess,
    LPSECURITY_ATTRIBUTES lpsa,
    DWORD cbStack, LPTHREAD_START_ROUTINE
    lpStartAddr, LPVOID lpvThreadParm,
    DWORD fdwCreate, LPDWORD lpIDTthread);.
```

The extra parameter that the **CreateRemoteFunction** expects is the **HANDLE** variable *hProcess*.

All information provided in this chapter about **CreateThread** is also applicable to **CreateRemoteThread**.

Parameters of the *CreateThread* Function

These are the parameters passed to the **CreateThread** function:

- *lpsa*: Points to a **SECURITY_ATTRIBUTES** structure that specifies the security attributes of the thread. If *lpsa* is **NULL**, the thread is created with a default security descriptor. The security attributes of a thread include an inheritance flag that determines whether the handle can be inherited by child processes. They also include a security descriptor, which the system uses to perform access checks on all subsequent uses of the thread's handle before access is granted.
- *cbStack*: Specifies the size, in bytes, of the new thread's stack. The new thread's stack is allocated automatically in the memory space of the current process and is freed when the thread terminates. If a value of zero is passed to *cbStack*, the new thread's stack is the same size as the stack used by the current process's primary thread. No matter what value is passed to *cbStack*, the new thread's stack size grows as needed.

- *lpStartAddr*: Points to an application-supplied function that the new thread executes as soon as it starts. The pointer that is passed to *lpStartAddr* is recognized by the system as the starting address of the new thread. The function that is referenced by the *lpStartAddr* pointer takes a single 32-bit argument and returns a 32-bit exit code. For more details on this topic, see "Terminating Threads" on page 457.
- *lpvThreadParm*: Specifies the single 32-bit parameter value passed to the user-supplied function that is the new thread's entry point (see the *lpStartAddr* parameter, above).
- *fdwCreate*: Specifies additional flags that control the creation of the thread. If the **CREATE_SUSPENDED** flag is specified, the thread is created in a suspended state, and will not run until the **ResumeThread** function is called. If this value is zero, the thread runs immediately after creation.
- *lpIDThread*: Points to a 32-bit variable that receives the thread identifier.

The CreateProcess *Function Creates Threads, Too*

As noted in "Creating and Using Threads" on page 421, the Win32 function **CreateProcess** also creates new threads. When an application creates a new process by calling **CreateProcess**, the **CreateProcess** function returns handles to both the new process and its primary thread.

How the *CreateThread* Function Works

When an application creates a new thread by calling **CreateThread**, a handle with full access to the new thread is created. If a security descriptor is not provided in the **SECURITY_ATTRIBUTES** structure that is passed to **CreateThread** as a parameter, the handle to the new thread can be used in any function that requires a thread object handle. If a security descriptor is provided, an access check is performed on all subsequent uses of the handle before access to the new thread is granted. If the access check results in the denial of access, the requesting process cannot use the handle to gain access to the thread.

Entry-Point Functions

The *lpStartAddr* parameter that is passed to **CreateThread** is the address of a function that is used as the thread's entry point. Typically, the starting address of the new thread is the name of a function that is defined by the application. When the new thread starts running, the function that executes is the function that is pointed to by the *lpStartAddr* parameter.

The input and output parameters of the entry-point function referenced by the *lpStartAddr* pointer are predefined; the function always takes a single 32-bit parameter and always returns a double word result.

The same function can be specified as the entry point for multiple threads.

Using Timers Instead of Multithreading

Windows 95, like Windows 3.*x*, comes equipped with a set of timers that can divide CPU time among various tasks. In some circumstances, you can use timers to schedule events instead of using threads.

There are differences, however, between the behaviors of events scheduled by timers and those of tasks schedules by threads. When you allocate CPU time to a task by using a timer, the task always receives the amount of time that it is allotted, regardless of the amount of CPU time that may be available. When you use threads to allocate time slices to multiple tasks, the Win32 operating system determines how much time to give to each thread depending upon how much CPU time is available.

Setting Thread Priorities

By default, every new thread created by **CreateThread** has a thread priority of **THREAD_PRIORITY_NORMAL**. An application can change a thread's priority by calling the Winb32 function **SetThreadPriority** function. An application can obtain the current priority of a thread by calling the Win32 function **GetThreadPriority**.

For more details about the **SetThreadPriority** and **GetThreadPriority** functions, see the *Microsoft Win32 Programmer's Reference.*

Signaled and Unsignaled States

When the application-supplied entry-point function of a thread terminates, the 32-bit value that the function returns value is an exit code. The system uses this code to terminate the thread by calling the **`ExitThread`** function.

When a thread is active, it is said to be in an *unsignaled* state. That means that any other threads that are waiting for the thread to terminate must keep waiting. When a thread terminates, its state changes to signaled. That setting alerts any waiting threads that the thread has terminated.

Even when a thread has terminated, the thread object (the object referenced by the thread's handle) remains in the system until all handles to the thread have been closed.

For more details on signaled and unsignaled states, see "Synchronization Objects" on page 439. For more about the termination of threads, see "Terminating Threads" on page 457.

Multithreading and the MFC Library

Version 2 of the Microsoft Foundation Class Library, which was released with Version 1.0 of Visual C++, did not support multithreading; the only way to implement its multithreading features was to call C-language functions or Win32 API functions.

With the release of Version 4.0 of Visual C++ and Version 4.0 of the MFC library, Microsoft has fnally introduced some basic MFC support for multithreading. But this support is still minimal; even MFC 4.0 provides only two thread-related classes.

One of the MFC library's new thread-support classes is the CWinThread class. The other MFC thread class is called CWinApp. Even with these two new classes, the MFC library is still a long way from encapsulating all the multithreading functions that are supplied in the Win32 API.

The MFC library still has no classes that deal with mutexes, semaphores, critical sections, or events. To incorporate these features into your Visual C++ applications, you still have to use functions provided by the Win32 API.

The example programs in this chapter show you to use Win32 API functions to implement all these multithreading capabilities in your programs.

Varieties of MFC Threads

The MFC library provides support for two kinds of threads: *worker threads* and *user-interface threads*.

Worker threads are typically used to perform operations that do not require user input—operations such as calculations, screen updating, and background printing.

User-interface threads are designed to handle user input and to respond to user events without affecting other threads that may be running in an application.

The MFC library provide a separate tools for writing worker threads and user-interface threads, and provides thread-related functions in that make distinctions between worker threads and user-interface threads. But the Win32 API makes no such distinctions.

The Win32 API does not know anything about the differences between worker threads and user-interface threads. All it needs to execute a thread is the thread's starting address.

Worker Threads and User-Interface Threads

The main difference between user-interface threads and worker threads is that user-interface threads have a "message pump." That means they can receive and process messages, and can therefore interact with the user of your application.

In contrast, worker threads have no message pump, so they cannot process messages. So, when you need to create a thread that does not require any input from the user, the easiest thing to do is to create a worker thread.

For example, if you wanted to create a thread to perform background calculations in a spreadsheet program, or to create a window display without requiring any input from the user, your easiest choice might be to write a worker thread.

But if you wanted to use MFC to create a thread that relied on keyboard input from the user, you would have to make it a user-interface thread.

One advantage of using user-interface threads is that the Visual C++ ClassWizard utility supports them. You can create a user-interface thread automatically with ClassWizard, and you can then use ClassWizard to add member functions to the class and to integrate the class with your program and with other MFC classes it contains.

The CWinApp class itself, and classes derived from it, are examples of user-interface threads. Your applications can also derive user-interface threads directly from CWinThread.

Worker Threads

Creating a *worker thread* in an MFC application is very similar to creating a thread using the Win32 API. To create a worker thread in an MFC program, you must write a C-style function (not a member function) that serves as an entry point to your thread.

Then, at the point in your program where you want the thread to be created, you must provide a pointer to the function that serves as the thread's entry point.

Creating an Entry-Point Function for a Worker Thread

In an MFC application, an entry-point function for a worker thread has this syntax:

```
UINT ThreadFunc(LPVOID pParam)
{
   // ...
}
```

Notice that the preceding statement is a definition of a C-style global function—not a definition of a member function. In a Visual C++ program, you cannot use a member function of a class as the entry-point function of a worker thread. If you try, the Visual C++ compiler returns an error message.

AfxBeginThread and CreateThread

Once you write a thread entry-point function using the syntax shown under the preceding heading, you can start the thread by calling the MFC function **AfxBeginThread**, as in this example:

```
CWinThread *pThread = AfxBeginThread(ThreadFunc,
   (LPVOID) this,
   THREAD_PRIORITY_BELOW_NORMAL,
   0,
   CREATE_SUSPENDED);
```

The procedure for calling an MFC worker thread in a Visual C++ program is much like the procedure for calling a thread in a Win32 (non-MFC) program. But there are some important differences. One difference is that a Visual C++ program can create a thread by using the MFC helper function **AfxBeginThread**, as shown in the preceding example, while a non-MCF program creates a thread by calling the Win32 **CreateThread** function:

```
m_hThread = CreateThread(NULL, 0,
   (LPTHREAD_START_ROUTINE)ThreadFunc,
   this, CREATE_SUSPENDED,
   (LPDWORD) &m_IDThread);
```

Another difference is that **AfxBeginThread** function used in Visual C++ creates and initializes a CWinThread object and returns a pointer to that object. From that point on, you can use the pointer returned by **AfxBeginThread** to access the thread object that the **AfxBeginThread** function has created.

In contrast, the MFC **CreateThread** function creates a handle to a thread and returns that handle. Subsequently, you access the thread you have created through the handle returned by the **CreateThread** function.

There are similarities, as well as differences, between the **AfxBeginThread** and **CreateThread** functions. Both functions, for example, accept the address of a thread entry point as a parameter. But for Visual C++ users, there is a second version of the **AfxBeginThread** function.

As you have seen, one overridden version of the **AfxBeginThread** takes a thread entry-point address as a parameter. The other overridden version of the function accepts the address of a CWinThread object as a parameter. When you create a thread by passing **AfxBeginThread** a pointer to a CWinThread object, the thread you wind up creating is a user-interface thread.

Parameters of the AfxBeginThread Function

This is the syntax of the version of **AfxBeginThread** that creates a worker thread:

```
CWinThread* AfxBeginThread(
   AFX_THREADPROC pfnThreadProc,
   LPVOID pParam,
   int nPriority = THREAD_PRIORITY_NORMAL,
   UINT nStackSize = 0,
   DWORD dwCreateFlags = 0,
   LPSECURITY_ATTRIBUTES lpSecurityAttrs = NULL );
```

To create an MFC worker thread, you pass the following parameters to the **AfxBeginThread** function:

- *pfnThreadProc*—a pointer to the address of the thread's entry-thread's entry-point function.
- *pParam*—the parameter to be passed to the controlling function.
- *nPriority* (optional)—the priority of the thread. The default is normal priority. For more information on the available priority levels, see **::SetThreadPriority** in the *Win32 Programmer's Reference*.
- *nStackSize* (optional)—the stack size for the thread. Default is the same size stack as the creating thread.
- *dwCreateFlags* (optional)—CREATE_SUSPENDED if you want the thread to be created in a suspended state. The default is 0, or start the thread normally.
- *lpSecurityAttrs* (optional)—the desired security attributes. The default is the same access as the parent thread. For more information on the format of this security information, see SECURITY_ATTRIBUTES in the *Win32 Programmer's Reference*.

AfxBeginThread creates and initializes a CWinThread object for you, starts it, and returns its address so you can refer to it later. Checks are made throughout the procedure to make sure all objects are deallocated properly should any part of the creation fail.

To see how you can call **AfxBeginThread** to create a worker thread, see "The MFCTHRDS Program" on page 467.

Advantages of Using the AfxBeginThread Function

The primary advantage of using the **AfxBeginThread** function is that **AfxBeginThread** returns a pointer to a CWinThread object, while a thread-creating function in a Win32 program returns a handle to a thread. In a Visual C++ program, a CWinThread object is more useful than a handle to a thread because the CWinThread class is an MFC class and therefore enjoys all the usual benefits of MFC class, such as smooth interaction with the Visual C++ framework and with other classes in the MFC library.

Creating a Worker Thread

A statement that creates a thread by calling **AfxBeginThread** is usually implemented as a member function of a class. When a Visual C++ application creates a thread by calling **AfxBeginThread**, the thread is created as soon as the calling function is executed. The MFCTHRDS program, one of the sample applications presented in this chapter, shows how the **AfxBeginThread** function can be used to create a worker thread in a Visual C++ program.

User-Interface Threads

A *user-interface thread* is an MFC thread that can handle user input and can respond to user events without affecting other threads that may be running in an application.

Although user-interface threads have capabilities that worker threads do not have, there is nothing to prevent an application from creating and using a user-interface thread without taking advantage of all the thread's capabilities. In other words, an application can always use a user-interface thread instead of a worker thread—but the opposite is not true. You can never use a worker thread in situations that require interaction between the thread and the user. User-interface threads are more smoothly integrated into the MFC environment than worker threads. My personal preference is to use only user-interface threads in MFC programs, avoiding the use of worker threads completely.

Advantages of User-Interface Threads

There are at least two reasons for using user-interface threads rather than worker threads in MFC applications whenever possible:

- When you use a worker thread in an application, its entry point is always a global C-style function, not a member function of a C++ class. So, when you use a worker thread in a C++ program, you wind up with a global C-style function floating around in your application, not directly tied to any object and not encapsulated in any class. That is not a desirable feature for a C++ program to have because it is not consistent with the object-oriented design requirements of code encapsulation and limited access to data. Generally speaking, well-designed C++ programs avoid the use of global non-member functions because free-floating functions have no means of encapsulating their code or data inside objects and cannot be transported from one application to another as readily as member functions.
- When you build an application using the Visual C++ Framework, you can use ClassWizard to create user-interface threads automatically. When you create a user-interface thread class using ClassWizard, your thread class becomes an integral part of your application's C++ framework. ClassWizard creates an implementation file (.CPP file) and a header file (.H file) for your thread class, and from then on you can use the ClassWizard tool to create

and maintain thread-related member variables, member functions, and events.

Deriving a Class from CWinThread

When you want to create a user-interface thread, the first thing you must do is derive a class from CWinThread.

You must declare this class using the **DECLARE_DYNCREATE** macro, and you must and implement it by invoking the **IMPLEMENT_DYNCREATE** macro. If you create your thread class using the Visual C++ ClassWizard utility, ClassWizard automatically constructs an object that invokes both these macros in accordance with the requirements of Visual C++ and the MFC library.

When you create a user-interface thread by calling the **AfxBegin-Thread** function, you must override some functions, and you can override others. Table 9.1 summarizes these functions.

Table 9.1 Functions to override with user-interface threads

Function Name	Purpose
ExitInstance	Perform cleanup when thread terminates. Usually overridden.
InitInstance	Perform thread instance initialization. Must be overridden.
OnIdle	Perform thread-specific idle-time processing. Not usually overridden.
PreTranslateMessag e	Filter messages before they are dispatched to TranslateMessage and DispatchMessage. Not usually overridden.
ProcessWndProcEx ception	Intercept unhandled exceptions thrown by the thread's message and command handlers. Not usually overridden.
Run	Controlling function for the thread. Contains the message pump. Rarely overridden.

Instantiating a User-Interface Thread

When you have derived a user-interface thread class from the CWin-Thread class, you must instantiate an object of your CWinThread-derived class. You can construct your thread object either on the stack or on the heap, using either of these standard styles:

```
CMyWinThread myThread;
```

or

```
CMyWinThread *pMyThread = CMyWinThread;
```

When you have instantiated a CWinThread-derived object, you can call the **AfxBeginThread** function to initialize your thread. To provide your thread's entry-point function with a pointer to the thread object you have instantiated, you simply place the **RUNTIME_CLASS** of your thread object in the **AfxBeginThread** function's *pThreadClass* parameter. You can obtain your thread object's runtime class by calling the CObject member function **GetRuntimeClass**. (To see how the **AfxBeginThread** function and the **GetRuntimeClass** function can be called to create a user-interface thread, see "The USRTHRDS Program" on page 466).

Constructing a User-Interface Thread

There are two ways to construct a user-interface thread. One way is to create an object derived from the CWinThread class, as explained under the preceding headings, and then to initialize the object by calling the MFC **CreateThread** function. This two-stage construction method is useful if you want to create a CWinThread-derived object that you can start and terminate at will—for example, between successive creations and terminations of thread executions.

The other way to create a user-interface thread is to execute the version of the **AfxBeginThread** function that is specifically designed to create objects derived from CWinThread. This is the format of the version of the **AfxBeginThread** function that creates user-interface threads:

```
CWinThread* AfxBeginThread(
   CRuntimeClass* pThreadClass,
    int nPriority = THREAD_PRIORITY_NORMAL,
    UINT nStackSize = 0,
   DWORD dwCreateFlags = 0,
   LPSECURITY_ATTRIBUTES lpSecurityAttrs = NULL );
```

To create a user-interface thread, you pass the following parameters to the **AfxBeginThread** function:

- *pThreadClass*—The **RUNTIME_CLASS** of an object you have derived from CWinThread.
- *nPriority* (optional)—The priority of the thread. The default is normal priority. For more information on the available priority levels, see ::SetThreadPriority in the Win32 Programmer's Reference, Volume 4.
- *nStackSize* (optional)—The stack size for the thread. Default is the same size stack as the creating thread.

- *dwCreateFlags* (optional)—**CREATE_SUSPENDED** if you want the thread to be created in a suspended state. The default is 0, or start the thread normally.
- *lpSecurityAttrs* (optional)—The desired security attributes. The default is the same access as the parent thread. For more information on the format of this security information, see **SECURITY_ATTRIBUTES** in the *Win32 Programmer's Reference*.

How AfxBeginThread Creates User-Interface Threads

With two exceptions, the user-interface version of **AfxBeginThread** works just like the worker-thread version; it creates and initializes a CWinThread object for you, starts it, and returns its address so you can refer to it later. Checks are made throughout the procedure to make sure all objects are deallocated properly if any part of the creation fails.

One difference between the worker version and the user-interface version of the **AfxBeginThread** function is that the first parameter passed to the user-interface version of the function is the **RUNTIME_CLASS** of the object being derived from CWinThread.

In a framework-based Visual C++ program, the **RUNTIME_CLASS** of an object is a data structure that contains information needed by an application framework to create an object of a class at runtime. You can obtain the **RUNTIME_CLASS** of an object by executing the CObject member function **GetRuntimeClass** (for more information about creating user-interface threads, see the "The USRTHRDS Program" on page 466; for more details about runtime classes, see your Visual C++ documentation).

There is one other difference between an **AfxBeginThread** function that creates a worker thread and an **AfxBeginThread** function that creates a worker thread: The version of **AfxBeginThread** that creates a user-interface thread has no *pParam* parameter.

How the AfxBeginThread Function Works

When a program contains an **AfxBeginThread** function that creates a thread, the entry-point function executes as soon as soon as the **AfxBeginThread** function is executed. When the entry-point function executes, the thread starts. When the entry-point function terminates, so does the thread. This series of operations applies both to worker threads and to user-interface threads.

When a process uses the **AfxBeginThread** function to start a thread—either a worker thread or a user-interface thread—the thread's entry-point procedure must have the following prototype:

```
UINT MyControllingFunction(LPVOID pParam);
```

As you can see, a thread entry-point function called by **AfxBeginThread** takes one parameter: a single 32-bit value. The value that is provided to the thread's entry-point function is the value of the **AfxBeginThread** function's *pParam* variable (see the syntax examples of the **AfxBeginThread** presented earlier in this chapter).

When an entry-point function is executed to create a worker thread, the *pParam* variable passed to the entry-point function by the **AfxBeginThread** function must be the constructor that instantiated the thread object when it was created.

The entry-point function that starts the worker thread can interpret the **AfxBeginThread** function's *pParam* variable in any manner it chooses. The entry-point function can treat the *pParam* variable as a scalar value, for example, or as a pointer to a structure containing multiple parameters. The entry-point function can even ignore the *pParam* parameter.

If the *pParam* parameter refers to a structure, the entry-point function can used the structure not only to pass data from the calling function to the thread, but also to pass data back from the thread to the caller. If an entry-point function uses the *pParam* variable to pass the address of such a structure to pass data back to its caller, the thread must notify the caller when the results are ready.

When a thread entry-point function terminates, it returns a **DWORD** value indicating the reason the function has terminated. Typically, an entry-point function returns an exit code of zero if it has successfully created a thread. It can return other values to specify different types of errors.

The CWinApp and CWinThread Classes

As explained earlier in this chapter, in "Multithreading and the MFC Library" on page 425, the MFC library provides two classes that support multithreading: CWinApp and CWinThread. Unfortunately, Version 4.0 of the MFC library does not encapsulate any thread-synchronization objects such as a mutex class or a semaphore class. The Win32 SDK does provide C-language functions for creating synchronization objects for multithreaded programs, but if you want to encapsulate those functions into C++ classes, you're on your own.

Under the two headings that follow, the two thread objects that the MFC library does provide are described.

The CWinApp Class

The CWinApp class is the base class from which Windows application objects are derived. In a Visual C++ program based on the AppWizard framework, an application object provides member functions for initializing and running the program.

In early versions of C++, the CWinApp class was derived from a class named CCmdTarget. The CCmdTarget class—which is still used in MFC programs—is derived from the mother of all MFC classes, CObject.

In Visual C++ 4.0, the CWinApp class is derived from a new class named CWinThread. Now it is the CWinThread class, not the CWinApp class, that is derived from the CCmdTarget class. Figure 9.3 shows this new class hierarchy.

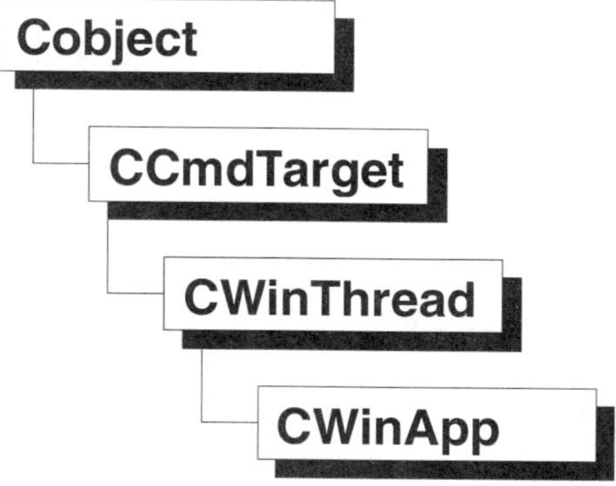

Figure 9.3 Hierarchy of the CWinApp class

In an application based on the Visual C++ AppWizard framework, you must create one and only one object derived from the CWinApp class. A Visual C++ program constructs its CWinApp-derived object when other C++ global objects have been constructed, so the program's CWinApp object is already available by the time Windows calls the **`WinMain`** function—the main function of a Visual C++ program.

When you derive an application class from the CWinApp class, you must override the Visual C++ **`InitInstance`** member function to create your application's main window object.

In addition to the CWinApp member functions, the MFC library provides the following global functions to access your CWinApp object and other global information:

- **AfxGetApp**—Obtains a pointer to the CWinApp object.
- **AfxGetInstanceHandle**—Obtains a handle to the current application instance.
- **AfxGetResourceHandle**—Obtains a handle to the application's resources.
- **AfxGetAppName**—Obtains a pointer to a string containing the application's name. Alternately, if you have a pointer to the CWinApp object, use **m_pszExeName** to get the application's name.

The CWinThread Class

Every framework-based Visual C++ program has a CWinApp object that is an encapsulation of the application's main thread of execution. This main thread of execution is usually provided by an object derived from CWinApp.

As shown in Figure 9.3 on page 435, CWinApp is an MFC-library class derived from CWinThread. You can create additional CWinThread objects to add multiple threads to an application.

Thread Local Storage

Thread local storage, sometimes abbreviated *TLS*, is a method that individual threads running under a process can use for storing private, thread-specific data. With thread local storage, every thread called by a process can access a set of variables that are used only when the thread is called by that process; they are not used when the thread is called from other processes.

When the thread is called from a different process, the thread uses a different set of variables that are unique to that process.

By storing variables in thread local storage, a thread can use those variables in much the same way that a C-language application uses local variables—or in much the same way that a C++ programs uses static member variables. As a process starts and terminate threads, any TLS variables that are provided for the thread remain persistent—that is, they remain in storage and retain their values even when the thread is not running.

If another process calls the same thread, any TLS variables that are provided for the thread are stored in a different area of memory and also retain their values when that thread is not running. This system prevents different sets of TLS variables used by the same thread from interfering with each other when the thread runs under different processes. By using thread local storage, a thread can save and retrieve private variables that cannot be accessed by other threads.

Using Thread Local Storage in DLLs

Dynamic-link libraries called by threads often store variables using thread local storage (see "How DLLs Use Thread Local Storage" on page 484). By using TLS, a DLL can access data maintained by multiple threads without requiring the calling thread to keep track of where the data is stored.

When a thread needs to share data in a DLL with another thread (or another process), it calls a Win32 SDK function named **`TlsAlloc`** to create a global variable called a *TLS index*. It then allocates a block of memory and places a pointer to this memory block in the TLS index.

When a process calls **`TlsAlloc`** to create a TLS index, every client that accesses the DLL's data is provided with the address stored in the TLS index. Then, when a client requires access to the DLL's data, it can attach itself to the data, preventing other clients from accessing the data. When the client has finished accessing the data, it can detach itself from the data, freeing the data for access by other clients. This system provides multiple clients with access to a DLL's data, while preventing multiple processes from attempting to modify the data at the same time.

When a DLL called by multiple threads stores variables using thread local storage, the DLL is required to keep track of just one TLS index. The system can use that index to determine which thread is calling the DLL.

Windows 95 can store at least 64 TLS indexes for any process. That guarantees that if enough memory is available, any single process can store up to 64 different DLLs using TLS in memory at the same time.

How Thread Local Storage Works

To illustrate how TLS works, suppose you write a DLL that can be called by multiple threads running under the same process. Also suppose that each thread has its own set of TLS variables.

When you call a function in your DLL from a particular thread, your DLL allocates a block of memory to hold that thread's global data. The DLL stores a pointer to the thread's data block in the thread's TLS area. From that point on, each time the DLL is called from that thread, it uses variables stored in the thread's TLS area.

Internally, Windows 95 stores TLS variables in an array inside a memory block called the thread control block. A process can allocate thread local storage areas in the thread control block by calling a Win32 function named **TlsAlloc**.

The Win32 SDK also provides several other functions for managing thread local storage. They include **TlsGetValue**, **TlsSetValue**, and **TlsFree**.

When a thread is active, the FS segment register in the 386/486/-Pentium processor points to a data block that holds the thread's TLS variables. Each time an application switches threads, Windows 95 updates the FS register to point at the appropriate TLS memory block.

The thread Attribute

To support TLS, an attribute named **thread** has been incorporated into Microsoft C and C++ and is supported by the Visual C++ compiler. The **thread** attribute, like the **dllexport** attribute used to export DLLs (see "Exporting Functions from VCPP 1.0 DLLs" on page 510), is an *extended storage class modifier*. You can declare TLS variable in the same way you declare the **dllexport** variable: with the **__declspec** keyword. For example, the following statement declares TLS integer variable and initializes it with the value 1:

```
__declspec( thread ) int tls_i = 1;
```

Thread Local Storage Step by Step

✔ These steps summarize how a DLL can set up and use thread local storage:

1. The DLL calls the **TlsAlloc** function to allocate a TLS index.
2. The DLL dynamically allocates a block of memory for a thread and calls **TlsSetValue** to store the starting address of the memory allocated to the thread.
3. Each time a subsequent thread is initialized, the DLL calls **TlsSetValue** to allocate an additional block of dynamic memory and calls **TlsSetValue** to store the starting address of each additional memory block. Windows 95 automatically resolves the process's TLS index and the thread's internal ID to return a

memory location that is different from the locations used by previous threads.

4. Each time the DLL needs to access the dynamic memory associated with a thread, it retrieves the address of the appropriate block of memory by calling **TlsGetValue**. Again, the system uses the thread's ID to determine which thread's memory address to return.
5. As each thread detaches from its calling process, it retrieves its TLS memory address and then explicitly releases the dynamic memory that it uses for thread local storage. If a thread fails to take this step, the system does not clean up the memory until the process exits, leaving unavailable resources hanging around.
6. When the process detaches from the DLL, the DLL releases the TLS index by calling the **TlsFree** function.

To see a sample program that uses thread local storage, see "The MFCTHRDS and USRTHRDS Programs" on page 466.

Synchronization Objects

In Windows 95 applications, threads often share resources. That means there's always a danger that a thread will modify a resource in a way that another thread does not expect. For example, it is quite possible for two threads to have write access to the same file or the same block of memory. In this kind of situation, if one thread writes to the file or memory area that it shares with the other thread, and the other thread doesn't know about it, the result can be a mess of corrupted data.

Things can also get messy when more than one thread attempts to use the same graphics (GDI) object at the same time. Windows 95 doesn't synchronize GDI objects—such as brushes, bitmaps, and the like—so your application has to make sure that threads don't trip up on each other's brushes and bitmaps in graphics-oriented programs.

Waitable Objects

To prevent these kinds of problems, the Win32 API provides three special synchronization objects called *waitable objects*. Actually, there are more than three kinds of waitable objects, but only three of them are also categorized as synchronization objects.

A waitable object is any object that can be in a signaled or unsignaled state. (If an object is currently in use, it is said to be in an unsignaled state. If it has terminated, it is said to be in a signaled state. For more details, see "Signaled and Unsignaled States" on page 425). Waitable objects include processes, thread handles, file handles, named pipes, console input buffer handles (see Chapter 8, "Programs and Processes"), and communication device handles.

To determine whether a waitable object is signaled or unsignaled, an application can call aWin32 function such as **WaitForSingleObject**, **WaitForMultipleObjects**, or **WaitForDebugEvent**. These "wait" functions, along with several others provided by the Win32 SDK, can halt the processing of a thread until the state of the thread changes to unsignaled or until there is a timeout. To illustrate how wait functions work, this is the syntax of the **WaitForSingleObject** function:

```
DWORD WaitForSingleObject(HANDLE hObject,
   dwTimeout);
```

When you call **WaitForSingleObject**, the *hObject* parameter identifies the object being waited for. The *dwTimeout* parameter is a timeout interval, expressed in milliseconds. If the specified timeout interval elapses before the specified object's state becomes unsignaled, the wait function returns. If the *dwTimeout* parameter is zero, the wait function tests the specified object's state and returns immediately. If *dwTimeout* has a value of INFINITE, the timeout interval never elapses.

For more details about the wait functions provided by the Windows 95 SDK, see "Wait Functions" on page 465.

When an application discovers that a waitable object is in a signaled state, it can call a "WaitFor" function to wait until the object's state switches to unsignaled. Processing of the program can then resume.

Waitable objects can be useful when an application needs to prevent a thread from executing until some specific event occurs. For example, a wait function can be used to block a console input buffer from being read until there is input from the user, such as the pressing of a key or the clicking of a mouse button. Wait functions can also be used to keep a process or a thread from starting until a currently executing process or thread terminates.

Waitable objects can also be useful in protecting shared resources from being accessed simultaneously by multiple threads or processes—a potentially disastrous occurrence.

One "WaitFor" function, **WaitForInputIdle**, causes a thread to wait until a specified process is initialized and is waiting for user input. This can be useful for synchronizing parent and child processes, because the Win32 function **CreateProcess** returns without waiting for any child processes to complete their initializations.

Critical Section Objects

A fourth kind of object, called a critical section object, is sometimes included in the category of synchronization objects. Critical section objects are sometimes used in place of mutex objects to protect shared resources from being unexpectedly modified by different threads that are being executed simultaneously. Critical section objects are a bit easier to implement than mutex objects are, but their capabilities are more limited.

Critical section objects are better tools for exception handling than for thread management. Strictly speaking, critical section objects are not synchronization objects because they do not have signaled and unsignaled states that can be detected by wait functions. Instead, they operate by declaring certain blocks of code to be critical code sections, and then blocking unwanted use of those sections by calling the Win32 functions **EnterCriticalSection** and **LeaveCriticalSection**. Only one thread can be granted access to a critical section at any given time.

Because critical sections do not meet the strict definition of synchronization objects, and because mutex objects are better tools for synchronizing threads, I will not go into detail about critical section objects in this volume. If you're interested in learning more about critical section objects, refer to Volume 2 of the *Microsoft Win32 Programmer's Reference*.

Categories of Synchronization Objects

Three kinds of objects that fall into the category of waitable objects are also considered *synchronization objects* because they can be used to synchronize threads. A synchronization object is an object whose handle can be passed to a wait function to coordinate the execution of multiple threads. The state of a synchronization object is always either nonsignaled—a state that means the object is in use and is thus unavailable to other threads—or signaled, which means that the object has completed its work and that other threads can claim it.

More than one process can have a handle to the same synchronization object, making interprocess synchronization possible.

In Windows 95, there are three kinds of synchronization objects:

- Mutex objects, which can protect shared resources by ensuring that only one thread can be modifying the resource at any given time
- Semaphore objects, which can limit the number of threads that can be executed simultaneously
- Event objects, which can prevent a thread from starting until the execution of another thread is complete.

Mutex Objects

A mutex (mutual exclusion) object is a synchronization object that can protect shared resources by preventing them from being accessed by multiple threads simultaneously. The state of a mutex object is signaled when it is not owned by any thread, and nonsignaled when it is owned by a thread.

To prevent multiple threads from writing to shared memory at the same time, a mutex forces a thread to "own" a block of code before it is granted access to the code. When a block of code is protected by a mutex, a thread that seeks access to the code must wait for the thread that owns the code to release it. When the code is released by the thread that owns it, the thread that is seeking access can be granted ownership. After the new owner of the code finishes accessing it, ownership of the code is again released—and so on.

The CreateMutex Function

An application creates a mutex object by calling the Win32 function **CreateMutex**. This is the syntax of the **CreateMutex** function:

```
HANDLE CreateMutex(LPSECURITY_ATTRIBUTES lpsa,
   BOOL fInitialOwner, LPCSTR lpszMutexName);
```

If a **CreateMutex** calls succeeds, it returns a handle to the mutex it has created. If unsuccessful, the function returns a **NULL** value.

The following parameters are expected by **CreateMutex**:

- *lpsa*: A pointer to a **SECURITY_ATTRIBUTES** structure (see "The SECURITY_ATTRIBUTES Structure" on page 353).
- *fInitialOwner*: If **TRUE**, the calling thread requests immediate ownership of the mutex object being created. If **FALSE**, the mutex is not initially owned.
- *lpszMutexName*: Points to a string specifying the name of the mutex object. If this parameter is **NULL**, the mutex is created without a name.

How Mutex Objects Work

This is a step-by-step overview of how a mutex object works:

1. A thread calls **CreateMutex** function to create a mutex object. The creating thread can request immediate ownership of the mutex, and can also specify a name for the mutex object.
2. If a thread in another process seeks access to the mutex that has been created, it opens a handle to the mutex object by calling the Win32 function **OpenMutex**. (For more information about the **OpenMutex** function, see the *Microsoft Win32 Programmer's Reference*.
3. Any thread that has obtained a handle the mutex object that has been created can call one of the Win32 SDK's wait functions to request ownership of the mutex.
4. If the mutex is owned by another thread (which is the case in this scenario), the wait function that has been called by the thread seeking access withholds access until the thread that owns the mutex releases it.
5. When the thread that owns the mutex is finished with it, the thread releases the mutex by calling the Win32 function **ReleaseMutex**.
6. If the **ReleaseMutex** function succeeds, the waiting thread is granted access to the released mutex and becomes the mutex's owner.

For more information on how mutex objects work in Windows 95 programs, see "The MUTEX Program" on page 459.

Semaphore Objects

A semaphore object is a synchronization object that maintains a count between zero and a specified maximum value. When a semaphore is created, it has a specified initial count. Each time a thread uses and releases the semaphore, the semaphore's count is decremented.

As long as a semaphore's count is greater than zero, the semaphore's state is signaled. When the semaphore's count is decremented to zero, the semaphore becomes unsignaled. From that point on, the semaphore can no longer be accessed by any thread.

Uses for Semaphore Objects

Semaphore objects can be useful when an application contains a shared resource that can support a limited number of users. Acting as a gate, a semaphore object can count threads as they enter and exit a controlled area and can limit the number of threads that share a resource to a specified maximum number.

Suppose, for example, that an application needs to conserve memory by placing a limit on the number of windows that it creates. The SEMAFORE application, which you can find in the SEMAFORE subdirectory on your bonus disk, shows how an application can use a semaphore object to accomplish that objective.

The CreateSemaphore Function

You create a semaphore object by calling the Win32 function **CreateSemaphore**. This is the syntax of the **CreateSemaphore** function:

```
HANDLE CreateSemaphore(LPSECURITY_ATTRIBUTES lpsa,
    LONG cSemInitial, LONG cSemMax, LPCSTR
    lpszSemName);
```

The CreateSemaphore function returns a handle to the semaphore that it has created. If the function does not succeed, it returns a **NULL** value.

CreateSemaphore takes the following parameters:

- *psa*: A pointer to a **SECURITY_ATTRIBUTES** structure (see "The SECURITY_ATTRIBUTES Structure" on page 353).
- *cSemInitial*: The semaphore's initial count.
- *cSemMax*: The semaphore's maximum count. Usually, the same value as *cSemInitial*. If this is the case, the semaphore can no longer be accessed when *cSemInitial* threads are running.
- *lpszSemName*: The semaphore's name, if any. If this value **NULL**, the semaphore is created without a name.

"The SEMAFORE Program" on page 462 explains how semaphore objects can be incorporated into Windows 95 programs.

Event Objects

An event object is a synchronization object that can delay the start of a thread until another thread has terminated. Event objects can be useful when an application contains a thread that should not start until another thread has terminated.

To illustrate the use of event objects, suppose you want to write a compiler that builds programs in three stages: preprocessing, compilation, and linking. You can design the program to do its work by running three threads sequentially: first a preprocessing thread, then a compilation thread, and finally a linking thread.

Sequential threads might also be useful in a program that manages serial communications; by using sequential threads, the program could wait for a client to finish a transmission before allowing another client (or a server) to start another transmission.

Event objects can manage sequential threads because an event object can be set to a signaled state, either with an explicit call to a Win32 function or by simply releasing a waiting thread.

To set an event object to a signaled state, an application can call either the Win32 function **`SetEvent`** or the Win32 function **`PulseEvent`**. The **`SetEvent`** function sets the state of an unsignaled event object to signaled. The **`PulseEvent`** function releases all threads that may be waiting for an event object, and then sets the event object's state to signaled.

Alternatively, an event object can be set to a signaled stated by merely releasing a waiting thread.

Auto-Reset and Manual-Reset Event Objects

There are two kinds of event objects: auto-reset and manual-reset. When an auto-reset event object that is in a signaled state releases a waiting thread, the release of the thread automatically toggles the state of the event object to nonsignaled. If no threads are waiting, the event object's state remains signaled.

Manual-reset event objects work differently. When a manual-reset event object that is in a signaled state releases a waiting thread, the release of the thread does not toggle the state of the event object to unsignaled.

When the state of a manual-reset event object is signaled, the only thing that can put the object into an unsignaled state is an explicit call to **`SetEvent`** or **`ResetEvent`**. Until **`SetEvent`** or **`ResetEvent`** is explicitly called, a manual-reset object that is signaled remains signaled, no matter how many waiting threads it releases.

The CreateEvent Function

To create an event object, an application calls the Win32 function **CreateEvent**, which has this syntax:

```
HANDLE CreateEvent(LPSECURITY_ATTRIBUTES lpsa,
    BOOL fManualReset, BOOL fInitialState,
    LPCTSTR lpszEventName);
```

A successful call to **CreateEvent** returns a handle to the event that has been created; an unsuccessful call returns a **NULL** value.

The **CreateEvent** function takes these parameters:

- *lpsa*: A pointer to a **SECURITY_ATTRIBUTES** structure (see "The SECURITY_ATTRIBUTES Structure" on page 353)
- *fManualReset*: **TRUE** if the object to be created is a manual-reset object; otherwise, **FALSE**
- *fInitialState*: **TRUE** if the initial state of the object to be created is signaled; otherwise, **FALSE**
- *lpszEventName*: a pointer to a name string if the object to be created is to have a name; otherwise, a **NULL** value.

To get some hands-on practice with event objects, see "The EVENTS Program" on page 464.

MFC Synchronization Classes

Version 4.0 of the Microsoft Foundation Class (MFC) library provides several *synchronization* and *synchronization access* classes to aid in solving this problem. This section explains the classes available, and when and how to use them to create thread-safe classes in a typical multithreaded application.

The six multithreaded classes provided with MFC fall into two categories: synchronization objects (CSynchObject, CSemaphore, CMutex, and CEvent) and synchronization access objects (CMultiLock and CSingleLock).

Synchronization classes are used when access to a resource must be controlled to ensure integrity of the resource. Synchronization access classes are used to gain access to these controlled resources.

Which class you choose to use in your application depends on how you need to restrict access to the resource. If only one thread can access your resource at a time, use CMutex. If more than one thread can access your resource at a time, use CSemaphore. CEvent is used to signal a thread that a particular event has occurred. (CSynchObject is never used directly. It is the base class for the other three synchronization classes.)

As an example, suppose you have written an application that maintains a linked-list of accounts. Assume that your application allows up to three accounts to be examined in separate windows, but allows only one account to be updated at any particular time. When an account is updated, the updated data is sent over the network to a data archive.

This kind of application uses all three types of synchronization classes. Because it allows up to three accounts to be examined at one time, it can use the CSemaphore class to limit access to three view objects. When an attempt to view a fourth account occurs, the application waits until one of the first three windows is closed.

When an account is updated, the application can use a CMutex object to ensure that only one account is updated at a time. After the update succeeds, the application can signal CEvent, which releases a thread waiting for the event to be signaled. This thread can then send the new data to the data archive.

Animation in the Example Programs

Each of the example programs presented in this chapter displays a bouncing ball that is drawn using a standard Windows bitmap. The bitmaps used in the sample programs are device-dependent bitmaps—the kind traditionally used in Windows programs—not the device-independent bitmaps that Microsoft now recommends for use in graphics programs.

In this chapter's example programs, the code that controls animation is encapsulated into a simple class named MAnimation. The MAnimation class was designed specifically for this book and does not rely on classes in the Microsoft Foundation Class (MFC) library. It is thread-safe and is also compiler-independent, so you can use it in programs that are built using any 32-bit compiler that is compatible with Windows 95.

The bitmap images that are used to create the bouncing balls in this chapter's programs are drawn in the usual Windows fashion. First, a GDI (graphics device interface) function is called to create a graphics object (in this case, a bitmap). Then the bitmap object is placed in (or, in Windows jargon, "selected into") a device context object, or DC. Finally, the bitmap object is drawn to the screen.

This process, which is as old as the Windows operating system, is explained in more detail in Chapter 10.

In the constructor of the MAnimation class, which appears in the ANIMWND.CPP file in each example program, the Win32 function

GetDC is called to set up a device context (DC). Later on in each program, in a member function named **MAnimation::MakeNewShape**, a bitmap object is created and is drawn into a memory buffer. The SDK functions that are called to draw the object are **CreateCompatibleDC**, **CreateCompatibleBitmap**, and **Ellipse**.

The animation in each example program is implemented by a member function named **MAnimation::AnimateShape**. Each time a thread orders an update in the position of the animated bouncing ball, the **MAnimation::AnimateShape** function calls the familiar Windows function **BitBlt** to copy the bouncing-ball bitmap from memory to the screen.

Example Programs: Using Multithreading

Eight example applications are provided on your bonus disk to demonstrate the topics introduced in this chapter. On your bonus disk, the source code for each example program is in a separate directory inside this chapter's directory.

The following are the eight example programs presented in this chapter:

- TIMER—A program that controls animation with a timer rather than threads
- THRDDEMO—A program that demonstrates the operation of threads
- MUTEX—A program that creates *mutex (mutual exclusion)* objects, which prevent threads from interfering with other
- SEMAFORE—An application that creates semaphore objects, which limit the number of threads that a process can run at the same time
- EVENT—An application that creates *event objects* to manage threads that run sequentially
- MFCTHRDS—An application that shows how to write multithreaded programs using worker threads
- USRTHRD—An application that shows how to write multithreaded programs using user-interface threads
- SHAREMEM—A program that demonstrates thread local storage.

All eight of these programs were written using Version 2.1of Visual C++, which comes with Version 3 of the MFC library. All six programs are equipped with Visual C++ makefiles, so you can build each program separately by choosing the **Build** command from the Developer Studio's **Project** menu.

The TIMER Program

In the first of this chapter's example programs—the TIMER program on your bonus disk—the Win32 function SetTimer is called to initialize a timer. That happens in the member function named CANimWnd::OnCreate, which appears in the ANIMWND.CPP file.

This is the code sequence in which SetTimer is called:

```
// Set up the shape parameters.
int CAnimWnd::OnCreate(LPCREATESTRUCT /* p */)
{
   if (!SetTimer(1, 0 /* start fast */, NULL)) {
      MessageBox("Not enough timers available for this window.",
           "CAnimWnd", MB_ICONEXCLAMATION | MB_OK);

      // If creation failed...
      return -1;

   } else {

      // Instantiate an animation object.
      m_pAnimation = new MAnimation(m_hWnd);
      ASSERT(m_pAnimation != NULL);
   }

   OnSizeStatic();

   return 0;
      }
```

Later in the ANIMWND.CPP file, in a member function named CAnimWnd::SetSpeed, the Win32 function SetTimer is called to set the timer's speed:

```
// Change the shape's speed
void CAnimWnd::SetSpeed()
{
   // Re-create the timer.
   KillTimer(1);
   if (!SetTimer(1, m_bFastSpeed ? 0 : 100, NULL)) {
      MessageBox("Not enough timers available for this window.",
        "CAnimWnd", MB_ICONEXCLAMATION | MB_OK);
      DestroyWindow();
```

```
   }
      }
```

Finally, in a member function CAnimWnd::OnTimer, the Win32 function OnTimer is called to synchronize the animation of an object with the speed of the timer. The name of the animation function is m_pAnimation->AnimateShape. The following code sequence is the section in which the animation function is synchronized with the timer:

```
void CAnimWnd::OnTimer(UINT nIDEvent)
{
   // TODO: Add your message handler code here and/or call default

   RECT rcClient;

   GetClientRect(&rcClient);
   m_pAnimation->AnimateShape(rcClient);

   CMDIChildWnd::CnTimer(nIDEvent);
      }
```

Although timers can be very useful in Windows programs, their usefulness is sometimes limited by the fact that they do not support preemptive multitasking. Timers control the execution of processes in a clockwork fashion; a timer receives control of the CPU each time a certain number of clock ticks has elapsed, and relinquishes control when a predetermined operation is complete. If an application requires a form of time management that's more sophisticated than that, threads are required.

The THRDDEMO Program

The THRDDEMO example program, in this chapter's directory on your bonus disk, demonstrates the use of the CreateThread function. In the THRDDEMO program, in the ANIMWND file, this statement calls CreateThread:

```
// Call CreateThread
m_hThread = CreateThread(NULL, 0,
   (LPTHREAD_START_ROUTINE)ThreadFunc,
   this, CREATE_SUSPENDED,
   (LPDWORD) &m_IDThread);
```

When the code fragment shown above calls CreateThread, a pointer to an entry-point function named ThreadFunc is passed to the CreateThread function in the *lpStartAddr* parameter. Notice that the pointer to `ThreadFunc` is cast as an `LPTHREAD_START_ROUTINE` data type. This casting operation ensures that the `CreateThread` function will recognize `ThreadFunc` as the entry point of a thread.

The thread entry point named `ThreadFunc`, which is referenced in the call to `CreateThread`, looks like this:

```
// ThreadFunc function
long ThreadFunc(CAnimWnd *pAnimWnd)
{
   long lEndThread = 0;
   pAnimWnd->SetSpeed(TRUE);
   DWORD exitCode;

   while (TRUE) {

      // Introduce a delay if speed is set to slow
      if(pAnimWnd->GetSpeed() == TRUE)
         Sleep(0);
      else
         Sleep(100);

      // When this thread's window closes, the lEndThread
      // variable becomes non-zero (see OnClose function, above).
      lEndThread = GetWindowLong(pAnimWnd->m_hWnd, GWL_USERDATA);
      if (lEndThread) {
         // Get this thread's exit code and exit the thread.
         GetExitCodeThread(pAnimWnd->m_hThread, &exitCode);
         ExitThread(exitCode);

         // Get rid of objects that won't be needed anymore.
         CloseHandle(pAnimWnd->m_hThread);
         delete pAnimWnd->m_pAnimation;
         delete pAnimWnd; // Created in mainfrm.cpp.
         break;
      } else {
         // perform tasks.
         if (pAnimWnd != NULL)
            pAnimWnd->Animate();
         else break;
      }
   }

   // Wait for thread to exit.
   DWORD dRetVal = WaitForSingleObject(pAnimWnd->m_hThread, 5000);

   // Message boxes used during debugging (might as well leave
   // them there).
```

```
    if (dRetVal == WAIT_FAILED)
        MessageBox(NULL, "WaitForSingleObject function failed!",
            "ThreadFunc", MB_OK);
    else if (dRetVal == WAIT_TIMEOUT)
        MessageBox(NULL, "WaitForSingleObject function timed out!",
            "ThreadFunc", MB_OK);

    // Get the thread's exit code again (in case it has changed),
    // and return it as this function's return value.
    GetExitCodeThread(pAnimWnd->m_hThread, &exitCode);
    return exitCode;
}
```

In the above code fragment, the value of a variable named *lEndThread* is set to 0 (false), and then the line

```
while (TRUE) {
```

executes an endless loop that calls a member function named `pAnimWnd->Animate`. The `pAnimWnd->Animate` member function, as you may guess from its name, is a member function of an object named `pAnimWnd`. In the THRDDEMO program, `pAnimWnd` is a window object. When the `pAnimWnd` object is instantiated, it opens a window that displays a bouncing ball.

The `while` loop in `ThreadFunc` causes the `pAnimWnd->Animate` function to be executed repeatedly until the value of the *lEndThread* variable is changed to a nonzero value (true).

The GetWindowLong Function

During each iteration of the `ThreadFunc` function's `while` loop, a Win32 function named `GetWindowLong` is called to reset the value of the *lEndThread* variable. In the preceding code fragment, this is the line that calls `GetWindowLong`:

```
lEndThread = GetWindowLong(pAnimWnd->m_hWnd,
    GWL_USERDATA);
```

Each time the statement shown above calls the `GetWindowLong` function, `GetWindowLong` returns a zero value (false). That continues to happen until the window displayed by the `pAnimWnd` object closes. As soon as the `pAnimWnd` window closes, a Win32 function named `SetWindowLong` resets *lEndThread* to a nonzero value (true), signaling the `ThreadFunc` function that it can now terminate.

The `SetWindowLong` call appears in the ANIMWND.CPP file, in a function named `CAnimWnd::OnClose`. The `CAnimWnd::OnClose` function overrides the MFC class `CMDIChildWnd::OnClose`. When the CAnimWnd::OnClose function ends, it calls the base function CMDIChildWnd::OnClose. This permits the CMDIChildWnd::-OnClose function to carry out certain procedures that are necessary to close a window.

This is the CAnimWnd::OnClose function:

```
void CAnimWnd::OnClose()
{
  // TODO: Add your message handler code here and/or call default
  // Pass close message to ThreadFunc by calling SetWindowLong.
  long lPrevLong = SetWindowLong(m_hWnd, GWL_USERDATA, 1);

  // Suspend the thread associated with this window. ThreadFunc
  // function will exit the thread (see ThreadFunc, below).
  SuspendThread(m_hThread);

  CMDIChildWnd::OnClose();
    }
```

When SetWindowLong resets the *lEndThread* variable to a nonzero true, the CAnimWnd::OnClose function returns to its calling function, ThreadFunc. ThreadFunc calls GetExitCodeThread to obtain the current thread's termination status, and then calls ExitThread to terminate the thread. That done, ThreadFunc calls CloseHandle and the delete operator to perform some housekeeping, and breaks out of the while loop that kept looping until the thread terminated.

Waiting for a Thread to Terminate

Before ThreadFunc terminates, it calls the Win32 function WaitForSingleObject to make sure that the thread which ThreadFunc controls has terminated. (As explained in "Synchronization Objects" on page 439, WaitForSingleObject halts processing until an object's state is signaled, and then moves on.) When WaitForSingleObject confirms that the thread's state is signal, ThreadFunc calls GetExitCodeThread again to obtain the thread's latest termination status, and then returns the thread's exit code to the CreateThread function. The processing of the thread created by CreateThread is then complete.

Thread Priorities

Windows 95 manages the activities of threads in accordance with priorities that are set when each thread is created. When the

CreateThread function creates a new thread, the thread's priority is set by default to THREAD_PRIORITY_NORMAL (see "Categories of Synchronization Objects" on page 441). However, an application can change the priority of a thread at any time by calling the Win32 function SetThreadPriority.

The THRDDEMO example program creates a thread with the default priority THREAD_PRIORITY_NORMAL but immediately resets the thread's priority to THREAD_PRIORITY_BELOW_NORMAL. That happens in the following code sequence, which appears in the ANIMWND.CPP file:

```
// Call CreateThread
m_hThread = CreateThread(NULL, 0,
    (LPTHREAD_START_ROUTINE)ThreadFunc,
    this, CREATE_SUSPENDED,
    (LPDWORD) &m_IDThread);

// Set the thread's priority
SetPriority(THREAD_PRIORITY_BELOW_NORMAL);

        ResumeThread(m_hThread);
```

To prevent the thread from starting until its priority is established, the thread is created in a suspended state (with its CREATE_SUSPENDED flag set). Then the Win32 function ResumeThread is called to start the thread.

Every thread has one of these five priorities:

- THREAD_PRIORITY_HIGHEST
- THREAD_PRIORITY_ABOVE_NORMAL
- THREAD_PRIORITY_NORMAL
- THREAD_PRIORITY_BELOW_NORMAL
- THREAD_PRIORITY_LOWEST

When an application is running, Windows 95 schedules the execution of each thread by going down a list of the application's threads, starting at the highest level and proceeding to the lowest. The first threads that execute are those with a priority of THREAD_-PRIORITY_HIGHEST. When no threads of the highest priority are demanding to be executed, Windows 95 allocates processing time to threads that have a priority of THREAD_PRIORITY_ABOVE_NORMAL. If no threads with above-normal priority are waiting to be processed, the system schedules threads with a priority of THREAD_-PRIORITY_NORMAL. Finally, threads with priorities of THREAD_-

PRIORITY_NORMAL and THREAD_PRIORITY_LOWEST get their turns.

For most uses in your applications, the THREAD_PRIORITY_-BELOW_NORMAL and THREAD_PRIORITY_NORMAL settings are probably adequate. For more time-critical operations, such as managing keyboard I/O or the operation of communications ports, it might be necessary to schedule threads to run at the above-normal priority or even at the highest priority. But threads with higher priorities should be allowed to run only for very short lengths of time; otherwise, they can consume all the processing time that a system has available, slowing down other processes or even halting them in their tracks.

At the other end of the scale, threads with the lowest priorities can run only when the system has nothing else to do. Operations such as printing or file indexing can be given low priorities so they will be carried out only when the CPU has idle time.

Suspending and Resuming Execution of Threads

No matter what priority a thread has, an application can control when the thread runs or does not run by calling the Wind32 functions SuspendThread and ResumeThread. As you might guess from their names, these two functions suspend and resume the execution of threads.

When you call CreateThread to create a new thread, you can create the thread in a suspended state by placing the CREATE_SUSPENDED constant in the *fdwCreate* parameter. You can then start the thread running at any time by calling ResumeThread.

If you place a zero in the *fdwCreate* parameter when you call Cre-ateThread, the thread starts running as soon as it is created.

Suspend Counts

When you call SuspendThread in an application, Windows 95 increments a "suspend count" that is maintained by the system for each thread. When you call ResumeThread, the thread's suspend count is decremented. During the execution of an application, whenever a thread's suspend count is greater than zero, execution of the thread is suspended. Subsequently, if the thread's suspend count is decremented to less than 1, the thread resumes execution.

A constant named MAXIMUM_SUSPEND_COUNT—coded to have a value of 7 in Visual C++—specifies the maximum value that any thread's suspend count can have. This constant was created to place a limit on multiple calls to SuspendThread that are not balanced by an accompanying ResumeThread, and vice versa.

The Sleep and SleepEx Functions

A thread can temporarily suspend its own execution for a specified interval by calling the Win32 functions Sleep or SleepEx. With these two functions, an application can specify a specific interval during which a thread is not scheduled for CPU time.

The Sleep and SleepEx functions can be useful when an application has a thread that responds to user action; they can delay the execution of a thread just long enough for the user to observe the results of an action.

The sleep functions have a side benefit, too; when they are used to slow down the operation of a thread, other active threads benefit by being allocated more CPU processing time.

In the THRDDEMO example program, the Sleep function is used to control the speed of the bouncing ball. A Boolean member function named m_bFastSpeed keeps track of the ball's speed. If the ball is currently bouncing rapidly, the value of m_bFastSpeed is TRUE. If the ball is bouncing slowly, of the bouncing ball, the value of m_bFastSpeed is FALSE.

In the THRDDEMO program, the Sleep function controls the ball's speed by introducing a delay in the ball's animation speed if the m_bFastSpeed variable is set to FALSE. If the m_bFastSpeed variable is set to TRUE, the Sleep function is called with a parameter of zero, which prevents the introduction of any delay.

The behavior of the Sleep function in the THRDDEMO program is determined by a member function named CAnimWnd::GetSpeed. The CAnimWnd::GetSpeed function is defined as follows in the ANIMWND.H file:

```
BOOL GetSpeed() {  return m_bFastSpeed; }
```

As you can see, CAnimWnd::GetSpeed merely returns the value of the m_bFastSpeed member function.

The Sleep function is called in three places in the THRDDEMO program. Its first occurrence is in the function named ThreadFunc in the ANIMWND.CPP file:

```
// Introduce a delay if speed is set to slow
if(pAnimWnd->GetSpeed() == TRUE)
```

```
    Sleep(0);
else
    Sleep(100);
```

In this code fragment, if `m_bFastSpeed` is set to `TRUE`, the `Sleep` function introduces a 100-millisecond delay in the thread that is currently executing. If the value of `m_bFastSpeed` is `FALSE`, the `Sleep` function introduces no delay. The `Sleep` call appears again in two functions that are executed when menu items are selected. Both functions appear in the ANIMWND.CPP file:

```
void CAnimWnd::OnSlow()
{
    m_bFastSpeed = FALSE;
    SetSpeed(FALSE);
    Sleep(100);
}

void CAnimWnd::OnFast()
{
    m_bFastSpeed = TRUE;
    SetSpeed(TRUE);
    Sleep(0);
}
```

The first of these functions, `OnSlow`, is called when the user of the THRDDEMO program selects the **Slow** item from the **Speed** menu. `OnSlow` introduces a 100-millisecond delay in the processing of the currently executing thread.

The `OnFast` function is called when the user selects the **Fast** item from the **Speed** menu. `OnFast` eliminates any delay that may be in effect and causes the currently executing thread to run at its normal speed.

Terminating Threads

A thread runs until one of the following events occurs:

- The Win32 function `ExitThread` is called.
- The thread function returns. This results in an implicit call to the Win32 function `ExitProcess` for a primary thread, or to `ExitThread` for other threads.
- `ExitProcess` is invoked explicitly or implicitly by any thread of the process.
- `TerminateThread` is called with a handle to the thread.

- `TerminateProcess` is called with a handle to the thread's process.

The `TerminateProcess` call is described in Chapter 8, "Programs and Processes."

When the application-supplied entry-point function of a thread terminates, the function returns a 32-bit exit code. The Windows 95 operating system uses this code to terminate the thread by implicitly calling the Win32 function `ExitThread`. This process is explained in more detail in "Creating and Using Threads" on page 421.

Terminating a Primary Thread

If a terminating thread is the primary thread of a process, the thread terminates in a special way. When a process's primary thread terminates, the `ExitThread` function is not called. Instead, when a primary thread terminates, the Win32 function `ExitProcess` is implicitly invoked.

The primary thread of a process can prevent other threads from terminating when it terminates by explicitly calling `ExitThread` before it exits. In this case, one of the remaining threads must explicitly call `ExitProcess` to ensure that all threads of the process are terminated. An application can use this technique when, for example, an attached DLL is implemented in a thread that does not terminate unless `ExitProcess` is invoked. DLLs are covered in Chapter 10, "Windows 95 DLLs."

When a thread terminates, the state of the thread object changes from unsignaled to signaled (see "Synchronization Objects" on page 439). This releases any other threads that may have been waiting for the thread to terminate. Then the thread's termination status changes from `STILL_ACTIVE` to an exit code signaling that the thread has been terminated. If a call to `ExitThread` terminates a thread, the entry-point function of each attached DLL is invoked with a code indicating that the thread is detaching from the DLL.

If a call to `ExitProcess` terminates a thread, the entry point function of each attached DLL is invoked once to notify the DLL that the process is detaching. DLLs are not notified when a thread is terminated by `TerminateThread` or `TerminateProcess`.

An application can call the Win32 function `GetExitCodeThread` to obtain a thread's exit code. The syntax and usage of this function are described in Volume 3 of the *Microsoft Win32 Programmer's Reference.*

For more information on how threads are terminated, see "Creating and Using Threads" on page 421.

The MUTEX Program

The MUTEX sample program, provided in the MUTEX subdirectory on your bonus disk, shows how a mutex object can be used in a Windows 95 program. The MUTEX program uses a mutex object to fix a bug you may have noticed in the THRDDEMO program.

In the THRDDEMO program, if you open a large number of windows and then start resizing windows with the mouse, the bouncing ball may become a large black rectangle, or more than one ball may appear in the window. When that happens, it's because the bouncing ball is a bitmap and two threads are accessing the bitmap's GDI object simultaneously.

In the MUTEX program, a mutex object keeps that from happening. This mutex object is implemented as a static member variable named `m_hMutex`. It prevents more than one thread from accessing the ball's bitmap at the same time, thus fixing the bug in the program.

The `m_hMutex` variable is declared in the ANIMWND.H file and is defined in the ANIMWND.CPP file as follows:

```
// Initialize m_hMutex, a static member variable.
   HANDLE CAnimWnd::m_hMutex = CreateMutex(NULL,
   TRUE,
   NULL);
```

Later in the ANIMWND.CPP file, in a member function named `AnimWnd::OnCreate`, the mutex that was initialized in the code fragment shown above is released for use by the first thread that claims it. The `AnimWnd::OnCreate` function releases the mutex by calling the Win32 function `ReleaseMutex` as soon as the program's child thread is created:

```
// Call CreateThread
m_hThread = CreateThread(NULL, 0,
   (LPTHREAD_START_ROUTINE)ThreadFunc,
   this, CREATE_SUSPENDED,
   (LPDWORD) &m_IDThread);
ASSERT(m_hThread != NULL);

// Release mutex.
ReleaseMutex(m_hMutex);
```

The first parameter that is passed to `CreateThread` is a pointer to a function that will serve as an entry point to the thread that is being created. In the code fragment shown above, the name of the thread's entry point is `ThreadFunc`. The function that is named `ThreadFunc` appears later in the ANIMWND.CPP file:

```
// ThreadFunc function
long ThreadFunc(CAnimWnd *pAnimWnd)
{
  long lEndThread = 0;
  pAnimWnd->SetSpeed(TRUE);
  DWORD exitCode;
  LPVOID lpvData;

  lpvData = (LPVOID) LocalAlloc(LPTR,4);
  ASSERT(lpvData != NULL);

  while (TRUE) {

    // Wait for mutex.
    WaitForSingleObject(pAnimWnd->m_hMutex, INFINITE);

    lpvData = TlsGetValue(dwTlsIndex);

    // Introduce a delay if speed is set to slow
    if (lpvData == &(pAnimWnd->m_bSlowSpeed))
      Sleep(100);
    else
      Sleep(0);

    // When this thread's window closes, the lEndThread
    // variable becomes non-zero (see OnClose function, above).
    lEndThread = GetWindowLong(pAnimWnd->m_hWnd, GWL_USERDATA);
    if (lEndThread) {

      // Get this thread's exit code and exit the thread.
      GetExitCodeThread(pAnimWnd->m_hThread, &exitCode);
      ExitThread(exitCode);

      // Get rid of objects that aren't needed anymore.
      CloseHandle(pAnimWnd->m_hThread);
      delete(pAnimWnd->m_pAnimation);
      delete(pAnimWnd);
      ReleaseMutex(pAnimWnd->m_hMutex);
      break;

    } else {
      // perform tasks.
```

```
        if (pAnimWnd != NULL) {
          pAnimWnd->Animate();
        } else {
          ReleaseMutex(pAnimWnd->m_hMutex);
          break;
        }
      }
      // Release mutex.
      ReleaseMutex(pAnimWnd->m_hMutex);
    }

    // Get the thread's exit code
    // and return it as this function's return value.
    GetExitCodeThread(pAnimWnd->m_hThread, &exitCode);
    return exitCode;
}
```

When the program's mutex object has been initialized and released, each thread that is created waits for the mutex to become available before the thread starts processing. This waiting period is established by the following statement, which appears near the beginning of the function named `ThreadFunc`:

```
// Wait for thread.
   WaitForSingleObject(m_hThread, INFINITE);
```

Each time a thread finishes accessing the mutex in the THRDDEMO program, it calls the `ReleaseMutex` function. Because `Release-Mutex` is called both inside and outside the wait loop that controls the program's threads, calls to `ReleaseMutex` appear several time in the function named `ThreadFunc`.

Each time a thread finishes using the mutex, it calls `ReleaseMutex` to free the mutex object:

```
// ...
     // Get rid of objects that aren't needed anymore.
     CloseHandle(pAnimWnd->m_hThread);
     delete(pAnimWnd->m_pAnimation);
     delete(pAnimWnd);
     ReleaseMutex(pAnimWnd->m_hMutex);
     break;

  } else {
     // perform tasks.
     if (pAnimWnd != NULL) {
       pAnimWnd->Animate();
     } else {
```

```
            ReleaseMutex(pAnimWnd->m_hMutex);
            break;
        }
    }
    // Release mutex.
    ReleaseMutex(pAnimWnd->m_hMutex);
}
```

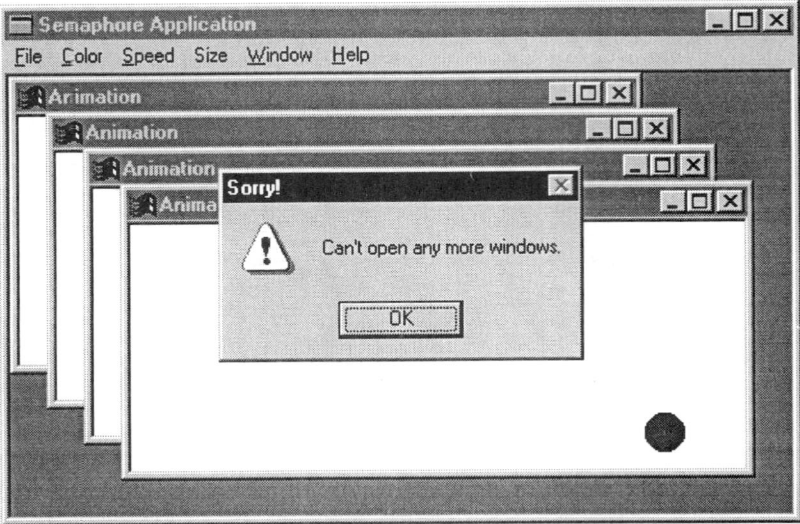

Figure 9.4 Message that says no more windows can be opened

The SEMAFORE Program

The use of semaphore objects is demonstrated in the SEMAFORE sample program, which is provided in the SEMAFORE subdirectory on your bonus disk.

The semaphore object used in the SEMAFORE application is implemented as a static member variable named `m_hSemaphore`. The `m_hSemaphore` variable is declared in the ANIMWND.H file and is initialized as follows in the ANIMWND.CPP file:

```
// Initialize m_hSemaphore, a static member variable.
HANDLE CAnimWnd::m_hSemaphore = CreateSemaphore(NULL,
    MAX_THREADS, MAX_THREADS, NULL);
```

In the preceding code fragment, the initial count of the `m_hSemaphore` object is declared to be a constant named `MAX_THREADS`. Later in the ANIMWND.H file the `MAX_THREADS` constant is initialized with a value of 4. Thus, when the program is executed, the `m_hSemaphore` object allows a maximum of four windows to be created.

When the `m_hSemaphore` object has been initialized, the `OnCreate` function uses the object by calling `WaitForSingleObject` every time it is about to create a thread:

```
DWORD dRetVal =
   WaitForSingleObject(CAnimWnd::m_hSemaphore, 0);
```

When the preceding statement is executed, if the `m_hSemaphore` object's countdown has not yet reached zero, a new thread is created. If the thread's count has been decremented to zero, a new thread is not created. Instead, the program displays an explanatory message box like the one shown in Figure 9.4 on page 462.

In the `ThreadFunc` function, each thread that is created releases the `m_hSemaphore` object before it terminates. To release the `m_hSemaphore` object, each thread calls `ReleaseSemaphore`, as follows:

```
ReleaseSemaphore(CAnimWnd::m_hSemaphore, 1, NULL);
```

In this call to `ReleaseSemaphore`, the parameter 1 specifies that the semaphore object's count is to be decremented by 1 when the semaphore is released. A `NULL` value is passed in the last parameter in lieu of an address that will receive the semaphore's previous (current) count. A `NULL` value means that no storage of a previous count is required.

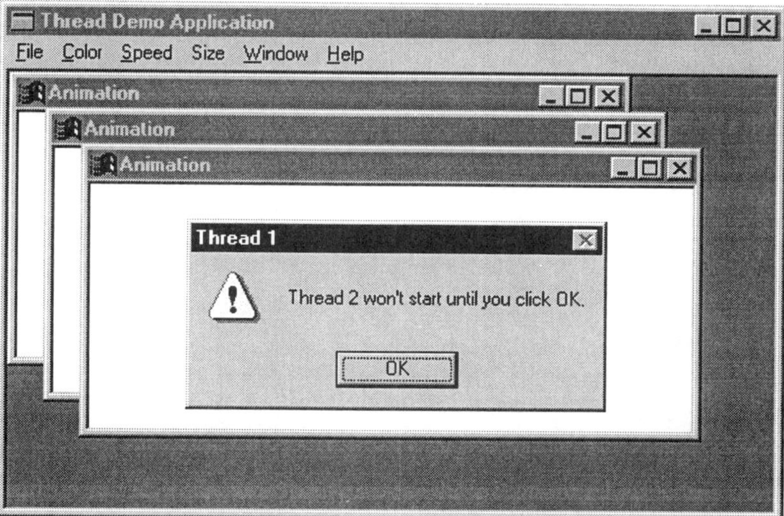

Figure 9.5 Output of the EVENTS program

The EVENTS Program

The EVENTS application, in the EVENTS subdirectory on your bonus disk, demonstrates the use of event objects. In the EVENTS program, two threads are created. One thread displays a window containing a bouncing ball, and the other displays a dialog box that contains the message, "Thread 2 won't start until you click OK."

Figure 9.5 on page 463 shows the pause message box that is displayed by the EVENTS program.

The event object used in the EVENTS program is implemented as a member variable named `m_hEvent`. The `m_hEvent` variable is initialized near the top of the ANIMWND.CPP file, in this statement:

```
// Initialize m_hEvent static member variable
HANDLE CAnimWnd::m_hEvent = CreateEvent(NULL,
   FALSE, FALSE, NULL);
```

When the user of the program selects the **New** item from the **File** menu, the program starts a thread that displays the dialog box containing the pause message. The program then calls the Win32 function `WaitForMultipleObjects`. The `WaitForMultipleObjects` function causes the pause message box to remain on the screen until the user closes it by clicking the OK button. The code that starts the message-box thread, and then waits until it terminates, appears in the `OnCreate` function in the ANIMWND.CPP file:

```
// Create Thread 1
m_hThread = CreateThread(NULL, 0,
   (LPTHREAD_START_ROUTINE)MsgFunc,
   this, 0,
   (LPDWORD) &m_IDThread);
ASSERT(m_hThread != NULL);

WaitForMultipleObjects(2, m_hTHREADS, TRUE,
   INFINITE);

return 0;
```

The event object used in the THRDDEMO program is an auto-reset object, so the thread that creates the pause message box does not have to call `ResetEvent` before it closes. As soon as the thread terminates, the message-box thread is set to an unsignaled state, and the thread that displays the bouncing-ball window is free to begin.

When the dialog box containing the pause message closes, the second thread starts, displaying the bouncing-ball window. The bouncing-ball thread is created in this section of the `OnCreate` function:

```
// Create Thread 2
m_hThread = CreateThread(NULL, 0,
   (LPTHREAD_START_ROUTINE)ThreadFunc,
   this, CREATE_SUSPENDED,
   (LPDWORD) &m_IDThread);
ASSERT(m_hThread != NULL);

// Set the thread's priority.
SetPriority(THREAD_PRIORITY_BELOW_NORMAL);

// Call ResumeThread to start the thread.
Resume();

OnSizeStatic();
```

Wait Functions

When an application calls a wait function, the function checks the state of the synchronization object (or objects) specified in its parameter list, and also checks for any other conditions that could cause it to return. If the wait function discovers no conditions that mandate a return, and if the function's timeout interval has not elapsed, the calling thread enters an efficient wait state, consuming very little CPU time while waiting for the conditions that can cause it to return to be satisfied.

When a program calls `WaitForSingleObject` or `WaitForSingleObjectEx`, it passes the wait function a handle to a synchronization object. `WaitForSingleObject` and `WaitForSingleObjectEx` return when the state of the specified object is signaled, or when the specified timeout interval elapses.

Three Win32 functions—`WaitForMultipleObjects`, `WaitForMul-tipleObjectsEx`, and `MsgWaitForMultipleObjects`—fall into the category of multiple-object functions. They allow the calling thread to specify an array containing one or more synchronization object handles.

Multiple-object functions accept parameters that can cause them to return when the state of any one of the specified objects is signaled. In such a case, the value returned by the wait function specifies the array index of the object that caused the function to return. Alternatively, a multiple-object function can be set to return only when the state of all objects is signaled at the same time. In this case, the return value simply indicates that the specified conditions were satisfied.

When a multiple-object function is waiting for all objects that it controls to be signaled, the function does not modify the state of the specified objects until all the objects are signaled simultaneously. For example, a mutex object can be signaled, but the calling thread does not become the owner of the mutex until the other objects are also signaled. In the meantime, some other thread may obtain ownership of the mutex, delaying satisfaction of all specified conditions.

The `MsgWaitForMultipleObjects` function is identical to the `WaitForMultipleObjects` function, except that it can also return when a specified type of input is available in the calling thread's input queue. For example, a thread could call `MsgWaitForMultipleObjects` to block its execution until either the state of a specified object is signaled, or there is mouse input available in the thread's input queue. When input is available, the thread can call `GetMessage` or `PeekMessage` function to retrieve it.

The `WaitForSingleObjectEx` and `WaitForMultipleObjectsEx` functions have a special characteristic: They can optionally perform an "alertable wait." During an alertable wait, a wait function can return when the specified conditions are satisfied, but it can also return if the system queues a completion routine for execution by the waiting thread.

The MFCTHRDS and USRTHRDS Programs

As explained in "Multithreading and the MFC Library" on page 425, the MFC library provides support for two kinds of threads: worker threads and user-interface threads. Worker threads are typically used to perform operations that do not require user input—operations such as calculations, screen updating, and background printing. User-interface threads are designed to handle user input and to respond to user events without affecting other threads that may be running in an application.

Two applications on your bonus disk—MFCTHRDS and USRTHRDS—show how worker threads and user-interface threads can be used in Visual C++ programs.

The USRTHRDS Program

The USRTHRDS program is similar to the MFCTHRDS program described under the previous heading. USRTHRDS also creates a user-interface thread by calling the `AfxBeginThread` function from inside the CAnimWnd::OnCreate member function in the ANIMWND.CPP file.The difference is that USRTHRDS program uses the overridden version of the AfxBeginThread that creates user-interface threads.

The user-interface version of AfxBeginThread does not take a variable that points to an entry-point function. Instead, it expects a variable that contains the RUNTIME_CLASS of a thread object derived from CWinThread. In the USRTHRDS program, the CObject member function GetRuntimeClass is called to retrieve the RUNTIME_-CLASS of the program's CWinThread-derived thread object:

```
CMyWinThread *pMyThread = AfxBeginThread(
   m_myThread->GetRuntimeClass(),
   THREAD_PRIORITY_BELOW_NORMAL,
   0,
   CREATE_SUSPENDED);
ASSERT_VALID(pThread);
```

The thread entry-point function is called by AfxBeginThread

The MFCTHRDS Program

The MFCTHRDS program creates a worker thread by calling the MFC helper function AfxBeginThread from the ANIMWND.CPP file. The program calls AfxBeginThread from inside the CAnimWnd::-OnCreate member function:

```
CWinThread *pThread = AfxBeginThread(ThreadFunc,
   (LPVOID) this,
   THREAD_PRIORITY_BELOW_NORMAL,
   0,
   CREATE_SUSPENDED);
ASSERT_VALID(pThread);
```

The thread entry-point function called by AfxBeginThread creates a thread synchronized by a mutex object (see "Mutex Objects" on page 442). This is the entry-point function called by AfxBe-ginThread:

```
// ThreadFunc function
UINT ThreadFunc(LPVOID pParam)
{
   CAnimWnd *pAnimWnd = (CAnimWnd*) pParam;
   long lEndThread = 0;
   pAnimWnd->SetFastSpeed(TRUE);
   DWORD exitCode;
```

```
  LPVOID lpvData;
  lpvData = (LPVOID) LocalAlloc(LPTR,4);
  ASSERT(lpvData != NULL);

  while (TRUE) {
    // Wait for mutex.
    WaitForSingleObject(pAnimWnd->m_hMutex, INFINITE);
    lpvData = TlsGetValue(pAnimWnd->m_dwTlsIndex);

    // Introduce a delay if speed is set to slow
    if (lpvData == &(pAnimWnd->m_bSlowSpeed))
      Sleep(100);
    else
      Sleep(0);
    // When this thread's window closes, the lEndThread
    // variable becomes non-zero (see OnClose function, above).
    lEndThread = GetWindowLong(pAnimWnd->m_hWnd, GWL_USERDATA);
    if (lEndThread) {
      // Get this thread's exit code and exit the thread.
      GetExitCodeThread(pAnimWnd->m_hThread, &exitCode);
      ExitThread(exitCode);
      // Get rid of objects that aren't needed anymore.
      CloseHandle(pAnimWnd->m_hThread);
      delete(pAnimWnd->m_pAnimation);
      delete(pAnimWnd);
      ReleaseMutex(pAnimWnd->m_hMutex);
      break;
    } else {
      // perform tasks.
      if (pAnimWnd != NULL) {
        pAnimWnd->Animate();
      } else {
        ReleaseMutex(pAnimWnd->m_hMutex);
        break;
      }
    }
    // Release mutex.
    ReleaseMutex(pAnimWnd->m_hMutex);
  }
  // Get the thread's exit code
  // and return it as this function's return value.
  GetExitCodeThread(pAnimWnd->m_hThread, &exitCode);
  return exitCode;
}
```

The SHAREDLL Program

As explained in "The MFCTHRDS and USRTHRDS Programs" on page 466, DLLs can use thread local storage to share memory. Listing 9.1, named SHAREDLL.CPP, is a source-code listing for a sample DLL that uses shared memory. To use the DLL, you must call it from a client application—for an example, one of the client applications presented in Chapter 10, "Windows 95 DLLs."

Listing 9.1 A DLL that uses shared memory

```
// shareddll.cpp
// A DLL entry-point function sets up shared memory using
// named file mapping.

#include <windows.h>
#include <memory.h>

#define SHMEMSIZE 4096

static LPVOID lpvMem = NULL; // Shared-memory address.

// LibMain() is the DllEntryPoint function for this DLL.

BOOL LibMain(HINSTANCE hinstDLL,    // DLL module handle.
        DWORD fdwReason,           // Reason called.
        LPVOID lpvReserved) {       // Reserved.

    HANDLE hMapObject = NULL;    // Handle to file mapping.
    BOOL fInit, fIgnore;

    switch (fdwReason) {


// Here the DLL attaches to a process, either when the
// procesas initializes or the client calls LoadLibrary.

          case DLL_PROCESS_ATTACH:

            // Create a named file mapping object.

            hMapObject = CreateFileMapping(
                (HANDLE) 0xFFFFFFFF, // Use paging file.
                NULL,  // No security attributes.
                PAGE_READWRITE, // Read/write access.
                0, // Size: High 32 bits
                SHMEMSIZE, // Size: Low 32 bits.
```

```
                "dllmemfilemap");     // Map-object name
            if (hMapObject == NULL)
                return FALSE;

// The first process to attach initializes memory.

            fInit = (GetLastError() !=
             ERROR_ALREADY_EXISTS);

// Get a pointer to the file-mapped shared memory.

            lpvMem = MapViewOfFile(
                hMapObject,      // Mapped object.
                FILE_MAP_WRITE, // Read/write access.
                0,               // High offset.

                0,               // Low offset.
                0);              // Map entire file.
            if (lpvMem == NULL)
                return FALSE;

// Initialize memory if this is the first process.

            if (fInit)
                memset(lpvMem, '\0', SHMEMSIZE);

            break;

// The attached process creates a new thread.

        case DLL_THREAD_ATTACH:
            break;

// The thread of the attached process terminates.

        case DLL_THREAD_DETACH:
            break;

// The DLL now detatches from a process, either when the
// process termination or when FreeLibrary is called.

        case DLL_PROCESS_DETACH:

// Unmap shared memory from the process's address space.

            fIgnore = UnmapViewOfFile(lpvMem);

// Close process's handle to the file-mapping object.
```

```
            fIgnore = CloseHandle(hMapObject);

            break;

        default:
          break;

  }

    return TRUE;
    UNREFERENCED_PARAMETER(hinstDLL);
    UNREFERENCED_PARAMETER(lpvReserved);

}


// This function sets the contents of shared memory.
VOID SetSharedMem(LPTSTR lpszBuf) {
    LPTSTR lpszTmp;

    // Get the address of the shared memory block.

    lpszTmp = (LPTSTR) lpvMem;

    // Copy the null-terminated string into shared memory.

    while (*lpszBuf)
        *lpszTmp++ = *lpszBuf++;
    *lpszTmp = '\0';
}


// This function gets the contents of shared memory.
VOID GetSharedMem(LPTSTR lpszBuf, DWORD cchSize) {
    LPTSTR lpszTmp;

    // Get the address of the shared memory block.

    lpszTmp = (LPTSTR) lpvMem;

    // Copy from shared memory into the caller's buffer.

    while (*lpszTmp && --cchSize)

        *lpszBuf++ = *lpszTmp++;
      *lpszBuf = '\0';
}
```

How the SHAREDLL Program Works

The DLL presented in Listing 9.1 on page 469 has an entry-point function named `LibMain`. The module-definition file for the DLL is named MYPUTS.DEF. It contains the following information:

```
LIBRARY myputs
EXPORTS
     myPuts
```

The DLL uses file mapping to map a block of named shared memory into the address space of each process to which the DLL is attached. Each time the DLL attaches to a new process, its entry-point routine calls the Win32 function `CreateFileMapping` to create a file-mapping object. The `CreateFileMapping` function either creates or opens a named file-mapping object, depending on whether a file-mapping object is already open.

The first process to which the DLL attaches creates the file-mapping object. Subsequent processes open a handle of the existing object. The `GetLastError` function triggers initialization of the shared memory because it returns NO_ERROR to the first process and ERROR_ALREADY_EXISTS to subsequent processes.

The Win32 function `MapViewOfFile` function maps the file-mapping object into the address space of each process, returning a pointer to the memory. But shared memory is not always mapped to the same address; it can be mapped to a different address in each process. Because the location of shared memory can be different for each process, each process has its own instance of a global variable named `lpvMem`.

The `lpvMem` variable is declared as a global variable to make it available to each function implemented in the DLL. The assumption is that the DLL's global data is not shared. Therefore, each attaching process has its own instance of the `lpvMem` variable.

Shared Data and Module-Definition Files

By default, DLL data is not shared. But you can change this default behavior by modifying the DLL's .DEF (module-definition) file.

When you execute the DLL, any memory it shares persists only as long as the DLL is attached to a process. In this example, the shared memory is released when the last handle of the file-mapping object is closed.

To create persistent shared memory, a DLL can create a detached process when the DLL attaches to the first process. If this detached process uses the DLL and does not terminate, it has a handle of the file-mapping object that prevents the shared memory from being released.

Summary

One of the most important new features of Windows 95 is support for preemptive multitasking—that is, the ability to run multiple processes simultaneously by allocating each process a slice of CPU time.

Windows 95 supports preemptive multitasking by using a method called multithreading. Multithreading is a technique for dividing processes into threads and allocating each thread an individual share of CPU time, depending upon preallocated thread priorities.

When a process has been divided into multiple threads, these threads must be synchronized if they are to operate properly. In Windows 95, several kinds of synchronization objects are provided to synchronize thread operations. These objects are mutexes (mutual exclusion objects), semaphores, and event objects.

Mutex objects prevent a thread from starting while another thread is running. Semaphores limit the number of instances of a single thread that can be running simultaneously. Event objects force a thread to wait for a specified event before it starts running.

This chapter explained how threads and synchronization objects are used in Windows 95 applications. Example applications were presented to demonstrate the use of timers, threads, mutex objects, semaphores, and event objects in Windows 95 programs. The example programs contain a thread class (named MThread) and an animation class (named MAnimation) that you can use in your own applications.

Chapter 10

Windows 95 DLLs

When you develop software for Windows 95, DLLs are even more important because they can be used in even more ways. In Windows 95, you can implement components and OLE controls as DLLs—so, under Windows 95, DLLs are an important gateway to code reusability.

Dynamic-link libraries were always important in the world of Windows programming, and they have become even more vital with the advent of Windows 95.

Dynamic-link libraries, or DLLs. DLLs are object-code libraries that let multiple programs share code, data, and resources. They are so important to the operation of windows that the Windows operating system owes its very existence to them. Windows itself is implemented as an enormous set of dynamic-link libraries, so any process that uses the Win32 API also uses DLLs.

Commercial Windows applications also use DLLs extensively. It is said that DLLs often make up 70 to 80 per cent of the code used by large, complex applications such as Microsoft Word and Microsoft Excel.

When you develop software for Windows 95, DLLs are more important than ever because they can be used in more ways than ever before. For example, in Windows 95, you can implement components and OLE controls as DLLs—so, under Windows 95, DLLs are an important gateway to code reusability. You can even create *MFC extension DLLs* that add new MFC-derived classes to Microsoft's MFC library.

About This Chapter

In this chapter, you will how to learn how to write three kinds of DLLs:

- *Windows 3.x DLLs*, which were designed for 16-bit versions of Windows are are likely to be around for some time to come.
- *VCPP 1.0 DLLs*, which were introduced with the premiere of Version 1.0 of Visual C++ and were the favored variety of 32-bit DLLs until the introduction of Visual C++ 4.0 and MFC 4.0.
- *MFC 4.0 DLLs*, which made their debut with the introduction of Visual C++ 4.0 and MFC 4.0. You can create MFC 4.0 DLLs using AppWizard. MFC 4.0 DLLs come in several flavors designed to meet specific requirements and demands.

This chapter covers all three kinds of Windows 95-compatible DLLs because developers of Windows 95 software are likely to encounter all three varieties of DLLs at one time or another in their day-do-day programming pursuits. In this chapter, each of the three main categories of Windows 95-compatible DLLs is described under a separate major heading. At the end of each major section, an example program is provided to show you how each kind of DLL works, and how you can use each kind of DLL in your Windows 95 programs.

In this chapter, MFC 4.0 DLLs receive more attention than the other two kinds of DLLs because they are the newest kind and are the type recommended for use in new Windows 95 programs.

The example program that demonstrates the use of MFC 4.0 DLLs in this chapter is an application named DLLTESTAPP. It is presented in the section titled "Example MFC 4.0 DLL: The DLLTESTAPP Program" on page 522.

When you execute the DLLTESTAPP program, it calls functions implemented in an MFC 4.0 DLL to create dialog boxes in which messages are displayed. Figure 10.1 on Page 477 shows one of the dialog boxes created by the DLLTESTAPP program.

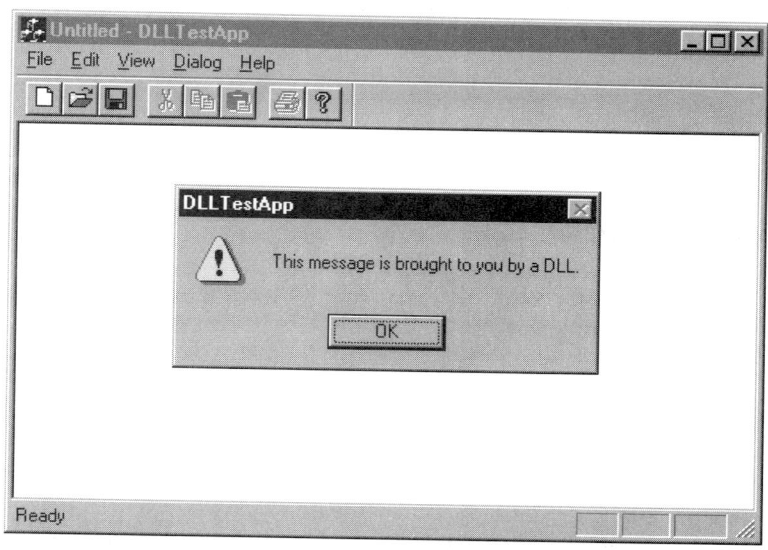

Figure 10.1 Dialog box displayed by the DLLTESTAPP program

The following is a complete list of the major topics are covered in this chapter:

- "About Dynamic-Link Libraries" on page 478
- "DLLs and Windows 95" on page 482
- "Static and Dynamic Linking" on page 484
- "Creating DLLs and Clients" on page 496
- "Varieties of Windows 95 DLLs" on page 499
- "Windows 3.*x* DLLs" on page 475
- "Example Windows 3.x DLL: The DLLMSG Program" on page 502
- "VCPP 1.0 DLLs" on page 506
- "Example VCPP 1.0 DLL: The WINHOST Program" on page 511
- "MFC 4.0 DLLs" on page 515
- "Defining _doserrmsg" on page 520
- "Example MFC 4.0 DLL: The DLLTESTAPP Program" on page 522
- "Summary" on page 534.

About Dynamic-Link Libraries

There are several major reasons for using DLLs in Windows 95 applications:

- When you implement a routine as a DLL, Windows can load the routine into memory automatically whenever it is needed, and can then unload it when the memory it occupies is needed for something else. Consequently, DLLs can conserve memory and improve program efficiency.
- A C++ routine implemented in a DLL can be used by multiple functions at the same time. When you have written and tested a DLL using Visual C++, you can use the DLL without modification in any Windows program.
- DLLs are useful for storing large numbers of resources—such as icons, dialog boxes, and bitmaps—that must be instantly accessible to applications and libraries.
- In the Windows 95 operating system, most of the code that registers and implements system-wide window classes is implemented as DLLs. Dynamic-link libraries are ideal for this purpose because the Windows messaging system gives DLLs preferential treatment over applications. In fact, the Windows 95 operating system virtually guarantees the availability of DLLs to any executing application or library at any time the DLL is needed.

In short, whenever you need a instantly usable library of functions or a collection of resources that can be called at any time by one or more executing applications, you should consider creating a DLL. Dynamic-link libraries can save enormous amounts of memory and disk space, and some Windows mechanisms—such as device drivers—must be implemented as DLLs. That's because DLLs are the only executables that are always loaded and are callable by any executing application or library.

Statically Linked Libraries and Dynamic-Link Libraries

Some kinds of object-code libraries are known as *statically linked* libraries. Statically linked libraries are linked with other functions in an application during the build process—specifically, when the application is being linked.

Dynamic-link libraries, in contrast, are object-code libraries that can be *dynamically linked* with other functions in an application. That means that functions implemented in DLLs can be linked with other functions in an application when the application is actually executing—not during the build process, when the application is being linked.

Because DLLs are linked with their clients at runtime, not at link time, you don't have to recompile—or even relink—an application to update a function implemented as a DLL. To modify code that is implemented in a DLL, all you have to do is overwrite the old DLL with the new one. Then, the next time you run an application that accesses the DLL, the application automatically uses the new DLL instead of the old one!

Here's another difference between a statically linked library and a DLL: When an application uses functions implemented in a statically linked library, all references to functions and data in the library must be resolved at link time, and they cannot be modified when the application is run. But when an application accesses functions implemented in a DLL, references to those functions do not have to be resolved until runtime, when the functions or data are about to be used. That feature is what makes it possible for applications to share code and data stored in DLLs. (Static and dynamic linking are examined in more detail in "Dynamic Linking" on page 486.)

Dynamic linking also makes it possible for an application to delay the loading of a DLL until the DLL is needed, and to unload the DLL when it is no longer needed. That can help an application use memory more efficiently.

For more details on static linking and dynamic linking, see "Static and Dynamic Linking" on page 484.

How DLLs Speed Development Time

One feature of DLLs can save you a significant amount of development time. When you write an application that contains DLLs, you can modify and enhance the parts of the program that are implemented in DLLs without having to rebuild the whole program. Instead of rebuilding your whole application, you can build an updated version by simply substituting new DLLs for the DLLs you are updating. In contrast, when you build an application using source code that is all statically linked, you must relink the whole application every time you make the slightest change in any function.

Code-sharing is another useful benefit of DLLs. As an illustration of this capability of DLLs, assume that your company marketed a spreadsheet, a word-processing program, and a graphics program. To support code-sharing, you could place text-editing routines used by both the spreadsheet and the word processor in the same DLL.

Drawing routines used in both the word processor and the graphics program could be placed in another DLL. Still another DLL could contain code for menus, dialog boxes, and window-manipulation routines used in all three applications.

If your company's three applications were designed in this way, you could potentially save enormous amounts of time in program development. Furthermore, because multiple programs can access the same DLL once it is loaded into memory, customers running your applications could save disk space and memory. And your programs would load faster, since each shared DLL would have to be loaded just once, not once for each application using it.

Still another interesting feature of a DLL is that it can be accessed from an application written in any language. So programs written using any Windows-compatible programming environment—even application generators such as Borland Delphi—can access your DLLs.

Functionalities that Must Be Implemented as DLLs

Sometimes DLLs aren't an optional convenience, but a requirement for writing Windows applications. Some of the functions and features supplied by Microsoft in the Windows API are accessible only from DLLs. For instance, the functions **SetWindowsHook** and **SetWindowsHookEx** can be called only from DLLs. Also, installable drivers for Windows —known as DRVs—must be implemented as DLLs.

This shouldn't be surprising, since most of the routines in the Windows API are implemented as DLLs. Every time an application makes a Windows call such as **CreateWindow**, **TextOut**, **MessageBox**, or **GetParent**, it is calling a DLL. For instance, the following call—even though it looks like any function call—is actually a call to a dynamic-link library:

```
HWND hWnd
hwndParent = GetParent(hWnd);
```

Windows 95 recognizes the preceding code fragment as a call to a DLL because the Windows function **GetParent** is implemented as a DLL in a file named USER32.DLL, which is found in your \WINDOWS\-SYSTEM directory.

Executable and Non-Executable DLLs

A DLL can be an executable file, but it doesn't have to be. For example, font libraries—which contain no executable code—can be (and are) stored as DLLs. DLLs can also be used to store other kinds of resource libraries—for example, libraries that contain icons, bitmaps, and strings. With the exception of font libraries, however, every resource library created by a developer must contain at least one code segment. Font-library DLLs are the only kind of DLLs you can implement that contain no executable code.

Although a DLL can be an executable file, it is never a full-fledged application. That's because a DLL is always controlled by the task (or, in Windows 95, the process) of its calling function. A DLL does not have its own stack, but shares the stack that is owned by its caller's process. Also, a DLL has neither a message processing loop nor a message queue, so it can't stand on its own as a full-fledged application.

DLLs Used by the Windows 95 Operating System

DLLs can have various filename extensions, depending on their uses. For example, DLLs used as font resources have the filename extension .FON; device-driver DLLs have the extension .DRV; and some DLLs used by the operating system have the extension .EXE. For example, these are the six DLLs that make up the Windows 95 subsystem:

- **KERNEL.EXE**—Handles 16-bit memory management, the loading and execution of programs, and scheduling.
- **KERNEL32.DLL**—Handles 32-bit memory management, loading and executing programs, and scheduling.
- **GDI.EXE**—Manages 16-bit graphics operations.
- **GDI32.DLL**—Manages 32-bit graphics operations.
- **USER.EXE**—Manages the 16-bit user interface and performs 16-bit window management.
- **USER32.DLL**—Manages the 32-bit user interface and performs 32-bit window management.

These six DLLs, as noted in "The Windows Subsystem DLLs" on page 124, contain most of the Windows 95 functions called by applications and by user-written libraries. They also pass communications back and forth between applications and subsystems that make up the Windows 95 operating system.

All six of these DLLs are loaded when Windows 95 starts up. The GDI (Graphics Device Interface) libraries are responsible for exporting the painting, drawing, plotting, printing, and color functions of Windows. The USER DLLs control almost everything in Windows involving window creation, communications, hardware, and messaging. And the KERNEL DLL handles Windows functions involving memory management, multitasking, and resources.

How Client Applications Use DLLs

Although a DLL can be an executable file, functions that a DLL contains cannot be executed independently. A function implemented in a DLL does not execute until it is called by an application or by another library, which can be either a statically linked library or another DLL. An application or library that calls a DLL is often referred to as a *client*. (There are other kinds of clients in Windows 95, too—for example, OLE clients and client workstations. But when the word client is used in this chapter, it refers to a DLL client.)

When a DLL has been loaded into memory, any function that the DLL exports can be used by any executing client. If a client calls a function in the DLL, the Windows 95 API directs the client's call to the correct DLL and then to the called function. As long as any client continues to use any function in a loaded DLL, the DLL remains in memory. But if the operating system discovers that the DLL is no longer being used by any client, and the memory that DLL occupies is needed for another purpose, the Win32 operating system unloads the DLL.

Besides providing clients with executable functions, DLLs can provide their clients with shared resources such as fonts, icons, cursors, and bitmaps. When a DLL contains resources that can be used by multiple clients, any number of applications can access the resources provided in the same DLL. In this way, a DLL can conserve the memory used to store resources, as well as the memory used to store executable code.

DLLs and Windows 95

As Windows has evolved, Microsoft has streamlined the procedures for creating and linking Windows DLLs. Many rules for DLL writing that worked in early versions of Windows—and some that still work in 16-bit Visual C++ programs—do not necessarily apply to DLLs written in Visual C++, or to DLLs written for Windows 95.

How DLLs Work in Windows 95

Some of the differences between Windows 3.*x* DLLs and Windows 95 DLLs are caused by the way Windows 95 manages memory. As explained in Chapter 3, "Windows 95 Architecture," the Windows 95 operating system allocates every Win32 application a private area of virtual memory within the lower 2GB of virtual address space.

All shared memory objects used by applications—including DLLs—are stored in an area of virtual memory that ranges from 2GB to 3GB. DLLs used by the Windows 95 operating system reside in a different area of memory: specifically, in the area above the 3GB boundary. Figure 10.2 illustrates this arrangement.

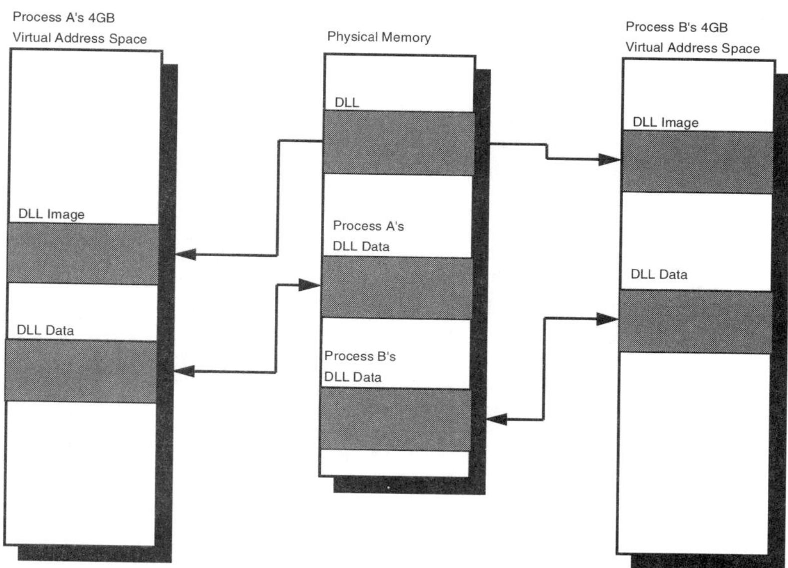

Figure 10.2 How DLLs are mapped into memory

How Applications Share DLLs

As Figure 10.2 shows, DLLs used by the Windows 95 operating system reside in their own protected area, above the 3GB virtual memory boundary. DLLs shared by applications reside in the 2GB-to-3GB area of virtual memory.

When applications share code and data—in DLLs or otherwise—memory conflicts can result. As noted in "Executable and Non-Executable DLLs" on page 480, DLLs can contain data as well as executable code. And, under ordinary circumstances, any application that accesses a DLL can modify any data that the DLL contains.

When multiple applications are accessing a DLL simultaneously and one of the applications modifies data stored in the DLL, a potentially dangerous situation can arise if special precautions are not taken. For example, if one application using a DLL deletes a data item stored in the DLL, and does not notify other applications that might also be using the DLL, some other application might try to access the deleted data without being aware that it had no longer exists. If this situation were allowed to arise, it could result in a disastrous accident—even a system crash.

Fortunately, Windows 95 has a built-in safeguard to prevent such catastrophes from occurring. The solution that Windows 95 uses is to map memory used by a DLL into the address space of each process to which the DLL is attached. This technique, called *file mapping*, is examined more closely in "Virtual Memory, Heap Management, and File Mapping" on page 147.

How DLLs Use Thread Local Storage

When the code and data provided by a DLL are stored separately to prevent data corruption, another potential problem arises. Sometimes it is desirable for a client application to modify data in a DLL in a way that is visible other clients. For example, if a DLL creates a window, and a client changes the window's size, you might want other clients to know what the new size of the window is.

Fortunately, Win32 provides a mechanism that makes it possible for clients to share data in a DLL. This mechanism is called *thread local storage*, or TLS. When a thread needs to share data in a DLL with another thread (or another process), it calls the SDK function **`TlsAlloc`** to create a global variable called a *TLS index*. It then allocates a block of memory and places a pointer to this memory block in the TLS index. "The MFCTHRDS and USRTHRDS Programs" on page 466 describes thread local storage in more detail.

When an application calls **`TlsAlloc`** to create a TLS index, every client that accesses the DLL's data is provided with the address stored in the TLS index. Then, when a client requires access to the DLL's data, it can attach itself to the data, preventing other clients from accessing the data. When the client has finished accessing the data, it can detach itself from the data, freeing the data for access by other clients. This system provides multiple clients with access to a DLL's data, while preventing multiple processes from attempting to modify the data at the same time.

Static and Dynamic Linking

Clients can call functions stored in DLLs in the same way they call other functions. But DLLs are not compiled and linked in the same way that applications and standard libraries are compiled and linked. As noted in "Statically Linked Libraries and Dynamic-Link Libraries" on page 478, applications and conventional libraries are *statically linked*, while DLLs are *dynamically linked*.

Static linking takes place at link time, when the linker assembles object-code modules produced by a compiler into an executable program. In contrast, dynamic linking takes place at runtime—that is, when an application is executed.

Static Linking

When an application calls a function stored in a statically linked library, the application must link with the library while the application is being built; specifically, during the linking process. In this kind of linking—called static linking—a copy of the library function that the application calls is placed in the application's executable file at link time. As a result, a separate copy of the library function is placed in the executable file of each application that uses the function.

Figure 10.3 on Page 486 illustrates static linking. When an application that uses static linking is compiled, the compiler generates references to the addresses of library functions that the program calls. When the program is linked, the linker resolves those references.

When the Visual C++ compiler performs the static linking process shown in Figure 10.3, the linker copies all object code from each object-code file and each library—including routines that are not called—into the executable file that it is compiling. Then the linker incorporates all the object code that it has found into the executable application (the .EXE file) that it compiles.

To accomplish this task, the linker searches each library file used in the compilation, resolves the remaining function references, and retrieves the code of each required function into the.EXE file that it is building. In this way, the linker replaces the addresses left unresolved by the compiler with real addresses and ensures that the code of every function that is called is included in the program.

If the linker can't find the code of a function that it needs, it generates an error message. If it finds the code it needs, it builds the application's .EXE file, and the role of the static library used in the compilation and linking process is then over. The code that the library has provided is now incorporated into the.EXE application that needed it, so the code that the static library contains is no longer required.

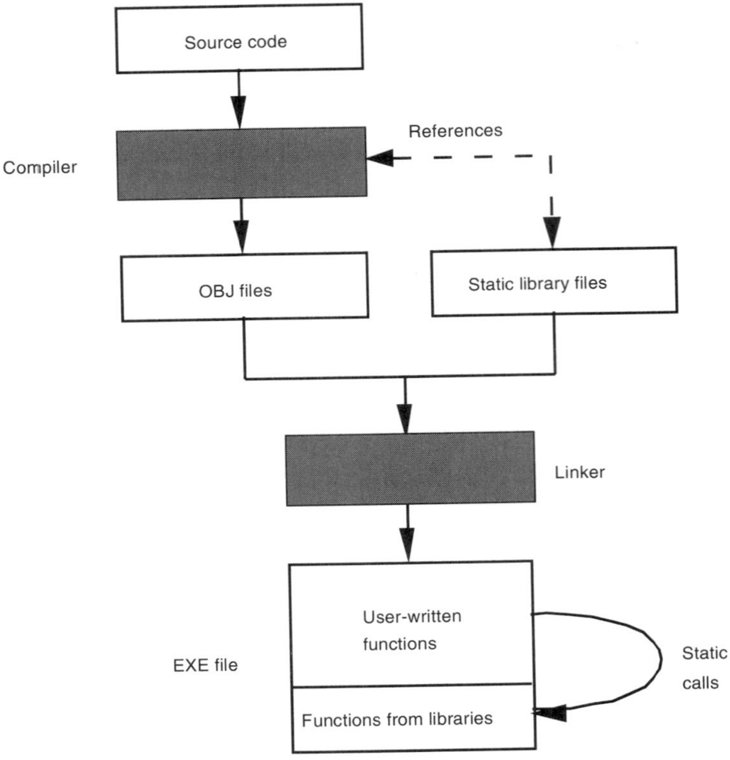

Figure 10.3 Static linking

Dynamic Linking

Dynamic-link libraries are linked dynamically, not statically. When an application calls a function that is stored in a dynamic-link library, the linker does not provide the application with its own copy of the function. Instead, at link time, a reference to the function is placed in a file that will be accessible to the application's executable file at runtime. Dynamic linking is illustrated in Figure 10.4 on Page 487.

To access a function in a DLL at runtime, the first thing an application has to do is find the DLL that contains the function. To track down functions implemented in DLLs at runtime, an application can consult three kinds of files, depending on the category of the DLL that is being linked.

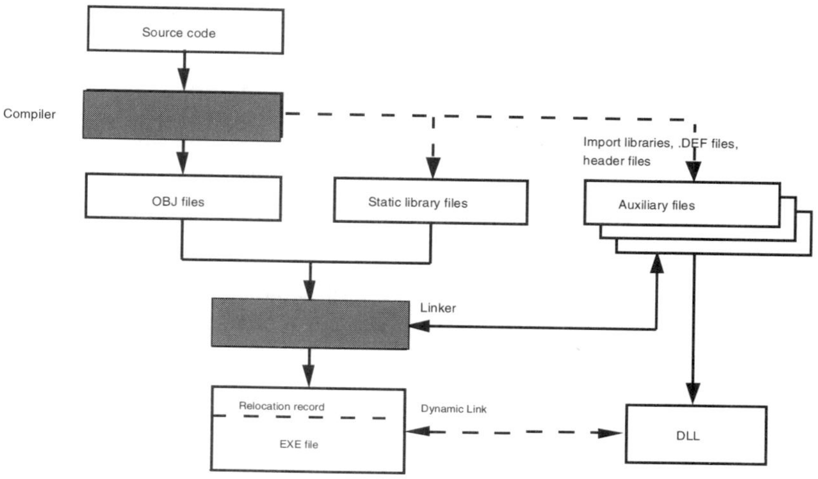

Figure 10.4 Dynamic linking

These three kinds of files are:

- Import libraries
- Module definition (.DEF) files
- Header files.

At runtime, when your application needs to access a function in a DLL, it uses one of the preceding kinds of files to locate the DLL and the function stored in the DLL.

Linking a Client with a DLL

When the Visual C++ linker links a client with a DLL, the linker searches the program's source files and statically linked library files for each external function in the program each time the function is called. If the linker finds the function in a library or object module that is statically linked with the application, it copies the function's code into the .EXE file that it is creating.

If the linker cannot find the function's code, it searches any available auxiliary files (such as import libraries) that may contain references to functions that are implemented in DLLs.

Each time the linker finds such a reference, it stores information specifying where the reference can be found in a *relocation record* in the application's .EXE file. A relocation record contains information that the Windows 95 operating system uses to access and execute the function's code dynamically. This record includes the name of the name of the function and the name of the DLL from which the function came.

At runtime, when the client calls a function exported by a DLL, the client looks through its relocation records for the information that needs to find the exported function. When it obtains the name of the DLL that implements the function, the Win32 operating system automatically loads the DLL that contains the function into memory (if it is not already in memory), and then calls the function. Windows 95 also adds a patch to the image of the program's code in memory so the program can access functions in the DLL whenever they are needed.

Loading and Executing DLLs

Before your application can use functions implemented in a DLL, the DLL must be loaded into memory. There are two ways to load a dynamic-link library into memory:

- An application can stockpile a set of DLLs by loading them at the same time the application itself is loaded. It can then access any DLL it has preloaded whenever a function implemented in the DLL is needed. This method is sometimes called *implicit loading.* (A longer and more confusing name for this technique is *load-time dynamic linking.)*
- A process can wait until a function in a DLL is needed, and can then load that specific DLL by calling the Windows API function **`LoadLibrary`**. This technique is sometimes referred to as *explicit loading*. (A longer and less user-friendly name for this method is *runtime dynamic linking*.) Explicitly loaded DLLs can be explicitly unloaded when they are no longer needed.

Which of these loading methods should you choose? That depends on how your DLL will be used during the execution of an application. If the application uses the DLL repeatedly, you might as well load the DLL implicitly, along with the application. Then you won't have to worry about explicitly loading the DLL by calling **`LoadLibrary`** the first time it is needed.

On the other hand, if the user of your application may not need to access a particular DLL while your application is running, you might want to load the DLL the first time it is called. For example, there may be a menu item that the user may or may not select while your application is running. That kind of menu item might be a good candidate for implementation as an explicitly loaded DLL.

Depending on which method you use to load a DLL, the DLL attaches to whatever process needs to access it as soon as the DLL is loaded. When a DLL attaches to a process, the Windows 95 operating system maps the DLL module into the address space of the process, making the DLL's executable code available to the process.

When the DLL detaches from a process (because the process terminates or because the **FreeLibrary** function is called), the DLL module is unmapped from the process's address space.

Implicitly Loading a DLL

A Windows 95 process can load a DLL by simply calling a function that is implemented in the DLL. This operation is called *implicit loading.*

When a process attempts to load a DLL implicitly, the first thing the operating system must know is where to find the DLL. To track down the DLL, the operating system uses a special kind of file called an *import library file.* Every time you create a DLL, your compiler creates an import library. Subsequently, when you build an application that requires access the DLL, you must link the application to the DLL's library. The application can then use the DLL's import library to locate functions that are implemented in the DLL. (For more information on import libraries, see "Import Libraries" on page 492.)

How Implicit Loading Works

Here is a closer look at how implicit loading works: At link time, when an application is preparing a process for the implicit loading of a DLL, the application performs two important operations.

First, it maps the DLL's code into the process's virtual address space. Then it creates an import library for the DLL, using the virtual address of each function implemented in the DLL as an entry function and recording that function in the DLL's import library. (For more information on import libraries, see "Generating Import Libraries" on page 492.)

Although an implicitly loaded DLL is mapped into an application's memory when the application is linked, it is important to note that the DLL's code is not actually loaded into memory until the DLL is needed. If a DLL is not being used and the memory that it occupies is needed for another purpose, the system can unload the DLL until it is needed again.

Thus, implicitly loaded DLLs do not require any more memory space than explicitly loaded DLLs. However, they do require a little extra baggage: a range of dedicated virtual memory and an import library.

Explicitly Loading a DLL

When a process does not load a DLL until the DLL is needed, that is called explicit loading. Explicit loading is a slightly more efficient method of loading DLLs than implicit loading because it doesn't require a dedicated range of virtual memory or an import library.

A process explicitly loads a DLL by calling the SDK function **LoadLibrary**. When the DLL is no longer needed, it can be freed with a call to the SDK function **FreeLibrary**.

If a DLL does not have any other clients when **FreeLibrary** is called, it is unloaded from memory. If the DLL does have other clients, it is not unloaded until all its clients have called **FreeLibrary**.

When an application has explicitly loaded a DLL, it can call the Win32 function **GetProcAddress** to obtain the starting addresses of any function implemented in the DLL. When the DLL is no longer needed, the process can explicitly unload it by calling the **FreeLibrary** function. This method eliminates the need to link with an import library.

If a process calls **LoadLibrary** to access a DLL module that is already mapped into the address space of the calling process, **LoadLibrary** simply returns a handle to the DLL and increments reference count that the process maintains. If the DLL is not already loaded into memory, **LoadLibrary** checks to see if the DLL has a **DllEntryPoint** function. If it does, the operating system calls the function in the context of the thread that called **LoadLibrary**.

If **LoadLibrary** succeeds in finding and loading a DLL, it returns a handle to the DLL that it has loaded. The calling process can then use this handle to identify the DLL in calls to other functions, such as **GetProcAddress** or **FreeLibrary**.

How Windows Programs Access DLLs

There are differences between the way DLLs are loaded and accessed in Windows 3.*x* programs and the way they are loaded and accessed in 32-bit DLLs written specifically for Windows 95 and Windows NT. For instance, in the Windows 3.*x* environment, the initialization function for DLLs is customarily named **LibMain**.

Usually, when a 16-bit Windows application creates a DLL, it calls the **LibMain** function to handle most of the DLL's initialization. When the **LibMain** function completes its job, it returns control to the **LibEntry** function. **LibEntry**, in turn, returns control to Windows. Then the DLL can be accessed.

When a Windows 3.*x* program needs to unload a DLL, a function named **WEP** (which stands for Windows Exit Procedure) is called. If any cleanup procedures are needed before the DLL is unloaded, they are managed by the **WEP** function. The **WEP** function performs a number of standard DLL cleanup operations before the DLL is unloaded.

DLL Entry Points in Windows 95

In a Windows 95 program, the **LibMain** function works just fine as an DLL entry point, just as it did under Windows 3.*x*. But the Windows 95 operating system also provides a more streamlined DLL entry-point function named **DllEntryPoint**. Windows 95 applications can use either **LibMain** or **DllEntryPoint** as an entry point for DLLs.

In Windows 95, **DllEntryPoint** is not an actual function, but a template that can be assigned any legal function name. When you create a **DllEntryPoint** function in a Windows 95 program, you can give it any name you like—including **LibMain**, as illustrated in this example:

```
link -entry:LibMain out:mydll.dll mydll.exp mydll.obj
    $(mylibs)
```

How the DllEntryPoint Function Works

The new **DllEntryPoint** function is a little easier to use than the **LibMain** function used to be. Under Windows 95, an application does not have to specify a **DllEntryPoint** function in order to access a DLL.

In fact, as you will see in "Varieties of Windows 95 DLLs" on page 499, applications that use **DllEntryPoint** functions are already fading from favor because newer, easier ways are now available for writing Windows 95 DLLs. If you do access a DLL using the **DllEntryPoint** function, the operating system calls **DllEntryPoint** whenever any one of the following events occurs:

- Your DLL attaches to a process.
- Your DLL detaches from a process.
- Your DLL attaches to a thread.
- Your DLL detaches from a thread.

Import Libraries

An *import library* is a statically linked library that provides a client with information it needs to locate a function implemented in a DLL. A .LIB file that contains information about one or more dynamic-link libraries (DLLs), but does not contain the DLL's executable code. Every time an application needs to locate functions or data stored in an implicitly loaded DLL, it consults the DLL's import library.

When you write a program using Version 2.0 or later of Visual C++, the compiler generates an import library automatically when it builds a DLL (earlier versions of Visual C++ provide a utility that you must use to write your own import libraries; see the box titled "IMPLIB Fades Away" on page 493).

What is an Import Library?

An import library is a statically linked library (usually with a .LIB extension) that can be read by the Visual C++ linker. When you link an application, you can create an import library for your program in the same way you would create an ordinary statically linked library.

When you build a client that implicitly references a DLL (see "Implicitly Loading a DLL" on page 489), you must link the client with your DLL's import library.

When an application accesses functions implemented in a DLL, the linker uses an import library to provide the information that is needed to resolve the external references to functions exported by the DLL. More specifically, the linker uses the import library to build any executable module that requires access to the DLL.

An import library is the recommended utility for resolving references from applications to DLLs. When an application without an import library needs to access a function exported by a DLL, an external reference to the exported function must be declared in an IMPORTS statement in the application's .DEF file or must be explicitly coded in the program.

Generating Import Libraries

In earlier versions of Windows, developers had to write import libraries when they wanted to use implicitly loaded DLLs. However, the Visual C++ compiler can generate an import library automatically each time it compiles a DLL.

Later, when you compile an application that accesses the DLL, all you need to do is link your application to the DLL's import library.

IMPLIB Fades Away

In 16-bit versions of Visual C++, Microsoft provides a special utility for creating import libraries. This tool, called IMPLIB, is an .EXE file that you must manually execute from a command line every time you compile a DLL. IMPLIB then creates an import file which you must link with every client that references your DLL.

Beginning with Version 2.0, Visual C++ stopped supplying the IMPLIB tool. The 32-bit versions of Visual C++ do not need an IMPLIB tool because 32-bit Visual C++ generates an import library automatically each time it compiles a DLL. It is still your responsibility, however, to link the import file that is generated by the compiler with each client of your DLL.

Module Definition Files

Another kind of file you may encounter in writing DLLs is a *module definition file,* or *.DEF file.* A module definition file is a text file containing one or more module statements that describe various attributes of a dynamic-link library.

Module definition files, often called .DEF files, provide the Visual C++ linker with the information it needs to make the functions in the DLL accessible to the DLL's client. Listing 10.1 shows the format of a module definition file.

Listing 10.1 Example of a Module Definition File

```
; Example of a module definition file.

LIBRARY Select
CODE MOVEABLE DISCARDABLE
DATA SINGLE
EXPORTS
    WEP                  @1 RESIDENTNAME
    StartSelection       @2
    UpdateSelection      @3
    EndSelection         @4
    ClearSelection       @5
```

Every module definition file for a DLL begins with a **LIBRARY** statement and also contains an **EXPORTS** statement. The **LIBRARY** statement identifies the .DEF file as a module definition file that is associated with a DLL and specifies the name of the DLL's import library.

The **EXPORTS** statement in a .DEF file lists the names of the functions exported by the DLL. Each **EXPORTS** statement can also contain an *ordinal number* written in the form **@***n*. In source files that access functions exported by DLLs, any exported function that has been assigned an ordinal number in a .DEF file can be accessed using either its name or its ordinal number.

The .DEF file shown in Listing 10.5—named DLLMSG.DEF—has an EXPORTS section that expresses a function as the ordinal number **@1**, as follows:

```
EXPORTS
   _ShowDLLDlg@4  @1 NONAME
```

As you can see, the **EXPORTS** section of a .DEF file is preceded by the word **EXPORTS** and is divided into three columns. The names of functions exported by the DLL appear in the first column. The ordinal numbers assigned to those functions appear in the second column. An alternative name, or *alias*, for the function can be placed in the third column. If the function has no alias, the word **NONAME** can appear in the third column.

In the preceding example, the function named **ShowDLLDlg** is identified by its full C++ name—or, in Microsoft jargon, its *decorated* name. When member function of a C++ class is used in a .DEF file, the class must be referred to by its decorated name. To obtain a list of decorated names while building an application, you can link the application using the /MAP option (for details, see Books Online or your Visual C++ documentation.) In this case, the name of the **ShowDLLDlg** function provided in the EXPORT S section is **_ShowDLLDlg@4**.

In the **EXPORTS** section shown in the preceding example, only one function is exported, so it is assigned the ordinal number **@1**. In a .DEF file, the ordinal number assigned to a function is always preceded by the character **@**. So the function **ShowDLLDlg** is identified by the ordinal number **@1**. If more functions were exported, they could be assigned the numbers **@2**, **@3**, and so on.

If a function in a DLL is expressed as an ordinal number, clients of the DLL can then use those numbers to refer to the DLL's functions, instead of using their names. Rules for referring to exported functions by the ordinal numbers specified in a .DEF file are spelled out in more detail in the Microsoft *Microsoft Win32 Programmer's Reference*.

In 16-bit versions of Visual C++—but not in 32-bit versions of Visual C++—there is an alternative method for exporting functions from DLLs. In a 16-bit Visual C++ program, you can export a function from a DLL by placing the **_export** attribute in the header of the function's definition. This technique does not work with 32-bit versions of Visual C++; beginning with Version 2.0 of Visual C++, the **dllexport** attribute replaced the **_export** attribute, as explained in the box titled "_export Is Obsolete in Win32" on page 509.

A module definition file can also contain statements that determine other attributes of a DLL. For example, a .DEF file can contain **SECTIONS** statements that change the default scope of global and static variables.

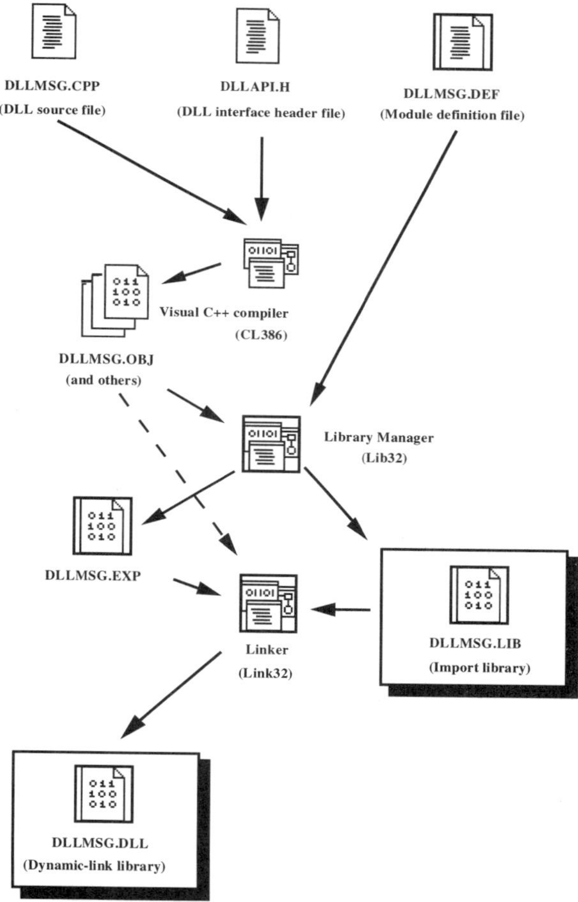

Figure 10.5 Building a DLL

Creating DLLs and Clients

The easiest way to build a DLL and a client to execute it is to a build two Visual C++ projects: one for the DLL and one for the client. To build a DLL, you use the same three tools that are used to build any other executable:

- The Visual C++ compiler, a tool with the command-line designation CL386
- The Visual C++ Library Manager, which has the command-line designation LIB32
- The linker, or LINK32 tool.

You can compile and link a DLL in the same way that you compile any executable, using either Developer Studio or a DOS command. However, there are some extra steps to take and some extra compiler and linker switches to pay attention to when you build a DLL.

Figure 10.5 on page 495 shows how a DLL is compiled and linked in 32-bit Visual C++. The compiling and linking of a DLL client is shown in Figure 10.6 on page 497.

Figure 10.5 illustrates the building of a dynamic-link library named DLLMSG.DLL. The client that is built in Figure 10.6 is named CLIENT.EXE. The two figures illustrate the complete build of a sample program named DLLMSG, which you can find in this chapter's folder on your bonus disk.

Building a DLL

Source files for a C++ DLL have the same filename extensions as those for a C++ application: .CPP and .H. In the DLL build shown in Figure 10.5, the source file that is used to build the DLL's main module is named DLLMSG.CPP. The DLL that is built in Figure 10.5 exports just one function, which is declared in a header file named DLLAPI.H (Listing 10.4). This same header file is included in the compilation of the DLL's client, as shown in Figure 10.6.

When you build a DLL, the compiler uses the DLL's .C, .CPP, and .H files to create an object-code (.OBJ) file. In Figure 10.5, the object file generated by the compiler is named DLLMSG.OBJ.

The method of building a DLL shown in Figure 10.5 also requires need a module definition file, or .DEF file. A .DEF file contains information about the functions that the DLL exports and about certain attributes of the DLL. A .DEF file named DLLMSG.DEF is used in the build shown in Figure 10.5. The source code of the .DEF file is shown in Listing 10.5, "DLLMSG.DEF."

When you build a DLL, your compiler also creates several other interim files that are used internally during the compiling and linking process—files with extensions such as .RES and .RBJ. Once a DLL file and an accompanying import library are produced, the .OBJ file and the other files interim files generated by the CL386 compiler are no longer needed, except as makefile targets to make recompiling unnecessary.

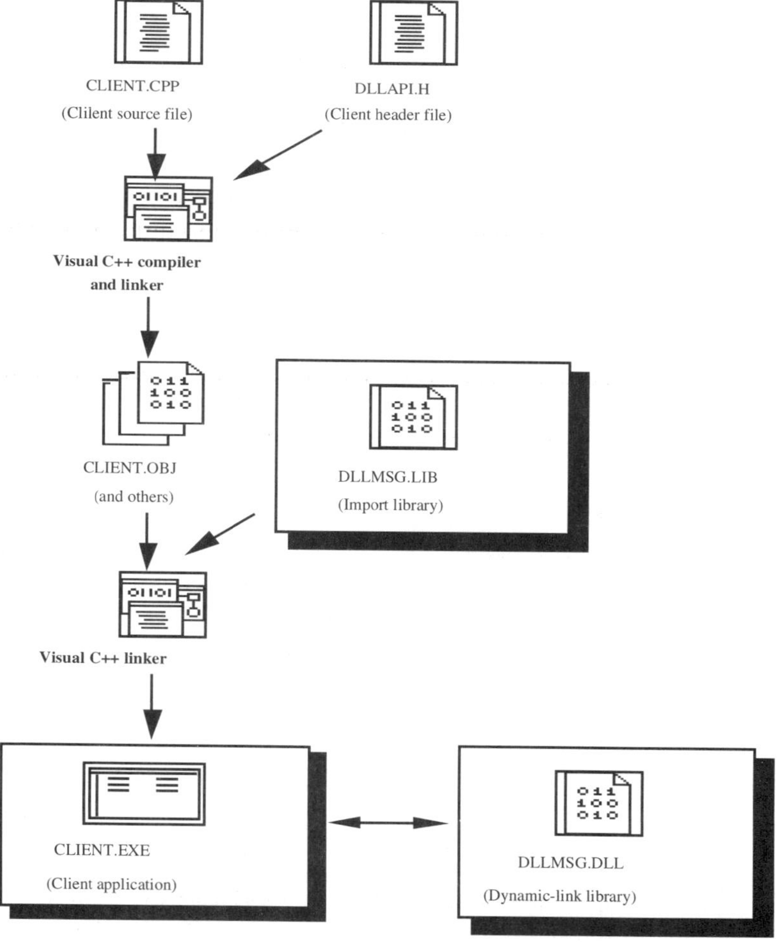

Figure 10.6 Building a client

When a DLL has a module definition (.DEF) file, that file is not passed to the compiler; instead, it goes directly to Library Manager (Lib32). The Library Manager uses this .DEF file, along with the .OBJ file and other interim files produced by the compiler, to generate an export library file and an import library file. In Figure 10.5 on page 495, these two files are named DLLMSG.EXP and DLLMSG.LIB.

Subsequently, when it is time to build a client for the DLL shown in Figure 10.5, the DLL's import library file is supplied to the client to help the client locate and obtain functions and data exported by the DLL. However, once the DLL has been built, there is no further need for the DLL's export library file.

When an .EXP file and an import library (.LIB) file have been created, the linker uses those files, along with the .OBJ file and other interim files produced by the compiler, to build the final object file for the DLL. In Figure 10.5, this file is named DLLMSG.DLL.

Later, when the DLL's client is built, the LIB file that was generated during the DLL's build is linked to the client. That happens because the client needs the contains information that the that the LIB file contains to resolve the external references to DLL functions.

When the client is linked with the LIB file, the client obtains the information that it needs to locate the DLL and the functions and data that the DLL exports at runtime.

Building a Client

You can't execute a DLL unless you have a DLL-aware client—that is, an application or a library that is equipped with an import library. That's because a DLL cannot be executed independently; it can be executed only indirectly, by a client.

The compiling and linking of a DLL client is shown in Figure 10.6 on Page 497. The diagram illustrates the procedures used to build the client application for a sample program named DLLMSG. The source code of the DLLMSG program is presented later in this chapter, in Listings 10.2 through 10.6.

As you can see, the client used in the DLLMSG program has one .CPP file (CLIENT.CPP) and one header file (DLLAPI.H). As shown earlier, in Figure 10.5 on page 495, the DLLAPI.H header file is also included in the compilation of the program's DLL.

To build a client, you use procedures similar to those used to build a DLL. Building a client is a little simpler, however. When you build a client, the Visual C++ compiler uses the client's source files to compile an OBJ file and several other interim object files. These files then go to the linker, along with the import library (.LIB) file that the client needs to reference functions and data exported by a DLL. In Figure 10.6 on Page 497, the .OBJ file produced by the compiler is named CLIENT.OBJ.

Figure 10.6 also illustrates the use of an import library file named DLLMSG.LIB. The DLLMSG.LIB file was generated earlier during the build of the DLL file DLLMSG.DLL, as shown in Figure 10.5 on page 495.

When the build shown in Figure 10.6 reaches the linking stage, the linker uses the .OBJ file generated by the compiler and the. LIB file provided by the client to generate the program's executable (.EXE) file. The executable produced by the build in Figure 10.6 is named CLIENT.EXE.

Once the build of the CLIENT.EXE file is complete, CLIENT.EXE can access functions, data, classes, and objects that are exported by the DLLMSG.DLL library. (DLLMSG.DLL was generated earlier, in the build shown in Figure 10.5 on page 495.)

At runtime, when the client built in Figure 10.6 needs to access to locate functions or data exported by the DLL built in Figure 10.5, the client uses the information that it obtained from its import library at link time to locate the functions or data that it needs from the DLL.For a detailed guide to building DLL clients, see "Building a DLL Client, Step by Step" on page 521.

Varieties of Windows 95 DLLs

There are many ways to write DLLs that work with Windows 95 programs, and there are many options for accessing and linking DLLs that can be called from Windows 95 programs. Rules for writing and accessing different varieties of Windows DLLs overlap in many ways and, unless you have some background on how DLLs work, the whole topic of Windows DLLs can get confusing.

To make it easier for you to sort out the complexities of writing and linking Windows DLLs, this chapter divides the many combinations of DLLs and DLL linkages used in Windows programs into three major categories:

- *Windows 3.x DLLs* can be compiled as 16-bit or 32-bit DLLs and can be called from any program written for any version of Windows. Windows 3.*x* DLLs are not written using the Visual C++ application framework, and they do not rely on the MFC library or on routines in the Win32 API. They are not guaranteed to work with programs written using the Visual C++ application framework or classes or classes implemented in the MFC library. But they are the only variety of DLLs that work as written with 16-bit versions of Windows, and you should know how they work and how to use them. There are still a lot of them around for a long them, and there probably will be for a long time. For a closer look at Windows 3.*x* DLLs, see "Windows 3.x DLLs" on page 500.

- *VCPP 1.0 DLLs* were introduced with the premiere of Version 1.0 of Visual C++. In their day, they were the most streamlined variety of DLLs available. VCPP 1.0 DLLs can be called from any Windows 95 or Windows NT application, including both Visual C++ programs and non-Visual C++ programs written using the MFC library. That means VCPP 1.0 DLLs can be used with applications written with Visual C++, Borland C++, Delphi, or any other development environment that generates code for Windows 95 or Windows 95. VCPP 1.0 DLLs are described in more detail in "VCPP 1.0 DLLs" on page 506.
- *MFC 4.0 DLLs* made their debut with the introduction of Visual C++ 4.0 and MFC 4.0. One of the most important features of MFC 4.0 DLLs is that AppWizard can generate them for you automatically when you write applications using Visual C++ 4.0. Another major feature of MFC 4.0 DLLs is that you can link them to the MFC library in different ways, depending on your preferences and the requirements of your application. To make this versatility possible, Visual C++ divides MFC 4.0 DLLs into three subcategories. Each of these subcategories is described under a separate heading in the section titled "MFC 4.0 DLLs" on page 515.

In the sections that follow, each of these main categories of DLLs is described under a separate major heading. At the end of each major section, an example program is provided to show you how each kind of DLL works, and to demonstrate how you can use each kind of DLL in your Windows 95 applications.

Windows 3.*x* DLLs

The *Windows 3.x DLL* is the most familiar kind of dynamic-linked library to designers of 16-bit Windows programs. A Windows 3.*x* DLL has an explicit entry-point function named **LibMain** and an explicit termination function called a Windows Exit Procedure, or **WEP**. (As you'll see in later sections, VCPP 1.0 DLLs and VCPP 1.0 DLLs also have entry-point and **WEP** functions, but you don't have to write

LibMain or **WEP** functions in framework-based Visual C++ programs; they are managed automatically by the compiler.)

Before the advent of Windows 95, Windows 3.*x* DLLs were generally compiled and linked using non-GUI-based compilers such as Version 7 of Microsoft C/C++. Windows 3.*x* DLLs are now considered obsolete, and are in the process of fading away. So they are not fully documented in the manuals that come with Windows 95, Windows NT, or current versions of 16-bit or of 32-bit Visual C++.

Windows 3.*x* DLLs do not make use of functions defined in the Microsoft Foundation Class (MFC) library, and are not guaranteed to work with MFC applications. But it's a good idea to know something about Windows 3.*x* DLLs because there are still a lot of them around.

The example program named DLLMSG, presented in Listings 10.2 through 10.6 later in this chapter, demonstrate how Windows 3.*x* DLLs work under Windows 95.

How Windows 3.*x* DLLs Work

A Windows 3.*x* DLL always contains two special procedures: an entry function named **LibMain** and a Windows Exit Procedure, or **WEP**. The **LibMain** function performs all initialization of a Windows 3.*x* DLL, and the **WEP** function performs all cleanup operations.

Format of the LibMain Function

This is the format of a **LibMain** function:

```
extern "C"
int FAR PASCAL LibMain(HINSTANCE hInstance, WORD
   segAddr, WORD heapize, LPSTR commandLine)
{
   return TRUE;
}
```

As the preceding example shows, a **LibMain** function takes four parameters:

hInstance An instance handle (the instance handle of the DLL)

segAddr In 16-bit Windows programs, the DLL's data segment address

heapSize The size of the DLL's heap

commandLine A command line (specified only when the DLL is manually loaded; otherwise, this parameter is **NULL**.

A **LibMain** function can do various things with the parameters that you pass to it, depending on what the **LibMain** function is designed to do. For example, if you're creating a DLL that registers a window class and creates a window, or if you want a DLL to load a resource, you can supply the required instance handle in the *hInstance* parameter.

When the **LibMain** function is successful, it returns a nonzero value. If a zero value is returned, Windows 95 unloads the DLL.

Format of a WEP Function

Just before Windows unloads a Windows 3.*x* DLL, the Windows API calls the DLL's **WEP** function. The **WEP** then performs any housekeeping that may be needed before the DLL is unloaded.

This is the syntax of a **WEP** function:

```
extern "C" int FAR PASCAL _WEP(int param)
{
   return TRUE;
}
```

A **WEP** function requires one parameter: an **int** data type (called *param* in the preceding example). If you call a **WEP** from an application, you can pass any value you like in the **param** argument. But when Windows calls a **WEP** function, it passes one of two specific constants to the function. When a DLL that has a **WEP** is unloaded, Windows passes the constant **_FREE_DLL** to the **WEP** function. Just before Windows unloads a DLL, it calls WEP and passes it the constant **WEP_SYSTEMEXIT**.

As the preceding example illustrates, you must use the name **_WEP** when you refer to a **WEP** in source code.

The specific cleanup functions that a DLL's **WEP** performs depend on the needs of the DLL. If a call to **WEP** is successful, a nonzero value is returned.

Example Windows 3.*x* DLL: The DLLMSG Program

DLLMSG, a sample application presented in Listings 10.2 through 10.6, is an example of a Windows 3.*x* DLL. Listing 10.2 is the source file for a DLL referenced in the program.

Listing 10.3, "CLIENT.CPP," presents the source code for the DLLMSG program's client application. Listing 10.6, "CLIENTDEF," is the client's .DEF file. Listing 10.5, "DLLMSG.DEF," is the DLL's module definition file.

DLLMSG is a straightforward program; the client calls a DLL, and the DLL simply displays a message box on the screen like the one shown in Figure 10.7 on Page 503.

Figure 10.7 The DLLMSG display

DLLMSG Source-Code Listings

Listings 10.2 through 10.6 present the source code of the DLLMSG program.

Listing 10.2 DLLMSG.CPP

```
// dllmsg.cpp
// A simple DLL
// Copyright 1994, 1995, Mark Andrews

#include <windows.h>
#include "dllapi.h"

extern "C"
int FAR PASCAL LibMain(HINSTANCE hInstance, WORD
    segAddr,
    WORD heapize, LPSTR commandLine)
0.{
   return TRUE;
}

extern "C"
int FAR PASCAL _WEP(int param)
{
   return TRUE;
}

//////////////////////////////////////////////////////////////
    //////////////////////
```

```
// Public DLL interface

LPSTR theMsg = "Your message goes here.";

extern "C"
BOOL FAR PASCAL ShowDLLDlg(LPSTR wintitle)
{

   MessageBox(NULL, theMsg, wintitle, MB_OK);
   return TRUE;
}
```

Listing 10.3 CLIENT.CPP

```
// hello.cpp
// Client module for a DLL demonstration
// modified to demonstrate the use of DLLs
// Copyright 1994, 1995, Mark Andrews

#include <windows.h>
#include "dllapi.h"

int PASCAL WinMain(HINSTANCE, HINSTANCE, LPSTR, int)
{
   LPSTR msg = "Your Message Here";

   ShowDLLDlg(msg);
   return 0;
}
```

Listing 10.4 DLLAPI.H

```
// dllapi.h
// Interface definition file for a demonstration DLL
// Copyright 1994, 1995, Mark Andrews

extern "C"
BOOL FAR PASCAL ShowDLLDlg(LPSTR wintitle);
```

Listing 10.5 DLLMSG.DEF

```
; dllmsg.def: Declares the module parameters for
; the DLL demo program.
;

LIBRARY DLLMSG

DESCRIPTION'DLL Demo'
```

```
CODE     MOVEABLE PRELOAD
DATA  SINGLE MOVEABLE PRELOAD
HEAPSIZE8192

EXPORTS
   _ShowDLLDlg@4@1NONAME
```

Listing 10.6 CLIENTDEF

```
; hello.def: Declares the module parameters
; for the application.


NAME CLIENT
DESCRIPTION 'DLL Demo'

STUB     'winstub.exe'
EXETYPE WINDOWS

HEAPSIZE 8192
STACKSIZE8192
```

Running the DLLMSG Program

When you launch the DLLMSG application, it executes a very simple `WinMain` function. This tiny `WinMain` function registers a window (which is never displayed), and calls a function named `ShowDLLDlg`, which is implemented as a DLL.

This is a complete listing of the DLLMSG program's `WinMain` function:

```
int PASCAL WinMain(HINSTANCE, HINSTANCE, LPSTR, int)
{
   LPSTR msg = "Your Message Here";

   ShowDLLDlg(msg);
   return 0;
}
```

The `ShowDLLDlg` function defined in the preceding example is declared in a header file named DLLAPI.H. The DLLAPI.H file is included in the compilations of both the client's implementation file (CLIENT.CPP) and the DLL's implementation file (DLLMSG.CPP).

The DLLAPI.H file contains one definition:

```
extern "C"
   BOOL FAR PASCAL ShowDLLDlg(LPSTR wintitle);
```

Most of the work in the DLLMSG program is done by the DLLMSG.CPP file, the implementation file for the program's DLL.

The DLLMSG.CPP file contains a `LibMain` function that returns a TRUE value if there are no errors, a WEP function that returns a TRUE value if there are no errors, and the function that displays the program's message box:

```
extern "C"
BOOL FAR PASCAL ShowDLLDlg(LPSTR wintitle)
{

   MessageBox(NULL, theMsg, wintitle, MB_OK);
   return TRUE;
}
```

VCPP 1.0 DLLs

With the introduction of Version 1.0 of Visual C++, Microsoft introduced a new and improved way to write DLLs. In this chapter, DLLs that fall into this new category are referred to as *VCPP 1.0 DLLs*. VCPP 1.0 DLLs are especially designed for use by applications written and compiled using Visual C++ 1.0 and Version 2.0 of the MFC library.

VCPP 1.0 DLLs had a short lifetime; they became obsolete with the double-barrelled release of Visual C++ 4.0 and MFC 4.0. But they still work fine with programs written for Windows 95 or Windows NT, and they are still useful because support the C++ classes implemented in the Microsoft Foundation Class (MFC) library. If you ever encounter a need to access a VCPP 1.0 DLL from an application, you can build the DLL using Developer Studio, in the same way you would build any other dynamic-link library.

One important characteristic of VCPP 1.0 DLLs is that they don't require the use of entry or exit procedures. Also, .DEF files are optional. VCPP 1.0 DLLs do support the single-threading, multi-threading, and preemptive multitasking capabilities of Windows 95.

Even though VCPP 1.0 DLLs don't require module definition files, supplying a VCPP 1.0 DLL with a .DEF file can provide certain advantages. For example, if you write a .DEF file for a VCPP 1.0 DLL, clients can refer to exported functions by their ordinal numbers rather than by their names. See the *Microsoft Win32 Programmer's Reference* for more details.

Linking VCPP 1.0 DLLs with the MFC Library

To understand how VCPP 1.0 DLLs work, it helps to know how Microsoft has implemented the MFC library. (Knowing how the MFC library is implemented can also help you understand how MFC 4.0 DLLs work. MFC 4.0 DLLs are described in "MFC 4.0 DLLs" on page 515.)

The Two Versions of the MFC Library

Microsoft ships two different versions of the MFC library with Visual C++. When you build an application (or a DLL) using Visual C++, you can specify which version of the MFC library you want your customers to use when you ship the release version of your application.

When you write an application that relies on the statically linked version of the MFC library, the MFC classes you use in your program are dynamically linked with your application at design time, so you don't have to distribute a copy of the MFC library with your application.

In contrast, when you create an application that makes use of the dynamically linked version of the MFC library, you must distribute a copy of the dynamically linked version of the MFC library along with your application.

When you create a Visual C++ a DLL using AppWizard, you can specify which version of the MFC library you want your application or DLL to access when AppWizard displays the dialog box shown in Figure 10.8 on Page 508. For more about selecting an MFC library to use with your DLL, see "How DLLs Work in Windows 95" on page 482.

MFC Pros and Cons

Each version of the MFC library—the dynamically linked version and the statically linked version—has its own advantages and disadvantages. Applications built with the dynamically linked version of the MFC library require considerably less memory and disk space and may also run faster than applications that are linked with the statically linked MFC library.

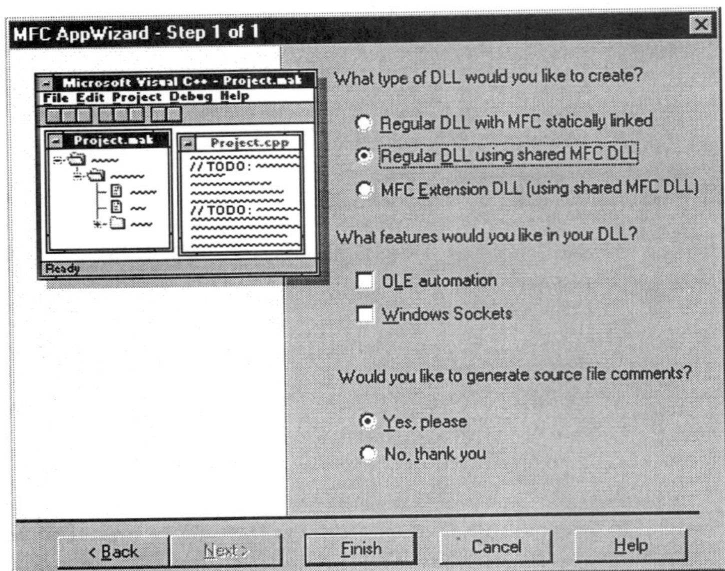

Figure 10.8 Choosing an MFC-library version for an application

However, if your application uses the dynamically linked version of the MFC library, you must supply a copy of the MFC DLL to each user of your program, and you must make sure that the MFC-library DLL is installed in each user's system, along with your application.

Fortunately, the dynamically version of the MFC library is redistributable. That means that when you create and build an application that uses the dynamically linked MFC library, you are free to distribute a copy of the MFC DLL along with each copy of your application. In fact, if you use MFC classes in an application, you must link your application with the dynamically linked versions of the MFC library.

VCPP 1.0 DLLs and the USRDLL Library

When Visual C++ 1.0 was introduced and the VCPP 1.0 DLL made its debut, the statically linked version of the MFC library was named USRDLL. (With the introduction of MFC 4.0, the term USRDLL became obsolete. What used to be called the USRDLL library is now called the static-link version of the "regular" MFC DLL; for details, see "MFC 4.0 DLLs" on page 515.)

Because the statically linked MFC library was named USRDLL when VCPP 1.0 DLLs were created, VCPP 1.0 DLLs accessed the statically linked version of the MFC library by defining the preprocessor symbol _USRDLL when they were compiled. (In MFC 4.0 DLLs, even though the name of USRDLL library has changed, you still access the statically linked MFC by defining the preprocessor symbol _USRDLL).

Linking with the MFC-Library DLL

The MFC library that is implemented as a shared DLL is named AFXDLL. That name has not changed with the introduction of Version 4.0 of the MFC library. So MFC 4.0 DLLs, as well as VCPP 1.0 DLLs, can access functions implemented in Version 4.0 of MFC library.

To link a VCPP 1.0 DLL (or an MFC 4.0 DLL) with the statically linked version of the MFC DLL, you define the preprocessor symbol _AFXDLL in your DLL's source code.

If you ship an application with a VCPP 1.0 DLL that accesses the AFXDLL version of MFC, you must distribute a copy of the AFXDLL library with your application, and you must make sure that AFXDLL library is installed in your customers' computer systems along with your program. If you ship your application with any MFC 4.0 DLLs that make use of classes implemented in the MFC library, those DLLs can access the same copy of the MFC DLL.

If you ship your application with a VCPP 1.0 DLL that supports OLE, you must also supply each user of your program with a runtime MFC library named MFCO30.DLL. Furthermore, if you ship your application with a VCPP 1.0 DLL that uses any of database classes implemented in the MFC library, you must provide each of your application's users with still another runtime library named MFCD30.DLL. And if you ship your program with any VCPP 1.0 DLLs that require Unicode support, there are other runtime DLLs you must supply. For more details on the various dynamically linked MFC libraries that are available, see Books Online or your Visual C++ 4.0 documentation.

_export *Is Obsolete in Win32*

In the Win32 SDK—and, consequently, in 32-bit Windows 95 DLLs—the _export keyword is obsolete. In Win32, the dllexport attribute replaces the keyword _export in DLLs and clients that call DLLs. If you use the _export keyword in a Win32 program or in a 32-bit Visual C++ program, you'll get an error message.

Exporting Functions from VCPP 1.0 DLLs

One of the most noteworthy features of VCPP 1.0 DLLs is that they export functions, data, classes, and object by using the keywords `dllexport` and `dllimport`. These two keywords are storage-class modifiers that are specific to Microsoft C and C++. They are very handy for DLL writers to have around because they eliminate the need for module definition files.

When you use a VCPP 1.0 DLL, you can identify any function in the DLL as an exportable function by simply declaring it using the `dllexport` modifier. Then you can access the function from a client by declaring the same function using the `dllimport` modifier.

When a VCPP 1.0 DLL uses the `dllexport` and `dllimport` attributes to identify a function, the DLL does not require a module definition file. However, clients of a VCPP 1.0 DLL—like clients of any other kind of DLL—must still be linked with an import library to obtain access to the function.

Using VCPP 1.0 DLLs

To identify a function in a VCPP 1.0 DLL as an exported function, you place the `dllexport` attribute in a function definition similar to this in your DLL's header file:

```
#define DLLExport __declspec(dllexport)
   DLLExport void DLLMessage(LPSTR dlltitle);
```

To reference this function from a client, you place a function definition like this in the client's header file:

```
#define DLLImport __declspec(dllexport)
   extern DLLImport void DLLMessage(LPSTR dlltitle);
```

When you have written a pair of definitions such as those in the preceding example, and have provided the DLL's client with an import library file, you can access the function from the DLL's client.

In the two preceding code fragments, you may notice that notice that the `dllexport` and `dllimport` attributes are used in conjunction with the keyword `__declspec`. That's because `dllexport` and `dllimport` are attributes, not keywords, and therefore cannot be used alone. The required syntax is:

```
__declspec(dllAttribute)
```

The DLLExport and DLLImport Macros

In the preceding examples, the keyword/attribute constructs `__declspec(dllexport)` and `_declspec(dllimport)` are defined as preprocessor macros and are assigned the names `DLLImport` and `DLLExport`. The `DLLExport` and `DLLImport` macros are defined merely for the sake of convenience; they make it easier to refer to the unwieldy constructs `__declspec(dllexport)` and `__declspec(dllimport)` in source code.

To export functions, VCPP 1.0 DLLs generally use the standard "`C`" interface. In other words the declaration of a function exported from a VCPP 1.0 is written in this format:

```
extern "C" EXPORT ExportedFunction();
```

Example VCPP 1.0 DLL: The WINHOST Program

The sample application presented in Listings 10.7 through 10.10, titled WINHOST, shows how a VCPP 1.0 DLL can be accessed from a Windows 95 program. It also shows how a C++ object can be exported by a VCPP 1.0 DLL.

When you execute the WINHOST program, it displays a console window that contains two messages, as shown in Figure 10.9. (A console window is a text window that an application can display using functions provided in the Win32 SDK. Console windows are described in detail in Chapter 8, "Programs and Processes."

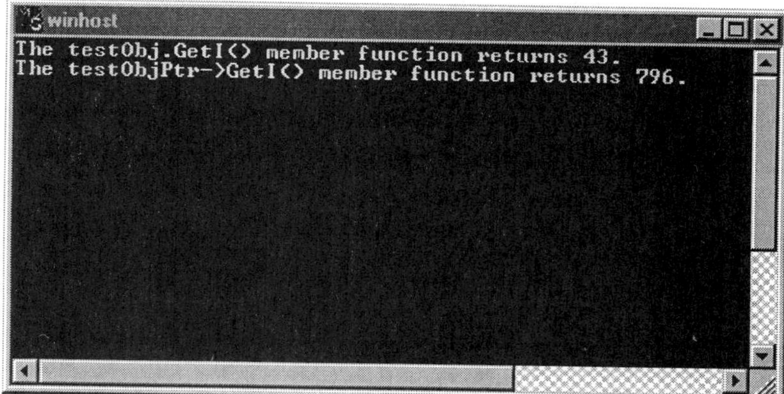

Figure 10.9 The WINHOST display

WINHOST Source-Code Listings

The following listings present some of the source code of the WINHOST program. For complete listings of the program's source code, refer to this chapter's folder on your bonus disk.

Listing 10.7 WINHOST.CPP

```
// WINHOST.cpp

#include <iostream.h>
#include <afx.h>
#include "dlllib.h"
#include "WINHOST.h"

int main()
{
   testObj.SetI(43);
   testObjPtr->SetI(796);

   cout << "The testObj.GetI() member function returns "
      << testObj.GetI() << '.' << endl;
   cout << "The testObjPtr->GetI() member function
    returns "
      << testObjPtr->GetI() << '.' << endl;

   while (TRUE);

   return 0;
}
```

Listing 10.8 WINHOST.H

```
// WINHOST.h

#define DLLImport _declspec(dllimport)

DLLImport TestClass testObj;
DLLImport TestClass *testObjPtr;
```

Listing 10.9 DLLLIB.CPP

```
// dlllib.cpp

#define DEFINING
#include "dlllib.h"

INTERFACE TestClass testObj;
```

```
INTERFACE TestClass *testObjPtr = new TestClass;
```

Listing 10.10 DLLLIB.H

```
// dlllib.h

#ifdef DEFINING
#define INTERFACE _declspec(dllexport)
#else
#define INTERFACE _declspec(dllimport)
#endif

class INTERFACE TestClass
{
private:
   int i;
public:
   TestClass() {}
   ~TestClass() {}
   void SetI(int mi){ i = mi; }
   int GetI( void ){ return i; }
};
```

Running the WINHOST Program

As noted in Chapter 5, "Console Windows," the entry point for a console window is a `main` function. The `main` function of the WINHOST program is defined in Listing 10.7, "WINHOST.CPP" as follows:

```
int main()
{
   testObj.SetI(43);
   testObjPtr->SetI(796);

   cout << "The testObj.GetI() member function returns "
      << testObj.GetI() << '.' << endl;
   cout << "The testObjPtr->GetI() function returns "
      << testObjPtr->GetI() << '.' << endl;

   while (TRUE) ;

   return 0;
}
```

The DLLLIB.H File

The main function shown in the preceding code fragment uses the C++ string operator cout to print two messages in a console window. It obtains the two numbers that are printed in the message by calling the function SetI, which is a member function of a class named TestClass. This class and its member functions are defined in Listing 10.10, "DLLLIB.H."

In Listing 10.10, TestClass::SetI is called twice: first by value and then by reference. This demonstration shows that a function exported by a DLL can be called either way.

This is the definition of TestClass, as it appears in Listing 10.10:

```
class INTERFACE TestClass
{
private:
   int i;
public:
   TestClass() {}
   ~TestClass() {}
   void SetI(int mi){  i = mi; }
   int GetI( void ){  return i; }
};
```

Along with the definitions of TestClass, the DLLLIB.H file contains definitions of a preprocessor macro that is used to access the attributes dllexport and dllimport. This macro, named INTERFACE, is defined as follows:

```
#ifdef DEFINING
#define INTERFACE _declspec(dllexport)
#else
#define INTERFACE _declspec(dllimport)
#endif
```

In the preceding code fragment, the INTERFACE macro is conditionally defined in two ways. If the macro is defined in a module that exports an object or a function—as the DLLLIB.H code module is—it is expanded as:

```
_declspec(dllexport)
```

If the macro appears in a module that imports a function—for example, the WINHOST.H function defined in Listing 10.8—it is expanded as:

```
_declspec(dllimport)
```

The DLLLIB.CPP File

In Listing 10.9, "DLLLIB.CPP" the macro named `DEFINING` is defined, so the `INTERFACE` macro is expanded as `_declspec(dllexport)`. The class named `TestClass` is then exported in two ways: on the heap, so that it can be called by value, and on the stack, so it can be called by reference:

```
#define DEFINING
#include "dlllib.h"

INTERFACE TestClass testObj;
INTERFACE TestClass *testObjPtr = new TestClass;
```

The WINHOST.H File

In Listing 10.8, "WINHOST.H" a macro named `DLLImport` is defined as `_declspec(dllimport)`.The class named `TestClass` is then imported in two ways: by value, as an object named `testObj`, and by reference, as an object pointer named `testObjPtr`:

```
DLLImport TestClass testObj;
    DLLImport TestClass *testObjPtr;
```

The WINHOST program does not require a module definition file because it references VCPP 1.0 DLLs using the attributes `dll-import` and `dllexport`. Although the program exports an object that is a member of a class, the object class is not derived from any class defined in the MFC library, so the program works with Win32 Visual C++, which shipped with Version 2.0 of the MFC library.

MFC 4.0 DLLs

With the twin releases of Visual C++ 4.0 and MFC 4.0, Microsoft unveiled a new AppWizard with some interesting new features. One new feature lets you use AppWizard to build dynamic-link libraries.

One important feature of MFC 4.0 DLLs is that you can link them to the MFC library in different ways, depending on your preferences and the requirements of your application.

To create a DLL using AppWizard, you simply choose the **MFC AppWizard (dll)** option in AppWizard's **New Project Workspace** dialog box, as shown in Figure 10.10. For a step-by-step demonstration of how AppWizard can be used to generate a DLL automatically, see "Defining _doserrmsg" on page 520.

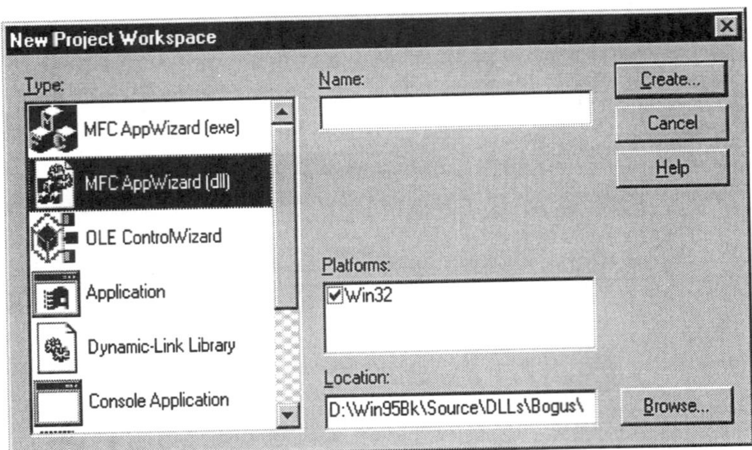

Figure 10.10 Using AppWizard to build a DLL

How MFC 4.0 DLLs Work

To understand how MFC 4.0 DLLs work, it helps to be familiar with some new terminology that Microsoft has now begun to use in its DLL documentation.

Microsoft still ships two versions of the MFC library with Visual C++. When you buy Visual C++, you still get a statically linked version of the MFC library and a dynamically linked version of the MFC library. But now some new terminology—and some new levels of complexity—have been added.

The Static-Link and Shared MFC Libraries

Microsoft now refers to the statically linked version of the MFC library as the *static-link* version of the MFC library. And dynamically linked version of the MFC library is now referred to as the *shared* version. So you should get used to hearing the terms *static-link MFC library* and *shared MFC library* from now on.

The Static-Link MFC Library

In MFC 4.0, the static-link MFC library has the same characteristics as the familiar statically linked MFC library that was used in earlier versions of Visual C++. In other words, the static-link version of MFC is the MFC 4.0 equivalent of what used to be called the USRDLL library before the advent of MFC 4.0.

As noted earlier in this chapter, the name USRDLL is obsolete in MFC 4.0. However, when AppWizard creates a DLL that links dynamically with the shared version of the MFC library, AppWizard still sets up the link by defining the `_USRDLL` preprocessor symbol in the DLL's source code.

The Shared MFC Library

In MFC 4.0, the shared MFC library has the same characteristics as the library that was called the dynamically linked MFC library, or the AFXDLL library, before the advent of MFC 4.0.

In MFC 4.0, as in previous version of MFC, the shared version of the MFC library is named AFXDLL. So, when you use AppWizard to create a DLL that links dynamically with the shared version of the MFC library, AppWizard defines the `_AFXDLL` preprocessor symbol when it builds your DLL.

Regular and Extension DLLs

Along with the new terms that have just been explained, Microsoft has created some new levels of detail that affect the creation and implementation of DLLs. In MFC 4.0, there are now two different kinds of shared (dynamically linked) MFC libraries: the *regular* shared MFC library and the *extended* shared MFC library.

In MFC 4.0, the regular shared MFC library has the same characteristics as the version of the MFC library that used to be called the statically linked version. When you equip an MFC 4.0 application with DLLs that access MFC classes, you can save memory and disk space by writing DLLs that access the regular shared MFC library. But you must ship a copy of the regular shared MFC library with your application.

When you link a DLL with the extended shared MFC library, you can create MFC-derived classes that actually become extensions to the hundreds of Microsoft classes implemented in the MFC 4.0 library. You can then make your own derived classes available to other applications that access the MFC-derived classes or functions implemented in your DLL.

Creating Extension DLLs

The extension version of the shared MFC library is a new kind of MFC library that made its premiere along with MFC 4.0. When you create a DLL that accesses the extended version of the shared MFC library, any new classes that you implement in your DLL become integral parts of the shared MFC library that you ship with your application. Other applications that are loaded into the user's computer system can then access your new classes without loading another DLL into memory.

When you create a DLL that links with the extension version of the shared MFC library, your DLL is called an *extension DLL*. You can create extension DLLs almost automatically using AppWizard.

To create an extension DLL using AppWizard, you click the radio button labelled **MFC Extension DLL (using shared MFC DLL)** when AppWizard displays the dialog box shown in Figure 10.11 on Page 519. (The process of creating a DLL with AppWizard is described in more detail in "Defining _doserrmsg" on page 520.)

Creating Regular DLLs

As noted earlier in this section, the term USRDLL is obsolete in Version 4.0 of Visual C++. In previous releases of MFC, USRDLL was the name of the statically linked version of the MFC library. To access MFC classes from one of your own DLLs, all you had to do was statically link your DLL to the statically linked version of the MFC library.

In MFC 4.0, you can obtain this same functionality by statically linking your DLL with the static-link version of what is now called the "regular" version of the MFC DLL. When you statically link a DLL to the regular version of the MFC library, your DLL is called a *regular DLL*.

When you create a regular DLL, functions exported by your DLL can be called by any Win32 application, as well as by programs that also use MFC.

In MFC 4.0, you can easily create regular DLLs using AppWizard. When AppWizard displays its first DLL-generation dialog box (shown in Figure 10.11), you can link your DLL to the regular version of MFC by clicking the radio button labelled **Regular DLL with MFC statically linked.**

When you select that option, AppWizard generates a regular DLL and statically links it with the static-link version of the MFC DLL by defining the `_USRDLL` preprocessor symbol when it builds your DLL.

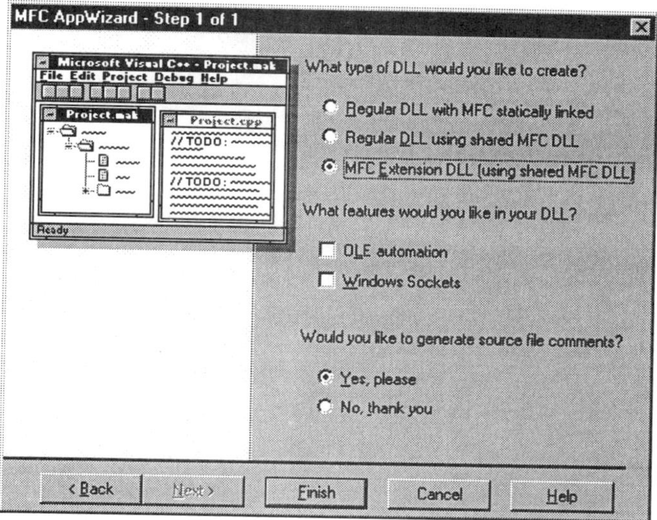

Figure 10.11 Choosing the kind of DLL you want to create

Linking with a Shared MFC Library

In MFC 4.0, as in earlier versions of MFC, you can save memory and disk space by dynamically linking your application's DLLs to a shared version of the regular MFC library. When you dynamically link a regular DLL to the shared version of the MFC library, multiple applications can access the same copy of the MFC library, saving disk and memory space.

When you want to create a DL that dynamically links with the shared version of the shared MFC library, you can easily create your DLL using AppWizard. When AppWizard displays its first DLL-generation dialog box (Figure 10.11), you can link your DLL to the regular version of MFC by clicking the radio button labeled **Regular DLL with MFC statically linked.**

When you dynamically link a DLL to one of the shared versions of the MFC library, functions in your DLL can be called only by MFC applications that are also dynamically linked to the shared version of the MFC library.

When you use AppWizard to link a DLL dynamically with the shared version of the regular MFC library, AppWizard simply refrains from defining the `_USRDLL` preprocessor symbol when it builds your DLL. Instead, AppWizard defines the `_AFXDLL` preprocessor symbol. (If AppWizard defined the `_USRDLL` preprocessor symbol in your DLL's source code, you would obtain a static link to the static-link version of the regular version of the MFC library.)

When you dynamically link a DLL to the regular shared version of the MFC library, functions in your DLL can be called by any Win32 application, whether or not the program uses MFC classes.

Defining _doserrmsg

If you try to build a DLL and get a link error complaining that something called `_doserrmsg` is not defined, select Options/Project/Linker from the Developer Studio menu bar and then select Input from the Category text box. When the libraries that are being used in the link appear in the Object/Library Modules text box, make sure that the name of the library `libc.lib` appears at the end of the list, right after the name of the `nafxdwd` library. If it doesn't, type it in. Then close the Linker Options dialog box and the Project Options dialog box by clicking their OK buttons. After you have done all that, rebuild your DLL by selecting Build or Rebuild All from the Project m.enu. That should solve your problem.

Creating DLLs with AppWizard

When you use AppWizard to generate an MFC 4.0 DLL, the AppWizard utility lets you choose what kind of DLL you want to create (Figure 10.11). These are the options that AppWizard offers:

- *Regular DLLs with MFC statically linked*: This choice creates a regular DLL that links with the static-link MFC 4.0 library. When you choose this option, the Visual C++ linker accesses functions in the static-link version of the MFC library and links your application to the MFC library at build time. Both Win32 applications and MFC applications can call functions exported from this kind of DLL.
- *Regular DLL using shared MFC DLL*: When you make this selection, the Visual C++ linker links your application to the dynamically linked (shared) version of the MFC library at runtime. Using this kind of DLL can reduce the disk and memory requirements of your application if your program has multiple executable files that access the MFC library. This variety of DLL can be used by both Win32 applications and MFC applications.
- *MFC Extension DLL (using shared MFC)*: If you make this choice, your application is linked to the shared version of the MFC library

at runtime. This option can reduce your application's disk and memory requirements if your program has multiple executable files that access the MFC library. Only MFC applications can call functions implemented in this kind of DLL.

Creating an MFC 4.0 DLL Step by Step

✔ To generate an MFC 4.0 DLL using AppWizard, follow these steps:

1. Choose the **File|New** menu item.
2. When the **New** dialog box opens, choose the **Project Workspace** item from the **New** list box.
3. Close the **New** list box by clicking **OK.**
4. When the **New Project Workspace** list box opens, you can build a DLL with AppWizard by simply selecting the **Dynamic-Link Library** item from the **Type** list box, as shown earlier in Figure 10.10 on Page 516.
5. Type a name for your DLL project in the **Name** text box.
6. Click the **Create** button.
7. When the first AppWizard dialog box opens, you can decide which kind of MFC 4.0 DLL you want AppWizard to generate: a regular DLL with MFC statically linked, or a regular DLL that uses a shared MFC DLL.
8. When you have specified what kind of DLL you want to create, click the **Finish** button. AppWizard then builds your DLL in the same way it builds any executable, creating both an object library (an .OBJ file) and a DLL (a DLL file).

Later, when you develop an application that accesses your DLL, you must link the application with the .OBJ file that is created during Step 8. And when you ship an application that accesses your DLL, you must also provide your customers with the .DLL file that is generated in Step 8.

Building a DLL Client, Step by Step

Building a DLL client is just like building an ordinary application, except for a few extra steps that involve linking with libraries.

✔ To build a Windows-based client application using Version 4.0 of Visual C++, these are the general steps to follow:

1. Build your client project, with or without AppWizard, in the same way you would build any other Visual C++ project. To use a

shared version of the MFC library, an application must be built as an MFC application.

2. Using Developer Studio, add your dynamic-link library's .DLL and .LIB files to your project.
3. Build and execute your client application.

For a more comprehensive guide to building a DLL client, see "Building a Program that Accesses an Extension DLL" on page 527.

Example MFC 4.0 DLL: The DLLTESTAPP Program

This chapter's main example program, named DLLTESTAPP, is shown in Listings 10.11 through 10.14. The DLLTESTAPP program has two parts: an MFC 4.0 DLL named WIN95DLL and an application that calls the DLL. The application is named DLLTESTAPP. Figure 10.12 shows the custom dialog box displayed by the DLLTESTAPP program.

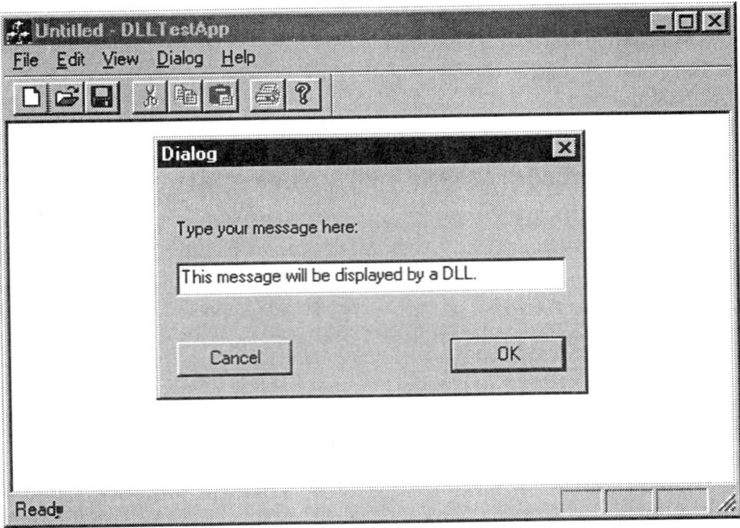

Figure 10.12 Output of the DLLTESTAPP program

The DLL that is implemented in the WIN95DLL file implements an MFC-derived class named CTestClass. CTestClass has several member functions, including one that displays a message box and one that displays a custom message box designed using Studio App. The custom message box contains an edit box in which the user can type text. The text that the user has entered can subsequently be displayed in the application's message box.

How the DLLTESTAPP Program Works

Both the DLLTESTAPP program and the WIN95DLL dynamic-link library were created using AppWizard. The WIN95DLL dynamic-link library is an extension DLL that was built using the second AppWizard option: **MFC Extension DLL (using shared MFC DLL).** For an explanation of this option, see See "Linking with a Shared MFC Library" on page 519.

When you execute the DLLTESTAPP program, the application calls member functions that are implemented in the dynamic-link library named WIN95DLL. The DLLTESTAPP program is a document-and-view application that calls the WIN95DLL dynamic-link library from its CView class, named DLLTestAppView. The application's DLLTestAppView object calls the WIN95DLL dynamic-link library using two menu commands: **Dialog | Send** and **Dialog | Recieve.**

When the user executes DLLTESTAPP and chooses the **Dialog | Send** menu item, the DLLTESTAPP program executes a member function named `DLLTestAppView::OnDialogSend`. The `DLLTestAp-pView::On-DialogSend` member function displays a custom dialog box titled **Send a Message** (shown in Figure 10.12 on Page 522). The user can then type a message inside the edit box labeled **Type your message here.**

When the user types a message and closes the **Send a Message** dialog box by clicking **OK**, the DLLTESTAPP program calls a member function implemented in the WIN95DLL dynamic-link library. That member function, named `CTestClass::SetMessage`, stores the user's message in a member variable named `CTestClass::m_msg`.

When the user chooses the **Dialog | Receive** menu item, the DLLTEST program calls another WIN95DLL member function named `GetMes-sage`. The `GetMessage` function retrieves the text stored in the `m_msg` member variable and returns the text to the DLLTESTAPP application. DLLTESTAPP then displays the user's message in a standard message box, as shown in Figure 10.13 on Page 524.

Figure 10.13 The DLLTESTAPP message box

Architecture of the DLLTESTAPP Program

Although AppWizard makes creation of MFC 4.0 DLLs almost automatic, there is still some work you have to do yourself. Listings 10.11 through 10.14 show how AppWizard helped create the DLLTESTAPP and WIN95DLL programs. The listings also show the extra work that had to be done to make the two projects work together.

Characteristics of Extension DLLs

The WIN95DLL dynamic-link library—as noted in the previous section—is an extension DLL that was built using the shared version of the MFC library.

In MFC 4.0, an MFC extension DLL is a DLL that typically implements reusable classes derived from existing MFC classes. Extension DLLs can also be used for passing MFC-derived objects to and from applications.

An MFC extension DLL uses a shared version of MFC in the same way an application uses the shared AFXDLL version of, with a few additional considerations:

- An extension DLL, unlike an MFC application, does not have a CWinApp-derived object.

- An extension DLL calls the MFC function `AfxInitExtension-Module` in its `DllMain` function. Your application should check the return value of this function. If `AfxInitExtensionModule` returns a zero value, your application's `DllMain` function should return 0 also.
- If an extension DLL is designed to export CRuntimeClass objects or resources to an application, it creates a CDynLinkLibrary object during the initialization process.

Building an Extension DLL

To create an extension DLL using AppWizard, you select the option **MFC Extension DLL (using shared MFC DLL)** in the AppWizard dialog box shown earlier in Figure 10.11 on Page 519. In an application that has already been compiled, you can change this option using the **Project Settings** dialog box.

When you create an extension DLL, you must also provide a header (.H) file. AppWizard generates a module definition (.DEF) file when it generates your DLL, but you don't have to do anything with AppWizard's .DEF file unless you want to access the functions in your DLL using ordinal numbers. If you want to use ordinal numbers to access functions, you must place the names of the functions in your DLL's .DEF file, and you must assign ordinal numbers to the functions listed in the .DEF file.

There are two methods for exporting functions from an extension DLL created by AppWizard. The first technique can export whole classes without requiring you to track down the decorated names of those classes and placing them in a .DEF file. The second strategy requires you to place decorated names in a .DEF file.

The second method is more efficient because it provides you with a way to export the names of symbols using their ordinal numbers. But you may prefer the first method because it doesn't require the use of ordinal numbers.

Exporting Classes Without Using Decorated Names

If you want to export a class from an extension DLL without using decorated names, you must use the `extern "C"` construct to initialize your DLL and register its classes with Windows 95. In the WIN95DLL.H file shown in Listing 10.11, this is the line that initializes the WIN95DLL.H file:

```
extern "C" AFX_EXT_API void WINAPI InitWin95DLL();
```

You must also insert the `AFX_EXT_CLASS` keyword into the heading of your class's definition. For example, in the WIN95DLL.H file shown in Listing 10.11, the class named CTestClass is defined this way:

```
class AFX_EXT_CLASS CTestClass : public CObject
{
private:
   CString m_msg;
public:
   CTestClass();
   ~CTestClass();
   void ShowMessage(CString msg);
   void SetMessage(CString s);
   CString GetMessage();
};
```

This technique allows you to export entire classes without placing the decorated names for all that class's symbols in the .DEF file.

Exporting Symbols Using Their Ordinal Numbers

There is another method you can use if you prefer to place the decorated names for all external symbols in your .DEF file. This method is most useful if you don't need to export many symbols from your DLL. If you have a lot of symbols to export, you might not want to use this method because it would require the use of a large number of decorated names.

To use the decorated-names method, place the following code at the beginning and end of your header file:

```
#undef AFX_DATA
#define AFX_DATA AFX_EXT_DATA
   // <body of your header file>
#undef AFX_DATA
#define AFX_DATA
```

The preceding code ensures that your DLL is compiled correctly for an extension DLL. Leaving out these four lines may cause your DLL to either compile incorrectly or link incorrectly.

When you have inserted the necessary code in your file, you must obtain the decorated names of all the classes you want to export (you can do that by linking your application using the /MAP option), and then you must place those names in your application's .DEF file.

Building a Program that Accesses an Extension DLL

A program that accesses functions in an MFC extension DLL must be an MFC application—that is, an application that contains a CWinApp-derived object.

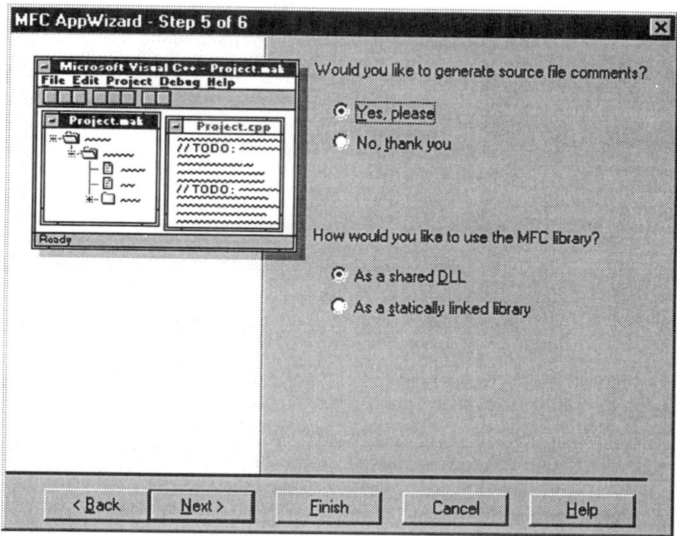

Figure 10.14 Building a program that accesses an extension DLL

The easiest way to create such an application is to generate a framework for it using AppWizard. When AppWizard displays the dialog box shown in Figure 10.14, select the **As A Shared DLL** option. Then AppWizard creates an application that can access functions in an MFC extension DLL.

In an application that has already been compiled, you can select this option by tabbing to the **General** property page in the **Project Settings** property sheet and and selecting the shared-DLL option from the **Microsoft Foundation Classes** list box.

When you create an application that is designed to access your extension DLL, you must add the your DLL's import library to your application's project. You can do that, follow these steps:

1. From the Developer Studio editor, choose the **Build | Settings** menu item.
2. When the **Project Settings** property sheet opens, tab to the **Link** property page.
3. Select the **Input** item from the **Category** drop-down combo box.

4. Type the name of your DLL's import library in the text box labeled **Output file name**, as shown in Figure 10.13.
5. Close the **Project Settings** dialog box by clicking **OK**.
6. Include the name of your DLL's header (.H) file in the file that implements your client application. In Listing 10.14, the following line includes the WIN95DLL.H file in the DLLTE-STAPP-VIEW.CPP file:

```
#include "Win95DLL.h"
```

7. Build your application by choosing Developer Studio's **Build | Build** menu item.

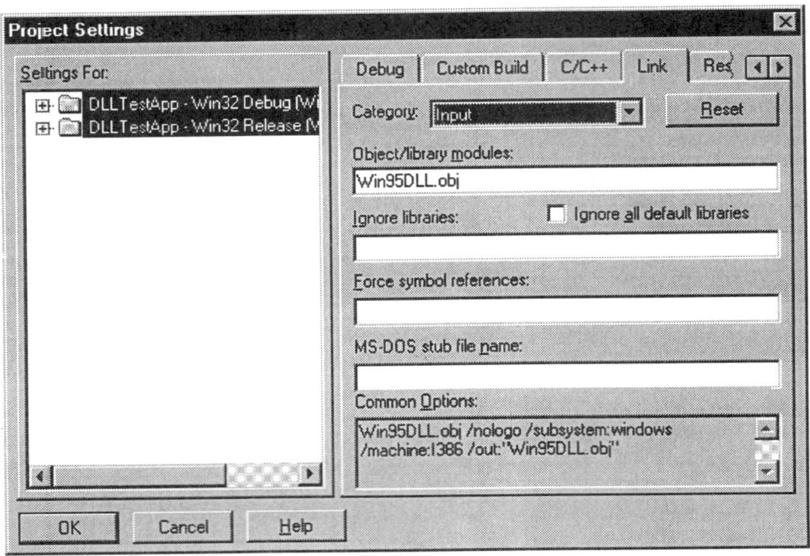

Figure 10.15 Linking an application with a DLL's .OBJ file

Listing 10.11 WIN95DLL.H

```
// Win95DLL.h

// Initialize the DLL, register the classes etc
extern "C" AFX_EXT_API void WINAPI InitWin95DLL();

class AFX_EXT_CLASS CTestClass : public CObject
{
private:
   CString m_msg;
public:
```

```
    CTestClass();
    ~CTestClass();
    void ShowMessage(CString msg);
    void SetMessage(CString s);
    CString GetMessage();
};
```

Listing 10.12 WIN95DLL.CPP

```
// Win95DLL.cpp : Defines the initialization routines
// for the DLL.
//
#include "stdafx.h"
#include "win95dll.h"
#include <afxdllx.h>
#ifdef _DEBUG
#define new DEBUG_NEW
#undef THIS_FILE
static char THIS_FILE[] = __FILE__;
#endif
///////////////////////////////////////////////////////////
    //////////////////////
// Initialization of MFC Extension DLL
static AFX_EXTENSION_MODULE Win95DLL = { NULL, NULL };

extern "C" int APIENTRY
DllMain(HINSTANCE hInstance, DWORD dwReason, LPVOID
    lpReserved)
{
    if (dwReason == DLL_PROCESS_ATTACH)
    {
        TRACE0("WIN95DLL.DLL Initializing!\n");

        // Extension DLL one-time initialization
        AfxInitExtensionModule(Win95DLL, hInstance);

        // Insert this DLL into the resource chain
        new CDynLinkLibrary(Win95DLL);
    }
    else if (dwReason == DLL_PROCESS_DETACH)
    {
        TRACE0("WIN95DLL.DLL Terminating!\n");
    }
    return 1;   // ok
}
// Exported DLL initialization is run in context of
// running application
extern "C" void WINAPI InitWin95DLL()
```

```
{
   // create a new CDynLinkLibrary for this app
   new CDynLinkLibrary(Win95DLL);
   // nothing more to do
}
/////////////////////////////////////////////////////////////////////////////
// CTestClass functions
//
CTestClass::CTestClass() {}
CTestClass::~CTestClass() {}
void CTestClass::ShowMessage(CString msg)
{
   AfxMessageBox(msg);
}
void CTestClass::SetMessage(CString s)
{
   m_msg = s;
}
CString CTestClass::GetMessage()
{
   return m_msg;
}
```

Listing 10.13 DLLTESTAPPVIEW.H

```
// DLLTestAppView.h : interface of the CDLLTestAppView
// class
//
#define VAR2CTRL FALSE  // These defines make DDX
                        // a little clearer.
#define CTRL2VAR TRUE

class CDLLTestAppView : public CView
{
protected: // create from serialization only
   CDLLTestAppView();
   DECLARE_DYNCREATE(CDLLTestAppView)
   void OnInitialUpdate();

// Attributes
public:
   class CDLLTestAppDoc* GetDocument();

// Operations
public:
// Overrides
   // ClassWizard generated virtual function overrides
   //{{AFX_VIRTUAL(CDLLTestAppView)
```

```
    public:
    virtual void OnDraw(CDC* pDC);  // overridden to draw
                                    //this view
    virtual BOOL PreCreateWindow(CREATESTRUCT& cs);
    protected:
    //}}AFX_VIRTUAL

// Implementation
public:
    virtual ~CDLLTestAppView();

#ifdef _DEBUG
    virtual void AssertValid() const;
    virtual void Dump(CDumpContext& dc) const;
#endif

private:
    CString m_msg;
public:
    void SetMessageString(CString s)
        { m_msg = s; }
protected:
// Generated message map functions
protected:
    //{{AFX_MSG(CDLLTestAppView)
    afx_msg void OnDialogReceive();
    afx_msg void OnDialogSend();
    //}}AFX_MSG
    DECLARE_MESSAGE_MAP()
};
#ifndef _DEBUG  // debug version in DLLTestAppView.cpp
inline CDLLTestAppDoc* CDLLTestAppView::GetDocument()
    { return (CDLLTestAppDoc*)m_pDocument; }
#endif
/////////////////////////////////////////////////////////
    //////////////////////
```

Listing 10.14 DLLTESTAPPVIEW.CPP

```
// DLLTestAppView.cpp : implementation of the
//CDLLTestAppView class
//
#include "stdafx.h"
#include "DLLTestApp.h"
#include "DLLTestAppDoc.h"
#include "DLLTestAppView.h"
#include "Win95DLL.h"
#include "DlgGetMsg.h"
```

```
#ifdef _DEBUG
#define new DEBUG_NEW
#undef THIS_FILE
static char THIS_FILE[] = __FILE__;
#endif

////////////////////////////////////////////////////////////
    //////////////////////
// CDLLTestAppView
IMPLEMENT_DYNCREATE(CDLLTestAppView, CView)
BEGIN_MESSAGE_MAP(CDLLTestAppView, CView)
   //{{AFX_MSG_MAP(CDLLTestAppView)
   ON_COMMAND(ID_DIALOG_RECEIVE, OnDialogReceive)
   ON_COMMAND(ID_DIALOG_SEND, OnDialogSend)
   //}}AFX_MSG_MAP
END_MESSAGE_MAP()
////////////////////////////////////////////////////////////
    //////////////////////

// CDLLTestAppView construction/destruction
CDLLTestAppView::CDLLTestAppView()
{
   // TODO: add construction code here
}

CDLLTestAppView::~CDLLTestAppView()
{
}

void CDLLTestAppView::OnInitialUpdate()
{
   // An initial message to start off with.
   m_msg = "This message is brought to you by a DLL.";
}

BOOL CDLLTestAppView::PreCreateWindow(CREATESTRUCT& cs)
{
   // TODO: Modify the Window class or styles here by
    modifying
   //  the CREATESTRUCT cs
   return CView::PreCreateWindow(cs);
}

////////////////////////////////////////////////////////////
    //////////////////////
// CDLLTestAppView drawing
void CDLLTestAppView::OnDraw(CDC* pDC)
```

```
{
    CDLLTestAppDoc* pDoc = GetDocument();
    ASSERT_VALID(pDoc);
    // TODO: add draw code for native data here
}

//////////////////////////////////////////////////////////
    //////////////////////
// CDLLTestAppView diagnostics
#ifdef _DEBUG
void CDLLTestAppView::AssertValid() const
{
    CView::AssertValid();
}

void CDLLTestAppView::Dump(CDumpContext& dc) const
{
    CView::Dump(dc);
}

CDLLTestAppDoc* CDLLTestAppView::GetDocument() // non-
    debug version is inline
{
    ASSERT(m_pDocument-
    >IsKindOf(RUNTIME_CLASS(CDLLTestAppDoc)));
    return (CDLLTestAppDoc*)m_pDocument;
}
#endif //_DEBUG
//////////////////////////////////////////////////////////
    //////////////////////
// CDLLTestAppView message handlers
void CDLLTestAppView::OnDialogReceive()
{
    // Show the last message that was
    // input by the user.
    CTestClass myTestObj;
    myTestObj.ShowMessage(m_msg);
}

void CDLLTestAppView::OnDialogSend()
{
    // Instantiate the get-message dialog box.
    CDlgGetMsg dlgGetMsg;
    // m_msg = dlgGetMsg.m_editMsg;
    // Display the get-message dialog box.
    dlgGetMsg.DoModal();
    // Copy the user's entry into this class's
    // local m_msg variable.
```

```
    m_msg = dlgGetMsg.m_editMsg;
}
```

Summary

There are three ways to write a DLL for a Windows 95 program: the Windows 3.*x* way (for Windows 3.*x* applications), the Visual C++ 1.0 way (for programs written after the introduction of Visual C++ 1.0 but before the premiere of Visual C++ 4.0), and the MFC 4.0 way (for Windows 95 and Windows NT programs written using Visual C++ 4.0 and Version 4.0 of the Microsoft Foundation Class Library).

Window 3.*x* DLLs are clunky but are likely to be around for a long time, so you never know when you'll encounter the need to use one. Similarly, if you ever encounter a Visual C++ 1.0 DLL, a knowledge of how it works could come in handy.

This chapter focused mainly MFC 4.0 DLLs—which come in several varieties—and showed you how you can use them in your applications. MFC 4.0 DLLs can be generated automatically by AppWizard, and can be used to create and export MFC extension classes—that is, classes that automatically become extensions to Microsoft's MFC library. When you create a Microsoft extension class in an extension DLL, any MFC-compatible application loaded into a computer system's memory can use your class.

This chapter concluded with an example application that showed how to create an MFC extension DLL using AppWizard, and how to access that class from a Visual C++ program.

Chapter

11

Windows 95 Networking

Windows 95 is superhighway-friendly and Internet-ready. The TCP/IP communications protocol, the most direct gateway to the Internet, is built right into Windows 95. And support for many other kinds of communications mechanisms is built in, too.

The information superhighway makes the headlines so often these days that it would be very strange if Windows 95 did not have support for the information superhighway (including the Internet) built in.

Well, there are no surprises. Windows 95 is superhighway-friendly and Internet-ready. The TCP/IP communications protocol, the most direct gateway to the Internet, is built right into Windows 95. And support for many other kinds of communications mechanisms is built in, too.

This chapter introduces the Windows Sockets API, which you can use to equip your Windows 95 applications with support for TCP/IP and other communications protocols. It also introduces the MFC classes CasyncSocket and CSocket, which make it easier to use the TCP/IP protocol. Finally, it presents an example program that demonstrates how you can use TCP/IP to set up communications between a pair of Windows 95 systems, a pair of Windows NT systems, or a mixture of Windows 95 workstations and Windows NT workstations or servers.The following are the major topics covered in this chapter:

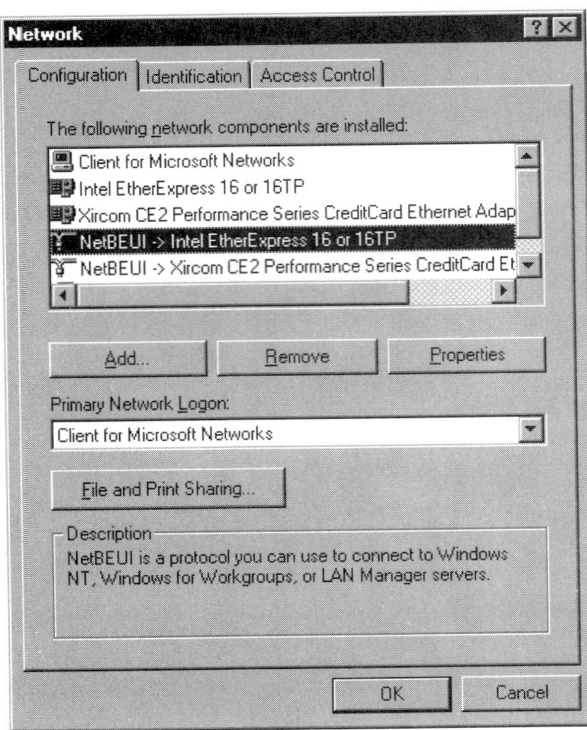

Figure 11.1 Network property sheet

Installing TCP/IP

The TCP/IP network protocol is one of several protocol services provided by Microsoft with Windows 95. You'll learn much more about TCP/IP in this chapter. If you're a Windows 95 user, one of the most important things to learn about TCP/IP is how to install it on your Windows 95 workstation.

If you need to install TCP/IP on a Windows 95 workstation, the chapter may provide you with a lot of help, because many important facts about the installation and use of TCP/IP are missing from the documentation provided with Windows 95.

This chapter provides a step-by-step guide designed to help you install TCP/IP on a Windows 95 workstation. You can install TCP/IP at the same time you install Windows 95, or you can do it later. It doesn't matter which kind of installation procedure you use; the steps are the same.

TCP/IP Installation Step by Step

✔ To install TCP/IP on your Windows 95 system, follow these steps:

1. From the Windows 95 Control panel, select the **Network** icon.
2. When the **Network** property sheet (Figure 11.1 on Page 536) appears, click the **Add** button.
3. The TCP/IP installer now opens a dialog box labeled **Select Network Component Type**. Double-click the **Protocol** icon, as shown in Figure 11.2.
4. Click the **Add** button.

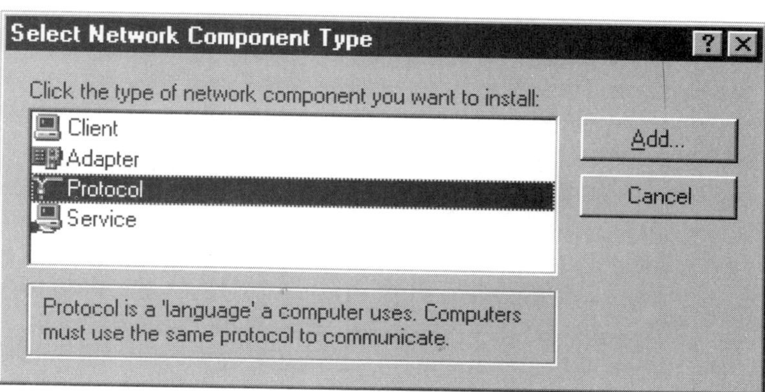

Figure 11.2 The Select Network Component Type dialog box

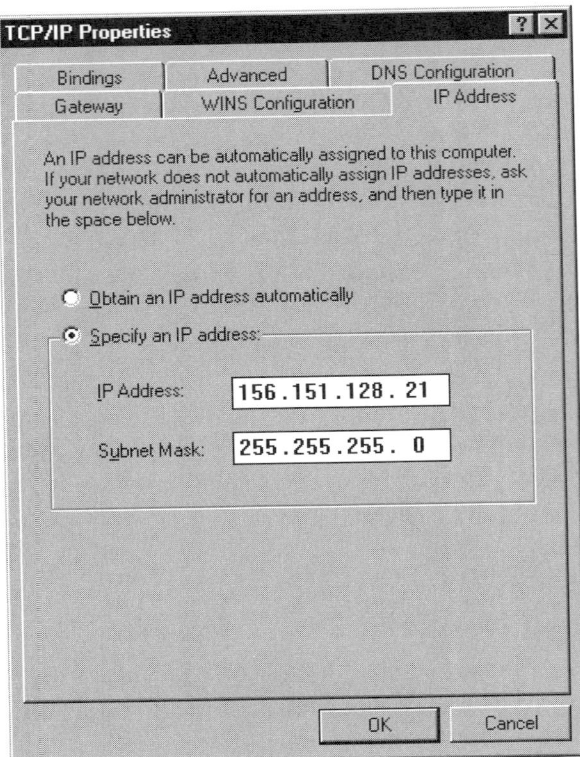

Figure 11.3 TCP/IP Configuration dialog box

5. When the **Select Network Protocol** dialog box appears, select the name of a vendor in the **Manufacturers** list box. Choose the vendor of the TCP/IP networking products installed at your site. For example, if you want to use the TCP/IP protocol that's built into Windows 95, select the **Microsoft** item. (If your Windows 95 workstation is connected to a network at your work site, you may have to ask your network administrator what manufacturer name you should select.)
6. In the **Network Products** list box, select **TCP/IP**.
7. Close the **Select Network Protocol** dialog box by clicking **OK**. When the Network property sheet regains the focus, notice that at least one new TCP/IP item has been added to the drop-down combo box that displays installed components. Select the TCP/IP item that appears to the network card you have installed and click the **Properties** button.

8. When the TCP/IP installer opens a property sheet titled **TCP/IP Properties** (shown in Figure 11.3 on page 538), tab to each property sheet that is available and fill in the requested information. You may have to obtain some of this information from your network administrator. On the items to be filled in are:
   - **IP Address**: Your Window's 95 server's IP address. (To learn about IP addresses, see "IP Addresses" on page 552.)
   - **Subnet Mask**: The subnet mask (see "Subnets and Subnet Masks" on page 555) that is used to access your server's IP address.
   - **Bindings**: the network components that will communicate using TCP/IP.
   - **Gateway**: The IP address of your system's default gateway (if there is one).
   - **DNS configuration**: Information related to DNS, a service for automatically locating IP addresses. You can disable DNS if your site doesn't use it. (For more about DNS addresses, see "Domain Name Services" on page 565).
   - **Advanced**: There's one entry on this property page that isn't really advanced: You can choose TCP/IP as your workstation's default protocol by checking the check box at the bottom of the **Advanced** property page.
9. Close the **TCP/IP Properties** dialog box by clicking the **OK** button.
10. When the **Network** dialog box comes back into focus, tab to the **Identification** property page and fill in your computer's name (assigned by your network administrator), you workgroup's name (also assigned by your network administrator), and an optional description of your computer.l
11. Close the **Network** dialog box by clicking the **OK** button.
12. Check to see whether your network administrator has installed the correct HOSTS, PROTOCOL, and SERVOICES files on your system. If not, you may have to open a **Notepad** window from the Windows 95 desktop and customize your computer's HOSTS, PROTOCOL, and SERVICES files. To learn more about these three files, see "The HOSTS File" on page 564, "TCP/IP Name Services" on page 564, and "Port Numbers and the SERVICES File" on page 559.
13. When you have configured your TCP/IP software, you'll have to shut down your computer and restart it to put your new configuration into effect. When your system starts up again, you'll have to log on.

Berkeley Sockets and Windows Sockets

The Windows Sockets API, which you will learn about later in this chapter, is based the Berkeley Software Distribution (BSD) Sockets design. In fact, the Windows Sockets API has incorporated into Windows Sockets, and is compliant with Release 4.3 of the Berkeley Software Distribution (4.3BSD). But the Windows Sockets API, as you will see, has a number of extensions that are not found in the BSD sockets protocol.

Windows Sockets are described in "The Windows Sockets API" on page 568.

Writing a TCP/IP-Aware Application

Once TCP/IP is installed on your Windows 95 system, it's easy to create a Visual C++ application framework that recognizes the TCP/IP protocol. And once you have an application framework that is TCP/IP-aware, you have all you need to start developing networking software for Windows 95.

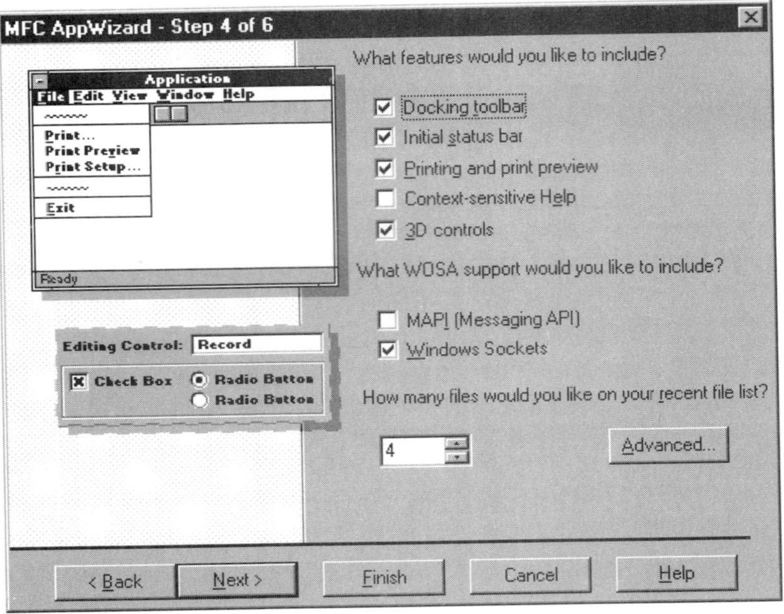

Figure 11.4 Creating a TCP/IP-aware application

To create an TCP/IP-aware application framework, follow these steps:

- Start Developer Studio if it isn't already started.
- Choose the **File | New** menu item.
- When the **New** dialog box opens, choose the **Project Workshop** list-box item and click OK.
- When the **New Project Workspace** dialog box appears, type a name for your application in the **Name** text box.
- When the fourth AppWizard dialog box opens, check the Windows Sockets check box, as shown in Figure 11.4 on Page 540.
- To finish creating your program, click the **Next** buttons in the sixth and seventh AppWizard dialog boxes and the **Finish** button in AppWizard dialog box No. 6.

TCP/IP and the Windows Sockets API

In the world of international politics, diplomatic protocols can smooth the relations between nations separated by cultural and historical differences. Similarly, in the world of computer communications, protocols make it possible for different kinds of hardware and software to get along together even though they might have different native languages.

TCP/IP is often referred to as a protocol, but it is actually a suite made up of many data-communications protocols. In fact, TCP/IP derives its name from two different protocols: the Transmission Control Protocol (TCP) and the Internet Protocol (IP). There are many other protocols in the TCP/IP suite, but TCP and IP are the two that are probably the most important.

To help you develop TCP/IP-related applications, Microsoft and other computer and communications companies use a special API called the Windows Sockets API. The Windows Sockets API has been around for a long time, and the complete API is built right into your Windows 95 system. Everything you need to write and use TCP/IP applications is right at your fingertips, supplied to you with Windows 95.

With the Windows Sockets API, you can create Windows 95 applications with full access to the Internet, and to many other kinds of computer networks, including Novell networks, Microsoft client-server networks, and many other kinds of wide-area networks (WANs) and local-area networks (LANs).

Windows Sockets Then and Now

Until Microsoft released Version 3.0 (that's right, Version 3.0) of the Microsoft Foundation Class (MFC) library, the only way to access the Windows Sockets API was to call its functions directly using C-style API function calls. And the Windows Sockets API is so full of gotchas that working with it was quite difficult—as you'll see later in this chapter. It required a lot of callbacks and the passing of some very strange parameters, so it was hard to work with the API using C++ programs.

Fortunately, MFC 3.0 came to the rescuers of Windows 95 developers who want to use the Windows sockets API. MFC 3.0 neatly encapsulates most of the functionality of the Windows Sockets API into two C++ classes, CasyncSocket and CSocket. Those two classes are also provided in MFC 4.0. You'll learn more about them later in this chapter.

Once you know what TCP/IP is and learn how to use it, you can start learning to write applications that make use of TCP/IP and several other popular protocols. Then you can connect to both the Internet and local-area networks using protocols built right into Windows 95.

The SOCKS Program and the Windows Sockets API

On the bonus disk that comes with this book, you'll find an example program named SOCKS, which can actually set up communications between a pair of Win32 systems. The SOCKS program demonstrates how you can use some of the most important functions in the Windows Sockets API in your Windows 95 programs.

Another bonus you'll find on your bonus disk is a public-domain online help file that contains the complete text of the Windows Sockets API, including the complete command set. It's hypertext-coded and ready for you to read, in the same way you read the online help files that come with Windows 95 and Visual C++.

How the SOCKS Program Works

The example program named SOCKS, which is listed at the end of this chapter, was written using the Windows Sockets API. The program starts the Windows Sockets TCP/IP and lets two users communicate with each other by sending messages across a network.

When you execute the SOCKS program, it opens a form-view window like the one shown in Figure 11.5 on Page 543. You can listen for incoming transmissions by clicking the **Listen** toolbar button (the ear glyph) or by selecting **Listen** from the sockets menu. By clicking the **Connect** toolbar button (the fingers) or selecting the **Connect** menu item, you can connect your workstation to another computer running the SOCKS program.

When the two machines connect, you and the user at the other end can send messages back and forth by typing them in the window labeled Input and clicking the Transmit toolbar button (the envelope blow an arrow). Whenever a message is received, or whenever you send one, it is displayed in the output window.

For more details on how the SOCKS program works, see the section titled "Example Program: SOCKS" on page 572.

If your Windows 95 system is not connected to a network, you can execute the program by launching two instances of it on the same machine.

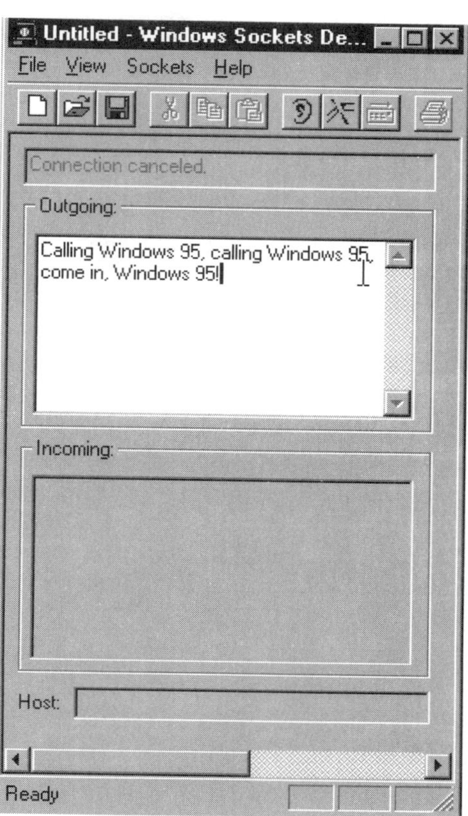

Figure 11.5 Output of the SOCKS program

The SOCKS program communicates directly with the Windows Sockets API, without any help from MFC or its CasyncSocket or CSocket classes. So you can run the program on compilers (such as the Borland C++ compiler) that do not support the use of the Microsoft Foundation Class library.

The user interface of the SOCKS program includes a set of toolbar buttons, a menu bar, and many other interesting features that you'll see when you start examining the program's source code. The source code for the program is provided, of course, in this chapter's directory on your bonus disk.

The TCP/IP Story

The TCP/IP story dates back to 1969. In that year, the Defense Advanced Research Projects Agency—sometimes fondly referred to as DARPA—funded a research and development project to create an experimental packet-switching network (packet-switching is how TCP/IP works—it moves data grouped into packets).

As part of its project, DARPA set up a computer network called the ARPANET to study techniques for providing reliable, vendor-independent communications that could interface a variety of client and host machines.

The Defense Department's ARPANET experiment was so successful that many other organizations both inside and outside the government were soon using it for day-to-day computer communications.

In 1975, ARPANET was promoted from experimental to operational status, and the Defense Communications Agency (DCA) took over the job of administering it. ARPANET kept on growing, and in 1983 it was split into two parts. Most of the network became MILNET, a military network used for unclassified communications. ARPANET remained on the network, but was considerably slimmed down. Together, MILNET and ARPANET were referred to as the Internet. ARPANET formally passed out of existence in 1990, but the Internet continued to grow, eventually becoming the monster it is today.

In 1983, the year the Internet was born, the first specifications for the TCP/IP protocols were published. They were part of a set of standards called the Military Standards (MIL STD). The government decreed that all host machines connected to the Internet were required to convert to the MIL STD protocols.

To make the conversion easier, DARPA bankrolled an effort by the firm of Bolt, Beranek, and Newman (BBN) to implement the TCP/IP in the Berkeley (BSD) version of the UNIX operating system. Since then, UNIX and TCP/IP have gone together like a horse and carriage. It's possible to have one without the other—as Windows 95 is proving—but UNIX and TCP/IP are so closely bonded that separating them successfully has never been a trivial operation.

Features of TCP/IP

TCP/IP did not achieve the fame it has today just because the government sponsored it—although that may helped (or maybe not). Anyway, it's also true that the TCP/IP protocols met an important need for worldwide computer communication, and they happened to have some features that made them especially suitable for fulfilling that need well.

These are three important features of the TCP/IP protocols:

- TCP/IP does not depend on any specific physical network hardware. This means that the TCP/IP protocols can integrate many different kinds of networks and can be run equally well using many different kinds of hardware. You can use TCP/IP on Ethernet, a token ring network, a dial-up line, an X.25 net, or almost any other kind of physical transmission hardware.
- The TCP/IP protocols provide open protocol standards, freely available and developed independently from any specific computer hardware or operating system. Internet aside, TCP/IP is so widely supported that it has proved to be a useful system for uniting different hardware and software.
- TCP/IP workstations and networks use a homogeneous and universally accepted addressing system that provides every TCP/IP network worldwide with a unique address. That makes every user's address accessible to every other user, regardless of any user's physical locations.

Networking Protocols

Earlier in this chapter, I mentioned that TCP/IP—although widely referred to a protocol—is actually a suite of protocols. The TCP/IP protocol suite is based on ISO reference model, a seven-layer communications stack developed by the International Standards Organization.

This architectural model, also called the Open Systems Interconnect (OSI) reference model, or OSI stack, has rarely (if ever) been implemented in its purest form by any hardware or software manufacturer.

But it does serve as a universally recognized model for communications systems. Figure 11.6 is a diagram of the OSI stack.

The TCP/IP protocol does not exactly match the OSI model. But the protocols that make up the TCP/IP protocol suite can also be arranged in a similar fashion, in a kind of stack that reflects some of the features of the OSI model.

Windows 95 and Windows NT make use of a protocol suite that is not exactly like the OSI model and is not exactly like the TCP/IP model. But it has elements in common with both, as you'll see later in this chapter.

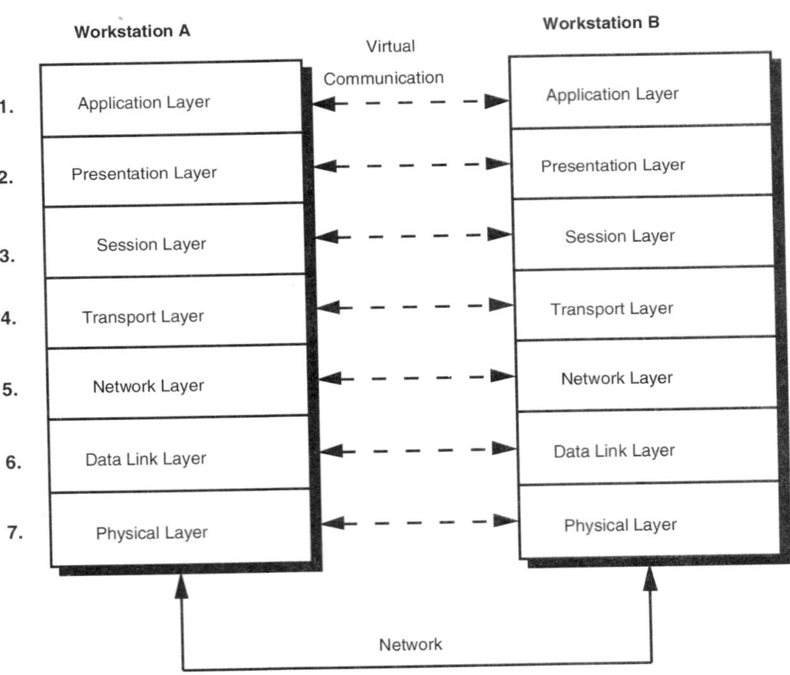

Figure 11.6 The OSI reference model

As Figure 11.6 illustrates, the OSI reference model is made up of seven layers of protocols that define the functions of data communications protocols. Each layer of the OSI model represents a function performed when applications or other software modules send messages to each other across a network.

When two software modules on the same layer of the stack communicate with each other across network, it appears to them as if they are communicating directly with each other. In fact, however, all their transmissions are being processed through lower layers of the stack—moving down the stack on the transmitting end, and moving up the stack on the end that is receiving.

Furthermore, a single services may span two or more layers of a stack. For example, in the Windows 95 stack, a mechanism called a *redirector* spans Layers 5, 6, and 7 of the OSI stack. Figure 11.7 illustrates the Windows 95 protocol stack.

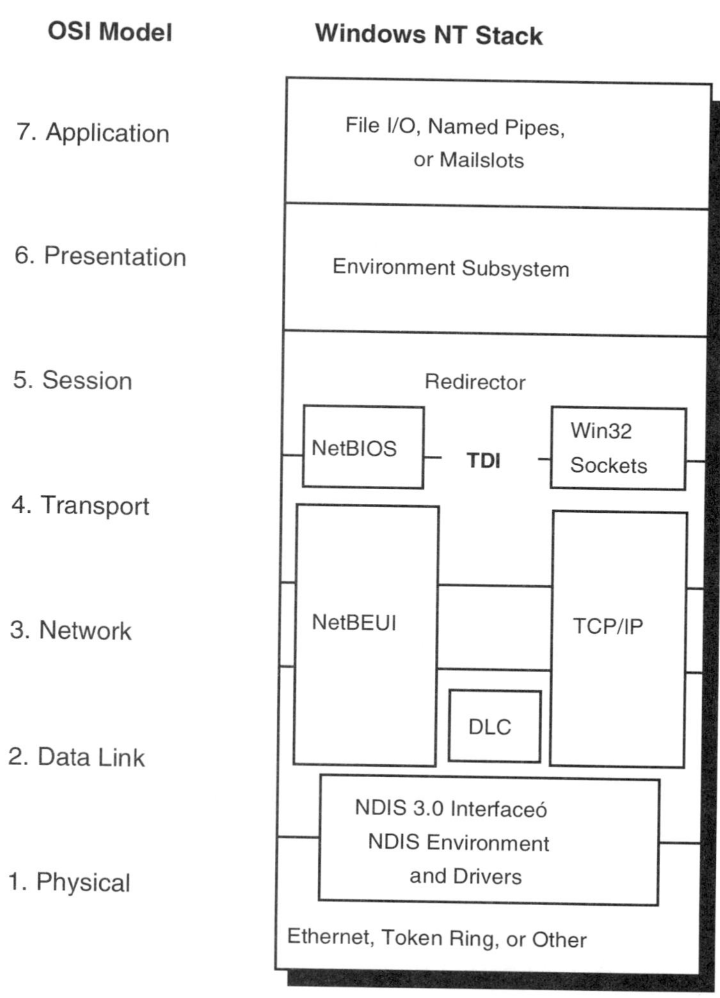

Figure 11.7 The Windows 95 protocol suite

As Figure 11.7 on Page 547 shows, a layer in a stack can contain multiple protocols, with each providing a service suitable to the function of that layer. For example, an electronic mail protocol and a file transfer protocol might occupy the same layer of the stack. Both provide user services, so both could be considered part of the application layer (Layer 7) of the OSI.

In the TCP/IP stack, as in the OSI reference model, data is passed down the stack when it is being sent to the net, and up the stack when it is being received from the network. In the TCP/IP model, each layer in the stack adds control information to the data that it handles to ensure proper delivery. This control information is placed at the beginning of the data being transmitted, and is therefore called a header. This addition of delivery information at every layer of the stack is called encapsulation.

The TCP/IP Protocol Suite

Although Windows 95 uses a protocol stack, the Windows 95 stack does not exactly match the OSI reference model. It should come as no surprise that although the TCP/IP protocols can also be grouped into a stack-like arrangement, that stack also differs from the OSI version.

In fact, the TCP/IP stack differs more from the OSI model than the Windows 95 protocol suite does. One reason is that the TCP/IP occupies only a portion of the OSI stack (a short stack?).

Experts differ on how the TCP/IP protocol stack should be represented. In fact, they even disagree on how many layers it has. Most descriptions of the TCP/IP stack say that it has three to five functional layers in the protocol architecture. The Department of Defense says there are four layers, and since the DOD set the original standard, that's the model used in this chapter.

Figure 11.8 on Page 549 shows how the TCP/IP protocol suite compares with the OSI reference model and the Windows 95 reference model.

When a computer using TCP/IP protocols receives data, it handles the data in the opposite fashion; each layer strips off the header that was added by its corresponding layer on the transmission stack. The receiving layer then passes the data along to the layer above it.

Let's look more closely at the function of each layer, working our way up from the network access layer to the application layer.

The Network Access Layer

The network access layer is the lowest layer in the TCP/IP stack. It can be seen as encompassing the functions of all three lowest layers of the OSI reference model: the network, data link, and physical layers. The protocols in this layer make it possible for the system to deliver data to the other devices on a directly attached network.

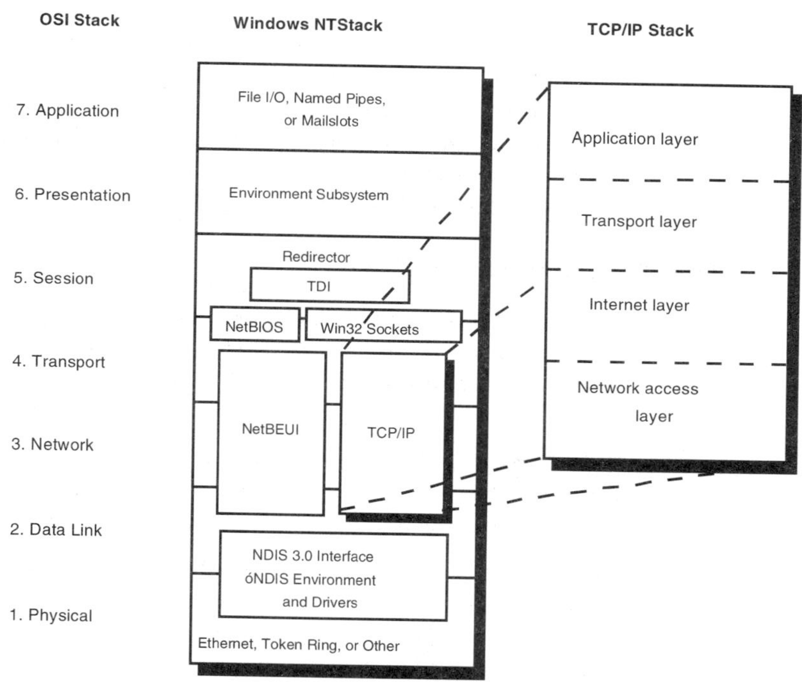

Figure 11.8 The TCP/IP protocol suite

The TCP/IP network access layer defines how the network transmits IP datagrams (see box titled "Streams and Packets" on page 551). APIs that reside at the network layer encapsulate IP datagrams into frames that can be transmitted by the network, and convert IP addresses into addresses appropriate for the physical network over which the datagram is transmitted.

The protocols in the network layer are often implemented as combinations of device drivers and related programs. Some network-layer modules encapsulate and deliver the data to the network, while others perform related functions such as address mapping.

The Internet Layer

The layer above the network access layer in the TCP/IP stack is the Internet layer. The Internet protocol, the basic building block of TCP/IP, is situated in the Internet layer. The Internet protocol, or IP, provides the basic packet delivery service on which TCP/IP networks are built. All other protocols—in the layers above and below IP—use the Internet protocol to deliver data. All TCP/IP data—incoming and outgoing—passes through the Internet protocol, regardless of its final destination.

Responsibilities of the Internet protocol include:

- Defining the datagram, which is the basic unit of transmission on the Internet
- Defining the Internet addressing system
- Breaking down datagrams and reassembling them into structures that can be transmitted across the network
- Moving data between the network access layer and the transport layer
- Routing datagrams to remote hosts.

The Transport Layer

The transport layer, also known as the host-to-host transport layer, lies just above the Internet layer in the TCP/IP stack. The two most important protocols in the transport layer are the transmission control protocol (TCP) and the user datagram protocol (UDP). Both protocols deliver data between the application layer and the Internet layer. When you write a network application, you can choose between the TCP protocol and the UDP protocol, picking the one you feel is best for your specific application.

If your application demands very reliable data delivery service with comprehensive error detection and correction, the protocol to pick is TCP. The transmission control protocol verifies that data is delivered across the network accurately and in the proper sequence.

If the application you are writing does not require a great deal of error checking—which may be the case if it provides its own error checking—you might decide to use the user data protocol. UDP is a less complex protocol that can send and receive messages with very little overhead.

UDP can come in handy in applications that transmit small amounts of data. When there is only a small amount of data to send, the overhead required for extensive error-checking may be greater than the work of simply retransmitting the data.

Streams and Packets

Different kinds of APIs send out data in different kinds of data structures. Different kinds of APIs also use different kinds of terminology to describe the structures they use for header encapsulation.

APIs that use the TCP/IP protocols are divided into main categories. Some APIs send data out in uninterrupted streams that work like file streams. When data is sent out in a stream, it goes to only one destination, and that destination cannot be changed without stopping the stream and then starting it up again.

Other APIs, sometimes called packet-driven APIs, divide data up into small packets before they send it out. By splitting a transmission up into packets, an API can send a transmission to any number of destinations by simply changing the transmission's destination address.

The most commonly used packet-based API used in TCP/IP communications is the User Datagram Protocol, or UDP. The most widely used stream-based API is the so-called Berkeley Software Distribution (BSD) Sockets API, which was developed at the University of California at Berkeley.

Packet-based protocols such as UDC have a couple of advantages over stream-based protocols in applications that need a convenient way to send short amounts of data over reliable transmission lines. UDC transmissions move fast and are easy to manage, but they are not as reliable as stream-based transmissions, especially when large amounts of data must be transmitted over facilities whose reliability is not guaranteed.

When you want to transmit considerable amounts of data over a network with guaranteed reliability, your best choice is a stream-based protocol—such as Windows Sockets, which you will learn more about in "The Windows Sockets API" on page 568.

Addresses and Port Numbers

TCP/IP transmits data in two steps. First, the data is transmitted over the network from a local machine to a remote machine. Then, within the machine that receives the data, the data is carried to the correct process.

To perform these two tasks, TCP/IP uses three mechanisms:

- *Gateways* that deliver data to the correct network.

- *IP addresses* that uniquely identify every network on the Internet and deliver data to the correct host.
- *Protocol addresses* and *port numbers*. When a transmission arrives at the workstation that is its destination, protocol addresses and port numbers deliver data to the correct software module within the host.

Network administrators are generally responsible for managing gateways; other Windows 95 users are more likely to be concerned with IP addresses and protocol and port numbers. So the following paragraphs focus on those topics.

IP and E-Mail Addresses

All Internet users have both a four-number IP address and an e-mail address, and they both mean the same thing. The e-mail address is written in the form *userName@ipName.extension*. For example, the IP address 156.151.128.21 is the same as the e-mail address: **marka@parvati.com**.

Most people put their e-mail addresses instead of their IP addresses on their business cards because most humans find it easier to remember words than to remember numbers. So most commercial e-mail software allows users to send and receive electronic mail using the character-based e-mail address system. When the user types in an e-mail address, the software converts the address to IP format automatically.

Even though e-mail addresses are used extensively in corporate and inter-office communications, online Internet directories almost always store user addresses in the IP format, so dedicated TCP/IP hackers also use IP addresses quite extensively.

IP Addresses

Every network on the Internet has a unique IP address. When you have an IP address, you're an Internet user, and any other Internet user can contact you.

Every IP address is written as four decimal numbers separated by periods, in this format:

156.151.128.21

Each of the four numbers in an IP address has a range of zero to 255, or 0x00 to 0xFF in hexadecimal notation. In hexadecimal notation, this is the range of possible values for one byte. So an Internet address is made up of four single-byte numbers, each one separated by a dot.

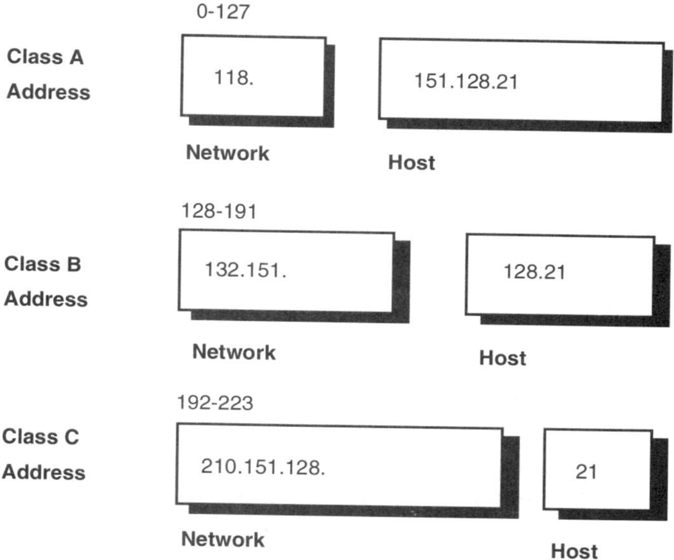

Figure 11.9 IP addresses

Classes and Categories of Internet Addresses

IP addresses are divided into four classes. The Internet maintains a limited number of addresses for very large networks—that is, networks with very large numbers of computers. There is a larger set of addresses for medium-size networks, and there is a still larger number of addresses for small networks.

The three categories of addresses are called Class A, Class B, and Class C. Class A is for very large networks, Class B is for medium-sized to large networks, and Class C is for small networks and individual users. Figure 11.9 shows the differences in Class A, B, and C addresses.

As Figure 11.9 illustrates, the first byte of an IP address determines the class of the address. This is how the three classes of IP addresses are divided:

- The first byte of a *Class A address* is always less than 128, or less than 0x80 in hexadecimal notation. In a class A address, the first byte is the number of a network, and the last three bytes are used designate the host computers on the network. The first address in Figure 11.9 is a Class A address.
- The first byte of a *Class B address* can range from 128 to 191, or from 0x80 to 0xBF in hexadecimal notation. The second byte can

have any value. The first two bytes identify the network and the last two bytes identify the host computers on the network. Because two bytes are used to designate the network, that leaves only the last two bytes to designate host machines. So a Class B address cannot accommodate nearly as many computers as a Class A address can. But a class B network can still include more than 65,000 computers. Subnet masks are described under the next heading. The second address in Figure 11.9 on Page 553 is a Class B address.

- The first byte of a *Class C address* can range from 192 to 223, or from 0xC0 to 0xDF in hexadecimal notation. The second and third bytes can have any values. The first three bytes identify the network and the last byte identifies the host. This arrangement of numbers restricts the number of a computers on a Class C network to around 250. (Some of the 256 individual integers are reserved and not available for use in addresses.) The third address in Figure 10.5 is a Class C address.
- If the first byte of an IP address is greater than 223 (0xDF), the address is reserved. You can ignore reserved addresses.

Figure 11.9 illustrates how the address structure varies with address class. The class A address is 26.104.0.19. The first bit of this address is 0, so the address is interpreted as host 104.0.19 on network 26. One byte specifies the network and three bytes specify the host. In the address 128.66.12.1, the two high-order bits are 1 and 0, so the address refers to host 12.1 on network 128.66. Two bytes identify the network and two identify the host. Finally, in the class C example, 192.178.16.1, the three high-order bits are 1 1 0, so this is the address of host 1 on network 192.178.16—three network bytes and one host byte.

There are some IP addresses that are not available for general use. It has already been noted that addresses with a first byte greater than 223 are reserved. There are also two class A addresses, 0 and 127, that are reserved for special uses. Network 0 designates what is known as a default route, and network 127 is known as a loopback address.

Default route 0 is used to simplify the routing information that IP must handle. Loopback address 127 simplifies network applications by allowing the local host to be addressed in the same manner as a remote host. You use these special network addresses when configuring a host.

Some host addresses are also reserved for special uses. In all network classes, host numbers 0 and 255 are reserved. An IP address with all host bits set to zero identifies the network itself. For example, 26.0.0.0 refers to network 26, and 128.66.0.0 refers to network 128.66.

Addresses in this form are used in routing table listings to refer to entire networks. An IP address with all bits set to one is a broadcast address. A broadcast address is used to simultaneously address every host on a network. The broadcast address for network 128.66 is 128.66.255.255. A datagram sent to this address is delivered to every individual host on network 128.66.

Subnets and Subnet Masks

A network manager can break a network down into subnetworks by applying subnet masks to the network's IP address. Subnet masks are recognized only by the networks that they apply to—not by the Internet.

When you apply a subnet mask to an Internet address, you shift the dividing line between the network portion of the address bits and the host portion of the address. This shift divides the network portion of the address into subnetworks. Some of the host workstations on the network can then belong to one subnetwork, and other workstations can belong to another.

Networks subnet for many reasons—often because subnetting permits the decentralized management of host addressing. Without subnetting, a single administrator is usually responsible for managing the host addresses on an entire network. By subnetting, the administrator can let subnet administrators handle portions of the network.

Geographical divisions and router allocation can also be reasons for subnetting. Routers and gateways can connect geographically separated subnets together if each physical network has a unique network address. Portions of networks that use different kinds of hardware can also be grouped together in subnets.

Creating a Subnet

To create a subnet, you apply a bit mask called a subnet mask to an IP address, as shown in Figure 11.10 on Page 556. If a bit is the mask is set, the equivalent bit in the IP address is interpreted as a network bit. If a bit in the mask is clear, the bit belongs to the host part of the address. Remember that this arrangement is recognized only within the affected network; to the rest of the Internet, the address is still interpreted as a standard class A, B, or C IP address.

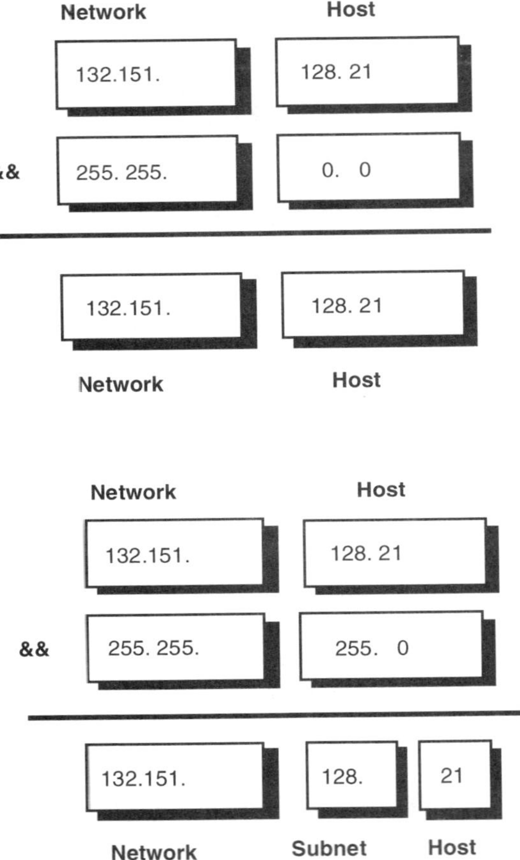

Figure 11.10 Subnet masks

Figure 11.10 shows how subnetting works. It illustrates the most commonly used kind of subnet mask, which extends the network portion of a class B address by an additional byte. As Figure 10.6 illustrates, the subnet mask that accomplishes this is 255.255.255.0

In the address 255.255.255.0, all bits are on in the first three bytes and all bits are off in the last byte. In Figure 11.10, two different subnet masks are applied to a Class B IP address.

In a Class B address, as noted earlier, the first two bytes define the network that the address belongs to, while the third and fourth bytes are used to identify the host machines on the net. Ordinarily, the subnet mask that is applied to a Class B address is 255.255.0.0, as shown in the top diagram in Figure 11.10. That results in a standard

Class B address, in which two bytes represent the user's network and two bytes represent the user's address.

When a different subnet mask is applied to a Class B address, it changes this arrangement, as shown in the lower drawing in Figure 11.10 on Page 556. When a subnet mask of 255.255.255.0 is applied to the same class B address, only the first byte of the user's address identifies the user's network. The second byte now identifies the use's subnet within the network, and the last byte is used to identify each workstation on that subnet.

Remember, though, that this change is visible only to workstations within the affected network. To the rest of the Internet, the address to which the subnet mask has been added is still a standard class B address—and still looks like the top drawing in the, just as before.

Subnet masks are often made up of only the numbers 0 and 255. However, that is not a requirement; other numbers can also be used. For example, you could divide a Class C address into four subnets by applying the subnet mask 255.255.255.192 (the number 192 is 0xC0 in hexadecimal notation). Applying this mask to a class C address defines the two high-order bits of the fourth byte as the subnet part of the address. That creates 16 subnets. Then the two low-order bits can be used to designate 16 host workstations on each subnet.

If you apply the mask 255.255.255.192 to a class B address, you create more than a thousand subnets, each of which can accommodate up to 16 workstations.

If don't want to bother with all this hexadecimal math, you can meet most networking needs by simply using a subnet mask of 255.255.255.0. If you have a Class C address, that usually means that you can connect more than 200 computers to your network without having to worry about subnetting.

Protocols, Ports, and Sockets

To find a computer on the Internet, all you need is a four-byte IP address. But when two computers start exchanging information, they need additional numbers to specify the kind of information that is being sent and received. These extra identifiers are called *protocol numbers* and *port numbers.*

The combination of an Internet address and a port number is called a *socket*.

When an API that resides on one computer needs to send data to an API on another computer, the transmitting API identifies itself to the receiving API by inserting a protocol number into the header of the datagram that it is sending.

To specify what kind of message it is sending, the transmitting API also sends the receiving API a second identifier called a port number. This number is also placed in the header of the datagram being sent.

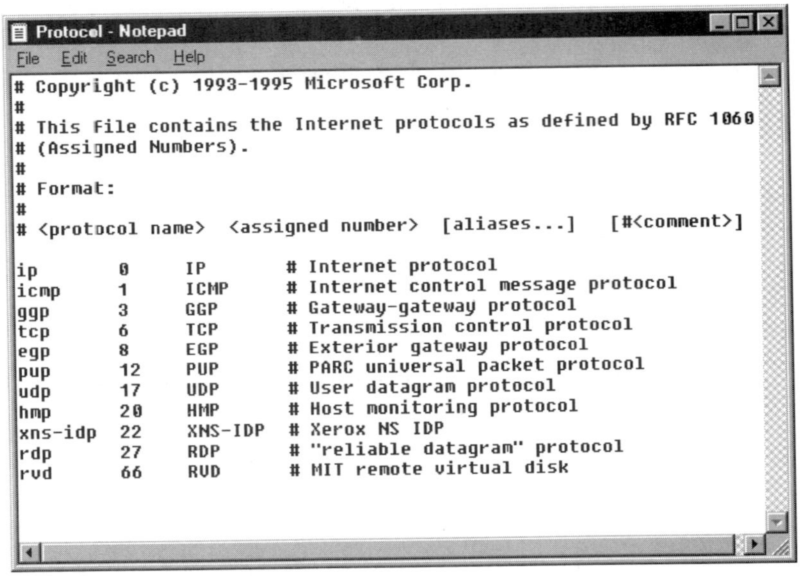

Protocol - Notepad

File Edit Search Help

```
# Copyright (c) 1993-1995 Microsoft Corp.
#
# This file contains the Internet protocols as defined by RFC 1060
# (Assigned Numbers).
#
# Format:
#
# <protocol name>  <assigned number>  [aliases...]   [#<comment>]

ip        0     IP        # Internet protocol
icmp      1     ICMP      # Internet control message protocol
ggp       3     GGP       # Gateway-gateway protocol
tcp       6     TCP       # Transmission control protocol
egp       8     EGP       # Exterior gateway protocol
pup       12    PUP       # PARC universal packet protocol
udp       17    UDP       # User datagram protocol
hmp       20    HMP       # Host monitoring protocol
xns-idp   22    XNS-IDP   # Xerox NS IDP
rdp       27    RDP       # "reliable datagram" protocol
rvd       66    RVD       # MIT remote virtual disk
```

Figure 11.11 The PROTOCOL file

Protocols and the PROTOCOL File

When your Windows 95 workstation receives a datagram from a remote computer, it interprets the protocol and port numbers in the datagram's header by consulting a text file named PROTOCOL. The PROTOCOL file is stored in the same directory as your Windows 95 system (by default, your WINDOWS directory). Figure 11.11 shows what the PROTOCOL file looks like when you first install TCP/IP on Windows 95.

The PROTOCOL file contains the name of each protocol that the Windows Sockets software recognizes, along with a number that represents each protocol name. Widely used protocols, often referred to as *well-known services*, have numbers that are recognized throughout the Internet. For instance, Protocol 0 is always the Internet protocol, which is officially named **ip**. And Protocol 20 is always the user datagram protocol, or **udp**.

There are many other well-known services on the Internet. They include standard network protocols such as FTP, which is used for file transfers, and TELNET, which is used to set up communications with IP addresses.

Briefly, this is how protocol numbers work:

1. When a datagram arrives at the correct IP address, the IP layer knows that the datagram must be delivered to one of the transport protocols situated above it in the TCP/IP stack. To determine which protocol should receive the datagram, the IP API checks the datagram's protocol number.
2. The IP API then delivers the datagram to the protocol that matches its protocol number. For example, if the protocol number is 6, IP delivers the datagram to TCP. If the protocol number is 17, the datagram goes to UDP.

Port Numbers and the SERVICES File

When the Internet protocol has passed incoming data to the transport protocol, the transport protocol passes the data to the correct application process. Application processes—also referred to as *network services*—are identified by16-bit values called *port numbers*.

Every datagram header contains two port numbers: a *source port number*, which identifies the process that sent the data, and a *destination port number*, which identifies the process that is to receive the data.

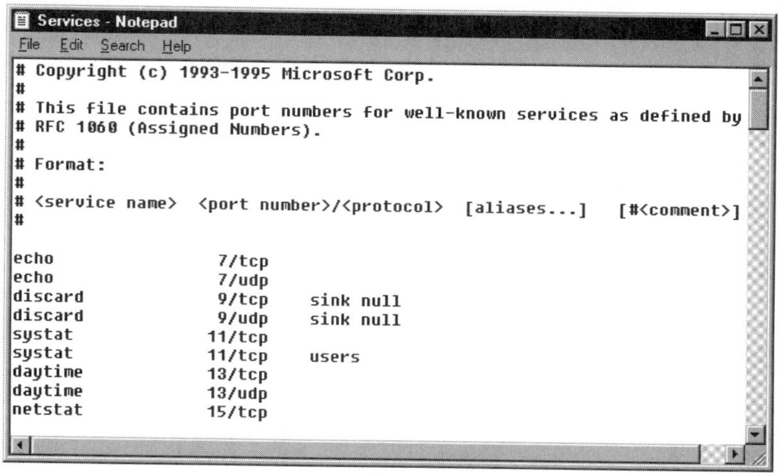

Services - Notepad

File Edit Search Help

```
# Copyright (c) 1993-1995 Microsoft Corp.
#
# This file contains port numbers for well-known services as defined by
# RFC 1060 (Assigned Numbers).
#
# Format:
#
# <service name>  <port number>/<protocol>  [aliases...]   [#<comment>]
#

echo                7/tcp
echo                7/udp
discard             9/tcp    sink null
discard             9/udp    sink null
systat             11/tcp
systat             11/tcp    users
daytime            13/tcp
daytime            13/udp
netstat            15/tcp
```

Figure 11.12 The SERVICES file

Port numbers, like protocol numbers, are kept in a text file that is placed in your Windows 95 directory (by default, your /WINDOWS directory when you install TCP/IP). The file in which port numbers are stored is called the SERVICES file. Figure 11.12 on Page 559 shows part of the SERVICES file that is installed in your system when you install TCP/IP.

The format of the SERVICES file is very similar to that of the PROTOCOLS file. The SERVICES file is formatted as a table. Each line contains four columns:

- The name of the protocol.
- The port number assigned to the service.
- An column in which you can place an optional alias for the protocol. When you have placed an alias for a protocol in your computer's SERVICES file, you can access the protocol from TCP/IP-aware applications using the alias you have defined. Alias stored on your workstations are private to your computer system. You can define multiple aliases for the same protocol by placing them on different lines in your SERVICES file.
- A column for comments. Each comment is preceded by a "**#**" symbol.

Port numbers are not unique between transport layer protocols; they are only unique within a specific transport protocol. TCP and UDP can, and do, both assign the same port numbers to different services. This system works because each protocol listed in the PROTOCOL file is assigned two numbers: one specifying its protocol number and the other specifying its port number. Together, these two numbers uniquely identify a specific process that data should be delivered to.

All port numbers below 256 are reserved for well-known services. Port numbers that range from 256 to 1024 are used for services such as **rlogin** (a remote login service) that were originally developed especially for UNIX systems. However, most of these services, including **rlogin**, are no longer UNIX- specific.

Sockets

When a computer on the Internet sends a datagram to another computer, the header of the datagram that is being sent not only includes the recipient's IP address; it also contains a second identifier that is made up of a protocol number and a port number. With this protocol/port identifier, the recipient's TCP/IP API can route the datagram to the appropriate protocol and to the correct port.

The protocol/port identifier that a TCP/IP workstation creates does not have any name that I know of. But when you add a protocol/port identifier to the end of an IP address, what you wind up with is a *socket*. A socket, then, is a combination of an IP address and a combination protocol/port number.

A conventional way to express a socket number is to follow a conventional three-byte IP address with an additional dot, followed by an additional number. For example, an IP address and a socket number could be expressed as follows:

156.151.128.21.3382

A Note on Terminology

Sometimes the terms "socket" and "port number" are used interchangeably. In fact, well-known services are frequently referred to as "well-known sockets." In this chapter, the word socket is used in its unambiguous sense: to identify the combination of an IP address and a port number.

The first four numbers in this example make up an IP address. The fifth number, 3382, is a socket number.

As you can see, a socket is a number that uniquely identifies a single network process within a single IP address. Thus, a socket uniquely identifies a single network process throughout the entire Internet.

Dynamically Assigned Sockets

When a workstation sends a datagram to another workstation, two different socket identifiers are needed: one for the transmitting workstation and another for the recipient. If only one socket number were used, it would identify the protocol and port at only one end of the transmission. Two socket numbers are needed because every transmission has two ends.

To distinguish between the protocol and port identifier used by a transmitting workstation and the protocol and port identifier used by the recipient of a datagram, the transmitting workstation dynamically allocates its own socket identifier and uses well-known protocol and port numbers to specify the identifier of the destination socket.

To allocate its own socket identifier dynamically, the transmitting station simply assigns its originating socket an arbitrary number. It then places that socket number in the header of the datagram that it is transmitting.

To identify the socket that it is transmitting to, the originator of the datagram uses a well-known socket identifier. To identify its own socket, the originating workstation uses the socket identifier that if has dynamically assigned. This procedure is illustrated in Figure 11.13 on Page 563.

In Figure 11.13, Workstation A—the originator of a datagram—is dispatching a message to a recipient, Workstation B. Workstation A is sending its message to Port 23.

Port 23 is the port number of **`telnet`**, a well-known API. The job of the **`telnet`** API is to send and receive messages.

To send its datagram to the telnet port, Machine A addresses its datagram to Port 23.

You can see from the diagram that Machine A has addressed its message to Port 23 on Workstation B. But you can't tell what port the message is originating from on Workstation A. It looks as if it is originating from Port 3024, but that can't be a real port because it lies outside the range of well-known port numbers.

Let's assume, though, that the message coming from Workstation A is being transmitted by Port 23, the **`telnet`** port number. Messages being transmitted from a particular port on one machine to the same port on another machine use identical port numbers, so Workstation A cannot use Port 23 to identify the origin of the datagram it is sending—even though the datagram is originating from Port 23. Therefore, Workstation A uses an arbitrary number—3024—as a return address for this particular datagram.

In the header of its datagram, Workstation A identifies the return address of its datagram as 3024. Workstation B has no way of knowing that this number is an alias for Port 23. However, Workstation B knows all it needs to know to send the datagram to its proper port—and, as we shall see, Workstation B also knows all it needs to know to address its reply to the correct port when it sends its reply back to Workstation A.

Workstation B knows that the datagram should go to Port 23 because Workstation B has addressed its datagram to Port 23, and Port 23 is a well-known port number. Workstation B also knows that when it replies to Workstation A's datagram, it should send its reply to Port 3024.

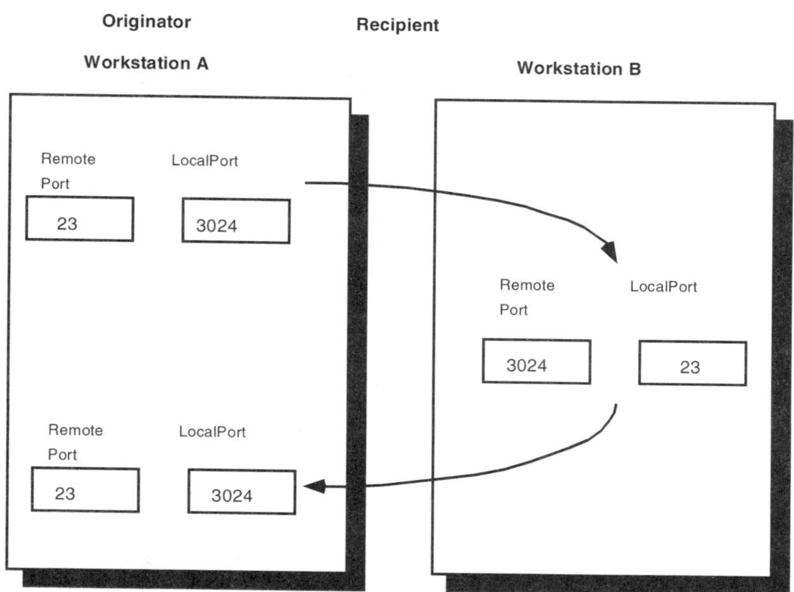

Figure 11.13 Sending and receiving a datagram

Workstation B has never heard of Port 3024 because it's a number that Workstation A made up. But that's OK. When Workstation B replies to the message, it simply sends its reply to Port 3024, even though it knows that's a phony port number.

When Workstation B's reply gets back to Workstation A, addressed to a port number that doesn't really exist, Workstation A knows that the reply is intended for Port 23 because Workstation A is the machine that made up the number 3024 in the first place. So Workstation B's reply finally makes it back to Port 23 on Workstation A, the port that sent out the original datagram.

Figure 11.13 illustrates this scenario. The operation is made possible by the fact that socket numbers don't always have to identify well-known sockets; when a workstation transmits a datagram to another workstation, TCP/IP rules allow the transmitter of the message to use a socket number that is dynamically assigned.

The TCP/IP API has built-in mechanisms for ensuring that it does not dynamically assign duplicate port numbers to multiple processes, and that the numbers that it assigns fall outside the range of standard port numbers.

TCP/IP Name Services

Recall that every network interface attached to a TCP/IP network has a unique 32-bit IP address. Unfortunately, the numbers that make up IP addresses are difficult to remember and type correctly. So sites often use pronounceable names rather than IP addresses to communicate over networks.

To provide easy-to-use aliases for IP addresses, the TCP/IP protocol provides a mechanism called *host names*. When an IP address has been associated with a host name, the host name can be used in place of its associated address in TCP/IP-aware applications.

There are two common methods for translating host names into IP addresses. One method is to use a *host table*—a text file that resides on your Windows 95 workstation. Another way to convert a host name into an IP address is to use a TCP/IP utility called the Domain Name Service, or DNS.

The HOSTS File

A sample HOSTS file, named HOST.SAM, is automatically placed in your system's Windows 95 directory (by default, the /WINDOWS directory) when you install TCP/IP. Figure 11.14 on Page 565 shows part of this sample Windows 95 HOSTS file. The Domain Name Service is a database that can be maintained by the administrators of your TCP/IP site. When you install TCP/IP on your Windows 95 workstation, you can configure it to use a DNS database by setting the appropriate options in the **TCP/IP Properties** property page (see "Installing TCP/IP" on page 537).

When you create aliases for IP addresses using a HOSTS file, your aliases are accessible only on your individual computer system—unless your machine is configured to be a DNS server. If your computer is a DNS server, other computers on your network can access your aliases. DNS servers are generally set up by network administrators.

A HOSTS file—like a PROTOCOL file or a SERVICES file—is formatted as a table. Each line contains either two or three entries. The first entry is always an IP address. The second entry is a host name that corresponds to the specified address. The third entry is an optional comment preceded by a "**#**" symbol.

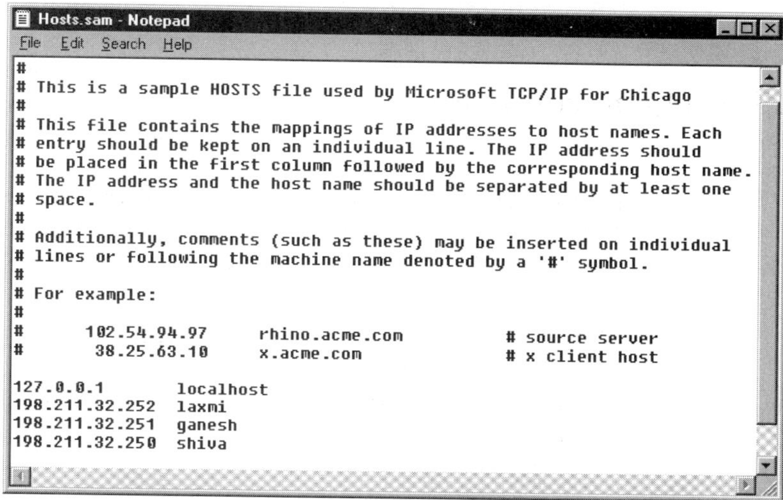

Hosts.sam - Notepad

File Edit Search Help

```
#
# This is a sample HOSTS file used by Microsoft TCP/IP for Chicago
#
# This file contains the mappings of IP addresses to host names. Each
# entry should be kept on an individual line. The IP address should
# be placed in the first column followed by the corresponding host name.
# The IP address and the host name should be separated by at least one
# space.
#
# Additionally, comments (such as these) may be inserted on individual
# lines or following the machine name denoted by a '#' symbol.
#
# For example:
#
#      102.54.94.97     rhino.acme.com          # source server
#       38.25.63.10     x.acme.com              # x client host

127.0.0.1       localhost
198.211.32.252  laxmi
198.211.32.251  ganesh
198.211.32.250  shiva
```

Figure 11.14 A Windows 95 HOSTS file

Domain Name Services

It can be difficult and time-consuming for sites to maintain individual HOSTS files stored on individual machines. An easier way to keep track of hosts that are used by a site is to provide a central DNS database in which the names of hosts can be stored. Generally, Domain Name Service databases are maintained by network administrators.

Fortunately, HOSTS tables and a Domain Name Services are not mutually exclusive mechanisms for storing host names. If you like, you can maintain a HOSTS table on your local Windows 95 workstation and also use one or more DNS databases. When you configure TCP/IP on your Windows 95 workstation, you can activate or deactivate Domain Name Services—and specify as many DNS servers you want to access—using the **DNS Configuration** page of the **TCP/IP Properties** property sheet (see Figure 11.15 on Page 566).

Obtaining an IP Address

If you want to become a TCP/IP user, you must obtain an IP address. There are four common ways to do that:

- Get your own Internet address directly from the Internet's administrators.

- Work for an organization or be affiliated with an organization or institution that has an Internet address.
- Rent an Internet connection from a commercial provider.
- Connect to the Internet through a commercial information system such as CompuServe, America Online, or Prodigy.

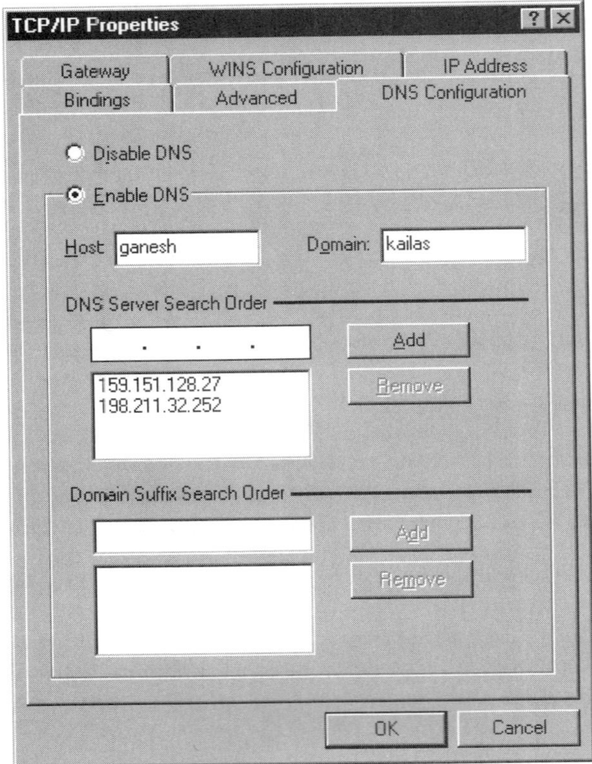

Figure 11.15 The CNS Configuration property page

Connecting Directly to the Internet

The most direct way is to obtain forms from the Internet's DDN Network Information Center (NIC), and to fill them out and send them in. That will get you a permanent Internet address that you can carry with you forever, like your Social Security number. But it won't connect you to the Internet.

To connect to the Internet, you'll still have to go to a commercial provider or (currently, at considerable expense for an individual computer user) obtain the hardware that it takes to set up a direct connection.

Obtaining a network address from the NIC is simple and costs nothing, and you can do it by either postal mail or electronic mail. The NIC'S mailing address is:

DDN Network Information Center
14200 PARK Meadow Drive
Suite 200
Chantilly, VA 22021

DDN's e-mail address is **hostmaster@nic.ddn.mil**. The organization's telephone numbers are 1-800-365-3642 and 1-703-802-4535.

Obtaining an IP Address through a Company or Organization

An easy way to obtain an Internet address is to work for an organization that has an Internet address, or to be affiliated in some other way with an organization or institution that has one. In this case, you can see your network or Internet administrator and request an e-mail address. Then you can use that to connect to the Internet.

This approach is simple and doesn't cost anything, but if you ever leave the company, organization, or institution that provides you with your e-mail address, you will lose it.

Connecting to the Internet through a Commercial Provider

There are several telecommunications companies that can provide you with your own connection to the Internet—and your own private Internet address—for a monthly fee. Although this method of getting an IP address costs money, it is probably no more expensive than signing up with a commercial (and more limited) commercial network such as CompuServe, America Online, or Prodigy.

Most companies that provide Internet connections offer at least two different kinds of services. You can choose what is known as a shell service, which offers a limited kind of access to the Internet, or you can select a full-service connection, which costs more but lets you take advantage of all the services that the Internet offers.

If you have an ordinary (non-TCP/IP) telecommunications program such as CrossTalk or ProComm Plus, a shell service is what you need. With a shell service, you can browse through files on the Internet, chat with other users, and read news items and bulletin boards. But you can't execute TCP/IP commands from your Windows 95 workstation.

If you own a real TCP/IP software package, such as Chameleon from NetManage or PC/TCP from FTP Software, you'll need a full-service

Internet connection to tap the power that your telecommunications software has.

With a full-service connection, you can execute TCP/IP commands such as **ftp** (for file transfers) and even run remote applications from your 95-equipped PC, just as if you were sitting at a UNIX workstation. (If you're communicating through a modem instead of over a direct wire, things will run more slowly, of course, but that will be a limitation on your end of the system, not a limitation of your Internet connection.

Companies that can provide you with an Internet connection include Netcom of San Jose, CA (408-554-8649 or **info@netcom.com**), Performance Systems International (PSInet) of Reston, VA (703-620-6551 or **info@psi.com**), Portal Communications of Cupertino, CA (408-973-9111 or **cs@cup.portal.com**), and Whole Earth 'Lectronic Link (the WELL), Sausalito, CA (415-332-4335 or **info@well.-sf.ca.us**).

These are not the only companies that provide Internet connections for a fee. There are dozens of others. You can obtain an up-to-date list of them from:

NSF Network Service Center (NNSC)
BBN Laboratories Inc.
10 Moulton St.
Cambridge, MA 02138

NFC's telephone number is 617-873-3361. The organization's e-mail address is **nnsc@nnsc.nsf.net**.

The Windows Sockets API

The Windows Sockets API defines a network programming interface for Microsoft Windows. This interface is based on the Berkeley Software Distribution (BSD) programming model, which is the *de facto* standard for TCP/IP networking. The Windows Sockets API contains all the functionality of BSD Sockets—often referred to as Berkeley Sockets— along with a set of extensions that provide extra features for Windows programmers.

The Windows Sockets API was originally engineered to work with the 16-bit Windows operating system. It was designed to appeal to software designers who were familiar with writing sockets applications for UNIX and other non-Windows environments, and to simplify the task of porting existing sockets-based source code to Windows.

The 16-bit Windows Sockets API contains all of the familiar Berkeley Sockets-style routines, plus a set of Windows-specific extensions designed to allow programmers to take advantage of the message-driven design of Window programs.

The Windows Sockets API for Windows 95 is a 32-bit version of the original Windows Sockets API. It is designed to be compatible within all implementations and versions of Microsoft Windows, from Version 3.0 onwards. It supports Windows Sockets implementations and Windows Sockets applications in both 16-bit and 32-bit operating environments. Windows Sockets for Windows 95 also supports multi-threaded Windows processes.

BSD Sockets and Windows Sockets

The Windows Sockets API contains two sets of functions: one set that corresponds to the functions defined in the BSD Sockets API, and another set that contains Windows-specific extensions.

It's easy to tell the difference between the BSD-style functions in the Windows API and the Windows-specific extensions that the API contains. The BSD-style functions are typed in all-lowercase letters. All the Windows-specific functions are typed in a mixture of upper-case and lowercase letters. Also, they all begin with the letters **WSA**, which stand for "Windows Sockets API."

Blocking and Nonblocking Functions

A more important difference between the BSD and Windows function sets is that the Windows set contains a group of functions that solve a common problem in TCP/IP programming: a problem called blocking.

Blocking occurs when a function starts an operation and does not return until the operation is complete. Blocking generally causes no problem when a function carries out a fast operation and returns immediately. But blocking can become a serious problem when a function takes a long time to finish what it is doing and return.

Blocking can become an extremely serious problem when a function has the task of sitting and waiting to receive a transmission from a remote system. When a blocking function is assigned this kind of role in a program, it simply stops the program until it receives the transmission it is waiting for. If the transmission never arrives, the system hangs up forever.

Windows Sockets has addressed this problem by adding a group of non-blocking functions to the function set provided by the BSD Sockets API. All these functions begin with the letters **WSAAsync**. For example, the **WSAAsyncSelect** function instructs Windows Sockets to send a message to a specified window when it detects a specified event.

WSAAsyncSelect is a nonblocking function, so it can wait for an incoming transmission without blocking other functions. That makes it an ideal alternative to the BSD function **recv**, which is a blocking function.

When you write applications that make use of Windows Sockets, you should always use the nonblocking functions provided by the Windows Sockets extensions rather than the BSD-style blocking functions inherited from the BSD Sockets API.

MFC and the Windows Sockets API

The Microsoft Foundation Class library now includes two classes that are designed to simplify the use of the Windows Sockets API. These two new functions are named CasyncSocket and CSocket.

A CasyncSocket object encapsulates the Windows Sockets API, providing an object-oriented abstraction that makes it much easier to use Windows Sockets in an MFC program. If you are working solely on the Win32 platform—that is, on either Windows 95 or Windows NT—you can take advantage of additional socket functionality built into those two operating systems.

Using Threads to Write Nonblocking Functions

In a Windows 95 application, there is an alternative to using non-blocking Windows Sockets functions to overcome the blocking limitations of BSD functions. The alternative is to write a multithreaded application that can prevent blocking functions from hanging the system by implemented blocking functions in threads.

While you may find it interesting to experiment with this approach, you should remember that multithreaded applications can't be ported to Windows environments that don't support threading, so an application that uses multiple threads is not as portable as one that doesn't. Also, threads are more difficult to manage than the nonblocking functions that the Windows Sockets API supplies. So I consider the Windows Sockets nonblocking functions to be the better alternative.

Using the CasyncSocket Class

To use a CasyncSocket object, you must include the AFXSOCK.H header file in your application. To instantiate a CasyncSocket object, call its constructor and then call the **CasyncSocket::Create** member function. The **CasyncSocket::Create** member function creates the a socket handle (type SOCKET) that provides the Casync-Socket class with its underlying functionality.

When you have instantiated a CasyncSocket object, you can create a server socket by calling the **Listen** member function, or you can create a client socket by calling call the **Connect** member function. Subsequently, when the server socket receives a connection request, it calls the **Accept** function. Other CasyncSocket member functions can be used to carry out communications between sockets.

When it's time to terminate your TC/IP communications, you must destroy your CasyncSocket object if it was created on the heap by calling its destructor. The CasyncSocket class's destructor automatically cleans everything up by calling a **Close** function.

Using the CSocket Class

The CSocket class is derived from the CasyncSocket class. CSocket inherits an encapsulation of the Windows Sockets API from Casync-Socket. CSocket, like CasyncSocket, requires you to include the AFXSOCK.H header file in your application.

A CSocket object represents a higher level of abstraction of the Windows Sockets API than that of a CAsyncSocket object. CSocket works with classes CSocketFile and CArchive to manage the sending and receiving of data.

A CSocket object also provides blocking (see "Blocking and Nonblocking Functions" on page 569), which is essential to the synchronous operation of the CArchive class. (You'll need to use the CArchive class if you want your application to support the serialization, or automatic saving and loading, of files.)

When you use CSocket, blocking functions—such as **Receive**, **Send**, **ReceiveFrom**, **SendTo**, and **Accept** (all inherited from CAsync-Socket)—do not return a an error when communications are blocked. (In contrast, a CAsyncSocket object does return an error message.) Instead, CSocket's blocking member functions wait until the operation completes. (An exception: the original call terminates with the error WSAEINTR if the **CancelBlockingCall** is called while a CSocket blocking function is blocking.)

To create a CSocket object, you follow the same procedure used to create a CAsyncSocket object: You call the object's constructor and then call **Create** to create the underlying socket handle (type SOCKET). The default parameters of the **Create** member function create a stream socket, but if you are not using the socket with a CArchive object, you can specify a parameter to create a datagram socket instead, or bind to a specific port to create a server socket.

When you have created a CSocket object, you can connect to a client socket using **Connect** on the client side and **Accept** on the server side. Next, you create a CSocketFile object and associate it with the CSocket object in the CSocketFile constructor.

After you have done all that, you can create a CArchive object for sending and one for receiving data, as needed. Then you can associate each of these archive objects with the CSocketFile object in the CArchive constructor.

When communications are complete, you must destroy the CArchive, CSocketFile, and CSocket objects.

Example Program: SOCKS

This chapter's sample program, SOCKS, demonstrates how you can use the functions provided in the Windows Sockets API to write your own TCP/IP-based applications.

The SOCKS program was written before Microsoft added the CSocket and CAsyncSocket classes. When CSocket and CAsyncSocket were introduced, I made one attempt to update the program to make use of the AsyncSocket class (I didn't try to write a version of the program that would use the CSocket class because it was immediately apparent that the functionality of the CSocket class was too limited to meet my needs.)

I soon discovered that the CAsyncSocket class also fell somewhat short of supplying the functionalities that I needed. As it turned out, I left the program the way it. I made that decision because the program's direct access to the Windows API provided a degree of versatility and expandability that I would have lost if I had rewritten the program to use the AsyncSocket class.

Unfortunately, the program is also more complicated and more difficult to understand than it would have been if I had gone ahead and modified it to use the AsyncSocket class. Because there were no MFC classes to rely on when I first wrote the program, I had to use a rather complex callback architecture to access functions provided in the Windows Sockets API.

When the SOCKS program creates its main window, the **`OnCreate`** message handler in the file SOCKSVW.CPP calls the Windows Sockets function **`WSAStartup`**. (The **`WSAStartup`** startup function is not used in programs that rely on CSocket or AsyncSocket. But in a program that directly accesses Windows Sockets, **`WSAStartup`** initializes Windows Sockets, and consequently is always the first socket function that you call.)

When the SOCKS application finishes using Windows Sockets, it calls the **`WSACleanup`** function—a requirement for applications that directly access the Windows Sockets API, but not for programs that rely on CSocket or CasyncSocket.

For more details about the operation of the SOCKS program, see "How the SOCKS Program Works" on page 575

Building the SOCKS Program

To compile and link the SOCKS program, simply launch Visual C++, navigate to the directory in which the program is stored, and build the program by choosing Build from the Options menu. Then you can execute the program from the Windows 95 desktop.

Because the SOCKS program has a prewritten makefile (generated by AppWizard), you don't have to build a makefile to compile and link the SOCKS application. However, to write your own programs with the Windows Sockets API, there are two essential steps that you must take.

First, you must include the WINSOCK.H file in your compilation. That is the header file that defines the functions in the Windows Sockets API.

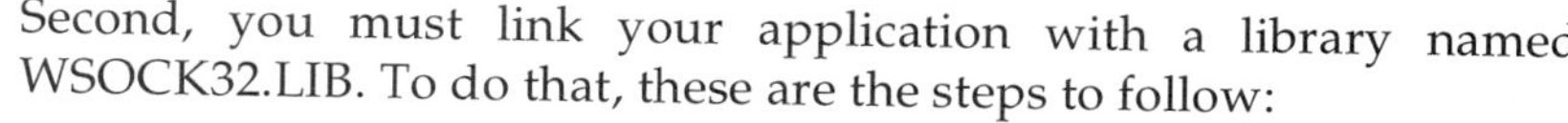

✔ Second, you must link your application with a library named WSOCK32.LIB. To do that, these are the steps to follow:

1. Choose the **Settings** item from Developer Studio's **Build** menu.
2. Tab to the **Link** property page in the **Project Settings** dialog box.
3. Select the **Input** item in the **Category** drop-down combo box.
4. In the **Object/library** modules text box, type **wsock32.lib**.
5. Close the **Project Settings** list box by clicking **OK**.
6. Build the SOCKS application by choosing **Build** from the **Build** menu.

Running the Example Program

✔ To execute the SOCKS program, follow these steps:

1. If possible, connect two Windows 95 or Windows NT workstations using the TCP/IP protocol.
2. On one Windows 95 or Windows NT workstation, launch the SOCKS application from the Windows 95 desktop or from Developer Studio. We'll call this machine Workstation A.
3. On the second Windows 95 or Windows NT workstation (or on the same workstation if you don't have access to a network), launch a second instance of the SOCKS program. We'll call this machine (or this instance of the SOCKS application) Workstation B.
4. When TCP/IP starts up, it displays a dialog box like the one shown in Figure 11.16. On both workstations, close this dialog box by clicking the OK button.

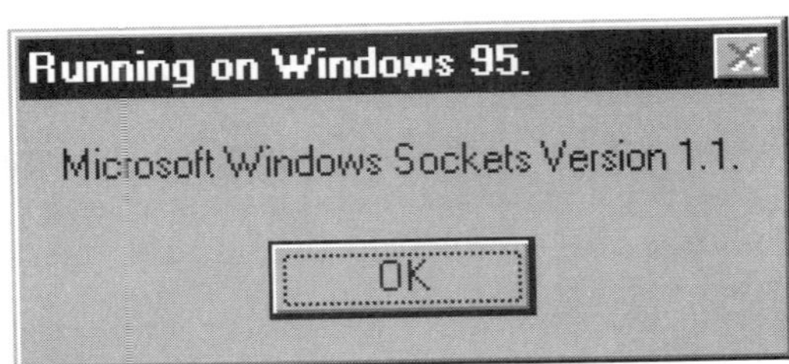

Figure 11.16 TCP/IP Startup dialog box

5. When the SOCKS application window appears on Workstation A, choose the Listen command from the menu or click the Listen button (the ear icon) on the toolbar.
6. The SOCKS program responds by displaying a dialog box titled **Port Number**. In the edit box labeled "Port number (try 12)," you can enter either a port number or the name of a service listed in your SERVICES file (for information about the SERVICES file, see "Protocols, Ports, and Sockets" on page 557.) Experiment with various port numbers and names.
7. Close the **Port Number** dialog box by clicking the OK button.
8. When the SOCKS window opens on Workstation B, click the Connect toolbar button (the fingers icon) or select the Connect command from the menu. The application responds by displaying a **Host Name** dialog box (Figure 11.16 on Page 574) that prompts you for the name of a remote host.

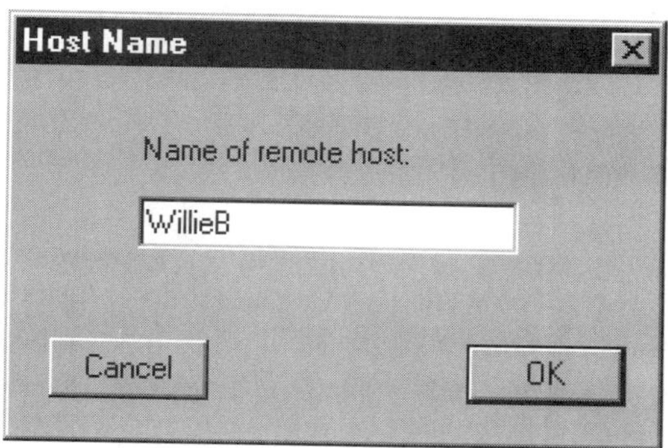

Figure 11.17 Host Name dialog box

9. If you are running the SOCKS program on two Windows 95 or Windows NT workstations, enter the name of the remote computer that you are connected to. If you are running the program on just one workstation, enter the name of your computer.
10. Close the **Host Name** dialog box by clicking the **OK** button.
11. The **Port Number** dialog box, described in Step 6, now appears on the machine making the connection. The user of this machine now types in a port number or the name of a service, as explained in Step 6.
12. When a TCP/IP connection is made, each workstation displays a "Connection accepted" announcement in the one-line message window just above the outgoing message panel. When the connect message appears in the windows both of both workstations, you clan start sending and receiving messages.
13. To send a message, type it in the outgoing pane and click the Transmit button (the envelope beneath the arrow). Read the replies to your messages in the window's incoming panel.
14. When you are finished sending and receiving messages, cancel your connection by selecting the Cancel Connection command from the Sockets menu.

How the SOCKS Program Works

The SOCKS program implements the Windows Sockets API, which imposes a host of special requirements applications. So some formidable challenges arose in the process of writing the SOCKS application.

For example, some Windows Sockets calls—such as **WSASyncSelect** and the **WSAGet** functions—require an application to respond to specific messages that are sent to a specified window. And messages sent to windows must be handled differently in framework-based Visual C++ programs from the way they are handled in non-Visual C++ Windows programs.

Traditional Windows API programs responding to messages triggered by user events by simply placing calling the appropriate message handlers from a main event loop. In Visual C++ applications generated by AppWizard, messages are dispatched to windows using a more indirect mechanism called message map. When you need to handle a message in a Visual C++ program, you must write a message handler and tell your application where your message handler is by placing an entry in a message map. (Message maps are not unique to Windows 95 but have been around since Version 1.0 of Visual C++; for more information about message maps, see your Visual C++ documentation.)

The SOCKS program relies extensively on custom-designed message handlers and message maps.

Starting the SOCKS Program

When you launch the SOCKS program, the **OnCreate** member function of the application's view object starts Windows Sockets by calling a function named **SockStartup**. **SockStartup** is called from the SOCKSVW.CPP, which implements the program's view object. The **SockStartup** function is impleCAsyncSocketCAsyncSocketmented this way in the WSOCK.CPP file:

```
// SockStartup member function.
void CMySocket::SockStartup(CView *pView)
{
  WSADATA WSAData;
  char szTemp[80];
  int status;

  if ((status = WSAStartup(MAKEWORD(1,1), &WSAData)) == 0) {
    MessageBox(pView->m_hWnd, WSAData.szDescription,
      WSAData.szSystemStatus, MB_OK);
  } else {
    sprintf(szTemp, "%d is the err", status);
    MessageBox(pView->m_hWnd, szTemp, "Error:", MB_OK);
  }
}
```

As you can see, **the SockStartup** function starts Windows Sockets by calling the **WSAStartup** function. When a client tries to connect, a member function named **CMySocket::FillAddr** is called. This function retrieves the client's IP address, gets the host's name, and locates the service to which the client is trying to connect. If the FillAddr member function returns successfully, the client is allowed to connect. This is the **CMySocket::FillAddr** function:

```
BOOL CMySocket::FillAddr(HWND hWnd, PSOCKADDR_IN psin, BOOL bConnect)
{
     DWORD dwSize;
     PHOSTENT phe;
     PSERVENT pse;
     char szTemp[200];
     int status;

     psin->sin_family = AF_INET;

 if (!bConnect) {

          // Retrieve user's IP address. We assume that the hosts file
          // in your Windows 95 directory contains your
          // computer name.

          dwSize = sizeof(m_szBuf);
          gethostname(m_szBuf, dwSize);
     }

     phe = gethostbyname(m_szBuf);
     if (phe == NULL) {
          sprintf(szTemp,
               "Error %d. Make sure '%s' is listed in the hosts file.",
                    WSAGetLastError(), m_szBuf);

          MessageBox(hWnd, szTemp, "gethostbyname function failed.",
               MB_OK);
          return FALSE;
     }
     memcpy((char FAR *)&(psin->sin_addr), phe->h_addr,
          phe->h_length);

// Retrieve the Port number

     CDlgPort dlgPort;
     dlgPort.m_editPort = "12";// Put suggested port number
                                // in edit box.
     status = dlgPort.DoModal();
```

```
    if (status == IDOK) {
        CString tempStr = dlgPort.m_editPort;
        char *cTempStr = tempStr.GetBuffer(BUF_LEN);
        strcpy(m_szBuf, cTempStr);

        if ((portno = atoi(m_szBuf)) == 0)
            status = 2;
        else
            status = 1;
    }

    switch(status) {
        case 0: // User cancelled request.
            return FALSE;

        case 1: // actual port number entered
            psin->sin_port = htons(portno); // Convert to network
                                            // ordering
            break;

        case 2: // Service name entered

            // Find the service name, m_szBuf, which is a type-tcp
            // protocol in the SERVICES file.
            pse = getservbyname(m_szBuf, "tcp");
            if (pse == NULL) {
                sprintf(m_szBuf,
                "Error %d. Make sure this is a valid TCP service.",
                WSAGetLastError());
                MessageBox(hWnd, m_szBuf,
                    "getservbyname function failed",
                    MB_OK);
                return FALSE;
            }
        psin->sin_port = pse->s_port;
        break;

        // Save port number.
        m_portNum = psin->sin_port;

        default:
            return FALSE;
    }
    return TRUE;
}
```

The SockProc Function

The **SockProc** function is a member function of the CMySocket class. **SockProc**, implemented in the WSOCK.CPP file, is structured much like a standard C-language Windows procedure. **SockProc** expects the same parameters that a standard windows procedure expects, and it handles them just like a standard window procedure: with a **switch** statement that detects messages and dispatches them to message handlers.

The SOCKS program implements WSA functions by calling the **SockProc** function and passing it parameters that cause it to perform specified tasks. Messages are passed to **SockProc** in a parameter named *message*. **SockProc** handles the *message* parameter by examining it in a series of **case** tests and taking whatever action the appropriate message requires.

Architecture of the SOCKS Program

Most of the functions that implement the client side of the application are implemented in the SOCKSVW.CPP file. A message map in the SOCKSVW.CPP file links client functions with a **switch** statement in a file named WSOCK.CPP. The message map in SOCKSVW.CPP looks like this:

```
BEGIN_MESSAGE_MAP(CSocksVw, CFormView)
   //{{AFX_MSG_MAP(CSocksVw)
   ON_WM_CREATE()
   ON_COMMAND(ID_SOCKETS_CONNECT, OnSocketsConnect)
   ON_COMMAND(ID_SOCKETS_LISTEN, OnSocketsListen)
   ON_COMMAND(ID_SOCKETS_TRANSMIT, OnSocketsTransmit)
   ON_COMMAND(ID_SOCKETS_CANCELCONNECTION,
    OnSocketsCancel)
   ON_WM_DESTROY()
   ON_UPDATE_COMMAND_UI(ID_SOCKETS_TRANSMIT,
    OnUpdateSocketsTransmit)
   ON_UPDATE_COMMAND_UI(ID_SOCKETS_CONNECT,
    OnUpdateSocketsConnect)
   ON_UPDATE_COMMAND_UI(ID_SOCKETS_LISTEN,
    OnUpdateSocketsListen)
   //}}AFX_MSG_MAP
   ON_MESSAGE(WSA_READ, OnWSARead)
   ON_MESSAGE(WSA_ACCEPT, OnWSAAccept)
   ON_MESSAGE(WM_ONSOCKLISTEN, OnSockListen)
   ON_MESSAGE(WM_ONSOCKCONNECT, OnSockConnect)
   ON_MESSAGE(WM_ONSOCKGETHOSTNAME, OnSockGetHostName)
   ON_MESSAGE(WM_ONSOCKSENDTCP, OnSockSendTCP)
   ON_MESSAGE(WM_ONSOCKDESTROY, OnSockDestroy)
```

```
   ON_MESSAGE(WM_ONSOCKCANCEL, OnSockCancel)
END_MESSAGE_MAP()
```

Each time a message implemented in this message map is dispatched, a member function associated with the message is executed. For example, when the user clicks the **Connect** toolbar button or chooses the **Connect** command from the **Sockets** menu, the message map in SOCKSVW.CPP detects an **ON_SOCKETS_CONNECT** message. As a result, a member function named **OnSocketsConnect** (also in the SOCKSVW.CPP file) is called:

```
void CSocksVw::OnSocketsConnect()
{
   // TODO: Add your command handler code here
   SendMessage(WM_ONSOCKCONNECT);
   m_tcpMsg = m_socket->m_msgString;
   UpdateData(FALSE);
}
```

As the preceding code fragment shows, the **OnSocketsConnect** function executes a **SendMessage** functions with a **WM_ONSOCK-CONNECT** argument. That argument causes another member function, named **OnSockConnect**, to be executed. This is the **OnSockConnect** function:

```
LRESULT CSocksVw::OnSockConnect(WPARAM wParam, LPARAM
    lParam)
{
   m_listenActive = FALSE;
   m_connectActive = FALSE;
   m_transmitActive = TRUE;

   (SockProc(m_hWnd, WM_COMMAND, IDM_CONNECT, lParam));

   m_tcpMsg = m_socket->m_tempCString;
   m_hostName = m_socket->m_tempCString2;
   UpdateData(FALSE);

   return TRUE;
}
```

Because the **OnSockConnect** function is executed as a result of a **SendMessage** function, the system passes a *wParam* parameter and an *lParam* parameter to **OnSockConnect**. The **OnSockConnect** function then passes the **lParam** parameter on to the **SockProc** function, along with an **IDM_CONNECT wParam**, a **WM_COMMAND** message identifier, and a handle to the SOCKS application's window. When the **SockProc** function executes, the **IDM_CONNECT** argument directs **SockProc** to the following **case** statement:

```
case IDM_CONNECT: {

   SOCKADDR_IN dest_sin; // DESTination Socket INternet

   // Get the name of the remote host and
   // STORE THE STRING IN m_szBuf.


   // Display dialog box that gets host's name.
   CDlgHostName dlgHostName;
   status = dlgHostName.DoModal();
   m_tempCString = dlgHostName.m_editName;
   m_tempStr = m_tempCString.GetBuffer(BUF_LEN);
   strcpy(m_szBuf, m_tempStr);
   m_tempCString = "Host name is: " + m_tempCString;
   m_tempCString2 = m_szBuf;// Host's name
   m_remoteHost = m_szBuf;// Save host name.

   // m_szBuf = tempStr.GetBuffer(BUF_LEN);

   if (!status) // User cancelled request from ...
      break; // ... previous dialog box.

   sock = socket( AF_INET, SOCK_STREAM, 0);
   if (sock == INVALID_SOCKET) {
      MessageBox(hWnd, "socket function failed",
         "Error:", MB_OK);
      break;
            }

   // Retrieve the IP address and TCP Port number.
   // (Global variable m_szBuf contains the remote
   // host's name).

   if (!FillAddr( hWnd, &dest_sin, TRUE)) {
      closesocket( sock );
      break;
   }

   if (connect( sock, (PSOCKADDR) &dest_sin,
      sizeof(dest_sin)) < 0) {
      closesocket( sock );
      MessageBox(hWnd, "connect function failed",
         "Error:", MB_OK);
      break;
   }
   // Now we have a connection --
```

```
        m_msgString = "Connection established.";

        // Send main window a WSA_READ when either data is
        // pending on the socket (FD_READ) or the connection
        // is closed (FD_CLOSE)

        if ((status = WSAAsyncSelect( sock, hWnd, WSA_READ,
            FD_READ | FD_CLOSE )) > 0) {
            wsprintf(m_szBuf, "%d (0x%x)");
            MessageBox( hWnd, "Error on WSAAsyncSelect()",
                m_szBuf, MB_OK);
            closesocket( sock );
        }
    }
    break; // IDM_CONNECT
```

When the preceding **case** statement is executed, it displays a dialog box that obtains the host's name. Most of the other sockets-related operations in the SOCKS program operate in a similar fashion. To see the **SockProc** function, refer to the WSOCK.CPP file.

Once you understand how the non-MFC SOCKS program works, figuring out the MFC version of the program is a breeze. In the MFC version of the program, almost all the API calls are encapsulated into MFC functions, making it much easier to understand the application.

Summary

This chapter described the Windows Sockets API, a utility that provides wide-area networking capabilities to Windows 95. With Windows Sockets, you can write applications that access computer bulletin boards and network services such as the Internet, the giant computer network that can connect you with millions of users across the United States and around the world.

With the Windows Sockets API, you can write applications that access TCP/IP, the Transmission Control Protocol and Internet Protocol. TCP/IP comes with Windows 95 and can be installed using the Control Panel. This chapter explained how to install TCP/IP, how to write TCP/IP applications, and how to use your applications to communicate with other Windows 95 or Windows NT workstations running TCP/IP.

To help you get started with TCP/IP, a complete copy of the Windows Sockets API is provided on your bonus disk, in the form of a Windows help file. You can access the file from the Windows 95 desktop or from Developer Studio.

This chapter also presented an example application, named SOCKS, that allows you to connect with other computer users and chat with them using TCP/IP.

SOCKS is a Visual C++ application that has two parts: a server program that manages communications, and a client program that you can launch once the server is running. The client program's main window is an interactive text window that was created using the MFC's CFormView class. This chapter presented the program in two versions: one version that uses the Microsoft Foundation Class library and one that does not.

The SOCKS application also shows how serialization—the automatic loading and saving of disk files—can be built into Visual C++ programs. When you run the SOCKS program, it automatically generates a log of all messages that are sent and received, and you can use serialization to load and save message logs that have been generated in TCP/IP sessions.

Bibliography

Andrews, Mark: *C++ Windows NT Programming*. New York: M&T Books, 1995.

Andrews, Mark: *Visual C++ Object-Oriented Programming*. Carmel, IN: Sams, 1993.

App Studio User's Guide. Redmond, WA: Microsoft Press, 1993.

Atkinson, Lee, Atkinson, Mark, and Mitchell, Ed: *Using Microsoft C/C++ 7*. Carmel, IN: Que Corporation, 1992.

Barkakati, Nabajyoti. *Microsoft C/C++ 7 Developer's Guide*. Carmel, IN: Sams, 1992.

Barkakati, Nabajyoti. *Object-Oriented Programming in C++*. Carmel, IN: Sams, 1989.

Booch, Grady. *Object Oriented Design*. Redwood City, CA: Benjamin/Cummings, 1991.

Brockschmidt, Kraig. *Inside OLE*, Second Edition. Redmond, WA: Microsoft Press, 1995.

C Language Refence (for Visual C++). Redmond, WA: Microsoft Press, 1993.

C++ Language Refence (for Visual C++). Redmond, WA: Microsoft Press, 1993.

C++ Tutorial (for Visual C++). Redmond, WA: Microsoft Press, 1993.

Christian, Kaare. *The Microsoft Guide to C++ Programming*. Redmond, WA: Microsoft Press, 1992.

Class Library User's Guide (for Visual C++). Redmond, WA: Microsoft Press, 1993.

Custer, Helen. *Inside Windows NT*. Redmond, WA: Microsoft Press, 1992.

Ellis, Margaret A. and Stroustrup. *The Annotated C++ Reference Manual*. Reading, MA: Addison-Wesley, 1990.

Faison, Ted. *Borland C++ 3 Object-Oriented Programming*. Carmel, IN: Sams, 1989.

Hansen, Augie. *C Programming: A Complete Guide to Mastering the C Language*. Reading, MA: Addison-Wesley, 1989.

Hansen, Tony L. *The C++ Answer Book*. Reading, MA: Addison-Wesley, 1990.

Hunt, Craig. *TCP/IP Network Administration*. Sebastopol, CA: O'Reilly and Associates, 1992/1993.

Hunter, Bruce H. *Understanding C*. Berkeley: Sybex, 1984.

Kernighlan, Brian W., and Ritchie, Dennis. M. *The C Programming Language*, Second Edition. Englewood Cliffs, NJ: Prentice-Hall, 1985.

King, Adrian: *Inside Windows 95*. Redmond, WA: Microsoft Press, 1995.

Klein, Mike. *DLLs and Memory Management*. Carmel, IN: Sams, 1992.

Kochmer, Jonathan. *NorthWestNet's Guide to Our World Online*, Fourth Edition. Bellevue, WA: NorthWestNet and Northwest Academic Computing Consortium, Inc., 1993.

User-Interface Guide. Redmond, WA: Microsoft Press, 1995.

Index

Symbols

Numerics

A

B

C

D

E

G

H

I

J

K

L

M

N

O

P

Q

R

S

T

U

V

W

Z

Load this diskette using Windows® 95 or Windows NT